Captives and Corsairs

Captives and Corsairs

*France and Slavery in the
Early Modern Mediterranean*

Gillian Weiss

STANFORD UNIVERSITY PRESS

STANFORD, CALIFORNIA

Stanford University Press
Stanford, California

© 2011 by the Board of Trustees of the Leland Stanford Junior University.
All rights reserved.

This book has been published with the assistance of the Case Western Reserve
University History Department and College Stimulus Fund for Faculty Research,
Scholarship and Creative Endeavors.

Printed in the United States of America on acid-free, archival-quality paper

Library of Congress Cataloging-in-Publication Data

Weiss, Gillian Lee.
Captives and corsairs : France and slavery in the early modern Mediterranean
/ Gillian Weiss.
p. cm.
Includes bibliographical references and index.
ISBN 978-0-8047-7000-2 (cloth : alk. paper)
ISBN 978-0-8047-9209-7 (pbk. : alk. paper)
1. Slavery—Africa, North—History. 2. French—Africa, North—History.
3. Slaves—Emancipation—Africa, North—History. 4. Slavery—Political
aspects—France—History. 5. Pirates—Africa, North—History. 6. France—
Relations—Africa, North. 7. Africa, North—Relations—France. 8. Africa,
North—History—1517–1882. I. Title.
HT1345.W45 2011
306.3'620961—dc22
2010028607

Typeset by Bruce Lundquist in 10/12 Sabon

Contents

Figures

Acknowledgments

I have been enslaved to this book for a very long time. Since its inception, I have also accumulated a tremendous number of debts. For putting me on the path of Mediterranean captives and corsairs, I credit a conversation with Daniel Gordon. For steering me toward rich sources, fruitful questions, and sharper arguments, I owe my advisors and mentors in the Bay Area. Dena Goodman helped me shape the project in its initial stages and has been generous with her time and intellect ever since. Keith Michael Baker offered support and erudition. Paula Findlen, a marvelously attentive reader, gave encouragement and criticism in equal measure. Peter Sahlins shared archival wisdom and astute suggestions. Aron Rodrigue provided pragmatic advice, both academic and culinary. I am also deeply grateful to my undergraduate professors, particularly Robert Shell, whose seminar first introduced me to the topic of comparative slavery and to the rigors of historical research and writing. Natalie Zemon Davis remains a tremendous inspiration.

Numerous institutions funded my research in France: the Bourse Chateaubriand, the Lurcy and Newhouse foundations, and the Dean's Office at Stanford University; as well as the Baker-Nord Center for the Humanities and the W. P. Jones Presidential Faculty Fund at Case Western Reserve University. Fellowships from the Stanford Department of History, the Mellon and Camargo foundations, the Rock Island Arsenal Historical Society, and the Geballe Family gave me four idyllic places to write: San Francisco, Paris, Cassis, and the Stanford Humanities Center. Afterward, support from the Case Western Reserve University History Department, the American Council of Learned Societies, and the John W. Kluge Center at the Library of Congress allowed me to complete the manuscript in snowier but no less congenial climes.

At Case, I am extremely fortunate to have a coterie of fantastic colleagues. Their camaraderie and intellectual dynamism have contributed immeasurably to this book, and I want to offer particular thanks to Jim Allegro, Robert Chase, Christopher Flint, Marixa Lasso, Ken Ledford, Jonathan Sadowsky, Ted Steinberg, and Angela Woollacott for engaging with a topic that is in some ways remote from their own. For additional comments and suggestions at various phases, I also gratefully acknowledge Megan Armstrong, Jana Bruns, Mitra Brewer, Malick Ghachem, Mark Hichman, Renate Kosinski, Ben Lazier, Mary Ellen Levin, Nabil Matar, Lara Moore, Marcy Norton, Tara Nummedal, Sue Peabody, Sara Pritchard, Jennifer Sessions, Marie-Pierre Ulloa-Pit, Nicolas Vatin, Nick Wilding, and Joe Zizek. For careful reading beyond the call of childhood friendship, I am beholden to Sarah Friedman and Judith Surkis. For thorough, challenging readers' reports beyond the call of professional duty, I am indebted to one anonymous reviewer and two initially anonymous ones, Suzanne Desan and Colin Jones.

Over the years, this book also benefited from conversations with Marc Bertrand, Rob Blecher, Robert Davis, Michel Fontenay, Michael John Gorman, Brad Gregory, Wolfgang Kaiser, Ben Kaplan, Kate Masur, Claire Schen, John Shovlin, Sarah Stein, Sarah Sussman, Balázs Szekényi, Miriam Ticktin, Lucette Valensi, and Bernard Vincent. I would like to express my appreciation to them and to audience members and conference participants on several continents who responded to my work.

Thank you to the staff of numerous French municipal and departmental archives and especially the Chamber of Commerce Archives in Marseille; to librarians at Stanford (Mary Jane Parrine), Case (Mark Eddy), and the Library of Congress (Carol Armbruster); and to the interlibrary loan offices at Stanford and Case (and to Google Books). Thank you to Jonathan Calkins, Carolyn Heine, and Allison Hirsch for research assistance. Finally, thank you to Norris Pope, Sarah Crane Newman, Carolyn Brown, and Jessie Hunnicutt at Stanford University Press for their patience and professionalism.

In sections of this book, I use material adapted from "Le Dernier esclave français" in *L'Esclavage, la colonisation, et après: France, Etats-Unis, Grande-Bretagne*, eds. Patrick Weil and Stéphane Dufoix (2005), 83–105; "Barbary Captivity and the French Idea of Freedom," *French Historical Studies* 28, 2 (2005): 231–264; and "Les Français enchaînés: lettres des captifs des pirates barbaresques aux XVIIe et XVIIIe siècles," in *Les Tyrans de la mer: pirates, corsaires & flibustiers*, ed. Sylvie Requemora and Sophie Linon-Chapon (2002), 71–81.

On both sides of the Atlantic and three coasts of the United States, I have been sustained by wonderful friends. For boundless hospitality in France, I thank the *famille* Lubo, Françoise Duvail, Sophie Bonnor and Christophe Soyer, Ange-Marie Acevedo, Michel Aznavourian and

Martine Amsili, Anne and Mokrane Oukhemanou, and Judith Surkis and Antoine Guitton. For exuberant fraternizing in San Francisco and Washington, DC, I thank Kevin Carey, Juliet Eilperin, Sarah Friedman, Andrew Light, Dan Mach, Kim Parker, Jen Sermoneta, Sara Sklaroff, Andrew Solomon, and Scott Wallsten. For not "let[ting] me freeze in that Lake Erie breeze," I thank Alexis Abramson, Florence Dore, Will Rigby, Renée Sentilles, and Chris Sklarin.

I could not have finished this book without my extended family. Carol and Norman Weiss, Marta Weiss and Alex Paseau, Bill and Lil Smalley, Edna Hersh, Mark Hersh and Megan MacMillan, and other relatives big and small provided love, succor, and babysitting. You have my eternal gratitude. Showing up midvoyage, Oliver Ames Weiss Posner has been a source of constant delight and questions about pirates. Happily, he can now stop asking, "What page are you on?" Last but not least, I thank Elliot Posner. My companion in captivity, he remains my partner in all of life's adventures.

Note on the Text

Arabic and Ottoman names and terms are transliterated without dia-
critical marks except for the hamza, *'ayn*, and macron over some long
vowels. The spelling of early modern European titles have not been modernized but are reproduced as in the original. Unless otherwise indicated, all translations from French are my own.

Captives and Corsairs

Introduction

The analogies started within twenty-four hours. Given one minute to address his colleagues on 12 September 2001, Representative Nick Smith of Michigan invoked the Barbary pirates. Then, just as Congress had done during the era of Thomas Jefferson, he proclaimed, "We must declare war on these new terrorists."[1] In the weeks that followed, radio, television, newspaper, and Internet commentators all seized on the apparent historical parallel between the Republic's first foreign conflict, which occurred from 1801 to 1805 with the polity that became modern Libya, and the battle against Al Qaʻida that now lay before the United States.[2]

To media analysts of various political stripes, the nineteenth-century experience combating sea bandits harbored by the Ottoman regencies of Tripoli, Tunis, and Algiers and the independent kingdom of Morocco provided a valuable object lesson for fighting Islamic militants in the new millennium, offering a strategic tutorial on the failure of appeasement and showcasing an elemental and enduring clash of civilizations.[3] Ironically, most modern observers credited the French—soon to be shunned for their refusal to join "coalition forces" in Iraq—for striking out alone and obliterating the North African criminals through invasion. Conservative pundit Paul Johnson was notably prescriptive. "It was France that took the logical next step, in 1830, not only of storming Algiers but of conquering the entire country," he wrote in a *Wall Street Journal* opinion piece titled "21st-Century Piracy." His piece was subtitled "The Answer to Terrorism? Colonialism."[4]

In fact, by the time France's army disembarked on Algerian soil, the mutual practice of Mediterranean abduction had already ended. For three hundred years before, however, just as French privateers had hunted Muslim quarry, North African corsairs of mixed background had preyed on French ships and shores, stealing away tens of thousands of men (and a few women). Condemned to a long life in servitude if they did not convert to Islam, escape, die early, or purchase their freedom, these seafarers and coastal denizens spent months to decades awaiting deliverance. Starting in the 1550s, they received it in different measure from families, municipalities, two regionally organized Catholic orders, and the government. Between then and 1830, liberating slaves from North Africa changed from an expression of Christian charity to a method of state building and, eventually, a rationale for imperial expansion.

Until the mid-seventeenth century, French monarchs paid relatively little attention to the fates of unlucky subjects from peripheral regions, whose religious and secular institutions were perforce selective in their rescue efforts. After that, royal disinterest gave way to more acute fear about the dangers enslavement by so-called infidels posed to French health, wealth, religious unity, and social stability. Not only did Louis XIV dread the loss of valuable mariners, merchants, and other breadwinners, but he also shared local anxiety about their exposure to North African "contagions," notably plague, sodomy, and Islam. Only in the 1680s and 1690s, however, did the king have the means to protect them effectively. Employing artillery in place of ransom, he repatriated most of the French Catholics and even some of the foreign ones held in Barbary. But during these decades spent purging his realm of Reformed Christianity, he intentionally abandoned France's Protestants in servitude.

Such shifts in royal ability to unshackle countrymen and judgments about whom to release from Muslim bondage had important consequences for ideas of French belonging. No longer was liberty the reward of a chosen few. Instead, from the possibility that all Frenchmen *could* be free flowed the notion that all Frenchmen *should* be. Thereafter, apart from associating French status with freedom, North African slave emancipation became an explicit way of incorporating geographic outsiders, while excluding diseased bodies and deviant souls from France. The crown used it to invite allegiance from natives of annexed territories—and to keep out both Muslim converts and Christian heretics. Bringing slaves back from Barbary thus became a vehicle for establishing that Frenchmen had to be Catholics and determining which Catholics counted as French.

The late seventeenth-century decline in Mediterranean slavery coincided with the growth of Atlantic slavery. Along with a drop in the number of captive Frenchmen in North Africa, therefore, came a surge in the number of sub-Saharan chattel in France's American colonies. This switch in the victims of enslavement was accompanied by new racial assumptions about which people deserved to be slaves. During the Revolution, principles of universal rights and common humanity purported to justify conquest in the guise of liberation. Yet the restoration of skin-color hierarchies and chattel slavery in the Caribbean under Napoleon soon confirmed that French freedom did not extend to blacks. In 1830, the two conflicting ideologies met when the abolition of "white slavery" formed a pretext for France's takeover of Algiers.

This book revises the standard picture of France's emergence as a nation and a colonial power, challenging static interpretations of slavery, binary conceptions of the Inner Sea, and both centrist and domestic portraits of French history. Rather than measuring all forms of servitude against the extreme version established in the New World, the book examines an Old World type, which I argue was initially understood in terms of religion and mischance, not race and destiny. Rather than embracing the usual stereotype of a clear division between Crescent and Cross, it confirms the presence of unstable loyalties in a Mediterranean contact zone and explores the ways French authorities tried to secure them. And rather than recounting the extension of monarchical authority from the perspective of Paris, it demonstrates how the interactions of France's Mediterranean seaports—especially Marseille—with Muslim lands fostered national sentiment. By working to ensure that captives did not succumb to physical or spiritual corruption in North Africa or introduce Barbary pollutants into France, municipal and royal institutions on the coast supported the crown's bid to construct a strong polity of subjects who were fit and faithful to Christ and country.

This book is indebted to several generations of fertile research on the Mediterranean and on comparative slavery, and to an emerging subfield in the study of corsairing and captivity. It is also predicated on a striking historiographical gap. Despite possessing an extensive Mediterranean shoreline that so enchanted Fernand Braudel, the modern scholar most responsible for conceptualizing a pan-Mediterranean world, France does not figure prominently in studies of the sea or the lands that surround it.[5] The country's status as a continental victor and centralized state seems to have precluded it from sharing the "common destiny" of less powerful coastal neighbors, positioning it within a master narrative of European history instead. Furthermore, despite France's eventual role as avenger of North African brigandage, professional historians and popular authors long shied away from the subject.[6] Until quite recently French readers interested in finding out about forebears in captivity had to search through obscure provincial journals and colonial periodicals. For much of the twentieth century, status as an imperial power seems to have fostered selective amnesia about an earlier time when the conquered enslaved their conquerors.

During the second half of the nineteenth century, by contrast, Barbary piracy and slavery were fashionable topics among the former military men and colonial bureaucrats who attempted to legitimate colonization with history. Foreign affairs attaché Eugène Plantet, for example, who compiled several volumes of Franco-Algerian and Franco-Tunisian diplomatic correspondence, portrayed the leaders of both regencies as unwilling or unable to live peacefully—and deserving of their subjugated fate. "Our government . . . tried more than all the others to civilize this evil race," he wrote in 1889, but "in the demonstrated impossibility of punishing [Algiers] effectively, [France] subdued it."[7] To retired admiral Jean Pierre Edmond Jurien de la Gravière, author of an 1887 study, French soldiers were modern crusaders who had battled the descendants of ancient enemies to stake a historical claim to North Africa, which "from the moment she escaped from the Arabs and could no longer belong to the Spanish . . . returned rightfully to France." In a chapter entitled "Gallia victrix" (Gaul Conqueror), he extolled "the immense service we have performed for Europe in establishing ourselves on the African beach."[8]

With one notable exception, it was only once the Algerian War had begun to dislodge France from its North African perch that members of the *Annales* school rediscovered Mediterranean sea roving and slave taking.[9] From the 1950s, these scholars and others offered a corrective to the crude jingoism and colonial triumphalism of their predecessors, finding evidence that Europeans had been agents as well as objects of abduction.[10] Through studies of merchant activity, diplomatic negotiation, and religious conversion, they followed Braudel's example in considering the totality of the region rather than the countries that composed it and in questioning the notion of an eternal, sharp division between warring Christian and Muslim civilizations.[11] Such historians, however, mostly overlooked his assertion that "slavery was a structural feature of Mediterranean society . . . by no means exclusive to the Atlantic and the New World."[12] Rather than embrace this inclusive perspective, they tended to adopt the extreme model of hereditary bondage that in the Caribbean and parts of Latin America and the United States turned people into pure commodities,[13] and to accept the dominant view that the Arab-Islamic world featured a notably benign, racially neutral type of servitude.[14] Accordingly, they tended to distinguish—semantically and substantively—the confinement of Christians and Muslims in Europe from that of sub-Saharan Africans in the Americas, and the experience of "captives" or "prisoners of war" from that of true "slaves."[15]

This study of captivity and redemption in an Old World frontier zone disputes the assumption that the primary reference point for slavery in the minds of Frenchmen and Frenchwomen from the seventeenth to the nineteenth century was the colonial chattel kind. Without suggesting that the Mediterranean system of seizure and detention for the sake of ransom bears direct comparison to the Atlantic system of brutal transport and violent exploitation to satisfy mass markets, it rejects seemingly universal, static typologies and takes Barbary slaves and their contemporaries at their word.[16] By acknowledging historical definitions and keeping diverse forms of servitude within a single field of vision, it uncovers a shift in French ideas of freedom and unfreedom over time and provides a fresh outlook on the intersection between Mediterranean and Atlantic slaveries. My goal is not to locate additional possible intellectual or technical antecedents to the American plantation complex.[17] Instead, it is to lay clear the ties between saving slaves and making Frenchmen, between destroying slavery and making colonies.

Such a project is by definition interdisciplinary. Besides drawing on multiple historical studies of North African enslavement from other geographical perspectives,[18] it borrows insights about Christian and Muslim encounters from the fields of literature[19] and art history,[20] whose practitioners have been particularly attuned to the specter of religious conversion and other anxieties of empire. My sources are similarly broad. They include the masses of administrative correspondence among French officials in North Africa, Versailles, and in Marseille and other port towns; the voluminous printed output of the friars devoted to redeeming captives; newspaper accounts; philosophical treatises; novels, plays, and paintings; as well as unpublished letters and published narratives by the French slaves themselves. The result is a blend of diplomatic, social, and cultural history that advances new arguments about the fluid nature of slavery, the association between liberation and state building, and imperialism's roots in abolition.

Contemporary France still bears the painful legacy of 1830, which led to more than a century of colonial occupation. Only in recent decades have journalists and historians begun to counter French collective "memory loss" about the Algerian War that ended in 1962, probing the logic behind the violence employed to delay relinquishing a North African region viewed as an integral part of France and exploring the political, social, and cultural repercussions of decolonization.[21] Meanwhile, the basis for France's initial foray into Algiers has remained largely unexamined.[22]

Since 9/11, an earlier American generation's resolve to protect its citizens and assets from Muslim outlaws has been entrenching itself as a foundation myth of the United States.[23] This book seeks to understand how France's ultimate response to a phenomenon that no longer posed a significant material threat came to form a foundation myth of the French empire. Presenting the Mediterranean as an essential vantage for studying the rise of France, the book reveals how efforts to liberate slaves in North Africa shaped French perceptions, both of the Muslim world and of the parameters of "Frenchness." It links captive redemption to state formation—and in turn to the still vital ideology of liberatory conquest.

CHAPTER ONE

Mediterranean Slavery

Before he became a sea rover, 'Arūj was a slave. The son of a onetime Turkish soldier and the grandson of a Greek Orthodox priest, by the early sixteenth century he had made a name for himself as a Muslim corsair captain, or *ra'is*, attacking Christian shipping from his base off the Tunisian coast. As his reputation for looting cargo and snaring captives grew, the inhabitants of Algiers recruited him to help expel their Spanish occupiers. Killed in battle in 1518, 'Arūj did not live long enough to see the territory become an Ottoman dependency in 1529 with his brother installed as its first pasha. But his brother, Kheir al-Din, later known as Barbarossa or Redbeard, continued the family legacy of conquest, briefly taking Tunis in 1534 before it fell to Holy Roman Emperor Charles V the following year.[1] When the long struggle over control of North Africa finally abated in the 1580s, Morocco had won complete autonomy and Algiers, Tunis, and Tripoli had emerged as reluctant "regencies" of the Sublime Porte in Constantinople (Figure 1).[2]

From these turbulent beginnings and mixed ancestries, the Barbary States developed into polities dependent on maritime plunder, whose reputation as "pirate republics" struck terror in the hearts of Europeans until the nineteenth century.[3] Even though Christian powers sponsored their own corsairs in the form of military orders like the Knights of Malta and Livorno—in addition to licensing private captains to steal Muslim merchandise and men—they tended to portray Mediterranean seizure and enslavement as a one-sided affair.[4] In fact, thousands of Ottomans and Moroccan rowers (sometimes Jewish or Orthodox yet indiscriminately known as "Turks" or "Moors") were captured and sold by various European powers[5] for service aboard Maltese,[6] Italian,[7] Spanish,[8] and French[9] galleys. Meanwhile, their compatriots of diverse geographic origin ravaged coasts and coves from Palermo to Valencia. These Berbers, Arabs, and Jews of various provenance; Muslim exiles

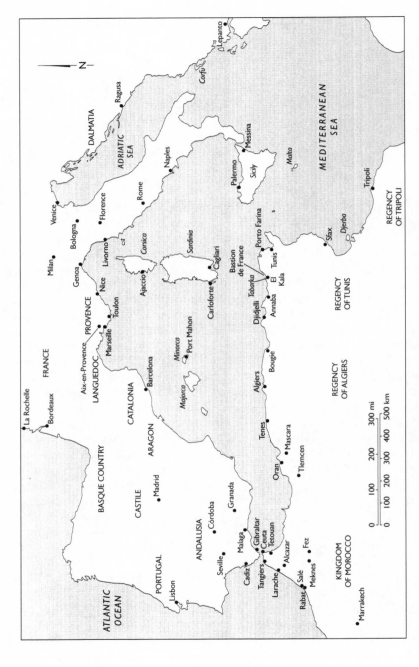

Figure 1. Map of the early modern Mediterranean.

from Iberia; and Christians who converted to become "Turks by profession"[10] carried off lone shepherds, entire villages, and boats of all shapes and sizes, turning even more Catholics (and some Protestants) into slaves.[11]

In 1530 and 1531, as Hungary surrendered to Ottoman advances, communities along the southernmost tip of France suffered incursions too.[12] Yet compared to their neighbors French subjects had relatively little to fear during the first half of the sixteenth century, because of an informal alliance between King Francis I and Sultan Suleiman I.[13] For the most part, rather than attack France's ships and shores, corsairs from North Africa brought military protection against the Habsburgs; for six months between 1543 and 1544, thirty thousand members of the Ottoman fleet wintered in Toulon.[14] Even a decade later, at least from a royal perspective, the presence of "Barbary pirates" on the Inner Sea remained more an annoyance to be handled diplomatically than a serious threat. In the 1550s, for example, ambassadors began forwarding occasional grievances to the Porte about raids, or *razzias*, on Provence and Languedoc.[15] A "maritime and limitrophe city" with long-standing ties to North Africa and relatively recent ones to France, Marseille (annexed in 1486) took separate measures to protect commerce and liberate natives, even as it petitioned regent Catherine de Medici about the seizure of vessels.[16] Nevertheless, in the five years prior to 1565, when Suleiman I formally ordered North African brigands away from French targets, Marseille had lost "ten or twelve *nefs* [large galleons]" and a "large number of boats."[17] It was partly to "keep an eye on these corsairs" that King Charles IX established the first consular outposts in North Africa and staffed them with Marseillais.[18]

Still, at a time when reports had it "raining Christians in Algiers," the number of French ones carried into captivity was bound to surge.[19] Expressing a widely shared conviction about the propensity of southern Europeans to "apostasy" (conversion to Islam)[20] and the propensity of neophyte Muslims to piracy and pederasty, court cosmographer Nicolas de Nicolay wrote in 1568 of the "renegade or Mahumatized Christians" from Spain, Italy, and Provence "all given to smut, sodomy, theft, and all the most detestable vices . . . [who] with their piratical art bring daily to Algiers an incredible number of poor Christians, whom they sell to the Moors and other Barbary merchants as slaves."[21]

Yet thanks to the Capitulations (*ahdnames*)—depicted as a bilateral agreement by the French but understood as a one-sided bequest by the Ottomans—officially signed in 1569, those claimed by France were not exposed to such alleged religious and sexual deviance for long.[22] A year after the Holy League's 1571 victory over the Ottoman Empire at Lepanto,[23] at the climax of France's Catholic-Calvinist Wars of Religion,[24] all five hundred Frenchmen in Algerian thralldom seem to have gone home.[25]

FRANCE'S FREE SOIL

The wholesale liberation of French subjects also coincided with the most cited articulation of a free soil principle for France. "France, mother of liberty, allows no slaves," the Parlement of Guyenne reportedly ruled after a Norman merchant attempted to sell several "Moors" he had purchased on the Barbary Coast.[26] Thereafter, illegally subjugated Turks prized for their strength at the oar notwithstanding, Muslims unbound became as central to political theories of freedom as captive Christians already were to everyday understandings of slavery.[27] With the demise of serfdom between the fourteenth and sixteenth centuries, a primary reference for conceiving personal status in France was the Mediterranean Sea, whose waves carried some to doom and others to deliverance. It would be another fifty years before French colonizers put down roots in the Caribbean and fifty more before French traders did more than pick occasional sub-Saharan Africans off the continent's Atlantic shores or steal them from Iberian and Dutch competitors. From a late sixteenth-century French vantage, the archetypal slave was either a Muslim abducted to Europe or a Christian abducted to North Africa.

In common usage, *captif* (from the Latin *captivus*) and *esclave* (from the medieval Latin *sclavus*, by way of the Byzantine Greek *sklabos* for Slav) were synonyms without modern racial or temporal distinctions. Heirs to conflicting classical views on the origins of human bondage, French subjects across the social spectrum generally ascribed the condition not to nature but to misfortune, even as they framed it as the outcome of an ongoing—if in their case theoretically suspended—clash between Crescent and Cross.[28] Though anxious that French corsair victims not switch religion or perish from disease, those most familiar with *captivité*, *esclavage*, *servitude*, and *esclavitude* assumed the possibility of a happy endpoint, based on a monotheistic tradition of redemption.[29] The French were attuned to physical difference and even inclined against blackness, but they did not yet categorically distinguish servitude by skin color.[30] What contemporary scholars have begun to term "ransom slavery," or *captivité de rachat*, whose fluidity reflected its watery genesis, was spatially conceived and spiritually inflected.[31] It was dependent on the reciprocal exploitation of multiethnic "infidels," not racial "others," and replenished via acquisition rather than reproduction. Its influence endured in metropolitan France for almost two more centuries.[32]

As an abstraction, Christian slaves in Muslim lands—given different literal and euphemistic appellations across North Africa—helped confirm the nature of French territoriality.[33] As an increasingly concrete reality, Christian slaves in Muslim lands spurred action from municipalities and—when not distracted by more pressing affairs—from monarchs. By 1585, for example, Marseille's commercial livelihood stood in sufficient jeopardy that the city organized an offensive league of Provençal ports to fight the Barbary corsairs. Concerned the following April about the bodily integrity and religious and political loyalties of vulnerable subjects, King Henry III had his ambassador in Constantinople protest the actions of five Algerian galleys that "took two French *saettias* [vessels with lateen sails] from Marseille and ransacked everything, killing the men and forcibly converting and circumcising a young boy," and wrote directly to the pasha and to the sultan about depredations by Tunis and Tripoli.[34]

Yet royal intercession on behalf of the kingdom's gateway to the Mediterranean stopped soon enough. When Marseille joined the secessionist Catholic League during the Wars of Religion, heir to the throne Henry of Navarre recognized the potential alongside the perils of North African corsairing; in 1590 he used his good offices with Sultan Murad III not to end physical captivity but to promote political vassalage. "We enjoin you to yield to your leaders and render obedience to that most magnanimous among the great and powerful lords," read the letter sent by the Ottoman sovereign to the city. "If you persist in your sinister obstinacy," it continued, "we declare that your vessels and their cargoes will be confiscated and your men made slaves."[35] The rebellious city decided to dispatch an emissary of its own to Algiers.[36]

Six years later Marseille resumed allegiance to the king. But by then the three Barbary regencies, chafing against authority from Constantinople, were pursuing ever more independent foreign policies,[37] making it increasingly difficult for sultans to enforce their security pledges to France.[38] Though French ambassadors inundated Ottoman authorities with intervention requests and French consuls advanced funds to captives, Muslim corsairs were apprehending seventy or eighty Christian ships per year by the turn of the century, and additional reports were circulating about "young men clipped and circumcised by force."[39] Therefore, the church, the crown, civic leaders, and expatriate communities had to adopt new strategies for shielding French people and property. In the 1590s, for instance, the *nation* of France in Tunis (constituted by resident traders and administrators) pooled their resources and then imposed a 1 percent merchandise tax to help buy back tens of compatriots.[40] Meanwhile, individuals with relatives in captivity, who had been commissioning special ransoming merchants—called *al-fakkakīn* by Muslims and, derivatively, *alfaqueques* by Christians—since the Middle Ages,[41] began taking greater recourse to two other Catholic institutions with medieval origins: the Frères de la Sainte Trinité (Trinitarians) and the Pères de la Merci (Mercedarians).[42]

The Trinitarians earned papal approval in 1198 after, as legend has it, the order's Provençal founder, Jean de Matha, and Pope Innocent III experienced identical divine visions. Known in France as *Mathurins*, or "donkey brothers," for the asses they rode as a sign of humility, they annually spent one third of their alms to ransom Christians from Muslim lands.[43] The Mercedarians, started by Pierre Nolasque, a Frenchman who settled in Perpignan, were established in 1218 or 1230 (historians disagree). Members of this second "redemptive order" were distinguished by a fourth vow.[44] Apart from promising poverty, chastity, and obedience, they swore to indenture themselves to liberate slaves, though in practice only a single French Mercedarian, Sebastien Bruyère, seems to have done so during the early modern period.[45] Instead, Henry IV granted the Mercedarians letters patent in July 1602, a month after confirming the presence of three thousand French captives in Algiers and receiving remonstrations about the "the ravages of the Turks" and "the young men and small children that they constrain and force with truly barbarous, unprecedented cruelties, to renounce Christianity to the great scandal of Christendom."[46] The friars then began competing viciously with the longer-established yet financially precarious Trinitarians for money and for souls.[47]

In the immediate aftermath of the 1598 Edict of Nantes, which accorded limited religious and political privileges to the kingdom's Calvinist (or Huguenot) minority, the French monarch who had once deployed the specter of Barbary captivity to bind insubordinate subjects to the realm began using it toward the goal of maintaining sectarian peace. Despite mutual recriminations of proclivity toward Islam and collusion with Muslims in political tracts,[48] ordinary Catholics and Protestants were equally haunted by visions of Christians compelled to change religion, just as both groups were affected by North African captures of merchant ships. Safeguarding Frenchmen from apostasy and French trade from brigandage was an endeavor even bitter rivals could support. Another of Henry IV's projects that promoted business and helped to prevent enslavement—and the accompanying perceived dangers of perversion and conversion—was the Marseille Chamber of Commerce. Founded in 1599 at the request of the city's business elite, this body served as intermediary between representatives in overseas trading ports (*échelles*) and ministers in the capital—and almost immediately became embroiled in the intricacies of repatriating captives. In its capacity as state enterprise, the Marseille Chamber of Commerce functioned as a kind of bank, advancing ransom money to the redemptive orders, transferring currency from the king to royal envoys, and reimbursing consuls for expenses. In an alternate role as municipal association, it responded to pressure to privilege the fate of natives.

The first decade of the seventeenth century brought a crucial diplomatic development too: official acknowledgment by the new sultan, Ahmed I, that he could not stop North African sea robbery, and explicit permission for Henry IV to engage the western Ottoman regencies directly.[49] After ordering, once again, that all pillaged French cargo be restored and all French captives be liberated, the Capitulations of 1604 allowed that if the Barbary corsairs did not obey, "the emperor of France [could] chase them down, punish them, and deprive them of his ports."[50] In Algiers the following summer, ambassador François Savary, seigneur de Brèves, secured only a tentative agreement for a slave exchange.[51] But with Tunis he negotiated a bilateral treaty, which among other measures promised safe passage and safe harbor to both sides and the trade of all "Turks and Muslims detained in Provence" for all French subjects held in the regency.[52]

For the first time committing mutual manumission to paper, this Franco–North African agreement also inaugurated a pattern of French obstruction in releasing promised galley slaves. After initially ordering the consuls of Marseille to turn over the rowers (who seem to have included some runaways from Spain), Henry IV added a qualification: to free "only the least useful . . . and least able to support work."[53] In Tunis, by contrast, the royal envoy claimed to have redeemed as many as 150 Frenchmen—though not without resistance.[54] There, despite the protests of interested parties "furiously seized by love (as they call the filthiest and infamous brutality that sullies human nature)," he wrote, the group to be repatriated included not just resolved Christians but also repentant converts to Islam. To those "young boys who had been circumcised and made Turk by force and already raised two, three, four years in the Mahometan Religion," yet who were willing to avow souls "unyielding in belief of our Lord Jesus Christ," the king had offered a blanket pardon.[55]

However, the accord apparently did not extend to French Knights of Malta. In 1606 the pasha of Tunis demanded so enormous a price for one such Marseillais (the subject of the first Barbary captivity narrative published in France) that the French consul would not pay. Embracing a genre already popularized in England and Portugal fifty years earlier,[56] the future author of a novel set in Turkey drew inspiration from martyrology and drama in this tale of Muslim travail and Catholic triumph. As the casualty of a raid on Mahomette (modern-day Hammamet), François de Vintimille reportedly passed numerous tests of faith while laboring on land and sea from Assumption to Pentecost. That "despite every agony" this knight never fell "slave to depravity"—that is, religious betrayal—seemed to testify not just to his own strength of spirit but to the charity and self-interest of onetime residents of France and members of the apostolic church.[57] First saved from slaughter by the "still half-Christian will" of Morat Aga, formerly of Rennes, "a Frenchman who still had pity in his heart and sincerity in his conscience," Vintimille paid his ransom with a loan from a Genoese renegade at 25 percent interest.[58] Like Henry IV, who twice traded Calvinism for Catholicism, slave and biographer seemed to reject the notion that conversion effectively severed all previous ties to God, king, and country. Perhaps influenced by older ideas about the inalienability of noble ancestry, they suggested that the blood of Gaul still pumped through an apostate's veins.[59]

Such optimism from a Catholic warrior notwithstanding, the outflow of French Christians—especially to Tunis—did worry coastal residents and royal officers, and during the four years before his assassination, the king heard repeated calls for violence against North Africa.[60] Especially given the idleness of the kingdom's proto-navy, "a descent on Barbary to take, sack, and ruin Bizerte and its port . . . with artillery" was in order, wrote the French ambassador to Constantinople in 1609.[61] Use your God-given firepower to wreak vengeance against the "pagans and infidels" of Tunis, recommended another Knight of Malta—Guillaume Foucques from La Rochelle—in two letters and a printed memoir composed the same year. For Foucques, the point of detailing his two months in Tunisian servitude was less religio-political inspiration than practical intelligence. Ten or twelve men-of-war and seven or eight galleys should suffice to destroy Tunis's slave-taking capacity, he asserted—on the condition that the inhabitants of Marseille whom he called "more Moor than French" not learn of the plans. Rather than believe in the enduring virtue of converted countrymen, Foucques adopted a conventionally negative attitude toward French renegades, blaming their complicity for the existence of a servile Christian population that had recently jumped from thirty to two thousand and included about three hundred captives from Provence, Languedoc, Gascony, Saintonge, Basque Country, Brittany, and Normandy.[62] His was not a tale of individual triumph over adversity, nor was it—like later narratives of North African bondage—an exposé of foreign culture, an homage to rescuers, an exhortation for charity, or an argument for colonization.[63] It was a call to arms.

ROYAL INATTENTION, LOCAL INTERVENTION

In the absence of royal military aggression against Muslim polities in North Africa—first by a king preoccupied with the fate of Muslim exiles (Moriscos) from the Iberian Peninsula, and then, after his death, by a regent preoccupied with the legacy of her eight-year-old son—French subjects had no choice but to continue searching for alternative solutions.[64] Marseille armed its own galleys, debated offering monetary incentives for merchants to fight rather than abandon ship, and, briefly, ordered departing vessels to travel in expensive and inconvenient convoy.[65] In the meantime, smaller coastal communities like Cassis stocked gunpowder to drive away "Turks" or were forced to fund rescues at the expense of other worthy objects of charity, as in the case of Fréjus, which "for the honor of God" voted to spend annuities meant to provide impoverished girls with dowries to emancipate a resident held by the "infidels" of Tripoli.[66] A coral fishing company received permission to ransom slaves.[67] Huguenots in maritime regions "complain[ed] loudly" to their synod "about the multitude of captives enchained in . . . Barbary,"[68] and Catholics founded new confraternities to raise money for ransom.[69]

When Queen Mother Marie de Medici finally did act, she resorted to familiar defensive measures, banning all trade with North Africa and instituting naval patrols.[70] Yet the royal fleet, decimated by a half century of religious war, proved an inadequate deterrent. Historically, corsairs operating out of what early modern Europeans called Salé (modern-day Rabat)—chiefly the product of two expulsions from the Iberian Peninsula—had been more interested in settling Spanish scores than seizing Frenchmen.[71] Between 1613 and 1618, however, at least 120 Frenchmen became captives in Morocco, whose sultan rebuffed peace proposals carried by a Provençal nobleman and a Norman Knight of Malta.[72] Relations with the Ottoman regencies did not fare much better. In Tripoli, a brief consular absence might have provided the initial pretext for slave taking (150 from 1610 to 1612), but nowhere across the Barbary States could diplomats establish or enforce an effective road map for release.[73] A second Franco-Tunisian accord negotiated in 1612 resulted in only a partial slave exchange and recriminations that the Marseille emissary cared more about exporting Arabian horses than saving French lives.[74] Persistent ambushes afterward brought renewed protests about merchandise pilfered;[75] "husbands, brothers, and cousins" captured; and "small children or cabin boys trimmed by force."[76] With nearly four hundred Frenchmen in chains in Tunis by 1615 and another fifty just captured in Tripoli, Marseille financed yet another offensive that the next year yielded new provisions for curbing conversion rates and swapping slaves.[77] Unfortunately, rather than thwart apostasy, a provision for registering at the French consulate seems only to have confirmed the presence of renegades, and Tunisians released only a quarter of the French slaves.[78] In the meantime, ever since Flemish renegade-cum-corsair Simon Dansa had resparked hostilities in 1609 by stealing two cannons from Algiers and taking asylum in Marseille, regency and city had traded diplomats with even less fruitful results: flight in the case of two Marseille deputies bearing a captive-exchange offer,[79] and murder in the case of two Algerian ambassadors and their retinue waiting to ratify a peace treaty.

MURDER IN MARSEILLE

In March 1619, France and Algeria signed an agreement reaffirming each party's intention to comply with the Capitulations, though neither displayed particularly good faith in the months that followed.[80] While French galley captains stalled—not wanting to turn over valuable Algerian rowers—Algerian corsairs cruised, taking two hundred new French slaves by February 1620. Then in March, two sailors straggled into Marseille and related a terrible tale of a Provençal *polacre* (three-masted merchant ship) overtaken, its goods confiscated and crew beheaded, then tossed, one by one, into the sea. Grief quickly turned to fury. "One man had lost a son with all his means . . . one a father, . . . one a brother, along with all hope of fortune," recorded a pamphlet printed later that year. Soon two or three thousand people surrounded the waterfront mansion housing the Algerian embassy and a group of North African and Levantine merchants. While the mob grew increasingly frenzied, the Muslims stayed barricaded inside. Early Sunday morning, a few attempted to escape. "Some cast themselves into the sea and were immediately killed or drowned. Some made it to the countryside but were soon beaten to death by peasants and gardeners, and others who ran after them," the report stated. Afterward the populace invaded the residence, "killing and massacring anyone they found, sparing neither the ambassadors nor the others." When it was over, at least forty-eight men were dead.[81]

Four months later, the Marseille city council gave another version of events and attempted to justify its inaction: "It was impossible to check the violence of such a multitude," wrote the deputies in a defensive letter to the Algerian pasha, acknowledging that though "the personal rights of ambassadors were supposed to be inviolable . . . it was a completely unexpected accident, and a tumult so sudden could hardly have been predicted."[82] Promising that justice would be served, even as Louis XIII ordered the royal galleys on an Algerian campaign,[83] city consuls forwarded a ruling from the Parlement of Aix, which had condemned the perpetrators—among them a tailor, a porter, two master carpenters, a butcher, a potter, a galley sergeant, and a "redhead"—to death, the galleys, or the whip.[84] These assurances did not placate Algerian authorities, however. After an August riot instigated by the families of the dead, according to testimony from a French captive, they immediately imprisoned all French subjects in their territories. Although the Franco-Algerian peace accord remained technically unbroken, for the next eight years the two powers were unofficially at war.[85]

SEIZURE AT SEA

North African corsairs unchecked by Constantinople swarmed France's Mediterranean coastline in the 1620s.[86] Strongly armed and adapted for speed, carrying the minimum in provisions, their oar-powered brigantines, frigates, and feluccas—as well as the rare galley or galliot—outran and outgunned French merchant vessels and fishing craft that could neither fit nor afford bulky weaponry and personnel. Crossing the Strait of Gibraltar, round-bottomed sailing ships, like xebecs and pinks, also began loitering in the Gulf of Gascony, at the mouth of the Garonne River, and at the entrance to the La Rochelle canal to pluck French "sardines and flying fish" straight from the ocean.[87] No region of France ever endured territorial assaults with near the frequency of Italy[88] or Spain,[89] or on quite the scale of Ireland[90] or Iceland,[91] which lost four hundred men, women, and children in a single heist. Yet they occurred often enough for leaders in Marseille to forward *cahiers de doléances* (lists of grievances) to King Louis XIII about "the pirates of Tunis and Algiers, who . . . devastate all the merchants of your said city and other maritime places of your kingdom . . . [and] devour the blood of your poor subjects"; and for the Parlement of Brittany to complain about waters "utterly infested with Turkish pirates who commit great thefts" on land.[92]

The frequent assaults of the 1620s resulted in upward of a thousand French subjects in chains across Algiers, Tunis, Tripoli, and Morocco.[93] Since the vast majority of captives had encountered corsairs on open water, and only the rare woman traveled aboard ships, they tended to be seafaring men.[94] Generally hailing from maritime areas remote from the capital, and disproportionately Protestant though mostly Catholic (given the location of the "Huguenot Crescent" of settlement along France's coasts), these sailors and fishermen, pilgrims and traders, speaking regional dialects and perhaps a smattering of the Mediterranean pidgin Lingua Franca, possessed stronger ties to communities of faith and geography than to France as a whole.[95] Before the mast, however, Provençals, Gascons, Basques, and Bretons had to be at least dimly aware that their lives and liberty depended on more than the navigational skills of shipmates or intercession from God.

During interludes of Franco-Barbary peace, bilateral treaties offered protection on the basis of sovereign—not provincial or civic—standing, judged by language, dress, and, to some degree, papers. While the monarchy did not require individual travelers to hold passports attesting to their personal status, some passengers carried letters of introduction and baptismal certificates, and at each port of call ships picked up safe-conducts, which were supposed to exempt bearers from attack.[96] During times of war, distinguishing friend from foe was crucial for avoiding hostile fire. Yet the various nautical badges of identity—credentials, salutations, flags, and architecture—were infinitely disposable, forgeable, and malleable. Documents could be faked or tossed overboard, Turkish and Arabic speakers hidden below, merchant vessels rigged with cannons, enemies camouflaged as allies. "But alas! No sooner did we come within a musket's range than the multicolored Dutch banners disappeared," related an aristocrat from Anjou, ambushed near the islands of Bayonne, and "the mastheads and stern castles . . . [were] immediately draped with taffeta flags of every color, decorated and embroidered with stars, crescents, and crossed swords and foreign emblems and writings."[97]

When vanquishers shouting in "diverse tongues," wearing "strange garments," and brandishing "unfamiliar arms" poured onto deck at the moment of surrender, soon-to-be captives had an interest in dissimulating identity too. In case documentary evidence of origin did not suffice to avert enslavement, they scrambled to conceal all signs of wealth and to hide a few coins on (or inside) their persons—a practice dubbed "chrysophagia"—hoping to rate a low ransom price and retain some money to pay it.[98]

ENSLAVEMENT ON SHORE

Though generally stunned by their abrupt reversal of fortune, Frenchmen seized at sea had, in fact, embarked on a highly ritualized and regulated process for transforming people into chattel. Beginning on board with the loss of clothing and valuables, it continued on shore as fresh catches were marched from the harbor, "amid laughter and infinite jeers" and "the blare of trumpets and *atabals*," to an audience with the North African ruler, attended by European consuls and, in some places, a special officer responsible for supervising the distribution of booty.[99] As long as their political attachments and circumstances of capture qualified these human spoils as valid prizes, a Quranic injunction allowed the pasha, dey, bey, or sultan a percentage for his own use.[100] He picked out beautiful women for his harem, young boys for his entourage, and strong or skilled men for his construction projects, medical team, shipyards, and workshops. Following the Ottoman tradition of putting ostensibly deracinated captives loyal only to the government into sensitive administrative and military posts, he chose lettered men as secretaries.[101] As for noblemen, he attempted to hold on to them in expectation of colossal ransoms.

Leftover individuals went up for sale. At the slave bazaar, or *badistan* (from the Turkish word for covered market) as it was known to Christians, vendors spent the morning parading half-naked new arrivals for inspection. Modesty may have allowed females to wait indoors, but males remained in the open, where prospective buyers tried to determine health and social standing, and prospective bondsmen tried to withhold any information that might result in a more uncomfortable or extended period of servitude. Unlike the pretentious Spanish, "who prefer[red] to spend longer or even die as slaves than lower themselves a little," as one interested observer claimed, the French evinced a pragmatic flair for deceit.[102] Thus even as within France legislation sought to fix rank with apparel, in North Africa a Knight of Malta already leveled by the social uniform of slavery tried to pass for a simple soldier, and a gentleman assumed "a perpetual affectation of rusticity and dirtiness."[103] In response, purchasing agents scanned physiognomies, and when they spotted "someone with a delicate complexion and hands . . . infer[red] that he is rich."[104] On the auction block by afternoon, prices stamped on their heads and shoulders, captive Frenchmen lost further remnants of their humanity. As Barbary slaves, their experience varied by place, time, and chance.

BARBARY CONDITIONS

One axiom held that suffering worsened from east to west. Certainly, Frenchmen in Morocco, whose sultans earned a name for gratuitous violence and demanded head-for-head exchanges rather than just ransom, often endured longer slaveries and, until late in the seventeenth century, a more isolated existence than their countrymen in Algiers, Tunis, and

Tripoli. Everywhere in North Africa, however, detained Christians belonged to one of two categories: those who worked and those who waited. Masters usually allowed highborn slaves to buy a work exemption. Among the laboring sorts—who lacked the means to pay for leisure—unfortunates dispatched to the galleys were by far the worst off. Chained to benches below deck for months at a stretch, allocated a bare minimum of hard tack, vinegar, and water, beaten if they did not keep up, and left to defecate where they sat, rowers regularly succumbed to hunger and thirst, the unrelenting pace, and the brutal stench. Even youth could not endure this "unbearable drudgery," several French slaves reported from Algiers, and many of them renounced their faith to escape it.[105] Luckily, this wretched destiny befell few Frenchmen, apparently counted among "people exempt from the oar because they are too feeble," even before the first third of the seventeenth century when the galley went mostly out of use in North Africa.[106] But captive mariners on sailing ships, "heaped with blows and in constant moral danger," perhaps fared only slightly better. According to a frequent stereotype about Muslim laziness and lack of naval skills, "when [Turks] go to sea, they do nothing but take tobacco and sleep; the poor Christians do all the work."[107]

Slaves who remained on land had somewhat improved chances for survival. The minority sent to the interior as agricultural and domestic workers may have toiled without succor. By contrast, water carriers, rope makers, stable hands, wood haulers, child minders, shopkeepers, welders, millers, quarriers, cooks, scribes, launderers, masons, weavers, surgeons, clerics, and jacks-of-all-trades in urban centers had the possibility of enjoying relative comfort in households. For them, the greatest variable was their master. Of the ethnic and religious groups in North Africa, Moriscos had the worst reputation, Jews—who circumvented prohibitions against slaveholding with silent Muslim partners—the best. French captives found renegade owners to be either particularly kind or callous, affording former coreligionists and compatriots special privileges or especially brutal treatment. Meanwhile, slaves of the state, though provided meager rations and a skimpy clothing allowance—no more than a shirt, shorts, and a pair of sandals per year and fifteen ounces of bread per day, according to one account; one outfit and two black rolls, according to another—received some material and spiritual support from resident consuls in most locations.[108]

Thus rather than experiencing "natal alienation" and "social death" associated with more extreme forms of servitude, French public and private slaves in North Africa maintained kinship ties and legal status.[109] They interacted with European traders. They registered acts at royal chanceries. Perhaps most important, they sent and received letters from home. Sanctioned as a means of soliciting ransom money, and addressed most often to relatives and civic leaders (though occasionally to the king), such correspondence invoked physical and spiritual suffering and offered tactics for restraining corsairs. In addition, during a period when enslavement remained an everyday hazard and emancipation a rare reward, for the most part locally arranged, pleas from captive subjects also attempted to show geographic loyalty, religious faith, social worth, and economic utility, all of which would be squandered should their authors die or convert to Islam. Generally produced by scribes, slave letters were transported by an ad hoc postal system operated by merchants, religious organizations, and, later, agents of the state. While one member of the educated elite paid a Moor "to give [him] paper and the arm of a quill," similarities in handwriting, phonetic spelling, and disparities between text and signature indicate that the mass of illiterate slaves depended on learned acquaintances—like a certain "François the Student," who was "always writing letters without payment, though he would accept a complimentary drink."[110] Back in France, one former captive went on pilgrimage to hand-deliver dispatches from comrades in servitude; from North Africa, associates of a Catholic secret society marked outgoing missives with small red crosses.[111]

At night, those male captives in Algiers, Tunis, and Tripoli belonging either to leaders or to prosperous owners who lodged them for a fee slept in special jails, known to the French as *bagnes* (from the Italian for bath). In the Moroccan capital of Meknes, after initially boarding them among Jews in the *mellah* (Jewish quarter), the sultan allocated Christian slaves a separate neighborhood popularly known as the Canot. Elsewhere in the Moroccan kingdom they lived in *matemores* (Arabic for subterranean silo).[112] Witnesses almost universally agreed that the round Moroccan structures, originally designed for storing grain, dug several feet underground and accessible only by rope ladders, were stinking, hot, dreadful places. Along their circumference, men separated by geographic origin lay shackled to the wall on damp rush mats occasionally covered with a piece of animal hide, and at the center stood a chamber pot.[113] But opinion was divided regarding the two-story freestanding buildings with small rooms around central courtyards that boarded captive Christians in the Ottoman regencies. Were they comfortable dwellings filled with drinking, polyglot conversation, and good cheer, or "sites of horror, where smoke from cooking fires . . . noise, cries, blows, and tumult reign"?[114]

A Mercedarian friar who described "the poor slaves . . . bedded much worse than horses and cows . . . in stables and cowsheds in France" was nevertheless impressed by the bagnes' Catholic, Protestant, and Orthodox chapels, which "were decently furnished . . . and did not lack for lavish

ornaments."[115] In these houses of God, captive clergymen excused from
work and free priests paid by donation led prayers. In slave-run taverns,
reportedly also patronized by Turks and renegades, inmates from Stock-
holm to Seville bartered stolen goods for extra food and home-brew, and
traded stories of the outside world. Despite such freewheeling charms,
this international, interfaith community did not live in perfect harmony.
Factions clashed and, on several occasions, revolted.[116] To check a potentially explosive situation and prevent breakouts, a staff drawn from
the captive population and society at large monitored behavior and
tracked movement. In Morocco, an elected majordomo represented the
interests of enslaved compatriots; elsewhere an *écrivain principal* occupied an analogous position. Converts to Islam often filled the post of
gardien-bashi, or concierge. His duties included punishing troublemakers,
distributing rations, and taking attendance at sunrise and sunset.

BARBARY DANGERS

The mere breath of hundreds of men disturbed some residents of the slave
prisons. Others complained of cramped quarters and noxious smells,
which, along with bodily disequilibrium and providence, they blamed
for contagion. Indeed, plague was endemic to the entire Mediterranean
region starting in the Middle Ages. Though it had mostly receded from
France by the late seventeenth century—until, in 1720, spectacularly
flaring in Marseille—outbreaks remained common across North Africa.[117] Hospitals opened by Catholic orders, which treated members of
all churches, could accommodate only a fraction of the sick, and scholars
estimate mortality rates from malnutrition, mistreatment, and malady at
17 to 20 percent annually.[118] Whatever number of enslaved Christians actually contracted pestilence, however, French observers believed it higher
for Muslims, whose allegedly sinful practices invited divine punishment
and whom superstition prevented from taking precautions.[119]

　　Like many early modern European polemicists, French captives commonly characterized Islam itself as an abomination—a false, depraved,
patchwork, and cruel religion. In personal letters and published accounts, they also regularly accused North Africans of indulging in the
aberrant vice of sodomy.[120] Therefore, they suggested, until God meted
out final retribution, Christians had to ward off not only plague but
also the dangerous sexuality of Muslims. And lest the same traits that
disseminated disease and deviance adhere to enslaved Frenchmen, they
had to guard against changing into what a consul of a later period labeled "an intermediate class of men who, like amphibious animals, seem

to comprise two elements. I speak of renegades, who have renounced Christianity to embrace *Mahometanism*."[121] Implying that polluted bodies engendered corrupted souls, they feared particularly for adolescent ship hands and language apprentices (*jeunes de langue*), whose tender age made them candidates both to satisfy "the disgusting brutality of these infidels" and to enter the Ottoman bureaucracy.[122]

According to French eyewitnesses, becoming a Muslim required just a few steps: pointing to the sky, proclaiming the existence of one God with Muhammad as his prophet, surrendering long hair, donning Turkish-style head covering and costume, taking an Arabic name, and submitting to circumcision. To gesture upward and utter the words commonly transliterated as "la illah la &c" was to commit to conversion, a process of putting on and casting off. The neophyte shaved his skull, drew on a white robe, and, most important, swapped his headgear, giving up his hat and "taking the turban," a symbolic act and an expression synonymous with apostasy—in most French minds tantamount to treason. Fitted out in fresh clothes, he ostensibly became what he wore.[123] If the convert was a Jew, he was supposedly required to pass through the intermediary religion of Christianity by eating pork and accepting Jesus.[124] Otherwise, all that remained to try on was a new moniker and to cut off was a foreskin. Public celebrations and almsgiving followed this "blood baptism," when—European observers recorded—the sumptuously attired convert was paraded through the streets.[125]

On paper, French slaves deemed it unthinkable that a Christian might accept out of conviction the teachings of a prophet sometimes branded the "great imposter."[126] Though regularly raising the threat of apostasy in redemption petitions, they also deemed unforgivable that anyone might take on an enemy faith as a direct response to captivity's travails, no matter how excruciating, let alone use religious defection as a means of social mobility. In practice, whether persuaded by dogma (which did happen), constrained by youth (most made the switch between the ages of ten and eighteen), or lured by opportunity (even if conversion did not bring immediate freedom), considerable numbers of captives with French origins did "turn Turk."[127] Rates in Algiers may have reached 20 percent.[128]

ANALYZING APOSTASY

For sailors and roustabouts destined for lives of salt pork and scurvy, not to mention social misfits, spiritual nonconformists, and economic go-getters stifled by French hierarchy and ever increasing orthodoxy, North Africa's relatively open, tolerant societies may have held considerable appeal. During the first half of the seventeenth century—and to a lesser extent before and after—renegades from Amiens to Antibes married Muslim women above their station, entered the janissary corps, and became powerful ra'is. Through conversion they sometimes escaped debt, criminal prosecution, and religious harassment. As entrepreneurs, physicians, engineers, and public servants, they accrued wealth and prestige. In Tripoli, one French convert briefly ascended to the position of dey.[129] Speaking multiple languages, renegades made excellent interpreters. Possessing foreign cultural knowledge and—as chancery records and naming practices attest—enduring bonds of affection, duty, and trust with family and friends from home,[130] they were well positioned to fill a role afterward taken over by Jews, Armenians, and Greeks as commercial, diplomatic, and intellectual brokers between Christian and Muslim lands.[131]

A notable French renegade who maintained a connection to Christendom was Thomas d'Arcos. Captured near Toulon by Algerian corsairs in 1625 at the age of about fifty-two, this native of either Rouen or La Ciotat and former secretary to a cardinal spent six months enslaved in Tunis before a Corsican merchant from Marseille paid at least a portion of his ransom. Perhaps the transaction did not go through or he was recaptured on his way home, but d'Arcos was still in North Africa three years later and converted to Islam four years after that, taking the name Osman and living as a Muslim until his death, probably in 1637.[132] Before and after his apostasy, d'Arcos communicated with associates in Toulon and Marseille, as well as the humanist magistrate Nicolas Claude Fabri de Peiresc in Aix-en-Provence. With this distinguished correspondent, he exchanged manuscripts, curios, and animal specimens—ostrich eggs, a fossilized elephant tooth, chameleons, and Roman medals—for books, eyeglasses, wine, and other French delicacies.

While not going so far as to try ejecting d'Arcos from the Republic of Letters, Peiresc did not accept his friend's religious transformation without comment. Writing in 1632, he affirmed himself "so scandalized that I do not know how best to express the sentiment of displeasure I feel." In his defense, the new Muslim proffered oblique assurances that he had remained Catholic at heart. "Excision has not yet gained anything over me," he asserted in 1633, "and the initial sign of salvation that the church gave me will never be erased from my soul, even though my dress has changed."[133] Echoing a favored inquisitorial distinction[134]—likewise justified by the Muslim doctrine of *taqiyya*, or prudential dissimulation[135]—this convert swore that his inner faith did not match his outward appearance. Such a message may have satisfied Peiresc, as it would have the episcopal tribunals that tried and most often pardoned French renegades wishing to reconcile with the church. But it did not necessarily accord with the material and geographical aspects of religious identification that less erudite Christian converts to Islam appeared to share.[136]

CREATING BINARIES

D'Arcos claimed to be a crypto-Turk, untouched by the place he inhabited, the prayers he said, the food he ate, the clothes he wore, and the circumcision he had undergone. Accepting such declarations at face value, some scholars have situated renegades—as others have analogous Jewish converts to Catholicism (*marranos*)[137]—at the vanguard of modernity, because of their seeming ability to disassociate belief from behavior.[138] Clearly, Mediterranean travel and its flip side Mediterranean captivity provided countless occasions for instrumental pretense.[139] At sea and in shackles, for the sake of self-preservation or self-promotion, travelers and captives lied, played tricks, and even committed apostasy. As important, these two politically messy, socially mixed, confessionally muddled, multiethnic, and multilingual contexts also created possibilities for less purposeful kinds of multivalence. They helped form individuals who straddled cultures and syncretized creeds. Such spiritual wanderers, culinary sophisticates, sartorial adventurers, and economic vagabonds could not always cleanly separate the various strands that made them.[140]

Evidence of hybridity in the seventeenth-century Mediterranean provides a refreshing antidote to contemporary "East vs. West" mythology. In the early modern period as today, however, a dualistic perspective better served the various people and institutions dedicated to reversing North African servitude and reintegrating Provençal, Breton, and other slaves with ties to France. Those involved in the double project of "redemption," like captives awaiting "salvation," found a useful parallel between unbinding the body and revealing an authentic soul. Thus while pragmatically operating in a world whose inhabitants may have, in fact, possessed manifold allegiances and malleable identities, concerned families, town councils, Catholic and Protestant associations, and, in later periods, French rulers sought symbolically to restore what they imagined to be the essential natures of relatives, neighbors, colleagues, brethren, subjects, and nationals caught on the wrong side of a clear Christian-Muslim divide. In other words, as Fernand Braudel put it, the permeability of that frontier and the "fraternal alliance" among the region's peripatetic denizens "would have been even more evident if . . . states had not required appearances to be preserved."[141]

In France, a state whose power and prestige rested on the success-ful incorporation of people and provinces, appearances were preserved through individual, diplomatic, legal, and evangelical means, intermit-tently military and often ritual—few of which were directly ordered by the crown. These strategies against contagion and transculturation, mostly devised by municipal bodies and religious organizations with disparate objectives, nonetheless furthered French political consolida-tion and religious convergence. Once released, according to the ideal suggested by private letters, printed accounts, and public processions, Barbary captives from low stations and marginal territories would be cleansed of sexual, miasmic, and spiritual contaminants. Out of slav-ery, they could reassume their rightful places in the social order: as pro-ductive professionals, heads of household, devout Christians, and loyal subjects.

CHAPTER TWO

Salvation without the State

In December 1622 "the poor afflicted and unfortunate captives" held in the Moroccan capital of Marrakech addressed Louis XIII by letter. In meticulous handwriting and florid prose, "remonstrating very humbly, with all possible honor, respect, obedience, and fidelity due to [his] very Christian and sacred majesty," the captives laid out their claim for deliverance. First, the seven signatories, taken from a twenty-gun, 108-man galleon armed in Marseille and bearing a royal commission to make war "against the Turkish corsairs and other pirates," suggested that liberty was just reward for aid and loyalty to the crown. After all, they had been fighting at their own expense "for the service of your majesty and the good and peace of our country." In addition, "clemency, piety, and . . . devotion" to suffering subjects were established attributes of good kings. Their king should preserve French bodies from "this cruel and insupportable captivity" and follow Christ in becoming "the second redeemer to so many poor languishing souls." Otherwise, these self-declared loyal subjects might commit the ultimate betrayal. Comparing Islam to a raging sea and themselves to sailors aboard an unworthy boat battered by a violent storm, they warned that some of their companions had already "sunk into the abyss of paganism."[1]

The king who would come to be known as "Louis the Just" may have accepted these arguments, predicated on notions of impermanent slavery and selective emancipation, not to mention contractual monarchy. Certainly he appreciated the dangers of religious heterodoxy and the accompanying perils of political subversion. For the previous year and a half, royal forces had been quelling resistance to increased restrictions on Huguenot autonomy, and in October he had celebrated the submission of the Protestant strongholds Poitou and Languedoc.[2] Louis XIII also appreciated the value of the captive seamen's home base, Marseille. Despite its historically contentious relationship with Paris, the city had long played a special role in both protecting and enriching his realm. During a tour only four weeks earlier, the king had admired Marseille's ancient harbor, where ships loaded and unloaded sheaves of grain, bolts of cloth, and crates of spices, oil, cheese, tobacco, soap, wood, coral, metal, salted fish, and dried fruit.[3] He had also admired Marseille's diverse population, ceremonially flanked by guards in costumes of savages, Americans, Indians, Turks, and Moors, displaying its openness to the outside world.[4]

Yet France's principal Mediterranean seaport was more than a transport hub for profitable commodities. For more than a century, Marseille had also taken the lead in keeping out those literal and figurative Barbary contagions—plague, sodomy, and apostasy—widely believed to threaten the kingdom as a whole. Not only did Marseille's galleys (partially powered by "Turks") patrol for sea rovers, but its grandees, merchants, and cleric-soldiers moonlighting as diplomats regularly spent personal funds to break the shackles of countrymen. The city's Trinitarian convent was the only one in France that never strayed from its redemptive mission.[5] Its Chamber of Commerce maintained a triangular correspondence with ministers in Paris and consuls across North Africa about the fate of French captives. And as of January 1622, the city—along with Toulon—had assumed responsibility for receiving every ship arriving from the Ottoman Empire and Morocco at its sanitation facilities (*lazarets*). There, inspectors screened passengers and cargo for disease, fumigated fabric with herbs and spices, dipped letters in vinegar, and prescribed varying periods of quarantine.[6]

Though this dual status as entry point and bulwark fit Marseille's independent streak and commercial orientation, its inhabitants and institutions still wanted more royal resources allocated to plague surveillance, corsair combat, and slave redemption. So while municipal sons held in North Africa implored their sovereign to fulfill his sacred and temporal duties, municipal fathers back in France addressed the heavens, praying that "this great king [who] has reduced the [Protestant] rebels to obedience . . . can stamp Africa and Palestine with the fleur-de-lys and strike terror in the hearts of infidel pirates."[7] By helping to finance French spiritual and material purification as well as North African submission via Marseille, Louis XIII would be recognizing the capacity of an unstable port to serve the cause of stability.

SLAVES INTO SUBJECTS

Neither God nor king paid immediate heed to these calls.[8] However much Louis XIII valued French health, wealth, religious unity, and sociopolitical concord, he directed resources to the problems of North African corsairing and captivity only when not distracted by anti-Huguenot warfare at home and anti-Habsburg warfare abroad. Therefore, apart from laying plans to expand France's tiny Mediterranean fleet and making brief shows of naval force, mild attempts at diplomacy, and limited payments, Louis XIII followed his predecessors and left slave liberation to those people and places affected most directly.[9]

Throughout his reign, responsibility continued to fall either to the victims themselves, their friends, families, and communities, the Frères de la Sainte Trinité and Pères de la Merci, or members of additional Counter-Reformation orders. None of these parties had an explicit stake in shoring up the French state. Yet by even grudgingly repatriating slaves with dependents, valuable skills, friends in high places, or proclivities toward Islam, all played a role in materially strengthening it. Starting in the 1630s, multimedia innovations introduced by the rival friars in a quest for royal patronage and ransom funds made even greater symbolic contributions.

These pictures, processions, and publications helped characterize "slavery" for ordinary French subjects. They also circulated images of North Africa as a diseased den of depravity whose inhabitants regularly seduced or compelled Christians to sin against nature and God. Conversely, they projected an idealized vision of France, whose church and king reigned over a harmonious polity. During a period of economic stagnation, confessional strife, civil unrest, and sporadic eruptions of pestilence, they demonstrated to a broad audience the positive effects of Catholic charity and Bourbon rule, while defining French belonging against the negative model of North African captivity.

Salvation without the state thus laid the groundwork for state building through redemption. Beyond a territorial negotiation between center and periphery—Paris and Marseille—the transformation of Barbary slaves into French subjects also depended on the interplay of policy and ritual across the Mediterranean.

SELF-THEFT AND SELF-PURCHASE

In North Africa, French captives who did not aspire to martyrdom or apostasy had just two options: attempting escape or paying ransom. Mutinies succeeded rarely—as when a sailor from the Breton oyster-producing town of Cancale and two others from nearby Saint-Malo led a pack of northern European Protestants brandishing pocket knives to take over an Algerian privateer cruising near Majorca, or when twenty-four captives apparently chained up twenty-five drunken crew members and sailed a thirty-six-cannon warship to Genoa.[10] Unable to abscond overland once Spain and Portugal lost their North African territories, slaves also tried—and most often failed—to escape by sea. From inland Moroccan cities, they paid guides known as *metadors* to lead them to the coast; from Ottoman ports, they launched stolen boats or hand-made rafts.[11] In spite of repeated French bans against boarding fugitives, a more popular flight technique was stowing away on visiting merchantmen, whose captains usually balked at turning over compatriots. Like their counterparts in France, North African authorities dealt severely with runaways, cutting off an ear, nose, or tongue as disincentive and example.

Self-purchase carried fewer risks, especially for the lucky few with insurance policies. Introduced to France by Italian, Spanish, and Flemish immigrants, maritime coverage initially indemnified only boats and cargo from "the sea, fire, the winds, Turks, friends and enemies and every other misfortune whether caused by God or man," for rates ranging from 8 to 14 percent of merchandise value.[12] Then, with the advent of personal protection during the seventeenth century (against the loss of liberty but not life), guarantors began promising the acquittal of ransom within fifteen days plus passage home.[13] As a precondition, underwriters expected ship captains to take reasonable precautions for avoiding corsairs and refused compensation in suspected cases of cowardice or negligence. One late seventeenth-century case involved a captain from Toulon who had abandoned ship with his crew for fear of imminent capture. Given that "captivity in the hands of Turks is worse than death . . . [and] it is always better to preserve the king's subjects and citizens than to lose them," the Parlement of Provence judged the Marseille insurers liable.[14]

Everyone else had to beg cash from France or borrow it in North Africa. Only rarely did captive Frenchmen accumulate enough capital through theft, trade, or tavern keeping to go free. For larger sums, they turned to consuls, merchants, and renegades whose advances to compatriots and former coreligionists generally stipulated repayment plus interest to designated colleagues or kin in France. A chancery act from Tunis, for example, shows one Ragep Vicard lending eighteen piastres in ransom money to André Pourquier of Six-Fours in Provence, with the provision that the slave reimburse the convert's father inside twenty days of arrival home.[15] Sephardic Jews, established in the Ottoman Empire and Morocco and possessing protected minority (*dhimmi*) status and contacts throughout the Mediterranean region and northern Europe, also made direct transfers to Christian captives of various geographical origins.[16]

CAPTIVES AND KINDRED

What they could not acquire abroad, slaves hoped to garner from home. Very occasionally North African masters granted captives provisional release to take collection in France. More often, municipal institutions stepped in, sending money set aside or bequeathed for the purpose.[17] Otherwise, relatives motivated by a combined sense of religious duty, familial honor, and legal obligation did their best to raise funds or, infrequently, procure a Turk for exchange. "I beg you to go to Livorno" (a major entrepôt for servile Muslims), wrote one Provençal captive to his father in Toulon, "and see if you can set free the sharif's son and another Moor to acquire my liberty."[18] In fact, both the Roman law guiding France's southern regions and the customary codes of some northern provinces compelled parents, spouses, siblings, and children to take all possible measures to deliver relations.[19] A son "must not lose a moment in pulling his father out of the hands of infidels," read one treatise on inheritance. "He must drop everything and borrow the necessary sum to buy him back from enemies of the Christian name," or else become not only *indigne* (unworthy) to receive any legacy but also *ingrat* (ungrateful), thus undeserving of any gifts from the person left in captivity. Another legist noted that the same penalty applied to a daughter.[20] Meanwhile, two seventeenth-century rulings required mothers and fathers to pay off ransom debts incurred by their children.[21]

Thus to rescue Barbary slaves, French households sold off possessions and shifted assets. Cousins called in loans. Wives, sisters, and daughters mortgaged communal property. Although under normal circumstances, codices and customs expressly forbade women from alienating their dowries, statutes made exceptions for those with family members in captivity.[22] This is precisely what Pierre Callabre from a town in the Vendée wanted his wife to do, asking her to sell her *propre* to free him from Algiers.[23] Jurists across the kingdom also agreed that married women and unmarried girls under the age of majority who ordinarily needed male consent either to buy or sell goods, or enter into valid contracts, could do so without permission in order to release family members from involuntary confinement.[24] Perhaps unaware of such explicit legal dispensations, however, enslaved Frenchmen frequently conferred power of attorney on female relatives to raise money and make ransom arrangements. From Tunis, for example, Laurens Arnaud hired two Livornese merchants as debt collectors, instructing them to turn over all proceeds to his wife, Marguerite Gantleaume, in the Provençal village of La Ciotat. Then he gave her proxy to deposit nine hundred livres with intermediaries for transfer to the French consul who would secure the slave's release.[25]

Not all women waited to receive instructions from afar before taking matters into their own hands (Figure 2). While a wealthy mother from Marseille chartered a ship to deliver her son, the Chevalier de Romilly, from Tunis, wives of more modest means who did not wish to become poorer widows, along with widows who could ill afford to lose wage-earning sons, sometimes hired agents to travel to North Africa.[26] In February 1625, for instance, Jane Bérard, wife of Halexandre Helbo; Nicolle Vinet, wife of Jan Janaud; and Michelle Ollivaud, wife of Jan Bertho—all from the village of Montoir-de-Bretagne in the parish of Saint-Nazaire—made an agreement with a royal notary in Nantes to return their husbands from Algiers. Together they entrusted him with about two thousand livres, not counting 250 in fees and expenses, on his pledge to ransom the men or, if they had escaped or died, return the money. Since the three women were illiterate, male witnesses signed in their stead.[27]

Figure 2. Women as intermediaries in slave ransoms. "Le Rachat de l'esclave," engraving by Jacques Aliamet (1785) from a painting by Nicolaes Berghem (ca 1675). © Musée national de la Marine, ph. 154 463.

During the early seventeenth century, French captives in North Africa sold for two to five hundred livres apiece, the price of a thousand chickens or ten years' salary for a valet.[28] Those women unable to come up with such large amounts petitioned religious and government officials, emphasizing the absence of male breadwinners to rhetorical advantage. For example, in 1634 the wives of several sailors captured by Saletian corsairs from vessels armed in Saint-Malo successfully solicited the Estates of Brittany for ten thousand livres in ransom.[29] By responding positively to such female requests, this regional body—like the Marseille Chamber of Commerce, town councils, and fraternal orders that also appropriated funds for redemption—prevented women in precarious financial straits from further calling on the resources of church and state.[30] By sanctioning females to act without male protectors, France's legal system actually encouraged the salvation of men—and in turn repaired the fractured hierarchical family unit at the basis of French society.

SLAVES AND STRANGERS

The suspension of gender disabilities for the sake of social stability found a parallel in the realm of religion. Though French Catholics and Protestants mostly relied on separate channels for rescuing brethren, both groups were occasionally willing to overlook confessional distinctions in saving slaves from Muslim lands.[31] Like members of the official church, Huguenots tended to assign local responsibility for gathering charity and then employ coreligionists to carry the combined proceeds to North Africa. A few families with commercial ties to Salé, in particular, regularly redeemed slaves. Over a twenty-five-year period in the seventeenth century, for example, traffickers from La Rochelle signed at least seventy contracts that spelled out terms for negotiating ransoms and assuming risk at rates of up to 22 percent. At least one document bound these Protestant traders to ferry currency on behalf of the Trinitarians.[32] Even after the so-called Reformed Religion was banned from France in 1685, Huguenot exiles in Morocco still helped the Mercedarians liberate French Catholics.[33] Conversely, the redemptive orders accepted alms from Protestants and may have spent Catholic charity on "heretics," if only to create opportunities for proselytizing.[34]

Diasporic settlement, proficiency in multiple languages, and, in North Africa, posts as government advisors made Sephardic Jews ideal ransom brokers too. Members of bicoastal families—many with ties to Livorno, some living in southwestern France—carried out orders from around Europe and received commissions of 14 to 15 percent plus interest.[35]

French slaves acknowledged the crucial role of Jewish go-betweens in issuing bills of exchange and interceding with rulers; French friars recognized them (not always positively) for providing credit, translation, and even lodging.[36] Inside the kingdom of France, Jews were religious aliens selectively tolerated in the service of economic prosperity; beyond its borders, however, they were commercial middlemen and cultural guides commonly (if unwittingly) engaged in the service of religious purity, bolstering French Christianity by helping to remove slaves from the influence of Islam. Like women, Huguenots, and renegades, who also aided erstwhile brethren, Jews were excluded figures who became agents of inclusion.

DEFINING FRENCHMEN, FINANCING DIPLOMACY

For consuls and envoys, a principal difficulty in freeing countrymen from Ottoman bagnes and Moroccan matemores was establishing who, at least for the purposes of redemption, counted as French. Generally, representatives of France—as often as not hailing from Marseille, and perhaps seeking to apply the exceptional privilege granted that seaport—favored an expansive definition. They claimed both longtime expatriates and foreigners either married in French territory or serving under French flag.[37] Not surprisingly, North African rulers sought to leave out not only members of those categories but even those slaves they acknowledged as French subjects seized during combat or while working on enemy ships. An additional hindrance to the recovery of French captives was the constant delays—and demands for monetary compensation—by the commanders of privately owned galleys before returning promised Muslim slaves.

After a decade of failed Marseille embassies, Sanson Napollon, a Corsican immigrant and experienced merchant-envoy, tried his hand at freeing Frenchmen. In 1624, with a two-year-long epidemic having killed off huge numbers of inhabitants in Tunis,[38] he obtained the release of what may have been the last 150 French subjects detained, paying more than half the cost of ransom, transport, and quarantine from his own pocket.[39] This servile French absence seems to have lasted five years. It might have lasted longer had Louis XIII enforced the timely repatriation of Tunisian rowers and the Parlement of Provence not ordered the execution of a captured renegade.[40]

Liberating eight hundred slaves, mostly Provençals, from Algiers proved a greater challenge. When Napollon reached that regency in June 1626, armed with orders from the Ottoman sultan and the French king, he found plague raging, captives dying, and a pasha tactically unwilling to release more than eighty men or finalize any treaty without the fulfillment of two lingering demands: the return of the cannons stolen by Simon Dansa, and the return of all Algerians enslaved in Marseille and Toulon.[41] Further adding to Napollon's difficulties, Louis XIII, perennially strapped for cash, had his own requirement: shifting the monetary onus for redemption off the royal treasury.

In late 1627, therefore, the king directed all communities "whence slaves in Algiers were native" to contribute two hundred livres a head to buy back their inhabitants.[42] Toulon took out several loans to pay its share, but other southern cities and towns showed less eagerness to comply.[43] The consuls of Fréjus and Martigues insisted they had no captives in Algiers; delegates from Six-Fours, Ollioules, and Cannes proposed giving a smaller amount, proportional to the scale of their North African trade.[44] In Marseille a *crie publique* went out for those with relatives in captivity to register their names at city hall. Clearly, families that might have scrimped and scrounged to liberate a single person hoped that in the case of a large group, the king would pick up the tab. In the end, a modest royal allowance and donations eked out locally provided Napollon with enough money both to reimburse a French galley commander for the cost of the disputed cannons and Algerian rowers and to liberate three hundred Frenchmen, though he far exceeded his budget paying off officials before he departed from Algiers.[45]

Such overspending on just a portion of the French slaves may have helped sour Louis XIII on state-sponsored, locally executed redemptions. Still, the resulting peace settlement—signed in September 1628 and published in the quasi-official *Mercure françois*—promised to be "highly useful" for French commerce, competition, and Catholicism. According to France's consul to Algiers, it not only benefited trade but encouraged "these corsairs to turn their forces against the English, Flemish, Italians, and Spanish," while liberating individuals "in danger of perverting their religion."[46] Furthermore, it afforded explicit legal protection against the perceived problem of forced conversion. Besides requiring voluntary renegades to make public declaration before the divan, the treaty stipulated that Algerians "may under no circumstances take boys and compel them to renounce their faith, nor have them cut or circumcised, using violence and threats against them."[47]

Algiers won some limited concessions too. One clause confirmed that France's "freedom principle," in practice inapplicable to Muslim slaves acquired by French arms or money, did in theory cover Algerians fleeing other countries. Another verified that French émigrés traveling on foreign vessels and French subjects initiating violence at sea were fair game for the regency's corsairs. This implied that until the negotiation of a more favorable accord, despite the many French captives officially reclaimed as invalid prizes, there would always be more with disputed origins left to procure their own freedom from Algiers. The largest threat to this paper peace, however, were France's own sea rovers—who repeatedly exploited their new ability to approach Algerian vessels by killing, enslaving, and selling Algerian crews.[48]

Tripoli also had plenty of its own "pirates," and from Constantinople the French ambassador registered his protests about them with the sultan.[49] But without representation on the ground, there was no one to challenge illegal enslavements. Thus in 1624, when yet another Marseille merchant crossed the Mediterranean to bring home one hundred captives, he put the gears in motion to leave behind a permanent French consul.[50] The appointed attaché, however, was not particularly effective. In 1631, during his second year in office, 250 French slaves were taken in a matter of six months. "There is more to fear from this place," wrote one frustrated Marseille envoy, "than from Algiers and Tunis together."[51]

COMPETING FOR RELIGIOUS PURITY
AND POLITICAL STATUS

In ten years, Marseille had not succeeded in ending Barbary slave taking. Nor could it keep France entirely safe from plague, which killed off a large portion of the kingdom's population between 1629 and 1630 and prompted the extension of the city's lazaret.[52] The seaport had, however, at least spearheaded the recovery of some southern subjects from Algiers, Tunis, and Tripoli. For westerners lingering in Morocco, the original éminence grise did the same. As Capuchin advisor to Richelieu, Joseph Le Clerc du Tremblay—"Father Joseph," as he was better known—had given up youthful dreams of launching a crusade against the Ottoman Empire in favor of planning evangelical missions to Muslim territories.[53] In 1624, he sent several Italian friars to Tunis with instructions to start consoling Catholics and (discreetly) proselytizing to Muslims, and arranged for three French friars to accompany Knight of Malta Isaac de Razilly, a veteran North African diplomat and future North American colonizer, on his third embassy to Morocco. Unfortunately, like previous forays to the region's sole independent kingdom, this one ended badly, with deportation for some members of the French entourage and enslavement for the rest.[54]

Yet Louis XIII gave scant consideration to Capuchin reports of famine, pestilence, and apostasy among several hundred French slaves in Moroccan cities.[55] Newly focused on Huguenot rebellion along the

Atlantic, he ignored the knight's calls for military intervention and redemption underwritten by taxes on Lenten meat and Parisian carriages, diverting Razilly to La Rochelle. It took another year for Father Joseph to procure a royal grant for a Capuchin-led rescue voyage, which failed. Only in February 1629, a few months after France's last Protestant holdout finally surrendered to royal forces, did Louis XIII acknowledge his Breton, Norman, Poitevin, and Bordelais subjects in servitude. With France's heretics crushed, he was ready to take on North Africa's infidels. On board the seven-vessel squadron bound for Salé that summer were Razilly, an Ottoman interpreter (bearing a variant of the name of his godfather Richelieu), a Capuchin friar, and a gentleman envoy (Priam-Pierre du Chalard) selected by Father Joseph, plus a member of the Mercedarian order.[56]

With the majority of its convents located in Iberian lands and colonies, the Mercedarians were eager to legitimate their presence in a kingdom dominated by the fiercely territorial if underfunded and underperforming Trinitarians. Earlier in the century, protection by influential families, construction of Parisian headquarters, and assertion of French pedigree had all helped counter accusations of Mercedarian hispanophilia.[57] Mercedarian founder Pierre Nolasque's canonization in 1628, four years before Trinitarian Jean de Matha's, was another feather in the order's cap.[58] But for the French branch of the Mercedarians, winning the ransom race in North Africa represented a still more significant coup, even if the deliverance of fifty slaves, judged soon-to-be renegades, required a year of wrangling and taking on a sizable debt.[59] From Salé, redeemers and redeemed, plus seventy other captives liberated under royal auspices, set sail in September 1630.[60]

ADVERTISING FREEDOM, FAITH, AND FIDELITY

They docked at Brouage. This salt-producing Atlantic seaport had accommodated royal troops during the siege against Huguenot La Rochelle. Now it played host to the first ceremony on French soil to commemorate the return of Catholic slaves from North Africa.[61] In future decades, processions from coast to capital that lasted one to three months would become the principal vectors for transmitting ideas about the horrors of Barbary slavery and the benefits of French belonging to inland areas.[62] On this occasion, implicitly honoring a victory over Muslims and Protestants, as well as a clause in the Mercedarian order's constitutions,[63] redemptive fathers and repatriated Frenchmen probably followed a medieval model elaborated in Spain, Portugal, and Italy during the sixteenth century.[64] There, highly choreographed performances featuring costumes, prayers, and song had been meant to impart spiritual edification and inspire charitable giving among spectators, while reintegrating freedmen into the social, religious, and political fabric. Here, an additional goal was to assert Mercedarian ties to Louis XIII and his church. Thus on 27 September 1630, 119 liberated captives gathered before the governor's mansion, where a provincial officer read off their names amid shouts of "Vive le Roi!" Afterward, at the town's main cathedral, the group prayed for "the prosperity of His Majesty's [and Cardinal's] arms."[65]

From France's freshly subdued western province, those who owed their freedom to the friars continued on to Paris. Although the Mercedarians had not yet started churning out pamphlets and books with the itinerary and iconography of slave marches, they had anticipated the spontaneous "joy and pleasure" expressed by clergy and the "upper and lower rank of people and faithful of all kind and condition" in every "Catholic place" they passed. After winding their way through the capital, the plan was to stop at the Mercedarian convent located near the ancestral home of one of the kingdom's leading Catholic families for a final round of feasting and thanksgiving. Only then, supplied with new clothes, special certificates, and travel fare, would the catechized captives disperse homeward, walking advertisements for the holy, state-sanctioned work of redemption.[66]

The Mercedarians had triumphed in France, but back in Morocco, the spiritual tenacity of Muslims and frailty of Catholics had left the Capuchins disillusioned. In August 1630, therefore, the order's emissary and those friars who had spent the preceding several years in captivity, plus eighty more freshly freed Frenchmen escorted by Razilly, left Salé for Safi. The knight's intent was to take on board additional slaves being held at the capital. But after a three-month wait during worsening weather, he steered his fleet homeward, only to miss the arrival of the "French subjects" from Marrakech whose letter to Louis XIII told of "many souls . . . lost, forced by a thousand labors . . . to renounce their faith."[67] A single compensation for the voyage's relative failure was the capture en route of a Dutch ship carrying a valuable cache of contraband arms. That it had been chartered by a Moroccan Jewish family with close ties to the sultan resulted in considerable intrigue,[68] but also the September 1631 negotiation of a short-lived peace treaty—and the ransom of 180 more French slaves.[69]

That year's edition of the *Mercure françois*, reflecting the concerns of its putative editor, Father Joseph, lavishly praised these limited diplomatic and redemptive accomplishments. The next year it also connected slave salvation to saving at least one Muslim soul, announcing the baptism of a "Barbarian from the kingdom of Morocco" at the Capuchin Church in Paris.[70]

AGITATING ON PAPER

Pierre Dan was a rising Trinitarian star in 1631 when he was tapped to lead his order's first early modern voyage to North Africa. But a deficiency in funds and the typical detention of pledged Muslim oarsmen delayed the liberation of any incarcerated Frenchmen—and stalled the order's advancement over its rivals. So while waiting to intervene physically, the Trinitarians campaigned with paint and ink. Their commission of twenty-four canvases for the main convent in Paris and a set of complementary engravings from one of Rubens's protégés, Theodor van Thulden, disseminated scenes from Matha's life, showing his sovereign loyalty and religious devotion expressed by the return of Catholics to France.[71]

Agents of the Marseille Chamber of Commerce and the crown took a more direct approach. In letters addressed to Paris, they griped about royal parsimony and private intransigence, which was preventing the release of North African galley slaves and the payment of ransoms.[72] And they forwarded captive correspondence that issued dire warnings about the perils of physical and spiritual corruption, as well as commercial domination, by Barbary corsairs. "They make slaves of sailors to sell in Modon or Tripoli," wrote a "poor Carmelite monk" from Tunisian thralldom, "and if they find some young boy, they force him to repudiate his faith." Without a solution, he continued, "the Barbarians will fill their prisons with Frenchmen and empty your storehouses of merchandise." Or as a collective petition to Louis XIII admonished, "the Turk will plant his flags in the middle of Provence, if his majesty does not take care." For some of the French slaves, it was already too late. They had embraced "the false law of Muhammad rather than languish at the discretion of the infidels," but lived to regret the decision, "tormented by their profanation, their souls plunged into the depths of hell because of these ministers of Satan."[73]

Whatever the accuracy of such testimonies and prophecies, attacks along the Mediterranean were once again a daily occurrence. In 1633, according to a coastal defense inspector, the hamlet of Martigues lost eighty seamen in the space of just four months; in the seven years prior to 1634, according to Father Dan, Algiers gained more than thirteen hundred French slaves, bringing the total across the Ottoman regencies and

Morocco to nine thousand—or one quarter of the Christians in chains. He estimated a third to be renegades.[74] Writing from Algiers that February, France's consul made a similar claim, informing the court that two hundred desperate compatriots had already converted to Islam. Should that news not spur action, he proposed a novel solution: exchanging the "Turks" stationed in French ports for five hundred captive Frenchmen, who "will bind themselves to serve his majesty in Canada for a period of five years." Freed from bondage in the Old World to enter servitude in the New, such indentured laborers would not only work in agriculture and construction but also "marry there and make alliances with savages to assure better trade."[75]

Louis XIII did not listen. That spring, rather than trade all his Algerian rowers or transport any French subjects to the colonies, he finally sent a Trinitarian-escorted delegation (including Dan) to Algiers. On royal orders, however, it brought only a few galley slaves "of mediocre condition" to create a bargaining advantage—which backfired, leaving disappointed captives, disgruntled parents, and an angry Algerian dey.[76]

FIGHTING MUSLIMS, BEFRIENDING PROTESTANTS

As for Morocco, misunderstanding rather than bad faith had broken the last treaty, and Louis XIII was eager to sign a new one, so long as its execution did not drain his coffers. The mission began promisingly in July 1635 with a re-ratification and a token slave exchange. But then the seasoned emissary du Chalard expended everything he had on just a third of more than six hundred French subjects detained, borrowing additional money for another portion and leaving a huge promissory note for the rest. Furious at this insubordination and unprepared to pay more, Louis XIII had du Chalard imprisoned, then banished from Paris; the next July, the king dispatched warrior-priest Henri d'Escoubleau de Sourdis, archbishop of Bordeaux, in the disgraced envoy's place.[77]

Squadrons from France's "fleet against the pirates of the Mediterranean," in the words of a royal declaration, reinforced by vagrants impressed into service, appeared at Salé and Algiers just as detachments from French land forces started fighting alongside Protestant allies against Catholic Spain and the Holy Roman Empire.[78] By showily if ineffectively taking a stand against the Barbary corsairs, Louis XIII may have been seeking to deflect attention from his subordination of religion to strategy in the Thirty Years' War, since in the words of a lieutenant general of the galleys, nothing more behooves "a very Christian king" or better suits "the majesty of his name than to avenge the cause of Christians [and] defend their belongings, their lives, and their souls from the oppression of infidels."[79]

Yet as much as victory over Muslims might have helped the king's international reputation, the demands of combat on multiple fronts were quickly overextending his already strained maritime and financial capacity. In Morocco, the capture of two Saletian corsairs and the intercession of two French renegades initially persuaded the sultan to negotiate. But as months passed without resolution, local slave owners grew impatient for the funds du Chalard had promised. Then sixty French slaves escaped, provoking a new diplomatic rupture, the arrest of the *nation*'s consul, and the reimprisonment of its entire servile population. Over the next few years, however, the number of French captives in Morocco dwindled into the single digits because of flight, individually arranged ransom, and death.[80]

France's tepid display of naval might at Algiers produced similarly disastrous results. Instead of inducing a peace renewal on better terms to protect French commercial and religious integrity, the arrival of twelve warships and a merchant deputized as a diplomat provoked a counter-assault on the kingdom's trading outpost, the Bastion de France, and the enslavement of 317 French inhabitants. Reports of daily apostasy reached Paris, but Louis XIII was in no position to retaliate.[81]

THE SYMBOLISM OF SHACKLES

Happily for the crown, the Trinitarians, pursuing their own competitive agenda, had finally completed a successful North African redemption, which occasioned a series of ornate processions. Mounted with the double aim of collecting alms for future voyages and demonstrating the order's utility to France, these rituals also promoted the kingdom's status as Eldest Daughter of the Church. A contemporaneous brochure and Dan's harrowingly illustrated *Histoire de Barbarie et de ses corsaires* (Figure 3), released by a popular Parisian publisher two years later, described throngs of well-wishers at Marseille's port in April 1635, jostling to glimpse forty-three Frenchmen freed from Tunis and deemed free of pestilence.[82]

What they saw (Figure 4) depicted a reality already imagined by Van Thulden (Figure 5) and evoked other ceremonies with related ends.[83] Singing Te Deum, a tune associated since the sixteenth century with royal births and military victories, the city's cathedral chorus came first.[84] Hundreds of confreres and clerics followed. At the parade's focal

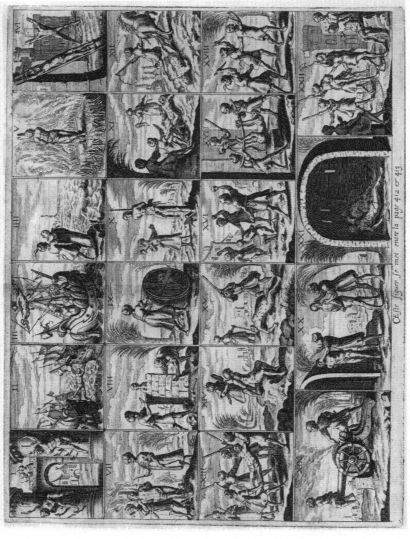

Figure 3. Torture of Barbary slaves. Engraving by Gilles Rousselet in Pierre Dan, *Histoire de Barbarie et de ses corsaires* . . . (Paris: Pierre Rocolet, 1637). Courtesy of Houghton Library, Harvard University, *FC6.D1907.637h.

Figure 4. A procession of freed slaves. "Processie des Verloste Slaauen," engraving by Jan Luyken in Pierre Dan, *Historie van Barbaryen, en des zelfs zee-roovers . . .*, trans. G. V. Broekhuizen (Amsterdam: Jan ten Hoorn, 1684). © Musée national de la Marine, ph. 92338.

Figure 5. An earlier slave procession. "Allapsi Christianorium littoribus Captiuos . . ." in Theodor van Thulden, *Revelatio ordinis s[anctis]s[i] mae Trinitatis redemptionis captivorum* (Paris: n.p., 1633). Bibliothèque nationale de France, Tolbiac H-1541.

point marched pairs of disheveled slaves with chains slung over their shoulders, while Trinitarians and city officials trailed behind.[85] With their backs to the Mediterranean, the group headed northward to hear mass and then to eat and rest at the order's convent. Like urban *processions générales* that annually displayed municipal hierarchies, and royal entries that intermittently displayed monarchical power, this pageant broadcast an ideal of a corporate society made up of coherent parts arranged in their proper order.[86] It also brought to mind penitential appeals to God during periods of famine, drought, and plague—and reportedly served the same function. "No sooner was the procession achieved," Dan later wrote, "than a gentle rain began to fall across the whole region. . . . Many attributed its cause to the prayers of these poor captives and the merit of this good work of redemption."[87]

Redemptive fathers and freed captives left Marseille by foot and passed through Aix-en-Provence, Lambesc, Arles, Tarascon, and Avignon before heading northward on the Lyon road to Nevers and Fontainebleau. Each place hosted its own performance, which took roughly the same periphery-to-center form, mirroring the overall route from France's outer limits to its sacred core. In Paris, which the group entered through an eastern gate in late May, the procession began along the right bank of the Seine. Several beadles, archers, and trumpeters walked first, then came eighty barefoot confraternity brothers wearing laurel garlands to denote victory and carrying candles to suggest divine light; they were followed by forty children in "small rochets of fine cloth," bearing a flag with two angels on bended knee.[88] Rather than preceding the host, as in Corpus Christi ceremonies, these youth introduced another sort of religious object: the slaves, whose manacles appeared on a banner emblazoned with the order's red and blue cross and eight fleurs-de-lys (on an azure field stamped with a royal crown). The friars and several more bowmen brought up the rear.

Completing a circuit that crisscrossed the river between the Trinitarian convent in the Latin Quarter and Notre Dame Cathedral on the Ile de la Cité took two days. With a nod to ceremonials of previous generations that had responded to political crisis or celebrated feats of war and peace by touring the island's monuments, Dan's spectacle transmitted two fundamental messages: one about the reversibility of servitude, the other about the alliance between Catholic faith and monarchical clout.[89] Not only had his order by the king's authority freed Frenchmen from North African detention, but back in France it also cleansed them of North African contaminants. By a process represented on chapel walls and made visible along country roads and urban streets, the Trinitarians symbolically replaced the shackles of infidels with the ties that bound all French subjects to altar and to throne. Then they provided the ex-slaves with new clothes to indicate their re-admission to the civic order.

Dan's 1637 account of voyages to Tunis and Algiers reviewed the drama that Muslims and Christians, slaves and saviors had earlier enacted. A judgmental guide to the "superstitions" and "ridiculous ceremonies" of Muslims, and the history, demography, government, fashion, diet, and naval capacity of the region, this tome dedicated to Louis XIII spawned a second edition and numerous imitators. It also detailed with words and engravings the "mortifications," "ruses," "outrages," "inhumanities," and "infamous lechery" that drove some Christian captives to apostasy and others to either dissimulation or martyrdom. "Barbary is a bloody theater where many tragedies are performed," wrote Dan.[90] In the Trinitarian imaginary, by contrast, France had become a stage for jubilation and religious, political, and social reconciliation.

FRIARS TO THE RESCUE

Continuing to vie for preeminence, the Mercedarians and Trinitarians traversed the Mediterranean ten more times over the next two decades and mounted as many processions.[91] While an ailing Louis XIII, followed by his wife as regent, concentrated on pan-European warfare, fiscal crisis, epidemic disease, food shortages, and a series of noble revolts known collectively as the Fronde, the orders also published countless brochures and broadsides, plus twelve full-length accounts, which showed divine grace and royal power as antidotes to Barbary servitude and its associated corruptions.[92] The Trinitarians and Mercedarians did have at least something to celebrate: more than five hundred Frenchmen freed—anywhere from 5 to 20 percent of the total in captivity.[93]

As for the rest of the captives, the crown had already given up on those in Morocco but made a final bid for subjects detained in Algiers and Tunis. "We must stay firm and create something solid and enduring with these people, or else make a complete break, the king having sufficient means to force them to come to reason," Richelieu bluffed in 1639, offering to donate twenty thousand livres of his personal fortune to the effort.[94] In Algiers, an ennobled merchant acting as royal emissary made some headway, managing to retake possession of the Bastion de France. However, backed by a diminished flotilla in 1640 and 1641, he fell short of settling the fate of twelve to fifteen hundred French captives in the plague-infested regency. A missive to Marseille's leaders from a group of enslaved aristocrats and commoners complained of hellish labor and sexual abuse that was leading the young to convert out of despair.

It labeled the French consul a perfidious letch gone native, who had sold free compatriots into slavery, raped a page from Grasse, and humiliated three knights who took up the boy's cause. Putting their liberation claim in terms of inheritance, they declared, "We do not believe that his Majesty wishes some of us to be bastards and only a few to enjoy the heritage of liberty."[95]

Louis XIII may well have viewed freedom as the proper recompense for legacy or allegiance, especially since approving the first deportations of black Africans without these qualities to the French Atlantic—reputedly as the best method for converting the nonbelievers to Catholicism.[96] Yet twice on the Mediterranean, the arrival of winter forced France's warships to depart.[97] Clearly, Marseille's Chamber of Commerce did not anticipate speedy progress in Tunis either; it made independent arrangements for captive Provençals. Forty Frenchmen from other provinces found liberty through an initial head-for-head exchange, but the usual foot-dragging over the release of another handful of Tunisian "Turks" blocked the achievement of any comprehensive agreement.[98] Afterward, friars and merchants continued to liberate Barbary slaves, but no state representative visited the Ottoman regencies for a generation.

Two more Catholic orders joined the Trinitarians and Mercedarians in taking up the cause of coreligionists in Muslim bondage five years later. First, the Franciscan-derived Recollet Fathers suspended operations in French Canada and sent two missionaries to Tripoli, where they ostensibly liberated fifty Christians.[99] Second, members of the Congrégation de la Mission, established by Saint Vincent de Paul, expanded their pastoral care from the rural poor and galley slaves of France to the Christian captives of North Africa. Popularly called "Lazarists" for the lazar house (or leper colony) they occupied in Paris, these priests purchased consular offices in Algiers and Tunis, holding them from 1646 to 1683 and 1648 to 1666, respectively. As consuls and *vicaires apostoliques* of the French merchant community, the Lazarists gave spiritual guidance to subjects in Barbary bagnes. In imitation of the apocryphal Tunisian captivity of their founder, they also devoted themselves to redemption, claiming to have set free twelve hundred Frenchmen in four decades.[100]

RANSOM PRIORITIES, ROYAL AUDIENCES

Every French institution engaged in delivering slaves had to be selective in the 1640s and 1650s. Unable to afford the comprehensive manumissions sometimes pursued by other European powers, French Lazarists, Trinitarians, and Mercedarians, like their secular counterparts, all tried to maximize numbers, while adhering to judgments about "worth." Men who fought back rather than go meekly into slavery were prized by the Marseille Chamber of Commerce, which created monetary incentives to take up arms against corsairs.[101] High rank and good connections made a difference all around: religious houses and municipal bodies in France were awash in correspondence urging aid for esteemed parishioners. Because the redemptive orders were regionally organized, and all the more so once royal edicts split the kingdom into distinct territories for building convents and collecting alms, they paid close attention to origin. Thus captives from Normandy, say, might be spurned by friars from Languedoc, and vice versa.

By contrast, the elderly and infirm, who commanded lower prices, received preferential liberation regardless of where they came from. So did heads of household, traders, and mariners, who filled especially vital social, commercial, or military roles. Tactically adopting local and royal government pragmatics, Trinitarians and Mercedarians privileged a merchant who claimed a "wife and six children" set to "die of hunger if I do not help them," or "patriots" who promised to "consecrate [our] liberty to the service of our prince and our homeland, for it is possible to say without vanity that the cream of Provençal sailors are slaves in this country."[102] A woman of any station, of course, always took precedence. However, single, middle-aged, low-born, inexpert men languished.

Corporal suffering in North African bondage was doubtless a reality and certainly a rhetorical strategy. Few French slaves, whether writing for private or public consumption, omitted details about inadequate food and clothing, dreadful housing, or cruel treatment. But relieving pain was not a motivation for holy men, let alone lay saviors, as an end in itself. Both sought to repatriate as many useful—but also loyal—individuals as possible. It might therefore appear counterintuitive to favor slaves on the brink of conversion over those steadfast in their beliefs. Yet given the ultimate goal of attracting souls to Catholicism, agents of the Gallican Church hesitated to lose any to Islam, especially those belonging to young, unlettered boys believed prone "to sins so horrible and despicable they cannot even be named, and which are not committed except among these monsters and infernal furies," as one Trinitarian wrote on his return from Algiers. Captives "who resist the . . . brutal passions" of Barbary masters "are flayed and ripped apart with blows, hung upside down naked on a plank, their fingernails torn out, the soles of their feet burned with blazing torches, so that often enough they die in agony."[103]

From a Catholic perspective, martyrs were far preferable to renegades, while Protestants made potential recruits to the one true faith.

As Louis XIII lay on his deathbed in 1643, for example, the Trinitarians freed thirty-three "captifs de la Religion" with money entrusted by the embattled Protestant community of La Rochelle.[104] Fitting with seventeenth-century notions of charity as "encompass[ing] both compassion and compression," all ransomed slaves were contractually required to lend out their dramatic services for up to three months, and there is no reason to suspect that Huguenots were exempted from trudging toward the seat of monarchical authority.[105] No matter how inclement the weather or little the desire, they presumably had to play grateful beneficiaries of religious and royal largesse like everybody else. Whatever their backgrounds or beliefs, identically dressed former captives (now led by boys in angel wings) presented themselves as equal children of Christ.

There is little record of any qualms among spectators. In a period when plague did regularly hit parts of France, however, it is no wonder that some onlookers, doubting the efficacy of quarantine, worried that Frenchmen back from Barbary were "full of bad air." Given chronic food shortages, it is also no surprise that others demanded reimbursement for refreshments.[106] Certainly, the redemptive fathers acknowledged a dampening in charitable enthusiasm[107]—a situation they took pains to correct.[108] But the *tours de France* they remembered in print met only fervent crowds whose very presence lent legitimacy to the emancipatory enterprise.[109] Chroniclers from both orders told of collection basins overflowing with coins, satisfying meals served by "virtuous ladies," and meandering voyages that culminated in rewarding interviews with the king.[110]

According to a Trinitarian pamphlet from 1643, the late Louis XIII had expressed "with a look of gentleness and compassion his joy at seeing partisans of Jesus Christ brought back from the cruelty and tyranny of the Barbarians," while his young son had "[taken] pleasure in seeing them and examining them for a good long time, seeming to form a plan in his heart to go himself (like another Saint Louis) to chastise the insolence of these Barbarians who treat his subjects so inhumanely."[111] On the occasion of this meeting between the king and around fifty slaves returned from Algiers, the royal gaze, like the "Royal Touch" alleged to cure scrofula, exerted a transformative effect: "It was . . . in this Royal Palace, or rather in this terrestrial Paradise, that these poor captives changed their miseries into bliss, through the eyes of the most perfect image of God on earth."[112] Eleven years later, when fifty more slaves from Salé reached the Louvre, a commemorative poem recalled the thaumaturgy Louis XIV had evidenced during his coronation: "Having been weakened in a harsh slavery / They regain vigor upon seeing your face / Where shine all the traits of a great Liberator."[113]

CAPTIVES INTO CONVERTS

For former captives, the act of seeing and being seen allegedly healed body and soul. According to the ideal sketched out in redemption narratives, having convalesced en route via the inspection of bystanders, they departed from the capital as from a baptismal font. Functioning as reconversion rites to generate robust Catholics, redemption marches thus provided dramatic counterpoints to celebrations for neophyte Muslims. In North Africa, the apostate wore a beautiful turban, rode a horse with lavish trappings, and carried an arrow to show his willingness to fight for Islam—or, in the case of a "nasty" Huguenot "from the region of Saintonge . . . who turned Turk to the great satisfaction of all the people," followed a drummer, "a bagpipe player resembling a shepherd from Poitou," and a pikeman wielding a decapitated head as a banner. Back home, the evangelist on foot and in a simple white shift exhibited peaceable humility rather than pride and aggression. On both sides, the faithful gave liberally for individuals rescued from erroneous beliefs.[114]

In France, however, it was not only latent renegades who experienced Catholic rebirth. In the 1640s and 1650s, handfuls of Muslims also abjured "the false religion of Muhammad" before and after Barbary slave ceremonies.[115] Twenty-nine-year-old Mustafa from Algiers, for example, received his baptism at Paris's Saint Sulpice Church in April 1641, a month ahead of the arrival of forty French slaves from Tunis. With large numbers of high- and low-born people in attendance and the king's brother as his godfather, he took a new name, Jean-Philippe, in honor of his new faith.[116] As a clearly timed riposte to the southwestern passage of 150 French captives from Algiers by the Mercedarians in May 1644, Trinitarian friars baptized two Muslims in the Gascon town of Orthez. Among ten "Moorish Turks" escaped from a Spanish galley captured near Bayonne and kept for exchange, the pair had been so "ravished by the gentleness and good treatment of their caretaker" that, reportedly, they repudiated Muhammad and accepted Christ before a mass of people.[117] Not to be outdone by papists, Huguenots sponsored Muslim conversions too. Thus in March 1655, seven months after the Trinitarians proceeded through La Rochelle with about fifty slaves from Salé, another native of Algiers, Mustapha, "publicly renounced the impieties of the impostor Muhammad and embraced the Christian religion." Significantly, he swore "to live and die professing the truth taught in *our* churches" (emphasis mine).[118] Protestant-Catholic rivalry continued to be played out through Muslims over the next three decades.[119]

INTO THE ROYAL VOID

During the first half of the seventeenth century, increasing numbers of French subjects were carried off to Barbary and most of them never returned home. Overall, the crown's failure to prevent enslavement or redeem slaves demonstrated its fundamental weakness. Overwhelmed by the defense of France's religious and territorial integrity against Christian enemies from within and without, neither Louis XIII nor Louis XIV in his minority had sufficient means to address threats posed by Muslims. The problem of seizure by corsairs and detention in Morocco, Algiers, Tunis, or Tripoli affected French coastal areas most directly, depriving families and communities of income and protection. But it also had the potential to undermine the French body politic, not only commercially and militarily but also through the physical and spiritual corruption of its constituent members.

Into this royal void stepped several marginal groups, religious associations, and civic bodies, each working to thrive or merely to survive. For Catholic orders and confraternities, ransoming slaves was a holy calling, which did not preclude them from profanely tussling for primacy. It was a sideline business for Jewish and Protestant merchants, an expression of sympathy or cupidity by renegades, and a matter of necessity to some women. Unfettering native seamen represented a practical response by town councils, especially in maritime regions with economies dependent on the sea. For disparate reasons, then, it was mostly inhabitants of geographically marginal places and relative outsiders (either by religious conviction or accident of birth) who worked to free the most indispensable and vulnerable captives. In so doing, they contributed to the monarchy's affluence and at least the projection of its influence both at home and abroad. Observed through the lens of slavery and liberation from North Africa, these early decades of French state building had less to do with decisions made in Paris than with initiatives taken in ports.

Of course, none of these wives in Saint-Nazaire and fathers in Toulon—let alone the Jews, Huguenots, and new Muslims belonging to transnational networks or Trinitarians and Mercedarians of whatever stripe—cared per se about empowering the French king or nurturing sovereign attachment. Yet they did so, because of the political contexts in which they operated. In North Africa, local origin did influence decisions about whom to liberate but not about who ultimately went free. The Capitulations signed in Constantinople and the bilateral treaties negotiated with North African powers made manumission conditional on proof of affiliation to France, not roots in the province of Normandy or the village of Cassis, giving slaves with ties to particular locales a reason to start presenting themselves in broader terms. Back in France, meanwhile, the need to justify demands for charity in lean times led to the organization of Barbary slave processions, which in turn charted a course for regional patriots to become Frenchmen and religious crossbreeds to become Catholics.

Along with rituals of quarantine—"ceremonial[s] of control for merchandise and men"—these much-described rituals of redemption were opportunities for disinfection and reattachment.[120] They were ways to rid French bodies of Barbary pathogens and French souls of Barbary perversions—as well as attempts to stir love of God and country in French hearts. By their very existence, isolation wards and reintegration marches acknowledged the Ottoman regencies and Morocco to be powerful sources of illness and iniquity, capable of robbing the king's subjects of freedom, fitness, fidelity, and faith. Yet at the same time they implied confidence that disease could be thwarted, French Catholic allegiance recovered, and North African bondage undone.

In the mid-seventeenth century, such trust was not misplaced. Plague had arrived overland, most notably in 1629–1630, but until the early eighteenth century it failed to traverse the sea. The ranks of black chattel held in perpetuity on colonial plantations were just beginning to swell, but Christian captives who could be ransomed were still the more familiar sorts of slaves in metropolitan France. Finally, Marseille's ongoing assertions of autonomy did culminate in outright rebellion in 1658.[121] Nevertheless, the city remained the kingdom's access point to the Mediterranean and its buffer against North Africa. This was a position that Louis XIII accepted implicitly and that Louis XIV would soon make official.

CHAPTER THREE

Manumission and Absolute Monarchy

In March 1660, Louis XIV entered Marseille through a breach in the ramparts, and fifty-seven former slaves with a Trinitarian escort filed into Paris.[1] With the first gesture, one usually reserved for a conquered city, the Sun King asserted dominion over a notoriously rebellious territory at the margins of his realm whose inhabitants had threatened to "give themselves over to the Turk" rather than submit to royal authority.[2] With the second, though it occurred in his absence, he claimed sovereignty over a group of potentially diseased, deviant, and disloyal subjects returned from "infidel" lands to France's sacred center. These two ceremonies of possession took place 486 miles apart, but they shared a common message: the ascendant power of a monarch poised for marriage and personal rule whose bid to construct a formidable, prosperous, and cohesive polity depended on the co-option of volatile places and peoples—and the symbolic expurgation of Islam.[3]

During the next ten years, Marseille received a monopoly over the kingdom's flagging Mediterranean trade, a new arsenal to accommodate royal galleys for patrolling French shores, and a modernized lazaret for quarantining suspected plague carriers. That is, it was transformed from a maritime outpost with suspect allegiances yet de facto responsibility for Franco–North African relations into a cosmopolitan port with an imposing citadel and formal oversight over all goods and individuals entering France from Muslim territories.[4] Over the same period, the number of Frenchmen and women detained in North Africa surpassed two thousand.[5] As in the past, a portion of the captives consisted of unlucky fishermen and ill-fated pilgrims. But now that the crown, under the influence of minister Jean-Baptiste Colbert, had pledged itself to naval, commercial, and colonial expansion, those abducted included ever more sailors, shipbuilders, merchants, explorers, and, occasionally, sub-Saharan African slave traders. Their servitude was thus a by-product of international development as well as a lingering sign of overseas vulnerability.[6]

The notion that Christian compatriots might succumb to plague, sodomy, and apostasy continued to provoke tangible anxiety during the 1660s and 1670s, especially among religious leaders and along France's littoral. From the court's vantage, the loss of valuable seamen in Algiers, Tunis, and Tripoli undermined French maritime strategy. Thus when not otherwise occupied by war on multiple fronts, ministers and admirals began charting a more aggressive course in the Ottoman regencies, which had the added benefit of giving yet another monarch allied with a sultan the chance to try on the role of anti-Muslim crusader.[7] Both labor and propaganda considerations in these decades also led to greater royal supervision over the liberation of Frenchmen and procurement of "Turks"— via Paris-ordered rescue voyages, purchasing schemes, and payment plans. Although unevenly executed and sporadically resisted by localities jealous of their privileges and purses, such pragmatic interventions to strengthen the kingdom's sea forces bore ideological fruit in the years that followed, as French belonging and Barbary captivity came to seem incompatible.

Until Louis XIV's capacities actually matched his pretensions, slaves and their saviors used performance as a compensatory means of definition and defense. Apart from witnessing ever more theatrical slave processions and the continued appearance of redemption chronicles, both of which stressed religio-royal restorations of French Christian identities, this period saw the flowering of first-person French-language captivity narratives with a new sort of protagonist. In most of these embellished memoirs (at least eleven composed if not published in the last quarter of the seventeenth century), inspired by romantic literary forms and blurring the line between fact and fiction,[8] survival depended less on outside intercession than on self-initiated imposture.[9] Whether circulated in manuscript or granted royal permission to be printed by a handful of established presses in Paris and Lyon, such accounts presented dissimulation as a path to authenticity.[10] Unlike writings aimed at intellectual dissenters and religious minorities that counseled deceit as a way to avoid the reach of persecuting European states, these envisioned duplicity as a counterweight to Mediterranean fluidity, fostering adherence to France.[11]

BORDER PATROLS

After their wedding on the Pyrenean border, Louis XIV and his new Spanish bride, Maria Theresa, began a two-month journey to the capital. This temporary revival of peripatetic kingship from June to August

1660, following decades of internal disorder and external hostilities, represented an attempt to delineate France's geographical boundaries. That summer, the effort to demarcate French status in subjects held outside these frontiers still relied on the conventional and relatively ineffective tactics of chasing down pirates and blockading ports while unlawfully detaining North African slaves.[12] Exasperated, Mediterranean commander Paul de Samur (also known as Chevalier Paul) dashed off a memorandum in 1661, outlining plans "to ruin Algiers, Tunis, and Tripoli"—and acquire fresh blood for the galleys. "It would be necessary," he wrote, "to attack these Barbary cities by land with an army of 20 to 30,000 men."[13] For the next three years, while king and minister urged naval officers to go on raids for Muslim rowers, engineers assessed the viability of a full-scale invasion of Muslim territory.[14]

In the interim, many incarcerated Frenchmen across the region sought solace and salvation in writing letters. While held in Tripoli, Antoine Quartier took notes. *L'Esclave religieux et ses avantures* appeared anonymously more than two decades after the young man from Chablis, discovering the "cost of curiosity," was ambushed on his way to Constantinople.[15] His book proffered "no other design than to excite the charity of Christians for the relief of captives." But as the title suggests, it primarily showcased the escapades of its leading man, starring in an account "which resembles a romance; [since] the country of corsairs is the theater for all sorts of events and novelties."[16] Like a character in a play of that genre, and following the example of previous putative autobiographies by Algerian captives from La Flèche and Bruges,[17] Quartier lost his bearings—and, in this case, his freedom—during a sea-tossed voyage to a foreign realm, where over a period of seven years and eight months he used trickery and transvestism to overcome bodily, religious, and political threats, before finding resolution via ransom and, eventually, the decision to take holy vows.[18]

Quartier's adventure began in July 1660 when four North African corsairs captained by European renegades chased down the Dutch cruiser he had boarded in Venice. Stripped of his clothes, reviewed by the pasha, and then sold at market, Quartier lost all anchors of his former self. As a laborer on a building site in the countryside, his body strained under the exertion of quarrying stone and his tongue struggled to learn Lingua Franca. Then he came down with plague and, he opined, might have perished if not for a captive surgeon from Antibes, a lucky bout of vomiting, his "dry temperament" and young age, and the consolation he received from the sole Catholic priest in the regency.[19] Combining several etiologies, Quartier credited his internal balance—humoral and religious—for safeguarding him against external pathogens. Conversely, he blamed the twin abominations of sodomy and Islam for bringing down "this scourge frequent to Africa."[20] For this French slave, sexual perversion in itself represented a step toward spiritual conversion, and those hobbled by youth or ignorance, avarice or impiety, or a burning desire for revenge were most vulnerable to apostasy.[21] But in Quartier's Tripoli even the most pious captives might fall victim to lingual or sartorial cons. A girl from La Ciotat, for example, believing she was reciting lines from an emancipation proclamation, inadvertently declared herself a partisan of Allah, and members of a multinational group who passed out from drink awakened to find themselves dressed in Turkish fashion.[22]

Quartier was no different from contemporaneous authors in identifying at least one renegade "who was Mahometan of lips only" and retained "the seeds of Christianity" within his heart—in this case, the Tripolitan pasha. Picking out impostor apostates—especially French ones—clearly comforted men who were otherwise unmoored and afraid. But hope for the triumph of Frenchness and Christianity over North African hybridity as often gave way to disdain for these "Turks by profession" who abjured one faith only to contravene the next, rarely praying and flouting prohibitions against liquor and lard. "With Turks he was Muslim, with Renegades impious and debauched, and in the presence of Roman Catholics he recited his rosary and spoke only of devotion," Quartier sneered of his Greek renegade master, a "Schismatic" he judged well on the way to Islam.[23]

For the sake of religious constancy and bodily purity, then, Quartier and his comrades summoned inner strength and used outward ploys against Tripoli's non-Christian populations. They found their easiest target in a reviled minority, the Jews. In one example, Quartier sounded the alarm near a synagogue while a Breton sidekick robbed the shop of a Jewish merchant.[24] In another instance in 1666, he related, with Jewish communities around the world swept up in messianic fervor, a captive from Lyon fluent in Hebrew and Arabic played the role of the Sabbatai Sevi. Bedecked in black, the supposed savior from Smyrna slipped aboard a boat arriving from Alexandria and greeted followers who rushed to welcome their "chimerical king" at the harbor. According to Quartier, that night the pasha, amused by this masquerade at the expense of unbelievers, sent emissaries to the Jewish quarter to pay their respects.[25] But in the morning, the bogus redeemer had vanished: "Everyone made fun of the Jews, who to cover up the flight of their Messiah, said that he had become invisible, having orders from the Eternal to continue his voyage through Barbary." None dared complain about the theft of a hundred ecus worth of silver, which helped pay the ransom of the French slave who had postured as the Jewish savior.[26]

More threatening to North African hierarchies than "passing down" as Jews, it seemed, was the manipulation of visual, sensual, or aural markers of belonging to ridicule Muslims. Nonetheless, Quartier apparently received no penalty for standing guard outside a mosque while a friend, "dressed as a Moor," absconded with fifteen pairs of slippers belonging to men at prayer. Though the "Turks who lost their *babouches* . . . demanded justice for this sacrilege," he wrote, the pasha ruled that pilfering shoes was pardonable for people who needed them.[27] But another of his antics invited more lethal consequences. In Quartier's tale, after his second master died of plague, he seized an opportunity for personal enterprise and began washing linens for Tripoli's Christian merchants, using the profits to hawk French cuisine at a cabaret. Claiming gastronomic as well as religious superiority, he bragged that most of the city's converts to Islam "left their bad fare to come eat my ragouts." Then he acknowledged, "[It] is true that I mixed in pork meat, which is forbidden by the Quran." Business was booming until a eunuch discovered Quartier's culinary blow below the belt and, aptly, went after him with a knife.[28]

Relations of such hoaxes and high jinks in the romantic mode potentially served a double function. First, they gave readers a voyeuristic glimpse of alien societies and the thrilling experience of movement without the risk of captivity that accompanied sea travel. Second, with liberation inscribed within their plot and, indeed, the very framework of this type of bondage—which always held out the possibility of deliverance—books like Quartier's tried to soothe worries about physical and spiritual corruption in Muslim lands with a guaranteed happy ending. Presenting North African confinement as the flip side of maritime adventure, they showed subterfuge as a form of resistance, halting the spread of contagion and relieving the pressures of transculturation. In decades before Louis XIV could even hope to attract religious and political allegiance through wholesale emancipation, they imagined a method of state building through make-believe.

ROYAL ELUSIONS

Whereas French slaves in Tripoli had only divine providence and devious ingenuity to protect them, farther to the west they had consuls who were also Lazarist priests. Between military strikes, rescue operations, and at least one planned slave revolt,[29] these members of the Congrégation de la Mission used their Algerian and Tunisian offices for comforting Christians in bondage.[30] As agents of the church who maintained chapels in consulates and bagnes, they worked to shield enslaved French subjects from Islam; as representatives of a Catholic monarch, they put particular energy into proselytizing to Calvinists. Apart from ministry, Lazarists pursued French religious discipline in North Africa through monetary advances to renegades and heretics judged susceptible to reconciliation with the apostolic faith.[31] To French chagrin, however, their methods found only partial success. Despite regular ransom payments, Catholic slaves still defected to Islam, and captive Huguenots in search of aid without catechism approached members of the Dutch and English diplomatic corps.[32] Competition for the souls of Barbary slaves, in other words, extended political sectarian rivalries from Europe across the Mediterranean.

Back in France, the redemptive fathers worked hard to reverse the direction of religious influence by linking salvation from Islam to the fight against reformed Christianity. According to one Mercedarian, in a published account with an impressive run of one thousand, his order meant for the poignant vision of parading captives saved from apostasy to encourage conversion among Protestant spectators. He testified that in early 1662, at least in Montpellier, showing Catholic charity as the proper response to Muslim corsairing had its desired effect: "There's no doubt that several heretics felt their conscience dictate that this one is the one true church."[33] Unfortunately, the reality of bodily pollution and bad weather upset plans to carry this tableau of religious unity galvanized by the threat of spiritual corruption to the capital. Quarantine at Marseille had apparently failed to cleanse ninety-six former slaves of plague contracted in Algiers, and scores died and fell ill while touring Mediterranean regions. Rather than guide a band of sick, inadequately clothed men through wintry ice and wind for the sake of a royal audience, the Mercedarians aborted the trip entirely.[34]

By July 1664, invading the regency of Algiers had been on the royal agenda for three years. Not until France strategically suspended its alliance with the Ottoman Empire to help defend Hungary against the Turks, however, did a fleet of fifteen galleys and fourteen warships, carrying fifty-two hundred men, descend on the coast between Bougie and Annaba. At Djidjelli (or Gigeri), Louis XIV's intent was to establish a commercial outpost and permanent base for combating Barbary corsairs on the model of the Spanish stronghold at Oran and the recently deserted Bastion de France. With a naval commander "bearing a crucifix in one hand and a naked sword in the other," the idea was also to right an ancestral wrong—against Holy Roman Emperor Charles V, routed from Algiers in 1541. In fact, the Bourbon expedition found no greater success than had the Habsburg. A surprise Algerian assault came after just two months and a few days, and France's retreating armada sank within sight of Provence.[35] According to a captive eyewitness, the inhabitants of Algiers greeted news of the withdrawal with jubilation and jeers, "hurling a thousand insults and spitting in our faces." While the king dreamed of revenge by conquest ("I tell you that the city of Algiers is not as strong as one imagines"), he fell back on siege warfare, which drew Tunis into the fray, instead.[36] It took another nine months and two treaties—one official, one secret—to end hostilities with that regency and provide for the release of 360 "natural subjects of France and Navarre, conquered lands, and generally all places in His Very Christian Majesty Louis XIV's royal dominion" through a combination of exchange and ransom.[37] Then in May 1666, a royal envoy finally reached a settlement with a new Algerian dey, stipulating the liberation of twelve hundred French slaves. Some were Protestants; most were natives of maritime regions.[38]

On the surface, these diplomatic provisions to unshackle thousands of captives from places such as Antibes, Quimper, Six-Fours, and Saint-Malo appeared to validate both French sovereignty over peripheral territories and French power in the Mediterranean. Yet conditions of reciprocity and cash payment after an embarrassing defeat actually showed the limits of France's ability to dictate terms to North Africa. Moreover, domestic difficulties in raising the necessary funds, besides suggesting hard economic times and waning religious zeal, highlighted the still contentious relationship between the king and his provincial subjects.[39] Between 1666 and 1668, regional assemblies, the Marseille Chamber of Commerce, municipal councils, and family members reluctantly obeyed royal edicts to contribute fixed sums for slaves.[40] While the Estates of Brittany earmarked a massive ransom for a Knight of Malta, for example, it left the deliverance of lower-born Bretons to parents, communities, and the redemptive orders, which struggled to collect sufficient alms.[41] The Estates of Provence called on the royal galleys to stop "the pillaging, sacking, and ravishing by Turks and sea pirates along the country's whole coast" and the resulting loss of "an infinity of poor subjects, women, and children, most of whom made to abjure their faith, the others put up for ransom."[42] Meanwhile, its constituent towns did their best to avoid the monetary burden. The warship base of Toulon, for example, impoverished by a recent outbreak of plague, requested dispensation, and the fishing village of Cassis complained about being forced into debt. Neighboring La Ciotat and Martigues, known as "la Venise provençale," objected to suffering disproportionately because their shipyards made inhabitants favored targets for North African corsairs in search of skilled labor.[43]

Of course, Louis XIV valued skilled labor too. Convinced that his galleys were "triumphant chariot[s]" and that "nothing manifest[ed] his sovereignty more than these ships, stern aloft and underfoot three hundred slaves in chains," the king used all means to avoid returning promised Algerian and Tunisian oarsmen, and he allocated money only for French captives with navigational ability and then impressed them into the royal fleet.[44] After quarantine, state emissary and future consul Laurent d'Arvieux escorted the seamen he ransomed directly to warships docked at Toulon. Prevented from visiting their families or even changing their clothes before re-embarking, he recalled, the bitter, louse-infected mariners "cursed me for having taken them out of slavery to put them into hell."[45]

SOVEREIGN ILLUSIONS

What authority eluded the Sun King in these international and domestic arenas he continued to claim ritually through slave processions organized in his name. Such seemingly universal pageants did not acknowledge the pragmatic exclusion of sea-ready sailors, regional opposition to paying out ransoms, or North African insistence on repatriating their own enslaved subjects. Instead, like earlier spectacles mounted by French Catholic orders, those of 1666 and 1667 glorified the collaboration of altar and throne in turning Barbary captives exposed to foreign maladies, proclivities, and beliefs into vital, devoted Frenchmen.

In Marseille, one Trinitarian described, crowds greeted fifty-five plague-free arrivals from Algiers with "such great signs of joy and admiration . . . it was as if we were returning from another world."[46] A local curate from Troyes in the region of Champagne used verse to observe that other world—Islam—still clinging to the ransomed slaves midvoyage: "These men out of slavery / (Though good and still human) / In face and hands / Retain a bit of Savagery," he wrote. "They need this cross / Where Jesus once died / To become recognizable."[47] Its traces, however, had vanished by the time the troop reached Paris. "Entering the city in civil fashion," according to a rhymed letter that appeared in a municipal gazette, "They had instead of chains / That caused them shameful pains / Only sweet golden bonds / With which they were but adorned."[48]

Like earlier fetes that wove from coast to capital, the slave processions of 1666 and 1667 evoked baptismal rites and penitential marches that brought heretics and sinners back to the church. They must also have reminded observers of another, less joyous sort of cortege that followed the opposite itinerary: *chaînes* innovated by Colbert for transferring convicts to the royal galleys. Shackled in pairs and accompanied by armed guards and a doctor, men condemned for crimes that ranged from salt smuggling to murder departed from Paris, Brittany, or Guyenne and took

a standard route to Marseille.[49] Rather than the golden chains that captives carried for dramatic effect on the northward journey from servitude
to freedom, these prisoners wore actual forty-pound irons during the
southward trek to serve sentences of hard labor.

As rites to break the bonds of slavery and reestablish ties with church
and crown, finally, ceremonials of the 1660s stood in dialogue with the
last royal entrances of the Old Regime. In the sixteenth century captivity
and redemption imagery had been incorporated into performances of
kingship: a Gallic Hercules, his tongue chained to the ears of the four
estates, civilizing his people through language; a review of English war
captives, offering proof of military virtuosity.[50] When Louis XIV took
over the northern city of Douai in the summer of 1667, the parade's
iconography linked the invasion of Flanders to the emancipation of Barbary slaves. Hailing the monarch as a great liberator, this celebration of
sovereign power featured a mock-up galley of Christian rowers guided—
rather than by the traditional children dressed as cherubs—by a Jesuit
outfitted as a Trinitarian.[51] Here, in a public triple entendre, a servant
of the pope did the bidding of the French king, relating manumission,
annexation, and establishmentarianism.

Official texts worked in tandem with this visual lexicon to project
an image of political strength and Catholic supremacy. In 1667, for the
first time, the *Gazette de France* printed the itinerary of a Barbary slave
procession. A few months later, a Trinitarian-authored chronicle, *Le
Tableau de Piété envers les Captifs*, which listed the names and geographical origins of Frenchmen recently returned from North Africa,
broadcast that Protestant captives from Saintes and Flanders had "converted to the Faith after [their] redemption."[52] Such spiritual bluster in
printed form sought to reinforce the linkage between saving slaves from
Muslim lands, establishing royal authority, and healing sectarian divisions in France. Evangelization through ransom, however, proved more
abstract than actual. In practice, Huguenots continued largely to use
separate channels for buying back coreligionists. Thus a 1670 missive
from nine Protestant captives held in Tripoli beseeched members of the
Reformed Church in Lyon to deliver them from "Babylon." No modern-
day Gibeonites wearing the cloak of Calvinism to attract charity, these
"brothers groaning for so long in the pitiless chains of the Turks in Africa" vowed to spend any alms they received solely on self-preservation—
from the hazards posed by both papists and Muslims.[53] One signatory,
the surgeon Pierre Girard of Seyne en Provence, whose "bad star" put
him in the clutches of the corsairs, survived for seven years, long enough
to be liberated by English arms, write a narrative of his experiences, and
join the king's Swiss Guard.[54]

Semiotics of liberation to the contrary, then, Louis XIV was still giving neither his full attention to the plight of his remaining captive subjects nor his full commitment to an enduring Franco-Barbary peace. Despite rhetoric about making waterways safe for travel and trade, French officials showed equal concern with making them unsafe for European competitors, especially England. Despite promises to unshackle Muslim rowers, furthermore, they showed greater concern with manning the royal galleys.[55] It was in this climate of distrust that open conflict with Algiers and Tunis again broke out during the 1669 Ottoman conquest of Crete. Although France officially supported the sultan's claims to the island,[56] an Algerian ship under Turkish command intercepted a French trader supplying the Venetians, and local sea rovers resumed preying on French vessels, including one ferrying 220 slaves from Cape Verde.[57] In response, French admirals cut off access to Algiers. There, the pasha temporarily defused the crisis by punishing the perpetrators.[58] In Tunis, however, the dey asserted the right to enslave enemies traveling under French flag, while insisting on the difficulty of distinguishing friend from foe. According to his version of events, Tunisian and French boats had mistaken one another for rival corsairs, and during the fighting that ensued several men were wounded or killed.[59] Louis XIV insisted that the Tunisians, like the Algerians, had simply violated the accord, and he ordered a siege on Tunis. Once French warships set in motion this new cycle of reprisal, North African privateers responded by impounding a new batch of ships and 150 Frenchmen.[60] One victim was a Provençal merchant, Jean Bonnet, who left an account of three years' captivity.

CIRCULATING FORTUNE

The narrative of Bonnet, though told in his voice, was actually composed by Antoine Galland, an Orientalist best known for translating *A Thousand and One Nights*.[61] Born in Cassis, Bonnet went to sea as a young boy, completed a stint as a ship's apprentice, and spent several years working for a relative before purchasing his own boat to provision Crete. He encountered corsairs on what was only his second independent journey. For this soon-to-be Barbary captive, the sight of two suspicious sails on the horizon and the pillage of his vessel "by soldiers armed with sabers" were terrifying. But thanks to crewmates and friends who had endured periods in servitude, he knew enough to take precautions, throwing his chest full of fancy clothes overboard "so they would not easily know who I was." Awareness also made these experiences comprehensible.[62] Rather than confront a jumble of foreign faces and an alien tongue, Bonnet discovered a multilingual hybrid culture—North African and European, Muslim and Christian. He recognized a relative among the other captives and learned that the corsair captain, Redjeb Ra'is, originally hailed from Antibes.[63] He also found out that his master would be none other than the legendary Dom Philippe, a Tunisian prince renowned for his flight to Christendom and reluctant return to Islam. In Porto Farino (now Ghar al-Milh), Dom Philippe addressed Bonnet in Italian.[64]

In some respects Bonnet found Barbary slavery strangely familiar, but in no way did he consider it fun. Crowded at night into an airless underground bunker with irons on his ankles and fleas gnawing at his legs, he spent the day as an agricultural laborer, harvesting olives, pulling weeds, and building dirt walls.[65] He judged exemptions from work or invitations to Dom Philippe's country estate to be schemes to lure him into apostasy.[66] Yet rather than gamble on ruse to protect his religious and sovereign loyalties, Bonnet hatched plans to escape. He succeeded three years after arriving in Tunis when he and eleven other Frenchmen, a Calabrese, a Maltese, a Trapanese, a Livornese, a Portuguese, a Dutchman, and a Greek stole a boat. From the coastal city of Soussa, they paddled to Malta and on to Sicily, boarded a ship to Genoa, and rowed a felucca back to France.[67]

Once reunited with his family, Bonnet decided to trawl the Mediterranean for Muslims. "I bought a vessel, half-merchant, half-armed for privateering, to avenge the cruelties I had suffered during my slavery," read the conclusion to Galland's text, approved by royal censors at the twilight of Louis XIV's reign. After reconnoitering with other French corsairs on the Persian Gulf, he loaded up with booty and "twenty slaves that I bought from the same corsairs by order of [galley intendant Nicolas] . . . Arnoul." Then satisfied that his actions had restored some moral balance to the seascape, helped the French navy, and lined his own pockets, the escaped slave "cho[se] a less turbulent lifestyle" and retired.[68] As it turned out, had he not taken the initiative to flee, Jean Bonnet would in any case probably soon have gained his freedom—through exchange for a "Turk" acquired by his parents or by virtue of a 1672 treaty signed after three seasons of French blockades. Within a month officers had rescued three hundred captive Frenchmen (over half the total), vowing to send home any servile Tunisians in France.[69]

At Tripoli, by contrast, the divan rejected liberation demands by a naval commander with neither the resources nor the time to insist. An expedition publicized for 1673 was aborted too. "So many threats without effect have made our condition worse," grumbled seven hundred enslaved subjects in a letter to the Secretary of State. "Not only Turks but captives from other nations who are our companions in suffering insult us, reproach us that we have only words . . . make us the butt of malicious gossip, as if our powerful monarch did not have forces strong enough to destroy the audacity of these pirates."[70] This appeal to sovereign pride might have worked had Louis XIV not been financially and militarily overextended. Those Frenchmen in Tripoli lucky enough to survive plague from 1675 to 1676 but not lucky enough to receive ransom funds from home had to wait another five years before the king took action.[71]

MOROCCAN IMPROVISATIONS

France was hardly more confrontational on the Atlantic coast of North Africa than it had been on the Mediterranean. In 1669, 1670, and 1671, warships appeared before Salé, the "pirate capital" of Morocco.[72] But the city's geography—set back from the water and protected by a sandbar—made effective bombardment nearly impossible. Meanwhile, Saletian corsairs posing as peaceable Algerians cruised in the waters of western France, carrying off vessels like the frigate *La Royale*, bound for the Caribbean with future chroniclers of Moroccan captivity, Jean Gallonyé and Germain Moüette.[73] With no accord between king and sultan forthcoming, and redemptive orders barred from the realm, a "native of La Rochelle and eleven other Frenchmen" held in Fez implored Colbert to release an equal number of "Turks" from the galleys and deputize a local merchant to negotiate their exchange.[74] Louis XIV was amenable despite the Protestant identities of all involved, but he did not rule out a more violent option for unfettering captive subjects. In March 1672, his commander in the region received orders to "make the harshest war possible" on Morocco. Besides hunting down sea bandits between the English Channel and the Strait of Gibraltar, French forces had instructions to relay smaller launches into Salé's harbor. In the end, however, chastising corsairs and freeing slaves took second place to defeating the Dutch: the fleet was diverted north before it could execute this ambitious plan.[75]

Then the ascension of Mulay Isma'il changed the dynamic of slavery in Morocco. In 1672, there were about twelve hundred Christians under public and private control in Salé, Fez, and Tetouan.[76] The new sultan, who would reign for the next fifty-five years, claimed dominion over the entire servile population, which within six years he started transferring first to Fez and then to Meknes to construct a new capital modeled on Versailles. He also reversed his brother's exclusion policy and welcomed the Mercedarians back into his territories. Between 1674 and 1676 convents in Bordeaux and Paris organized voyages that freed seventy-five men and two women, mostly native to Atlantic provinces.[77] Gallonyé, from a village near Montpellier, was an exception. He had hoped to reach Saint Christopher (now Saint Kitts), where sub-Saharan African slaves were already cultivating sugar cane. But when the redemptive fathers arrived, he was the one loaded with irons—and an exorbitant price tag.[78] Unlike published forerunners who supplied entertaining vignettes about outwitting Muslims and humiliating Jews, this would-be planter claimed "absolutely no intention of giving pleasure." Rather Gallonyé's account of brute labor, brutal punishment, and bravery through five masters and two failed escape attempts was a paean to his rescuers and a plea "for true Christians to think occasionally about the infinite number of their brothers who still groan under the same chains and in the same prisons today."[79]

As miller, mason, and menial in various Moroccan cities from 1670 to 1681, Moüette—who hailed from a town near Chartres—also experienced heavy shackles and numerous owners. But his prose was punctuated by humorous digressions about the stratagems slaves used to gain the upper hand over masters. According to this gentleman explorer, private owners treated him with relative kindness, but his condition worsened once he passed to the state. "Our galley slaves are less unhappy than are those who labor on the castles in Meknes," wrote Moüette, insisting that "the matemores of Salé, Alcazar, and Tetouan surpass the darkest and filthiest prisons. And the tortures with which murderers and assassins in France are punished do not compare to those invented by the Moor."[80] Indeed, his tome provided a litany of "persecutions" and "travails" that put captives in constant bodily and spiritual jeopardy. While starvation, overwork, and contagion killed off the physically weak, he maintained, those with deficient religious armor submitted to the dangerous sexuality and seductive proselytizing of Muslims. Mulay Isma'il, "irreconcilable enemy of Christians," employed ugly women in his harem "at the basest of work," Moüette recounted, promising the pretty ones great favors "if only they agreed to make themselves Mahometans."[81] Naturally devout, most females stood firm. But assurances of earthly wealth and heavenly bliss sufficed to convert a group of "young people, nearly all valets and cabin boys, and consequently little schooled in the Catholic Religion, most of them even heretics." By implication prone to homosexuality, these likely apostates had already drifted from the tenets of their creed.[82] Slaves who trusted in God and themselves, he suggested, had a better chance of survival.

In Moüette's telling, Catholic prayer saved many captives from disease and delivered at least one prospective martyr from the jaws of death.[83] But in the absence of a permanent consul, artifice seemingly also shielded enslaved French subjects from religious and material impurities and helped them transcend their lowly positions in Morocco. In one example, the crafty wife of a Rochelais ship surgeon conspired with Moüette to contact a royal envoy in Salé by baking a note into a loaf of bread. In another, an Arabic-speaking merchant from Bordeaux trekked out of slavery in the guise of a dervish (eventually to divulge his true origins by cursing a dog in French).[84] Meanwhile, Moüette asserted that French slaves not hoodwinking North Africans used costume to cuckold them instead. According to two sides of a common stereotype reiterated here, Muslim mistresses found Christians sexy, but masters considered them sexless. Although Islam required strict separation of the sexes, "the grandest lords were not in the least scandalized when [we] came across their wives in an indecent state"; they did not even bother to hide their wives' nakedness, "saying that we are blind to the body as well as to the soul."[85] Asserting the capacity for discernment—whether of feminine beauty or divine truth—as well as virility, French slaves thus cross-dressed to pursue illicit rendezvous across religious lines. In Meknes, a Norman nobleman "with a natural inclination for debauchery" sneaked into the *bains* (public baths) "disguised as a girl" and played the guitar among the nudes. "If anything else specific took place during these gallantries," Moüette coyly remarked, "I have no knowledge of it."[86]

Whatever the case, such erotic adventures upended Barbary power relations along with visual signs of gender. By wearing a skirt, captives unmanned their masters; through camouflage, slaves confined to bagnes at night penetrated bains by day. As in ancient Saturnalia, they violated the most intimate boundaries that distinguished superiors from subordinates.[87] Rather than draw strength from sexual conquest, however, Moüette boasted of remaining sexually impervious. Eighteen years old and unattached in Salé, he must have seemed a good catch to his first master's wife, who reportedly plied him with delicacies, protected him from her husband, and, in Moüette's description, "solicited me to make myself a renegade so she could show me greater marks of her affection by wedding me to her niece, who was very beautiful and very rich." Fortunately, he extricated himself with such eloquence that she exempted him from sleeping in the disease-ridden matemore thereafter. Where other Christian captives played with fashion, Moüette substituted rhetoric. Disingenuous speech, not deceptive garb, inoculated him against Muslims infections. With "tender and touching words," he claimed to have sidestepped seduction, deflected the turban, and repelled the plague, which flared again in 1678.[88] It helped that he had become fluent in Arabic.

ALGERIAN PERFORMANCES

During the eleven years of Moüette's captivity, up to four hundred French slaves "languishing in the hands of barbarians, working more than beasts of burden," as one petition put it, awaited military or missionary salvation from Moroccan limbo.[89] Meanwhile, two incidents involving runaways imperiled the fragile truce between France and Algiers. First, in violation of ordinances that forbade captains to allow fugitives on board, French vessels had sneaked off with forty-six enslaved countrymen, leaving behind irate masters deprived of ransom.[90] Second, in violation of an asylum principle recapitulated in previous treaties, local authorities had arrested members of a fifty-six-man Algerian crew that took refuge in Roussillon and sent them to the royal galleys.[91] After some debate the king consented to repatriate the disputed "Turks and Moors." But ignoring concerns about the legality, let alone advisability, of detaining committed converts to Islam, he also gave orders that several renegades among their number "serve on my galleys as slaves until they make profession of the Catholic, apostolic, and Roman religion."[92] Then Mezzomorto, the indomitable corsair destined to head the regency, further aggravated Franco-Algerian relations by arresting two dozen French passengers aboard a Livornese craft. (One was royal numismatist Jean Foy-Vaillant, noted for swallowing twenty gold coins at the moment of capture and later excreting them with a spinach purgative.) Defending his prerogative—rejected by France as illegitimate—to keep human and material spoils from enemy vessels, the dey threatened to sell off the French captives to buy back the Algerians.[93]

Diplomatic acrimony at the highest levels did not preclude local ransom arrangements, however. Mercedarian redemptors freed thirty-nine French subjects from Algiers in 1674, and the following fall, a trader from Marseille used funds supplied by the Trinitarians to mediate the release of ninety-one others, including three women, displayed ritually in Aix-en-Provence and Arles.[94] But an unknown number of additional French slaves, whom sex, geographical origin, lack of patronage, or high cost rendered less desirable, did not make the cut—to the dismay of a factotum in the marine ministry. Rather than allow Catholic orders to "pompously process" a few cheap captives while abandoning everyone else to Islam, he proposed an overhaul that, as in Protestant kingdoms, would turn fund-raising and redemption duties over to secular authorities.[95] That did not happen. Diplomacy and religion remained intertwined. In 1675 Pope Clement X ordered France's bishops to start delivering biannual sermons on the redemption of Barbary captives, and it ultimately fell to French consul–cum–apostolic vicar Jean Le Vacher to broker the exchange of half the unlawfully seized French travelers for twenty-two "Turks."[96] Yet his efforts did not resolve the matter either: to the dey's consternation, the men who disembarked in Algiers in early 1676 composed only a portion of the promised rowers, along with a motley selection of invalids.[97]

Pressure to staff an expanding galley fleet had set France on a dangerous course. To maximize numbers at the oar, French commercial agents scoured Mediterranean markets for "Turks" (carefully sifting out any Orthodox Christians);[98] local leaders plucked several more Algerian sailors from a shipwreck; and galley intendants continued resolutely to dissimulate the identities of the Muslims they possessed.[99] Disregarding warnings from merchants and consuls about allowing the pursuit of rowers to spark another war, the king refused to acknowledge any infraction. Now that the 1678 treaty of Nijmegen had brought temporary peace to Europe, he could better afford to stake a hard position on Barbary. Instead of releasing the illegally detained Algerians, Louis XIV demanded restitution of around sixty of his own subjects taken off non-French boats and dispatched warships to Algiers in 1679, 1680, and 1681.[100]

However these belligerent performances played in the capital, they fell flat on the coast, where experience had taught residents to expect neither freedom on the sole basis of Frenchness nor liberation through firepower. Thus a group of mothers in La Ciotat pressured the town council, not the throne, to apportion funds for Algerian ransoms, and Pierre Choland, from the same town, begged his father for three hundred piastres to end what he termed "mon esclavitude." Choland's letter from April 1679, written in unschooled French tinged with Provençal, described his daily struggle to avoid conversion. "My master tries incessantly to persuade me with threats and flattery, and though I have resolved to die rather than consent to his evil designs," he averred, "I fear that time and the punishments . . . he inflicts on me . . . will in the end lead me to desperation."[101] Family and friends may have come up with the cash to save a single native soul from apostasy. But given Choland's southern roots, a Trinitarian mission to Algiers that year organized in Normandy and Champagne may well have left him behind.[102] Naval posturing and diplomatic custom notwithstanding, place still often trumped both Catholic faith and sovereign ties in determining redemption priorities.

ROMANTIC ROLES

Higher-born captives from areas closer to Paris—like the nobleman Claude Auxcousteaux de Fercourt and the playwright Jean-François Regnard, taken from an English vessel during a voyage from Genoa to

Marseille in 1678—knew to make independent provisions. As Fercourt registered in his journal, once posing as impoverished mercenaries proved untenable, both men readily signed promissory notes for hefty ransoms.[103] In the eight-month interim before the money arrived, Fercourt ground wheat and wound wool under the gaze of a vindictive Morisco. But he acknowledged that "not all slaves meet as unhappy a fate as ours; those lucky to fall into the hands of a true Muslim or natural Turk suffer only insofar as they have lost their liberty." Such masters, he wrote, offered their chattel comfort by reflecting on the temporary nature of Mediterranean servitude. "Don't worry; God is great, the world so-so; God will lead the way; an occasion will arrive for you to return home," they said, speaking in Lingua Franca.[104] The cruelest trial the hero of Regnard's posthumous novel, *La Provençale*, endured was competition for the heart of his beloved. The wheel of fortune that thrust Zelim into Algiers, exposing him to the typical Barbary perils, also provided a ruler with "nothing barbarous but his name," approved the Frenchman's amorous exploits, and relatively quickly restored his freedom.[105]

For the protagonist of *La Provençale*, as for the leading men of roughly contemporaneous narratives written in the romantic style, enslavement resulted from mischance, and the possibly transformative effects of North African detention could be thwarted and, if necessary, undone. In the fluid, mercantile, and largely male world of circulating goods, peoples, beliefs, and diseases that Jean Bonnet inhabited, for example, ship captains became chattel, Frenchmen "turned Turk," and a Tunisian lord metamorphosed into a Catholic penitent and back again. By acquiring twenty Muslims for the galleys after his escape, Bonnet was trying on the role of privateer, settling the score for his own seizure, and garnering points in the competition between Crescent and Cross. For him, slavery had nothing to do with destiny or race and everything to do with bad luck. By taking on transvestite parts on the North African stage, Antoine Quartier, Germain Moüette, and their enslaved companions acted out masculinity and vigor, fidelity to Christ, and fealty to the crown. Making love and making trouble in female guise and Turkish habit, they transgressed the bounds of slavery and preserved the traits that bonded them to France. Together their writings depicted pretense, at least on foreign soil, as a weapon in the service, not the subversion, of French health, wealth, and socioreligious stability; showed Barbary dangers as frightening but largely reversible, like Barbary slavery itself; and proposed French identity as externally signified and mutable but internally unwavering.

Responding to the anxiety engendered by the constant flow of commodities and pathogens in the Mediterranean, the continuous uncertainty of diplomatic and social standing, the perpetual mixture of languages and creeds, the insatiable appetites of corsairs, and the permanent risk of captivity, these texts prescribed not stubborn stasis but further motion: liberatory imposture and redemption through fraud.

RESOLUTION THROUGH RITUAL

In the case of Quartier and Moüette, final resolution entailed another sort of circulation: ransom payments, by a Marseillais merchant and four Mercedarians, respectively. Since Quartier had devolved to the pasha of Tripoli by the time a trader with a sideline buying back captives arrived in March 1668, fixing his price required a trip to the palace and the same knack for concealment that had earlier proved useful at the slave bazaar. "Youth, talent, strength, social rank, and birthplace are so many obstacles to the liberty of a Christian, who cannot break his chains without paying doubly for his condition or merit," Quartier affirmed, "unless he had the prudence to hide them"—a prospect made more difficult by lurking renegade spies.[106] Though a Jew from Tetouan who noticed him writing almost blew "Sieur Moüette's" doltish cover, Mulay Isma'il ultimately allowed this noble slave to be included among a group of ostensibly poor, unskilled, old, or sick men (and one woman) brought out of Moroccan bondage. Predominantly Breton but "entirely French," as advertised in a pamphlet distributed by the redemptive fathers, they set sail in May 1681.[107]

Quartier took pride in his ability to maintain purity of body, heart, and soul in Barbary. But neither officials nor ordinary residents in his mother country initially received him as the unadulterated French Catholic he believed himself to be. As soon as the former slave neared French territory, the experience of North African captivity marked him as a possible carrier of religious and physical contagion. Before he could disembark in Marseille and make his way home, therefore, he had to participate in at least one of two reintegration rituals demanded of redeemed slaves: quarantine. Despite receiving a clean bill of health after several days on an island outside the city harbor, the people he encountered in southern France remained fearful of pestilence. Rather than touch letters he delivered from relatives in servitude, "according to custom," addressees cautiously "dipped [them] in boiling vinegar before they were opened." Rather than accept a few coins from him as payment, one woman gave him fruit "out of charity."[108]

As the beneficiary of an individual rather than group redemption, Quartier was not required to reenact his North African ordeal for spectators throughout the kingdom. Nor, except on the page, was he obliged to play the role of grateful subject and pious Catholic to assure the repudiation of Islam and inspire the return of Protestants to the church. But his pilgrimage to towns and hamlets around France to deliver mail from compatriots still enslaved in Tripoli, then to Chablis to greet his family, and finally to Paris to become a Mercedarian actually resembled one of these religious pageants, becoming an orderly land journey to right the tumultuous sea voyage that had originally led him astray.[109] Thirteen years later, following a two-week quarantine, Moüette paid homage to his predecessor in chains with a stopover in "the birthplace of father Cartier [*sic*] . . . whose parents plied us with all sorts of refreshments for two days."[110] According to the route printed in the *Mercure galant*, the Mercedarians marched Moüette and his fellow redeemed captives from Marseille to Toulon, Avignon, Lyon, Saulieu, Avalon, Chablis, Auxerre, Joigny, and Paris. For Moüette, an interview with Louis XIV represented the culmination of a restorative homecoming that had lasted over eleven months. "Being brought to Versailles," he wrote, "we had the honor of greeting His Majesty, the view of whom did not give us any less consolation than the recovery of our liberty."[111]

This encounter between slaves and sovereign took place in July 1682. As the climax of the second reintegration rite undergone by church-claimed captives, it symbolically erased competing allegiances, cemented loyalty to God and country, and confirmed royal authority over even the farthest-flung subjects. By completing the circuit from servitude to freedom, estrangement to Frenchness, Moüette's troop also mirrored the king's own quarter-century-old peregrination and the kingdom's ongoing struggle between commerce and orthodoxy, between opening international markets and clamping down on religious nonconformity, and between enriching and purifying the state. Over the previous decades, Louis XIV had strengthened the navy, regulated manufacturing, established chartered companies, sponsored scientific expeditions, encouraged overseas trade, and even invited foreign Protestants and Jews to bring their financial expertise and capital to the realm. But he had also exercised cultural, legislative, and judicial means to rein in the consequent "France of movement" that threatened to introduce alien values, including Islam, to French society along with bullion and useful outsiders.[112] Instead of straightforwardly rehearsing colonial possession through commercial expansion, therefore, the Most Christian King acquisitively surveyed the globe and then patrolled his borders.[113]

Relation de la captivité du Sr Moüette, which received a royal privilege and a Parisian publisher in 1683, concluded with a glossary of useful Arabic terms and a treatise on commerce. It lauded the minister whose "tireless zeal, sublime and vast genius . . . vigilance, exactitude, prudence, and marvelous talents" had sent abroad merchants and brought home skilled production, "making [France] today the happiest and most abundant part of the world." Now Moüette looked across the sea to "one of the most fertile countries on earth" and envisioned harmonious exchange with Barbary as a replacement for disruptive corsairing, with traffic in dates, ostrich feathers, wool, mirrors, leather, velour, grapes, combs, sugar, and tobacco as a substitute for traffic in Christians and Muslims. France's future prosperity, he suggested, depended on Mediterranean peace.[114] But Louis XIV had other plans. In an attempt to keep the maximum number of Ottoman oarsmen and free the most French subjects, the monarchy had finally unleashed its full naval arsenal against Algiers, igniting a new era of state violence against the Barbary States that would last for the next forty years.

CHAPTER FOUR

Bombarding Barbary

Louis XIV had lied. The dey found out in the fall. Despite assenting to a captive exchange, the Sun King never intended to free able-bodied Algerians from the royal galleys. As one rower complained, "We are told after this campaign liberty, and this liberty never comes. Now we all believe we are being mocked, that it is only imaginary liberty [they promise]."[1] In October 1681, his country declared war on France, and in the course of six weeks the number of French slaves in Algiers burgeoned by three hundred.[2] "There are already twelve French prizes in this port: four ships and eights boats from Provence and Brittany," testified an enslaved Marseille merchant, Laurent Gracier, cautioning that if the monarch did not quickly mend relations, "commerce will be gravely damaged . . . and many poor people among whom I unfortunately number will suffer."[3]

In the short term, he was right: France's initial offensives proved destructive yet ineffective. But repeated salvos against Algiers and Tripoli in the 1680s and 1690s did release a flood of slaves. Just as important, they demonstrated the crown's newfound ability to impose its will on the Ottoman regencies, which in turn helped shift the power dynamic between France and the eastern portion of North Africa. An ascendant France in the Mediterranean enhanced Louis XIV's crusading credentials and intensified the symbolic insult of Barbary captivity. Meanwhile, further royal over local involvement in saving Christians from Muslim lands broadened expectations of who deserved to be free, even as redemption by the king's command became a more explicit means of establishing who counted as French.

ASSAULT ON ALGIERS

In 1682 Louis XIV picked the Huguenot naval officer Abraham Duquesne to bomb North Africa into submission. That a Protestant spent the years before the Revocation of the Edict of Nantes fighting Muslims in the service of his Most Christian King was an irony not lost on contemporaries.[4] As second in command of the Mediterranean fleet, Duquesne had been cruising against North African sea rovers for more than a decade. The year before, a deadly strike against Tripolitan corsairs hiding out at the island of Chios had yielded a favorable treaty with provisions for unfettering eight hundred French captives.[5] Still buoyed by that victory, he arrived in Algiers toward the end of August, heading up an armada composed of fifteen galleys, eleven warships, two fire ships, and five bomb ketches, newly invented for launching explosive shells at sea. Despite its destructive potential, the two-week "earthquake"[6] brought upon a city already ravaged by plague and famine[7] accomplished little more than killing five hundred inhabitants and blowing up fifty houses: most of the missiles fell into the water before hitting their mark, and relatively few privateers were at port.[8] Suspicions that Jews in Marseille had passed intelligence on French naval maneuvers to coreligionists in Algiers led to the community's temporary expulsion.[9]

The onslaught started up again the following June. This time, after only two days, the dey called a twenty-four-hour armistice to round up the French slaves. On 29 June 1683, Algerian boats delivered 142 men to Duquesne's warships; over the next three days they rowed out groups of 180, 152, and 83, who were sent on to quarantine in Toulon.[10] On shore pandemonium reigned. With a death toll of one thousand and the port reduced to rubble, the regency's political factions split over whether to negotiate with France. Backed by the militia, Italian renegade and former ra'is Mezzomorto staged a coup. In the meantime, an angry mob, believing laundry drying on the French consulate terrace had given a signal to the squadron, dragged off Lazarist consul Jean Le Vacher. Some accounts have him receiving the choice of apostasy or a gruesome demise; all describe his body being blasted into the harbor from the mouth of a cannon before twenty-two other Frenchmen met the same fate.[11]

Yet whatever their horror, these casualties paled in light of France's victory, which along with harassing Protestants helped further stoke Louis XIV's international reputation as religious warrior and distract some attention from the alliance between Sun and Crescent that endured even as Ottoman troops advanced on Vienna.[12] A commemorative medal minted in 1683 likened the Bourbon monarch to the Greek goddess of wisdom, defeating pirates with one hand and saving slaves with the other (Figure 6). A tribute by a repentant Huguenot lawyer praised his sovereign's "just revenge," which "transformed Christian shackles into corsair chains," and his "fiery bombs," which "changed [Algiers] into [a] blazing tomb."[13] Copying the phrasing of a former Spanish captive in Morocco,

Figure 6. Announcement of medal commemorating the bombardment of Algiers, 1683. © Musée national de la Marine, ph. 135002.

champion of absolutism Jacques Bossuet exalted the king in a funeral oration for the queen: "You will fall to this conqueror, Algiers, rich with the spoils of Christendom. You have already turned over your slaves. Louis has smashed the irons with which you loaded his subjects, who are born to be free in his glorious empire."[14]

Indeed, the articles of peace secured in April 1684 by a French rear admiral and a *capidji* (ambassador) from Constantinople did provide for the liberty of all French subjects and protected foreigners still detained in the regency.[15] Yet they actually fell short of the king's expectations by conceding an equal number of his precious galley slaves.[16] After making what French propagandists depicted as a contrite visit to Versailles that summer ("Africa supplex, confecto bello piratico" [Africa is suppliant, since the pirate war has been concluded] boasted a medal showing him prostrate before Louis XIV), an Algerian ambassador accepted various jewel-encrusted presents.[17] In November he embarked with four hundred Turks—if not Algerians—aboard a naval vessel, which returned to Toulon a month later with four hundred seemingly French sailors and one ship captain.[18] Flaunting his power over infidel foes to heretic rivals England and Holland (themselves at war with Algiers, despite having pressured the regency to fight France instead), Louis XIV used a second Algerian embassy the next spring to trade another group of (most likely crippled) Ottoman rowers for a number of non-French Christians, which included some English and Dutch Protestants.[19]

During the months that followed, the redemptive orders ransomed several dozen more slaves from Algiers and Tunis, some of who trudged the path to Paris as Huguenots streamed out of France (Figure 7). These men, it seems, reached their sovereign on the very day he outlawed Protestantism from the kingdom—to the consternation of one likely participant, arrested as a *relaps* (convert to Catholicism relapsed to Protestantism) (Figure 8). Certainly an eyewitness to the 20 October procession recognized a parallel between redeeming Christians from North Africa and extinguishing Christian heresy at home. He wrote, "They were delivered like the poor Huguenots, and the whole world sang the glory of the king, their liberator."[20] All together, crowed an issue of the 1685 *Mercure galant*, "these different restitutions took away more than 1200 slaves from the Algerians. Thus not only is their state depopulated of French slaves, but it has very few others, such that there is hardly a nation in Europe whose subjects are not publicizing at home the good it received from His Majesty, this Prince having spared neither care nor expense for the liberty of so many unfortunates, from whatever nations they came."[21] By saving slaves, Louis XIV was now trying to cement the status he had cultivated by fighting corsairs.

Figure 7. French Christian slave in Algiers in Barbary. "Esclave chrétien
français à Alger en Barbarie," engraving by Alexandre Leroux (c. 1690).
© Musée national de la Marine, ph. 159013.

Figure 8. Mercedarians present ransomed slaves to Louis XIV. Engraving by Franz Erlinger, in *Histoire de l'ordre sacré, royal et militaire de Notre-Dame de la Merci . . .* (Amiens: Guislain Le Bel, 1685). Paris, Bibliothèque Mazarine, 5432 F; photo by Jean-Loup Charmet.

BRAWN AND BELIEF

Of course, once the bagnes of Algiers had emptied of Frenchmen, ministers and intendants drew up the plank on the royal galleys, delaying the release of additional Algerians, and dispatching elderly and infirm "Turks" of indiscriminate origin instead.[22] Geography mattered profoundly to the dey of Algiers, but as concerned Ottoman rowers, the French ruler privileged brawn and belief: he wanted Muslims at the oar to manifest his sea power and converts from Islam to manifest his newly unified Gallican Church. What he did not want was any publicity about the two combined, which would put him in the awkward position of having either to rationalize the servile labor of Catholics who committed no crime or else lose valuable manpower.[23] Nor did he want tales of involuntary baptisms to threaten French interests. When a rumor of a Tunisian woman kidnapped to Marseille for this purpose began to circulate in 1685, therefore, galley officials rushed to quash it. "My lord, I have been a slave in France and living in Marseille for five years," Agy Abdallah was made to address his dey, "and never have I seen or heard about . . . anyone bringing girls from Tunis or anywhere to Marseille or making a single Turk Christian by force."[24]

As for voluntary baptisms, they had better be to the apostolic faith. Pre-1685, *parlements* throughout France had registered an ordinance for "Mahometans and idolaters" who switched religion to be instructed only in the tenets of Catholicism rather than the "false doctrine" of "the said R.P.R. [*Religion Prétendue Reformée*]."[25] Post-1685, while France's almanacs advertised "the triumph of the church over Calvin and Muhammad," its periodicals heralded infidel conversions, exhorting "charitable" readers to work toward converting Muslims.[26] At the news, albeit false, that a renegade captain had abjured in October 1687, the king reportedly announced that he valued the "salvation of one soul" over the "capture of many warships." A month later, the Marseille city council had occasion to make good on this claim when several officers and crew from a Tunisian vessel declared that "God had inspired them to re-enter the Christian religion."[27] Contrasting France's open doors to its Catholic neighbor's closed ones, municipal magistrates remarked that Aly Raix (formerly Pierre Terragon of Majorca) and Romadon (otherwise known as Jean Gueydon of Marseille) had wisely chosen their port of call. In Spain, inquisitors would have confiscated the boat and arrested everyone on board.[28] It was royal policy to deal harshly with relapsed heretics—whether Protestant or Muslim—but, as the marine minister later put it, a reflection of "royal bounty to receive [renegades] with kindness and charity."[29]

TROUBLE IN TRIPOLI

The ink was hardly dry on the accord between France and Tripoli when a diplomatic insult and a maritime incident again started the two powers down the road to war. In November 1682, nine months after the relay of 340 captives to Toulon and ransom promises for the rest, a Tripolitan corsair commandeered a Marseillais freighter heading home from Syria.[30] Louis XIV had slighted the regency by failing either to buy back his leftover subjects or even correspond with his supposed ally, a group of ra'is complained to the divan. In any case, they argued, peace with France was economically untenable, since it put any vessel with legitimate—or, as often, sham—French colors, passes, or captains off limits to attack. Whether convinced or cowed, the dey locked up the French consul and declared French ships and crew valid prizes. Over the next two years, Tripoli's three bagnes gained 164 new French inmates, among them an agent from the Marseille Chamber of Commerce bearing a conciliatory missive from the king.[31]

Fresh from Algiers in the fall of 1683, Duquesne reportedly turned his guns on Tripoli. According to the recollections of Laurent d'Arvieux (then consul to Aleppo), the Protestant commander dispatched five thousand bombs and disembarked twelve hundred troops, setting buildings and fortifications on fire. But even as the city smoldered, much of the Tripolitan fleet remained at large.[32] Their capture of two more French boats triggered another expedition, led by a Catholic admiral, Jean d'Estrées. On this occasion, two days of shelling sufficed. "The torpedoes exploded red from the mouths of cannon and rose into the air like flaming brands, and then others followed, more and more numerous," recounted a Moroccan pilgrim en route to Mecca. Though thousands of would-be martyrs poured in from the countryside, he wrote, "in the city panic took hold; the infidels did not stop raining bombs. Finally, it was decided to parley."[33] On 25 June 1685, a nonagenarian envoy transmitted a message of surrender and heard France's conditions, which went beyond anything demanded thus far: the indemnification of French losses for 500,000 livres, the establishment of French consular preeminence, the implementation of a three-day waiting period for French conversions to Islam, the provision of ten hostages, and the liberation of all Christian captives in the realm.[34]

With gold jewelry expropriated from Tripoli's women and gold lamps confiscated from its Jewish synagogue, the dey began payment and the release of twelve hundred slaves—half French, half victims of raids along the Italian coast. "What is remarkable," noted the mission's royal interpreter, "is that they gave us back all the French and foreign slaves taken under our flag . . . without our returning a single one, or even promising to give back any in the treaty."[35] Naval muscles flexed, France was now in a position to extend physical protection to Christians whom it could previously offer only spiritual comfort.[36] To avoid the brunt of French artillery, Tunis signed a preemptive "one hundred year" accord at the end of August.[37]

SNARING PROTESTANTS

The composition of the French slave population in North Africa had always reflected domestic and foreign developments. While opportunity overseas had landed greater numbers of aspiring Caribbean colonists in servitude during the 1660s, twenty years later, religious persecution drove ever more Huguenots into the traps of corsairs. "Disappear[ing] without so much as paying the baker," a Breton official noted with satisfaction in July 1686, "these people are being punished more severely than if they had been arrested in France."[38] In fact, hundreds of fugitive *religionnaires* (Huguenots) carried off to the Ottoman regencies after the Revocation of the Edict of Nantes found themselves enmeshed in a three-way power struggle among Catholic, Protestant, and Muslim leaders, and caught between developing official policy and varying personal sympathies. At stake were money, religion, and politics. To a dey, bey, or pasha, captive Huguenots represented a new source of revenue; to missionaries, a ready pool of converts. Dutch and English agents, meanwhile, perceived suffering coreligionists and potential allies against France. Finally, French diplomats, admirals, and friars, whether they saw vulnerable Christians or treacherous heretics, recognized the symbolic and practical dangers in relinquishing sovereignty over Protestant subjects in chains.

Until the resumption of Franco-Algerian hostilities the next summer, therefore, consul André Piolle repeatedly demanded liberty for any refugees picked off Dutch and English boats—not only those individuals prepared to abjure.[39] As Frenchmen, whatever their faith, enslaved Huguenots discovered aboard an intercepted Algerian vessel "should be free according to the treaty," galley general Louis Victor de Rochechouart, duc de Mortemart, told the divan.[40] Pasha and dey Hajj Hussein, formerly ra'is Mezzomorto, disagreed. Demanding the return of all his subjects found serving on the Algerian *Croissant d'Or* that crashed in Brittany, he refused to cede thirty-six Christians whom he judged "no longer French since they were fleeing France and all Lutherans."[41] Muslims were not the only ones who put up barriers to repatriation, however. Rather than betray their religious convictions or risk condemnation to what had after 1685 become floating vehicles for forced conversion—the royal galleys—many Huguenots chose "irons in Algiers or Tunis" over "hard slavery" in France. At least in North Africa, émigré minister Jean Claude declared, "they [did] not have their conscience oppressed and might still entertain some hope of liberty by way of ransom."[42] Indeed, over French objections to foreign Protestant intercession, which undermined Louis XIV's efforts to control his subjects, numerous such men and women were bought out of Barbary with alms forwarded from England and the Netherlands.[43]

Isaac Brassard arrived in Algiers after a fittingly precise forty days at sea. One of "sixty-three French Protestants" on a 614-passenger captured Dutch packet boat who "[ran] a large risk of being sold as slaves," the *Gazette de Haarlem* reported, this pastor from Montauban endured eighteen months as a construction worker and a cook, and witnessed a third cycle of French bombardments before being delivered by English and Dutch brethren. According to a narrative he composed in exile and afterward had smuggled into France, Brassard felt no religious pressure from Muslims. Instead, in July 1687, it was the resident father of the Congrégation de la Mission who solicited his conversion, promising that "by such means, I would assure my salvation . . . and render a great service to the king, who would reward me well." Brassard's defiant answer was that he "abhorred the Roman religion," and his loyalty lay with God, "king of kings." Once rejected, Brassard maintained, the Lazarist cooked up assorted torments to inflict on the obstinate Protestant, whom he nicknamed "Ducaine" to stir "the furor of the populace."[44]

French Catholics in North Africa could be as cruel as any Turk, suggested another captive Huguenot abducted with fifty coreligionists on the English Channel. "As French subjects we are hated and extraordinarily badly treated by the nation to which God has subjugated us," Daniel Poyen informed the leadership of the banned Protestant church, "and as Reformed we are hated and insulted by almost all the slaves and particularly by the French ones . . . so that we find ourselves simultaneously heaped with blows, work, abuse, curses, and threats." Like his Catholic countrymen, he feared for the youths of both sexes, whose "bodies are abused . . . to stifle in their hearts the feeling of Christian faith." Unwilling to compromise his own religious convictions, he followed Brassard in seeking help from Protestants abroad.[45]

War between France and Algiers broke out again in August 1687 for the same reason it had six years before: the king's attachment to his galleys and the Ottoman rowers who powered them. Fed up with government stonewalling over Algerian slaves withheld from the last treaty, Hajj Hussein set his corsairs on French vessels.[46] Intent on punishment rather than peace, Louis XIV aimed his mortars at Algiers. A battle of nerves preceded the start of hostilities. While the pasha-dey threatened to assassinate a second French consul and sacrifice 372 newly enslaved French residents, Estrées, back for another round, swore to kill an equal number of Algerian hostages brought along precisely for that purpose.[47] When the first of ten thousand bombs began crashing into buildings in early July 1688, Hajj Hussein started shooting Frenchmen. The captives were positioned "head down and feet up, attached by their arms to the cannon, ripped apart by the fire of the powder alone, which propelled limbs far and wide," Brassard recalled.[48] The admiral retaliated in kind, casting the remains of several Muslims ashore by raft.

After watching scores of seamen hideously executed and the apostolic vicar tortured, mutilated, and finished off with a knife, Brassard wrote, he himself prepared to die. Impressed by such bravery, the pasha-dey reportedly vowed to spare Protestants and kill Spanish and Italian Catholics once he had finished off the French. If accurate, his response to a group of Catholic captains and merchants who volunteered to apostatize was even more bizarre. According to several accounts, he called the men unworthy of Islam but offered mercy if they converted to Judaism instead.[49] By mid-July, Algiers stood in ruins, debris from collapsed houses blocking the streets. But Hajj Hussein did not capitulate. Experience had taught that French resolve against North Africa lasted only as long as weather, ammunition, and peace in Europe held out.[50]

REDEEMING CATHOLICS

This time revolution in England and skirmishes in the Rhineland brought the Mediterranean armada home. With the War of the Grand Alliance under way, which pitted France against a coalition of England, Holland, Austria, Spain, and several German principalities, Louis XIV wanted to settle with Algiers.[51] In April 1689 he organized a secret mission to feel out Algerian intentions, and then in September he deputized naval commissary Guillaume Marcel to make a new accord. Negotiated under pressure and not ratified until December 1690, its terms were far less advantageous than those of the preceding treaty. Although France did succeed in inserting clauses imposing a three-day waiting period for apostasy and recognizing Lazarist monks as French subjects, the kingdom also agreed to pay Algiers an indemnity, refrain from sailing near North African shores, suffer the enslavement of foreigners traveling under French flag, provide the regency with artillery to assault the Spanish bastion at Oran, and, finally, release about one hundred Algerian slaves for a fixed sum but ransom as many as thirteen hundred French slaves at market value.[52]

The original instructions for freeing these captives had blended expediency and dogma in prioritizing sailors, young boys, and Huguenots—that is, likely cannon fodder, possible renegades, and prospective *nouveaux convertis* (new converts from Protestantism), or *forçats* (convict oarsmen). Yet when Algerian masters responded to a public call to bring French slaves in their possession to the consulate and bargain over prices in December 1689, the royal envoy seemed to disregard profession, age, and creed. Apparently, he picked out 250 of the cheapest ones.[53] Bastion de France director Denis Dusault put a stop to such indiscrimination. Extending the principle of "one faith, one law, one king" to Barbary captives, the man who had earlier objected to the prominence of Duquesne now convinced the marine ministry to make Catholicism a prerequisite for release. Thus by early 1690, while France continued to extend diplomatic protection to all Christians of *foreign* origin in North Africa, the Eldest Daughter of the Church theoretically cut off committed Protestants with French roots. The redemptive fathers who arrived in Algiers that spring, however, did not necessarily examine their objects of charity too closely. Deterred from channeling funds toward anyone but sea-ready mariners, the Trinitarians bought back 54 captives and the Mercedarians up to 150, whom they may have shown off in Marseille before delivering to a warship in Toulon.[54] "Indeed, these slaves were all sailors," explained a retrospective pamphlet, "and consequently necessary to the service of his Majesty, who was then supporting the weight of a tough war by land and by sea."[55]

But even these ransom efforts on behalf of the navy and the flight of as many as thirty additional slaves aboard French warships still left up to eight hundred subjects of both sects in Algerian bagnes.[56] In letters to be transported by a new dedicated postal boat, two such remaining captives appealed for salvation on the grounds of regional fealty, Catholic devotion, and filial love—and received it in pursuit of religious purity and social stability.[57] Identifying himself as a "child of Marseille," as well as one of many enslaved Provençals in the summer of 1690, Antoine Broglia likened himself to a soul in purgatory, imploring city leaders to accept paternity and deliver a native son. Then he provided the names of his parents as proof. Three months later Jean-François Finier told his father that if the king delayed redemption much longer, "not a single French slave will remain, since a day does not go by when plague does not kill two or three." He begged him to pray to Saint Roch for protection and send two hundred piastres as soon as possible. The Marseille city council had a simple motivation for Finier's release: "head of household," reads a marginal note in a distinct hand.[58]

By averting the death of one resident abroad, municipal authorities hoped to save a whole family at home. By sheltering "honest folk" among the captive population in his own residence, consul René Lemaire (who had himself spent five years interned in Algiers) hoped "to exempt them from contagious disease as much as the rigors of slavery." As per usual, however, the release of Algerian galley slaves was a sticking point, and when Dusault finally returned to the regency as "royal advisor, sent by H.M. to execute the peace treaty," accompanied by an Algerian ambassador, three redemptive fathers and a token offering of "Turks" in May 1691,[59] pestilence had taken the lives of 350 French captives and driven up prices.[60] It took until the end of October to renegotiate the exchange of 257 Algerian galley slaves for 452 Catholic survivors and 15 new converts from Calvinism. (Dusault abandoned 8 Huguenots "who persevere in their stubbornness, preferring it to liberty.")[61] Then it took another year for two ships carrying a portion of the rowers and another bringing some of the currency to pull into port.[62]

The Trinitarians paid for fewer than fifty ostensibly Catholic slaves.[63] Under orders from Louis XIV, relatives and maritime communities picked up the tab for the rest: about three hundred seamen whose price varied by rank. Marseille, for instance, provided funds for 112 carefully identified natives but denied responsibility for mere inhabitants—despite what one official deemed the obligation "to take care of people who leave their country to come and settle in France."[64] By royal decree Saint-Malo, Brest, and Nantes began remitting three deniers for every livre of revenue derived from state-licensed corsairing to redeem Bretons.[65] In the context of centrally directed, regionally funded redemption, French status was now restricted to Catholics and the limits of local identity determined by cash.

As implementation of the 1689 treaty dragged into the next century, royal agents continued to monitor the behavior and beliefs of Huguenots who arrived in Algiers, noting ones for sale at the *badistan* (slave bazaar) and others set free by Protestant powers.[66] Some French redemptive fathers had a harder time turning their backs on fellow Christians—even heretical ones. Seeming to view Islam as a greater evil than Reformed Christianity, the Trinitarians who ransomed forty-six French and foreign subjects from Algiers (plus ten from Tunis and eight from Tripoli) in the summer of 1700 also intended to rescue two Norman "Calvinists." But the women apostatized before they could intervene. "All the others were redeemed, and these ones surely would have been too," wrote the friars in a published account that went through multiple editions, "if they had not been held by chains that cannot be broken, having renounced Christianity and given themselves over to the Moors."[67] Other redemptive fathers, like the Trinitarians of Dunkirk, however, resisted royal interference by withholding funds for "foreigners" who "do not directly concern us."[68]

In fact, the first slave procession in a generation, which journeyed from Marseille to Paris after a difficult quarantine (one ex-captive succumbed to plague at the lazaret), did feature a multinational and even multireligious group from, besides France, the United Provinces, the Spanish Netherlands, Ireland, Genoa, Malta, and the Holy Roman Empire, but not Flanders. Once again burnishing the Sun King's image as defender of Christendom, they appeared at Fontainebleau, where Louis XIV was hosting the monarchs of England and Spain just a month before Charles II's death set off the War of the Spanish Succession.[69]

TAMING TRIPOLI AND TUNIS

In Tripoli, the aftereffects of France's earlier assault lingered. With the regency dispossessed of all its Christian slaves and a good portion of its wealth by the punishing 1685 accord, dey Ibrahim Tarzi initially tried to maintain peaceful relations with Louis XIV, releasing several more captives in 1686 and sending an ambassador to Paris with exotic animals in 1687 as a sign of goodwill.[70] Still, Franco-Tripolitan amity hardly ran deep—certainly not deep enough to withstand the pressures of European politics. Swayed during bleak economic times following a plague epidemic by English and Dutch commitments of money, supplies, and defense (not to mention the prospect of new prizes) if he cut off ties with France, a new dey, Muhammad Pasha al-Iman, imprisoned the generally despised French consul and declared war at the end of January 1692. Writing from "the hell of Tripoli" in March, Louis Lemaire informed a colleague that corsairs had seized eleven French ships and made 215 new slaves. "They took all my clothes, sold my rags at auction and left me for several days without deigning to send me a piece of bread," he complained two weeks later. "Without one of our so-called friends, I would be dead of hunger. I finally accustomed myself to eating locusts like everyone else." Lemaire's misery only increased when, in anticipation of another bombardment, Tripolitan authorities put him and the other French captives to work rebuilding the city's fortifications.[71]

Two thousand French bombs catapulted from the harbor in July did not move the dey, who reportedly declared he would rather see the city in ashes than accept another humiliating treaty with France. By early the following March, however, after rebuffing a peace messenger from Constantinople, he did free the consul and allow an enslaved priest to take his place. "The powers of Tripoli, sirs, have resolved to make peace if our great monarch would be amenable," a captive ship captain from Toulon advised the Marseille Chamber of Commerce, though he warned of English schemes to block any accord and so prevent France from becoming "master of the sea."[72] Luckily for France, the ever-ready envoy Dusault had schemes of his own. Arriving in Tripoli in May, he pressured the dey to align with France and sever relations with England and Holland instead. Among other concessions, he exacted the release of 350 French slaves and the acquisition of thirty horses, along with some antique statues and columns from the city of Lebda. As in 1685, France yielded little, save the exchange of 250 Tripolitan galley slaves, which Louis XIV delayed as long as possible and then executed in dribs and drabs.[73] Only after the dey, under pressure from the rowers' families, threatened to make the detention of his subjects a casus belli in 1696 did officials in Versailles and Marseille act, repatriating what might have been the last twelve men.[74]

Unlike its two neighbors, whose experiences of bombardment left them ill disposed toward France, Tunis stayed mostly faithful to the preemptively signed 1685 peace treaty. The regency's sole violation followed the capture of an English vessel transporting a highly placed Tunisian and his retinue by French sea rovers disguised as Portuguese. After Tunisian ambassadors failed to receive full satisfaction for this transgression in January 1690, Tunisian corsairs ran down two more French privateers cruising under false flag, yielding 175 technically illegal French slaves.[75] For six months consul Auger Sorhainde, under instructions from Versailles, lobbied for their release and rebuffed proposals to sell them back. But in May 1691, desperate for experienced seamen, Louis XIV yielded. Though the agreement signed in mid-December certified that "all French slaves, of whatever quality and condition they are, even foreigners married in France . . . be given full and entire liberty without any ransom," the consul secretly paid approximately two hundred livres a head with money he advanced personally and allocated from the treasury of the chartered company for which he also worked.

With his naval ranks partially replenished and this North African rift temporarily mended, the king urged Tunis to break ties with England. Saving slaves from North Africa was not only a means of impressing sailors, protecting commerce, asserting authority, seeking loyalty, projecting orthodoxy, and promoting Catholicism. At the end of the seventeenth century, it was also a strategy for shifting the European balance of power in the Mediterranean.[76]

TRIPPING UP IN MEKNES

Louis XIV met his match in Mulay Isma'il. Having aggressively blitzed and successfully bargained with a succession of comparatively weak pashas, deys, and beys in the Ottoman regencies, he expected more of the same in Morocco. Instead, he deadlocked with the similarly autocratic and long-reigning ruler of North Africa's sole independent kingdom. Direct talks had produced a peace accord in July 1681. But before the document even reached court, news of several victories at sea changed the diplomatic geography. The sinking of one Saletian ship (by the celebrated Dunkirk pirate Jean Bart) and the capture of three others both weakened Morocco's corsairing capacity and replenished France's galleys.[77] With his relative naval strength improved and 350 fresh Moroccan rowers more than compensating for fewer than 200 incarcerated French seamen, the king refused to ratify the settlement or even receive the sultan's ambassador Muhammad Tamim, who came bearing peaceful overtures and an epistle exhorting the French monarch's conversion.[78] Rather than embrace Islam, Louis XIV decided to keep fighting Muslims.

Yet within a month, he had a change of heart about diplomacy, if not Catholicism. Article seven of the treaty signed at Saint-Germain-en-

Laye in January 1682 provided for the reciprocal ransom of slaves for a fixed individual price of three hundred livres. The royal plan was to buy back all the French subjects held in Morocco—with locally raised funds, of course—without letting any Moroccans go free.[79] Thus, when Tamim left for Marseille and Toulon the next month, set on visiting his incarcerated countrymen and tallying their number, the intendant of the galleys had strict orders to keep Moroccan oarsmen out of sight and to ensure that none passed on any correspondence to the ambassador. One officer claimed the whole fleet was at sea; another declared, implausibly, that he knew of no Saletian slaves in France. As Moroccan galley slave Muhammad ibn Ha'ider put it in a confiscated letter, the French "stroked [Tamim] on one side and stole his shirt on the other, for they prevented him from seeing a single one of us."[80]

Baron de Saint-Amans was appointed to confirm the 1682 articles of peace, to insert a new clause requiring a waiting period before the validation of French apostasies, and to determine the number of enslaved Frenchmen in Morocco. He received similarly duplicitous instructions: "Since His Majesty did not want to hear a single proposal about the restitution of slaves, subjects of the king of Morocco, who are at present on the galleys, [the French envoy] should use all his skill to avoid responding on this subject and if necessary [say] he does not have any power to deal with this article."[81] Saint-Amans departed in July, accompanied by an interpreter and a single Saletian oarsman, released from Toulon at the request of a highly placed uncle but detained on board until the mission's conclusion, for fear he would reveal the content of petitions from Moroccan galley slaves found on his person.[82] But such precautions made little difference, since the sultan was already disinclined to abide by the terms of the treaty, let alone make any new concessions. Three hundred livres, Mulay Isma'il had decided, was below market value. He pushed for a head-for-head exchange, which the French ambassador had no sanction to accept.[83]

The three Mercedarians who traveled to Ceuta in 1683 and the new consul to Salé who took office in 1684 found their hands similarly tied, since Mulay Isma'il would not surrender any Frenchmen without obtaining an equal number of Moroccans in return. "The poor French slaves in these parts" suffer enormously, one of them, Gabriel de Blandières, informed the marine minister, "because they live under ferocious masters . . . in awful poverty, so that many die in misery or are forced to renounce the faith." Unmoved, marine minister Jean-Baptiste Colbert, marquis de Seignelay, advised the friars to ransom captives from Tunis and Tripoli instead. Another liberation bid failed in 1685.[84] While the redemptive orders were floundering, French representatives in Moroccan cities made futile attempts to forge agreements with local leaders, and more or less

discreetly railed against royal intransigence. Exasperated by the way
brute strategic calculation was trumping religious concern, consul Jean
Périllé pointed out the hypocrisy of proselytizing to French Protestants
while ignoring the fate of Barbary captives whose number had doubled to
four hundred in the space of three years. "His majesty provides funds on
a daily basis to bring the heretics of his kingdom back into the bosom of
the Church," he opined, adding, "The least his employees and ministers
can do . . . [is] work to ensure that his subjects in slavery do not abandon
[Catholicism] and become renegades."[85]

The king turned a deaf ear to this critique, but he did entertain a
peace proposal carried to France in 1688 by a slave from Saint-Malo,
Luc Trouin de la Barbinais, which renewed calls for a captive exchange.[86]
Accordingly, he sent a new envoy to Meknes. However, this mission,
like subsequent ones over the next few years, ended in failure. In any
case, by the early 1690s, French officials in Morocco were less concerned
about apostasy than starvation, for as a collective petition informed the
next marine minister, Louis Phélypeaux, comte de Pontchartrain, "about
sixty Frenchmen have died from an excess of misery and a deficiency of
food."[87] Indeed, according to a Franciscan registry, overall captive death
rates, whether from malnourishment, disease, or other factors, climbed
from 48 in 1688 to 162 in 1689 to 276 in 1690 before starting to decline.[88] With negotiations stalled, a handful of wealthier French slaves
bought freedom with substitutes; the remainder could only pray for a
state or religious redemption.[89] Yet sudden Moroccan demands (four
rowers per captive plus the wholesale liberation of every North African
and Levantine in France) thwarted a 1693 embassy by François Pidou de
Saint-Olon, and for seven years thereafter the servile French subjects in
Meknes received nothing but a few alms from their monarch.[90]

Even that charity was selectively allotted. After learning in 1695 of an
opportunistic Huguenot ("wicked man, enemy of France") who claimed
to be English in the presence of English redemptors, and then asked the
French consul to attest that he was French, Pontchartrain ordered that
religious affiliation be noted on the slave rolls sent to Versailles. A 1696
census with 279 names identified 10 Protestants; one from 1698 with 254
names also identified 11 relaps and spared no affection for representatives of the French crown.[91] Still, France's Reformed Christians stood a
better chance of deliverance than its Catholics, since in 1699 Louis XIV
spurned another Moroccan ambassador, along with his proposal for a
marriage alliance between Mulay Isma'il and a French princess.[92] For the
next two decades, even as the English government ransomed 29 Huguenots (4 others escaped on their own), the majority of "the poor French,"
like Germain Cavalier of Honfleur, were left, as he put it, "in suffering

and deplorable misery to work day and night and die of hunger and nakedness."[93] The letter this Norman slave wrote to his mother in 1702, circulated by a local priest to the king's confessor, did inspire a joint mission
by the redemptive fathers. But the Trinitarians and Mercedarians faced
the same difficulties with the sultan as had their secular counterparts.[94]

Between 1704 and 1712, cooperative efforts first in Salé and Meknes,
then in Ceuta and Marrakech, achieved only modest success—and that
thanks to a favored Huguenot merchant in Moroccan exile who, as a
Mercedarian author acknowledged, "though of a religion no longer recognized in France displayed on our behalf all that the most perfect charity would inspire among the most zealous Catholics."[95] In eight years
the redemptive fathers liberated at most eighty French Catholics (and it
seems, at least, one Protestant),[96] the majority either elderly or infirm,
and corralled just a dozen into abbreviated processions, one of which
featured "little boys dressed in Turkish style with mustaches and turbans
. . . and little girls dressed as queens and nuns."[97] It was more through
publishing than performance that the friars contrasted Muslim and
Christian realms and advocated for redemption. Trinitarian Dominique
Busnot's *Histoire du règne de Mouley Ismael* (1714), for example, provided an exceptionally horrific portrait of Sultan Mulay Isma'il, spending
pages on the tortures he allegedly inflicted on those French slaves he did
not gratuitously slaughter. Echoing a scene from Rabelais, which plays
on the elision between circumcision and castration, and the attribution
of canine traits to Muslims, Busnot described a native of Frontignan who
was dismembered then fed naked to a pack of starving dogs.[98] Two years
later, the king of England may have saved some French Protestants[99]
and the Mercedarians a dozen French Catholics from this presumed fate
through another less highly regarded Huguenot "refugee" (who subsequently "traded his black hat for the red turban" to become pasha of
Salé).[100] The large-scale liberation of French subjects, however, awaited
new regimes on both sides of the Mediterranean. Only in 1737, ten years
after the death of Mulay Isma'il, did the friars free the last seventy-five
Frenchmen held in Morocco, with a gift of gunpowder, a sizable payment of cash, and the services of another expatriate trader suspected of
Calvinism. And that did not solve the problem permanently.[101]

FRONTIERS OF FRENCHNESS AND FREEDOM

During the brief interlude between the 1678 Peace of Nijmegen and a
fresh eruption of pan-European warfare, Louis XIV had tried to humble
the Barbary States. Relative success in Algiers, Tunis, and Tripoli—if not

Morocco—freed several thousand captives, whose repatriation presented new opportunities for self-promotion and state building, new questions about the religious parameters of French belonging, and new ideas about the relationship between Frenchness and freedom. The decision to expend naval resources in the Mediterranean did not derive from sudden royal sympathy for individual suffering. As in previous eras, the crown remained more than willing to sacrifice Frenchmen for the sake of an ideal one-to-four balance of Turks aboard its galleys.[102] Nevertheless, the French-sponsored exodus of Christians from Muslim lands, whether forced or surreptitiously purchased, did help foster the illusion that France's sovereign privileged crucifix over sword. In conjunction with the Revocation of the Edict of Nantes, it made him appear the enemy of both heretics and infidels.

In the 1680s and 1690s, the liberation of slaves had become an *affaire d'état*. At the same time, civic and religious leaders had reluctantly ceded authority to choose particularly worthy recipients of salvation. Though Louis XIV still expected towns and provinces to pay for their own people—including those with ties of marriage and circumstance—he no longer wanted geography to determine precedence. Instead, his goal was to remove *all* French subjects from bondage. With the Sun King at the helm, the Trinitarians and Mercedarians also had to forfeit control over whom, when, and where to ransom. They did occasionally sidestep royal instructions. Overall, however, members of the two orders had to stop initiating their own missions or applying their own ransom priorities. Instead, they began crossing the Mediterranean at the monarch's command, subordinating their operations to his domestic and foreign policies. Initially, one of these policies was using redemption to win over enslaved religionnaires. But when North African rulers refused to treat religious refugees as French fugitives, Louis XIV withdrew his outstretched arm from "stiff-necked Huguenots." Afterward, his representatives had to overcome their aversion to giving ex-compatriots over to English and Dutch adversaries or leaving them to Islam and be content with merely tracking the former slaves' activities.

Imperfect execution notwithstanding, deluge, decree, and diplomacy had left France mostly free of Protestants and most Frenchmen freed from North Africa. But with upward of two thousand North Africans (and several hundred recalcitrant Huguenots) laboring on Mediterranean galleys and more than ten times that many sub-Saharan Africans laboring on Atlantic plantations, greater France had hardly been transformed into a land of liberty.[103] Not even French dictionaries systematically kept up the pretense. In 1694, nine years after the promulgation of the *Code noir* to regulate colonial slavery, the entries *esclave* and *esclavage* in the *Académie française*'s first lexicon still made no mention of blacks, only Moors, Turks, and Christians.[104] However, Antoine Furtière's compendium from four years earlier had finally acknowledged not just that "slaves in Algiers are captives taken by corsairs" but that "in America is conducted a big traffic in Negro slaves." The dictionary had also insisted that "as soon as a slave arrives in France, he is free."[105] Though in the Caribbean dark pigmentation operated as a rationale for subjection, in late seventeenth-century metropolitan France a black stowaway could fruitfully petition for freedom.[106]

Likewise, heresy as treason might be offered to justify condemnation to the galleys or abandonment in Barbary captivity in the case of Protestants. But it did not provide an adequate justification for the detention of Muslims who had violated no laws—and whose liberation in a previous century had bolstered France's commitment to territorial freedom. Rejecting the gift of a *nègre* rower his predecessors might have accepted even fifteen years earlier during an abortive trial of sub-Saharan Africans at the oar, marine minister Pontchartrain attempted to explain why Ottomans and Moroccans could be slaves: "Every man who has touched the soil of the kingdom once is free. One is not exempt from following this law, except [in the case of] the Turks and Moors who are sent to Marseille for service to the galleys, because, before arriving there, they are purchased in foreign countries where this kind of commerce is established."[107] Stressing custom and contract, the minister's account of North African servitude in France left out the issue of religion. Four years later, the Sorbonne addressed the theological perspective. Christians may not enslave other believers seized in combat, ruled presiding judge Germain Fromageau. "In a just war," however, Christians have every right "to deprive [unbelievers] of their liberty and make them slaves."[108] By the logic of reprisal against infidels, Muslims had every right to deprive Christians of liberty too. Only now, everywhere but Morocco, Louis XIV had become strong enough to stop it.

France's ascendancy vis-à-vis the Ottoman regencies, its centralization of slave redemption, and its criminalization of Protestantism during the final decades of the seventeenth century had another important effect too. Representatives of the crown had long employed selective deliverance from North Africa to integrate useful residents of peripheral regions and to protect vulnerable souls from Islam. Now, the potential for collective manumission had given the king an additional tool for excluding confessional nonconformists. Bringing captives back from Barbary had become a way of associating freedom with loyalty—to both the king and his Catholic faith.

CHAPTER FIVE

Emancipation in
an Age of Enlightenment

Bombarding Barbary did not obliterate the region's slave-making capacity. But, helped by disease, it did radically diminish the number of French subjects in chains.[1] With a gradual contraction of the galley fleet and a corresponding willingness to return Muslim rowers, especially after Louis XIV's death in 1715, most Catholic captives outside Morocco able to demonstrate ties to France could anticipate relatively speedy release. Except for mariners and merchants snatched during brief interludes of war—1728–1729 and 1741–1742—those who lingered in Algiers, Tunis, and Tripoli possessed one of four sorts of disputed identity. Early in the century, they lacked the proper papers, or they had mixed or alien parentage but a connection to the kingdom via employment or emigration. Later, they had deserted the French or a foreign army, or they had come under French dominion through conquest. They were, in other words, unlucky, undocumented, unfaithful, or unintentional Frenchmen.

For one regent (Philippe d'Orléans) and two monarchs (Louis XV and Louis XVI), freeing slaves in even these marginal categories remained a tactic for binding individuals to the state and jockeying for preeminence over European competitors. For the Trinitarians and Mercedarians, redemption remained a holy calling whose pursuit promoted allegiance to the Gallican Church and crown. Over the course of several decades, however, such continuity in purpose was undermined by a divergence in context. Besides the greater scarcity and ambiguous status of victims carried to the Ottoman regencies, the eighteenth century saw—among many other developments—the rapid expansion of human trafficking to the Caribbean, the failure of Marseille's quarantine system, and the further loss of autonomy and standing for the two Catholic orders.

Operating less frequently and under increasingly restrictive conditions, the Trinitarians and Mercedarians still tried with processions and publications to champion themselves as the kingdom's essential guardians against Muslim bondage and its associated infections. But their claims began to ring hollow after plague struck southern France and the drive to seize slaves from one part of Africa dwarfed the need to unshackle them from another. With liberty becoming the norm for loyal French Catholics, and slavery just starting to be acknowledged as the fate of ever more black pagans, eighteenth-century friars faced anticlerical suspicion that they exaggerated the horrors of Barbary servitude in order to bolster their own declining legitimacy.[2] In part predicated on a new understanding of slavery, this hostility to the spiritual rationale for deliverance gradually undercut its political function.

Meanwhile, naval success bred a new sort of diplomatic vulnerability. Forced to recognize the power of French kings—to offer freedom and protection even to non-French Christians in Muslim lands—North African leaders now held them responsible for the treatment of Muslims throughout Christendom. Thus in the eighteenth century, France's bid for Mediterranean dominance depended not just on the liberation of particular Turks held inside the kingdom but also on its defense of their far-flung countrymen.

UNCERTIFIED SUBJECTS

France entered the War of the Spanish Succession against England, Holland, Austria, Prussia, and the Holy Roman Empire partly to gain access to the slave trade in Spanish America. It abandoned this pretense after fighting on two continents between 1701 and 1713. In the course of those twelve years, the number of sub-Saharan African slaving voyages embarking from French ports and the number of black chattel laboring in French colonies nonetheless tripled.[3] Given this Atlantic orientation, plus the financial and human strains of warfare and a horrific famine following a cold winter, Mediterranean matters once again became an afterthought. In any case, the size of the French servile population in the Ottoman regencies had plummeted from three digits to two or one.[4]

Among a mere forty Catholic captives from France left in Algiers in 1708, for example, were two Knights of Malta whose standing as "enemy combatants" overrode any privilege of Frenchness. The rest, seamen from Provence and Basque Country, had used poor judgment in traveling without French passports, then "by accursed habit" asserted roots in "Cassis, Senay, or another unusual place that might be unknown."[5]

Pierre Burin came from a village in the Pyrenees. Captured on a privateer out of Saint-Jean-de-Luz, he used his native tongue to inform his mother and father about his master: "a magician" who "wants to force me like a girl." Had he immediately "declared himself French," noted French consul Antoine-Gabriel Durand, he might have been reclaimed, for "the word 'French' is known by all." Instead, Basque freedom was contingent on Algerian. A head-for-head exchange took two years.[6]

In Tripoli in 1707, the French slave count stood at five. There, as in Algiers, it was the previous century's bilateral treaties backed by the threat of violence that facilitated the release of captives and kept the corsairs mostly in check. Not so for Tunis, whose sea rovers started going after French vessels under the false assumption that an elderly, over-extended monarch would not intervene.[7] A squadron of three warships in the fall of 1710 convinced the bey otherwise. He apologized for the violations, released an unknown number of French slaves, and signed a new treaty. But relations did not improve, and a six-month ban on Franco-Tunisian trade imposed in 1714 only made matters worse.[8] The next year the Sun King's nephew put North African affairs under the command of a new Navy Council and reverted to a traditional, pecuniary approach.[9] Perhaps responding to warnings about counterfeit monks pocketing donations for captives, he restored royal privileges to genuine ransom collectors (*marguillers*).[10] Then he directed their sponsoring orders to instigate a new fund-raising campaign—with the cooperation of every bishop in France and the pope, who had instructed his Gallican flock to preach the redemption of captives every Advent and Lent.[11]

The regent's intent, however, was not to buy back well over one hundred Frenchmen in Morocco "groan[ing] alone in the irons of the cruelest barbarians," nor to buy back tens of non-elites elsewhere in Barbary.[12] Instead, the money—which was painfully extracted, whether from France's impoverished faithful or in some regions from reluctant new converts from Calvinism—was to reimburse outlays for subjects captured during the Ottoman conquest of the Peloponnesian Peninsula and to pay out an enormous sum for the Knights of Malta held in Algiers.[13] In neither case were the Trinitarians and Mercedarians able to take public credit. The Chevalier Louis Castellane d'Esparron, for one, ransomed in 1717 after ten years of slavery, refused to appear with the redemptive fathers who raised much of his ransom. Distinctions of rank may have been blurred in Barbary, where captives still pretended to be lowborn in the hopes of commanding a low price. But back in France a nobleman resented dressing as a commoner and being required to walk alongside plebeian sailors.[14]

INFECTIOUS SLAVES

The friars got a chance at self-promotion only in March 1720 after accompanying seasoned emissary Denis Dusault on another mission to reconfirm ties with the Barbary States. From Algiers, where he signed a new accord,[15] the Trinitarians bought back around sixty slaves.[16] A simultaneous Mercedarian voyage ransomed thirty, emptying the regency of servile French subjects.[17] These men (and a few women) could not have uniformly obeyed the 1718 injunction to carry certificates showing themselves "French and *regnicole* [native-born resident]" when venturing onto the Mediterranean Sea or else give up the prospect of redemption.[18] Most had spent at least four years in captivity, and one native of Dunkirk thirty-five years. Some had been seized from enemy ships. Others, including Mademoiselle du Bourk, the ten-year-old daughter of a well-connected French mother and the Spanish ambassador to Sweden, had been shipwrecked and then enslaved by indigenous Kabyles along the Algerian coast. Sensitive to the propaganda value of an aristocratic girl saved from sexual and religious pollution in a harem, the Trinitarians featured her story in a brochure that advertised an impending procession and a laudatory narrative published afterward.[19]

The majority of freed slaves, however, did not come from France at all. They were Catholic, Protestant, and perhaps even Jewish foreigners, whose deliverance cast another French monarch as Christendom's defender against physical and spiritual contamination from Islam.[20] This time the Mercedarians seem not to have mounted a procession. The Trinitarians, however, began theirs in Marseille, just two months before a shipment of cloth from Syria sparked the worst (and last) plague epidemic the city had ever known. On the way to Paris, where soon-to-be-crowned Louis XV watched from the Louvre, the troop reportedly received enthusiastic welcomes from viewers still adept at reading the message of a slave march.[21] "All the people felt moved and stirred up by the sight of these poor victims, escaped from the furor of the Barbarians, rescued from the peril of renouncing their faith, and returned to their liberty," the organizers avowed. In Lyon, multilingual clerics stood ready to hear confession, city fathers distributed wine and alms, and residents from all walks of life poured into the streets to witness "a spectacle no less original than touching, finding enough to satisfy the eyes where only interesting the heart had been intended."[22]

No sooner had these festivities ended than another set began. At the end of May 1720, following a ten-day quarantine outside Marseille, forty-five French slaves and fifteen other Christians released from Tunis set off for the capital.[23] In that regency, Dusault had successfully soothed tensions about the enslavement of almost two hundred North African pilgrims traveling to Egypt aboard a French vessel that crashed on Sicilian shores.[24] While promising to intervene on behalf of Turks of both sexes, he took care to insert an article in the new Franco-Tunisian treaty to ensure that an inability to do so would not threaten the peace. He also agreed to a reciprocal captive release.[25] Ransom was paid with money supplied by the Trinitarians and left over from the Mercedarians.[26] Following a geographical division confirmed in new letters patent, these ex-slaves appeared with ersatz Ottomans and Roman soldiers throughout southern France. But authorities halted the pageant in Dijon.[27] Highly choreographed scenes of disinfection and reconciliation might have convinced some audiences of performers' spiritual purity. However, with the death toll in Marseille on an alarming rise, their bodily hygiene now stood in doubt.

Afterward, the Trinitarians remained silent about the fortunes of possibly tainted former slaves. Just back from signing a new accord with Tripoli, however, Dusault did not.[28] Identifying the freed Frenchmen as deserters from royal troops captured in the service of Venice, with deviant sexual preferences and political allegiances, he called them "libertines, who will for the most part return to foreign lands, accustomed to the libertinage of the Venetians."[29] His chance to free more worthy candidates might have come only posthumously. When Dusault died of plague, he left thirty thousand livres for redemption.[30]

FRAUDULENT MONKS

The year of his coronation, Louis XV ordered the Trinitarians to Algiers and Meknes. Two years later, in 1725, two groups of French and foreign slaves docked separately in Marseille and Le Havre and then met up in Fontainebleau. While the king oversaw the October parade from his study window, it was newly betrothed Queen Marie Leszczyska who encountered the friars and sixty-three freed captives in the flesh. Touched by "the spectacle, [which] was new to her," recalled a commemorative account, "her Majesty gave fifty gold *louis* and chose the Princess of Chalais to take collection." Once "the King signaled his charity," it continued, "the whole court followed his example." Buoyed by this mark of royal approval, the Trinitarians took their show to Champagne, Burgundy, Normandy, and Flanders. According to official reports, traditional representations of Muslim barbarity, Catholic devotion, and sovereign attachment aroused charity on every level of society in every corner of France.[31] In the Republic of Letters, by contrast, neither organizers nor participants were earning straightforward approbation.

Already French-language, first-person Barbary captivity narratives had vanished. Replacing romantic tales that celebrated imposture as a means of self-protection against contagions from North Africa were satires that appropriated Muslim characters and Mediterranean plotlines to identify political, religious, and sexual degeneracy in France itself. The *Mémoires de madame la marquise de Frêne*, attributed to Gatien Courtilz de Sandras and published in Amsterdam in 1701, for example, was, to judge by its numerous editions, a best seller. It featured an evil aristocrat who sells off his wife to a renegade corsair who turns out to be a kindhearted ex-Huguenot.[32] Other writings took aim at the redemptive fathers, either as foolish optimists or opportunistic leeches. Alain-René Lesage's *Diable boiteux* (1707) gave the lie to a Mercedarian procession. Although the "Spanish Moses" at its head, with "a long gray beard that helped to give him that venerable look," had an air of "inexpressible joy at bringing back so many Christians to their country," he wrote, the participants "in their slaves habit with their chains about their necks" were not "equally transformed at recovering their liberty." Unlike the heroes of seventeenth-century slave chronicles, these men back from Barbary found not happy reunification with their families but estates squandered, wives remarried, and loves betrayed.[33]

A onetime French consul went further. In his 1725 description of Algiers, also printed in the Dutch center of France's literary underground, Jacques Philippe Laugier de Tassy called slave performances a sham and accused the Trinitarians and Mercedarians of lying for money. Spectators see captives with beards down to their waist, which "the monks take care to prevent them from cutting . . . laden with chains they have never worn," stirring compassion they should not feel and charity they should not give, he asserted.[34] With no French autobiographies available to refute such claims, a compatriot took it upon himself to translate a decade-old one from English. "I do not think one can suspect either the English slave whose relation I give here, nor Mr. Ockley, one of England's most knowledgeable Protestants . . . of colluding with our Catholics and clerics to authorize the deception," he wrote.[35] Nevertheless, Marseille naturalist and physician Jean-André Peyssonnel found reason to question the friars' portraits too. "Based on the accounts I had read I expected to find these wretches in a state to draw tears of blood," he reflected in epistolary observations of Algiers and Tunis from 1724 to 1725. "But what I saw did not all correspond to the ideas I had developed from reading the books that the religious of the Redemption of captives take care to put forth." Noting that "of all slaveries, this one is the least harsh," he continued, "For me, who has been to the Americas and the Levant, I have been witness to plenty of cruelty and even inhumanity by

Christians to their Negro slaves, and much affability and good manners by Turks toward their Christian slaves."[36]

He might have added that French subjects actually now stood less chance of being made a slave than owning one. Even accepting the redemptive fathers' most inflated figures, the number of black slaves in France's colonies had surpassed the number of Christian captives across North Africa by a factor of ten.[37] Perceptions of scale might have lagged, but these two forms of bondage had started to share mental as well as physical space. Thus the Protestant refugee Jean Barbot urged his fellow slave traffickers to recognize sub-Saharan Africans as "men as well as themselves tho' of a different colour, and pagans." "They ought to do to others as they would be done by in like circumstances," he wrote, "as it may be their turn if they should have the misfortune to fall into the hands of Algerines or Sallee men, as it has happen'd to many after such voyages perform'd."[38] That whites and blacks, heretics and infidels might share the common fortune of seizure and slavery suggested to this former Frenchman that everyone on earth might possess a common humanity.

TRANS-OCEANIC PARALLELS

Numerous eighteenth-century intellectuals from across the political spectrum agreed. From their perspective, France's ever-greater role in transporting and exploiting human beings from the sub-Saharan portion of Africa barred it from playing the victim in the continent's north. Voltaire, for example, condemned American plantation slavery with a portrait of a mutilated Surinam runaway in *Candide*, while mocking the conventions of Barbary captivity narratives with a richly embroidered and racially charged vignette about the daughter of a pope and a princess raped by an "abominable negro" pirate captain, sold into Moroccan slavery, and then saved and betrayed by an Italian eunuch. An article in his *Dictionnaire philosophique* reviled Algerians, Moroccans, Tunisians, papal soldiers, and the Knights of Malta as "birds of prey that feast on one another" by carrying on "the custom of pillaging and enslaving anyone encountered at sea." Yet this Mediterranean tradition found its Atlantic analogy, he sardonically proposed, when "those who call themselves white go to buy Negroes cheaply in order to resell them expensively in America."[39]

Even Simon Linguet, opponent of philosophes and physiocrats, challenged the double standard that made heroes of captives who fled Tunis and Algiers and villains of Caribbean maroons who "prefer[red] the company of snakes . . . over that of Europeans who whip them; and the pleasure of eating wild sugar canes to the fatigue of crushing what they have cultivated."[40] In an unfinished sequel to the famous work *Emile*, Jean-Jacques Rousseau's protagonist found true freedom in chains and noted that "Negroes would be only too happy in America if the European treated them with the same fairness" as the Algerian dey treated him.[41] Henri Bernardin de Saint Pierre, better known for his utopian love story *Paul et Virginie*, conveyed a similar lesson in a play about a Guinean bondsman risen to power in Marrakech, who enslaved and then liberated his former master from Saint-Domingue under the influence of his equality-spouting French-born wife.[42]

But it was Denis Diderot, seemingly as inspired by Pierre Joseph André Roubaud on the subject of Christian servitude as on colonial bondage, who lashed out most directly. His anonymous contribution to the fourth edition of Guillaume Raynal's *Histoire des deux Indes* berated readers for sympathizing with the casualties of North African corsairing over those of imperial greed: "Those of our neighbors whom the inhabitants of Barbary have weighed down with irons obtain our pity and assistance. Even imaginary distress draws tears to our eyes . . . especially at the theatre. It is only the fatal destiny of the Negroes that does not concern us. They are tyrannized, mutilated, burnt and put to death, and yet we listen to these accounts coolly and without emotion. The torments of a people to whom we owe our luxuries are never able to reach our hearts."[43] None of these thinkers made a categorical distinction between slavery in the Old World and the New. Rather, they drew parallels to inveigh against misplaced compassion and further an argument for abolition.[44]

RECIPROCITY AND RIVALRY

For French political leaders, abolishing slavery—whether of Christians or blacks—was nowhere on the agenda, despite proposals for collaborative efforts among Christian powers.[45] Instead, competing with antipapists, the Holy Roman Emperor, and the pope, Louis XV sought Mediterranean ascendancy in liberating French slaves—and in preserving the liberties of indigenous Christians, missionaries, and other expatriate Catholics under France's diplomatic mantle. Whereas great-grandfather Louis XIV had risked warfare to maintain the royal galleys as symbols of anti-Muslim majesty, great-grandson regularly unshackled Turks at the request of North African rulers. Though not always quickly, his ministers investigated complaints about mistreated Ottoman diplomats, traders, and rowers, whether in Marseille, Livorno, or Malta, and protested Spanish or Italian captures from French vessels. They knew that even rumors of blocked access to Muslim cemeteries, disrupted worship, insulted holy men, or forcible conversion imperiled French standing and both actual and honorary Frenchmen.[46]

In Tripoli it was a letter from the Tyrrhenian seaport of Civitavecchia that had this effect. After learning in 1721 that his subjects laboring there had been beaten and their *qadi*'s (Islamic judge) beard shaved, pasha Ahmad Qaramanli responded in kind, ordering the Capuchins in his dominion fettered, paraded, and imprisoned. He also started turning a blind eye when Tripolitan corsairs fired on French boats or, say, intercepted a valuable silk shipment, tore up the commander's passport, then claimed he was Genoese. Early in his reign, Louis XV met such violations with small squadrons and mild shows of force. But by 1728, concerned that Italians protected by Austria were gaining a trade advantage, he changed tactics.[47]

On the morning of 16 July, two men-of-war, four frigates, three bomb ketches, two galleys, and two line ships anchored before Tripoli. The 3,600-man fleet had just imposed a harsh new treaty on Tunis.[48] Now, France's consul rowed out to the flagship and received a list of extreme demands for the Tripolitan pasha, including a large indemnity for the loss of merchant vessels and the emancipation of a dozen Christian slaves taken under French flag. His treasury depleted and his pride ruffled, Qaramanli offered a smaller sum, which the royal commissary summarily rejected before issuing a noon deadline for the declaration of war. The pasha responded, after meeting with his divan, "As to payment, no one consents to make it, and no one will give it. As for your bombs, we do not fear them; you can throw them if you wish." The assault lasted a week and destroyed hundreds of buildings, including the French consulate, but inflicted few casualties, since most of the population had retreated to an oasis east of the city. Once the pasha rejected another peace overture, the flotilla, low on provisions and ammunition, withdrew.[49]

No longer constrained by any pretense of respecting the fleur-de-lys, Tripolitan corsairs seized twenty-one French ships between July and November, making about 150 new French slaves. One was Joseph Antoine Roux of Saint-Tropez, en route from Alexandria and the Libyan city of Bengazi with a consignment of cloth. Clapped in irons, thrown into an underground cell, and put to work quarrying stone with thirty-four other Frenchmen, he doubted he would survive a month. "Please have the grace to say a *pater* and an *ave maria* for the poor slave that I am to [Marseille's patron saint] *la Vierge de la Garde*," he begged his parents in a letter home.[50] Other Provençal captains pleaded on behalf of "children and nephews . . . of a tender age . . . in peril of changing their religion and serving the brutalities of their masters."[51] Their missives to the marine minister and the Marseille Chamber of Commerce reviled the French consul, whom they blamed for the rupture, insisting that "the pasha never wanted war." Do not bombard Tripoli a second time, they warned, lest he make good on the threat to "put all the French into the mouth of a cannon."[52]

In fact, plans were afoot for a full-scale land raid, and only Ottoman opposition averted its execution. Instead, starting in January 1729, seven French battleships cut off access to the harbor. This time, facing interior threats of civil war and famine, the pasha surrendered. In the six months it took to complete negotiations, however, he sold off more than a dozen French ship hands, inducing the captains to grouse that "little by little the slaves will disappear if this business drags out for long."[53] It did not. The final agreement, signed in June after two ambassadors visited Versailles, stated imperiously that "in consequence of the repentance that the pasha-dey, the divan, and the militia of Tripoli have shown for the infractions they have committed since the last peace treaty and the pardon they request, [the king] is content to grant them peace."[54] Commemorated by a silver coin declaring Louis XV "king of Christendom" and depicting him as a hawk assaulting a flock of lesser birds,[55] the treaty made provisions for monetary compensation and the mutual release of captives,[56] which took place through a mixture of escape, ransom, and donation.[57]

Only one French slave, it seems, had been forced "to take the turban," and he was soon allowed to re-don "his original clothing and be left free in the Christian religion."[58] Yet renewed anxieties about the corruption of French youth had evidently struck a nerve. "No cabin boy may be left in the ports of the Levant and Barbary," read a royal declaration from 1730, establishing in law what could not be entirely prevented in practice.[59]

These persistent worries aside, with Tripoli's sea rovers curtailed but not crushed, friendly to French ships but poised to attack those belonging to European foes, Louis XV had achieved equilibrium. "We are well aware that it is not in our interest for all the corsairs of Barbary to be destroyed," wrote an anonymous Marseillais that year, for without them "we would be on par with all the Italians and peoples from the North."[60]

FRAGILE PEACE

After the redemptions of 1720, France and Algiers enjoyed a decade of relative calm, interrupted by occasional disputes about new passport standards and odd slaves: victims of trickery, like a passenger from Antibes in Provence captured by a Greek renegade sailing an English vessel with

Catalan flags, or of ignorance, like a captain from Granville in Normandy carrying an out-of-date travel permit.[61] In April 1729, the Mercedarians freed about twenty leftover Basques, Provençals, Bretons, and Flemish, along with assorted elderly Italians and Spaniards and a stray Englishman, all of whom had presumably been made to "swear on the gospel that . . . they will follow you everywhere for three months."[62] Having failed to celebrate publicly during Louis XV's minority, members of this order now took the opportunity to show off their accomplishment with processions and pamphlets—eight hundred listing the names of ex-slaves requisitioned for Montpellier alone.[63] Not to be outdone, a Trinitarian delegation advertised plans to parade eighteen natives of Flanders through the capital.[64]

When famine, plague, and poverty drove Algerian sea rovers back into French waters during the fairs at Beaucaire that attracted Italian and Spanish traders to the kingdom, Louis XV sent a royal frigate to patrol the coast of Provence and Languedoc,[65] then a flotilla to repatriate fifteen natives of Sète gone fishing without identity papers and various Genoese sailors taken too close to French shores.[66] In the 1730s and 1740s, France's consul reclaimed diverse merchants and at least one Breton slaver,[67] while Marseille's Trinitarian confraternity bought back thirty-six native sons.[68] Whether by oversight or negligence, however, a few individuals with valid claims to French protection or belonging slipped through the cracks. André Stanya, for example, at sea at the time of France's naval stopover, somehow failed to rouse successive consuls to take up his cause. Though in 1733 the captain begged France's marine minister to be a "father and liberator" to him and his wretched crew, their deliverance was eventually paid with alms from Genoa.[69] Jean-Victor-Laurent, baron d'Arreger, born in Switzerland, raised in France, but employed by Spain, also alerted the court about his enslavement by a Portuguese renegade and his slavery under a Provençal one. The French consul kept tabs on his situation, but it was his family, not the king, that ultimately sent the nobleman's large ransom via an English merchant. The Spanish Mercedarians transported him to Madrid.[70]

Yet by this time it was not so much these occasional failures to redeem Catholics that threatened France's standing in Algiers. Rather, as in Tripoli, it was the possibility of not adequately enforcing the negotiated privileges of free and servile Muslims around the Mediterranean. When "Turks and Moors" who expected refuge in Toulon instead "faced the approbation of the population who spat in their faces, threw stones, and insulted their religion," the Algerian dey confiscated the rudders of all French ships in his harbor and imprisoned fifty-four Frenchmen plus the French consul. There were rumblings of a rupture. But in the end, the two powers stayed nominally at peace.[71]

TEMPORARY BREAK

Tunis was a different story. Reflecting on his 1729–1733 tenure as consul in a memoir published three years after retirement, Jacques Boyer de Saint-Gervais wrote laconically of tavern-keeping captives who bought their own freedom and his role in "ransom[ing] . . . a few slaves chosen by the court."[72] Yet revolution and the installation of a new bey eager for profits and hostile to France soon pushed the two states toward war. Starting in 1737, they clashed over matters of etiquette (bey 'Ali's insistence that, contrary to custom, the French consul kiss his hand), religious expression (the barring of Catholic slaves from mass on news of Muslim slaves in Livorno denied access to a hospital), and corsairing (the capture and enslavement of a Toulon merchantman with fourteen passengers and crew).[73] Finally, in the fall of 1741, just as he was opening all French ports to the sub-Saharan slave trade, Louis XV suspended commerce with Tunis and ordered a blockade. The bey countered by sending out armed galliots.[74] Their victims included twenty-seven traveling French actors who staged pantomimes while awaiting ransom.[75]

The spark that ignited open conflict, however, was the invasion of Tabarka, a strategically located island that one of France's chartered companies was trying to purchase from Genoa. In order to halt this profitable transaction, Tunisian forces attacked, carrying off eight hundred men and women[76] before laying waste to the neighboring commercial outpost of Cap Nègre and taking all of its inhabitants prisoners.[77] A surprise French counterattack failed miserably. Of three hundred soldiers who made the descent in July 1742, only twenty escaped alive. As France's vice-consul informed the court, "the heads of 27 Frenchmen killed on Tabarka" were displayed for two days "on a small square next to our *fondouk* [an inn and warehouse for merchants]." Of 224 Frenchmen enslaved, only officers were spared work. According to one witness, soldiers and sailors had to dig a pit by the palace under the watchful eye of a renegade Spanish priest.[78]

Luckily, their ordeal did not last long. Instructed to resolve the conflict quickly in anticipation of England's entrance into the War of the Austrian Succession, a royal commissary negotiated a new accord in November.[79] Many of its terms were identical to those in the 1685 treaty. New additions gave Tunisians the right to search French ships for runaway slaves and required France to release any remaining Tunisians on its galleys. A secret convention also conceded that France's consul "will kiss [the bey's] hand every time he goes to see him."[80] Through ceremony during the Tunisian embassy to Versailles, Louis XV tried to recover symbolically what he had lost diplomatically by signing such an unfavorable treaty.[81]

FREEING FUGITIVES

During the second half of the eighteenth century, the pragmatic desire for both North African peace and European precedence also drove policy relating to army deserters in Barbary captivity. Some of these men had crossed paths with corsairs while fleeing French regiments. Most had joined the Spanish military on promises of lucrative postings in Mexico and Peru only to be confined to dismal, isolated presidios along the North African coast, then had deliberately fallen into Muslim hands with the hope of winning freedom through redemption or apostasy. Seized primarily from Oran and detained primarily in Algiers,[82] such "voluntary slaves"—also known as *bienvenidos* (welcomed) or *carneros* (sheep)[83]—had mixed into French servile ranks earlier in the century, even before 1708 when Spain lost possession of its oldest North African outpost. But after its recapture in 1732, their number soared.[84] As a group, enslaved defectors had wider geographical origins than countrymen carried away from boats and maritime villages in earlier centuries and an especially vulnerable status. Since private investors hesitated to buy slaves that the Spanish government seldom showed interest in aiding, escapees tended to become state property—manual laborers considered poor bets for sincere conversion. In the dey's judgment, captive turncoats had forfeited French standing, thus their freedom depended on charity rather than diplomacy. The crown's response vacillated between utilitarian leniency and purposeful neglect.

Following his great-grandfather's policy of commuting punishments for battle-ready fugitives, Louis XV occasionally directed the redemptive orders to ransom individual deserters.[85] In 1750, however, on the urging of the Mercedarian general and the apostolic vicar—who warned that 145 French Oraners stood on the brink of Islam, and that in "turning Turk" these "proven rascals . . . can cause the state more harm than one would think"—the king ordered a joint mission to repatriate *all* remaining French captives in Algiers plus any foreigners taken under French flag.[86] Thus in Paris that December, the Frenchmen escaped from Oran, along with a few Genoese, Mantuans, and Sardinians, marched side by side for four days during the orders' respective pageants.[87] Afterward, the Bretons among them struck out to fund-raise in their region's principal cities, the invalids received new clothing and travel money, and most of the others seem to have been left to their own devices. Only the runaways from royal troops had to endure suspension in an intermediary state between emancipation and confinement at Mercedarian headquarters while they awaited word of clemency or penalty—permission to travel home or banishment to the Caribbean.[88]

The removal of volatile slaves may have improved the commercial, political, and religious prospects of the French *nation* in Algiers, providing a respite from anxiety about latent renegades plotting against its interests. But their delivery to France in the later throes of the "great confinement" introduced new concerns about yet another type of marginal people whose circulation threatened the public order. Presumably because some of the returned captives did wander off and cause disturbances during their journey from coast to capital, Trinitarians and Mercedarians had to sign an agreement in April 1751, establishing that "there are only two routes by which the disembarked slaves may go, in general, to Paris [and that] the religious who accompany the slaves will not deviate from the ordinary route, whatever itinerary they follow." A year and a half later, a royal ordinance linked ex-captives from North Africa with so-called "Oriental Christians" from the Levant as half-foreign elements who brought unspecified chaos into the kingdom. Limiting the validity of consular passports and begging permits to a year and six months, respectively, the edict warned that members of either group without proper papers would be treated as vagabonds and imprisoned.[89]

In any case, no sooner was Algiers emptied of Oran fugitives than the influx resumed. Writing that November, France's consul notified the court that one hundred deserters from various European countries had entered the regency during the previous two months alone. Spain was well advised to start returning captured soldiers to the garrison, he mused, in order to dissuade others from taking the same route. Alert to the "dangerous augmentation" of desperate slaves possessed of state secrets, the Spanish crown did in fact buy back a large number that December, including—exceptionally—the majority of Frenchmen seized in its service.[90] Over the next several years, Oran's lid better sealed, fewer defectors made it to Algiers, and pestilence, famine, and earthquake wiped out scores who did.[91] But, at least according to the *Gazette de France*, those who survived caused havoc. In September 1753, it reported, a Genoese clockmaker led Algiers's principal bagne in rebellion.[92]

By 1760, in an attempt to protect both Catholic souls and French merchants by keeping the peace, an interim consul was supporting at least half of the regency's Christians in captivity, whose number had more than doubled in size when Algerian soldiers plundered Tunis.[93] He was also trying to repair diplomatic relations strained by claims both on behalf of and by slaves. His predecessor's expulsion followed a dispute over the provenance of Basques captured aboard foreign vessels;[94] continuing popular antipathy stemmed from the unfounded rumor, disseminated by an Algerian runaway from France's galleys, that authorities in Toulon had destroyed the municipal mosque and disfigured its imam.[95] Meanwhile, thirty deserters (out of forty-six French captives) in Algiers hoped the exigencies of the Seven Years War might sway Louis XV toward benevolence. Thus in 1761 they asked to benefit from the newest amnesty aimed at attracting fresh recruits to shorthanded warships. But whereas in the mid-seventeenth century the prospect of adding hundreds of seamen to the naval corps had influenced policy decisions, this time the slaves lacked power in numbers. Furthermore, Versailles was unprepared to jeopardize a critical alliance with Spain by publicly acknowledging through redemption the detention of French subjects in Oran.[96]

The *Gazette de France*, now bearing the subtitle *Organe officiel du gouvernement royal*, did not acknowledge French Oraners either. Instead, it described the January 1763 uprising of "more than four thousand Christian slaves," brutally crushed by janissaries until the "streets ran with blood."[97] Whether because of precision or prudence, France's consul remained silent about any slave revolt. But he did alert his superiors when, to avenge a mistaken French attack on an Algerian galliot, he was sent to labor in the quarries—with his secretary, three servants, the French chancellor and apostolic vicar, two priests, two missionaries, five traders, the sailors from four vessels that happened to be at port, and the French deserters already enslaved. The group of fifty-three spent forty-six days loaded with eighty-pound chains. A naval captain with orders to remove all fellow subjects from the regency made little progress in November. By the following January, however, France's gunpowder diplomacy bore fruit: the dey released his hostages and several slaves, in recognition of which Louis XV emancipated twenty Algerians from his now out-of-use galleys.[98]

REPATRIATING REBELS

When news of the brief Franco-Algerian rupture reached Tunis in 1763, France's consul initially feared war.[99] In fact, that regency's bey, while fighting and enslaving Christians from Genoa, Malta, Portugal, and Spain, had only broken ties with France a single time during his twenty-three-year reign.[100] For the most part, he maintained good commercial and political relations, awarding the kingdom a monopoly on coral fishing and gifting two islands to the chartered Compagnie d'Afrique, disciplining ra'is who assaulted French boats, and releasing captives who proved French status.[101] The major areas of contention had to do with his insistence that Saletian corsairs cruising in Tunisian waters could take legal French prizes and his refusal to validate French imperialism via slave redemption.[102] While French officials had long extended protection—and even paid ransoms—for individual foreigners demonstrating emotional, religious, and useful affinities to France, the takeover of Corsica from Genoa in 1768 provided the first of several future occasions to claim sovereignty over an enslaved people en masse.[103]

For the crown, delivering islanders from North African servitude was a chance both to win international recognition for territorial expansion and to earn fidelity from new subjects. It also gave French Trinitarians and Mercedarians, in Paris judged drunkards and elsewhere under pressure to merge and ordered to close understaffed convents, an opportunity to salvage their reputation.[104] Of course, neither Tunis (with eighty-four Corsican slaves) nor Algiers (with about thirty) relished the prospect of turning over men and women who had seemingly become French overnight. Rejecting protestations that "it is current subjection that forms the right of prince and flag and not the origin of people and provinces,"[105] bey 'Ali of Tunis maintained he would only manumit for money.[106] To assert his dominion, therefore, Louis XV dispatched a naval fleet to Tunis and, after negotiations faltered in May 1770, ordered a barrage on Porto Farina, Sousse, and Bizerte.[107] Tunis capitulated, agreeing both to accept "the reunion of the island of Corsica and the states of the Emperor of France" and "to return all the slaves of this nation who were seized and taken into [that] kingdom under French flag."[108] By the fall, with a treaty signed and an ambassador dispatched to Versailles,[109] the Corsicans in captivity won provisional freedom.[110]

In the four years before his death, however, the king neglected these newly French captives, and the resident consul in Tunis overlooked them too when, to mark Louis XVI's ascension to the throne, he renewed the Franco-Tunisian peace.[111] By the end of 1774, mortality, conversion, and individual ransom had diminished their number by a third.[112] Still, the bey steadfastly refused to let the rest go. In 1777 another Tunisian emissary presented the twenty-three-year-old French monarch with six Corsican fathers and daughters plus a fugitive soldier from Grenoble to suggest largesse, along with six horses and two lions to evoke sovereign dignity.[113] Meanwhile, relatives of the enslaved Corsicans had migrated to Tunis and begun supporting themselves through the sale of wine.[114] Thus in 1778, when bey 'Ali finally bowed to French pressure and released the last thirty-five slaves he possessed at an elevated price, it was a coed, mutigenerational group that two pairs of Trinitarians and Mercedarians and a Tunisian envoy escorted back to France.[115] They departed in June 1779 aboard a Swedish vessel and picked up three dozen compatriots in Algiers,[116] before sailing on to Marseille and spending eighteen days in quarantine.[117]

The well-advertised procession of musicians, standard-bearers, confraternity brothers, redemptive fathers, guards, collectors, and slaves in rags, along with their wives and children wearing angel wings, followed a route along the seaport's major boulevards, past the municipal cathedral and the residences of long-established Corsican families to the order's respective convents on 11 August, officially touting the "triumph of humanity and the defeat of irreligion." According to organizers, "the spectacle of young children, infirm women, [and] elderly men" produced in viewers "sentiments of tenderness, pity, and joy, which were manifest by their tears, and by the thousands of blessings they showered upon the captives and those who had . . . br[oken] their chains." Besides honoring the church's success in saving bodies from ruin and souls from Islam, the parade celebrated historical Valois and Bourbon support for Corsican immigrants. It also highlighted the crown's recent achievement in adhering new territory to the realm and inculcating royal allegiance in the hearts of "new Frenchmen," who, the friars testified, exultantly shouted, "Long Live the King!" What it deliberately concealed, by focusing attention on the emancipation and integration of Corsicans, was the release of nine French deserters of metropolitan origin. Rather than receiving an invitation to a join a pageant to French faithfulness, these men received a small sum of transit money.[118]

While the disloyal former captives traveled furtively homeward, the accredited band of ransomed slaves, their families, and clerical chaperones undertook a monthlong, clockwise circumnavigation of Corsica. From Calvi, the former Genoese presidio, they journeyed to Bastia in the north, sailed on to Bonifacio on the southern tip, and continued around to Ajaccio. In each town, the Trinitarians and Mercedarians recounted, relatives with streaming eyes packed the streets to cheer France's monarch and its Catholic institutions. Like mainland processions of an earlier era, which echoed royal, civic, penitential, and thanksgiving displays, these island festivals blended the iconography of liberation and conquest. This time the goal was more than binding participants and spectators with shaky loyalties to the polity and its official creed. It was inducing submission among a potentially rebellious people. Having used redemption to impel North African recognition of French sovereignty over Corsica, Louis XVI now banked on ritual to build Corsican loyalty to France. As the king's Trinitarian and Mercedarian delegates boldly predicted, the sight of peace-loving, grateful captives would "inspire sentiments of fidelity and obedience among their fellow citizens."[119]

Such confidence in the transformative power of ceremony turned out to be misplaced. Rather than continue to set an example of royal and religious fealty for compatriots, within a year a large portion of the freed

Corsicans returned to North Africa. Private bonds clearly trumping political ones, they rejoined tavern-keeping family members living on the margins of the expatriate community, suffered by French authorities who feared they might otherwise further sever ties to the kingdom by changing their religion.[120]

AVERTING DISASTER

The monarch to be known as Louis the Last did not seek further conflicts with the Ottoman regencies. Saddled with debts from the Seven Years War and poised to take on new ones to help finance the American Revolution; facing poor harvests, rising prices, and high levels of crime and vagrancy; and hoping to avert a new political crisis, he valued stability and prosperity where he could find it—and trod particularly softly with regard to Rome's granary and Marseille's trading partner, Algiers. As in the past, that meant granting asylum to refugees or even buying freedom for natives enslaved on foreign galleys, and offering physical protection, monetary support, and spiritual resources to Muslim merchants and travelers.[121] Together these efforts may have provided some safeguard to French-Algerian relations. Yet Louis XVI's decadelong neglect of captive deserters—whose number climbed toward four hundred in the 1770s—posed an ongoing danger.[122]

Appeals from fugitive soldiers, their advocates, and, increasingly, their mothers inundated the marine ministry during that decade and the beginning of the next. Such pleas, while keeping the familiar tropes of corporal pain, social necessity, and Catholic piety, placed particular emphasis on love of king and country. Instead of stressing local connections as in the period before buying back slaves became a matter of state, they offered paeans to the *patrie* (fatherland) and either expressed remorse about, made excuses for, or glossed over the betrayal of desertion. Enslaved after an ill-fated attempt to return to France during a general amnesty, Jean-Eléanore Dumont, for example, plainly acknowledged absconding from his company in Lyon and crossing into Spain, but was now "pierced by the sharpest repentance for having failed his Prince and his *patrie*."[123] By contrast, Jean-Baptiste La Croix, identified in consular correspondence as a runaway from Strasbourg, portrayed himself as no more than the luckless victim of a corsair attack on a Genoese ship.[124]

Other slaves used the capriciousness and susceptibility of youth as defense. Alexandre Mercier insisted that he was "absolutely not a deserter from France," but rather an orphan from Lorraine who had left for Spain to seek his fortune at the age of nine and had gone "over to the Algerians to get back to [his] *patrie*." Now he called on Louis XVI to be "a heroic victor similar to Moses[,] conductor of the people Israel" by dividing the Mediterranean "so that we might pass into the promised land" of France.[125] Rémi Conor of Clermont-Ferrand likewise made clear that he "never knew what it was to enjoy the true bliss of being French," having been pressed into Spanish service at fourteen. Such was "the unhappy situation" of a "French subject . . . with a heart stirred only by sentiments of his noble *patrie*."[126] Guiltless captives among the French ranks resented associations with runaways whom even the consul described as "almost all thieves . . . capable of the most hideous crimes . . . schemers . . . and rhymesters, extremely insolent and very menacing people."[127] Jean Mauri from the region of Chartres had been imprisoned in Spain as a Jesuit spy, a charge he stoutly denied along with any suggestion of disloyalty to his country. Declaring himself "neither deserter nor criminal," he begged the marine minister to instruct the Trinitarians to redeem him.[128]

Over a fifteen-year period, the crown did approve the secret ransom of a few dozen enslaved fugitives on good behavior and with good connections.[129] But overall it followed a policy of abandonment. "These slaves have never been considered French," insisted a brief from the foreign affairs ministry. Those freed were "the exception that proves the rule." To a Provençal father's plea to buy back his son, the marine minister responded, "I am very angry that he left his country to pass under foreign rule. His majesty has decided to leave to other powers the care of ransoming those of his subjects who accorded them such blameworthy preference."[130] Louis XVI's eventual reversal stemmed less from a change of heart than from fear of insurrection.

THE BREAKING POINT

For several years consular reports to Versailles had noted rising despair and fury among the French slaves in Algiers and urged first Louis XV, then Louis XVI, to ransom his subjects.[131] Those Oran escapees enslaved ten, fifteen, or twenty years who anticipated grace from a new king were disappointed by royal indifference; fresher arrivals who expected freedom via conversion were thwarted by a dey wary of deserters and dependent on captive labor.[132] With no end in sight to their ordeal, "they incriminate the Chamber of Commerce, which, according to them, feeds on their blood," wrote Robert-Louis Langoisseur de La Vallée. "They incriminate the consul, who doubtless betrays them and sells them out, by keeping the court ignorant of their lot. They incriminate the curate, who colludes with the consul to keep them languishing in chains; finally, when they seem well convinced that it is not the consul's fault, they incriminate the minister, and it is thus that they give themselves over to all the blindest and most frantic lapses of despair. Since there's nothing to hope for, let's kill, massacre, exterminate! We'll die! At least then we won't suffer any more!—Such is their everyday language."[133] In October 1781 the situation exploded when a French slave and two accomplices lured the apostolic vicar into a vestry to hear confession and then stabbed him thirteen times with a knife. Thanks to the heroics of three captive bystanders, the Lazarist priest survived, and the guilty men hanged. But three months later the consul uncovered another plot—against his own life—and began traveling under armed escort. The bagne's atmosphere simmered ominously.[134]

Until then it had been "dangerous to stray too far from the maxim that has been followed," wrote the marine minister in June 1782, explaining France's neglect of captive fugitives, "but their number has become so big that I would not be far removed from proposing . . . to carry out a sizable redemption." Notably, he instructed the consul to draw up a list of all French slaves present in Algiers, taking care to distinguish between actual subjects and natives of frontier regions who merely spoke the French language.[135] The primary eighteenth-century ransom criterion—Frenchness, established by birth in royal dominions and allegiance to the king, not common humanity as critics might have preferred—had in this context lost its grounding. Instead of weighing particular religious, social, and professional value as had his predecessors during most of the seventeenth century, or freeing all those with convincing emotional or practical claims to French belonging, Louis XVI decided to buy back everyone, including men his forebears might have deemed undeserving or might have excluded as not even French.

Not surprisingly, the Trinitarian and Mercedarian orders also pressed to buy back the kingdom's last servile subjects. With phony alms collectors undermining the status of real ones and charity drying up in the absence of clear outcomes, the redemptive fathers were eager for work.[136] The marine ministry continued to toe the official line that "properly speaking there are no slaves reputed French in Algiers," but by May 1783 even it conceded that those who "have lost in the eyes of the Algerians and almost in ours the quality of subjects of the king" should come home.[137] This time, no one suggested conscripting liberated fugitives into the navy or sending them to the colonies. These sons of Saint-Jean-de-Luz, Cahors, Amiens, Limoges, Metz, Bayonne, Dijon, and Lyon would cross the Mediterranean, dock at Marseille, and then continue through the French countryside to Paris. They would demonstrate Louis XVI's majesty and the Gallican Church's sanctity to adoring crowds. The only issue was how to pay for it.

THE LAST REDEMPTION

In Algiers a new consul started counting slaves—315 adolescents and old men, 94 percent Oran runaways.[138] In France foreign ministry bureaucrats began projecting the full cost of freeing, transporting, feeding, and clothing them. For over a year, the Marseille Chamber of Commerce consolidated donations and loans trickling in from local confraternities, the Parisian headquarters of the redemptive orders, the royal treasury, and the Compagnie d'Afrique and worked to convert various currencies and bills of exchange into gold coinage.[139] At the end of May 1785, longshoremen at Toulon heaved forty-two sacks containing 573,094 livres and change onto a royal frigate. Reduced to figureheads in this last, state-organized redemption, the Trinitarians and Mercedarians made a quick turnaround, disembarking their charges—some diagnosed with fevers, others with leg ulcers, but none with plague—at Marseille's lazaret in early July.[140]

Anticipating a less than warm welcome for repatriated deserters, whose violent reputation preceded them, the friars spent the month's quarantine making preparations and sending assurances. They wrote to municipal officers and religious leaders along two routes to Paris. They told the commerce deputies about the "permanent calm . . . which has reigned" and the "devotion and fervor" with which their charges, pardoned by the king, receive religious instruction and "pray for the long life of his majesty." Good Catholics and loyal Frenchmen despite previous betrayals, "all of them give us hope," stated an August letter, "that they will become useful citizens."[141] Apparently, the intendant of Provence had his doubts: he ordered the mounted police to provide protection to the new arrivals—and "arrest those slaves who stray from the route."[142] Local authorities seem also to have resisted housing and feeding so many people, for in response the fathers explicitly defended their vocation in terms of both religion and value to humanity.[143]

The anonymous author of the first French captivity narrative published in a generation also did his part to universalize the meaning of redemption. His epistolary tale in a sentimental mode described the usual cannon fire, clanging bells, and applause at the harbor. Where previous observers had seen only the victory of Catholicism, however, he recognized the triumph of the human spirit. This soldier claimed to have fought "zealously to defend liberty oppressed" before his enslavement and now to care first and foremost about embracing his beloved fiancée. For him, generous almsgiving was less an indicator of godliness than a sign "that man is good, and that the sensitivity of his heart never appears better than during big spectacles." In flag-waving priests, tattered slaves, and winged children, he found a shared emotional experience that temporarily united curious throngs and turncoats arguably unfit for salvation.[144] Jacques Grasset de Saint-Sauveur, in possible collaboration with Sylvain Maréchal, employed similarly lachrymose rhetoric to different ends. His thinly disguised retelling of the trials and tribulations of Mademoiselle du Bourk, while paying homage to the redemptive fathers and appealing for charity, also blamed consumers of luxury products for exposing Christians to enslavement and demanded why "Europe *policée*" did not "go arm in hand . . . to impose on these pirates the heart's first law: *humanity?*" (emphasis in original).[145]

Local newspapers, charting the troop's progress through cities and towns along the Rhône and Garonne rivers, framed the release of captives in terms of civic and social reincorporation. The *Affiches et annonces de Toulouse*, for example, cast the processions that wound through that city on 7 and 8 September 1785 as a human-interest story, dwelling less on the religious meaning of men in sailor outfits and boys dressed as angels than on the abundant meals and hearty toasts that followed. It also described the jubilant return of a native son after forty-two years to claim an enormous—legally contested—inheritance.[146] In Grenoble, where a Trinitarian confraternity provided beds and food for ninety men, the *Affiches du Dauphiné* told of residents coming out in force and expressing a mix of pity and fascination with the freed slaves, who were seen not as traitors but as quasi-savages: "The majority of these unhappy souls, even those whom nature had best constituted, were completely disfigured by thinness and tinged by the horrors they had suffered. Most had entirely forgotten their religion and even any idea of civilization."[147]

The bishop of Paris had coached his flock to evince a suitable response before the victims of "peoples blinded by fanaticism and ferocity" to whom "the progress of humanity" had not yet extended. "When [these Christians] pass before your eyes, when you see the traces of their chains imprinted on their withered limbs, you will not be able to refuse them your tears, and you will feel compelled to participate in the merit of their deliverance through your alms and good deeds," he told them.[148] Songbooks distributed beforehand affirmed the religious and political commitments of returning slaves and the barbarism of their onetime masters. "Brave soldiers of Jesus Christ / Come back to see your *patrie*," declared one tune; another evoked "the cruel Algerian / Who trades in humans /

... In a country [where] the Christian / ... Is regarded as a dog."[149] Associating Christianity with humanity, civilization with France, and visible deformity with internal transformation, these sermons and songs discerned Muslim inhumanity and North African incivility upon the bodies of suffering slaves, while interpreting the choreographed interaction between observers and observed as a means of reabsorbing the latter into the body politic.

After the October processions (Figure 9), some Catholics insisted on the piety of participants and spectators. "At the sight of these noble martyrs of faith, hearts were deeply moved with tenderness," recorded a man identified only as Brother Déduit. "Promenaded in triumph through the capital, [the redeemed captives] saw in their heads an image of God that torments had not made them disavow. Who would not be touched hearing their canticles of grace, and who would be barbarous enough to refuse to join their aid with that of the generous liberators?" The pres-

ORDRE ET MARCHE DE LA PROCESSION DES CAPTIFS FRANÇOIS RACHETÉ PAR LES 2 ORDRES DE LA REDEMPTION

Figure 9. The last slave procession. "Ordre de la marche de la procession des captifs rachetés ..." (1785). © Musée national de la Marine, ph. 149471.

ence of Louis XVI, in spirit if not in body, he suggested, completed the process of reintegration as chanting bystanders put themselves in the place of marching slaves:

> Seeing LOUIS THE SIXTEENTH
> For the first time,
> How our heart rests easy!
> He is the best of Kings . . .
> Who among us is not honored
> To be good Frenchmen.[150]

Another writer—hawking anecdotes, poems, morality tales, and "history submitted to opinion" to profit the two orders—concurred. To him, the parades were "spectacles that can only be envisaged with the eyes of a citizen."[151]

Yet where one such citizen saw piety or humanity, others saw decadence and hypocrisy. The *Mémoires secrets* described a scene more carnivalesque than devout, with a large banquet following the traditional parade and alcohol raising the spirits of the former slaves: "Such a long promenade necessarily required many pauses, and consequently refreshments or wine flowed abundantly, so much so that a number of captives and a few monks were seen in a hardly decent state, which caused this pious and charitable ceremony to degenerate into farce."[152] Raynal was outraged. "Upstanding people were indignant to see so many villains return to France with so much ostentation," he noted in a 1789 manuscript, before blaming royal ministers who "directed the most important affairs of this unhappy empire."[153] If the sovereigns of Europe simply united "to stop [Mediterranean] brigandage" rather than "mak[ing] treaties with the pirates of Algiers and Tunis," the vaunted utility of the Trinitarians and Mercedarians would become quickly unnecessary, noted a contemporaneous tract. "One dares to say that millions of men [from the Congo and Monomotapa] are far unhappier" than Christians trafficked by Muslims, continued this attack on religious orders. Yet "one does not see the divinity procuring visions for any founders of new orders to buy back these other captives from Saint-Domingue, Martinique, and Guadeloupe."[154]

For Alexandre Moreau de Jonnès, child revolutionary and adult abolitionist, who beheld the fanfare at seven years old—accompanied by his nurse in the rue du Temple—friars brandishing rusty swords and "bearded, ruffled, sun-burned, half-naked men depicting Christians who had been held in slavery by the Barbaresques" seemed neither spiritual nor dissolute but simply macabre: "They noisily dragged the chains that had bound them . . . and cracked the whips that had thrashed them.

They showed off other instruments of torture and displayed backs scarified by cuts they had received from their masters." From the jaded vantage of middle age, he lambasted the redemptive fathers. "These so-called Barbary slaves," he asserted, were but riffraff imported from the suburbs, "men rented out and made up to fill this role," whose trickery worked "to abuse public humanity" and "to fill the [monks'] outstretched purses."[155] Whether ill-begotten spoils or innocent charity, the alms gathered en route and in Paris hardly offset the huge expenses—for banners and music, food and lodging—incurred during a month's quarantine and two months' travel. By the time they reached their destination, sixty-one slaves had worn out their shoes and together the orders had accrued more than a hundred thousand livres in debt, which they had not fully repaid seven months later, nor even at the start of the French Revolution.[156]

EMANCIPATION AND SENTIMENT

To think about Barbary captivity and redemption during the final decades of the Old Regime is to confront a widening gap between modern sensibilities and early modern phenomena and the eternal challenge of aligning perception with performance. During the reign of Louis XIV, the repatriation of enslaved Catholics from maritime regions through the efforts of religious orders and royal envoys may not have actually produced legions of fit and faithful Frenchmen. But nor did seventeenth-century captive liberation as state building stir antagonism comparable to that of the eighteenth century. The Sun King's exclusion of Protestants and impression of sailors certainly drew protest, and his assessment of ransom funds from coastal towns resistance. Snide judgments about the Trinitarians and Mercedarians likewise predated the late eighteenth century. Yet the chorus of criticism attending these last state-directed, church-executed rescue missions reached an unprecedented pitch. Though freedom had been established as a perquisite of French belonging, never before had freedom's beneficiaries seemed so indifferent to France.

The confluence of Corsicans who preferred Tunisian residence to French colonial rule, intemperate deserters who made poor poster children for a vulnerable monarchy, faux-friars who compounded the declining status of real ones, and writers who questioned the entire premise of redemption helped undercut the project of emancipating slaves in order to strengthen France. The effect of these proximate factors, however, depended on at least two underlying developments: a broad shift in narrative expectations and a new mode of human classification. That is, stories of French Christian servitude and scenes of religio-political salvation made less sense in a society that was coming to understand slavery as racially based and permanent, and to seek pleasurable feelings for themselves, not the purification and reintegration of others, by watching and reading. Clumsy attempts to reconcile these two visions from the 1760s to the 1780s failed.

In 1783 the poet and essayist Laurent Pierre Bérenger's nostalgic description of a slave procession came the closest to providing a useful interpretive guide. According to his recollection, the men—outfitted like oarsmen from the royal galleys "in red or brown jerseys and still wearing the chains of slavery"—"show off, imploring public pity, the cruel mutilations that the Turks made them suffer for the smallest faults. Some have cheeks branded with hot irons; others are torn up with deep incisions on the head and arms . . . one no longer has a tongue, and opening his mouth, proffers only inarticulate sounds; almost all are bald and blackened like carbon by the strength of the vertical African sun and consumed, dried out, by harsh agricultural labor." He lauded the "monk-citizens" who looked after the welfare of Frenchmen whom climate and captivity had turned into virtual sub-Saharan Africans, "strangers in the bosom [of their country] . . . unrecognized by their mothers . . . similar to men from another century or another hemisphere." From his vantage, the appearance of racially ambiguous figures gave onlookers the opportunity to show solidarity with slaves everywhere and revel in personal emotion. "Humanity, generosity, all the virtues that ennoble man, shine on [everyone's] face," he declared, "and half the spectators cannot hold back, frankly losing themselves to the sweet pleasure of shedding tears of tenderness without other awkwardness than to wipe them away."[157]

CHAPTER SIX

Liberation and Empire
from the Revolution to Napoleon

With the suppression of France's religious orders between 1790 and 1791, responsibility for freeing captives shifted completely from the church to the state. Deprived of their vocation, the Trinitarians lodged a plea that "with all its acts intended for the establishment of liberty," the National Assembly not forget those Frenchmen still enslaved in North Africa.[1] But more than a year passed before the deputies began to consider the fate of more than 150 deserters,[2] petty outlaws, shipwreck victims, and casualties of mistaken identity[3] still lingering in Barbary. In a December 1791 address, marine minister Antoine-François Bertrand de Molleville reminded the "representatives of a generous and free nation" of "our ill-fated brothers languishing in irons" and outlined possible ways of carrying out and financing the "humanitarian work" of deliverance. Apart from appropriating any surplus funds from the Trinitarians and Mercedarians and allocating additional moneys from the public treasury to fulfill this secular goal, he floated the idea of adopting the Catholic practice of alms taking, from which the redemptive fathers had only ever garnered significant sums when "they excited the commiseration of parishes with processions that afforded a spectacle of the unfortunates they had released."[4]

Over the next several months, therefore, national agents investigated not only the residual assets of Trinitarian and Mercedarian convents but also the number of slaves the orders had rescued, the methods they had used, and the ransoming priorities they had embraced during the previous two centuries.[5] By March 1792 the Committee on Public Assistance had prepared a report that linked the liberation of France to the liberation of Barbary slaves. Given that "in these happy times . . . the antique colossus of despotism has been forever banished from the French empire," declared

Jean-Baptiste Jamon, delegate from the department of Haute-Loire, "to break the chains of these unhappy victims of ignorance and the most revolting barbarity . . . would be an act of humanity and benevolence." He proposed buying back residents held over from the last treaty (who, delicately, he declined to identify as fugitives), foreigners apprehended while in French employ, and crewmembers recently seized by tribal Kabyles over whom the Algerian dey held little influence—for as the preamble to the draft emergency decree proclaimed, "there is nothing more important, nor more pressing, for the representatives of a free people than to ensure that every individual enjoy this noble and proud liberty to the full."[6]

To resolve this acknowledged contradiction between North African servitude and the French idea of freedom, six articles ordered negotiations with the Barbary powers and ransom payments at the charge of the nation. Former alms collectors were instructed to turn over any surplus cash, and, perhaps reflecting secular discomfort with the spiritual basis of charitable giving, all future collections were banned.[7] There is no evidence to suggest, however, that either the marine ministry or the revolutionary legislature took any immediate measures to unfetter Frenchmen—for even ardent emancipatory rhetoric could not breach bureaucratic gridlock. As the redemption legislation slowly wound its way through the diplomatic, finance, and naval committees, therefore, slaves and their backers continued to resort to a traditional means of persuasion: petitioning government officials.

While pointing to a liberation rationale grounded in a conception of common humanity, such correspondence nonetheless alternated bids to national and universal sentiment with religiously inflected appeals for compassion. Between the Revolution and the Napoleonic era, this mixed legacy of the Old Regime and the Enlightenment was recrafted in the service of empire. As ideas of Christian salvation gave way to an ideology of secular deliverance—as "redemption" continued to evolve into "regeneration"—saving slaves became less a method of asserting sovereignty over individuals than a manifestation of France's still controversial imperial project: its "civilizing mission" on both shores of the Mediterranean.[8]

CHARITY WITHOUT CHRISTIANITY

In April 1792, five self-identified Marseillais and "true citizens with the love of their *patrie* engraved on their hearts," who happened also to be tobacco smugglers, were caught off the coast of Provence without passports and transported to Algiers. What irony, they lamented to their city's Chamber of Commerce, "to have wiped the first sweat from [our bodies] to enjoy the fruit of liberty; and having tasted it to lose [our] homeland forever . . . to [be] . . . reduced to permanent captivity and at the height of wretchedness, overburdened with work and beatings, and then deprived of all that is necessary [and] natural."[9]

This plea, which played up the incongruence of people recently freed from the metaphorical chains of tyranny now wearing the literal chains of servitude, fell on sympathetic ears in Marseille and Paris. In Algiers, however, the long-standing French consul, though likewise convinced of France's mission to substitute "justice, humanity, and reason" for "ancient wrongs," was unimpressed.[10] Even so, he followed orders to settle their ransom price, in theory to be paid by a newly nationalized municipal redemption agency, funded through the "patriotism" of local inhabitants.[11] Another letter from the five slaves, composed two days after the abolition of the French monarchy, conveyed gratitude for his intervention. In a style better suited to recipients who still regarded the liberation of captives as a holy calling, it lauded the directors' "bounty" and the court's "grace," which promised to "end our pain and deliver us from this awful slavery."[12]

As it turned out, by this point Louis XVI was hardly in a position to offer clemency or anything else to his former subjects.[13] At least in the short term, a power vacuum in the Mediterranean and the dismantling of the Old Regime's redemption apparatus had stranded captive citizens and mounting numbers of other captive Christians with fewer resources and less hope of deliverance than they previously possessed.[14] While the demise of the French branches of the Trinitarian and Mercedarian orders deprived enslaved nationals of passionate advocates, the fall of the Congrégation de la Mission left all detainees without much of the material and spiritual assistance on which they depended. Indeed, with the cessation of customary alms distributed by four resident Lazarists, "seven to eight hundred unfortunates . . . often lack bread and clothing," the French consul to Algiers advised his superiors, asking permission to advance money reimbursable with annuities from the order's confiscated property. He further requested that the fathers, despite rejecting the Civil Constitution of the Clergy, still be allowed to minister to slaves. "Their position is becoming extremely deplorable," he maintained, and at stake were French affiliation and influence. Articulating in fresh terms an earlier period's anxiety that desperation would drive captives to apostasy, he warned of the imminent threat of the men "no longer being considered French and seeking foreign protection."[15] Delegates from the Beaugency district of the Loire Valley imagined a more useful role for nonjuring friars. The following spring, they proposed simply trading the slaves for "this useless horde of priests."[16]

While it is doubtful that the National Convention acceded to either request, its leaders were certainly sensitive to the difficulty of alleviating the plight of enslaved nationals and protected aliens who, regardless of institutional desacralization and civil status secularization at home, continued by inclination and necessity to self-identify and be identified as Christians abroad.[17] The deputies also confronted the more general problem of trying to uphold France's traditional role as guardian of Latin Christians, pilgrims, and holy sites in the religiously constituted Ottoman Empire without the support and sanction of the church. Accordingly, the ambassador to Constantinople was told to continue attending Catholic services and to convey to his hosts that the switch in government had not altered France's interests in the region or its time-honored privileges.[18]

REVOLUTIONARY FREEDOM

Regime change had, however, appreciably transformed official attitudes toward servitude in North Africa. For most of the seventeenth century, the capture and captivity of Frenchmen in the lands of Islam represented an undesirable side effect of commerce. By the end of Louis XIV's reign it became an intolerable insult to the king's glory. In the eighteenth century Barbary slavery was a fate reserved mostly for subjects without clear French credentials. During the Revolution it stood as a stark challenge to republican ideology.[19] Although politicians debated whether in an Atlantic context sub-Saharan Africans of any faith deserved complete access to freedom, they agreed that the slavery of European Christians in the Mediterranean clearly violated the principles of liberty, equality, and fraternity.

By November 1792, just months after bestowing political rights on some free blacks and mixed-race people—in a divide-and-conquer effort to strengthen opposition to the slave rebellion in Saint-Domingue that began the previous summer—the Republic officially extended its emancipatory (possessive) vision far beyond the borders of France and the bodies of French citizens and other Christians to "all peoples who want to recover their liberty" through the occupation, annexation, and founding of satellite "sister republics" in neighboring territories.[20] This process required reconciling, or at least fudging, seemingly contradictory goals: political liberation and territorial expansion.[21] Thus while ostensibly offering "brotherhood and aid" to inhabitants living under oppressive regimes from the Alps to the Pyrenees, revolutionary troops also began overseeing the manumission of Muslim galley slaves.

This action, which demonstrated the dwindling significance of religious difference as a justification for slavery, served both symbolic and pragmatic ends. In the newly subjugated ports of Nice and Villefranche, for example, the marine minister recognized opportunities for establishing goodwill around the Mediterranean, as well as economizing on ransom funds. "These men must be returned to their homeland," he directed Marseille's interim commerce bureau, "but they also must be exchanged for an equal number of French and even Christians who groan in Barbary irons."[22] Friendly relations with the North African powers—for which the government was at least temporarily prepared to give presents[23] as well as unshackle captives—brought the additional benefit of helping to assure a steady inflow of grain to feed a hungry populace and provision a new conscription army.[24]

Within a year and a half, practical considerations and the same revolutionary credo that had propelled the nation on a European crusade for liberty that encompassed Muslims as well as Christians led it to end slavery in the colonies. Abolition had never been a high priority in metropolitan France.[25] Still, residents of port cities and inland towns met news of the February 1794 decree with jubilation and pageantry, including dramatic parades that employed *gens de couleur* (free people of color) in costume and whites in blackface to reenact emancipation and that resembled nothing so much as prerevolutionary, Catholic redemption processions.[26] Having set free the Caribbean's slaves of sub-Saharan African lineage, the Committee of Public Safety dispatched a special envoy to Barbary with a directive to release any remaining French ones—and monitor royalist sympathies inside the diplomatic corps. In Tripoli, where there were no captive citizens, the government had already replaced France's loyalist consul;[27] in the other regencies, Louis-Alexandre d'Allois d'Herculais successfully impugned the reputations of two state servants and shut down the consular chapels. But he made no progress delivering a handful of incarcerated Corsicans in Tunis or almost 150 enslaved deserters in Algiers.[28]

Over the next several years these men, mostly Oran fugitives, continued to supplicate Jeanbon Saint-André, the Protestant revolutionary appointed to the Algerian consular post. With a blend of mawkish secular vocabulary and old-fashioned religious metaphors, their collective petitions described longing for the patrie and provided assurances that no one on earth "can extirpate from our hearts the vigorous root [that makes us want] to live and die for the Republic." Appealing to the consul's "brotherly, just, and human sentiments," they begged him to show pity and "serve as father" to the "poor unhappy Frenchmen."[29] By revealing feelings and appealing to emotion, these epistles (like eighteenth-century epistolary novels) encouraged identification with their authors as fellow human beings.[30] In fact, personal sympathy and philosophical conviction (along with fear for his life) did sway Saint-André, who repeatedly urged his superiors toward manumission. It hardly befits "France, large, powerful, and victorious," he wrote in 1796, "to let languish just a few unfortunates in irons."[31]

Yet the slaves' submission to universal values, which suggested liberty for all, did not cleanly replace either the now-illegal skin-color divisions that had rationalized chattel slavery in the Americas or the religious beliefs that had once inspired redemption from North Africa. Even as France strategically invoked emancipatory arguments during the Directory, assuming a role as global savior of subjugated, incapacitated peoples of all complexions and creeds in order to swallow up more and more European land and position itself as a colonial power superior to Great Britain, the possibility remained that French citizens deserved special consideration as patriots, as Christians, and even as whites. The advent of Napoleon Bonaparte in the roles of general, first consul, "consul for life," and then emperor ultimately unraveled the fiction of France's race-blind freedom project and helped buttress the link between liberation and conquest.

LIBERATORY CONQUEST

During the Italian campaigns of the late 1790s, as France extended its "natural frontiers" to the north and to the east, the ritual for unshackling Muslim oarsmen grew more elaborate and the anticipated recompense—further advancement of France's imperial status in both Europe and the Ottoman Empire—more grand. In May 1797, one of the first acts of Jacobin insurgents in Genoa, for instance, was to throw open the naval arsenal doors. Two months later, a festival celebrating both the establishment of the Ligurian Republic and the storming of the Bastille featured sixty-eight North African slaves who exchanged chains for Phrygian caps and then received instructions to spread word of French bounty back home.[32]

This gesture fell flat in Algiers.[33] In Tunis, it earned the release of over a dozen Genoese but did not convince the bey to acknowledge as French those slaves from other newly subject lands. Calling France's repossession of Corsica from Britain illegitimate and Corsicans "rebels [who] we need not regard as Frenchmen," he asserted the prerogative of "Tunisian corsairs . . . to take them when they encounter them." Meanwhile, bey Hammuda authorized stepped-up attacks against the ex-colonies of the Venetian Republic, ceded to France by the October 1797 treaty of Campo Formio, on the grounds that the takeover had rendered any standing peace accords invalid, a position he reversed only under duress.[34] Such intransigence, along with France's mounting grain requirements and a desire to make up for defeats in North America, produced at least one proposal for invasion cloaked in the language of liberation and regeneration. "Our vengeance, directed . . . against these tyrants," the ex-consul to Tunis wrote of the regency's inhabitants, "will be converted into blessings in making them free, honest, and happy."[35]

Algiers greeted France's continental expansion with even greater hostility, since accepting its sovereignty over a large swath of western Europe, including the Low Countries, the Cisalpine Republic (composed of the former Duchy of Milan, parts of Venice, Modena, Piedmont, and the Papal lands), and the Ionian Islands (from whose galleys the vanquishing army had released scores of Muslims),[36] also meant granting freedom to hundreds of Christian slaves.[37] Thus in a diplomatic endgame played out on two sides of the Mediterranean, the Algerian dey withheld recognition, French bureaucrats demanded it, and, under the suspicious gaze of British officials, savvy captives from previously Italian city-states and their dominions feverishly swore allegiance to the Republic of France.

In an attempt to thwart such maneuvers, the dey had forbidden on pain of death all contact with the French consul, reported Christophe Visovick of Venice in March 1798. Nevertheless, "on the first day of Pluviôse," he informed the Directory, "I presented myself to our Consul Jeanbon Saint-André and gave him a vow of fealty, along with my friends in misfortune from the [Ionian] islands of Corfu, Zante, and Cephalonia." Then he begged in revolutionary and religious terms for the "most capable, republican zealous citizen consul . . . [to] liberate me from this martyrdom."[38] Meanwhile, Pietro Giovanni Vigo, a veteran of fifteen and a half years of Algerian captivity from the Milanese city of Pavia, was well aware that "we French" had conquered his homeland, as his letter put it in Italian, and that he was "among the fortunate French citizens who will soon be liberated." He credited the Lord as much as France for the promise of redemption and prayed that once "charity and love of God moved [Saint-André's] heart" to help him, the consul would receive "temporal and spiritual benediction" from on high.[39]

Unfortunately for the three dozen French-credentialed Italians left in the regency, neither providence nor the Directory had sufficient clout to alter their enslaved status[40]—though Bonaparte kept up the pressure when, charged with leading an invasion of Egypt to cut off British access to India, he elected in June 1798 first to land at Malta.[41] There, just days after dispossessing the Christian knights of their Mediterranean outpost, he issued an edict eradicating slavery from the island and trumpeting the liberation of "two thousand Barbary and Turkish slaves that the order of Saint-John-of-Jerusalem held on the galleys." Then he declared that from that day forward Algiers, Tunis, and Tripoli "must respect the Maltese, since they now find themselves subjects of France."[42] Yet despite the repatriation of, more accurately, about six hundred male and female captives from different parts of the Ottoman Empire, the dey of Algiers still balked at the suggestion that he match with Venetians and French deserters the number of Algerians discharged from Maltese prisons.[43] The somewhat more compliant bey of Tunis, by contrast, had on news of the conquest instantly let loose "sixty-six Maltese and foreign slaves taken under the flag of this nation." Before departing, the freedmen "will attend the celebration of the *14 juillet* festival," the French consul reported, and on returning home after absences of fifteen to twenty years, he assured Bonaparte, will doubtless "bless the liberating regime under which they are going to have the happiness to live."[44]

Though undercut by naval defeat at the hands of British admiral Horatio Nelson within less than a month, Bonaparte cast his triumph over Egypt's Mameluke overlords at the Battle of the Pyramids in July 1798 as another victory over despotic rule, another act of deliverance— this time of a people held in thralldom by what he called a "pack of slaves, bought in Georgia and the Caucasus."[45] Whether the landing of French forces had a liberatory effect inside the Ottoman regency of Egypt, it clearly had a confining one in the Barbary States, whose respective leaders, albeit grudgingly, obeyed a directive from Istanbul to declare war on France and lock up its resident nationals. "To everyone's surprise, all the French were arrested; and all of us were sent to the naval armory where we were shackled one-to-one and lined up by the big cannon, expressly to satisfy public curiosity," wrote a chartered company agent from one of the Algerian bagnes on Christmas Day. The French consul and his entourage—approximately sixty-four people—"are currently slaves," a Spanish diplomatic report confirmed, describing efforts to win them exemptions from work and the chain. Over the course of the spring and summer of 1799, more than three hundred men, women, and children abducted from France's commercial concessions in Annaba and La Calle (now El Kala) and its garrison on Corfu joined the captive ranks, not to be released until the signing of a final armistice and peace the following fall.[46] In retaliation, the French government ordered the arrest of all Algerians in the nation's southern regions and the imprisonment of the dey's envoy in the notorious royal prison, the Temple.[47]

Bonaparte's assault on Muslim territory, combined with his obliteration of the Knights of Malta, also provided Tripoli and Tunis with new motives and opportunities for increasing attacks on European ships and shores.[48] Most of the fresh victims came from annexed Italian and Greek areas, but some hailed from metropolitan France. One, a physician on the Egyptian expedition whom ill health had driven homeward, was captured by Tripolitan corsairs and held for two years in the Peloponnesian Islands.[49] France's ex-ambassador to Naples was carried off to Tunis. There, Frenchmen and women had a more gentle captivity than elsewhere.[50] Thus despite the consul's urging to throw any Tunisians on French soil into internment camps (just months after promising the bey that his subjects "were free like the air over the Republic's whole territory"), the Directory decided first to curtail their movements and then to have a portion deported.[51] In fact, what raised greater ire in France than the temporary custody of up to 150 citizens in Tunis was the regency's corsairs' September 1798 pillage of Carloforte, a town on Saint Peter's Island located off the coast of Sardinia, a vestigial Savoyard possession temporarily shielded from Napoleonic occupation by the British navy. Of a scale and brutality unknown since the seventeenth century, this raid swept almost a thousand civilians into Barbary captivity.

Mostly the descendants of Genoese coral fishermen resettled in Carloforte a generation before from the island of Tabarka, the throngs of half-naked women with infants clinging to their breasts, elderly men, and children stricken by smallpox and fever that disembarked in Tunis also included some Corsicans, along with Spanish, Danish, Swedish, Dutch, and Ragusan consular families. According to European witnesses, their pitiful state moved Christian and even Muslim residents to charity but the bey only to avarice. While acceding to pressure to release any diplomats, asylum seekers, and acknowledged French nationals among the haul, he distributed the attractive girls and boys as prizes to his corsairs and fixed a high ransom price for everyone else. It would take five years of Sardinian fund-raising and French-led negotiation before the majority returned home. In the meantime, reports of suffering male and female captives reaffirmed fading notions of North African barbarity, which gave credence to France's purported duty to civilize and even colonize the region in the decades to come.[52]

FREEING WHITES, RE-ENSLAVING BLACKS

In the months after seizing power on the eighteenth of Brumaire (9 November 1799), Bonaparte moved authoritatively to grant some groups and deprive others in the French polity of liberties and liberty. Notably, he continued making bellicose demands for the release of whites held in North Africa, while moving to reverse the manumission of blacks in the Caribbean. Indeed, the 1801 and 1802 accords that concluded another bout of Franco-Barbary conflict—and freed captives with French standing by the hundreds—had still not altogether settled the fate of sister republicans and additional Europeans to whom France strategically extended diplomatic protection.[53] Nor had the successful slave uprisings of the previous decade convinced the first consul that men and women of sub-Saharan African descent merited full French citizenship. Thus despite initially pledging not to withdraw the hard-won freedom of ex-slaves, in the wake of peace with Britain and Saint-Domingue's bid for constitutional autonomy, Bonaparte decreed the restoration of chattel slavery and racial hierarchies throughout the empire.[54] As he had earlier argued, identifying parallel Atlantic and Mediterranean hazards to France's and Europe's colonial order, "the interest of civilization is to destroy the new Algiers [an independent Saint-Domingue] that is being organized in the middle of America."[55]

Bonaparte was also giving serious consideration to destroying (then rebuilding) the original Algiers and its allegedly piratical neighbors. In an 1801 memoir, Jacques-Philippe Devoise, consul to Tunis, had exhorted "the leader of a free and warlike nation" to fight the Tunisian "barbarians" and topple the regency's abusive government in order to instigate a popular revolution and "the regeneration of this portion of Africa."[56] North African banditry represented "the shame of Europe and the century in which we live," the first consul concurred nine months later, putting his weight behind a proposition discussed during the Amiens peace talks that France join its new allies in shielding more vulnerable states from attack.[57] What the London *Times* later branded an example of flagrant hypocrisy from a ruler holding France's entire population in slavery and filling its national museum with plundered objects, the *Mercure de France* judged a troubling double standard and inadequately sharp response from an otherwise pugnacious leader. "In the Antilles we unchain Africans born slaves and ready to massacre their liberators," intoned an April 1802 editorial, "and we do nothing to safeguard against the awful slavery with which Africans menace us . . . in the Mediterranean."[58]

In fact, while publicly supporting the idea of cooperative patrols, Bonaparte in his quest for empire was privately exploring options for separate action. Responding to a set of pointed queries from marine minister Denis Decrès, onetime Algerian envoy Jeanbon Saint-André referred to a still germane decade-old memorandum that had confidently affirmed France's capacity for "annihilating the Regency of Algiers," before providing current demographic information and military intelligence and making his own recommendations for the project's execution.[59]

From winter to summer of 1802, when his autocratic leadership was confirmed by plebiscite, Bonaparte actually adopted a moderate stance in pushing for the release of Cisalpinese and Ligurians from Tunis.[60] But he pursued a more aggressive one in claiming putative French citizens and other Europeans from the symbolic center of Barbary piracy and slavery, Algiers. "I destroyed the empire of the Mamelukes because after having outraged the French flag, they dared to demand money from me for the satisfaction I had the right to expect," Bonaparte thundered in a July missive to the dey of Algiers composed within days of the colonial re-enslavement diktat, warning him to expect the same fate at the hands of eighty thousand soldiers unless his corsairs started to respect Italian colors and his Arab tributaries agreed to liberate 150 Frenchmen recently seized from a wrecked Saint-Domingue-bound vessel.[61]

Menaces of imminent Algerian conquest notwithstanding, violent Caribbean insurrection had forced a tactical choice, between trying to fulfill what one former Barbary slave and future diplomat called France's "lofty destiny" to stop the ravages of North Africans against Europeans and attempting to reinstate sub-Saharan African bondage and retain possession of lucrative sugar-producing islands.[62] Opting in the end for known over prospective returns, conservation over invasion, Bonaparte dispatched just three warships to the regency, which achieved only some of his stated goals—including, notably, the release of the disputed captives.[63] He devoted the greater part of the Consulat's financial and military resources to reasserting French dominion over its American colonies.

COMPENSATORY COLONIZATION

Metropolitan armies did succeed in crushing rebellion in Guadeloupe. But in January 1804 Saint-Domingue declared itself an independent nation called Haiti. With the definitive loss of his most valuable colony in the New World, Bonaparte once again sought to fortify and expand French holdings in the Old. Besides intervening diplomatically on behalf of weaker polities like the United States,[64] which he wanted to draw into his sphere of influence, the self-crowned emperor attempted to strengthen control over France's continental dependencies through nepotism and emancipation.[65] He installed one brother, Joseph, on the throne of Naples, vowing not to permit "eight thousand of your subjects" detained in Algiers and Tunis to remain "slaves of the *Barbaresques*."[66] Another brother, Jérôme, he sent to Algiers.

"The object of your mission is to withdraw all the Genoese, Italian, and French slaves found in the bagnes," Bonaparte wrote to Jérôme in July 1805, a month after transforming the Ligurian Republic into three imperial departments, and enjoined him upon his homecoming "to disembark [the captives] with pomp."[67] In mid-September, after a fourteen-day quarantine, enthusiastic festivities and a traditional "Te Deum" did attend the entrance into Genoa of 231 rescued natives, along with 13 debtors and 43 deserters furloughed from prison and the galley. While spectators reportedly wept, participants rejoiced in their collective deliverance and full integration into the French empire. This outcome pleased both the emperor and his marine minister, who praised Jérôme for "having shattered the chains of a large number of Ligurians who long suffered the horrors of captivity" and were now "marked by the blessings of new Frenchmen."[68]

Such modest achievements in saving captives and making patriots, however, sufficed neither to force full North African recognition of France's satellite states nor to halt Britain's consolidation of its Mediterranean toehold. Only the promise of a sizable cash gift on Bastille Day 1806 persuaded the Tunisian bey to hand over 172 subjects of annexed lands and foreigners seized in imperial employ.[69] Only another naval demonstration two years later convinced the Algerian dey to accept as French and thus set free one hundred or so Genoese and erstwhile citizens of the Cisalpine Republic (enlarged and renamed the Kingdom of Italy)—possibly including the female captive who inspired Rossini's opera *La Italiana in Algeri*. And he still refused to relinquish any of the several hundred Neapolitans he possessed.[70]

Further frustrating Bonaparte's aspiration to become "master of the Mediterranean," the British had evicted France from its Algerian trading posts, taken over Malta, established a protectorate in Sicily, and would soon occupy the Ionian Islands. The 1807 ban on the slave trade had also brought them significant international prestige.[71] Given these factors, the western Ottoman regencies became for France ever more appealing sites for compensatory colonialism that might be presented as a strike against slavery on behalf of civilization. "A foot in Africa would give England something to think about," mused Bonaparte in April 1808, giving his marine minister a month to prepare a report based on the discreet observations of a military engineer on where, when, and how to land French forces. Then he began plotting a public relations campaign. An article placed in the official *Moniteur universel* would "make well known the horrors committed by the government of Algiers and the vexations it wreaks on all of Europe." That *Les Captifs d'Alger*, a play by Jérôme's personal secretary, was performed in French-occupied Ghent that November could not have been a coincidence.[72]

Two centuries before, French monarchs had tried by waging war on Barbary to deflect Catholic indignation over the Franco-Ottoman alliance. Now the French emperor, encouraged by various underlings, hoped by taking a stand against North Africa to recoup territorial losses and refocus humanitarian outrage away from the Caribbean. It was not blacks but whites that warranted "staggering pity," wrote consul Devoise in 1809, describing the scene at Tunis's slave market, where "squatting Negroes await their new master laughing and gaily leave with him, whoever he is . . . but Christians . . . find themselves in tears and profound dejection." His "afflicted soul" could not countenance the idle standing by of a government that could "by spitting make the *Barbaresques* tremble," and he urged France to assume the duties of the now-obsolete Knights of Malta.[73]

Fifteen hundred overworked, underfed, poorly clothed, vermininfested Christians in Algiers and another three thousand in Tunis prayed that God and Napoleon would take vengeance on "a power that, for centuries, has ridden roughshod over the most sacred of nations and humanity," agreed Charles-François Dubois-Thainville, consul to Algiers. "Their gaze is constantly turned toward the hero who governs France: they put all their confidence in him." Colonization, he argued, would accomplish three liberations at once. Apart from unfettering Europeans "condemned . . . to the most awful slavery," Bonaparte's wrath and rule would release indigenous, freedom-loving Kabyles from Ottoman tyranny. Finally, it would free the region's rich soil, so long depleted by "a handful of brigands, recruited from the Levant, unfit to possess these beautiful countries."[74] The promise of liberatory conquest was France's imperial fulfillment and North Africa's organic rebirth.

Instead of the potential corruption of bodies and souls via disease, sexual deviance, and religious perfidy that impelled salvation from North African captivity and reintegration into the French polity for much of the prerevolutionary period, or the ideological contradictions that motivated opposition to servitude of any sort during the Revolution, it was the physical suffering and political oppression of some but not all peoples, along with the perceived waste of fertile land, that justified plans for selective emancipation and empire building in the age of Napoleon. By the early nineteenth century, the Judeo-Christian tradition of redemption previously aimed at Catholics and occasional Protestants from coastal regions had been redefined, then redeployed. Promises of freedom and regeneration offered to accidental and self-proclaimed Frenchmen in farther-flung realms now embraced individuals in the overlapping categories of Christian, European, and white. Through the strategic adaptation of religious discourse and methods to the secular end of Great Power status in the Mediterranean, and through the cynical reinstatement of sub-Saharan African bondage in the Atlantic, Bonaparte had helped further racialize Barbary slavery and, in turn, connect the advent of French liberty to the colonization of North Africa.

CHAPTER SEVEN

North African Servitude
in Black and White

Measured numerically rather than imaginatively, French enslavement in North Africa was largely a seventeenth-century affair. One variety of Barbary servitude, however, spanned the Old Regime to the Restoration. It derived not from corsairing but from crashing—on remote strips of the Algerian and Moroccan coast. In those regions, indigenous tribes that rejected centralized government authority—and the treaties they forged—may have seized hundreds of Frenchmen and women (plus additional British, French, Spanish, Portuguese, Dutch, Scandinavians, and Americans) between the reigns of Louis XV and Charles X.[1] As in urban centers, a portion of these shipwreck victims died, primarily from deprivation of food and water in a harsh environment. Likewise, a few converted to Islam and stayed behind.[2] It seems, however, that most trekked through miles of rugged terrain before making contact with compatriots either in Algiers or Mogador (now Essaouira), the Moroccan trading port constructed for Europeans in 1764.[3] In the interim, slaves collected wood, herded goats, carried water, dragged plows, prepared meals, drove camels, and, on occasion, provided medical services for masters they judged inhumane and possibly cannibal.

Disproportionately the fate of Caribbean colonials, sub-Saharan slave traffickers, and West African explorers sailing close to notoriously treacherous shores, such bondage became more common as France expanded its role in the Atlantic slave trade and retook possession of Senegal from Great Britain.[4] From the last quarter of the eighteenth century, it preoccupied various iterations of the French government and fascinated the French reading public. At least eight French accounts—plus additional translations—of death, depravity, and transculturation in the Atlas Mountains and Saharan Desert appeared before 1824, replacing discredited redemption pageants and captivity narratives about plague, sodomy, and apostasy in North African cities.[5] Reflecting the hybrid sensibilities and colonial aspirations of their authors, these descriptions helped forge stronger associations between Old and New World slaveries, while supporting bolder arguments for territorial expansion on the African continent.

By the second decade of the nineteenth century, in fact, not only had religious motives for freeing captives lost legitimacy but also, at least in European eyes, the previous era's rationales for corsairing were deemed obsolete. With modernizing western states now possessed of relatively strong navies, it had become easier to denigrate polities that still relied on "extraterritorial violence" as criminal threats to the world order. At the same time, the inclusion of abolition as an element in the Anglo-French competition for international prestige and imperial supremacy was inviting explicit, racialized parallels between white and black slavery and calls for either multi- or unilateral action against North Africa.[6] According to an argument that gained greater traction in this period, curtailing the ravages of Barbary pirates once and for all would not only alleviate the individual suffering of "Christians"—now understood as white Europeans—unsuited to thralldom but also spark the regeneration of lands misused by Ottoman occupiers.

CURTAIN CALL IN MOROCCO

France's final military conflict with Morocco and last experience buying back sea captives (rather than coastal ones) followed the Seven Years War. While the royal navy was fighting abroad, privateers from Salé had stepped up attacks on French shipping. It was only once the Treaty of Paris of 1763 brought peace, debt, and colonial dispossession, however, that Louis XV revisited the situation closer to home. The next year he ordered the Trinitarians and Mercedarians on a joint voyage and—perhaps as a way to arm against Britain without rousing suspicion—a large coterie of battleships on patrol.[7] After conventional tactics of hurling shells brought mixed results, a French admiral tried to inflict greater damage on the northern Atlantic port (and former Spanish outpost) of Larache by sending gunners into its tributary, exposing them to unexpected enemy fire. Three hundred sailors and officers were killed or captured as they scrambled from sinking boats.[8]

Waiting to conclude ransom arrangements in Mogador, the friars feared retribution. But with the help of a local Jewish trader and a resident French merchant, they managed to free ninety-two men, less than half the captive French subjects. All but one rescued came from France proper. Jean-Baptiste, otherwise known as "Neptune," identified as a valet to a naval officer and a "creole negro" from Martinique, found himself in the peculiar situation of being liberated from one sort of servitude only to be reintroduced to another.[9] François Joseph Hippolyte Bidé de Maurville was one of fifty-odd officers and sailors seized during the disastrous assault. "I would have preferred to throw myself into the water and drown than fall alive into the hands of people from whom I expected only the most horrific death," he wrote a decade later. Instead, a dark-complexioned man he mistook for a fellow slave drove him with a whip to Salé and Marrakech, where the sultan made him "work like a negro." But Bidé de Maurville soon found relative comfort among books and consolation from letters.[10] After declining a post as Moroccan admiral, this French aristocrat remembered no pressure to renounce his faith and spent the rest of his two-year detention in Safi immersed in self-directed studies and correspondence, interrupted only by "horseback riding, hunting, and strolling."[11]

Like Moroccan rulers before him, Sīdi Muhammad ibn ʿAbdallah was less interested in money than in removing Muslims from the *dar al-harb* (domain of disbelief). Thus negotiations over two hundred French captives held in Marrakech, Tetouan, Meknes, Salé, Larache, and Mogador initially centered on their possible exchange for enslaved North African oarsmen in France.[12] Since the royal galleys had been put out of service, however, and officials in Toulon and Brest could assemble a mere sixteen suitable men, the sultan pressed the king to substitute rowers from the arsenals of Spain and Malta. It was only when that tactic failed in 1766 that peace talks led by a fleet commander finally turned to ransom price.[13] Deeming redemption "incompatible with his dignity," Louis XV delegated the Trinitarians and Mercedarians to buy everyone back in his name. The friars turned to the Marseille Chamber of Commerce, the Assembly of the Clergy, and the provincial estates of Brittany, Languedoc and Provence.[14] Bishops in these regions, in turn, printed up pastoral letters to be read aloud and distributed to diocesans, inviting contributions "to an effort so worthy of touching the hearts of good citizens . . . who will have this interior and pleasing satisfaction . . . to have worked together for the deliverance of their fellow countrymen."[15]

Appealing to patriotism and empathy, such writings by slaves and priests asked French readers (and listeners) both to identify and to distinguish—to imagine themselves in the place of Barbary captives who occupied diverse socioeconomic positions yet shared a homeland, and, at least in Bidé de Maurville's case, to recoil instinctively at the thought of a white man subservient to a black. By the 1760s, approximately three hundred thousand men and women of sub-Saharan descent labored in France's Caribbean colonies and French dictionaries consistently equated the word *nègre* with slave.[16] With this linkage between physiognomy and slavery better established, mental divisions according to belief system and skin color blurred.[17] Indeed, apart from the Larache casualties, most of the subjects held captive in Morocco had been abducted from ships headed to chattel-run, sugar-producing islands in America. When these would-be colonials and ill-fated mariners—with the exception of one woman who stayed behind to marry a resident Genevan—gained their freedom and boarded three ships bound to Marseille, Brest, and Saint-Domingue, a troubling power reversal seemed to have been put right definitively.[18]

SLAVERY IN THE SAHARA

After 1767 Sīdi Muhammad did effectively block corsairs in northern Morocco from capturing French subjects. However, he could not restrain populations of his southern territories, then known as the *bilad al-siba* (lands outside the sultan's control) and now composing the Western Sahara. These mixed descendants of Berbers, Arabs, and "black" Africans lived by transhumance and trade—partly of goods and people from vessels pulled inward by intense currents from the Canary Islands, which shattered on jagged rocks around Cape Bojador (Figure 10).[19]

In many respects, desert pirates at the Atlantic's edge elicited similar responses and stirred similar anxieties as had sea rovers in the Mediterranean. On the French side, diplomats and merchants lodged protests at the Moroccan court, either directly or via Jewish intermediaries, and occasionally hired special agents to undertake independent rescue missions. During the 1770s, for example, consul Louis de Chénier fretted about the fate of sixteen-year-old Nicolas Crochemare of Havre-de-Grâce, a sailor on a rubber expedition captured when he went ashore for fresh water, "exposed to all the vicissitudes of human misery and sold and re-sold in several markets."[20] With unwelcome help from a French businessman in Salé, who later petitioned the abolitionist Société des amis des noirs (Society of the Friends of the Blacks) and the Directory that "the cause of whites should be no less dear than the cause of blacks,"[21] the consul also lobbied tirelessly for the deliverance of twenty Breton men forced to abandon a Nantes-built, West Africa–bound slave ship.[22] As captain Pierre-Julien Dupuy noted without irony in an unpublished journal detailing two years of scorched peregrinations and

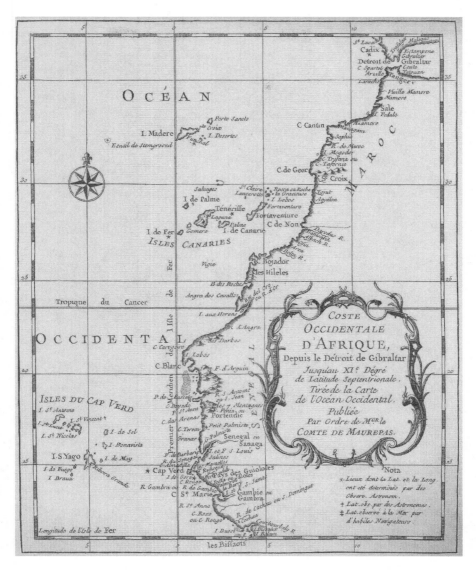

Figure 10. Map of the Atlantic coast of Africa. Jacques Nicholas Bellin, "Coste occidentale d'Afrique" (1754). University of Florida George A. Smathers Libraries, AMD8232, www.uflib.ufl.edu/ufdc/?b=UF00072322.

mistreatments among wandering Arabs, he and his crew had "escaped death only to fall into slavery."[23]

On the Moroccan side, successive sultans attempted through the strategic custody or discharge of Saharan captives to gain diplomatic capital, which they used to push for the release of their own subjects and other Muslims still employed on the galleys of a few European principalities. For instance, having dispatched two envoys to buy back Dupuy and his crew in 1776, Sīdi Muhammad considered the sailors "my slaves . . . to give or to refuse." He put them to work in Marrakech and Meknes and held out for an equal number of Moroccans from Malta or Livorno in recompense. Although Louis XVI rebuffed this demand as a violation of the last bilateral accord, the king did recognize a Moroccan ambassador—sent to accompany home sixteen of the stranded sailors, the missing adolescent, and three deserters from Ceuta—with a rich trousseau of presents.[24] This give-and-take dynamic continued over the next several decades when Sultan Mulay Suleiman gradually abandoned "jihad at sea" in favor of another sort of sacred work—with temporal benefits. Apart from signaling piety, his attempt to liberate *all* Muslim captives from Christian lands invited appreciation and amity from Tunis, Tripoli, and Constantinople, potentially at the expense of rival Algiers.[25]

Negotiations over Crochemare, the crew of Dupuy, and, later, Jacques Audibert of Marseille—who took a fourteen-month detour into servitude on the way to Guadeloupe[26]—depended on assumptions about the social and political order primarily developed in the Mediterranean. Yet by the late eighteenth century the ideological underpinnings and practicalities of Atlantic commerce and conquest were rapidly encroaching, transforming the way subjects and citizens of France thought about Barbary slavery. Whereas authors from an earlier period had written of being disrobed and disoriented on board by turbaned barbarians shouting in a cacophony of foreign tongues, this generation wrote of being stripped naked on shore by "half-black savages" emitting "terrible howls."[27] While slaves in Algiers, Tunis, Tripoli, and Meknes had feared homosexual rape by unintelligible, lascivious Muslims, their successors feared ingestion by ferocious, speechless, racially indeterminate man-eaters.

DEMISE OF THE *DEUX-AMIS*

Two eyewitnesses recounted the demise of the three-hundred-ton *Deux Amis* en route from Bordeaux to Senegal on 17 January 1784: Adrien-Jacques Follie, who intended to take up a post as colonial clerk, and a man identified only as Saugnier, who fled a career in the church to seek his fortune in Africa.[28] According to both men's accounts, published in 1785 and 1791, respectively, the first intrepid sailor to reach dry land was snatched, buried in sand, then suspended over a fire (Figure 11).[29] Despite assurances that no primitive "anthropophagi" inhabited the area, passengers and crew raised on legends about cannibalism practiced in uncharted parts of the globe believed their captors were preparing to feast.[30] As it turned out, they were preparing the young man's feet—for a long march into slavery in the Great Desert. Subsequent experiences further confounded their expectations about the mores of northwest Africans, if not their judgments about the ethics of slavery itself.

Once the twenty-one-year-old Saugnier recovered from the initial shock of capture by "barbarians he thought to be his executioners,"[31] he began to distinguish among his sequential owners along the route from the Rio de Oro region to the commercial outpost of Goulimine, some of whom, he acknowledged, demonstrated compassion, plying him with camel milk and dates. In fact, the closer he came to the population

Figure 11. Enslavement in the Sahara. "Deschamps sort de son tonneau . . . ," René Claude Geoffroy de Villeneuve, *L'Afrique, ou histoire, moeurs, usages, et coutumes des Africaines* (Paris: Nepveu, 1814). Photo © 2010, Musée du Quai Branly / SCALA, Florence.

centers of Morocco, the worse he endured. Echoing contemporaneous two-sided stereotypes about Bedouins as "good savages" and hospitable thieves, he noted that "the more civilized, the crueler men are."[32] Meanwhile, Follie at thirty-five cast himself as his shipmates' moral compass by dissuading them from the "barbaric" act of collective suicide. He wrote of beatings, temporary blindness, and near starvation among nomadic tribes but relative kindness and bounty from sedentary Moors and Jews.

In any case, the Saharan portion of their odyssey lasted just three months. Mistrusting the sultan to buy back this latest batch of French captives in a timely manner, France's vice-consul and the English directors of a Mogador commercial house hired a ransom agent of their own. By turns identified as an Arab, a Moor, and a Jew, Mohamed/David Bentahar paid 1,250 livres for Follie, 900 livres for Saugnier, and an unreported sum for several others.[33] Then he handed out Moorish-style coats and led the group through the cold Atlas Mountains to Mogador. No sooner had the liberated Frenchmen arrived, however, than Sīdi Muhammad ordered them re-enslaved. Apparently, he had sent a directive for their release a few months before and was furious that his subjects would obey European merchants more readily than him. But within a month the sultan had a change of heart, perhaps in response to news that a ship from Marseille had just rescued two hundred Moroccans.

Furnished with a proper French wardrobe of a blue jacket and shorts, three shirts, two handkerchiefs, a silk tie, a hat, a bonnet, and two pairs of shoes, the former slaves departed by mule for Marrakech, from which the sultan sent them with military escort to Salé. Then they continued on to Tangiers, took a boat carrying chickens and grain to Cadiz, and submitted to an unpleasant week's quarantine. Here their geographical and narrative paths diverged. Angling (futilely, as it turns out) for an indemnity and a less-dangerous domestic assignment, Follie gave over the remainder of *Mémoire d'un françois qui sort de l'Esclavage* to sentimental and patriotic reverie. "What keen pleasure, what sweet emotion seized me on entering the lands of France," he wrote of disembarking in Marseille. "I felt more joy during that too short moment than I suffered during my entire slavery," he declared of meeting his mother in Paris. His journey ended in Versailles, where his tale of woe reportedly "moved [the marine minister] to pity."[34]

Meanwhile, Saugnier's homeward voyage took him from the ports of Ostende and Dunkirk to the cities of Lille and Saint-Quentin. But his published story did not end there. Commensurate with its original title, scrapped in a later edition, promising travelogue alongside "interesting details for those destined for the trade in negroes, gold, and ivory," the book went on to describe its protagonist's post-liberation job as a sub-Saharan African slave trafficker.[35] Greed trumping reservations about participating in "a commerce disgraceful to humanity," Saugnier argued that his own ordeal in the Sahara had given him useful linguistic and cultural skills. Thus eight months after reuniting with his largely unsympathetic family, he departed for Senegal once again, this time aboard a Bordelais slaver, whose captain pledged a commission on "the negroes that I traded."[36]

The key to mastering this new colonial endeavor was knowledge.[37] "I was persuaded that I would never succeed without knowing deeply the people with whom I had to trade," Saugnier explained, writing admiringly of one merchant who "spoke negro like the negroes themselves, even living in their manner."[38] So for the benefit of would-be slave dealers among his readers, he appended a handy instruction manual, listing commodities to exchange, customary prices, directions for outfitting a slave ship, and, finally, pointers for keeping slaves docile, a matter in which the former captive Saugnier considered himself particularly expert.[39] Such was his power over his charges, he bragged, that many embarked for the Americas "with joy, having been assured that they would be happy where I was sending them."[40] Half Barbary captivity narrative, half how-to apologetic, Saugnier's account showcased the coexistence of two forms of servitude: a first that stemmed from mischance, a second that was implicitly justified by the color of his skin.

CAPTIVITY, CANNIBALISM, COLONIALISM

Like Follie, whom poverty compelled to accept another bureaucratic posting to Senegal, Saugnier chose to eat rather than even contemplate being eaten.[41] In an attempt to reestablish their French credentials and better their social and economic standing during the final decades of the Old Regime, both former captives embraced a system of brutal transportation and colonial exploitation designed to satisfy growing metropolitan appetites.[42] Indeed, the twofold increase in European sugar consumption between the mid- and late eighteenth century depended in part on French maintenance of slave depots off the coast of Senegal and slave plantations in the Caribbean.[43] Until the National Convention's 1794 suspension of slavery, and from its reinstitution under Napoleon in 1802 to 1809, when Britain reconquered France's Senegalese outposts, therefore, it was not uncommon for seafaring Frenchmen wary of captivity and cannibalism on West African shores to themselves be traders in human flesh.

At least one additional first-person, French-language recital of maritime misadventure and desert detention came out during the late eighteenth century. Written by Pierre-Raymond de Brisson and published in 1789, it recounted the year this high-ranking colonial officer of noble stock had spent in the possession of two rival Saharan tribes. The narrative he provided for the sake of "truth, patriotism, and humanity" followed his predecessors in describing "the dreadful cries, the horrible roars" of savages "unfamiliar with the appearances of Europeans" who ripped off his clothes on the African beach; the beatings suffered at the hands of masters with "prickly hair and long nails like beasts"; and the even worse torments inflicted by their wives, women allegedly so barbarous they even hit and pinched their own nursing babies.[44] But readers were not left wanting for such stories between the Revolution and the Restoration, because of the translation from English of other narratives—about a Liverpool captain headed for "the Guinea trade" but instead taken by "wild Arabs," for instance[45]—and the recycling of older, homegrown tales for the sake of education and persuasion.[46] Reaffirming images of bloodthirsty nomads prowling northwest African coasts, these early nineteenth-century retellings depicted Saharan slavery in more starkly racial terms and served both to recommend safer sailing routes and to champion imperial ambitions.

In 1802, for example, at precisely the moment that Napoleon was reintroducing chattel bondage to Caribbean territories, the director of the chartered Compagnie du Sénégal, Jean-Baptiste-Léonard Durand, used his compendium of historical, philosophical, and political memoirs about the discoveries, establishments, and commerce of Europeans in the Atlantic Ocean to warn readers of the "most terrible slavery" in African wilds due to incompetent navigation.[47] Twelve years later, just after the Treaty of Paris stipulated that Britain turn over Senegal, which it had governed for the previous six years, and the Congress of Vienna began debating the suppression of slave trades worldwide, René Claude Geoffroy de Villeneuve's treatise on the history, mores, and customs of Africans recounted the terror of wayward "whites" involuntarily conducted into the Sahara. At the same time, it promoted the virtues of "new colonization" based on settlement and agricultural production with free labor.[48] For France, expansion into Senegal would be a way of economically compensating for the recent loss of Saint-Domingue to independence, while fulfilling the humanitarian aim of regenerating black African lands and people ravaged by centuries of the commerce in human beings.[49] Such a proposal acknowledged the commingling and cannibalism engendered by slavery in all its forms and sought to reestablish violated boundaries through empire.

DISASTER ON THE *MEDUSA*

The four-ship convoy ferrying 365 teachers, priests, commissioners, pharmacists, gardeners, surveyors, soldiers, naturalists, bakers, and their wives and daughters to reclaim Senegal departed from the French port of Rochefort on 17 June 1816. In the name of the recently restored Bourbon monarch Louis XVIII, and through the application of abolitionist principles, these pioneers intended to establish a peaceful colony, in order to bring profit to the home country and civilization to the natives. Whereas the three smaller boats made it to Senegal without incident, the much larger frigate *Medusa* foundered just nineteen days after departure. Immortalized on canvas by Théodore Géricault and in print by two survivors (ship surgeon Jean-Baptiste Henri Savigny and engineer Alexandre Corréard), the fate of the 150 men and 1 woman denied space aboard lifeboats and abandoned on a makeshift raft is well known.[50] All but fifteen succumbed to thirst, desperation, mutiny, and cannibalism. Less familiar than this tale of self-destruction and self-consumption at sea, however, were the perils, real and imagined, encountered by those passengers who made it to land.

Corréard's and Savigny's reports of French inhumanity afloat—as much on the part of unfeeling commanders as animalistic passengers— spawned a public outcry led by the liberal opposition and a judicial trial with negative political consequences for the new regime. In response, several survivors composed exculpatory counternarratives from a conservative, or royalist, perspective that emphasized the greater African inhumanity lurking ashore. According to lieutenant Paulin d'Anglas de Praviel, for example, his "companions in misfortune," their minds overwhelmed by images of cannibalism and captivity from literary and historical sources, did not initially dare to disembark. "Everyone refused," he wrote, "to traverse an awful wasteland without any means of sustenance, to give themselves up to attacks by ferocious beasts and bad treatments by Moors . . . [members of] a perfidious and cruel nation." Once disgorged by the Atlantic onto the "sandy ocean" of the Sahara, however, anxieties about cannibalism seemed more inwardly than outwardly directed. Rallying his compatriots as they set out on the overland trek, Praviel cautioned, "Let no one ever say of us: Frenchmen drank the blood of their brothers, that they sated themselves with their flesh." Yet a few days in the desert sufficed to transform at least some of them into walking cadavers, mute monsters that sucked blood from their own fingers in a vain attempt to stay alive. These French nationals had expected dispossession and even dismemberment at the hands of preverbal, itinerant savages; instead, it was their "own tongues which could no longer articulate," their own cravings that greedily hungered for wrongful meats.[51] As fellow passenger and African adventurer Gaspard-Théodore Mollien remarked, "it was not from the Moors that we had the most to fear: those that would prolong our miseries were among ourselves."[52] Charlotte-Adelaïde Picard (who published under her married name, Dard), the daughter of a clerk to the appointed governor of Senegal, also recognized cannibalistic impulses among her shipmates, "who looked at one another with wild eyes, as if ready to tear each other to pieces and feed on the flesh of their fellow creatures." Nonetheless, she too preferred to suffer dehydration and starvation on open water than risk "being taken by the desert Moors."[53]

Necessity eventually compelled passengers on the grounded lifeboats to overcome their trepidations about bestial Arabs. As naval ensign Paul Charles Léonard Alexandre Rang des Adrets, otherwise known as Sander Rang, calculated, "captivity among the Moors . . . was the only means of procuring water and food."[54] Ironically, as all soon appreciated though perhaps did not readily admit, the wandering peoples they encountered in the Sahara actually had neither the means nor the inclination to enslave them. Thus the corvette captain Brédif recorded in his journal that a cry to arms at the approach of some "Negroes and Moors" was unnecessary, as the men in fact "came as friends to offer to lead us to Senegal."[55] Mollien concurred, recollecting the unpleasant sensation of timidly stepping foot on a continent "we should have entered as masters," only to discover that the anticipated hordes amounted to "three skinny women no less frightened than ourselves."[56] Received wisdom had distorted French perceptions, concluded Picard after realizing that an ominous caravan in the distance was actually composed of her own countrymen. "The Moors who caused us such alarm," she wrote, "became our protectors and our friends, so true is the old proverb: *there are good people everywhere*" (emphasis in original).[57]

Only Praviel unequivocally rejected this interpretation, which projected an image of successful French imperial domination but also hinted at a disturbingly permeable frontier of identity and the instability of binaries that had long divided civilized from barbarian, Christian from Muslim, and now increasingly distinguished white from black, man from beast. Rather than acknowledge common humanity or universal values in the desert, he persisted in depicting his journey to Senegal as a kind of bondage and in referring to the Arab guides as his masters. Thus he described his dashed hopes for manumission on what he called "the fourth day of our captivity," when a ship on the horizon seemed to be turning inland. And he described his joy and relief when on the sixth day after being "captured by the Moors," a marabout on camelback finally brought news from the capital of the imminent arrival of an English officer bearing ransom money. But it was not until the "ninth day, to date our slavery," he wrote, that the brave envoy in Moorish garb finally located the marooned troop. Escorted with his fellow sufferers to the capital Saint Louis, Praviel presented a sorry picture. Emaciated, practically naked, and covered with scars, he resembled not so much a triumphant colonial avatar as a tainted precolonial slave.[58]

Like earlier objects of Barbary captivity, this self-styled casualty of Saharan servitude would seem to have required purification and acculturation prior to homecoming. Unfortunately, early modern rituals of reintegration—from wardrobe replacement to medical quarantine to religious processions—intended to wash away any traces of plague, sodomy, and apostasy that adhered to redeemed captives did not prove adequate to obliterate all signs of cannibalism and racial mixing that a rescued shipwreck victim acquired in a modern context. Praviel, along with other privileged *Medusa* survivors, had adopted vocabulary and imagery from an earlier era when slavery represented a misfortune of Christian merchants rather than the destiny of black Africans, a side effect of mercantilist trade rather than an instrument of mass markets, a reversible status rather than a potentially permanent condition. With origins in a period of overseas vulnerability, however, North African slavery had different implications at a time of colonial ascendancy. Besides eliciting new concerns about bodily pollution, it provided additional fodder for abolition and additional rationales for empire building.

AN ALGERIAN RIP VAN WINKLE

Pierre Joseph Dumont was another shipwreck survivor whose experiences and sensibilities straddled eras.[59] Enslaved in 1782 at age fourteen and liberated thirty-four years later, he initially disbelieved tales of regicide and Restoration and failed to recognize Napoleon's face on a twenty-franc piece. His account, *Histoire de l'esclavage en Afrique*, dictated to Jacques Salbigoton Quesne and published simultaneously in French and English in 1819, presents the man and his tale as odd throwbacks to a former, vanished world.[60] However, Dumont's judgments about his captors and solutions to the problem of Barbary captivity bear the marks of the early nineteenth century.

Dumont was born in Paris to a coachman and livery overseer and enrolled as a young boy in the service of a French naval commander whom he accompanied to the Caribbean. He had boarded the same warship en route to Minorca when a violent storm dashed it against the coast between Algiers and Oran. Sixty men drowned and eighty reached land, only to be attacked by men Dumont called "Kabouls," that is, Algerian Kabyles. Members of this "ferocious nation," he reported, like the lions, tigers, leopards, panthers, bears, and wild boars that supposedly roamed the mountainous region, preyed on Christians with animalistic cruelty. After "butchering like sheep" the majority of Dumont's shipmates, they led the remainder on an eight-day journey to the residence of sheikh 'Uthman, "a sort of papal warrior king" whose dominion extended over much of the North African interior. "French! without faith, lawless, spiteful, malignant, and devils," he shouted upon learning the origins of the new arrivals, and ordered them loaded with sixty-pound chains.[61]

For Dumont such terms and worse applied to his captors. Skipping the ethnographic passages common in earlier accounts, he directed an unblinking gaze on Kabyle atrocities and the agonies of rural Algerian slavery: nights spent on a bit of straw crawling with vermin, shackled to the wall in a filthy prison with raw sewage flowing through its center; days passed dragging a plow, carting wood, and turning a mill under the supervision of abusive, vaguely cannibalistic guards. "When the blood, at times, streamed from our bodies, in consequence of the blows," he recalled, "the Kabouls would gather it with their fingers, and apply it to their lips, exclaiming, 'How sweet is the blood of Christians!'" Lacking meat, Dumont and his fellow slaves devoured rotting carcasses; denied utensils, they made cups from skulls; deprived of water, they quenched their thirst and treated their wounds with urine from horses and men.[62]

Such graphic descriptions of corporal suffering, common to late eighteenth- and nineteenth-century Saharan captivity narratives but not earlier urban Barbary renditions, infused Dumont's story with more than a trace of the macabre. In the estimation of its ghostwriter Quesne, gory details also lent it authority (though he acknowledged excising a few out of consideration for public decency). So did its slapdash style. To establish Dumont as a reliable witness, he offered additional material and emotional evidence: the former slave's "physiognomy and his candor," illustrated in before and after portraits (Figures 12 and 13); letters of introduction from prominent citizens; and a facsimile of Dumont's sworn statement written in an appropriately unschooled hand. Within the text he used footnotes to corroborate, expand upon, and in some instances correct Dumont's memories with reference to contemporary newspaper articles and biographies and to report on his interlocutor's emotional state (he wept at all the sad parts).[63] Yet the ultimate proof of his ordeal derived not from journals but from scars, which Dumont described and exposed to stir sympathy for the past and garner benevolence in the present.

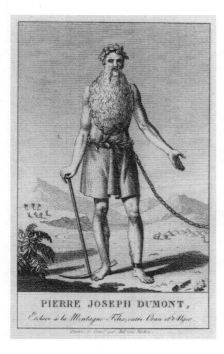

Figure 12. Pierre Dumont (before). Ambroise Tardieu, "Pierre Joseph Dumont, esclave à la Montagne Félix, entre Oran et Alger," in Pierre Joseph Dumont, *Histoire de l'esclavage en Afrique* . . . (Paris: Pillet ainé, 1819). Widener Library, Harvard College Library, Afr. 1947.10.

Figure 13. Pierre Dumont (after). Ambroise Tardieu, "Pierre Joseph Dumont, maintenant à l'hospice royale des incurables à Paris," in Pierre Joseph Dumont, *Histoire de l'esclavage en Afrique* . . . (Paris: Pillet ainé, 1819). Widener Library, Harvard College Library, Afr. 1947.10.

A body "covered with lacerations" did more than give credence to Dumont's story (eventually winning him a place in the Royal Hospital of Incurables). It also helped establish Kabyle barbarism. According to Quesne's and Dumont's collaborative logic, by physically abusing European captives, the inhabitants of inner Algeria revealed an utter lack of humanity. Their violation of old age and incest taboos, filial ties, and the bond between mother and child did the same: "The fathers sell their sons, the mothers their daughters, and the husbands their wives; the sons frequently redeem their mothers, and are even allowed to marry them." Once a wife grew too old to please the sheikh, he tossed her out of his harem to be eaten alive. Women described as being as heartless as those in the Sahara allegedly cast off even their own nursing infants: "The women give suck to their children three times a day; in the night if the latter cry, the she-goats are made to suckle them."[64]

Like previous narratives, this one reflected on the disturbing transformations wrought by North African captivity. Where Dumont boasted of multilingualism, Quesne identified a "Frenchman . . . who had almost forgot the language of his native country." As for apostasy, Dumont maintained that the Kabyles generally showed more interest in tormenting slaves than in converting them. Still, he refused several invitations to embrace Islam. Others displayed less resolve, yet he claimed—like redeemed captives and redemptive fathers before him—that French renegades kept national traits. Thus Manet from Dauphiné, who renounced Catholicism and took the name Aly, had "not lost the curiosity natural to his countrymen," which tempted him to spy on the sheikh's harem, leading to punishment, exile, and, through a complicated series of events, Dumont's eventual liberation.[65]

Rather than dwell on the religious hazards he evaded, Dumont focused primarily on the physical mutations he underwent. A beard down to his waist gave him some protection against heat, wind, and rain, but years of toil under a blazing sun accompanied by constant blows, he affirmed, still turned his skin "a deep chocolate color" and covered his back with a maze of scars. Manual labor left his hands so callused he could not close them even halfway. Indeed, for Dumont the ultimate risk posed by North African slavery was not spiritual death but suicide. Twice an Italian neighbor attempted to hang himself with a length of hemp. Filled with rage and despair after a series of unmerited beatings, even Dumont "resolved on death"—and assaulted the prison wardens. Although he had expected to be killed for this insubordination, the sheikh only ordered one of his hands crushed in a special machine, leaving it permanently crippled.[66]

In Dumont's telling, the land of the Kabyles offered far more in agricultural bounty than civilization; its produce alone inspired as much extravagant description as its inhabitants' cruelty. "The fruits of the garden and orchard are inconceivably fine; the peaches are tender and savory," he declared. "Vine-stalks are so large that a man cannot grasp them in his arms, and their bunches of grapes are not less than a foot and a half in length." In such an environment domestic animals grew fat and succulent. And when Dumont managed to abscond with a gigantic cabbage and a single elephantine lamb, he and five other captives feasted for eight days. In addition to crops and livestock, the interior of Algiers afforded commodities in abundance. "The chief articles of trade," he enumerated, "are oil, honey, wax, wool, skins, elephants' teeth, different sorts of grain [and] carpets"—exchanged via Jews for European manufactured goods since, he noted, Arabs refused to deal directly with Christians.[67]

Taking up what would become a common nineteenth-century refrain, Dumont's narrative maintained that trade alone would not suffice to prevent "these nests of barbarians" from "desolat[ing] one of the finest countries in the world." The only antidote, it insisted, was religious conversion. "It would be a vain attempt to attack hordes so numerous, or even to civilize them, so long as they continue attached to the Alcoran," began the English translation of Quesne's introductory remarks. "Could they be proselytized to the principles of Christianity, civilization would engender humanity, and regenerate their character." The original French was less discreet. "Make Christians of them if you can," it advised, "and you will see them human like the French."[68] If Christian doctrine separated man from beast, Frenchness—vested even in a bearded, disfigured, worn-out captive—provided the ultimate model of humanity.

CRUSADE AGAINST WHITE SLAVERY

The idea of establishing a Christian alliance to fight the Barbary powers dates to the seventeenth century, but political and religious divisions stood in the way. Though schemes to besiege, invade, or even colonize North African territories had flowed in from French admirals, consuls, and slaves, after the one unsuccessful attempt to descend on the Algerian coast in 1664, successive French governments opted to take on Algiers, Tunis, Tripoli, and Morocco individually and at a distance, launching bombs from the water before sending in envoys to sign new peace accords.[69] The 1767 debacle at Larache seemed only to have strengthened this resolve. By the early nineteenth century, however, voices from around the Mediterranean and both sides of the Atlantic were clamoring for the formation of a "universal league"—a modern crusade led by either France or England—that would extirpate Barbary piracy and slavery forever. The idea was not merely to limit the religious, commercial, political, and physical damage North Africans inflicted on Europeans but to end corsairing once and for all, and to stop the practice of capturing and keeping Christians—now commonly dubbed, by analogy to its American counterpart, "white slavery."

The person who lobbied hardest for such joint measures was a retired English vice-admiral and Napoleonic foe, Sir William Sidney Smith. Advocating the cessation of North African privateering and Christian slavery at the twilight of his career, he established two organizations: the Society of Knights Liberators of the White Slaves in Africa, and the Antipiratical Society. In August 1814 he brought his case to the Congress of Vienna. "While we discuss the means of bringing about the abolition of the Negro Trade on the western coast of Africa . . . it is surprising that we pay no attention to the northern coast of this same country," read a memorandum distributed to delegates, coauthored with royalist émigré and future marine minister Jean Guillaume Hyde de Neuville. Linking England's national project to Smith's personal mission, it gave familiar arguments about the depredations wrought by "Turkish pirates" a new twist: "This shameful banditry not only revolts humanity, it hinders commerce in the most harmful way, since today a sailor cannot navigate on a merchant vessel in the Mediterranean nor on the Atlantic, without fear of being carried off by pirates and taken as slave to Africa. . . . It is useless to demonstrate that such a state of affairs is not only monstrous but absurd, and outrages religion no less than humanity and honor. The progress of Enlightenment and civilization must necessarily make it disappear."[70]

For Smith the obligation to wipe out Barbary corsairing and captivity, supposedly committed by tyrannical Ottomans against Muslim vassals and Christians alike, did not stem from parochial concerns for one country's shipping or social stability, especially given that the strongest European states had already exempted themselves from attack. Making the seas safe for travel and trade was a matter of universal interest; converting "pirate states" into "governments useful to commerce and in harmony with all civilized nations," he wrote, served the common good. With the goal of creating a secular version of the Knights of Malta— busy agitating to reclaim their pious qua military vocation—he solicited all interested parties to help patrol Europe's coasts and keep North African brigands under constant surveillance.[71]

For the next two years the vice-admiral lost no opportunity to publicize and fund-raise for his cause, holding subscription picnics and banquets;[72] mailing out multilingual broadsides; inserting notices in the domestic and international press;[73] and inviting sundry heads of state, royalty, and people of means to support him.[74] These various appeals to both chivalric nostalgia and collective benevolence elided distinctions of geography, religion, and race, while drawing a connection between Mediterranean and Atlantic slaveries, fighting infidels and freeing captives. One account detailed brutal attacks committed against residents and fishermen on the Adriatic coast; another exposed the plight of German and Italian slaves and, in a peculiar analogy, urged readers to expend as much emotion contemplating servitude as art.[75]

Inspired by Smith's vision, princes and pundits from Florence, Rome, and the Vatican proposed the creation of an Italian alliance. The governor of Genoa lent his warm support to plans for an international version. "Compassion for the blacks is worthy of praise; but there are other men," he wrote, "who claim it against Africans more barbarous than the Europeans who carry [the slave trade] out in the former." The king of Sardinia also gave his backing, "whether for the abolition of the slave trade, or for the suppression of the piracies of the Barbaric States."[76] Indeed, one of his own subjects, the jurist Domenico Alberto Azuni, became a staunch admirer, styling himself another "protector of humanity suffering in African irons and of commerce devastated by pirate excursions." He too advocated a "general union of maritime powers," led by England, to carry out a war of disarmament and regeneration. By expelling the Turks, whose "unbridled passion for banditry" had corrupted the souls of North Africans, such a confederation would realize its natural calling to civilize, turning "monsters of the sea" into "our fellow creatures."[77]

In Britain, opinion split. One side accepted Smith's parallel between white and black slavery and his premise that the agonies of Europeans in North Africa represented a humanitarian crisis requiring immediate action. The other side maintained that the mild captivity of several hundred Italians hardly warranted English expense and bloodshed. The Whiggish *Edinburgh Review*, for example, cited a letter to Parliament by a naval officer who had described the bagnes of Algiers as "most resembl[ing] a house where the negroes of the West-India Islands keep their pigs." Noting that mortality rates in Algerian jails surpassed those on the Middle Passage, and that "the slave trade of the Africans in the Mediterranean is considerably worse that that of the Europeans in the Atlantic," the article urged the British government to fight the one as resolutely as it had the other.[78] A sharply worded rebuke in the Tory-leaning *Quarterly Review*, by contrast, maintained that for reasons both moral and self-preserving "it would be an act of madness" to get involved in the quixotic enterprise. "Certainly, if the quantum of individual misery was to determine the propriety of the measure, the abolition of white slavery would naturally obtain preference over that of the blacks," the editorial intoned, yet "Sir Sidney Smith, in his endeavours to excite a general feeling of hatred in the powers of Europe against the Barbary States, [has not] succeeded in bringing forward any thing very atrocious." Furthermore, even if "the treatment of Christian prisoners, or slaves, were more harsh than it is, what has England to do with it, that she must stand foremost as the avenging power, and sacrifice her seamen to evince her humanity towards Sardinians, Neapolitans, and Sicilians." If anyone should "stand forward as the champion of Christendom," it asserted snidely, surely "his *Most Christian* Majesty [of France] is the proper 'knight-president'" (emphasis in original).[79]

France's response was lukewarm. Before the Hundred Days, Louis XVIII had reportedly joined Smith's society and entertained one proposal to support a united front against North Africa, "for in making war on the pirates, we shall eventually prevent the escape of Bonaparte."[80] In another proposal future foreign affairs minister and premier Jules de Polignac, calling the idea Napoleon-worthy in scope, approved it as "directed by a great sentiment of Good whereas the plans of the usurper were always birthed by the genius of Evil." In his September 1814 memoir, Polignac listed several potential moral, political, and utilitarian benefits: "the deliverance of Christians languishing in the most shameful slavery," the protection of Europe's trade, the redirection of its warlike impulses, and, more pragmatically, French access to commercial resources and a secure passage to Egypt.[81] The next year, another Smith supporter, revolutionary cleric and abolitionist Henri Grégoire, lamented that since the demise of the redemptive orders, "Europe . . . has not yet employed vigorous measures for the repression of this brigandage that has become more calamitous." "Do we dare acknowledge that Algerian, Tunisian, and other pirates have committed assaults comparable to those of Europeans against Africa?" demanded his 1815 treatise, *De la traite de l'esclavage des noirs et des blancs.*[82]

After Napoleon's flight from Elba and the restoration of the Bourbon monarchy, the government endorsed in principle the objective of eradicating slavery in North Africa and purging the Mediterranean of pirates. Already mistrustful of English motives in the ongoing campaign to end black slave trafficking, however, it remained wary of joining another international effort with England at its helm, suspecting a play for greater dominance at sea. Jacques-Philippe Devoise, consul to Tunis, who had been rallying for land strikes against that regency, questioned the true purpose of English plans to head up "a crusade destined to abolish white slavery." Writing to foreign affairs minister Charles Maurice de Talleyrand-Périgord in March 1816, he noted the use of "philanthropic maxims" to "disguise . . . the real aim" of political maneuverings: "commercial and navigational interest," or in this case, access to fertile North African soil to provision their relatively barren new possessions, the islands of Corfu and Malta.[83]

The politician and writer René de Chateaubriand, also a member of the Anti-piratical Society, came out in favor of Smith's general ideas but called on France to go it alone. "The English Parliament, by abolishing the slave trade in blacks, seems to have indicated for our emulation the object of an even more splendid triumph: putting an end to the slavery of whites," he told the Chamber of Peers the following month, proclaiming, "It was in France that the first crusade was preached; it is in France that the standard of the last should be raised."[84]

ASSAULT ON ALGIERS

Nonetheless, the nations represented at the Congress of Vienna delegated the British navy to take action[85]—in large part because of the U.S. success in compelling Algiers, Tunis, and Tripoli to release all their American captives in 1815,[86] and because of reports of another terrible raid on Saint Antioche, an island off the coast of Sardinia.[87] In April 1816, three months before the sinking of the *Medusa*, Admiral Edward Pellew, Lord Exmouth, commander of the Mediterranean fleet, set sail with orders to negotiate new treaties on behalf of Sardinia and the Kingdom of the Two Sicilies and to push for the abolition of white slavery. The deys of Tunis and Tripoli turned over hundreds of Sicilians, Genoese, Neapolitans, and Sardinians and forswore future slave taking—even while reserving the right to keep prisoners of war, a distinction that eluded France's consul.[88] The dey of Algiers also released several hundred Italians at inflated prices, but he refused to give up his prerogative to capture more.[89] This intransigence, combined with news of the massacre of two hundred Corsican, Sicilian, and Sardinian coral fishermen under French and English protection attending mass in the Algerian port of Annaba, provoked a violent response.[90]

At the end of August, while the Great Powers met in London to debate the wisdom of international patrols against the trade in sub-Saharan Africans, a heavily armed combined English and Dutch squadron assaulted.[91] By then a war settlement with the Kabyles had assured Dumont's transfer to Algiers. From a hilltop outside the city, he recalled, fifteen hundred evacuated slaves watched artillery explode and buildings burn, and waited petrified while Algerian officers began exacting revenge. Thirty-two heads had fallen before news of European victory arrived.[92] The official Algerian capitulation stated, "The practice of condemning Christian prisoners of war to slavery is hereby formally and forever renounced." Or as the dey later put it, "The prisoners in Algiers were liberated without ransom, and because we are their prisoners, their conditions were accepted, may they go to hell."[93] Dumont related that "with hearts enlivened by hope," the captives ran toward the waterfront, where "we were taken in by a number of English boats, and there it was that our last chains fell off." He claimed to be among thirty Frenchmen freed, although more reliable sources put the number at only two—in

addition to eleven hundred Sicilians and Neapolitans, sixty-two Sardinians and Genoese, six Piedmontese, one hundred seventy-four Romans,
six Tuscans, two hundred twenty-six Spaniards, one Portuguese, seven
Greeks, twenty-eight Dutch, eighteen English, and two Austrians.[94]

In Britain, patriotic poems, songs, and narratives extolled Exmouth's
feat as confirmation of the nation's racially inclusive humanitarian bent
and its diplomatic and naval preeminence.[95] In the words of the royal interpreter for "Oriental Languages," Abraham V. Salamé, who accompanied
the expedition, "The same impulse, which induced the arbitress of the civilized world to stretch forth her protecting arm in behalf of the suffering
African, led her to teach the savage ruler of Algiers, that the blood of her
European brethren was too precious to be drawn by the whip of slavery:
and their freedom too costly to be submitted to the nod of a barbarian."[96]
Championing the eventual Christianization, colonization, and civilization
of a region governed by "monsters" and "piratical hordes" as an aim even
worthier than "abolish[ing] the iniquitous traffic of our black fellow creatures," Florentine poet and former Barbary slave Filippo Pananti praised
the attack on Algiers too. But the Italian and English versions of his book,
though not the French one, also extended due credit to the philanthropic
work and "heroic liberality" of the man most responsible for drawing
attention to the issue and defining the terms of the debate: Smith, passed
over for a new naval commission and pushed to the sidelines as his colleague accepted sole glory for "banish[ing] . . . the slavery of the whites."[97]

BARBARY SLAVERY RESURGENT

In fact, the trumpeted finale to Barbary corsairing and captivity did not
last. Algiers quickly rebuilt its fortifications and its fleet, and soon North
African privateers were back at sea—to the dismay of Europe's maritime
countries, which once again quaked before the prospect of abduction
and, because of a renewed outbreak of plague, contagion.[98] In June 1817,
for example, the London *Times* reprinted a memorandum to the German
Diet from the cities of Lubeck, Frankfurt, Bremen, and Hamburg, which
registered concern about "German fellow-citizens, whom the African
pirates plunge into the gloomy dungeons of slavery." But what it judged
even more worrisome were "the incalculably mischievous consequences
which may ensue, if these African pirates are permitted without interrup-
tion to sail from their infected coasts, and to spread among distant countries the diseases which they carry along with them."[99] Although rumors
that all the European consuls in Algiers had been slaughtered—spread
by Smith—proved unfounded,[100] by the time the Congress of Aix-la-

Chapelle convened in the fall of 1818, deputies who had already agreed on further measures to suppress the Atlantic "scourge which has for so long desolated Africa, degraded Europe, and afflicted humanity" once again debated the merits of forming either an offensive or defensive coalition in the Mediterranean.[101]

In a speech delivered to a local literary society, a Marseille merchant pleaded for leaders who "have again and again defended . . . the cause of Negroes" not to "abandon the cause of Whites." He found it utterly preposterous that around the world "the children of Europe reign and dominate, and on the septentrional coasts of Africa, two or three degrees from this Europe . . . they are slaves!" Once the Barbary pirates were finally destroyed, he envisioned the region being "subjected to one or several European governments"; sheltering the continent's excess population; producing sugar, coffee, and spices; and being "returned to civilization, agriculture, and commerce."[102] Despite such allures, France initially protested on the grounds of excessive cost and self-interest. As prime minister Armand-Emmanuel du Plessis, duc de Richelieu, put it, France, "having nothing to fear from the *Barbaresques*, had really no interest in pressuring other powers to unite against them."[103] Still, along with representatives from England, Austria, Prussia, and Russia, he assented to an Anglo-French sortie bearing a warning to the Barbary States "that the guaranteed effect of their perseverance in a system hostile to peaceful commerce would be a general league of European powers, the result of which might well be annihilation." The following year, French and English warships called at each of the three regencies, bringing yet another ultimatum to stamp out piracy and slavery, a document that Tripoli alone did not scorn.[104]

Dumont's recommendations for how to deal with North Africa responded directly to these contemporary proposals and political realities. "For the last two years, a theme has been in agitation, that the nations of Europe must coalesce," he announced. He then rejected out of hand the idea of transferring all Barbary pirates to Europe or the American colonies—"so as to civilize and assimilate them to our manners"—as seductive but unrealistic. He also cautioned against invasion. "My opinion is that at present a million soldiers would not suffice to subjugate these roving robbers," for rugged terrain, sparse roads, and abundant wildlife would make moving troops, weapons, and supplies treacherous. But there were more fundamental challenges to infiltrating the Algerian interior: custom and religion. How does a standing army fight nomads? he asked. How does it quell a people whose creed encourages martyrdom? "A military expedition against them would only provide another romantic instance of the results of a European crusade," he warned.

From Dumont's perspective, Europeans had only three options: accept North Africans as they are; wait for the sort of revolution that remade France to take its natural course; or, more vaguely, pursue the civilizing mission.[105] For Dumont, sponsoring a military expedition to Algiers may have seemed too daunting, but this last French slave left his readers in no doubt about France's indispensable role, not only in saving slaves from North Africa but in saving North Africa from itself.

BARBARY SLAVERY RACIALIZED

Neither Dumont nor the *Medusa* chroniclers were the last heirs to the shipwreck variety of the Barbary slave narrative. In 1821, a Parisian press released the final French account of crash and captivity in southern Morocco. Charles Cochelet, rerouted from Nantes to Brazil and stranded on the same band of coast that had foiled so many of his compatriots, clearly took his cues from translations of analogous American and British tales then circulating in France with more overtly racial lenses. The 1817 French version of an as-told-to memoir of desert slavery by African American New Yorker "Robert Adams" (commissioned by a committee of former black slave traffickers in London), for example, was dedicated to Smith, known for the "noble zeal with which you are animated for the cause of Christians who groan under the hardest slavery."[106] An 1818 account by Connecticut captain James Riley—whose publisher had promoted both the "knight liberator" (Smith) and the *Medusa* survivors—combined judgments about simian-like masters in the Sahara with pleas for ending the bondage of "a half million individuals of the human species" in the United States.[107] Rather than motley Muslims, Cochelet's captors were described as "negroes" whose black color contrasted sharply with the white sand and reminded him of nothing so much as "ourang-outangs." That they should possess him rather than the other way around filled him with revulsion and outrage. "Could I ever have imagined the empire these creatures would exercise over us," he demanded, "and that beings, who certainly form the last link in the chain that joins man to beasts, should become our masters and treat us as their property?"[108]

Over the first decades of the nineteenth century, such blunt associations between hereditary servitude justified by skin color and temporary bondage resulting from poor steering had, in part thanks to the publicity surrounding the sinking of the *Medusa*, become more pronounced and more common. So had the conviction that slavery of any sort represented an unacceptable fate for any white European, let alone for any Frenchman—in part thanks to the campaign of Smith (most likely responsible for the publication of Dumont's account).[109] Yet the previous eras' tools of limited warfare, bilateral diplomacy, and ritual cleansing no longer sufficed to guard against captivity or the various types of corruption believed to accompany it. Nor were they up to the task of satisfying new expectations for the comprehensive abolition of slavery or longer-standing hopes for the effective regeneration of territory. Judgments about North African barbarism—based on their mistreatment of slaves and debasement of one another, as well as their stubborn adherence to an outmoded system of stealing away people and pilfering merchandise—provided one of several rationales for liberatory conquest. Its eventual implementation in Algiers against considerable resistance got its impetus from both domestic politics and foreign developments, notably the Greek War of Independence.

CHAPTER EIGHT

The Conquest of Algiers

Hippolyte Lecomte designed lavish costumes for the theater. He also painted historical subjects and military themes. In 1827 he completed a canvas that combined his talents in an imagined abduction scene (Figure 14). *The Kidnap* depicts a raven-haired shepherdess in pouf sleeves and colorful skirts, arms flailing, as a man in a red turban carries her toward a waiting boat. On the beach, a swarthy accomplice stifles another girl's screams, as dogs howl and sheep flee. Although a cluster of white houses and a few angular sails rising in the distance provide the only geographical cues, French viewers would have immediately recognized the picture's locale and its context. Passionately committed to Greece's struggle for autonomy from the Ottoman Empire, they would have placed the action somewhere in the Aegean, identified the villains as Turks and Egyptians, and pegged the female victim as Greek.

In 1820s France, the resonance of Mediterranean corsairing and captivity had shifted once again. The expansion of Atlantic slave trafficking, the growth of abolitionism, the spread of colonial revolution, and, finally, the independence of Haiti had already raised the profile of black slavery. Numerically diminished and practically forgotten until imperial competition and philanthropic activism pushed it onto the international agenda, the detention of Christians had become the slavery of *blancs*. Then during a conflict that lasted from 1821 to 1829, women (and children) from rebellious provinces flooded Ottoman slave markets, and the archetypal victim of Muslim warfare changed sex. In the course of this decade, French political discourse and popular imagery conflated the causes of Greek insurgents, sub-Saharan Africans, and European mariners.

By the time "the abolition of white slavery" became a rallying cry for the invasion of Algiers in 1830, long-standing fears about boys lured into sodomy had been largely supplanted by fears about mothers, wives, and daughters defiled, and the specter of apostasy had melded with the spec-

Figure 14. A Greek woman abducted. *The Kidnap* (1827). Oil on canvas by Hippolyte Lecomte. Sotheby's Picture Library.

ter of miscegenation. The decision by the last Bourbon king, Charles X, to send troops across the Mediterranean probably derived from proximate factors—fiscal, diplomatic, and political—but its justification came from an ideology of liberatory conquest elaborated since the Revolution in multiple geographic contexts, in registers both real and imagined.[1] For France, the road to empire in North Africa passed by the "sister republics" of western Europe, traveled from the Caribbean to the Sahara, and then wound its way through Greece.

ABOLITIONIST ODYSSEYS

When the War of Greek Independence broke out, Louis XVIII sat on the throne, the Charter protected a bicameral legislature, and French citizens were roughly divided between royalists and liberals. The opposition, imbued with republican fervor and Romantic ideals, immediately supported efforts to free an oppressed nation from Ottoman thralldom and return the fount of civilization to classical splendor. Bourbon loyalists, especially the reactionary faction or "ultras" that dominated government ministries and the hereditary Chamber of Peers, by contrast, remained wary of a struggle that bore a frightening resemblance to the French Revolution. In their estimation, Sultan Mahmud II might be a tyrant but he was also a legitimate ruler and an ally of France. The weight of public opinion, fueled by liberals in the elected Chamber of Deputies and their media organs, eventually brought the government around. Drawing some of its leadership and inspiration from earlier campaigns to halt black and white slave trafficking,[2] and its followers from the worlds of literature, art, politics, and high society, philhellenism emphasized the corrupting effects of both political and physical slavery within the Ottoman Empire.[3] In so doing, it provided a new gendered and racialized prism for viewing the enslavement of European Christians, particularly in Algiers.

Chios was a turning point. The ruthless suppression of Greek rebellion on an island known for producing Homer, beautiful girls, and chewing gum horrified French readers during the spring and summer of 1822. Newspaper accounts of entire families massacred in cold blood confirmed notions of Turkish savagery; descriptions of women carried into slavery transposed enduring memories of North African *razzias* (raids) from the western Mediterranean to the east. According to a widely reprinted letter by one survivor, "Every day women from the best families are on sale in the public markets. . . . Our good friend has been killed in his own house in front of the eyes of his wife. . . . This poor woman was then sent as a slave to Algiers."[4] An official tally recorded the enslavement of forty-one thousand inhabitants, including five thousand sold on street corners in Constantinople, and diplomatic reports from Smyrna described the daily disembarking of hundreds of Chian women "reserved for the Harems or domestic servitude." Sixty or seventy, among them the widow and daughter of a former Danish vice-consul, ended up in Tunis.[5] Interpreting a Barbary enslavement image from a pro-Greek perspective the same year, the playwright and art critic Victor-Joseph Jouy and his colleague Antoine Jay recalled the "vultures infesting the seas" who "snatch our daughters and wives" and vituperated conservative writers who "declaim against those noble Greeks who battle for cross and liberty, [while] brigand Turks hang in their mosques sabers stained with Christian blood." The painter of the image, Horace Vernet (brother-in-law to Hippolyte Lecomte), would later record French military triumphs in Algeria. His *Combat of Corsairs at Sunrise* (1819) centers on the sexual vulnerability of a female captive.[6]

Loath to disturb Franco-Ottoman relations, Louis XVIII initially tiptoed around this latest manifestation of "white slavery." In response to Chios, a royal ordinance issued in January 1823 banned French merchant vessels from boarding Greek slaves for Ottoman clients, a practice which, as one liberal daily put it, "sullied the national flag." But a consular directive circulated in March insisted on the law's narrow application to captured rebels, and not to "slaves that the Turks have the custom of buying, as much in Cairo as in Tripoli in Barbary, in Circassia, and in Georgia, for their personal and household service."[7] While serving the cause of diplomacy, these distinctions meant little to the French journalists, artists, and urban elites flocking to philhellenism. In promoting the emancipation of Greece, they opposed servitude in all its varied forms: Old and New World, chattel and domestic, literal and metaphoric. It was their confusion and purposeful merging of these categories that connected the suppression of the *traite des noirs* (black slave trade), the salvation of female chastity, the freedom of Greece, and, within seven years, the invasion of Algiers.

After Chios, French Protestants who had just reinvigorated the abolitionist movement by founding the Société de la morale chrétienne (Society for Christian Morality)—an outgrowth of the older Société des amis des noirs—now spun off a Comité grec (Greek Committee) to aid the Greek revolutionaries.[8] Eugène Delacroix insinuated in paint the link his compatriots suggested through organization. When the Salon of 1824 opened in August, two months after Charles X's coronation, its catalog listed a work with the following description: "Scenes from the Massacres of Chios; Greek families awaiting death or slavery, etc. (See the diverse accounts and newspapers of the period)." To the consternation of critics, who preferred to see clearly opposed virtue and vice, the canvas portrayed its subjects as double slaves: a people already degraded by political oppression now headed for physical servitude. With clashing colors and crude brushstrokes, creating a mini-composition of rape and allusions to plague, Delacroix simultaneously evoked religious conversion and blood mixing. By suggesting that "turning Turk" might also engender a racial transformation, he brought the Orient and the Caribbean into the same frame.[9]

René de Chateaubriand also melded references to Mediterranean and Atlantic slaveries to rhetorical ends in 1825, soon after Charles X recognized the nation of Haiti. An early defender of French leadership in the battle against North African captivity, Chateaubriand initially toed the conservative line as foreign affairs minister during the Chios massacre. Within three years, however, he had left behind any reservations about supporting a national insurgency to become French philhellenism's staunchest promoter and president of the new Société philanthropique pour l'assistance aux Grecs (Philanthropic Society to Aid the Cause of the Greeks). Drafted in July 1825 as a prospectus for the group, "Note sur la Grèce" invoked white slavery as poetic metaphor. Drawing on a common trope, it likened the war against Greece to the abduction of an odalisque. "Bands of Negro slaves, transported from the depths of Africa," the essay begins, alluding to sub-Saharan troops in the Ottoman army, "rush up to finish in Athens the work of black eunuchs in the harem. The first come in force to knock over ruins that the second, in their impotence, allowed to stand." Then, quickly shifting geography, it asks, "Will Christendom calmly allow Turks to slit the throats of Christians?"[10] In Chateaubriand's mental landscape, violating the cradle of Western civilization amounted to an act of racial and sexual, as well as religious, transgression.

Officially neutral, France was complicit in the massacre of innocents, "the enslavement of women, the prostitution of children . . . the compulsion of circumcision, and the taking of the turban," Chateaubriand raged before the Chamber of Peers in December.[11] The following March, he denounced a semantic loophole by which a prohibition against the "trade in blacks" actually gave cover to what he termed the "trade in whites." Although not wishing to "diminish the horror that inspires the black slave trade," he argued that making slaves of "these women, these children, these elderly [who] are of the same white race as we" constituted a "monstrous anomaly" of a different proportion: "When a Negro is torn from the forest and transported to a civilized country, he finds himself in irons, it is true, but religion . . . at least consoles the poor Negro and assures him of deliverance in another life. . . . But the inhabitant of the Peloponnese and the Archipelago, torn from the flames and ruins of his homeland; the wife taken from her murdered husband; the child ripped from the mother in whose arms he was baptized, this whole race is civilized and Christian. And to whom is it sold? To barbarity and Islam!" In order to stop, or at least stem, the traffic in Greeks, he put forward an amendment modifying the law's language to protect peoples across the color spectrum by banning the *traite des esclaves*.[12]

Although Chateaubriand's proposal did not lead to concrete action, news of bloody surrender in Missolonghi to Ottoman forces and fresh tales of women and children carried off in chains, which reached France in mid-May 1826, spurred a rush of charitable giving, artistic production, and political debate. During budget discussions at the Chamber of Deputies the next week, Alexis de Noailles, a liberal deputy from central France, called the sale of sixty thousand Christians at Mediterranean slave markets "the shame of our age" and proposed a 30,000-franc allocation for buying them back. His motion failed by a two-thirds margin, despite support from colleagues on both sides of the aisle. One liberal delegate, remembering the redemptive institutions of previous eras, noted that "this would not be the first time that France has brought aid to the wives and children of unhappy warriors fallen into irons." William Sidney Smith collaborator, royalist parliamentarian, and future marine minister Jean Guillaume Hyde de Neuville urged "those with French [and] . . . Christian heart[s]" to think about 150 "modest virgins, all belonging to the principal families of Greece . . . delivered for a *piastre* to the public market and the ferocious brutality of Muhammad's most vile sectarians."[13]

On this occasion a majority voted to protect the Franco-Ottoman alliance rather than the sexual virtue, religious loyalty, and generative purity of Greece. But mounting public outrage was swiftly turning even the most faithful ultras into philhellenes. Charles X would opportunistically switch sides the following year, committing France to a pro-Greek military coalition and launching an independent expedition to the southern peninsula. But in 1826, campaigning for Greek self-rule and slave redemption was still the domain of opposition politicians and committed individuals: idealistic young men who shipped off to the front and fashionable women who took the lead in fund-raising at home. Besides soliciting door-to-door, the redemptive fathers' female successors helped arrange concerts and exhibitions, and in Paris organized biweekly bazaars of Greco-themed artwork and ephemera on the rue Saint Honoré (near the headquarters and home of the Society of Knights Liberators of the White Slaves in Africa and its eccentric steward).[14] "What happiness to think that the price of her work might contribute to the ransom of a slave of her sex," one man reflected regarding his wife's donation of two original engravings in early June.[15] At a charity art show that month—featuring another Delacroix painting—three-quarters of the entrance fee paid for Greek ransoms.[16]

Like his picture of Chios, Delacroix's *Greece on the Ruins of Missolonghi* brought to life newspaper reports of "women and children sold for low prices like livestock" and conjured both physical and figurative slavery.[17] Here, rather than hinting at blood mixture already achieved, the contrast between the pale, defenseless body of Greece in the foreground and the turbaned black warrior behind her intimated defilement about to occur.[18] The sexual appetites of dark-complexioned soldiers and the vulnerability of Greek maidens also preoccupied French poets that summer. On the pages of provincial and Parisian journals, heads fell to "Nubian swords" and virgins succumbed to "somber envoys."[19] And aftershocks from the latest Greek disaster rippled into the following year. Describing a local festival held for the Greek cause, the liberal Bordeaux daily *L'Indicateur* expressed regret that "those that we wanted to save have just succumbed to the murderous blade of barbarians and those who remain are destined, perhaps forever, to slavery worse than death." A painting at the 1827 Salon depicted "Frenchmen sent by the *Comité grec* to ransom women and children who escaped death during the siege on Missolonghi."[20] Though still committed to "the repression of the Black Slave Trade," the Marseille chapter of the Société de la morale chrétienne continued working to release three hundred Greek orphans held in an Egyptian arsenal. It counted the salvation of youth from "white slavery" as a "beautiful triumph . . . [for] the sacred cause of humanity."[21] In 1830, the liberation of white slaves would provide a premise for another triumph: this one for the cause of French imperialism.

INVASION DEBATED

What ended in France's takeover of the westernmost Ottoman regency began with a dispute over a debt contracted during the Revolution. Strapped for cash and starved for grain in the 1790s, the National Convention and the Directory had borrowed heavily from two prominent Jewish merchant families long involved in the redemption of captives.[22] A generation afterward, the outstanding loan to the Busnach and Bacri heirs remained a source of Franco-Algerian tension and provoked a diplomatic incident when, during an argument over repayment at the end of April 1827, dey Hussayn purportedly hit consul Pierre Deval with a utensil otherwise reserved for airborne insects. In response to the notorious *coup d'éventail* (strike of the fly whisk), Charles X sent a squadron to Algiers with orders to demand a formal apology and, if rebuffed, enforce a blockade. Three years later, in a futile attempt to improve his domestic standing with a foreign coup, an already unpopular king authorized the conquest that resulted in a colony.

During the intervening period, the merits of besieging or invading Algiers had been debated in the Chamber of Deputies and the press. At first, the decision to cut off access to a North African city remained a matter of relative indifference to politicians and writers who, while viewing struggles in the eastern and western Mediterranean of a piece, remained more focused on Greek independence. Rather than immediately accepting France's role as lone avenger of Algerian insolence, for example, the editor of the philhellene *Revue encyclopédique* noted that once possessed of its own amphibious force, Greece could join other Christian nations in contributing "to the eventual fulfillment of philanthropists' wish to one day see the Mediterranean freed from the incursions of these Barbary pirates"—though he noted that establishment of European (not necessarily French) colonies might be the only way of stopping North African corsairing.[23]

At the October 1827 Battle of Navarino when a combined French, English, and Russian fleet routed the Ottoman navy, however, royalists and liberals heard echoes of the sixteenth-century Battle of Lepanto. The liberal newspaper the *Constitutionnel* noted that while French diplomats agitated to halt "the massacres of our [Greek] brothers in the Orient . . . our fellow citizens, despite the annual tributes to which we have the cowardice to submit, are dragged into slavery in Tunis and Algiers, [and] in Morocco." If France accepted Ottoman supremacy over Greece as just, an article in the *Gazette de France* sarcastically observed, "it must hasten to recognize the legitimacy of Algerian domination, [and] it must be wary of breaking the chains of the unfortunate Christians crammed into *bagnes* on the coast of Barbary."[24] Victor Hugo summoned Louis XIV's favored admiral in France's seventeenth-century stand against North Africa to classify Barbary corsairs and Egyptian soldiers as equivalent religious and racial foes: "There, Egypt of the Turks, this African Asia / These indestructible pirates, unvanquished by Duquesne, / Who stamped on these nests of vultures in vain."[25] The converse effect of such historical and geographical fusion was to continue implicitly recasting the Christian victims of Muslim depredations as female and white.

Notable exceptions in disassociating the two reaches of the Ottoman Empire and insisting that attention be paid to Algiers were a cavalry officer on the Egyptian campaign and a delegate from the commercially implicated port of Marseille. René Julien Chatelain published his 1828 pamphlet on behalf of what he mistakenly believed were thousands of Italians, Spaniards, Germans, Britons, and French still captive in the Barbary States. In it he rehearsed analogies between Atlantic and Mediterranean servitude and invoked heroes of previous battles between Crescent and Cross, calling on "the descendants of Charles V and Saint Louis . . . to abolish the white slave trade." Based on his experience fighting Muslims, he advocated force over ransom and predicted success, writing, "Iron, not gold . . . must shatter their chains."[26] In a speech to his colleagues that spring, Marseillais representative Pierre-Honoré de Roux lambasted the blockade for its deleterious effect on maritime trade and his fellow parliamentarians for turning their backs on suffering compatriots. The liberty of Greeks, he asserted, should not come at the expense of "our fellow citizens, our brothers! . . . It is the slavery of *Francs* that must be abolished before anything else!!!"[27]

Though still caught up in the Greek rebellion, by 1829 the opposition had begun to recognize in the ongoing Algerian standoff a useful weapon against the king. While conservative ministers counseled patience in wearing down the dey's resolve against French demands, liberal deputies derided the costly and ineffective diversion of naval vessels. Not only was Charles X wasting money and manpower, they suggested, but he was also overstepping his authority to make war. During debates in July, adversaries assailed the character and questioned the word of the French consul, challenging the grounds upon which the Restoration government had transformed what amounted to a personal insult into a national crisis. A moderate emissary sent to Algiers two months later could not resolve the stalemate, nor did ultraroyalist Jules de Polignac manage, after taking office as prime minister, either to broker a deal through back channels or to interest the viceroy of Egypt in jointly conquering the whole region.[28] Thus in a bid to stem mounting criticism of the regime (and, as always, counter English naval supremacy), Polignac took advantage of that winter's parliamentary recess to announce military preparations for a solo land invasion. His stated goal was liberation and regeneration: to achieve "the destruction of slavery [and] piracy along the whole coast of Africa . . . [and] return the northern shores of [the Mediterranean] to production, civilization, and commerce."[29]

When the Chamber of Deputies reconvened in early March 1830, a new spate of book publishing was stoking Algiers's reputation as a pirate haven and a maelstrom for white slaves. With no recently released captives on hand to provide fresh material, editors had commissioned new translations of nineteenth-century works and recycled portions of even older narratives, one arguing that "in Barbary as in almost all the Ottoman states, nothing has changed . . . except for the men: there are still the same institutions, the same religion, the prejudices, the same mores, the same despotism."[30] Meanwhile, philhellene-honed arguments about France's religious and humanitarian duty to liberate Ottoman-held territories from such tyranny continued to hold broad appeal. Indeed, the beleaguered French monarch sought to refract some of the glow of Greek national fulfillment in a speech inaugurating the new session. He blamed "the grave events that have occupied Europe" for having stayed his hand in North Africa and suggested that Greece's recent success in throwing off the Turkish yoke presaged France's, promising through conquest to vindicate his people's sullied honor "for the profit of Christianity."[31]

While largely sympathetic to such motives, antigovernment partisans still met news of the Algerian expedition with hostility. Addressing a secret committee meeting two weeks later with a tirade he would publish the following month, liberal deputy and ardent philhellene Alexandre de Laborde allowed the possibility that "the standard of Saint Louis should be carried onto African soil and the great voice of Louis XIV heard." But he denounced the mobilization of forces without parliamentary consent as illegal and the reputed pledge to England of a hasty troop withdrawal as ill advised. If France sacrificed blood and treasure to invade Algiers, he argued, it should at least maintain the occupation long enough to inculcate civility in a savage people.[32] Throughout the spring and early summer, the country's major liberal newspapers also dismissed the project "to deliver France and Europe" from what marine minister Charles Lemercher de Longpré, baron de Haussez, called "the triple scourge that the civilized world is outraged to still have to endure: piracy, the slavery of prisoners, and the tribute that a barbarous state imposes on all Christian powers," calling it a chivalrous daydream masking a shameless attempt to influence electoral politics.[33]

Rejecting the crown's emancipative rationale as disingenuous, the *Journal des débats* upbraided "bad ministers without a majority who inanely expect to avoid their fate with noise and smoke." Their "insane hope," it editorialized, was less to free North Africa from Ottoman despotism, or the Mediterranean from Barbary corsairing, or white slaves from Muslim confinement, than "to make a victory over Algiers into a victory over our liberties."[34] Like-minded periodicals and pamphlets, basing their arguments on historical example and pragmatic considerations, focused less on the consequences of success than the likelihood of defeat. Not only had leaders from Saint Louis onward failed to subdue North Africa, but raising an immense fleet at the eleventh hour to make a Mediterranean crossing so late in the season could easily end in disaster. To predictions of badly equipped warships foundering in treacherous currents and unseasoned infantry succumbing to tropical disease, fanatical Arabs, and blazing heat, Restoration ministers made assurances of excellent French weaponry and janissaries supplied with inferior gunpowder.[35] Charles X also countered resistance to the Algerian invasion with Old Regime–inspired rhetoric and ritual, including royally ordered public prayers throughout the kingdom and serial processions involving divisions from the Armée d'Afrique.[36]

Expedition enthusiasts from elsewhere on the political spectrum based their support on financial calculation and imperial design. Residents of French port cities concluded that maritime commerce stymied by the Greek insurgency and the Algerian blockade could only benefit from invasion. "Better that Algiers is razed under a Polignac," opined the *Journal du Havre*, "than remain intact to pillage us further." Writing in the *Revue encyclopédique*, noted abolitionist, colonial theorist, and early advocate of European imperialism in North Africa Jean-Charles-Léonard Simonde de Sismondi spoke of the alleged presence of two thousand Christian slaves, forced to work if unwilling "to share the shameful favors of their masters," as "a scandal to the social order." He believed that France, liberator of the United States, progenitor of Haiti, and savior of Greece, had a special calling to "return civilization to the homeland of Saint Augustine." However, as important in his mind was turning the Ottoman regency into a market for French goods and depository for surplus population.[37] A retired consular guard shared this view in a brochure emphasizing the glory and income within French grasp. Boasting rich terrain perfect for cultivation and a labor force primed for enlightenment, Algiers could produce the colonial cash crops Europeans craved with less danger and more convenience than "those unwholesome islands of America," asserted M. Renaudot. Rather than attempt to exploit rebellious slaves in the Atlantic, France stood poised to free an oppressed people from servitude in the Mediterranean. "It is to you, oh my dear homeland," he wrote, "that I assign this great task."[38]

ALGIERS UNCHAINED

The fleet that assembled in Toulon during the month of May 1830 comprised 675 warships, thirty-seven thousand soldiers, forty interpreters, and a bevy of writers and artists prepared to chronicle military maneuvers and, on the model of Napoleon's expedition to Egypt, lay out "piratical" Algiers for "rational" French scrutiny.[39] Furnished with a hastily compiled *Aperçu historique, statistique et topographique sur l'état d'Alger* and Napoleonic-era reconnaissance, the expeditionary force sailed for Sidi Ferruch, a lightly fortified headland twenty-seven miles west of Algiers. Two bricks, the *Silène* and the *Aventure*, which foundered en route and crashed in Kabyle territory, lost about two hundred men to death or captivity: within a week, the dey took delivery of eighty-five heads and locked seventy-five survivors in an out-of-use bagne.[40] For the rest of the convoy, however, the Mediterranean crossing went smoothly. At the embarkation, General Louis de Bourmont had rallied his troops. "Soldiers! The civilized nations of two worlds have their eyes on you," he proclaimed. "The cause of France is the cause of humanity. . . . Too long oppressed by a greedy and cruel militia, the Arab will see us as liberators."[41]

Instead, Arabs, Berbers, and Ottomans attempted to repel what they clearly perceived as enemy invaders at the Battle of Staouéli. For the French army, victory over the Algerians and the looting of their encampment offered a less abstract if equally fantastical incentive for fighting. Bourmont's personal secretary, the playwright Jean-Toussaint Merle, noted that the sight of rich fabrics, carved swords, and bejeweled uniforms made him feel like "an actor in one of the marvelous tales of *A Thousand and One Nights*." Vague oriental visions reignited, he recalled that "from that moment, the conquest of Algiers offered itself to every imagination in the most brilliant colors. We dreamed only of treasures, harems, and palaces."[42] The offensive on Algiers, which began on 29 June, took only six days. From batteries named after French kings and naval heroes (notably Saint Louis and Duquesne), French bombs flew toward the sixteenth-century Emperor's Fort. With its walls lying in rubble, the dey surrendered.

On 5 July 1830, French soldiers penetrated the dey's compound. They pillaged decorative objects and impounded large quantities of gold and silver. Contrary to expectations, however, they did not find "millions of captives who groan in the bottom of deep and dank dungeons, mines and quarries, weighed down by chains and work of overwhelming oppression."[43] Nor did they discover an inner sanctum of lily-skinned beauties held against their will. Early that morning, the English consul had escorted eighty lice- and dysentery-ridden shipwreck victims out of the bagne's former chapel.[44] Army officer Théodore de Quatrebarbes recalled that the building also held 200 Greek, Spanish, and Italian captives, though Algerian registers put their number at 122. Later reports identified a single French national: a man from Toulon named Béraud, who had been enslaved for twenty-nine years.[45] According to George Simon Frederick Pfeiffer, a naval surgeon from the Palatinate restored to freedom as a reward for treating wounded janissaries, the Algerian defeat meant that "slaves who had languished for years were now set at liberty to walk about town at pleasure." Some of them rushed to the harbor, hoping "to obtain a passage to their native country," he wrote, while "others haunted the Jewish ale shops, and spent the first days of their rejoicing in rolling their drunken carcasses ('walking swill tubs') about the streets."[46] By every account, all those manumitted were men.

News of the conquest—transported by steamship and transmitted via telegraph—reached France on 9 July. Around the country, newspapers crowed victory. "Algiers is taken! . . . The honor of France is avenged! Piracy is suffocated in its den: the outrages of Europe are erased," declared the *Journal des débats*, accepting a pretext for invasion it had previously scorned and calling the deliverance of French captives the expedition's "sweetest recompense." In recognition of the king's crusading lineage, it proclaimed, "Muslim society recoils before Christian civilization. . . . Louis XIV punished piracy; Charles X abolished it." Another erstwhile critic, the *Constitutionnel*, found the seduction of empire difficult to resist. With Algiers fallen, it pronounced "the start of a new era for world civilization" and dreamily envisioned "Africa . . . covered with laboring populations" and "the Mediterranean . . . nothing but a big lake." Meanwhile, the *Sémaphore de Marseille* sketched out a hopeful postwar settlement: the incorporation of Algiers, Oran, and Constantine as departments of France.[47]

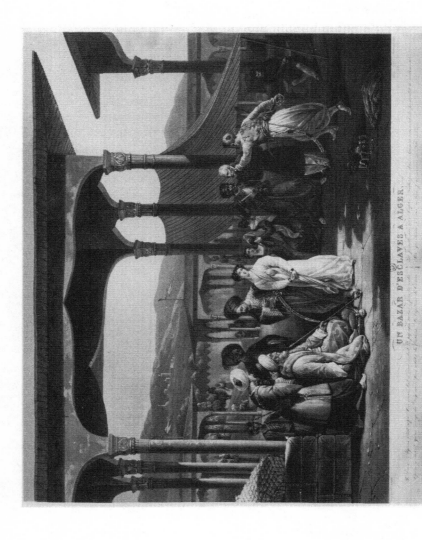

UN BAZAR D'ESCLAVES À ALGER.

Figure 15. A white woman for sale. "Un Bazar d'esclaves à Alger," engraving by Jean-Pierre-Marie Jazet (24 July 1830), based on a painting by Hippolyte Lecomte. © Musée national de la Marine, ph. 152 866.

At the French gateway to the Mediterranean, euphoria engulfed every level of society. There, municipal officers, dockworkers, and fishwives, republicans and ultras, rejoiced side by side.[48] But for citizens in the capital, overseas victory did not allay animosity against the regime of Charles X. Ominous silence greeted the royal cortege on its way to hear Te Deum at Notre Dame. "A few shouts, obviously purchased, coming from isolated groups in the midst of an impassive populace," remembered marine minister Haussez, "were the only signs of public joy." Fittingly, one of the few figures on hand to celebrate what the *Gazette de France* called "the triumphs of the French army, and the glory of the Monarch who has just accomplished in three weeks the wish of six centuries," was Sidney Smith.[49]

WHITE WOMEN ENSLAVED

The invasion of Algiers saved neither very many white slaves nor the Bourbon crown. But it did fix an image of Barbary servitude that lingered into the next century. Three days before Parisians took to the barricades in the July Revolution, Charles X authorized the publication of an engraving based on an earlier canvas by Hippolyte Lecomte (Figure 15). *Un Bazar d'esclaves à Alger* depicts a pale woman in a modest white robe, eyes averted and hands clasped as a turbaned man with a scimitar offers her up for inspection and a dark-complexioned soldier wearing an embroidered vest restrains her male protector with a dagger. Against a landscape of camels and minarets, her female companions weep, while off to the side sits another male figure in European dress, wrists bound in his lap. In the lower right corner, jewels spill suggestively from an open case. A legend explains: the dey has sent an envoy to select among the latest seizures of an Algerian corsair, and a father threatened by "Africans" is unable to stop him.

With allusions to sexual violence and intimations of racial mixing, this portrayal of a slave market in Algiers—a seeming sequel to his Greek kidnap scene transposed to a different geographical setting—represents an endpoint in French thinking about Mediterranean corsairing and captivity. After two hundred years of experience and reverie, the primary locus of anxiety had shifted from the souls of men to a white, female body. Now, however, it was the Ottoman regency, not a maiden, being plundered. Blending iconography from colonial bondage and harem servitude, made familiar by the Greek War of Independence, Lecomte's picture projected a fantasy to validate and commemorate France's recent conquest in North Africa.[50]

Conclusion

☾

Colonial and postcolonial Algeria continues to haunt French domestic affairs. Crisis in the *banlieues* (suburbs), a disputed law about textbooks, and debates about headscarves all manifest the nation's unease with addressing discrimination, acknowledging violence, and accommodating diversity born of a nineteenth- and twentieth-century past. The previous chapters have suggested that understanding the relationship between North Africa and France, in fact, requires a longer lens—back to the early modern period, and toward a shared history of galleys and bagnes, captives and corsairs.

For about two hundred years Mediterranean slavery was a reciprocal, religiously justified reality. It made tens of thousands of French Christians and North African Muslims into coerced laborers and speculative investments—with horrific personal, familial, and social consequences. During that period and for much longer, Mediterranean slavery was also a figment of the French imagination. It inspired fears and aspirations—about subjection and domination, defilement and decontamination—which friars, kings, consuls, and emperors drew on first to foster sovereign allegiance and then to defend territorial expansion.

From the sixteenth century onward, targeting particular captives from coastal areas, ransom efforts sought primarily to avert plague, sodomy, and apostasy and to establish attachment to France. After the mid-seventeenth century, targeting all French (and some foreign) Catholics, deliverance by salvo also attempted to demonstrate resolve against heretics and infidels, buttressing the monarch's reputation as protector of Latin Christendom and establishing a link between Frenchness, faith, and freedom. By the Revolution, targeting new nationals, diplomacy backed by force served as a tool for the secular goal of regeneration, personal and political. Turning foreign captives into loyal Frenchmen, while asserting dominion over not just contiguous provinces but also independent countries, France set a precedent for combining the seemingly contradictory goals of emancipation and colonization.

Other scholars have argued that Mediterranean slavery was a prototype whose system of exploitation and means of production—transported across the Atlantic, then racialized and enlarged—forced millions of sub-Saharan Africans into permanent, hereditary bondage. This book has pointed to a trajectory in the opposite direction. It shows how, at the dawn of the modern era, traces of the new form of dependence instituted in the Americas returned home, reshaping how the French understood the servitude of Europeans, whether army deserters and sister republicans in North African cities, hopeful colonists and human traffickers along the western coast of the Sahara, or Greek women taken from rebellious portions of the Ottoman Empire. Perceptions of slavery did not stand still. Between the mid-eighteenth and nineteenth centuries, New World thralldom became a lens for viewing Old World captivity. Once that happened, France adopted the abolition of "white slavery" as an even stronger excuse for overseas imperialism.

Regeneration and racial servitude, brought together in a broader discourse about liberation, helped make possible France's takeover of Algiers. Even opponents of the invasion largely agreed with its ideological premise: that the polity needed release from Turkish tyranny and Muslim misbelief. Common conviction held that spending three centuries under Ottoman rule and much longer under Islam had rendered the regency's population servile and superstitious, its seas and soil barren. But it was not just barbaric people and places that ostensibly clamored for freedom, concurred politicians and political theorists, artists and writers. The "civilized world" also required deliverance from North African corsairing and captivity. In the lead-up to 1830, they maintained that breaking the shackles of suffering European, Christian (thus white, perhaps female) slaves represented a service for all of humanity.

The Algerian expedition was thus more than the whim of a weak king, an accidental prelude to empire spurred by a series of unfortunate economic and political events. Besides the result of an ill-aimed fly whisk, it was the expression (though hardly preordained) of deep-rooted notions about the mission to civilize and the imperative to conquer. One of the many ways this set of ideas developed was through depictions of Mediterranean slavery in memoranda and memoirs, processions, poems, paintings, and plays. On one level these various media expressed anxiety about the corrupting effects of Islam. On another they expressed confidence in the restorative powers of France.

Reference Matter

Abbreviations

The following abbreviations are used in the appendixes and endnotes:

AAE	Archives des Affaires étrangères
ACC	Archives communales de Cassis
ACCM	Archives de la Chambre de Commerce de Marseille
ACT	Archives communales de Toulon
ADAM	Archives départementales des Alpes-Maritimes
ADAU	Archives départementales de l'Aude
ADBR	Archives départementales des Bouches-du-Rhône
ADCM	Archives départementales de la Charente-Maritime
ADF	Archives départementales du Finistère
ADG	Archives départementales de la Gironde
ADH	Archives départementales de l'Hérault
ADIV	Archives départementales d'Ille-et-Vilaine
ADV	Archives départementales de la Vendée
AE	Affaires étrangères
AESC	*Annales: economies, sociétés, civilisations*
AMM	Archives municipales de Marseille
AMN	Archives municipales de Nantes
AN	Archives nationales
AP	*Archives parlementaires de 1787 à 1860: recueil complet des débats législatifs & politiques des chambres françaises, imprimé par ordre du Sénat et de la Chambre des députés*, 2 ser., 99 vols. (Paris: P. Dupont, 1879–1914)
APF	Archives of the Propaganda Fide
AT	Charles Féraud, *Annales tripolitaines publiées avec une introduction et des notes par Augustin Bernard* (Tunis: Tournier; Paris: Vuibert, 1927; reprint with an introduction by Nora Lafi, Saint-Denis: Bouchène, 2005)

ATN	Alphonse Rousseau, *Annales tunisiennes, ou Aperçu historique sur la régence de Tunis* (Algiers: Bastide, 1864)
BN	Bibliothèque nationale
BSHPF	*Bulletin de la Société de Histoire du Protestantisme français*
CA	Consulat d'Alger
CADN	Centre des archives diplomatiques de Nantes
CB	Daniel Panzac, *Les Corsaires barbaresques: la fin d'une épopée, 1800–1820* (Paris: CNRS Editions, 1999)
CBT	Eugène Plantet, ed., *Correspondance des beys de Tunis et des consuls de France avec la cour, 1577–1830*, 3 vols. (Paris: Félix Alcan, 1893–1899)
CC	Correspondance consulaire
CCM	Chambre de commerce de Marseille
CDA	Eugène Plantet, ed., *Correspondance des deys d'Alger avec la cour de France, 1579–1833*, 2 vols. (Paris: Félix Alcan, 1889)
CM	*Cahiers de la Méditerranée*
CN	*Correspondance de Napoléon 1er*, 32 vols. (Paris: H. Plon, J. Dumaine, 1858–1870)
CPF/SOCG	Congregazione "De Propaganda Fide"/Scritture originali riferte nelle Congregazioni generali
CR	Calixte de la Providence, *Corsaires et rédempteurs: ou Récit des souffrances des anciens captifs et des travaux entrepris pour leur délivrance* (Lille: Desclée de Brouwer, 1884)
CSPD	Calendar of State Papers
CT	*Cahiers de Tunisie*
FA	François Charles-Roux, *France et Afrique du Nord avant 1830: les précurseurs de la conquête* (Paris: Félix Alcan, 1932)
FF	Fonds françaises
FT	Pierre Grandchamp, ed., *La France en Tunisie*, 10 vols. (Tunis: J. Aloccio, 1920–1937)
HA	Henri Delmas de Grammont, *Histoire d'Alger sous la domination turque (1515–1830)* (Paris: Ernest Leroux, 1887; reprint, Paris: Bouchène, 2002)
HCRT	[Pierre Girard], *Histoire chronologique du royaume de Tripoly*, 2 vols. (1685), BN, FF 12199–12200
LC	Bonifacio Porres Alonso, *Libertad a los cautivos: actividad redentora de la Orden Trinitaria*, 2 vols. (Córdoba: Secretariado Trinitario, 1998)
MD	Mémoires et documents
MS	Manuscrits françaises
NAF	Nouvelles acquisitions françaises

OC	Old classification
OT	Paul Deslandres, *L'Ordre des Trinitaires pour le rachat des captifs*, 2 vols. (Toulouse: Privat, 1903)
"PM"	Hugues Cocard, "Les Pères de la Merci dans le royaume de France depuis le Concile de Trente jusqu'à la fin de l'Ancien régime," 2 vols. (Thèse troisième cycle, Université d'Angers, 1982)
RA	*Revue africaine*
ROMM	*Revue de l'Occident musulman et de la Méditerranée*
SIHM	Henry de Castries, Philippe de Cossé Brissac, and Pierre de Cenival, eds., *Les Sources inédites de l'histoire du Maroc de 1530 à 1845*, 30 vols. (Paris: Paul Geunther, 1905–1960)
TF	Edgard Rouard de Card, *Traités de la France avec les pays de l'Afrique du Nord: Algérie, Tunisie, Tripolitaine, Maroc* (Paris: A. Pedone, 1906)

Appendix 1:
Slave Numbers

Year	French	Christian	Source
1530		7,000	*Ghazawât*, BN, MS 5754, f. 43 v, cited in Merouche, *Recherches sur l'Algérie*, 1: 213.
1533		7,000	Tonnelé, "Les Corsaires algériens," 31–32.
1550		30,000	Grammont, *HA*, 132.
1572	500		François de Noailles to Charles IX, Constantinople, 27 April 1572, BN, MS 16142, f. 138 r, cited in Poumarède, "La France et les barbaresques," 122.
1575		20,000	Bonet-Maury, "La France et la rédemption," 906.
1578–1581		25,000	Haëdo, *Topographie et histoire*, 55.
1587		20,000	Knights of Malta Francesco Lanfreducci and Gian Otto Bosio, "Costa e discorsi di Berberia," (1 September 1587), cited in Cresti, "Descriptions et iconographie," 8.
1597		32,000	Giovanni Antonio Magini, *Geographiae universae* . . . (Cologne: Petrus Keschedt, 1597), 185–187, cited in Gramaye, *Alger*, 139.
1598		Almost 15,000	Magini, *Geographiae universae*, cited in Cresti, "La Population," 480.
1602	3,000		Henri IV to ambassador Brèves, 10 June 1602, cited in Masson, *Histoire du commerce*, xxiv.

NOTE: A blank cell indicates that no data are available. A zero indicates that no slaves were present.

Year	French	Christian	Source
1619	36 (suspected in Spanish service)	+32,000–[50,000]	36: Vice consul François Chaix, "Attestation relative aux captifs," Algiers, 19 August 1619, and "Ordonnance royale," Cassarrubios, 25 December 1619; +32,000 Catholics: Jean-Baptiste Gramaye, "Informations recueillies . . . adressés à Rome" [1619]; 35,000: Gramaye, *Africa illustrata*, II: 10–11; "more than 50,000": Clergy of Algiers, 15 August 1619, all reprinted and cited in Gramaye, *Alger*, 138–139, 421, 479, 503.
1620	200–[1,000]		200, +1,000: Chaix to Marseille consuls, Algiers 27 February and 20 July 1620, reprinted in Grammont, "Relations," 23, 96.
1621	300–500	18,000–20,000	300, 500: Chaix to Marseille consuls, Algiers, 16 January and 1 May 1621, reprinted in Grammont, "Relations," 99, 103; 18,000–20,000: M. de Guillermy to Nicholas Claude Fabri de Peiresc, Marseille, 18 October 1623, Bibliothèque de Carpentras, Collection Tissot, 1777, ff. 61–62, cited in Grammont, "Relations," 136.
1621–1626		8,000 (Catholics)	Mascarenhas, *Esclave à Alger*, 72
1623	300–[3,000]	[36,000]	300: Chaix to Marseille consuls, 1623, ACCM, AA462 (OC), cited in Plantet, *CDA*, 1: 23 n. 3; 3,000/36,000: Garrot, *Histoire générale d'Algérie*, 458–459.
1625	[6,000]	25,000	6,000: *Cahiers de doléances* from Marseille to Louis XIII, 15 July 1625, AN, Marine B7 49, p. 60; 25,000: Giovanni Battista Salvago, *Africa overo Barbaria*, cited in Grandchamp, "Une Mission délicate," 492.
1626	800–[4,100]		800: Sanson Napollon to [Richelieu], Algiers, 14 December 1626, CADN, CA, vol. 1, f. 18; 4,100: "Instructions au S. Napollon," Paris, 14 February 1626, AN, Marine B7 49, pp. 67–68; 3,000 English: May 1626, CSPD, Charles I, 1625–6, 1: 343, cited in Matar, *Britain and Barbary*, 51.
1628		15,000	*Fourth Report of the Royal Commission on Historical Manuscripts*, Part I (London: Her Majesty's Stationery Office, 1874), 14, cited in Matar, "The Barbary Corsairs," 242.

Year	French	Christian	Source
1629	2		Napollon, 5 September 1629, cited in Grammont, "Relations," 371 n. 1.
1631		[20,000]	+20,000: Serefin de Freytas, Biblioteca Nacional Madrid, MS 3536, f. 11, cited in Friedman, "Christian Captives," 617 n. 4.
1632	150–400		150: Napollon to Richelieu, Bastion, 26 April 1632, CADN, CA, vol. 1, f. 60; to Louis XIII, Bastion, 26 April 1632, BN, Collection Brienne, vol. 78, cited in Grammont, "Relations," 371 n. 1, 372 n. 1; 400: "Esclaves d'Alger" to Charles de Lorraine, duc de Guise, Algiers, 3 November 1632, CADN, CA, vol. 1, f. 91 r, quoted in Poumarède, "La France et les barbaresques," 119.
1633	2,300		Blanchard to Marseille consuls, Algiers, 26 June and 7 July 1633, ACCM, AA463 (OC), reprinted in Grammont, "Relations," 390, 391, and cited in Teissier, *Inventaire des archives historiques*, 202.
1634	1,500	25,000	Dan, *Histoire de Barbarie* (1637), 284.
1637	1,200	60,000	1,200: Sanson Le Page to Chavigny, Marseille, 22 December 1637, CADN, CA, vol. 1, ff. 69–70; 60,000: Knight, *A relation of seaven yeares slaverie*, 51.
1640	1,500	40,000	1,500: "Ordre du Cardinal . . . pour délivrer les esclaves d'Alger," cited in Plantet, *CDA*, 1: 46 n. 1; 40,000: Father José de Tamayo, cited in Gramaye, *Alger*, 140; 750 English: Fisher, *Barbary Legend*, 207; 3,000 English: 3 October 1640 slave petition, CSPD, Charles I, 1641–1643, 17: 134, cited in Matar, *Britain and Barbary*, 65.
1640–1642		30,000–40,000	Aranda, *Les Captifs d'Alger*, 98.
1641	2,000–[5,000]	30,000–40,000	2,000: Trinitarian Hérault to Louis XIII and his mother, [early 1641], BN, MS 15721, f. 409, cited in Deslandres, *OT*, 2: 271; 5,000: Wolf, *The Barbary Coast*, 212.
1642			5,000 English: Henry Robinson, *Libertas, or, Reliefe to the English Captives in Algier . . .* (London: Richard Cotes for John Sweeting, 1642), 5, cited in Matar, *Islam and Britain*, 7.
1643	2,000–[10,000]		2,000: Hérault, *Les Larmes et clameurs*, 6, 14; 10,000: Chastelet des Boys, "L'Odyssée," 157.

Year	French	Christian	Source
1644	2,000		Egreville, *La Vive Foy*, 83; François Favre, *Le Véritable récit de la rédemption faite en Alger* . . . (Paris: L. Feugé, 1645), 47, cited in Turbet-Delof, *Bibliographie critique*, 133–134.
1650		8,000	Bono, *I Corsari barbareschi*, 220.
1653		10,000	Juan de Quincoces, Archivo Histórico Nacional, E, leg. 858, cited in Torres, *Prisioneros de los infieles*, 47.
1656		35,000	Slave Felipe Palermo, Algiers, 5 September 1656, Archivo General de Simanca, Cruzada, legs. 286, cited in Friedman, *Spanish Captives*, 192 n. 1.
1657		20,000	[Perboyre], *Mémoires*, 2: 205.
1660		20,000–35,000	20,000–25,000: Wolf, *The Barbary Coast*, 225; 35,000: Pierre d'Avity, *Description générale de l'Afrique* . . . (Paris: Claude Sonnius, 1637), cited in Cresti, "La Population," 480.
1660–1661		20,000–30,000	Chevalier Paul, cited in Charles-Roux, *FA*, 145.
1662		30,000–40,000	Including 12,000 Catholics: [Auvry], *Le Miroir de la charité*, 84, 250; 300 English: CSPD, Charles II, 2: 285, cited in Matar, *Islam and Britain*, 9.
1663	1,179–1,319		List compiled by consul Jean-Armand Durbordieu, Algiers, 3 December 1663, BN, CCC 483, ff. 551–553.
1664			AAE, MD Alger, vol. 12, f. 146, cited in Masson, *Histoire des établissements*, 154 n. 3.
1665	131 (Marseillais)	40,000	131: Deliberations of CCM, 17 December 1665, B3 (OC), f. 559, cited in Fournier, *Inventaire*; +40,000: Pierre du Val, *La Carte générale et les cartes particulières des costes de la mer mediterranée* . . . (Paris: author, 1665), cited in Cresti, "La Population," 480; 80 English: CSPD, Charles II, 5: 88, cited in Matar, *Islam and Britain*, 9.
1666	129 (Marseillais)		ACCM, G40.
1667	900–1,500		Marine minister Jean-Baptiste Colbert to general commissary André-François Trubert, Saint-Germain-en-Laye, 7 October 1667, AN, AE BI 115, f. 1003, cited in Touili, *Correspondance*, 9.

Year	French	Christian	Source
1669		14,000–15,000	Includes 100 women, 300–400 children: Mirella Mafrici, *Mezzogiorno e pirateria nell'eta moderna (secoli XVI–XVIII)* (Naples: Edizioni scientifiche italiane, 1995), 98, cited in Davis, "Counting European Slaves," 98; 400 English: SP 71/I/pt. 4, ff. 450–453, cited in Matar, "Introduction," in Vitkus, *Piracy, Slavery, and Redemption*, 14.
1670	23		14 from Djidjelli, 5 from before treaty, 4 bought in Salé, cited in [Perboyre], *Mémoires*, 2: 253; 378 Britons: Henry Printall, *A list of the English captives . . .* (London: William Bradly, 1670), and CSPD, Charles II, 10: 186, cited in Matar, *Islam and Britain*, 9.
1672		14,000	Consul Jean Le Vacher in *Relation véritable*, 1.
1675		10,000–12,000	10,000–12,000: Arvieux, *Mémoires*, 5: 525; 12,000, 200,000: Rocqueville, *Relations des moeurs*, 17; 31,000: English consul Samuel Martin in Pennell, *Piracy and Diplomacy*, 36.
1676	[9,000]	18,000	*The Present state of Algiers* (1682), cited in Cresti, "La Population," 480.
1680–1681		5,000	Apostolic missionary Francesco Gatta, cited in Aurora Romano, "Schiavi siciliani," 278.
1681	66–366	5,000	66, 366: Colbert to royal commissary Hayet, 16 June 1681, 29 November 1681, cited in [Perboyre], *Mémoires*, 2: 338, 341; 5,000 "or a few more": Congregazione "De Propaganda Fide," Rome, Scritture riferite nei congressi [CPF/SRC]-1, f. 503, cited in Davis, "Counting European Slaves," 98.
1682	300–400	17,000	300: "Capitaines des vaisseaux marchands françois esclaves à Alger" to Colbert, Algiers, 12 December 1682, AN, AE BI 115, ff. 341–343, cited in Touili, *Correspondance*, 29; 400: Sue, *Histoire de la marine*, 3: 410; 17,000: ex-slave Antonio Tedaldi Barbarella, Biblioteca Museo Correr, Venice, Carte Mocenigo, b. 515, f. 77, cited in Davis, "Counting European Slaves," 98.
1683	550	35,000–40,000	550: Bonet-Maury, "La France et la rédemption," 906; 35,000–40,000: Alain Manesson Mallet, *Description de l'univers . . .* (Paris: D. Thierry, 1683), 20, cited in Cresti, "La Population," 480.

Year	French	Christian	Source
1684	300		Royal envoy Denis Dusault to marine minister Jean-Baptiste Colbert, Marquis de Seignelay, Algiers, 1 August 1684, cited in [Perboyre], *Mémoires*, 2: 376.
1685	0		Peter, *Les Barbaresques*, 63.
1686	12		Divan and dey of Algiers to Louis XIV, 21 September 1686, AN, Marine B7 210, reprinted in Plantet, *CDA*, 1: 122, 125.
1687	372	10,000	372: Dusault to Seignelay, Algiers, 19 September 1687, cited in Plantet, *CDA*, 1: 148 n. 1; 10,000: Vicar apostolic Michel Montmasson to Seignelay, Algiers, 16 January 1687, cited in Bombard, "Les Vicaires apostoliques," 2: 273.
1688	460		460: Dusault to Seignelay, Algiers, 14 April 1688, AN, AE BI 116, ff. 118–121, cited in Touili, *Correspondance*, 44.
1689	350–1,370 (18 Marseillais)	1,033	350, 1033: Consul Barthélemy Mercadier to CCM, Algiers, 3 and 16 November 1689, ACCM, AA469 (OC), cited in Teissier, *Inventaire des archives historiques*, 206, and Plantet, *CDA*, 1: 178 n. 1; 1,370: dey Hajj Sha'bān to Louis XIV, Algiers, 23 July 1691, AN, Marine B7 214–215, reprinted in Plantet, *CDA*, 1: 306; 18: AMM, GGL105.
1690	700–850 (154 Marseillais)		700–800: Consul René Lemaire to CCM, Algiers, 11 December 1690, cited in Grammont, *Correspondance*, 14; royal envoy Guillaume Marcel to Seignelay, cited in Plantet, *CDA*, 1: 244 n. 1; 850: Bonet-Maury, "La France et la rédemption," 907; 154: AMM, GGL105.
1691	440	[36,000]	440: Bonet-Maury, "La France et la rédemption," 907; 36,000: Dey Sha'bān to Louis XIV, AN, B7 214, f. 115, cited in Plantet, *CDA*, 1: 310.
1693	8	4,000	8: Bonet-Maury, "La France et la rédemption," 907; 4,000: Vicar apostolic Yvon Lorance (APF), cited in Cresti, "La Population," 480; "more than 4,000": CPF/SRC-3, f. 144, cited in Davis, "Counting European Slaves," 98.
1693–1694		[10,000]	"More than 10,000": CPF/SRC-1, f. 54, cited in Davis, "Counting European Slaves," 98.

Year	French	Christian	Source
1696		1,600	Lorance (APF), cited in Cresti, "La Population," 480.
1697	30		Dusault to marine minister Louis Phélypeaux, comte de Pontchartrain, Algiers, 11 June 1697, AN, AE BI 117, ff. 307–314, Touili, *Correspondance*, 82.
1698		2,600–2,800	2,600: Lorance (APF), cited in Cresti, "La Population," 480; "2,800 Christians": CPF/SRC-3, f. 377, cited in Davis, "Counting European Slaves," 98
1700		8,000–10,000	Jean de La Faye to his uncle, 6 August 1700, in [Comelin and de La Motte], *Etat des Royaumes*, 332.
1701	7 (Huguenots)	3,000–[20,000]	7: Consul Philippe-Jacques Durand to Pontchartrain, Algiers, 14 October 1700; census of 12 *religionnaires* seized from a Dutch boat, 14 April 1701, AN, AE BI 118, ff. 109–112, 131–133, cited in Touili, *Correspondance*, 98; 3,000: Grammont, *HA*, 221; Lorance (APF), cited in Cresti, "La Population," 480; [Perboyre], *Mémoires*, 2: 512; "more than 20,000 Christians" / "not more than 3,000 Christians": CPF/SRC-3, ff. 408, 414, cited in Davis, "Counting European Slaves," 98.
1709	38 (25 from Martigues, 4 from Cassis, 9 Basques)		"Rôle des matelots . . . qui sont esclaves," Chancellor Thomas de Jonville to Pontchartrain, Marseille, 29 January 1709; Basque slave Harristeguy to Pontchartrain, Algiers, 4 March 1709, AN, AE BI 119, ff. 249, 250–251, cited in Touili, *Correspondance*, 144.
1711	15		"Liste des françois esclaves à Alger," Algiers, 11 June 1711, AN, AE BI 119, f. 386, cited in Touili, *Correspondance*, 156.
1719		4,000	Henri Chatelain, *Atlas historique . . .* , ed. Nicolas de Gueudeville (Amsterdam: L'Honore & Chatelain, 1721), cited in Cresti, "La Population," 480.
1720	0		Consul Jean Baume to CCM, Algiers, 28 December 1719, cited in Grammont, *Correspondance*, 156.
1721		5,000	Fewer than 5,000, mostly Protestants and Orthodox: CPF/SRC-3, f. 491, cited in Davis, "Counting European Slaves," 98.
1727–1732		2,000	Shaw, *Travels or Observations*, 1: 84.

Year	French	Christian	Source
1729		5,000– [10,000]	+5,000: Pieter van der Aa, *La Galerie agreable du monde* . . . (Leiden, Netherlands: author, 1729), cited in Cresti, "La Population," 480; 9,000–10,000: Fau and La Caze, *Rédemption*, 238, 239.
1730	0	2,000	0: ADAU, 5J42, cited in Cocard, "PM," 2: 343; 2,000: Monlaü, *Les Etats barbaresques*, 97.
1731	22		Dey Abdi to Maurepas, Algiers, 21 June 1731, reprinted in Grammont, *Correspondance*, 153.
1732	10 (without passports)		Dey Abdi to Maurepas, Algiers, 15 May 1732, AN, Marine B7 321, reprinted in Grammont, *Correspondance*, 168.
1732–1737		6,000	Jean-Victor Laurent, baron d'Arreger, in Arreger, "Un Captif à Alger," 334.
1734		4,000	"Exceeding 4,000": CPF/SRC-5, f. 516, cited in Davis, "Counting European Slaves," 98.
1735	42–122 (Oraners)		Jonville to marine minister Jean-Frédéric Phélypeaux, comte de Maurepas, Algiers, 30 June 1735; consul Alexis-Jean-Eustache Taitbout de Marigny to Maurepas, Algiers, 7 December 1735, AN, AE BI 123, ff. 269–274, 318–319, cited in Touili, *Correspondance*, 281, 284.
1736		1,063	Devoulx, *Tachrifat*, 86.
1737		931	Devoulx, *Tachrifat*, 86.
1738		705	Devoulx, *Tachrifat*, 86.
1739		569	Devoulx, *Tachrifat*, 86.
1740		412	Devoulx, *Tachrifat*, 86.
1741	54	499	54: Grammont, *HA*, 299; 499: Devoulx, *Tachrifat*, 86.
1742	11	530	11: Jonville to CCM, Algiers, 20 January 1742, reprinted in Grammont, *Correspondance*, 282; 530: Devoulx, *Tachrifat*, 86.
1743		582	Devoulx, *Tachrifat*, 86.
1744		739	Devoulx, *Tachrifat*, 86.
1745		741	Devoulx, *Tachrifat*, 86.
1746		783	Devoulx, *Tachrifat*, 86.
1747		821	Devoulx, *Tachrifat*, 86.
1748		1,003	Devoulx, *Tachrifat*, 86.

Year	French	Christian	Source
1749	160 (145 Oraners and 15 taken under foreign flag)	950– [7,000]	160, 5,000 (3,000 Spanish, 2,000 other European): memorandum by Lemaire, Algiers, 5 October 1749, AN, AE BI 126, ff. 281–282, and to marine minister Antoine-Louis Rouillé, comte de Jouy, ff. 288–294, cited in Touili, *Correspondance*, 371–372; 15 taken under foreign flag: "Observations sur le Royaume d'Alger," Vallière, 10 March 1749, cited in Chaillou, *Textes pour servir*, 75; Devoulx, *Tachrifat*, 86; 6,000–7,000 Catholics, CPF/SRC-6, f. 210, cited in Davis, "Counting European Slaves," 99; 7,000: Consul André-Alexandre Lemaire, Algiers, 28 May 1749, AN, AE BIII 27, f. 67.
1750	172	1,063	172: Lemaire to Rouillé, Algiers, October 1750, AN, AE BI 126, ff. 115–116, cited in Touili, *Correspondance*, 387; 1,063: Devoulx, *Tachrifat*, 86.
1751	0	1,773	0: Note on the Trinitarian and Mercedarian redemptions from Lemaire, Algiers, October 1750, AN, AE BI 126, ff. 115–116, cited in Touili, *Correspondance*, 387; 1,773: Devoulx, *Tachrifat*, 86.
1752		609	Devoulx, *Tachrifat*, 86.
1753		632	Devoulx, *Tachrifat*, 86.
1754		591	Devoulx, *Tachrifat*, 86.
1755		564	Devoulx, *Tachrifat*, 86.
1756		694	694: Devoulx, *Tachrifat*, 86; 34–75 Neapolitans: Lemaire to marine minister Jean-Baptiste Machault d'Arnouville, Algiers, 25 June 1756; Lemaire to marquis d'Ossun, French ambassador to Naples, Algiers, 13 September 1756, AN, AE BI 129, ff. 79–83, 103–105, cited in Touili, *Correspondance*, 434, 436–437.
1757		1,561	Devoulx, *Tachrifat*, 86.
1758		1,571	1,571: Devoulx, *Tachrifat*, 86; 400 Tabarkans: Consul Joseph-Barthélemy Pérou to secretary of state François-Marie Pierenc de Moras, Algiers, 20 March 1758, AN, AE BI 129, ff. 278–279, cited in Touili, *Correspondance*, 450.
1759		1,753	Devoulx, *Tachrifat*, 86.

Year	French	Christian	Source
1760		1,941–3,000	1,941: Devoulx, *Tachrifat*, 86; 3,000: Vicar apostolic Théodore de Groiselle to marine minister Nicolas-René Berryer, Algiers, 12 June 1760, AN, AE BI 130, ff. 109–114, cited in Touili, *Correspondance*, 470.
1761	46 (30 Oraners, 10 Genoese and Tabarkans, 6 taken at sea)	1,993	46: Groiselle to Berryer, Algiers, 28 January 1761, AN, AE BI 130, ff. 174–175, cited in Touili, *Correspondance*, 478; 1,993: Devoulx, *Tachrifat*, 86; 1,200–1,500 Neapolitans and Oraners: Devoulx, *Les Archives*, 86–94.
1762		1,902–3,000	1,902: Devoulx, *Tachrifat*, 86; 3,000: Groiselle to secretary of state Etienne-François de Choiseul, duc de Stainville, Algiers, 30 September 1762, AN, AE BI 130, ff. 342–343, cited in Touili, *Correspondance*, 501.
1763		1,900–[4,000]	1,900: Devoulx, *Tachrifat*, 86; 3,000: CPF/SRC-7, f. 122, cited in Davis, "Counting European Slaves," 99; 4,000: *Gazette de France* (8 March 1763): 98.
1764		1,920	1,920: Devoulx, *Tachrifat*, 86.
1765	46 (34 Oraners, 8 Genoese and Tabarkans, 4 taken under foreign flag)	1,904–[2,500]	46: List by consul Jean-Antoine Vallière, Algiers, 3 January 1765, AN, AE BI 132, f. 31, cited in Touili, *Correspondance*, 532; 1,904–1,944: Devoulx, *Tachrifat*, 86; 2,500 Spaniards: Vallière to marine minister César Gabriel de Choiseul-Chevigny, duc de Praslin, Algiers, 4 October 1765, AN, AE BI 133, f. 162, cited in Touili, *Correspondance*, 542.
1766		2,004	Devoulx, *Tachrifat*, 86.
1767		2,062–3,000	2,062: Devoulx, *Tachrifat*, 86; 2,662: Bono, *I Corsari barbareschi*, 220; 2,900 (1500 Spanish, 200 Portuguese): Vallière to Praslin, Algiers, 24 November 1767, AN, AE BI 133, ff. 114–118, cited in Touili, *Correspondance*, 562; 3,000: Gorani, *Recherches sur la science*, 2: 246.
1768	100–150 Oraners	1,131	100–150: Vallière to Praslin, Algiers, 18 and 24 September 1768, AN, AE BI 133, ff. 197–202, 203–205, cited in Touili, *Correspondance*, 568, 569; 1,131: Devoulx, *Tachrifat*, 86.

Year	French	Christian	Source
1769	180 (150 French and ~30 Corsicans)	1,226–3,000	150, ~30: Vallière to Praslin, Algiers, 2 and 4 October 1769, AN, AE BI 133, ff. 291–292, 298–299, cited in Touili, *Correspondance*, 577–578; 1,226: Devoulx, *Tachrifat*, 86; 3,000: Masson, *Histoire des établissements*, 302 n. 1.
1770	200 (Oraners, recruits en route to Spain, Corsicans)	1,323	200 (and 300 Portuguese): Vallière to Praslin, 20 November 1770, AN, AE BI 134, ff. 80–90, cited in Touili, *Correspondance*, 588; 1,323: Devoulx, *Tachrifat*, 86.
1771	160 (French and Corsicans)	1,320	160: Trinitarian general to marine minister, 1771, AN, AE BIII 319, f. 122; 1,320: Devoulx, *Tachrifat*, 86.
1772	199 (128 Oraners, 34 recruits en route to Spain, 37 Corsicans)	1,190	199: Slave list, Algiers, 20 March 1772, AN, AE BI 135, ff. 67 v–70, cited in Touili, *Correspondance*, 607; 1,190: Devoulx, *Tachrifat*, 86.
1773		1,326–2,000	1,326: Devoulx, *Tachrifat*, 86; 1,500: all Oraners, mostly Spanish, Merouche, *Recherches sur l'Algérie*, 2: 265; 2,000 Catholics?: CPF/SRC-7, f. 591, cited in Davis, "Counting European Slaves," 99
1774	80–229 (50 Oraners and 15–30 Corsicans)	1,376–1,900	19 Corsicans: Feuille approved by marine minister, December 1774, AN, AE BIII 13, f. 265; 50 Oraners/30 Corsicans: La Vallée to marine minister Pierre-Etienne Bourgeois de Boynes, Algiers, 30 June 1774, AN, AE BI 136, ff. 108–111, cited in Touili, *Correspondance*, 634; 1,376/1,378 (214 French, +144 Portuguese, 15 Corsicans, 7 Livornese, 29 Piedmontese, 5 Romans, 42 Austrians, 191 Neapolitans, 34 Genoese, 17 Tabarkans, 11 Sardinians, 5 from Palma, 4 Maltese, 4 Greeks, 656 Spanish): Devoulx, *Tachrifat*, 86; 1,900 Catholics: CPF/SRC-7, f. 653, cited in Davis, "Counting European Slaves," 99
1775	232–400 (14 Corsicans)	1,373–1,496	400: Grammont, *HA*, 333; 1,373/1,496 (218 French, +14 Corsicans, 3 Livornese, 161 Portuguese, 29 Piedmontese, 5 Romans, 1 from Doubra, 42 Austrians, 286 Neapolitans, 34 Genoese, 12 Tabarkans, 14 Sardinians, 5 from Palma, 3 Maltese, 3 Greeks, 666 Spanish): Devoulx, *Tachrifat*, 86, 87.

Year	French	Christian	Source
1776		1,468	Devoulx, *Tachrifat*, 86.
1777		1,501	Devoulx, *Tachrifat*, 86.
1778	268–400 (mostly Oraners, +20 Corsicans)	1,369–2,038	400, 2,038: Renaudot, *Alger*, 174; 1,369/1,640 (248 French, +781 Spanish, 195 Neapolitans, 40 Sicilians, 5 Dutch, 4 Greeks, 13 Sardinians, 155 Portuguese, 20 Corsicans, 32 Genoese, 55 Livornese, 12 Tabarkans, 38 Austrians, 6 from Palma, 25 Piedmontese, 4 Romans, 2 Maltese, 5 Prussians): Devoulx, *Tachrifat*, 86, 87.
1779		1,481–3,000	1,481: Devoulx, *Tachrifat*, 86; 3,000: Thédenat, "Mémoires," 159 n. a.
1780	249 (1 Corsican)	1,340–1,494	1,494/1,340 (248 French, +830 Spanish, 161 Neapolitans, 15 Portuguese, 3 Sicilians, 38 Austrians, 1 Corsican, 42 Piedmontese, 2 Prussians): Devoulx, *Tachrifat*, 86.
1781	317 (10 Corsicans, 3 missing passports)	1,586	317: Plantet, *CDA*, 2: 368 n. 2; 10, 3: Consul Robert-Louis Langoisseur de La Vallée to marine minister Charles-Eugène-Gabriel de La Croix, marquis de Castries, Algiers, 30 May 1781, AN, AE BI 139, ff. 138–142; 1,586: Devoulx, *Tachrifat*, 86.
1782	400 (seized serving foreign powers)	1,532	400: "Décisions du roy du conseil d'état et des ministres de la marine," 24 November 1782, AN, AE BIII 18, p. 53; 1,532: Devoulx, *Tachrifat*, 86.
1783	307–317 (288 Oraners, +19 recruits en route to Spain)	1,507–1,548	317: "Liste des François esclaves à Alger provenant d'Oran," Algiers, 1783, AN, AE BI 140, ff. 121–125, cited in Touili, *Correspondance*, 713; 1,507: Devoulx, *Tachrifat*, 86; 317, 1,548: Grammont, *HA*, 336.
1784	315–350 (299 Oraners)	1,520	315, 299: Consul Jean-Baptiste Michel Guyot de Kercy to Castries, Algiers, 30 September 1784, AN, AE BI 141, ff. 110–126, cited in Touili, *Correspondance*, 732; 350: AN, AE BIII 19, p. 73 ss; 1,520: Devoulx, *Tachrifat*, 86.
1785	246–313 (226 Oraners)	1,372–3,000	313 (254 public/19 private): Kercy to Castries, Algiers, 30 June 1785, f. 41; 226 Oraners: Kercy to Castries, Algiers, 17 February 1785, AN, AE BI 142, ff. 13–18, cited in Touili, *Correspondance*, 736;

Year	French	Christian	Source
			1,900 (1,800 Italian, Spanish, Portuguese; 100 Greek): Vicar apostolic Giovanni Alasia, cited in Bombard, "Les Vicaires apostoliques," 584; 1,924: Grammont, *HA*, 340; 2,000: Johan Adam von Rehbinder, *Nachrichten und Bemerkungen über den algierschen Staat*, 3 vols. (Altona, Germany: Johann Friedrich Hammerich, 1798–1800), cited in Cresti, "Population d'Alger," 478; 3,000: American State Papers 1: 29, cited in Parker, *Uncle Sam in Barbary*, 19.
1786		1,200–3,000	1,200: English observer, cited in Blyth, *History of the War*, 51; 1,426: Devoulx, *Tachrifat*, 86; 2,200: Thomas Jefferson to Congress, 30 December 1790, American State Papers 1: 100–108, reprinted in Parker, *Uncle Sam in Barbary*, 223–224; 3,000: Richard O'Bryen to Matthew and Thomas Irwin, Algiers, 20 December 1788 (enclosed in Matthew Irwin to George Washington, 9 July 1789), National Archives, Papers of the Continental Congress, item 59, reprinted in Twohig, 3: 158–165.
1787		572–2,000	572/1,041 (886 Spanish, 21 Americans, 18 Russians, 40 Piedmontese, 8 Romans, 2 Corsicans, 3 Sicilians, 54 Austrians, 9 Prussians): Devoulx, *Tachrifat*, 86, 87; 1,800–2,000: Venture de Paradis, *Tunis et Alger*, 258.
1788		574–1,000	574: Devoulx, *Tachrifat*, 86; 600: O'Bryen to Irwin and Irwin, Algiers, 20 December 1788, National Archives, Papers of the Continental Congress, item 59, reprinted in Twohig, *The Papers of George Washington*, 3: 158–165; 700–800: Raynal, BN, FF 6429, f. 121 v, cited in Deslandres, *OT*, 2: 471; 1,000: Julien, *History of North Africa*, 320.
1789		500–659	500: Venture de Paradis, *Tunis et Alger*, 154; 655: Jefferson to Congress, 30 December 1790, American State Papers, 1: 100–108, reprinted in Parker, *Uncle Sam in Barbary*, 223–224; 659: Devoulx, *Tachrifat*, 86.
1790		715	Devoulx, *Tachrifat*, 86.

Year	French	Christian	Source
1791	150–170 Oraners, +5 Marseillais	700–762 (²/₃ Oraners)	150 (mostly deserters): Kercy, "Mémoire sur l'Alger," in Esquer, *Reconnaissance des villes*, 110–111; 160–170 Oraners, +5 Marseillais: Vallière to CCM, Algiers, 28 July 1791, and to marine minister Bertrand de Molleville, Algiers, 3 December 1791, AN, AE BI 144, ff. 144, 188–189, cited in Touili, *Correspondance*, 780, 785; 700 (²/₃ Oraners): American State Papers 1: 29, cited in Parker, *Uncle Sam in Barbary*, 9; 762: Devoulx, *Tachrifat*, 86.
1792		700–832	700–800: Vallière to marine minister Jean de La Coste, Algiers, 25 July 1792, AN, AE BI 145, f. 175 bis; 832: Devoulx, *Tachrifat*, 86.
1793	150–200 (+2 Marseillais)	600–755	150: Slaves to foreign affairs ministry, Algiers, 20 August 1793; 202: Vallière to foreign affairs ministry, Algiers, [1793], AAE, CC, Algiers, vol. 32, f. 29; 600: Letter from American slaves, cited in Dupuy, *Etudes d'histoire d'Amérique*, 73; 755: Devoulx, *Tachrifat*, 86; 120–130 Americans: Carey, *A Short Account of Algiers*, 36, 39.
1794		896	896: Devoulx, *Tachrifat*, 86.
1795	47–144 in city (132 Oraners) and 50 more elsewhere in regency	603–730	144: List of French slaves and "those reputed to be," Vallière, Algiers, 7 October 1795, AAE, CC, Algiers, vol. 32, ff. 139–141; 730/603 (47 French, 217 Spanish, 59 Genoese, 40 Portuguese, 28 Americans, 12 Livornese, 2 Corsicans, 24 Maltese, 1 Roman, 2 from Doubra, 40 Piedmontese, 54 Austrians, 8 Sardinians, 11 Greeks, 40 Flemish, 8 Danish, 10 Prussians): Devoulx, *Tachrifat*, 86, 87; 630: Panzac, *CB*, 98–99.
1796	146 (130 Oraners and 16 taken at sea)	659–1,200	146: Note . . . en faveur des français esclaves à Alger," AAE, CC, Algiers, vol. 33, f. 47; 195 Corsicans released by British: Merouche, *Recherches sur l'Algérie*, 2: 267, and Elliot, *Correspondance*, 334; 659: Devoulx, *Tachrifat*, 86; 700: Alasia in Cresti, "Quelques réflexions," 159; 1,200 (includes 500 Oraners): John Foss, *Journal of the Captivity and Suffering . . .* (Newburyport, MA: A. March, 1798), in Baepler, *White Slaves, African Masters*, 87.

Year	French	Christian	Source
1797	146–210 (130 Oraners; 16–80 French and Italians taken at sea)	546	146: Envoy Louis-Alexandre d'Allois d'Herculais to foreign affairs minister Charles de la Croix, Algiers, 20 April 1797, AAE, CC, Algiers, vol. 32, ff. 320–321; 80 French and Italians: Foreign affairs minister Charles-Maurice de Talleyrand-Périgord to dey Sīdi Hassan, Paris, 28 September 1797, reprinted in Grammont, *Correspondance*, 467; 546: Devoulx, *Tachrifat*, 86.
1798	125 (89 Oraners, 17 Venetians, 18 Italians)	1,168	89: Talleyrand to consul Dominique-Marie Moltedo, CADN, CA, vol. 22, ff. 118–119; 17, 18: Talleyrand to Moltedo, CADN, CA, vol. 22, ff. 130–131; 1,168: Devoulx, *Tachrifat*, 86.
1799	315 (64 French and 251 more from Corfu garrison)	1,019–1,342	251 (236 men, 12 women, 3 children): Berbrugger, "La Régence d'Alger," 15, 90 (1871): 411; 1,019/1,050 (64 French, 95 Genoese, 44 Austrians, 193 Spanish, 95 Portuguese, 4 Sardinians, 4 Romans, 377 Greeks, 25 Corsicans, 77 Maltese, 72 Prussians): Devoulx, *Tachrifat*, 86, 87; 1,050 (372 from Ionian islands): Panzac, *CB*, 98–99; 1,342: Parker, *Uncle Sam in Barbary*, 9.
1800	0–315	860–1,050	1,050 (same breakdown as above)/o: "Recensement des esclaves d'Alger par Naha," in *Tachrifat*, 87, cited in Berbrugger, "La Régence d'Alger," 19, 109 (1875): 29–30; 16, 91 (1872): 4; 860: Devoulx, *Tachrifat*, 86.
1801	0	500–545	500: Vicar apostolic Jean-Claude Vicherat cited in Cresti, "La Population," 478; 545: Devoulx, *Tachrifat*, 86.
1802	150 (shipwreck victims)	772–1,500	150: Napoleon to the dey of Algiers, Paris, 18 July 1802, *Correspondance de Napoléon*, 7: 521–522; 772 (47 Austrians, 365 Neapolitans, 366 Portuguese, 89 Genoese, 33 Spanish, 8 Sicilians, 16 Corsicans, 8 Greeks, 5 Romans): Devoulx, *Tachrifat*, 86, 87; 937: Panzac, *CB*, 98–99; 1,500: Blyth, *History of the War*, 97; Parker, *Uncle Sam in Barbary*, 9.

Year	French	Christian	Source
1803	0	910–946	910: *Tachrifat*, 87, cited in Berbrugger, "La Régence d'Alger" (1875): 143; 946: Devoulx, *Tachrifat*, 86.
1804		901	Devoulx, *Tachrifat*, 86.
1805		1,022–1,200	1,022: Devoulx, *Tachrifat*, 86; 1,200: Vicar apostolic Joussouy in Cresti, "Quelques réflexions," 159.
1806		1,228	Devoulx, *Tachrifat*, 86.
1807		1,267	Devoulx, *Tachrifat*, 86.
1808		1,422	Devoulx, *Tachrifat*, 86.
1809	0	1,500–1,545	1,500: Consul Charles-François Dubois-Thainville, "Mémoire sur l'Alger," in Esquer, *Reconnaissance des villes*, 134, 147; 1,545: Devoulx, *Tachrifat*, 86, cited in Cresti, "La Population," 478.
1810		1,357–[6,000]	1,357: Devoulx, *Tachrifat*, 86; 6,000: Laranda, *Neapolitan Captive*, 30; Nicholson, *An Affecting Narative*, 16–17.
1811		1,345–1,494	1,345/1,494 (360 Portuguese, 634 Neapolitans, 6 Austrians, 34 Sardinians, 53 Romans, 116 Greeks, 242 Sicilians, 49 Spanish): Devoulx, *Tachrifat*, 86, 87; 1,494: Panzac, *CB*, 98–99.
1812	52	1,475–1,645	1,475/1,645 (52 French, 52 Romans, 625 Neapolitans, 24 Americans, 8 Spanish, 372 Greeks, 10 Austrians, 34 Sardinians, 285 Sardinians, 5 from Doubra, 159 from Melilla, 19 Flemish): Devoulx, *Tachrifat*, 86–87.
1813	52	1,645–1,669	1,645: Panzac, *CB*, 98–99; 1,656/1,645 (52 French, 52 Romans, 625 Neapolitans, 24 Americans, 8 Spanish, 372 Greeks, 10 Austrians, 34 Sardinians, 285 Sardinians, 5 from Doubra, 159 from Melilla, 19 Flemish): Devoulx, *Tachrifat*, 86, 87; 1,669: Verdier, "L'Esclavage musulman," annex.
1814		1,487–2,000	1,525/1,487 (693 Neapolitans, 325 Sicilians, 30 Greeks, 159 from Melilla, 174 Romans, 33 Sardinians, 10 Americans, 26 Flemish, 26 Austrians, 6 Mallorcans, 5 from Taboulsa): Devoulx, *Tachrifat*, 86, 87; 1,600: Document annexed to report presented at the Congress of Vienna, 29 December 1814, reprinted in London *Times*, 11 January 1816, 4; 2,000: Shaler, *Sketches of Algiers*, 124.

Year	French	Christian	Source
1815		1,450–1,487	1,450/1,487 (693 Neapolitans, 325 Sicilians, 30 Greeks, 159 inhabitants of Melilla, 174 Romans, 33 Sardinians, 10 Americans, 26 Flemish, 26 Austrians, 6 Mallorcans, 5 from Taboulsa): Devoulx, *Tachrifat*, 86, 87; 1,487: Panzac, *CB*, 98–99.
1816	2–30	1,016–1,200	2: Playfair, *The Scourge of Christendom*, 274; 30: Dumont, *Histoire de l'esclavage*, 110; 1,016/1,606/1,065 (434 Neapolitans, 154 from Melilla, 10 Sardinians, 26 Flemish, 21 Austrians, 5 from Trabelsa, 4 Mallorcans, 234 Sicilians, 19 Greeks, 158 Romans): Devoulx, *Tachrifat*, 86, 87–88; 1,065: Panzac, *CB*, 98; 1,100: Boyer, *La Vie quotidienne*, 250; 1,200: Verdier, "L'Esclavage musulman," annex.
1830	1–2	122–400 [1,400]	1: *Journal des débats*, 22 July 1830; 122: *Beylik* registers, cited in Boyer, *La Vie quotidienne*, 24; Julien, *History of North Africa*, 320; Serval, *La Ténébreuse histoire*, 276–277; Gaffarel, *La Conquête de l'Algérie*, 110; Deslandres, *OT*, 1: 24; 200: Quatrebarbes, *Souvenirs de la campagne d'Afrique*, 63; 400: Grammont, "Etudes algériennes: la rédemption," 37; 1,400: Deslandres, *L'Eglise*, 63.

TUNIS

Year	French	Christians	Source
1535		7,000–[22,000]	7,000: Morgan, *A Complete History*, 308; 22,000 (a number Morgan discounts): Vertot d'Aubeuf, *Histoire des Chevaliers de Malte*, 201.
1592	19		Pignon, "L'Esclavage en Tunisie," 376.
1593	30		Grandchamp, *FT*, 1: 136–140.
1594		1,600	Ricard, "Ibero-Africana," 194.
1605	140–150		140–150: Savary de Brèves to CCM, ACCM, BB247 (OC), Paris, 24 October 1616, cited in Plantet, *CBT*, 1: 12; 150: Brèves, *Relation des voyages*, 305–353.

Year	French	Christians	Source
1608	600		Ambassador Jean-François de Gontaut-Biron, baron de Salignac, 22 May 1608, BN, MS 16146, f. 182, cited in Heinrich, *L'Alliance franco-algérienne*, 211.
1609	260–300	2,000	260: Foucques, *Mémoires*, reproduced in Grandchamp, *FT*, 3: 395; 300: Foucques to Henri IV, 21 and 24 May 1609, reproduced in Grandchamp, *FT*, 3: 384.
1613	300		Jan Jacomo Belegno, Flemish dragoman, to the States General of the United Provinces, Tunis, 8 January 1613, cited in Pignon-Reix, "Un Document inédit," 110 n. 20.
1615	377–380		377: List of slaves, ACCM, AA514 (OC), cited in Teissier, *Inventaire des archives historiques*, 222; 380: Anonymous slave letter, ACCM, G43, reprinted in Pignon-Reix, "Un Document inédit," 105–130.
1625		10,000	10,000: "In Urbe Tuneti . . . ," *Acta Sacra Congregatione de Propaganda Fide*, 20 January 1625, p. 188, cited in Mesnage, *Le Christianisme en Afrique*, 3: 203; Salvago, *Africa overo Barbaria*, reprinted in Grandchamp, "Une Mission delicate," 493.
1634		7,000	Dan, *Histoire de Barbarie* (1637), 285.
1640	41	7,500	41: Envoy Jean-Baptiste Coquiel to Richelieu, Marseille, 31 January 1640, AAE, MD, Afrique, vol. 8, f. 66, reprinted in Plantet, *CBT*, 1: 135; 7,500: Jean Coppin, *Le Bouclier de l'Europe, ou La Guerre Sainte . . .* (Lyon: Antoine Briesson, 1686), 407, cited in Debbasch, *La Nation française*, 113.
1643	150		Consuls to comte de Brienne, 17 November 1643, cited in Masson, *Histoire du commerce*, 38 n. 3.
1651		6,000	Bombard, "Les Vicaires apostoliques," 388.
1654		6,000–8,000	6,000: Consul Jean Le Vacher, cited in Debbasch, *La Nation française*, 113; 8,000: Francesco di San Lorenzo, *Breve relatione del calamitoso stato . . .* (Rome, 1654), cited in Davis, "Counting European Slaves," 100.
1659		10,000–12,000	Thévenot, *Relation d'un voyage*, 1: 549.

Year	French	Christians	Source
1660		6,000	Guénot and Vasquez in Galland, *Histoire de l'esclavage*, 8.
1664		4,000	CPF/SOCG, f. 65, cited in Davis, "Counting European Slaves," 100.
1665	360		List of French captives, 1665, BN, CCC 483, ff. 534–535.
1666	300–360 (48 Marseillais)		300 (after departure of Marseillais): Envoy Dumolin to admiral Beaufort, Tunis, 3 July 1666, AE, *CT*, reprinted in Plantet, *CBT*, 1: 228; 360: Instructions to Dumolin, Saint-Germain-en-Laye, 9 February 1666, AAE, MD, Afrique, vol. 8, f. 124, cited in Plantet, *CBT*, 1: 199; 48: "Rolle des esclaves de Marseille qu'il faut racheter . . . ," Marseille, 28 May 1666, AMM, GGL 105.
1670		5,000–6,000	CPF/SRC-1, f. 176, cited in Davis, "Counting European Slaves," 100.
1671	590		Memorandum by Sieur de Lormes, Marseille, 5 February 1671, AAE, MD, Afrique, vol. 6, f. 167, cited in Plantet, *CBT*, 1: 259.
1673	3		Consul Jean Ambrozin to Colbert, Tunis, 6 July 1673, AE, Tunis, reprinted in Plantet, *CBT*, 1: 285.
1680		2,300	2,000 "Christians" and "300 schismatics and heretics," CPF/SRC-1, f. 478, cited in Davis, "Counting European Slaves," 100.
1680–1681		2,000	Apostolic missionary Francesco Gatta, cited in Romano, "Schiavi siciliani," 278.
1681		2,200	In Tunis and ports: CPF/SRC-1, f. 583, cited in Davis, "Counting European Slaves," 100.
1683	27–41		27: Consul Claude Le Maire to Seignelay, Versailles, September 1683, AE, *CT*, reprinted in Plantet, *CBT*, 1: 374; 41: Colbert to Intendant of Provence Thomas-Alexandre Morant, Versailles, 24 February 1683, cited in Plantet, *CBT*, 1: 309.
1686		7,000–8,000	Mafrici, *Mezzogiorno e pirateria*, 97, cited in Davis, "Counting European Slaves," 100.
1690–1692	175–179		Consul Auger Sorhainde to Pontchartrain, Tunis, 15 December 1691, 14 January 1692, AE, Tunis, cited in Plantet, *CBT*, 1: 457–461.

Year	French	Christians	Source
1720	45–48		45: BN, NAF 22136, Providence, *CR*, 350; 48: Dusault to Conseil de Marine, cited in Plantet, *CBT*, 2: 132 n. 1.
1721		5,000	Catholics: CPF/SRC-4, f. 491, cited in Davis, "Counting European Slaves," 100.
1722		3,000	Catholics: CPF/SRC-4, f. 485, cited in Davis, "Counting European Slaves," 100.
1742	224–530		224: Vice-consul Louis Crozet to Maurepas, AE, *CT*, reprinted in Plantet, *CBT*, 2: 344–345; 530: Summary of April 1743 letter about Tunis, AN, AE BIII 27, 8.
1743	0		Summary of April 1743 letter about Tunis, AN, AE BIII 27, 8.
1749	3		Provincial de la Merci in Montpellier, 10 February 1749, AN, AE BIII 318, f. 146.
1752	0	~1,400	~1,400 (Genoese, other Italians, Maltese, Spanish, Portuguese): Serres, *Mémoires*, 17; 540 Genoese and Tabarkans: Bono, *I Corsari barbareschi*, 315.
1756		870–1,200	870: Krieken, *Corsaires et marchands*, 113; 944 (306 women and children): Journal of consul Vallière, Algiers, 29 November 1756, reprinted in Chaillou, *Textes pour servir*, 141; 1,100–1,200: Plantet, *CBT*, 3: 514.
1757		0 (taken to Algiers)	Sebag, *La Course tunisienne*, 42; Bono, *I Corsari barbareschi*, 315.
1767		+267	267 Catholics and "a few schismatic Greeks": CPF/SRC-7, f. 281, cited in Davis, "Counting European Slaves," 100.
1770	84 (Corsicans)		AN, AE BI 1144, cited in Valensi, "Esclaves chrétiens," 1282 n. 1.
1771		483	Catholics: CPF/SRC-7, f. 560, cited in Davis, "Counting European Slaves," 100.
1773		600	320 Catholics and 280 Greeks: CPF/SRC-7, f. 585, cited in Davis, "Counting European Slaves," 100.
1774	49 (Corsicans)	240	49: Consul Etienne-Lazare-Barthélemy de Saizieu to marine minister Antoine-Raymond-Jean-Gabriel de Sartine, Tunis, 12 December 1774, reprinted in Plantet, *CBT*, 3: 37; 240 Catholics: CPF/SRC-7, f. 653, cited in Davis, "Counting European Slaves," 100.

Year	French	Christians	Source
1776	42 (Corsicans)		Sheet approved by minister on ransoming Corsicans in Algiers and Tunis, December 1777, AN, AE BIII 13, f. 265 v; AN, AE BI 1147, cited in Valensi, "Esclaves chrétiens," 1282 n. 1.
1778	37 (21 Corsicans)		Extracts of decisions from king and ministers, 1778, AN, AE BIII 14, f. 102 v.
1779	35 (Corsicans)		Santoni, "Le rachat des Corses," 2.
1780		2,000	Arcs, *Mémoires*, 89.
1781	1		Bishop of La Rochefoucauld to Castries, 2 February 1781, CADN, CA, vol. 9, ff. 103–106.
1783		60–80	Desfontaines and Peysonnel, *Voyages dans les Régences*, 2: 38–39.
1786		200	+200: Venture de Paradis, *Tunis et Alger*, 69.
1793	8 (Corsicans)		Consul Jacques Devoise to François-Louis-Michel Chemin Deforgues, Tunis, 10 December 1793, reprinted in Plantet, *CBT*, 3: 225.
1797	13–18 (13 Corsicans)	600–1,500	13: Devoise to Talleyrand, Tunis, 20 November 1797, reprinted in Plantet, *CBT*, 3: 331; 18: AN, AFIII 74; 600: Riggio, "Un Censimento di schiavi"; 1,500: Grandchamp, cited in Riggio, "Mariano Stinca," *Archivio storico per la Calabria e la Lucania* 13 (1943–1944): 171–183, all cited in Valensi, "Esclaves chrétiens," 1282 n. 1 and 1278.
1798	136 (Corfiotes, Maltese, Corsicans)		Devoise to Talleyrand, Tunis, 31 December 1797, 8 July 1798; to Bonaparte, Tunis, 15 July 1798, reprinted in Plantet, *CBT*, 3: 340, 353, 354.
1799	74–145		74: Devoise to Talleyrand, Tunis, 26 February; 82: Devoise to Talleyrand, Tunis, 11 March; 106: Devoise to Talleyrand, Tunis, 10 May; 145: Devoise to bey Hammuda, Tunis, 17 June 1799, all reprinted in Plantet, *CBT*, 3: 381, 382, 388, 391.
1800	136–150		136: Devoise to Talleyrand, Tunis, 1 September; 150: Devoise to Talleyrand, Tunis, 16 June 1800, reprinted in Plantet, *CBT*, 3: 408, 411.
1802	66 (Piedometese from Elba and Caprera)		Rousseau, *ATN*, 239.

Year	French	Christians	Source
1803	23 (17 Romans, 6 Swiss)	2,750	23: Talleyrand to Devoise, Paris, 20 February 1803, reprinted in Plantet, *CBT*, 3: 449; 2,750 (750 from Saint-Peter's Island raid): Rousseau, *ATN*, 247–248.
1806	172 (39 Genoese, 16 Swiss, 3 Elbanese, 36 Corsicans and Cisalpinese, 73 Neapolitans, 5 Romans)	1,000	172: "Liste des sujets dey pays réunis à l'Empire français ou pris au service des princes de l'Empereur . . . ," reprinted in Plantet, *CBT*, 3: 465 n. 1; 1,000: Gaborieau, "Corsaires barbaresques," 143; Panzac, *CB*, 98.
1807		1,500–2,000	²/₃ Neapolitan: Holk, Danish consul 1801–1807, cited in the London *Times*, 2 December 1815, 2.
1809		2,600–3,000	About 2,600 (mostly Sicilian, also Roman, Sardinian, Neapolitan, and some Greek): Loth, *Arnoldo Soler*, 74; 3,000: Dubois-Thainville, "Mémoire sur l'Alger," in Esquer, *Reconnaissance des villes*, 147.
1810		1,050–1,618	1,050: Riggio, "Un Censimento di schiavi," 334; 1,600: as of January, Panzac, *CB*, 98; 1,618 (1,500 Sicilians and Neapolitans, 118 subjects of the Papal States): Vice-consul François-Joseph Billon to Conte de Champagny, 8 January 1810, reprinted in Plantet, *CBT*, 3: 486.
1811		1,200–2,000	1,200 as of March: Panzac, *CB*, 98; nearly 2,000, mostly Neapolitans: MacGill, *Nouveau voyage à Tunis*, 79, 82.
1812		500	500 (400 Neapolitans, 100 Romans): Billon to duc de Bassano, Tunis, 27 April 1812, reprinted in Plantet, *CBT*, 3: 502; 500: Gaborieau, "Corsaires barbaresques," 144; Rousseau, *ATN*, 278.
1815	2–3	600	2–3: Talleyrand to Devoise, Paris, 26 December 1815, cited in *CBT*, 3: 546; 600: Noah, *Travels*, 368; 400 Neapolitans: Panzac, *CB*, 99.
1816		781	781: Gaborieau, "Corsaires barbaresques," 154; Pey, "Tripoli de Barbarie," 127; 300 Sardinians: Devoise to Talleyrand, *CBT*, 3: 547.
1817		0	Gaborieau, "Corsaires barbaresques," 154.

TRIPOLI

Year	French	Christians	Source
1550		3,000	Féraud, *AT*, 56.
1553		450	[Girard], *HCRT*, vol. 1, f. 61 v.
1564	0	4,025	[Girard], *HCRT*, vol. 1, f. 61 v.
1572		2,200	[Girard], *HCRT*, vol. 1, f. 61 v.
1584		700	[Girard], *HCRT*, vol. 1, f. 61 v.
1612	150		French slaves to Marseille consuls, Tripoli, 18 February 1612, ACCM, G44.
1613		240	[Girard], *HCRT*, f. 61 v.
1629	150		French slaves, Tripoli, 30 April 1629, ACCM, AA555 (OC), cited in Masson, *Histoire du commerce*, 42.
1631	400		200 taken in January 1631, another 50 in March, ACCM, AA555 [OC], cited in Masson, *Histoire du commerce*, 42–43.
1634		400–500	Dan, *Histoire de Barbarie* (1637), 285.
1635		500	[Girard], *HCRT*, vol. 1, 61 v.
1641	10 (Marseillais)		10 Marseillais slaves to CCM, Tripoli, 18 May 1641, ACCM, G44.
1642	130		Apostolic vicar Cauto, AE Tripoli, 1642–1698, cited in Masson, *Histoire des établissements*, 61 n. 1.
1649		650	[Girard], *HCRT*, vol. 1, f. 61 v.
1655	400		Pierre Roman to CCM, Tripoli, 20 March 1655, ACCM, G44.
1658		1,000	"1,000 and more Christians": CPF/SOCG, f. 88, cited in Davis, "Counting European Slaves," 100.
1659		2,500	+2,500: CPF/SOCG, f. 90, cited in Davis, "Counting European Slaves," 100.
1660	186	1,150	186: Chevalier Paul to Mazarin, 27 July 1660, AN, Marine B4 2, f. 86, cited in Bachelot, *Louis XIV en Algérie*, 58; 1,150: [Girard], *HCRT*, vol. 1, f. 61 v.
1665		1,500	CPF/SOCG, f. 95, cited in Davis, "Counting European Slaves," 100.
1669	106 (Marseillais)	1,370	106: "Etat des esclaves . . . ," Algiers, 16 November 1669, ACCM CC156 (OC), cited in Masson, *Histoire des établissements*, 168 n. 3; 1,370: CPF/SRC-1, f. 166, cited in Davis, "Counting European Slaves," 100.

Year	French	Christians	Source
1671		1,559–1,650	1,559: [Girard], *HCRT*, vol. 1, f. 65 r; 1,650: Alonso, *LC*, 1: 271.
1672		1,658	[Girard], *HCRT*, vol. 1, f. 61 v.
1673	700		French slaves to Le Tellier, 12 October 1673, in [Girard], *HCRT*, vol. 2, f. 202 r.
1674		2,000	[Girard], *HCRT*, vol. 1, f. 61 v.
1675		2,130	[Girard], *HCRT*, fol. 1, f. 61 v.
1676	800	1,275	800: Arvieux, *Mémoires*, 5: 416; 1,275: [Girard], *HCRT*, vol. 1, ff. 61 v, 65 r.
1677		950	[Girard], *HCRT*, vol. 1, 65 r.
1679		1,700 (700 Catholics and 1,000 Greeks)	700 "our people" and 1,000 "schismatic Greeks," CPF/SRC-1, f. 457, cited in Davis, "Counting European Slaves," 100.
1680	800		Féraud, *AT*, 151.
1680–1681			Apostolic missionary Francesco Gatta, cited in Romano, "Schiavi siciliani," 278.
1681		1,000–1,200	1,200 made Easter confession / "a few more than 1,000": CPF/SRC-1, ff. 455, 503, cited in Davis, "Counting European Slaves," 100.
1682	313		Colbert to naval commander Abraham Duquesne, Versailles, 23 June 1682, AN, Marine, Dépêches concernant la marine 1682, f. 269, reprinted in Clément, *Lettres*, 3: 230.
1685	192–900	2,150	192: Admiral Jean d'Estrées, 2 July 1685, AAE, MD, Tunis, 1685, ff. 4–9, cited in Boutin, *Anciennes relations*, 99; 600 (200 in the city, 400 at sea): Elie de La Primaudaie, "Le Littoral de la Tripolitaine," 304; Peter, *Les Barbaresques*, 90; "900 French slaves and an infinity of Greeks, Maltese, Spaniards, and Italians, and no English or Dutch" / "2,150 Christian slaves of all nations": BN, NAF 7488, ff. 300, 295 v, reproduced in Berthier, "Tripoli de Barbarie," 13–30.
1686		1,500–2,000	Mafrici, *Mezzogiorno e pirateria*, 98, cited in Davis, "Counting European Slaves," 100.
1688	265		26 September 1688, AN, Marine B2 64, f. 198.
1689		500	"Barely 500": CPF/SRC-2, f. 378, cited in Davis, "Counting European Slaves," 100.

Year	French	Christians	Source
1691		270	Mafrici, *Mezzogiorno e pirateria*, 99, cited in Davis, "Counting European Slaves," 100.
1693	350		Dusault to Pontchartrain, 17 January 1693, CADN, CA, cited in Plantet, *CDA*, 1: 396–397 n. 3.
1704		194	Mafrici, *Mezzogiorno e pirateria*, 99, cited in Davis, "Counting European Slaves," 100.
1707	5		Rolle des esclaves françois, AN, AE BI 1090, f. 20.
1709		400	Féraud, *AT*, 204.
1728	34		Slave Joseph-Antoine Roux to parents in Saint Tropez, Tripoli, 30 July 1728, AN, AE BIII 317, f. 271.
1760	6		Berryer to CCM, 10 March 1760, ACCM, AA76 (OC), cited in Teissier, *Inventaire des archives historiques*, 54.
1765		30	Catholics: CPF/SRC-7, f. 274, cited in Davis, "Counting European Slaves," 100.
1766		25	Catholics: CPF/SRC-7, f. 299, cited in Davis, "Counting European Slaves," 100.
1767		30	Catholics: CPF/SRC-7, f. 364, cited in Davis, "Counting European Slaves," 100.
1783	0	?	Only Maltese, Genoese, Spanish: Tully, *Letters Written during a Ten Years' Residence*, 61.
1785		100	"100 around 1785": Anciennes Amies de Vieux Toulon, Fonds Vallière, Liasse 7, Mémoire sur Tripoli de Barbarie, 30 December 1785, p. 16, cited in Pey, "Tripoli de Barbarie," 123.
1786		100	Féraud, *AT*, 277.
1803		308	Americans on *The Philadelphia*: Dearden, *A Nest of Corsairs*, 165.
1805		500	Americans and Italians: Pey, "Tripoli de Barbarie," 123.
1815		400–500	400: Deliberation of consuls in Tripoli, 24 July 1815, reprinted in Howard, *Memoirs of Sir Sidney Smith*, 2: 330–333; 500: French consul Natal-Henri Mure d'Azir, 4 December 1815, cited in Micacchi, *La Tripolitania*, 191; 62 Genoese: cited in Folayan, *Tripoli*, 68.

Year	French	Christians	Source
1816	0	554–596	554: Douglas-Morris and Perkins, *Gunfire in Barbary*, 68; 580 (422 Neapolitans and Sicilians, 144 Sardinians and Genoese, 10 Romans, 4 Hamburgers): Playfair, *The Scourge of Christendom*, 72; Panzac, *CB*, 98; Rossi, *Storia di Tripoli*, 272; 590: Féraud, *AT*, 305; 594–596: Chater, *Dépendance et mutations*, 254–255.

MOROCCO

Year	French	Christians	Source
[1512]		3,000 (Tetouan)	Africanus, *Description de l'Afrique*, 268.
1550		1,000 (Fez)	Diego de Torres, *Relation de l'origine et succez des Cherifs . . .* (Paris: Jean Camusat, 1636), 418, cited in Meakin, *The Moorish Empire*, 304.
1578		2,000 (Marrakech)	Godard, *Description et histoire du Maroc*, 496.
1618	120 (Marrakech)		Penz, *Les Captifs français*, 23.
1619		30,000	Mesnage, *Le Christianisme en Afrique*, 3: 206.
1625			600 English (Salé): CSPD, Charles I, 1625–6, 1: 84, cited in Matar, *Islam and Britain*, 6–7; 1,500 English (Salé): Slave Robert Adams to his father, Salé, 4 November 1625, reprinted in Vitkus, *Piracy, Slavery, and Redemption*, 350.
1626			1,500 Britons (Salé): CSPD, Charles I, 1625–6, 1: 343, cited in Matar, *Britain and Barbary*, 51.
1627	270	2,000	Penz, *Les Captifs français*, 280.
1629	150 (Salé)		Slaves Le Floc et al. to Razilly, Salé, 9 August 1629, reprinted in Castries, Cossé Brissac, and Cenival, *SIHM* (1911), 1st ser., 3: 234.
1631	0 (Salé), 180 (Marrakech)		Penz, *Les Captifs français*, 40, 55.

Year	French	Christians	Source
1632			38 English (Marrakech) and 7–8 (Salé): Slave petition to Charles I, Marrakech, [fall–winter 1631–1632], reprinted in Vitkus, *Piracy, Slavery, and Redemption*, 359–360.
1634	300–430 (Salé), 20 (Marrakech)	1,500 (Salé)	300, 20: Antoine Cabiron, cited in Penz, *Les Captifs français*, 48; 430: Dan, *Histoire de Barbarie* (1637), 285.
1635	637		Penz, *Les Captifs français*, 49–50.
1639	150		Penz, *Les Captifs français*, 56.
1645	650		*Histoire de l'ordre sacré.*
1653		30 (Marrakech)	18 Catholics, 11–12 English Protestants: Franciscan Superior in Marrakech, cited in Koehler, "Quelques points," 182.
1660		30 (Marrakech)	Father Antonio de la Cruz, cited in Koehler, *L'Eglise chrétienne*, 109.
1662	5–6 (Tetouan)		Penz, *Les Captifs français*, 64.
1671	12 (Fez)	300	Jacques Gosse to brothers and sisters in La Rochelle, Fez, 20 August 1670, 1671, AAE, CC, Carton: Rachat des esclaves, reprinted in Castries, Cossé Brissac, and Cenival, *SIHM* (1922), 2nd ser., 1: 324.
1672	130 (Fez)	300–400 (Fez)	Francisco de San Juan de El Puerto, cited in Koehler, "Quelques points," 177–187; Moüette, *Relation de la captivité*, 139.
1672–1676		1,200 (200 Marrakech, 500 Fez, 200 Meknes, 300 Salé)	Father Luis de San-Augustin, cited in Nékrouf, *Une Amitié orageuse*, 25, and Koehler, *L'Eglise chrétienne*, 150.
1676	200		Marseille consuls, Marseille, 27 April 1676, AMM, HH 347 bis.
1678		200 (Meknes)	Moüette, *Relation de la captivité*, 66.
1680	130–400 (moved to Meknes thereafter)		130: Penz, *Les Captifs français*, 89; 400: P. Calault de Villalain to the marquis de Villars, Meknes, 29 June 1680, reprinted in Castries, Cossé Brissac, and Cenival, *SIHM* (1924), 2nd ser., 2: 494.
1681	120		Desmay, *Relation nouvelle et particulière*, 87, cited in Koehler, "Quelques points," 182.

Year	French	Christians	Source
1682	200		200: Penz, *Les Captifs français*, 123.
1684	200	700	200: Penz, *Les Captifs français*, 129; 500 (not counting French): Slaves in Meknes, APF, vol. 2, f. 181, cited in Maziane, "Les Captifs européens," 3.
1685		800–2,000	800: Phelps, *A True Account of the Captivity*, 12; 2,000: Miège, "Les Aspects de la course," 52 n. 32.
1687	270–400	1,300–1,500	270: Nékrouf, *Une Amitié orageuse*, 264–265; 400: Galley general Louis de Rochechouart, duc de Mortemart, to Seignelay, Bay of Cadiz, 20 July 1687, cited in Penz, *Les Captifs français*, 153, 157, 280; 1,500: Estelle to Seignelay, Meknes, 10 June 1687, cited in Koehler, *L'Eglise chrétienne*, 173.
1688	365		Penz, *Les Captifs français*, 171.
1689		3,000	Including 1,700 captured from Larache in November: Koehler, *L'Eglise chrétienne*, 151, 173; also including 400 English: Rogers, *A History of Anglo-Moroccan Relations*, 65.
1690	260	1,500–2,000	1,500 (700 Spanish, 300 Portuguese, 220 English): "The Captivity Narrative of John Whitehead" [c. 1697], Ms. Sloane 90, British Library, reprinted in Matar, *Britain and Barbary*, 186; 2,000: Miège, "Les Aspects de la course," 52 n. 32; Pellow, *La Relation de Thomas Pellow*, 19.
1691	286		"Liste des 286 esclaves François à Miquenez des différentes provinces de la France," 12 February 1691, cited in Castries, Cossé Brissac, and Cenival, *SIHM* (1927), 2nd ser., 3: 344 n. 1.
1692	324		Penz, *Les Captifs français*, 195.
1693	264 (5 Protestants removed)		Mémoire from Consul Jean-Baptiste d'Estelle, Salé, 16 and 23 October 1693, AAE, Maroc, CC, vol. 2, ff. 146–151, reprinted in Castries, Cossé Brissac, and Cenival, *SIHM* (1931), 2nd ser., 4: 217.
1694	285 (243 Meknes, 22 Salé, 12 Tetouan and Alcazar, 4 Tafilalet, 3 Fez, 1 Taroudant)		Census by Estelle, AAE, Maroc, CC, vol. 2, ff. 269–271, cited in Castries, Cossé Brissac, and Cenival, *SIHM* (1931), 2nd ser., 4: 383.

Year	French	Christians	Source
1696	279 (10 Protestants)		Census by Estelle in AAE, Maroc, CC, vol. 2, ff. 269–271, cited in Castries, Cossé Brissac, and Cenival, *SIHM* (1931), 2nd ser., 4: 376–388.
1698	254 (20 Protestants)		Census by Estelle, AAE, Maroc CC, vol. 2, ff. 428–429, cited in Castries, Cossé Brissac, and Cenival, *SIHM* (1931), 2nd ser., 4: 630–632.
1701	(34 Protestants)		224 English, 34 French Protestants: Rogers, *A History of Anglo-Moroccan Relations*, 70.
1702	(34 Protestants)		0 English, 34 French Protestants: Rogers, *A History of Anglo-Moroccan Relations*, 71.
1703	240 (34 Protestants)		Castries, Cossé Brissac, and Cenival, *SIHM* (1960), 2nd ser., 6: 13, 14 n. 1.
1704	150		*Relation succincte de plusieurs avantures*; ADH 50H50.
1705	174 (34 Protestants transferred to Tangiers)		174: 11 April 1705, cited in Castries, Cossé Brissac, and Cenival, *SIHM* (1960), 2nd ser., 6: 14 n. 1; 34: Rogers, *A History of Anglo-Moroccan Relations*, 74.
1706	133 (29 Protestants)		133: 16 June 1706, cited in Castries, Cossé Brissac, and Cenival, *SIHM* (1960), 2nd ser., 6: 14 n. 1; 29: Rogers, *A History of Anglo-Moroccan Relations*, 74.
1707	158–160 (0 Protestants)		160, 158: 20 May, 30 August, cited in Castries, Cossé Brissac, and Cenival, *SIHM* (1960), 2nd ser., 6: 14 n. 1; 0: Rogers, *A History of Anglo-Moroccan Relations*, 76.
1708	143–150	800–883	143 (more exact): AN, AE BI 828, pp. 244–247, cited in Castries, Cossé Brissac, and Cenival, *SIHM* (1960), 2nd ser., 6: 14 n. 1, 713; 800: Mathiex, "Trafic et prix de l'homme," 164 n. 1; Penz, *Les Captifs français*, 280; Pellow, *La Relation de Thomas Pellow*, 19; 883 (150 French, 400 Spanish [+107 just ransomed], 200 Portuguese, ~20 Italians, 6 Dutch): Néant, *Relation de ce qui s'est passé*, 203.
1709	130–139		Under 130, 139: 15 May, 3 August 1709, cited in Castries, Cossé Brissac, and Cenival, *SIHM* (1960), 2nd ser., 6: 14 n. 1; 130: Néant, *Relation de ce qui s'est passé*, 295.

Year	French	Christians	Source
1710	129–138		Around 129, 138: 12 June, 7 September 1710, cited in Castries, Cossé Brissac, and Cenival, *SIHM* (1960), 2nd ser., 6: 14 n. 1.
1711	120–130 (2 women)	839–1,000	127, 120, 130 French: 31 January, 20 August, 30 November 1711, cited in Castries, Cossé Brissac, and Cenival, *SIHM* (1960), 2nd ser., 6: 14 n. 1; 839: Castries, Cossé Brissac, and Cenival, *SIHM* (1960), 2nd ser., 6: 14 n. 1; 1,000: Juan de la Concepción, *Relación veridical . . . de las santas Misiones de Mequinez, Fez, Zalé, y Tetuán . . .* [1712], 16, cited in Maziane, "Les Captifs européens," 4; 2 women: Penz, *Personnalités et familles*, 162.
1713	114 (19 Salé)		114: Castries, Cossé Brissac, and Cenival, *SIHM* (1960), 2nd ser., 6: 14 n. 1; 19: 7 September 1713, M. Lempereur, Saint-Malo, 23 December 1714, AN, Marine B3 221, f. 372.
1714	110 (10 Larache)	[5,000–6,000]	110: Castries, Cossé Brissac, and Cenival, *SIHM* (1960), 2nd ser., 6: 14; 10: M. Lempereur, Saint-Malo, 23 December 1714, AN, Marine B3 221, f. 372; 5,000–6,000: Busnot, *Histoire du regne de Mouley Ismael*, 169.
1716			125 English: Rogers, *A History of Anglo-Moroccan Relations*, 84.
1717			153 English: Rogers, *A History of Anglo-Moroccan Relations*, 84.
1718	122–123		122: Castries, Cossé Brissac, and Cenival, *SIHM* (1960), 2nd ser., 6: 14 n. 1; 123: Penz, *Personnalités et familles*, 202–203.
1719			188 English: SP 71/16/304–305, cited in Matar, "Introduction," in Vitkus, *Piracy, Slavery, and Redemption*, 15
1720	130 (13 Marseillais)		130: 13 Marseillais slaves to CCM, Meknes, 12 August 1720, ACCM, G45.
1721	152	1,100–[25,000]	1,100/1,114 (152 French, 300 English, 400 Spanish, 165 Portuguese, 69 Dutch, 25 Genoese, 3 Greeks): Windus, *A Journey to Mequinez*, 99; 25,000: al-Zayyani, *Le Maroc*, 54; 293 English: Rogers, *A History of Anglo-Moroccan Relations*, 86.

Year	French	Christians	Source
1723	170–179	660–748	170/748: Genoese slave Andres Mayo, cited in Maziane, *Salé et ses corsaires*, 273; 179: Archives Marine Toulon 1S2, cited in Cocard, *Les Pères de la Merci*, 230; 660: Mathiex, "Trafic et prix de l'homme," 164 n. 1; 0 English: Rogers, *A History of Anglo-Moroccan Relations*, 86.
1724	130	734	130 French, 350 Spanish, 160 Portuguese, 70 Dutch, 4 English, 20 Genoese: La Faye et al., *Relation en forme du journal*, 79–80.
1727	117–130 (Meknes)		117: [Adrien-Maurice de Mairault], *Relation de ce qui s'est passé* . . . (Paris: Chaubert, 1742), cited in Penz, *Journal du consulat*, iii; 130: Castries, Cossé Brissac, and Cenival, *SIHM* (1960), 2nd ser., 6: 14.
1730	92–93		92: Trinitarian general Massac to marine minister, Paris, 26 March 1730, AN, AE BIII 318, f. 5; 93: La Véronne, *Documents inédits*, 2: 1.
1734	68		68: Penz, *Personnalités et familles*, 35; 142/0 English: Rogers, *A History of Anglo-Moroccan Relations*, 91.
1737	88–89 (75 Meknes, 13–14 Marseillais in Tangiers)		75: Koehler, *L'Eglise chrétienne*, 151; Penz, *Personnalités et familles*, 58; 13: Bureau de la redemption des pauvres esclaves de la ville de Marseille, Marseille, 28 February 1738, AN, AE BIII 318, f. 73; 14: Number of sailors redeemed from Tangiers, Intendant de la marine Villeblanche, Toulon, 29 January 1739, AN, Marine B3 393, f. 48.
1738	17 (0 Meknes, 17 Marseillais in Salé and Tangiers)		0: Koehler, *L'Eglise chrétienne*, 151.
1739	6 (Ceuta deserters in Tangiers)		Trinitarian Massac (8 April) and Mercedarian Deverny (10 April 1739) to marine minister, AN, AE BIII 318, ff. 83–84.
1740	9 (0 Tangiers, 9 Meknes)	150–250	9: Masson, *Histoire des établissements*, 360; 150–200: Pellow, *La Relation de Thomas Pellow*, 19; 250: Miège, "Les Aspects de la course," 52 n. 32.

Year	French	Christians	Source
1743	22 (13 Marseillais in Tangiers, 9 Bretons in Meknes)		Trinitarian Massac to marine minister, Paris, 18 July 1743, AN, AE BIII 318, ff. 91, 102–103.
1746			87 English: Rogers, *A History of Anglo-Moroccan Relations*, 92.
1748–1749			52 English: Rogers, *A History of Anglo-Moroccan Relations*, 93, 94.
1750			90 English: Rogers, *A History of Anglo-Moroccan Relations*, 95.
1751			0 English: Rogers, *A History of Anglo-Moroccan Relations*, 95.
1753	60		Summary of information about Morocco, AN, AE BIII 29, f. 23.
1754	36		Letter from liberated captives, 1755, AN, AE BIII 318, f. 200.
1755	75 (66 Fez, 9 Meknes)		31 December 1755, AN, Marine B7 403, cited in Masson, *Histoire des établissements*, 617 n. 2.
1756		A few dozen	A few dozen: Pellow, *La Relation de Thomas Pellow*, 19; 19 British: Rogers, *A History of Anglo-Moroccan Relations*, 97.
1757	53		Jean Olive, Mercedarian vicar general, Paris, 28 January 1757, AN, AE BIII 318, f. 208.
1758	52 (throughout Morocco), 23 (Salé)		52: Mémoire from the Trinitarians and Mercedarians, 20 January 1758, AN, AE BIII 318, f. 274; 23: Captain Pierre-Julien Dupuis, slave in Salé, to M. Marck, merchant in Hâvre de Grace, 16 September 1672, ADF, B4687, cited in inventory; 350 British: Rogers, *A History of Anglo-Moroccan Relations*, 102.
1760		100–150	100–150: Miège, "Les Aspects de la course," 52 n. 32; almost no British: Rogers, *A History of Anglo-Moroccan Relations*, 102.
1762	120 (Salé)		120: Slave Dupuis, ADF, B4687.

Year	French	Christians	Source
1763	118–128		118: List of all crews and ships seized, AN, AE BIII 319, f. 26; 128: BN, NAF 6236, p. 9, cited in Cocard, *Les Pères de la Merci*, 230; memorandum from Mercedarian general Pierre-Gaspard Toustain and Trinitarian general Gabriel Lefebvre, November 1763, AN, AE BIII 319, f. 4.
1764	100		Trinitarian and Mercedarian vicar generals to Praslin, January 1764, AN, AE BIII 319, f. 13.
1765	260 (Salé)		Slave Joseph Roza to his wife, Algiers, 5 January 1765, AN, AE BI 132, ff. 34–35, cited in Touili, *Correspondance*, 532.
1766	223		223: Secretary of state Louis-Phélypeaux, comte de Saint Florentin, to bishop of Dol, ADIV G164, cited in Thomassy, *Des Relations politiques*, 150; "over 200": AAE, Maroc, vol. 3, ff. 62 and 65 v, cited in Deslandres, *OT*, 2: 430–431.
1767	300 (115 Mogador)		"over 300": Décisions du roy du conseil d'état et du ministre de la marine, 13 August 1774, AN, AE BIII 10, f. 110; 115: Penz, *Personnalités et familles*, 182.
1774	300		Memorandum from slave Dupuis, AN, AE BIII 193, IV, f. 44.
1786		6–7 Spaniards (shipwreck victims)	Thomas Barclay, Report on Morocco, Tangiers, 10 September 1786, reprinted in Roberts and Roberts, *Thomas Barclay*, 286.
1815	0	0	Noah, *Travels*, 101.

Appendix 2:
Religious Redemptions and
Processions

Year	Order[a]	Destination	Number redeemed	Procession?[b]	Source
1505	T	Tunis	?	N	Alonso, *LC*, 1: 195, 198.
1539–1540	T	Algiers	54	N	Dan, *Histoire de Barbarie* (1637), 283; Providence, *CR*, 74; Alonso, *LC*, 1: 195–196, 198.
1544	T	Algiers	64	N	Alonso, *LC*, 1: 196, 198.
1589–1603	T	Algiers and others	57	?	Alonso, *LC*, 1: 200, 230.
1602	T	Gran, Hungary	74–80	Y (2 months)	Michelin et al., *Le Tableau de Piété*, 53–54; BN, NAF 22136; Providence, *CR*, 313–316; Alonso, *LC*, 1: 201–202, 230.
1610–1628	T	Algiers, Tunis, Constantinople	158	?	Michelin et al., *Le Tableau de Piété*, 54; Alonso, *LC*, 1: 200–201, 230.
1629–1631	M	Salé	50	Y	*Histoire de l'ordre sacré* (1685), 808–811; Penz, *Les Captifs français*, 57; Armand, *Voyages d'Afrique*, 33, cited in Cocard, "PM," 2: 345.

[a] T = Trinitarians, M = Mercedarians
[b] Indicates whether a procession took place. Length, if known, is indicated in parentheses.

Year	Order[a]	Destination	Number redeemed	Procession?[b]	Source
1635	T	Tunis	42–44	Y (2 months)	Dan, *Histoire de Barbarie* (1637), 67–68; *L'Eminente charité* (1641), 11; Michelin et al., *Le Tableau de Piété*, 54; Providence, *CR*, 253–282; Alonso, *LC*, 1: 203–207, 230.
1637	T	Tunis	36	Y (1 month)	Michelin et al., *Le Tableau de Piété*, 55; Providence, *CR*, 292–293; Alonso, *LC*, 1: 208, 230.
1641	T	Tunis	40–41	Y (1 month)	*L'Eminente charité* (1641); Michelin et al., *Le Tableau de Piété*, 58–59; BN, NAF 22136; Providence, *CR*, 289–292; Alonso, *LC*, 1: 208–210, 230.
1642	T	Salé	41	Y (1 month)	BN, NAF 22136; Providence, *CR*, 308–312; Alonso, *LC*, 1: 210, 230.
1643	T	Algiers	47–51	Y (3 months)	Hérault, *Récit veritable*; Hérault, *Les Larmes et clameurs*, 21; Providence, *CR*, 295–298; Alonso, *LC*, 1: 211–212, 230.
1644	M	Algiers	[69]–163	Y	Egreville, *La Vive Foy*, 4, 13, 46, 69–70; [Auvry], *Le Miroir de la charité*, 214–223; *Catalogue des esclaves* (1681); *Histoire de l'ordre sacré* (1685), 878–881; Lambert, "L'Oeuvre de la rédemption," 366; François Favre, *Le Véritable récit de la rédemption faite en Alger* . . . (Paris: L. Feugé, 1645), 47, cited in Turbet-Delof, *Bibliographie critique*, 133–134; AMM, GG108, cited in Cocard, "PM," 2: 345.
1645–1646	T	Algiers	108–110 (2 groups)	Y (1–2 months)	Providence, *CR*, 302–307; Alonso, *LC*, 1: 213–220, 230.
1651	M	Algiers	10	N	*Catalogue des esclaves* (1681); *Histoire de l'ordre sacré* (1685), 919.

Year	Order[a]	Destination	Number redeemed	Procession?[b]	Source
1653	M	Tunis	?	?	Boussion, "Les Ordres religieux à Toulon," cited in Cocard, "PM," 2: 345.
1653	T	Tunis	31	Y (1 month)	BN, NAF 22136.
1654	T	Salé	43–55	Y (1 month)	Michelin et al., *Le Tableau de Piété*, 59–60; Héron, *Relation du voyage*, 70; BN, NAF 22136; Penz, *Les Captifs français*, 53–62; Alonso, *LC*, 1: 220–222, 230.
1655	M	Algiers	13–18	Y	[Auvry], *Le Miroir de la charité*, 225–227; *Catalogue des esclaves* (1681); Germain, "Oeuvre de la rédemption," 173 n. 1. Also Fasion and Gillon, *Catalogue des esclaves* (1655); AN, S4291 (2nd folder), and *Gazette de France* (1656), all cited in Cocard, "PM," 2: 345.
1658	M	Tunis, Tripoli, Algiers	24	Y	[Auvry], *Le Miroir de la charité*, 229–232; *Catalogue des esclaves* (1681); *Histoire de l'ordre sacré* (1685), 919, 926.
1659–1660	T	Algiers	57	Y (2½ months)	Michelin et al., *Le Tableau de Piété*, 60; Héron, *Relation du voyage*, 70–79; BN, NAF 22136; Alonso, *LC*, 1: 222–223, 230.
1662	M	Algiers	95–96	Y (1½ months)	[Auvry], *Le Miroir de la charité*, 150–162; ADG, H159, and *Gazette de France* (1662), both cited in Cocard, "PM," 2: 345.
1666	M	Tunis	17–48	Y	*Catalogue des esclaves* (1681); *Histoire de l'ordre sacré* (1685), 945.
1666	T	Algiers, Tunis	60	Y (2 months)	Michelin et al., *Le Tableau de Piété*, 62–144; Alonso, *LC*, 1: 223–225, 230.
1667	M	Algiers	38–39 (and 500 by king)	Y (1 day)	*Catalogue des esclaves* (1681); *Histoire de l'ordre sacré* (1685), 946; *Gazette de France* (1667), cited in Cocard, "PM," 2: 345.

Year	Order[a]	Destination	Number redeemed	Procession?[b]	Source
1667	T	Algiers	55–57	Y (1½ months)	Michelin et al., *Le Tableau de Piété*, 159–166; BN, NAF 22136; Alonso, *LC*, 1: 225, 230.
1669	M	Tunis, Tripoli, Algiers	17–25	Y	*Catalogue des esclaves* (1681); *Histoire de l'ordre sacré* (1685), 947; Germain, "Oeuvre de la rédemption," 178 n. 1; Féraud, *AT*, 130.
1670	T	Algiers	31	Y	Providence, *CR*, 315 n. 1; Alonso, *LC*, 1: 226, 230.
1671	T	Tripoli	90	?	BN, NAF 22136; Alonso, *LC*, 1: 271.
1674	M	Algiers	39	?	*Catalogue des esclaves* (1681).
1674–1676	M	Salé, Fez, Tetouan	52–75 (incl. 2 women)	Y	*Histoire de l'ordre sacré* (1685), 957; Gaudin, "Le Rachat des captifs," 113–114; Germain, "Oeuvre de la rédemption," 173; Penz, *Les Captifs français*, 77–79; Castries, Cossé Brissac, and Cenival, *SIHM* (1960), 2nd ser., 6: 615 n. 2; *Gazette de France* (1674), cited in Cocard, "PM," 2: 345.
1675	T	Algiers	91	Y	*Liste des esclaves françois*; Alonso, *LC*, 1: 226–227, 230.
1677	T	Algiers	19	?	BN, NAF 22136.
1679	T	Algiers	50	?	BN, NAF 22136; Alonso, *LC*, 1: 227, 230.
1680–1681	M	Ceuta, Salé, Meknes, Tetouan	72–79	Y (2½ months)	*Catalogue des esclaves* (1681); Moüette, *Relation de la captivité*, 134–160; Penz, *Les Captifs français*, 87–92; *Mercure galant* (1681): 237–257, cited in Turbet-Delof, *La Presse périodique*, 74–82; Desmay, *Relation nouvelle*, cited in Cocard, "PM," 2: 345.
1685–1686	T	Tunis, Algiers	53–55	Y	BN, NAF 22136; Alonso, *LC*, 1: 228, 230.

Year	Order[a]	Destination	Number redeemed	Procession?[b]	Source
1690	M	Algiers	113–150	Y (1 day)	AN, AE BIII 316, p. 33; Néant, *Relation de ce qui s'est passé*, 4; *Histoire de l'ordre* (1691), cited in Turbet-Delof, *Bibliographie critique*, 232; *Gazette de France* (1692): 263, cited in Jameson, *Montesquieu et l'esclavage*, 28; AN, S4291 (2nd folder), and ADG H146(3), cited in Cocard, "PM," 2: 345.
1690	T	Algiers	54	?	BN, NAF 22136; Alonso, *LC*, 1: 228–229, 230.
1692	T	Algiers	44–49	Y	BN, NAF 22136; *Gazette de France* (1692): 263, cited in Jameson, *Montesquieu et l'esclavage*, 28; Alonso, *LC*, 1: 229, 230.
1700	T	Tunis, Tripoli, Algiers	64	Y (1 month)	*Mercure galant* (October 1700): 56–62; [Comelin and La Motte], *Etat des Royaumes*; BN, NAF 22136; Providence, *CR*, 380–382; Grimaldi-Hierholtz, *Les Trinitaires de Fontainebleau*, 105; Alonso, *LC*, 1: 231–233, 264.
1704–1705	T, M	Salé, Meknes	9–12	N	*Avis au public*; *Relation succincte*; Néant, *Relation de ce qui s'est passé*, 409–418; Cocard, "PM," 2: 345; Alonso, *LC*, 1: 233–235, 264.
1708–1709	T, M	Salé, Meknes	34–45	N	*Avis au public*; *Relation succincte*; Néant, *Relation de ce qui s'est passé*, 409–418; Providence, *CR*, 341, 382; Cocard, "PM," 2: 345; Alonso, *LC*, 1: 235–237, 264.
1712	T, M	Ceuta, Marrakech	20–22	Y (less than a month)	*Avis au public*; *Relation succincte*; Néant, *Relation de ce qui s'est passé*, 409–418; BN, NAF 22136; Providence, *CR*, 338–343; Alonso, *LC*, 1: 237–239, 264; Cocard, "PM," 2: 345.

Year	Order[a]	Destination	Number redeemed	Procession?[b]	Source
1716	M	Marrakech	12–13	N	*Avis au public*; Néant, *Relation de ce qui s'est passé*, 409–418; Alonso, *LC*, 1: 239, 264.
1719–1720	M	Algiers	26–35	Y	Providence, *CR*, 348; ADG, H 162 (4) and H 146 (2), cited in Cocard "PM," 2: 345.
1719–1720	T	Algiers	58–63	Y (2 months)	*Ordre de la Procession* (1720); BN, NAF 22136; Providence, *CR*, 353–355; Alonso, *LC*, 1: 239–241, 264.
1720	T	Tunis	45–60	Y (2 months)	*Relation de la Procession*; [Comelin, La Motte, and Bernard], *Voyage*, 155–169; BN, NAF 22136; Germain, "Oeuvre de la rédemption," 188–191; Providence, *CR*, 355–359; Alonso, *LC*, 1: 242–243.
1724–1725	T	Meknes, Algiers	63–65 (17 from Meknes; 46, including many foreigners, from Algiers)	Y (2 months)	AN, Marine B3 317, pièce 246; *Ordre de la Procession* (1725), 8; BN, NAF 22136; Providence, *CR*, 383–386; Alonso, *LC*, 1: 243–245, 264; La Faye et al., *Relation en forme du journal*, 152–161.
1729–1730	M	Salé, Meknes, Algiers	46–47 (only 2 from Salé and Meknes)	Y (1 month)	*Liste des Esclaves Chrestiens*; *Ordre de la Procession* (1729); ADAU, 5J42, cited in Cocard, "PM," 2: 345; Durand to Maurepas, Algiers, 20 April 1729, AN, AE BI 121, ff. 385–390, cited in Touili, *Correspondance*, 228.
1729–1730	T	Algiers	17–18 (Flemish)	Y	*Ordre de la procession* (1730); BN, NAF 22136; Providence, *CR*, 386; Deslandres, *OT*, 2: 392; Alonso, *LC*, 1: 245–246, 264.

Year	Order[a]	Destination	Number redeemed	Procession?[b]	Source
1730	T	Algiers	43–53 (possibly in cooperation with M in 1729–1730, above)	?	BN, NAF 22136; Devy, "Le Couvent narbonnais," 64.
1732	T	Constantinople	40	Y (3 months)	Jehannot, *Voyage à Constantinople*, 395–401; *Ordre de la procession* (1732); BN, NAF 22136; Providence, *CR*, 373–378; Alonso, *LC*, 1: 247–248, 264.
1732	T	Meknes	6	?	BN, NAF 22136; Providence, *CR*, 387; Alonso, *LC*, 1: 248–249, 264.
1735	T	Algiers	1	?	BN, NAF 22136; Providence, *CR*, 387.
1735–1748	T	Algiers	34–36	?	BN, NAF 22136; Providence, *CR*, 390–39; Alonso, *LC*, 1: 250–251, 264.
1737	M	Meknes, Fez	37	Y	Germain, "Oeuvre de la rédemption," 193 n. 1; "Liste de la rédemption générale," ADH, 50H30, cited in Cocard, "PM," 2: 345.
1737	T	Algiers	1	?	Providence, *CR*, 387.
1737	T, M	Salé, Tangiers	72–98 (14 from Tangiers, remainder from Salé)	Y (2 months)	BN, NAF 22136; Teissier, *Inventaire sommaire*, 319 n. 421; Providence, *CR*, 387–390; Alonso, *LC*, 1: 249–250, 264.
1750	T, M	Algiers	105–106 (incl. 20 Oraners)	Y	*Noms des cent cinq esclaves*; *Ordre de la Procession* (1750); *Liste des captifs françois* (1751); BN, NAF 22136; Providence, *CR*, 391–394; Deslandres, *OT*, 2: 415; Gaudin, "Le Rachat des captifs," 118–120; Cocard, "PM," 2: 345; Alonso, *LC*, 1: 251–252, 264.

Year	Order[a]	Destination	Number redeemed	Procession?[b]	Source
1754	T, M	Fez	27–36	Y	*L'Ordre et la Marche* (1754); *Liste des LXX captives*; BN, NAF 22136; Providence, *CR*, 395; Gaudin, "Le Rachat des captifs," 118–120; *L'Ordre et la marche* (1765), cited in Cocard, "PM," 2: 345; Robert A. Schneider, *The Ceremonial City*, 114–116; Alonso, *LC*, 1: 252–253, 264.
1756–1758	T, M	Fez, Salé, Marrakech	50–70	Y	*Liste des LXX captives*; BN, NAF 22136; Providence, *CR*, 395–397; Alonso, *LC*, 1: 253, 264.
1756–1765	T, M	Algiers	5–7	?	Providence, *CR*, 398; Alonso, *LC*, 1: 254, 264.
1759	T, M	Algiers	1	N	BN, NAF 22136; Providence, *CR*, 398.
~1760	T, M	Morocco	70	N	Penz, *Personnalités et familles*, 7, 19; and Mercedarian Migard, Toulouse, 7 April 1782, AN, AAE BIII 321 f. 8.
1763–1765	T, M	Mogador	72–98	Y (3 months)	Forestz, "Journal de ce qui est passé" (1765), BN, NAF 6236; *Rédemption des quatre-vingts captifs* (1765); *L'Ordre et la marche* (1765); Fleury, *Mandement de Mgr. l'Eveque* (1766); BN, NAF 22136; Penz, *Personnalités et familles*, 188; BN, NAF 6236 and MS 6680, cited in Cocard, "PM," 2: 345; Alonso, *LC*, 1: 256–257, 264.
1767	T, M	Safi	145–194	N (?)	BN, NAF 22136; Alonso, *LC*, 1: 258–259, 264.
1779	T, M	Tunis, Algiers	74–78 (incl. 6 women, 13 children)	Y (1 month)	*Liste des Esclaves rachetés a Tunis*; BN, NAF 22136; Deslandres, *OT*, 1: 419, 2: 457; AN, S 4285 (62), cited in Cocard, "PM," 2: 345; Alonso, *LC*, 1: 259–260, 264; Santoni, "Le Rachat des Corses," 15–16.

Year	Order[a]	Destination	Number redeemed	Procession?[b]	Source
1785	T, M	Algiers	313–316	Y (2 months)	*Voyage dans les états barbaresques*; Ordre de la marche; BN, NAF 22136; Providence, *CR*, 398–411; Deslandres, *OT*, 1: 419; Raynal, "Mémoires divers," BN, FF 6429, f. 21, cited in Cocard, "PM," 2: 345; Alonso, *LC*, 1: 263, 264.
1786	T, M	Algiers	1	N	BN, NAF 22136.
1789	T, M	Algiers	2	N	BN, NAF 22136.

Notes

INTRODUCTION

1. Representative Nick Smith of Michigan, "America's Enemies Will Be Brought to Justice," *Congressional Record* 147, 117 (11 September 2001): 5497. An extremely suggestive analysis of the "Barbary analogy" in post-9/11 America and its relevance to contemporary France is Paul A. Silverstein, "The New Barbarians: Piracy and Terrorism on the North African Frontier," *New Centennial Review* 5, 1 (2005): 179–212.

2. The initial responses include "Cries of 'War' Stumble over the Law," *Los Angeles Times*, 13 September 2001; interview with military expert James Dunnigan, *Today in New York*, WNBC-TV, 13 September 2001; interview with retired army strategist Ralph Peters, WTOP-AM, 18 September 2001.

3. Samuel Huntington, "The Clash of Civilizations," *Foreign Affairs* 72, 3 (1993): 22–49. See also, among others, Richard Leiby, "Terrorists by Another Name: The Barbary Pirates," *Washington Post*, 15 October 2001, C01; Chris Mooney, "The Barbary Analogy," *American Prospect Online*, 16 October 2001, http://www.prospect.org/cs/articles?article=the_barbary_analogy; Berry Craig, "Bin Ladin, His Followers Remind Historian of Barbary Pirates," Associated Press, 5 December 2001; Rand H. Fishbein, "Echoes from the Barbary Coast," *National Interest* (Winter 2001–2002): 47–51.

4. Paul Johnson, "21st-Century Piracy: The Answer to Terrorism? Colonialism," *WSJ.com Opinion Journal*, http://online.wsj.com/public/page/news-opinion-commentary.html, 6 October 2001. With the American military project in the Middle East well under way two years later, the Pentagon considered another French model for the "war on terrorism" when it screened Gillo Pontecorvo's 1967 film about the moral ambiguities of colonial rule and resistance, *The Battle of Algiers*.

5. Anthropologist Michael Herzfield, searing critic of the Mediterranean unity thesis, wondered if France gets excluded from ethnographies of the region because it "belongs to a different category of countries—imperial, northern, universalist, and rationalist" and is "a country that—unlike Portugal, Spain, Greece and sometimes Italy—does not generate 'ethnic food' in North America but is instead the authoritative source of *haute cuisine*." "Practical Mediterraneanism: Excuses

for Everything, from Epistemology to Eating," in *Rethinking the Mediterranean*, ed. William Vernon Harris (Oxford: Oxford University Press, 2005), 60.

6. By contrast, Spanish schoolchildren still learn that Cervantes was a prisoner in Algiers. On that subject, see Maria Antonia Garcés, *Cervantes in Algiers: A Captive's Tale* (Nashville: Vanderbilt University Press, 2002). Meanwhile, Italian scholars inspired by the research Salvatore Bono pioneered with *I Corsari barbareschi* (Turin: ERI, edizioni RAI radiotelevisione italiana, 1964) continue to detail the economic and religious impact of Ottoman privateering on the city-states.

7. Eugène Plantet, ed., *Correspondance des deys d'Alger avec la cour de France, 1579–1833* (hereafter *CDA*), 2 vols. (Paris: Félix Alcan, 1889), 1: lxxv. Other major contributions to what Edmund Burke III calls the "French colonial archive on Islam" ("The Sociology of Islam: The French Tradition," in *Islamic Studies: A Tradition and Its Problems*, ed. Malcolm H. Kerr [Santa Monica, CA: Undena, 1980], 73–99) include Plantet, ed., *Correspondance des beys de Tunis et des consuls de France avec la cour, 1577–1830* (hereafter *CBT*), 3 vols. (Paris: Félix Alcan, 1893–1899); Pierre Grandchamp, ed., *La France en Tunisie* (hereafter *FT*), 10 vols. (Tunis: J. Aloccio, 1920–1937); and Henry de Castries, Philippe de Cossé Brissac, and Pierre de Cenival, eds., *Les Sources inédites de l'histoire du Maroc de 1530 à 1845* (hereafter *SIHM*), 3 ser., 30 vols. (Paris: Paul Geuthner, 1905–1960).

8. Jean Pierre Edmond Jurien de la Gravière, *Les Corsaires barbaresques et la marine de Soliman le Grand* (Paris: E. Plon, Nourrit, 1887), 286, 301, 313. For similar pronouncements, see Charles de Rotalier, *Histoire d'Alger et de la piraterie des Turcs dans la Méditerranée à dater du seizième siècle*, 2 vols. (Paris: Paulin, 1841); Henri Delmas de Grammont, "Etudes algériennes: la course, l'esclavage, la rédemption," *Revue historique* 25–27 (1884–1885): 1–42, 1–44, 1–37; Grammont, *Histoire d'Alger sous la domination turque (1515–1830)* (hereafter *HA*) (Paris: Ernest Leroux, 1887; reprint, Paris: Bouchène, 2002); and Ernest Mercier, *Histoire de l'Afrique septentrionale (Berbérie) depuis les temps les plus reculés jusqu'à la conquête française*, 3 vols. (Paris: Ernest Leroux, 1888–1891).

9. See, for instance, Jean Mathiex, "Trafic et prix de l'homme en Méditerranée au XVIIIe siècle," *Annales: economies, sociétés, civilisations* (hereafter *AESC*) 9 (1954): 157–164; and Lucette Valensi, "Esclaves chrétiens et esclaves noirs à Tunis au XVIIIe siècle," *AESC* 6 (1967): 1267–1288. The exception is Paul Masson, scholar of Mediterranean commerce—thus necessarily corsairing and captivity—from the perspective of Marseille. Masson's contributions include *Histoire du commerce français dans le Levant au XVIIe siècle* (Paris: Hachette, 1896) and *Histoire des établissements et du commerce français dans l'Afrique barbaresque (1580–1793): Algérie, Tunisie, Tripolitaine, Maroc* (Paris: Hachette, 1903).

10. Besides challenging France's victim status, historians from the 1950s onward helped debunk the idea that the kingdom harbored no slaves within its borders beyond the medieval period. Belgian historian Charles Verlinden was one of the first to document the persistence of servile labor in southern Europe. *L'Esclavage dans l'Europe médiévale: péninsule ibérique-France* (Bruges: De Tempel, 1955). In France, Pierre Boyer and Michel Fontenay, among others, began

investigating the diverse sponsors of early modern piracy and refocusing attention on the Knights of Malta and their role in supplying Levantine and Maghrebi captives to the French royal galleys. Boyer, "La Chiourme turque des galères de France de 1685 à 1687," *Revue de l'Occident musulman et de la Méditerranée* (hereafter *ROMM*) 6 (1969): 53–74; Fontenay, "La Place de la course dans l'économie portuaire: l'exemple de Malte et des portes barbaresques," *AESC* 43, 6 (1988): 1321–1347. The horrendous experience of rowers aboard these multipurpose vessels, which functioned simultaneously as warships, prisons, and Catholic reformatories, detailed by Masson in *Les Galères de France, 1481–1781: Marseille, port de guerre* (Paris: Hachette, 1938), became the object of more detailed studies from both inside and outside France: Paul Bamford, *Fighting Ships and Prisons: The Mediterranean Galleys of France in the Age of Louis XIV* (Minneapolis: University of Minnesota Press, 1973); André Zysberg, *Les Galériens: vies et destins de 60,000 forçats sur les galères de France, 1680–1748* (Paris: Editions du Seuil, 1987); Moulay Belhamissi, *Les Captifs algériens et l'Europe chrétien, 1518–1836* (Algiers: Enterprise nationale du livre, 1988).

11. Important studies based on inquisitorial documents about Christians who chose to convert to Islam include Lucia Rostagno, *Mi faccio turco: esperinze ed immagini dell'Islam nell'Italia moderna* (Rome: Istituto per l'Oriente, 1983); Bartholomé Bennassar and Lucille Bennassar, *Les Chrétiens d'Allah: l'histoire extraordinaire des renégats, XVIe–XVIIe siècles* (Paris: Perrin, 1989); Anita Gonzalez-Raymond, *La Croix et le croissant: les inquisiteurs des îles face à l'Islam, 1550–1700* (Paris: Editions de CNRS, 1992); and Lucetta Scaraffia, *Rinnegati: per una storia dell'identita' occidentale*, 2nd ed. (Bari, Italy: Laterza, 2002).

12. Fernand Braudel, *The Mediterranean and the Mediterranean World in the Age of Philip II*, 2 vols., trans. Siân Reynolds (New York: Harper and Row, 1966; reprint, Berkeley: University of California Press, 1995), 2: 755 (first published in French, 1949). In fact, Mediterranean servitude—whether of Ottomans, Europeans, or sub-Saharan Africans—has been largely excluded from surveys of world slavery. It is, for example, conspicuously absent from Paul Finkelman and Joseph Calder Miller's monumental *Macmillan Encyclopedia of World Slavery*, 2 vols. (New York: Simon & Schuster Macmillan, 1998). Orlando Patterson, who does include Barbary captives in his purview (117, 277), might logically have excluded them, according to his restrictive definition of slavery as "the permanent, violent domination of natally alienated and generally dishonored persons." Patterson, *Slavery and Social Death: A Comparative Study* (Cambridge, MA: Harvard University Press, 1982), 13.

13. On a comparable propensity to discount varieties of Native American unfreedom as "slavery," see William A. Starna and Ralph Watkins, "Northern Iroquoian Slavery," *Ethnohistory* 38, 1 (1991): 34–57.

14. Bono charged North African historians with overcompensating for past colonial bias and neglecting the subject of slavery in their regional surveys to avoid implicating their ancestors in the traffic of human beings. "Le Maghreb dans l'histoire de la Méditerranée à l'époque barbaresque (XVIe siècle–1830)," *Africa: notiziario dell'Associazione fra le imprese italiane in Africa* 54, 2 (1999):

182–192. For further discussions of this historiographical gap, see, among others, Ehud R. Toledano, *As If Silent and Absent: Bonds of Enslavement in the Islamic Middle East* (New Haven, CT: Yale University Press, 2007), chap. 1; John Hunwick, "The Same but Different: Africans in Slavery in the Mediterranean Muslim World," in *The African Diaspora in the Mediterranean Lands of Islam*, ed. John Hunwick and Eve Troutt Powell (Princeton, NJ: Markus Wiener, 2002), ix–xxiv; Eve Troutt Powell, "The Silence of the Slaves," in Hunwick and Powell, *African Diaspora*, xxv–xxxvii; and Chouki El Hamel, "'Race,' Slavery and Islam in Maghribi Mediterranean Thought: The Question of the Haratin in Morocco," *Journal of North African Studies* 7, 3 (2002): 29–52.

15. For explicit discussions of this question, see Fontenay, "Le Maghreb barbaresque et l'esclavage méditerranéen aux XVIe et XVIIe siècles," *Cahiers de Tunisie* (hereafter *CT*) 44, 3–4 (1991): 7–43; Claude Larquié, "Captifs chrétiens et esclaves maghrébins au XVIIIe siècle: une tentative de comparaison," in *Captius i esclaus a l'antiguitat i al món modern: actes del XIX colloqui internacional del GIREA*, ed. María Luisa Sánchez León and Gonçal López Nadal (Naples: Jovene, 1996), 347–364.

16. Here I follow the example of Steven A. Epstein, *Speaking of Slavery: Color, Ethnicity and Human Bondage in Italy* (Ithaca, NY: Cornell University Press, 2001), who examined the language of slavery in medieval and early modern Italy on its own terms.

17. Verlinden was the first to posit the transmission of sugar production methods from the Mediterranean to Atlantic islands. See "The Transfer of Colonial Techniques from the Mediterranean to the Atlantic," in *The Beginnings of Modern Colonization*, trans. Yvonne Freccero (Ithaca, NY: Cornell University Press, [1970]), 3–32. On the Old World intellectual origins of New World racial slavery, subject of an immense literature, see in particular the special edition of *William and Mary Quarterly* 54 (1997), featuring articles by Benjamin Braude, "The Sons of Noah and the Construction of Ethnic and Geographical Identities in the Medieval and Early Modern Periods," 103–142, and James H. Sweet, "The Iberian Roots of American Racist Thought," 143–166.

18. There are a number of English-language historical studies in book form. On the United States, see Lawrence A. Peskin, *Captives and Countrymen: Barbary Slavery and the American Public, 1785–1816* (Baltimore: Johns Hopkins University Press, 2009). On Italy, see Robert C. Davis, *Christian Slaves, Muslim Masters: White Slaves in the Mediterranean, the Barbary Coast, and Italy, 1500–1800* (New York: Palgrave Macmillan, 2003). On Britain, see Linda Colley, *Captives: The Story of Britain's Pursuit of Empire and How Its Soldiers and Civilians Were Held Captive by the Dream of Global Supremacy, 1600–1850* (New York: Pantheon Books, 2002); Nabil Matar, *Turks, Moors and Englishmen in the Age of Discovery* (New York: Columbia University Press, 1999); and Matar, *Britain and Barbary, 1589–1689* (Gainesville: University Press of Florida, 2005). On Spain, see Ellen G. Friedman, *Spanish Captives in North Africa in the Early Modern Age* (Madison: University of Wisconsin Press, 1983); and Jarbel Rodriguez, *Captives and Their Saviors in the Medieval Crown of Aragon* (Washington, DC: Catholic University of America Press, 2007).

19. Publications on images of the "Turk" in French literature date to World War II, when Clarence Dana Rouillard, an American, released *The Turk in French History, Thought, and Literature* (Paris: Boivin, 1941). Notable examples from the late colonial and postcolonial period are André Vovard, *Les Turqueries dans la littérature française: le cycle barbaresque* (Toulouse: Privat, 1959); and Guy Turbet-Delof, *L'Afrique barbaresque dans la littérature française au XVIe et XVIIe siècles* (Geneva: Droz, 1973). Within a large and growing corpus of scholarship on British and American renditions of the Barbary captivity narrative, see especially Hester Blum, *The View from the Masthead: Maritime Imagination and Antebellum American Sea Narratives* (Chapel Hill: University of North Carolina Press, 2008), chap. 2; Daniel J. Vitkus, ed., *Piracy, Slavery, and Redemption: Barbary Captivity Narratives from Early Modern England* (New York: Columbia University Press, 2001); Joe Snader, *Caught between Worlds: British Captivity Narratives in Fact and Fiction* (Lexington: University Press of Kentucky, 2000); and Paul Michel Baepler, ed., *White Slaves, African Masters: An Anthology of American Barbary Captivity Narratives* (Chicago: University of Chicago Press, 1999).

20. Art historians treating some of these themes include Albert Boime, *Art in an Age of Counterrevolution, 1815–1848*, vol. 3 of *A Social History of Modern Art* (Chicago: University of Chicago Press, 2004); and Darcy Grimaldo Grigsby, *Extremities: Painting Empire in Post-Revolutionary France* (New Haven, CT: Yale University Press, 2002).

21. Apart from a large body of writing inspired by revelations of torture during the Algerian War—see Neil MacMaster, "The Torture Controversy (1998–2002): Towards a 'New History' of the Algerian War?" *Modern and Contemporary France* 10, 4 (2002): 449–459—a spate of recent books and articles have followed the lead of Benjamin Stora, *La Gangrène et l'oubli: la mémoire de la guerre de l'Algérie* (Paris: La Découverte, 1998), in examining France's memory of decolonization. For a broader argument about the long-term effects of the loss of Algeria in France, see Todd Shepard, *The Invention of Decolonization: The Algerian War and the Remaking of France* (Ithaca, NY: Cornell University Press, 2006).

22. Exceptions include Ann Thomson, "Arguments for the Conquest of Algiers in the Late Eighteenth and Early Nineteenth Centuries," *Maghreb Review* 14, 1–2 (1989): 108–118; and, most recently, Jennifer Sessions, *Empire of Virtue: Colonialism and Political Culture in Nineteenth-Century France and Algeria* (Ithaca, NY: Cornell University Press, forthcoming), chap. 1.

23. Recent books include Joseph Wheelan, *Jefferson's War: America's First War on Terror, 1801–1805* (New York: Carroll & Graf, 2003); and Frederick C. Leiner, *The End of Barbary Terror* (New York: Oxford University Press, 2006).

CHAPTER ONE

1. Kheir al-Din's memoirs—shown to be accurate by Nicolas Vatin, "A propos de la captivité à Rhodes d'Oruç Re'îs dans les Gazavât-ı Hayrü-d-dîn Pasa," in *Turcica et Islamica: studi in memoria di Aldo Gallotta*, 2 vols. (Naples:

Università degli studi di Napoli "L'Orientale," 2003), 2: 995–1011; and Svet Soucek, "Remarks on Some Western and Turkish Sources Dealing with the Barbarossa Brothers," *Güney-Doğu Avrupa Araştırmaları Dergisi* 1 (1972): 63–76—confirm his birth on the Greek island of Lesbos, captivity of several months on the island of Rhodes, and arrival in North Africa in 1513.

2. Spain retained several coastal outposts called *presidios*; the most important ones were Ceuta and Oran. The "Sublime Porte," or simply the "Porte," was a European appellation for the Ottoman government.

3. As Géraud Poumarède notes in *Pour en finir avec la croisade: mythes et réalités de la lutte contre les Turcs aux XVIe et XVIIe siècles* (Paris: Presses universitaires de France, 2004), 1–2, this commonplace neglects the attraction some western Europeans felt toward Islam and the welcome some areas in eastern Europe gave to Ottoman expansion.

4. The Knights of Saint John (of Jerusalem, then Rhodes, then Malta) obtained two-thirds of their ranks and considerable financial support from France. Claire-Eliane Engel, *L'Ordre de Malte en Méditerranée (1530–1798)* (Monaco: Editions du Rocher, 1957); Fontenay, "Corsaires de la foi ou rentiers du sol? Les chevaliers de Malte dans le 'corso' méditerranéen au XVIIe siècle," *Revue d'histoire moderne et contemporaine* 35 (1988): 361–384. Cosimo de Medici founded the Knights of the Order of Saint Stephen in 1561–1562, specifically to fight the Barbary corsairs. They operated actively until 1642 and claimed to have made fourteen thousand Muslim slaves. Franco Angiolini, "Slaves and Slavery in Early Modern Tuscany (1500–1700)," *Italian History and Culture* 3 (1997): 74–76; Angiolini, *I Cavalieri e il principe: l'Ordine di Santo Stefano e la società toscana in età moderna* (Florence: Edifir, 1996).

5. In *Turks, Moors and Englishmen*, 57, and *Britain and Barbary*, 118–132, Matar provides examples of Britons making and selling North African slaves from the 1590s onward.

6. Godfrey Wettinger, who provides figures of fifteen hundred to two thousand for later periods, claims that "not a shred of evidence of any kind has been found on the size of the slave community during the first thirty-five years of the Order's rule (1530–1565)." *Slavery in the Islands of Malta and Gozo ca. 1000–1812* (San Gwann, Malta: Publishers Enterprises Group, 2002), 32–33. Nevertheless, extrapolating from the number of galleys and the number of slaves required to row them, Anne Brogini puts the size of the Maltese slave population at around four hundred in 1548, reaching about 1800 by 1599. "L'Esclavage au quotidien à Malte au XVIe siècle," *Cahiers de la Méditerranée* (hereafter *CM*) 65 (2002), http://cdlm.revues.org/index26.html.

7. Bono, *Schiavi musulmani nell'Italia moderna: galeotti, vu' cumpra', domestici* (Naples: Edizioni scientifiche italienne, 1999), 35, estimates the average presence of twenty thousand household and galley slaves in Italian seaports—primarily Livorno—during the sixteenth century. For specific numbers on the galleys of Tuscany, Sicily, and Naples, see Angiolini, "Slaves and Slavery," 78; and Maurice Aymard, "Chiourmes et galères dans la seconde moitié du XVIe siècle," in *Il Mediterraneo nella seconda metà des '500 alla luci di Lepanto*, ed. Gino Benzoni (Florence: L.S. Olschki, 1974), 83–85.

8. While the uprisings of 1568–1570 put twenty-five to thirty thousand Iberian Muslim converts to Christianity into domestic and penal servitude, by the late sixteenth century Spanish kings were staffing their galleys with ever more North Africans. Bernard Vincent, "La Vie affective des esclaves de la péninsule ibérique XVIe–XIXe siècle," in *Familia y mentalidades*, ed. Angel Rodríguez Sánchez and Antonio Peñafiel Ramón (Murcia, Spain: Universidad de Murcia, 1997), 31. For the numbers and origins of enslaved rowers, see Alessandro Stella, *Histoires d'esclaves dans la péninsule ibérique* (Paris: Editions de l'EHESS, 2000), 68–70; Stella, "Les Galères dans la Méditerranée (XVe–XVIIIe siècles): miroir des mises en servitude," in *Esclavage et dépendances serviles: histoire comparée*, ed. Myriam Cottias, Stella, and Vincent (Paris: L'Harmattan, 2006), 271; and Ruth Pike, *Penal Servitude in Early Modern Spain* (Madison: University of Wisconsin Press, 1983), chap. 1, esp. 5–14.

9. France, like other Mediterranean states in the sixteenth century, had difficulty recruiting voluntary oarsmen (*bonevoglies*) to an expanding galley fleet and began using condemned criminals and servile Ottoman and Moroccan subjects instead. According to inventories from 1526 to 1545, Moors, Turks, and Greeks were already numerous on the galleys of Marseille (ADBR, B1261). According to a 1544 inventory, of 420 *esclaves* (as opposed to convicts, known as *forçats*), there were 210 *turcs* and 79 *mores*, serving on approximately 25 galleys. Masson, *Les Galères de France*, 20–21, 82–87; Jean Bérenger, "La Politique française en Méditerranée au XVIe siècle et l'alliance ottomane," in *La Guerre de course en Méditerranée (1515–1830)*, ed. Michel Vergé-Franceschi and Antoine-Marie Graziani (Paris: Presses de l'Université de Paris-Sorbonne, 2000), 24. Writing from Roville to his naval commissaries for the Levant on 7 October 1562, Charles IX promised to pay compensation to galley captains in Marseille for the sixty slaves he would return to Algiers. BN, NAL 1324, ff. 397–398, reprinted in Paul Deslandres, *L'Ordre des Trinitaires pour le rachat des captifs* (hereafter *OT*), 2 vols. (Toulouse: Privat, 1903), 2: 198–200.

10. Berbers inhabited much of North Africa before the seventh-century Arab invasions. Jewish exiles from the Iberian Peninsula who settled in the Ottoman regencies and Morocco post-1492 discovered communities dating from Roman times, as well as groups from other parts of the Mediterranean basin and Northern Europe. Muslim refugees (Moriscos), sometimes converts to Christianity, began arriving from Spain and Portugal in the late sixteenth century. Janissaries were members of the Ottoman military corps, usually converts to Islam, recruited though a levy (*devşirme*) on conquered populations in the Balkans; their children with local women were called *kuloglus*. Western Europeans who switched religion were commonly called "Turks by profession," "renegades," or less often "apostates."

11. Sixteenth-century estimates for the number of Christian captives range from 7,000 to 32,000 for Algiers, 1,600 to 22,000 for Tunis, 450 to 4,025 for Tripoli, and 1,000 to 3,000 for Morocco. See app. 1 for details.

12. In response to assaults by Algerian galleys on Hyères, Toulon, and La Valette in 1530, and the Gulf of Caqueiranne, La Garde, and La Valette the next year, Francis I had fortifications built and imposed taxes to bolster mari-

time patrols. Ernest Watbled, "La France et les barbaresques au XVIe siècle," *Nouvelle Revue* 84 (1893): 51; Vergé-Franceschi, *Toulon, port royal, 1481–1789* (Paris: Tallandier, 2002), 31. See also "Ordonnance de François I contre les corsaires barbaresques," Angoulême, July 1530, reprinted in Ernest Charrière, ed., *Négociations de la France dans le Levant, 1515–1589*, 4 vols. (Paris: Imprimerie nationale, 1848–1860), 1: cxxxiii–cxxxiv. A decade later there were at least fifty-four French slaves in Algiers, since in 1540 the Trinitarians apparently brought back that many, redeeming another sixty-four in 1544. See app. 2.

13. An enduring historiographical fiction has the Ottoman Empire granting France "Capitulations" in 1535 (or 1536 according to the Gregorian calendar). Gilles Veinstein reminds us, however, that the proposal tendered by the French ambassador was never promulgated. "Le Mythe des capitulations de 1536," in *Histoire de l'islam et des musulmans en France du Moyen Age à nos jours*, ed. Mohammed Arkoun (Paris: Albin Michel, 2006), 354. A bilateral accord between France and Algiers lasted from 1534 to 1537. BN, Collection Dupuy 44, f. 30; *Calendar of State Papers, Spanish*, V: 2: 327, cited in De Lamar Jensen, "The Ottoman Turks in Sixteenth Century French Diplomacy," *Sixteenth Century Journal* 16, 4 (1985): 454.

14. A smaller squadron had already spent a winter in Marseille in 1536. Bérenger, "La Politique française," 13. On the Toulon stopover, see Christine Isom-Verhaaren, "'Barbarossa and His Army Who Came to Succor All of Us': Ottoman and French Views of Their Joint Campaign of 1543–1544," *French Historical Studies* 30, 3 (2007): 395–425. On his return trip the following spring, Barbarossa turned his destructive potential against Sicily. A French eyewitness recounted the enslavement of ten thousand inhabitants of Lipari and the slaughter of old men and women for their gallbladders. Jérôme Maurand, *Itinéraire de Jérôme Maurand d'Antibes à Constantinople (1544)*, ed. Léon Dorez (Paris: Ernest Leroux, 1901), 129.

15. Ambassador Jean Cavenac de la Vigne, seigneur d'Auvilliers, to King Henry II, Andrinople, 28 December 1557, and Constantinople, 21 June 1559, cited in Watbled, "La France et les barbaresques," 59–60.

16. As Wolfgang Kaiser points out, the absence of institutional sources before the seventeenth century "gives the false impression of a more marginal phenomenon," but in Marseille by the 1560s, capture by North African corsairs had already become "an almost everyday risk" to which individual merchants and other intermediaries responded with ransom and negotiation. "Les Paradoxes d'une ville frontière: conflits et compromis à Marseille au XVIe siècle," in *La Ville à la Renaissance: espaces, représentations, pouvoirs*, ed. Gérald Chaix, Marie-Luce Demonet, and Robert Sauzet (Paris: H. Champion, 2008), 298–299. See also Marseille consuls, 1561, AMM, BB40, f. 156 r; "Mission de Fouquet de Vega en Barbarie (1561–1565)," ACCM, J1861; and notarial records from ADBR, 357 and 390E, cited in Kaiser, "Les Paradoxes," 287–301.

17. Marseille consuls to Catherine de Medici, Marseille, 29 December 1560, reprinted in Louis Paris, ed., *Négociations, lettres et pièces diverses relatives au règne de François II, tirées du portefeuille de Sébastien de l'Aubespine, évêque de Limoges* (Paris: Imprimerie royale, 1841), 780; Jacques Billioud, "Le Com-

merce de Marseille de 1515 à 1599," in *Histoire du commerce de Marseille*, 8 vols., ed. Gaston Rambert (Paris: Plon, 1949–1966), 3: 269; ambassador Antoine de Pétremol to Catherine de Medici, Constantinople, 15 July 1561, BN, MS 7092, f. 4 r, cited in Poumarède, "La France et les barbaresques: police des mers et relations internationales en Méditerranée (XVIe–XVIIe siècles)," *Revue d'histoire maritime* 4 (2005): 118, 119, 122. Also see Braudel, *The Mediterranean*, 2: 272 n. 160, who cites, among other documents, deliberations from Marseille (27 September 1561, AMM, BB40, f. 197 ff.) and Bayonne (28 June 1565, AN, K11504, B19, no. 24). During the 1560s Pétremol was also working for the release of over a hundred *esclaves françoys* in Constantinople (Pétremol to France's ambassador to Venice Jean Hurault de Boistaillé, Constantinople, 8 and 16 June 1562, reprinted in Charrière, *Négociations*, 2: 696), a project held up by the detention and conversion of a Turkish girl serving the queen. See Susan A. Skilliter, "Catherine de' Medici's Turkish Ladies in Waiting: A Dilemma in Franco-Ottoman Diplomatic Relations," *Turcica* 7 (1975): 188–204.

18. Pétremol, Constantinople, 15 July and 27 September 1565, cited in Watbled, "Aperçu sur les premiers consulats dans le Levant et les états barbaresques," *Revue africaine* (hereafter *RA*) 16 (1872): 20–25, 30–31. Port cities such as Marseille had been sending *consuls à l'étranger* across the Mediterranean since the Middle Ages. See Plantet, *CBT*, 1: v–vii, 1–2.

19. Avisos de Marsella, 2 May 1564, Simancas E° 1393, quoted in Braudel, *The Mediterranean*, 2: 882.

20. The most comprehensive historical study of French converts to Islam in the early modern Mediterranean remains Bennassar and Bennassar, *Les Chrétiens d'Allah*, 165–177. They found traces of 172 converts—with origins almost equally divided between the southern (mostly from Provence) and western (mostly from Brittany) coasts of France—who appeared before the Maltese Inquisition from 1560 to 1566. The majority had switched religion in Algiers, and 98 had participated in corsair raids against Christians. Gabriel Audisio demonstrated the preponderance of Provençals among renegades from the other direction. Of 116 in North Africa between 1560 and 1600, he identified 34 slaves and 34 renegades from Marseille. "Renégats marseillais (1591–1595)," *Provence historique* 46, 185 (1996): 326, citing ADBR, Fonds de l'amirauté de Marseille 9B171, and Grandchamp, *FT*, vol. 1.

21. Nicolas de Nicolay accompanied the French ambassador to Constantinople in 1549, but his influential, illustrated travel account (translated into English, Italian, and German) took almost two decades to be published: *Les Quatre premiers livres des navigations et pérégrinations orientales . . .* (Lyon: G. Roville, 1568), 16–17. He repeatedly dwells on the issue of sodomy elsewhere in the book.

22. This first friendship and commerce treaty was renewed at least twelve times over the subsequent three hundred years. For the text see Ignace de Testa, *Recueil des traités de la Porte Ottomane, avec les puissances étrangères, depuis le premier traité conclu, en 1536, entre Suléyman I et François I, jusqu'à nos jours*, 11 vols. (Paris: Amyot, Muzard & Leroux, 1864–1911), 1: 15–21. Article 13 *allowed* the retrieval of slaves, the chastising of corsairs, and the liberation

of renegades. Presumably, Algiers received some sort of compensation in money or in kind.

23. Among the slew of new books about the Battle of Lepanto of 1571, which pitted the Ottoman Empire against the Habsburgs, the papacy, and Venice, see Niccolò Capponi, *Victory of the West: The Great Christian-Muslim Clash at the Battle of Lepanto* (Cambridge, MA: Da Capo Press, 2007). Though France officially stood on the sidelines, numerous subjects did fight (Jacques Heers, *Les Barbaresques: la course et la guerre en Méditerranée, XIVe–XVIe siècle* [Paris: Perrin, 2001], 274–275; Rouillard, *The Turk*, 132), and many others celebrated the Christian victory (Jensen, "The Ottoman Turks," 459).

24. The French Wars of Religion lasted from 1562 until 1598. Catholics in Paris slaughtered about three thousand Huguenots (Calvinists) during the Saint Bartholomew's Day Massacre of 24 August 1572. In the months that followed, thousands more died in other parts of France.

25. Ambassador François de Noailles to Charles IX, Constantinople, 27 April 1572, BN, MS 16142, f. 138 r, cited in Poumarède, "La France et les barbaresques," 122. According to Watbled ("La France et les barbaresques," 63), Noailles' successor, Chevalier Jacques de Germiny, baron de Germolles, also successfully interceded with the sultan for the redemption of an unknown number of French captives in 1577, with more liberating themselves over the next several years. Records of debts and proxies registered before the French Chancery in Algiers appear in ADBR, 9B171, discussed in Pierre Grillon, "Origines et fondation du Consulat de France à Alger (1564–1582)," *Revue d'histoire diplomatique* 78 (1964): 97–117; those in Tunis are reprinted in Grandchamp, *FT*, 1: 9. Ransom contracts signed with Marseille merchants in the 1570s–1590s are held in ADBR, 353, 357, and 360E, cited in Kaiser, "Les 'Hommes de crédit' dans les rachats de captifs provençaux," in *Le Commerce des captifs: les intermédiaires dans l'échange et le rachat des prisonniers en Méditerranée, XVe–XVIIIe siècle*, ed. Kaiser (Rome: Ecole française de Rome, 2008), 300–303. Between 1572 and 1597, two Provençals also received pontifical bulls (*litterae hortatoriae*) granting permission to collect alms for redemption from North Africa. Wipertus H. Rudt de Collenberg, *Esclavage et rançons des chrétiens en méditerranée, 1570–1600 d'après les "litterae hortatoriae" de l'Archivo Segreto Vaticano* (Paris: Le Léopard d'Or, 1987), 237.

26. A municipal tradition of territorial liberation common to Toulouse, Saint-Malo, and Bourges was here applied to the entire kingdom. Sue Peabody, *"There Are No Slaves in France": The Political Culture of Race and Slavery in the Ancien Régime* (New York: Oxford University Press, 1996), 12, 21. Regarding the so-called Moors, commonly cited twentieth-century scholars (Charles de La Roncière, *Nègres et négriers* [Paris: Editions des Portiques, 1933], 15–16; Shelby T. McCloy, *The Negro in France* [(Lexington): University of Kentucky Press, 1961], 12) assume sub-Saharan origins for the slaves freed in February 1571 based on two versions of the *Chronique bordeloise*: the first, by Gabriel de Lurbe ([Bordeaux: S. Millanges, 1594], 47 v; 2nd ed. [Bordeaux: Simon Boé, 1703], 33), which refers to *nègres et mores*; and the second, by Jean de Gaufreteau (2 vols. [Bordeaux: Charles Lebfèvre, 1877], 1: 158–159), which

notes that inhabitants of Bordeaux called the slaves *mores* because of the black color of their bodies and faces and white undersides of their hands. The slaves' complexion may well have been dark, but in the sixteenth century the term "Moor" was commonly understood simply to mean Muslim.

27. Additional sixteenth-century articulations of what Peabody calls the "Freedom Principle" also involved the liberation of Muslims. Pierre de Bourdeille recounts the refusal of the duc de Guise to turn over the "Moorish or Turkish slave" of a Spanish general during the 1552 siege of Metz, according to "the privilege of France from time immemorial . . . that the least barbarian or foreigner, having put only his foot on French soil, is immediately free and removed from all slavery and captivity." *Oeuvres complètes de Pierre de Bourdeille, seigneur de Brantôme*, 11 vols., ed. Ludovic Lalanne (Paris: Veuve J. Renouard, 1864–1882), 4: 193. According to Pierre de Saint-Romuald, Henry III also set a precedent for liberating Turks from a Spanish galley shipwrecked on a sandbar near Calais, declaring that in France only criminals served at the oar. *Annales chronologiques et historiques* . . . (Paris: Clouzier, 1665), cited in Ernest Nys, *Etudes de droit international et de droit politique*, 2 vols. (Brussels: Alfred Castaigne, 1896–1901), 1: 257. In an account of his law school days in Toulouse, however, Jean Bodin failed to indicate the geographical origin of a slave whom he witnessed a Genoese merchant en route to Spain being forced to manumit. Jean Bodin, *Les Six livres de la République* (Lyon: Jean de Tournes, 1579), 45.

28. Despite the modern influence of Aristotle's theory, sketched out in the first book of *Politics*, that some men were "slaves by nature," many Roman thinkers embraced the Stoic doctrine that slavery resulted from fortune. On this point, see David Brion Davis, *The Problem of Slavery in Western Culture* (Ithaca, NY: Cornell University Press, 1966), chap. 3. "When a man has been made a prisoner of war, it was found more expedient to keep him than to kill him," wrote Estienne Pasquier in *Les Oeuvres d'Estienne Pasquier: contenant ses recherches de la France* . . . , 2 vols. (Amsterdam: Aux depens de la compagnie des librairies associez, 1723), 1: 373, a compendium compiled between 1560 and 1615, explaining the ancient rationale for reversing man's natural state of freedom.

29. *Servitude* derives from the Latin *servus*, which as a noun took on the connotation of serf rather than slave in the Middle Ages. The term *esclavitude* enjoyed its greatest currency in the sixteenth century. Appearing frequently in liberation petitions, it may have come from the Provençal and Occitan spoken by a large portion of the French captive population, or else from one of the Romance dialects spoken by literate captive scribes. On the duty to ransom captives in Judaism, see Eliezer Bashan, *Shivyah u-fedut ba-hevrah ha-yehudit be-artsot ha-Yam ha-tikhon (1391–1830)* (Ramat-Gan, Israel: Hotsa'at Universitat Bar-Ilan, 1980); Bashan, "Le Rachat des captifs dans la société juive méditerranéenne du XIVe au XIXe siècle," in *La Société juive à travers l'histoire*, ed. Shmuel Trigano (Paris: Fayard, 1993), 4: 463–472; and Yvonne Friedman, *Encounter between Enemies: Captivity and Ransom in the Latin Kingdom of Jerusalem* (Leiden, Netherlands: Brill, 2002). On the theory and practice in Islam, see Pieter Sjoerd van Koningsveld, "Muslim Slaves and Captives in Western Europe during

the Late Middle Ages," *Islam and Christian-Muslim Relations* 6, 1 (1995): 5–23; Mohamed Moudine, "Le Rachat des esclaves musulmans en Europe méridionale du XIIIe siècle à la fin du XVIIIe siècle: le cas du Maroc" (Doctorat, Université de Provence, Aix-Marseille I, 1996), 151–152, 309; Debra Blumenthal, *Enemies and Familiars: Slavery and Mastery in Fifteenth-Century Valencia* (Ithaca, NY: Cornell University Press, 2009), 104–105, 135–136, 200–201.

30. On early modern French ideas about skin color, see William B. Cohen, *The French Encounter with Africans: White Responses to Blacks* (Bloomington: Indiana University Press, 2003), 7–15.

31. Fontenay uses the term *captifs de rachat* in "Routes et modalités du commerce des esclaves dans la Méditerranée des Temps modernes (XVIe, XVIIe et XVIIIe siècles)," *Revue historique* 640, 4 (2006): 824; see also Géza Dávid and Pál Fodor, eds., *Ransom Slavery along the Ottoman Borders: Early Fifteenth–Early Eighteenth Centuries* (Leiden, Netherlands: Brill, 2007).

32. Claude Meillassoux's definition of slavery as a "social system based on the exploitation of a class of producers or persons performing services, primarily through acquisition," applied by James T. Brooks to his analysis of the American Southwest, also makes sense for the frontier societies around the Mediterranean. Not coincidentally, Brooks finds roots of Iberian–Native American servitude as practiced in the New World in Christian-Muslim servitude as experienced in the Old. Meillassoux, *The Anthropology of Slavery: The Womb of Iron and Gold* (Chicago: University of Chicago Press, 1991), 343; Brooks, *Captives and Cousins: Slavery, Kinship and Community in the Southwest Borderlands* (Chapel Hill: University of North Carolina Press, 2002), chap. 1, esp. 23–24, 32–33.

33. The most general word for slave in Arabic is *'abd*. But in most parts of North Africa, when not indicating "servant of God," this male form was applied only to a person procured south of the Sahara. Robert Brunschvig, "'Abd," in *Encyclopedia of Islam*, 2nd ed. (Leiden, Netherlands: Brill, 1960), 1: 24–40; Bernard Lewis, *Race and Slavery in the Middle East: An Historical Enquiry* (New York: Oxford University Press, 1990), 55–59; Fatima Harrak, "Mawlay Isma'il's Jaysh al-'Abīd: Reassessment of a Military Experience," in *Slave Elites in the Middle East and Africa: A Comparative Study*, ed. Toru Miura and John Edward Philips (London: Kegan Paul, 2000), 177–196. Not so in its female form, *ama*, which in Algerian and Moroccan documents, at least, signified a slave of any race. Lemnouar Merouche, *Recherches sur l'Algérie à l'époque ottomane*, 2 vols. (Paris: Bouchène, 2002–2007), 1: 211; El Hamel, "The Register of the Slaves of Sultan Mawlay Isma'il of Morocco at the Turn of the Eighteenth Century," *Journal of African History* 51, 1 (2010): 96. According to Matar (*Britain and Barbary*, 114–115), Arabic-language sources of North Africa employed only two terms for unfree people, referring to a European slave of either sex as an *asīr* (Ottoman for captive). Other scholars and contemporaries, however, note the use of additional words, including but not limited to *nusrani* (that is, Nazareen or Christian), *'ilj* (meaning infidel but also apparently used to designate converts to Islam), and *mamlūk* (meaning tradable object in full possession of a master, even though applied to freed members of the Egyptian

cavalry). [Pierre Girard], *Histoire chronologique du royaume de Tripoly*, 2 vols. (1685), BN, FF 12199–12200 (hereafter *HCRT*), vol. 1, f. 61; Miriam Hoexter, *Endowments, Rulers and Community: Waqf al-Haramayn in Ottoman Algiers* (Leiden, Netherlands: Brill, 1998), 12; Eyal Ginio, "Piracy and Redemption in the Aegean Sea during the First Half of the Eighteenth Century," *Turcica* 33 (2001): 140; Asma Moalla, *The Regency of Tunis and the Ottoman Porte, 1777–1814: Army and Government of a North-African Ottoman Eyālet at the End of the Eighteenth Century* (New York: Routledge, 2004), 14, 24; Dávid and Fodor, *Ransom Slavery*, xiv.

34. Frédéric Mireur, "Ligue des ports de Provence contre les pirates barbaresques en 1585–1586," *Mélanges historiques* 5 (1886): 601–638; quotation from Ambassador Jacques de Savary, seigneur de Lancosme, April 1586, cited in Watbled, "Aperçu sur les premiers consulats," 33 n. 3.

35. It was another French ambassador to the Ottoman Empire, Lancosme's nephew François Savary, seigneur de Brèves, who obtained the letter threatening to use the Barbary corsairs against Marseille. Quotations from Public Record Office, Turkey, S.P. 97/2, f. 26, cited in Jensen, "The Ottoman Turks," 469; see also Michel Lesure, "Les Relations franco-ottomanes à l'épreuve des guerres de religion (1560–1594)," in *L'Empire ottoman, la République de Turquie et la France*, ed. Hâmit Baru and Jean-Louis Bacqué-Grammont (Istanbul: Isis, 1986), 54–55 (for a discussion of another letter on the same subject).

36. AMM, BB52, f. 10, 10 v, 29, cited in Braudel, *The Mediterranean*, 2: 883. See also Kaiser, *Marseille au temps des troubles, 1559–1596: morphologie sociale et luttes de factions* (Paris: Editions de l'EHESS, 1992).

37. A pasha named in Constantinople for a three-year term ruled Algiers during much of the seventeenth century. Meanwhile, beys administered the interior provinces, and a divan (general council of Ottoman soldiers or janissaries) shared power with the *ta'ifa* (assembly of ra'is). In 1659 a revolution turned the pasha into a figurehead, replacing him first with a military commander (*agha*), and then in 1671 with an elected dey, a post that carried lifetime tenure but no guarantee of political stability, since ten of eleven subsequent deys were killed in office. After 1711 a weakened sultan accorded the dey the additional title of pasha, but his status remained precarious until midcentury. The last North African area to become an Ottoman dominion in 1574, Tunis was the first to oust its pasha at the end of the sixteenth century. After two decades under a dey, a former slave founded a dynasty of army officer beys in 1613 that lasted until 1705. The pashas installed in Tripoli following its annexation in 1551 became ceremonial stewards by 1603, and deys selected from among janissaries or ra'is reigned for the next several generations. In the eighteenth century a line of hereditary pashas seized power in Tripoli and Tunis and governed until the nineteenth and twentieth centuries, respectively. Charles-André Julien, *History of North Africa (Tunisia, Algeria, Morocco) from the Arab Conquest to 1830*, trans. John Petrie (New York: Praeger, 1970), 302–305; C. R. Pennell, ed., *Piracy and Diplomacy in Seventeenth-Century North Africa: The Journal of Thomas Baker, English Consul in Tripoli, 1677–1685* (Rutherford, NJ: Fairleigh Dickinson University Press, 1989), 29–36; Daniel

Panzac, *Les Corsaires barbaresques: la fin d'une épopée, 1800–1820* (hereafter *CB*) (Paris: CNRS Editions, 1999), 13–14.

38. With the Capitulations of 1597, the Ottoman sultan agreed to return pillaged French cargo and punish responsible North African corsairs. Jensen, "The Ottoman Turks," 469.

39. Of 169 official acts solicited from the sultan between 1593 and 1604, 73 had to do with the suppression of North African corsairing. "Mémoire des capitulations, commandements, privileiges . . . que le seigneur du Brèves a obtenuz tant de Grands Seigneurs Amourat, Mehemet et Amat," BN, MS 16146, ff. 27 r–51 r, cited in Poumarède, "La France et les barbaresques," 124. Regarding the funds advanced to captives, see, for example, the 1 and 3 August 1593 documents from Tunis attesting to a loan from French consul Philippe Pena to thirty French captives hailing from Frontignan, Toulon, Nans-les-Pins, Six-Fours, and Cannes and the plan for three of their number to return home to raise funds, reprinted in Grandchamp, *FT*, 1: 136–140. The figure for Christian ships apprehended by Muslim corsairs, for the years 1592 to 1609, is from Alberto Tenenti, *Naufrages, corsaires, et assurances maritimes à Venise, 1592–1609* (Paris: SEVPEN, 1959), 27.

40. Pena to Brèves, Tunis, [June 1594] (on the repatriation of fifteen to twenty French captives and the forced conversion of several others); members of the French *nation* in Tunis (voting to contribute ten to twenty écus apiece on 12 August 1595 and for a tax on 12 October 1598), both reprinted in Grandchamp, *FT*, 1: 152–158. See also app. 1.

41. Koningsveld, "Muslim Slaves," 6–7. Heers, *Les Barbaresques*, 248–249, notes multiple agreements notarized in Marseille between Provençal or Catalan merchants and relatives of captives in the late fourteenth and early fifteenth centuries. For a 1595 example involving a French one in Marrakech, see Charles Bréard, *Documents relatifs à la marine normande et ses armements au XVIe siècles, pour le Canada, l'Afrique, les Antilles, le Brésil et les Indes* (Rouen: A. Lestringant, 1889), 39.

42. Of the numerous societies dedicated to fighting Muslims and both defending and delivering Christians during the Crusades, only the Trinitarians and Mercedarians extended operations throughout Western Europe. Heers, *Esclaves et domestiques au Moyen Age dans le monde méditerranéen* (Paris: Fayard, 1981), 244–245.

43. One morning while saying mass in Paris, Matha saw either Christ or an angel wearing a white tunic with a red and blue cross on the chest, poised to exchange a Christian and a Muslim slave. Then a few days later in the forest near Meaux, he encountered a deer with the same cross in place of antlers. Roseline Grimaldi-Hierholtz, *L'Ordre des Trinitaires: histoire et spiritualité* (Paris: Sarment-Fayard, 1994), 22–23.

44. James Brodman, *Ransoming Captives in Crusader Spain: The Order of Merced on the Christian-Islamic Frontier* (Philadelphia: University of Pennsylvania Press, 1986), 15–20.

45. Bruyère was held hostage in Algiers from 1643 to 1652. For details, see Hugues Cocard, *Les Pères de la Merci en France (1574–1792): un ordre voué*

à la libération des captifs (Paris: L'Harmattan, 2007), 187–188; Grammont, "Certificat des souffrances du Père Sébastien," *RA* 35 (1891): 98–108.

46. Marseille consuls to Henry IV (with his response from Paris), 24 June 1602, ADBR, B3341, f. 462 v, cited in Poumarède, "La France et les barbaresques," 118. Henry IV's second wife, Marie de Medici, became the Mercedarians' greatest patron, helping the order set up a Parisian base at the Chapelle de Braque, near the Hôtel de Guise in the Marais. *Histoire de l'ordre sacré, royal et militaire de Notre-Dame de la Merci, rédemption des captifs, dédiée au roi: Composée par les révérends Pères de la Merci de la congrégation de Paris* (Amiens: Guislain Le Bel, 1685), 731–732; Emile Ledermann, "Les Frères de N.D. de la Merci et la rédemption des captifs" (Bachelor's thesis, University of Paris, 1898), 38–39.

47. Louis IX founded the Trinitarian convent in Fontainebleau. His Valois successors acknowledged the order's presence in France by accepting payments on their ecclesiastical acquisitions. Deslandres, *OT*, 1: 166–167, 185–194. The French branch may have made a successful voyage to Tunis in 1505 and bought back the first slaves from Algiers in 1540. Bonifacio Porres Alonso, *Libertad a los cautivos: actividad redentora de la Orden Trinitaria* (hereafter *LC*), 3 vols. (Cordoba: Secretariado Trinitario, 1998), 1: 195–198. By contrast, the Mercedarians seem not to have ransomed any French slaves from North Africa before 1629. Cocard, *Les Pères de la Merci*, 224, 226. On the legal battles between the two orders in the early seventeenth century, see Erwan Le Fur, "La Renaissance d'un apostolat: l'Ordre de la Trinité et la rédemption des captifs dans les années 1630," *CM* 66 (2003), http://cdlm.revues.org/index110.html.

48. Rouillard, *The Turk*, 412–416. The term *calvinoturcism* was coined in 1597 with the publication in Latin of William Reynolds's treatise of the same title; Matthew Sutcliffe responded with the term *turcopapism* two years later. See Lesure, "Les Relations franco-ottomanes," 38–43; and Kaiser, "Les Paradoxes," 285.

49. An Algerian ambassador visited Marseille the year before, but the pasha he represented lacked enough authority over the *ta'ifa* to stop their assaults. René Pillorget, "Un Incident diplomatique franco-turc sous Louis XIII: le massacre d'une ambassade de la Régence d'Alger (14 mars 1620)," *Revue d'histoire diplomatique* 88 (1974): 45–46.

50. See Testa, *Recueil des traités*, 1: 141–151, for the text.

51. Brèves discusses the (unrealized?) plan for a captive exchange with Algiers in *Relation des voyages de Monsieur de Breves tant en Grece, Terre-Saincte et Aegypte, qu'aux royaumes de Tunis & Arger . . .* (Paris: Nicolas Gasse, 1628), 364–377.

52. For the text, see Edgard Rouard de Card, *Traités de la France avec les pays de l'Afrique du Nord: Algérie, Tunisie, Tripolitaine, Maroc* (hereafter *TF*) (Paris: A. Pedone, 1906), 113–115. Though the 1605 accord with Tunis was the first for France, Marseille had signed a treaty with the city in 1230.

53. Henry IV to Marseille's consuls, 28 September 1607, AMM, BB59, f. 15 v, cited in Jean Pignon-Reix, "Un Document inédit sur les relations franco-tunisiennes au début du XVIIe siècle," *ROMM* 20 (1975): 107–108, 120 n. 27, 121–122 n. 29.

54. Brèves to Marseille's consuls, Paris, 24 October 1616, ACCM, BB247 (OC), reprinted in Plantet, *CBT*, 1: 12.

55. On Henry IV's inclination to deal generously with the French renegades in Tunis, as he did in 1609 with Simon Dansa, see Brèves, *Relation des voyages*, 344–345; [François Comelin and Philémon de La Motte], *Etat des Royaumes de Barbarie, Tripoly, Tunis et Alger* . . . (Rouen: Guillaume Behourt, 1703), 65; and Pierre Dan, *Histoire de Barbarie et de ses corsaires* . . . (Paris: Pierre Rocolet, 1637; 2nd ed., 1649 [here citing the 1637 edition]), 166–167.

56. Portuguese shipwreck tales—many of which featured slavery in North Africa—started appearing in cheap editions called *folhetos* in the mid-sixteenth century. In the eighteenth century, an edited collection of them, *História Trágico-Marítima*, became a classic of Portuguese literature. João de Carvalho Mascarenhas, *Esclave à Alger: récit de captivité de João Mascarenhas (1621–1626)*, ed. Paul Teyssier (Paris: Chandeigne, 1993), 7–9. The first English narrative of North African captivity—John Fox, "The Worthy Enterprise of John Fox, in Delivering 266 Christians Out of the Captivity of the Turks" (in the Egyptian city of Alexandria)—was first printed in 1579 and included in Richard Hakluyt, *Principal Navigations* . . . (London: George Bishop & Ralph Newberry, 1589). Reprinted and discussed in Matar and Vitkus, *Piracy, Slavery, and Redemption*, 55–69.

57. According to the narrative of Knight of Malta Alonso de Contreras (1582–1633), a 1602 raid carried out by members of his order disguised as Turks had reaped seven hundred slaves. *The Life of Captain Alonso de Contreras, Knight of the Military Order of St. John, Native of Madrid, Written by Himself (1582 to 1633)*, trans. Catherine Alison Phillips (New York: A. A. Knopf, [1926]), 39–40.

58. Henry du Lisdam, *L'Esclavage du brave chevalier François de Vintimille* . . . (Lyon: Claude Morillon, 1608), 38–39, 103–109. On this text, see Christian Zonza, "Henri du Lisdam: la captivité au carrefour du roman et de la philosophie dans les premières années du XVIIe siècle," in *Captifs en Méditerranée (XVIe–XVIIIe siècles): histoires, récits, légendes*, ed. François Moureau (Paris: Presses de l'Université de Paris-Sorbonne, 2008), 227–242.

59. On this idea, see Arlette Jouanna, *L'Idée de race en France au XVIe siècle et au début du XVIIe siècle, 1498–1614*, 3 vols. (Paris: H. Champion, 1976); and Jonathan Dewald, *Aristocratic Experience and the Origins of Modern Culture: France, 1570–1715* (Berkeley: University of California Press, 1993).

60. Sadok Boubaker, "Négoce et enrichissement individuel à Tunis du XVIIe siècle au début du XIXe siècle," *Revue d'histoire moderne et contemporaine* 50, 4 (2003): 36–37.

61. Ambassador Jean-François de Gontaut-Biron, baron de Salignac, to Henry IV, Constantinople, 27 March 1609, BN, MS 16146, f. 236 r, cited in Poumarède, "La France et les barbaresques," 127.

62. Guillaume Foucques to Henry IV, 21 and 24 May 1609; Foucques, *Mémoires portants plusieurs advertissemens presentez au Roy par le Cappitaine Foucques* . . . (Paris: Guillaume Marrette, 1609), all reproduced in Grandchamp, *FT*, 3: 383–396.

63. I have identified twenty-two full-length French-language slave accounts, composed between 1608 and 1821, of which fifteen saw immediate publication, five were excerpted in modern journals, and two were circulated in manuscript (see Bibliography).

64. Jules Mathorez, *Les Etrangers en France sous l'Ancien régime: histoire de la formation de la population française*, 2 vols. (Paris: Edouard Champion, 1919), 1: 160–171; Louis Cardaillac, *Morisques et chrétiens: un affrontement polémique, 1492–1640* (Paris: Klincksieck, 1977); Pierre Santoni, "Le Passage des Morisques en Provence (1610–1613)," *Provence historique* 46, 185 (1996): 333–383.

65. Masson, *Histoire du commerce*, xxvii–xviiii, citing Marseille city council deliberations from 1606, 1608, 1609, and 1610. The next year, having convinced the crown to ban trade with North Africa, the city nonetheless agreed "to prepare to make war against the said corsairs." Marseille city council deliberation, 13 May 1611, AMM, BB60, ff. 38 v–39 v, reprinted in Pignon-Reix, "Un Document inédit," 126.

66. Cassis town council deliberations, 27 May 1616, ACC, BB7, at ADBR, 139E; Fréjus town council deliberations about Bertrand Mourgues, captive in Tripoli, 1614, Archives municipales de Fréjus, BB10, f. 89 v, cited in handwritten inventory.

67. Arrêt de parlement, Aix-en-Provence, 15 October 1614, ADBR, 9B1, f. 407, cited in Raoul Busquet, ed., *Inventaire sommaire des Archives départementales antérieures a 1790, Bouches-du-Rhône*, 4 vols. (Marseille: Archives des Bouches-du-Rhône, 1932), 4: 28.

68. Acts of the "Synode national de Jargeau" (1610), cited in Gaston Bonet-Maury, "La France et la rédemption des esclaves en Algérie à la fin du XVIIe siècle," *Revue des deux mondes* 35 (1906): 898.

69. For example, the *Pénitents blancs* of Provence took collection every Wednesday and the kingdom-wide *Sainte Trinité* distributed the texts of papal indulgences and prints depicting the sufferings of slaves. Grimaldi-Hierholtz, *L'Ordre des Trinitaires*, 48–49. Mercedarian confraternities had names like the "Frères et soeurs de la rédemption des captifs." *Notre Dame de Miséricorde*, established in 1616 by a former slave for the benefit of others from La Ciotat, had an unusually large endowment of ten thousand livres in 1666. Memo attached to a letter to the bishop of Marseille, 1 February 1708, AAE, MD, Alger, vol. 14, ff. 15–16.

70. Royal bans on trade with North Africa date to 1604, 1607, and 1611 (Registres de l'amirauté, ADBR, cited in Masson, *Histoire du commerce*, 28 n. 3). The letters patent issued on 5 October 1613, which came in response to remonstrances from Marseille (ADBR, Amirauté 9B1, 2nd ser., f. 354 v, cited in Pignon-Reix, "Un Document inédit," 110 n. 21; ACCM, HH4 [OC], cited in Octave Teissier, *Inventaire des archives historiques de la Chambre de commerce de Marseille* [Marseille: Barlatier-Feissat, 1878], 423), barred shipowners from trading with North Africa "to punish the corsairs for the cruises, ravages, and pillages that they regularly exercise on the Mediterranean" (Plantet, *CBT*, 1: 28 n. 3).

71. Despite European insistence that corsairs operated out of Sala (transliterated as Salé by the French, Sallee by the English) on the north bank of the Wadi Bu Raqraq, their harbor was actually on the south bank in Rabat. Jerome B. Bookin-Weiner, "The 'Sallee Rovers': Morocco and Its Corsairs in the Seventeenth Century," in *The Middle East and North Africa: Essays in Honor of J. C. Hurewitz*, ed. Reeva S. Simon (New York: Columbia University Press, 1990), 310 n. 4.

72. Provençal nobleman Robert Boniface de Cabane traveled back and forth to Morocco in 1617–1618. Knight of Malta Isaac de Razilly conveyed future consul Claude du Mas with proposals for Sultan Zidan Abu Maali in 1619 and 1624. Charles Penz, *Les Captifs français du Maroc au XVII siècle, 1577–1699* (Rabat, Morocco: Imprimerie officielle, 1944), 23–24. The letter from slaves Berenguier et al. to Louis XIII (Marrakech, 4 December 1622, AAE, Maroc, Correspondance consulaire (hereafter CC), vol. 1, printed in Castries, Cossé Brissac, and Cenival, *SIHM* [1911], 1st ser., 3: 86) asserts that the authors had already been in slavery for nine years.

73. French slaves to Marseille consuls, Tripoli, 18 February 1612, ACCM, G44. According to Masson, *Histoire du commerce*, 41, they were seized after Tripoli lost its consul in 1610.

74. The Franco-Tunisian accord of 1612, written in Spanish and signed by Jehan de Forbin, sieur de la Marthe, sieur de la Barben, is absent from most historical accounts with the exception of Antoine de Ruffi, *Histoire de la ville de Marseille*, 2nd ed., 2 vols. (Marseille: Henri Martel, 1696), 1: 456. It was, however, read and translated before a city council session on 29 May (AMM, BB60, f. 133) and is mentioned in numerous archival sources, including an anonymous slave letter from Tunis, dated 29 September 1615 (ACCM, G43). According to Jan Jacomo Belegno, Flemish dragoman, France's envoy had traded 132 Turks for 84 Frenchmen, leaving 300 behind. Belegno to the States General of the United Provinces, Tunis, 8 January 1613, cited in Pignon-Reix, "Un Document inédit," 106, 110, 114–125.

75. Sixteen French vessels between 1611 and the first six months of 1614, plus twenty-two boats off the Provençal coast in the month of June alone, fell to Tunisian corsairs, according to the following documents: French slaves to Marseille consuls, Tripoli, 18 February 1612, ACCM, G44; CCM to Admiralty, ACCM, AA544 (OC); consul Thomas Martin to CCM, Tunis, 15 March 1614, ACCM, AA509 (OC); slave Corniglia de Turrel to Marseille consuls, Tunis, 15 August 1614, ACCM, G43, cited in Masson, *Histoire du commerce*, 36–37, 41–42.

76. Wives, brothers, and cousins of Marseillais slaves in Tripoli to Parlement of Provence, 1615, ACCM, G44, excerpted in Kaiser, "Négocier la liberté: missions françaises pour l'échange et le rachat de captifs au Maghreb (XVIIe siècle)," in *La Mobilité des personnes en Méditerranée de l'Antiquité à l'époque moderne: procédures de contrôle et documents d'identification*, ed. Claudia Moatti (Rome: Ecole française de Rome, 2004), 508 n. 24; anonymous slave letter, Tunis, 29 September 1615, ACCM, G43, reprinted in Pignon-Reix, "Un Document inédit," 114–125, 127.

77. See app. 1 for slave numbers. Knight of Malta Alexandre de Vincheguerre

renewed the peace with Tunis on 12 August 1616 (ACCM G43, excerpted in Kaiser, "Négocier la liberté," 525–526, and Grandchamp, *FT*, 3: 401–402, 4: xiv), leaving his son, Philandre, as a hostage until the captive exchange was completed. A Tunisian envoy, Baba Drevis, traveled to France to ratify the treaty, bearing horses, ostriches, leopards, and other animals as gifts for Louis XIII. ACCM, AA544 (OC), reprinted in Plantet, *CBT*, 1: 11–13. Masson (*Histoire du commerce*, 42) maintains that a treaty with Tripoli was signed at the same time, though I have found no corroborating evidence.

78. Temporary consul to Tunis Hercule Tamagni claimed to have freed eighty-seven French slaves, including three renegades during his 1615–1616 tenure (Tamagni to Marseille consuls, Tunis, 3 December 1616, ACCM, AA544 [OC], reprinted in Plantet, *CBT*, 1: 14). Vincheguerre and additional envoys repatriated groups of Tunisian and French subjects over the next two years (ACCM, AA544 [OC], reprinted in Plantet, *CBT*, 1: 18–31, 28 n. 1, 29 n. 1), though in 1619 the dey was still demanding additional "Turks" and "women slaves" (Dey Yusuf to CCM, Tunis, 14 March 1619, ACCM, AA544 [OC], reprinted in Plantet, *CBT*, 1: 29–30). See also Masson, *Histoire du commerce*, 37, 50; Jean Pignon, "Une Expédition marseillaise sur les côtes barbaresques (1616). L'armement Vincheguerre," in *Maghreb et Sahara: études géographiques offertes à Jean Despois*, ed. Xavier de Planhol (Paris: Société de géographie, 1973), 307–320.

79. Grammont, "Relations entre la France et la Régence d'Alger au XVIIe siècle . . . ," *RA* 23 (1879): 5–32, 95–114, 137–138. A total of 193 French ships and 60 boats were seized by Algerian corsairs between 1613 and 1621. A year after an Algerian embassy to Marseille in 1616 (Pillorget, "Un Incident diplomatique," 47), two Marseillais deputies, Jean de Glandèves and Antoine Bérengier, made a fruitless attempt to exchange perhaps forty Algerian galley slaves for an equal number of French captives, and had to flee for their lives (Plantet, *CDA*, 1: xxxvii, 8 n. 2). In response, Louis XIII ordered ambassador Achille de Harlay, baron de Sancy, to lodge a protest with the sultan (Denis Louis Martial Avenel, ed., *Lettres, instructions diplomatiques et papiers d'Etat du Cardinal de Richelieu*, 8 vols. [Paris: Imprimerie impériale, 1853–1877], 7: 359). On 11 May 1617 France's consul reported the arrival of nine Muslims and the return of a "small child" that an Algerian "ra'is in Bône [now Annaba] made apostatize and had circumcised by force" (ACCM, AA460 [OC], cited in Teissier, *Inventaire*, 198).

80. During a short period of peace from 1617 to 1618, Jean-Louis du Mas de Castellane, baron d'Allemagne, went at the sultan's behest to renew French claims over the Bastion de France (established in 1560 on a site near Annaba where Marseille fishermen had traditionally trawled for coral; captured and retaken in 1568, then destroyed in 1604). Instead, the peace broken, he was taken captive along with one hundred of his men, and released only to negotiate the 1619 Franco-Algerian treaty. François Charles-Roux, *France et Afrique du Nord avant 1830: les précurseurs de la conquête* (hereafter *FA*) (Paris: Félix Alcan, 1932), 61–69, 102–103. For the French text of the treaty, signed in Marseille on 21 May 1619, see Rouard de Card, *TF*, 11–15.

81. "Histoire du massacre des Turcs à Marseille en 1620," in *Documents*

de l'histoire de Provence, ed. Edouard Baratier (Toulouse: Privat, 1971), 191–
193. Originally published as *Histoire nouvelles du massacre du Turcs fait en
la ville de Marseille en Provence le 14 de mars mil six cent vingt . . .* (Lyon:
Claude Armand, 1620), and reprinted in Grammont, *Histoire du massacre
des Turcs à Marseille en 1620* (Paris: H. Champion, 1879). On the massacre and its diplomatic implications, also see Pillorget, "Un Incident diplomatique," 44–58; Grammont, "Relations," 25–28; and Dalinda al-Arqash et
al., eds., *Muqadimmat wa Wathaiq fi tarikh al-Maghrib al-Arabi al-Hadith*
(Mannouba, Tunisia: Kulliyat al-Adab Manubah, 1995), 295, cited in Matar,
Britain and Barbary, 116.

    82. Consuls and governors of Marseille to Hussein, pasha of Algiers, Mar-
seille, 25 July 1620, ACCM, AA508 (OC), reprinted in Plantet, *CDA,* 1: 7–12.
See the 15 March 1620 deliberations of the AMM, register 30, f. 127, reproduced in Grammont, *Histoire du massacre,* 47–49, which uses similar language
to describe the massacre and the deputies' inability to stop it.

    83. Galley general Philippe-Emmanuel de Gondi, comte de Joigny, launched
a seven-galley fleet in July 1620, taking two Algerian corsairs and 160 Muslim
slaves. *Lettre d'un gentilhomme à un sien amy, contenant les exploits faicts
ès costes d'Espagne et Barbarie par M. le comte de Joigny . . .* (BN, Portefeuille Fontanieu 473, f. 15), cited in Vergé-Franceschi, *Chronique maritime de
la France d'Ancien régime, 1492–1792* (Paris: Sedes, 1998), 293–294. A year
later, Louis de Prévot, sieur de Beaulieu, commander of the duc de Guise's galley,
working on behalf of Marseille, captured three more Algerian vessels and made
530 more slaves. AMM, Délibérations, 18 December 1621, cited in Masson,
Histoire du commerce, 31.

    84. Although the *arrêt* (court decision), dated 22 May 1620, condemned four-
teen men to death, only one was executed. AMM, FF32, reproduced in Grammont, *Histoire du massacre,* 50–56. The rest ran away and were punished in
effigy. Others received lesser sentences, according to Ruffi, *Histoire de la ville,*
cited in Plantet, *CDA,* 1: 11 n. 2. With an edict from Fontainebleau dated 23
June 1623, the king ordered all charges dropped against those implicated in the
violence. ADBR, B3346, f. 584, cited in Busquet, *Inventaire sommaire,* 4: 199.

    85. Grammont, "Relations," 28, citing the "Mémoires journalières d'un cap-
tif," ACCM, AA508 (OC). According to La Roncière, the Algerians took revenge by burning alive the French consul. *Histoire de la marine française,* 6 vols.
(Paris: E. Plon, Nourrit, 1899–1932), 4: 403. Grammont, however, notes only
that "for an instant there was a question of burning [him and the other French
residents] alive."

    86. In the fall of 1622, ambassador Philippe de Harlay, comte de Césy, did
convince the sultan to send a *capidji* (ambassador) to the three Ottoman regencies with orders to halt all attacks against French shipping and release all French
slaves on pain of being treated as rebels. But warnings from Constantinople had
little effect between 1623 and 1627. Césy to Louis XIII and CCM, Pera, 4, 13,
and 18 September 1622, ACCM, AA143 (OC), reprinted in Plantet, *CBT,* 1: 58
n. 1. See also Masson, *Histoire du commerce,* 32.

    87. Joseph-Marie Danigo, "Chrétiens aux prises avec les Barbaresques,"

Mémoires de la société d'histoire et d'archéologie de Bretagne 31 (1951): 49–63. The phrase is Razilly's in a letter to Richelieu, which also notes the captivity of "more than 6,000 Christians and 15,000,000 livres of which France suffered two thirds the loss." Pontoise, 26 November 1626, cited in Castries, "Le Maroc d'autrefois: les corsaires de Salé," *Revue de deux mondes* 13 (1903): 846.

88. Within a large literature, see especially Bono, *I Corsari barbareschi*; Tenenti, *Piracy and the Decline of Venice, 1580–1615* (Berkeley: University of California Press, 1967); and, more recently, Giuseppe Bonaffini, *Cattivi e redentori nel Mediterraneo tra XVI e XVII secolo* (Palermo: ILA Palma, 2003).

89. Friedman, *Spanish Captives*; José Antonio Martinez Torres, *Prisioneros de los infieles: vida y rescate de los cautivos cristianos en el Mediterráneo musulmán, siglos XVI–XVII* (Barcelona: Ediciones Bellaterra, 2004).

90. On the 109 people carried off one night in 1631 from Baltimore in West Cork, Ireland, see Des Ekin, *The Stolen Village: Baltimore and the Barbary Pirates* (Dublin: O'Brien Press, 2006).

91. The 1627 raid on Iceland, organized by Jan Jansz—also known as ra'is Murad—and a Danish slave known in sources as Paul, was described in the seventeenth century by Dan, *Histoire de Barbarie* (1637), 276, and several other French authors. Modern studies include Jules Leclercq, "Les Corsaires algériens en Islande en 1627," *Bulletin de la Classe des lettres et des sciences morales et politiques (Académie royale de Belgique)* 12 (1926): 312–324; Lewis, "Corsairs in Iceland," *ROMM* 16 (1973): 139–144; and, more recently, Thornsteinn Helgason, "Historical Narrative as Collective Therapy: The Case of the Turkish Raid in Iceland," *Scandinavian Journal of History* 22 (1997): 275–289. Helgason also wrote and directed a film, *Atlantic Jihad* (2003).

92. Cahiers de doléances to Louis XIII, Marseille, 18 January 1620, AN, Marine B7 49, f. 25; *Procès-verbal* (official account) of Charles Lhonore, lieutenant du présidial de Quimper, 17 October 1624, in "Arrêt de la grande chambre du parlement de Bretagne . . . ," reprinted in Hervé Tigier, *La Bretagne de bon aloi: répertoire des arrêts sur remontrance du parlement de Bretagne, 1554–1789* (Rennes: Archives départementales d'Ille-et-Vilaine, 1987), 102.

93. French slave counts for Algiers increased from about 200 to 800 (discounting the improbable 6,000) between 1620 and 1626. In Tunis they rose from 140 to 380 between 1605 and 1615, but I have found no estimates for the twenty-five years afterward. Tripoli reportedly had 150 French captives in 1629, as in 1615; Morocco 150–270 from 1626 to 1629. See app. 1 for details.

94. Anecdotally, female names almost never appear on slave registers. One study of sixteenth-century records found that women represented almost half of Christians seized during land raids and a miniscule number of those taken at sea. Rudt de Collenberg, *Esclavage et rançons*, 303–304, 323–324. Among those slaves who registered acts at the French Chancery in Tunis from 1591 to 1700, an average of 3.25 percent were women. The only two French ones were native to Marseille. Leïla Blili, "Course et captivité des femmes dans la régence de Tunis aux XVIe et XVIIe siècles," in *Captius i esclaus*, 262–263. Dan (*Histoire de Barbarie* [1637], 313) noted the very small portion of female renegades from France. On British women as Barbary slaves, see Matar, *Britain and Barbary*,

92–110; and Colley, *The Ordeal of Elizabeth Marsh: A Woman in World History* (New York: Random House, 2008), chap. 2.

95. Jocelyne Dakhlia, *Lingua Franca* ([Arles]: Actes sud, 2008); Alan D. Corré, *A Glossary of Lingua Franca*, 5th ed. (2005), http://www.uwm.edu/~corre/franca/go.html.

96. On the history of passports in France, see Daniel Nordman, "Sauf-conduits et passeports," in *Dictionnaire de l'Ancien régime: royaume de France, XVIe–XVIIIe siècle*, ed. Lucien Bély (Paris: Presses universitaires de France, 1996), 1123–1124; Daniel Roche, *Humeurs vagabondes: de la circulation des hommes et de l'utilité des voyages* (Paris: Fayard, 2003), chap. 7; and Vincent Denis, *Une Histoire de l'identité: France, 1715–1815* (Seyssel: Champ Vallon, 2008). On the variety of passes employed in the early modern Mediterranean, see Peter Earle, *Corsairs of Malta and Barbary* (London: Sidgwick & Jackson, 1970), 40–41, 90–91. In Europe more generally, see Jane Caplan and John Toppey, eds., *Documenting Individual Identity: The Development of State Practices in the Modern World* (Princeton, NJ: Princeton University Press, 2001); and Valentin Groebner, *Who Are You? Identification, Deception and Surveillance in Early Modern Europe* (New York: Zone Books, 2007), chaps. 6 and 7.

97. René Chastelet des Boys, "L'Odyssée ou diversité d'aventures, encontres en Europe, Asie et Afrique par le sieur du Chastelet des Boys [1665]," ed. Louis Piesse, *RA* 10 (1866): 95.

98. Emanuel d'Aranda, *Les Captifs d'Alger*, ed. Latifa Z'Rari (Paris: Jean-Paul Rocher, 1997), 32; Chastelet des Boys, "L'Odyssée," *RA* 10 (1866): 97. On methods of identifying captives, see Kaiser, "Vérifier les histoires, localier les personnes: l'identification comme processus de communication en Méditerranée (XVIe–XVIIe siècles)," in *Gens de passage en Méditerranée, de l'Antiquité à l'époque moderne: procédures de contrôle et d'identification*, ed. Moatti and Kaiser (Paris: Maisonneuve & Larose, 2007), 369–386.

99. Jean-Baptiste Gramaye, *Alger XVIe–XVIIe siècle: journal de Jean-Baptiste Gramaye, 'évêque d'Afrique,'* ed. Abd El Hadi Ben Mansour (Paris: Editions de Cerf, 1998), 296, 299; Chastelet des Boys, "L'Odyssée," *RA* 10 (1866): 159.

100. The idea that the state should take one fifth of any booty comes from the Quran 42: 28. A special official partitioned corsair loot among various interested parties, including a special fund to ransom Muslims held in Christian lands. Hoexter, *Endowments, Rulers and Community*, 12–14; Albert Devoulx, "Le Registre des prises maritimes," *RA* 15 (1871): 73–77. This slave tax (*pencik*) could be paid either in kind or in currency. Hakan Erdem, *Slavery in the Ottoman Empire and Its Demise, 1800–1909* (New York: St. Martin's Press, 1996), 19–20. In practice, the deys and beys of Algiers and Tunis took one eighth or even one eleventh of each batch of Christian captives. Until 1673, the pasha of Tripoli kept them all; afterward they were divided equally between the dey and the marketplace. [Girard], *HCRT*, vol. 1, 60 v; Pennell, *Piracy and Diplomacy*, 50. The opposite occurred in Morocco, where corsairs paid out a 10 percent tribute until 1678 when Sultan Mulay Isma'il appropriated every slave in the realm. Penz, *Les Captifs français*, 11; Henry Koehler, "Quelques points d'histoire sur les captifs chrétiens de Meknès," *Hésperis* 8 (1928): 177–178.

101. Despite the ideal of loyalty to the sultan alone, scholars like Metin Ibrahim Kunt and Suraiya Faroqui have argued that recruits, in fact, maintained ties to their previous homeland and faith. Kunt, "Ethnic-Regional (*cins*) Solidarity in the Seventeenth-Century Ottoman Establishment," *International Journal of Middle East Studies* 5, 3 (1974): 233–239, and Faroqui, "In Search of Ottoman History," *Journal of Peasant Studies* 18 (1991): 216; both cited in Eric R. Dursteler, *Venetians in Constantinople: Nation, Identity, and Coexistence in the Early Modern Mediterranean* (Baltimore: Johns Hopkins University Press, 2006), 126–127.

102. Laurent d'Arvieux, *Mémoires du chevalier d'Arvieux . . .*, ed. Jean-Baptiste Labat, 6 vols. (Paris: Charles-Jean-Baptiste Delespine, 1735), 5: 267–268.

103. Lisdam, *L'Esclavage*, 63 (the Knight of Malta); Chastelet des Boys, "L'Odyssée," *RA* 11 (1867): 162–163 (the gentlemen). For a discussion of sumptuary law in early modern France, see Etienne Giraudias, *Etude historique sur les lois somptuaires* (Poitiers: Oudin, 1910), 76–104; and Roche, *The Culture of Clothing: Dress and Fashion in the Ancien Régime*, trans. Jean Birrell (Cambridge: Cambridge University Press, 1996).

104. Quotation from Germain Moüette, *Relation de la captivité du Sr Moüette dans les royaumes de Fez et de Maroc . . .* (Paris: Jean Cochart, 1683), 22; phenomenon discussed in Aranda, *Les Captifs d'Alger*, 41.

105. Slaves chevaliers du Saillant et al. to CCM, Algiers, [1639], ACCM, AA507 (OC), in Grammont, "Relations," 3: 31.

106. Grandchamp, "Une Mission délicate en Barbarie au XVIIe siècle: Jean-Baptiste Salvago, drogman vénitien à Alger et à Tunis (1625)," *Revue tunisienne* 8 (1937): 485.

107. Moüette, *Relation de la captivité*, 115; [François] le sieur de Rocqueville, *Relations des moeurs et du gouvernement des Turcs d'Alger . . .* (Paris: Olivier de Varennes, 1675), 20.

108. [Girard], HCRT, vol. 1, f. 59 v; Lisdam, *L'Esclavage du brave chevalier*, 83.

109. Patterson, *Slavery and Social Death*.

110. Many slave petitions were endorsed with marks rather than signatures. Gramaye, *Alger*, 326–327; Aranda, *Les Captifs d'Alger*, 149–150.

111. Antoine Quartier, *L'Esclave religieux et ses avantures* (Paris: Daniel Hortemels, 1690), 275–276. On the Compagnie du Saint-Sacrement's role in transporting slave mail starting in the 1640s, see Raoul Allier, *Une Société secrète au XVIIe siècle: la Compagnie du Très-Saint-Sacrement de l'Autel à Marseille, documents publiés* (Paris: H. Champion, 1909), 158–171. For more details on Franco–North African epistolary mechanics, see my "Barbary Captivity and the French Idea of Freedom," *French Historical Studies* 28, 2 (2005): 235–239.

112. Algiers had six bagnes in 1634, four in 1675, and three in 1830, while Tunis, with many fewer slaves, had nine in 1635 and as many as thirteen later in the century. In Tripoli construction kept pace with the captive population: the first bagne was built in 1615, a second in 1640, and a third in 1664. Bono, *Les Corsaires en Méditerranée*, trans. Ahmed Somaï (Paris: Editions Paris-Méditerranée, 1998), 219. Before the ascension of Mulay Isma'il in 1672,

matemores were scattered throughout Morocco, but with the centralization of slave holding in Meknes, the sultan built three new prisons, with the last one, built underground, completed in 1695. It suffered significant damage during the 1755 earthquake. During Mulay Isma'il's reign single female slaves entered the harem, whereas married ones lived with their husbands in separate abodes. Younès Nékrouf, *Une Amitié orageuse: Moulay Ismaïl et Louis XIV* (Paris: Albin Michel, 1987), 265–267; Audisio, "Recherches sur l'origine et la signification du mot 'bagne,'" *RA* 101 (1957): 363–380; Koehler, *L'Eglise chrétienne du Maroc et la Mission franciscaine (1221–1790)* (Paris: Société d'éditions franciscaines, 1934), 151–155; Jean de la Faye, Denis Mackar, Augustin d'Arcisas, and Henry Le Roy, *Relation en forme du journal du voyage pour la redemption des captifs aux roiaumes de Maroc et d'Alger pendant les annees 1723, 1724 et 1725 par les pères Jean de la Faye, Denis Mackar, Augustin d'Arcisas, Henry Le Roy*, ed. Ahmed Farouk (Paris: Bouchène, 2000), 71.

113. Moüette, *Relation de la captivité*, 116–117; Aranda, *Les Captifs d'Alger*, 69–69; Jean Gallonyé, *Histoire d'une esclave qui a été quatre années dans les prisons de Sallé en Afrique . . .* (Lyon: Rolin Glaize, 1679), 20–21; Antoine Galland, *Histoire de l'esclavage d'un marchand de la ville de Cassis, à Tunis*, ed. Catherine Guénot and Nadia Vasquez (Paris: Editions de la bibliothèque, 1992), 36.

114. Arvieux, informant to Molière, envoy to Tunis, and briefly consul to Algiers, described the two cities' bagnes in radically different lights. *Mémoires*, 4: 8; 5: 228–229. This discrepancy suggests the work of two different authors, one writing in the seventeenth century, the other (his posthumous editor) in the eighteenth. Denise Brahimi, *Opinions et regards européens sur le Maghreb aux XVIIe et XVIIIe siècles* (Algiers: Société nationale d'édition et de diffusion, 1978), 73; Turbet-Delof, *Bibliographie critique du Maghreb dans la littérature française (1532–1715)* (Algiers: Société nationale d'édition et de diffusion, 1976), 93.

115. [Michel Auvry], *Le Miroir de la charité chrétienne ou Relation du voyage que les religieux de l'Ordre de Nôtre Dame de la Mercy . . .* (Aix: Jean-Baptiste & Etienne Roize, 1663), 66, 253. Other descriptions by redemptive fathers include Dan, *Histoire de Barbarie* (1637), 405–407; [Comelin and La Motte], *Etat des Royaumes*, 49–50, 57–58.

116. The *Gazette de France* reported slave revolts in the bagnes of Algiers in 1662, 1753, and 1763; Dan (*Histoire de Barbarie* [1637], 393) discusses a rumor of one in 1629. See also Ahmad ibn 'Ali Zahhar, *Mudhakkirat al-Hajj Ahmad al-Sharif al-Zahhar, naqib ashraf al-Jazza'ir, 1246–1168 H./1754–1830 M.* (Algiers: al-Sharikah al-Wataniyah lil-Nashr wa-al-Tawzi', 1980), 18 n. 3, cited in Belhamissi, *Alger, l'Europe et la guerre secrète (1518–1830)* (Algiers: Dahlab, 1999), 46.

117. Jean-Noël Biraben provides a list of plague years for France and North Africa, respectively. *Les Hommes et la peste en France et dans les pays européens et méditerranéens*, 2 vols. (Paris: Mouton, 1975–1976), 1: 377–388, 433–438.

118. Friedman, "Trinitarian Hospitals in Algiers: An Early Example of Health Care for Prisoners of War," *Catholic Historical Review* 66, 4 (1980):

551–564; François Arnoulet, "L'Oeuvre hospitalière des Trinitaires et des Capucins dans la Régence de Tunis," *CT* 26, 105–106 (1978): 35–47; Charles L. Féraud, *Annales tripolitaines publiées avec une introduction et des notes par Augustin Bernard* (hereafter *AT*) (Tunis: Tournier; Paris: Vuibert, 1927; reprint, Paris: Bouchène, 2005), 192–193. On mortality rates, see Fontenay, "Le Maghreb barbaresque," 22; and Davis, *Christian Slaves, Muslim Masters*, 18.

119. Maurice de Toulon exemplifies seventeenth-century commentary on Muslim resignation to plague. *Le Capucin charitable . . .* (Paris: La Veuve Thierry, 1662), 25, cited in Colin Jones, "Plague and Its Metaphors in Early Modern France," *Representations* 53 (1996): 115.

120. On early modern European stereotypes of sodomite Muslims, see Matar, *Turks, Moors and Englishmen*, chap. 4; and Rudi C. Bleys, *The Geography of Perversion: Male-to-Male Sexual Behaviour outside the West and the Ethnographic Imagination* (New York: New York University Press, 1995), 19–22, 65–68, 79–81. For an analysis of Arab-Muslim and Ottoman ideas about sex and love (and practices) between men during the same period, see Khaled El-Rouayheb, *Before Homosexuality in the Arab-Islamic World, 1500–1800* (Chicago: University of Chicago Press, 2005); and Dror Ze'evi, *Producing Desire: Changing Sexual Discourse in the Ottoman Middle East, 1500–1900* (Berkeley: University of California Press, 2006).

121. Louis de Chénier, *Recherches historiques sur les Maures, et histoire de l'empire du Maroc . . .*, 3 vols. (Paris: author, 1787), 3: 130. On English responses to "turning Turk," see Claire S. Schen, "Breaching 'Community' in Britain: Captives, Renegades, and the Redeemed," in *Defining Community in Early Modern Europe*, ed. Michael J. Halvorson and Karen E. Spierling (Aldershot, UK: Ashgate, 2008), 229–246; Vitkus, *Turning Turk: English Theater and the Multicultural Mediterranean, 1570–1630* (New York: Palgrave Macmillan, 2003); Jonathan Burton, "English Anxiety and the Muslim Power of Conversion: Five Perspectives on 'Turning Turk' in Early Modern Texts," *Journal for Early Modern Cultural Studies* 2, 1 (2002): 35–67; and Matar, "'Turning Turk': Conversion to Islam in English Renaissance Thought," *Durham University Journal* 86, 55 (1994): 33–41. In the Spanish context, see Barbara Fuchs, *Passing for Spain: Cervantes and the Fictions of Identity* (Urbana: University of Illinois Press, 2003); and Fuchs, *Mimesis and Empire: The New World, Islam, and European Identities* (Cambridge: Cambridge University Press, 2001).

122. See the case of eighteen-year-old French renegade Luis Cadiera [Gadier?], tried by the Inquisition in Majorca, captured by Christians while accompanying a ra'is "he had as his friend." Archivo Histórico Nacional, Inquisición, Lo 898, f. 503 r–v, 1589, cited in Gonzalez-Raymond, *La Croix et le croissant*, 216.

123. On clothing as a crucial marker of Christian and Muslim identity, see Giovanni Ricci, "Crypto-identities: Disguised Turks, Christians and Jews," in *Finding Europe: Discourses on Margins, Communities, Images*, ed. Anthony Molho and Diogo Ramada Curto (New York: Bergham Books, 2007), 39–54. On its role for renegades from Marseille, see Audisio, "Renégats marseillais," 305–331.

124. Several redemptive fathers and former slaves make the same claim about

the special exemptions (circumcision) and additions (ingesting pork and accepting Christ) undergone by Jewish proselytes to Islam. See, for example, Dan, *Histoire de Barbarie* (1637), 327; and Aranda, *Les Captifs d'Alger*, 101.

125. Dan, *Histoire de Barbarie* (1649), 352; Boyer, "Continuation des mémoires des voyages du feu Père Hérault en Barbarie pour la rédemption qu'il a escrit luy même estant à Alger l'an 1645 ainsi qui s'en suit," *ROMM* 19 (1975): 38, reproducing AMM, MS 1212; Moüette, *Relation de la captivité*, 58, 288; Quartier, *L'Esclave religieux*, 113.

126. On early modern English authors' refusal to acknowledge the appeal of Islam, see Burton, "English Anxiety." On the appeal it actually had for significant numbers of Europeans, see Bennassar and Bennassar, *Les Chrétiens d'Allah*, esp. 237–266, 414–426.

127. Gonzalez-Raymond, *La Croix et le croissant*, 141–142; Bennassar and Bennassar, *Les Chrétiens d'Allah*, 168. Islam, like Judaism and Christianity, forbade the enslavement of believers. Numerous Christian slaves attested, however, that though conversion sometimes brought improved treatment, it did not necessarily lead to freedom.

128. According to Bennassar and Bennassar (*Les Chrétiens d'Allah*, 165–177), 11 percent of the renegades who appeared before the Inquisition in Malta had origins in France. Of those tried on another three Mediterranean islands, Gonzalez-Raymond (*La Croix et le croissant*, 138, 297) found that 8.8 percent in Sicily, 16 percent in Majorca, and 15 percent in Sardinia were French.

129. References to French renegades in high positions include Diego de Haëdo, *Topographie et histoire générale d'Alger*, trans. Dr. Monnereau and Adrien Berbrugger (Paris: Bouchène, 1998), 99–100; *Mercure françois* (1646): 361–365; [Girard], *HCRT*, vol. 2, ff. 10–11; Pennell, *Piracy and Diplomacy*, 32; and Boubaker, *La Régence de Tunis au XVIIe siècle: ses relations commerciales avec les ports de l'Europe méditerranéenne, Marseille et Livourne* (Zaghouan, Tunisia: CEROMA, 1987), 169.

130. Grandchamp, *FT*, 5: x, 154, 212; 6: xi–xii, 60–61, 124. On this point, among other Europeans, see Scaraffia, *Rinnegati*, 23; and Dakhlia, "'Turcs de profession'? Réinscriptions lignagères et redéfinitions sexuelles des convertis dans les cours maghrébines (XVIe–XIXe siècles)," in *Conversions islamiques: identités religieuses en islam méditerranéen*, ed. Mercedes García-Arenal (Paris: Maisonneuve & Larose, 2001), 167–169.

131. Fontenay, "Le Maghreb barbaresque," 23 n. 41; Grandchamp, *FT*, 7: xix.

132. French Chancellery acts from Tunis (reprinted and discussed by Grandchamp, *FT*, 4: xv n. 14, 156, 162, 166, 173, 174, 237, 308, 321, 350, 352–356; 5: ix, 11, 17, 23, 118, 143) offer details about d'Arcos's biography, captivity, and apostasy. The last sign of him dates to 1 August 1637 (ACT, vol. 11, f. 652). For a recent analysis, see Jane Tolbert, "Ambiguity and Conversion in the Correspondence of Nicolas-Claude Fabri de Peiresc and Thomas D'Arcos, 1630–1637," *Journal of Early Modern History* 13, 1 (2009): 1–24.

133. Nicolas Claude Fabri de Peiresc to Honoré Aycard, 26 December 1632, in Peiresc, *Lettres de Peiresc*, 7 vols., ed. Philippe Tamizey de Larroque (Paris:

Imprimerie nationale, 1888–1898), 7: 287. Additional correspondence reproduced in Thomas d'Arcos, "Lettres inédites de Thomas d'Arcos à Peiresc," ed.
Larroque, *RA* 32 (1888): 161–195, 289–302.

134. Rostagno, *Mi faccio turco*, 52.

135. On taqiyya as practiced by Iberian Mudejars and Moriscos, Shi'ites, and,
perhaps, Leo Africanus/al-Hassan al-Wazzan, see Kathryn A. Miller, *Guard-
ians of Islam: Religious Authority and Muslim Communities of Late Medieval
Spain* (New York: Columbia University Press, 2008), 141; Devin J. Stewart,
"Taqiyyah as Performance: The Travels of Baha' al-Din al-'Amili in the Otto-
man Empire 991–93/1583–85," in *Law and Society in Islam*, ed. Stewart, Baber
Johansen, and Amy Singer (Princeton, NJ: Markus Wiener, 1995), 1–70; and
Natalie Zemon Davis, *Trickster Travels: A Sixteenth-Century Muslim between
Worlds* (New York: Hill and Wang, 2006), 188–189. That European renegades
might have resorted to this Muslim practice is suggested by Gonzalez-Raymond,
La Croix et le croissant, 112–115.

136. Audisio, "Renégats marseillais," 318–331.

137. Followers of the Marranos-as-modern-men interpretation include Rich-
ard H. Popkin, "Epicureanism and Skepticism in the Early Seventeenth Cen-
tury," in *Philomathes: Studies and Essays in the Humanities in Memory of
Philip Merlan*, ed. Robert B. Palmer and Robert Hamerton-Kelly (The Hague:
Martinus Nijhoff, 1971), 353; Yosef Hayim Yerushalmi, *From Spanish Court to
Italian Ghetto: Isaac Cardoso, a Study in Seventeenth-Century Marranism and
Jewish Apologetics* (Seattle: University of Washington Press, 1981), 44; and José
Faur, *In the Shadow of History: Jews and Conversos at the Dawn of Modernity*
(Albany: SUNY Press, 1992), 142.

138. For a convincing critique of this tendency—as exemplified in Scaraffia,
Rinnegati, among others—see E. Natalie Rothman, "Becoming Venetian: Conversion and Transformation in the Seventeenth-Century Mediterranean," *Mediterranean Historical Review* 21, 1 (2006): 39–75.

139. See chap. 3 of this book, as well as Dakhlia, "Ligne de fuite: impostures et reconstructions identitaires en Méditerranée musulmane à l'époque moderne," in Moatti and Kaiser, *Gens de passage*, 427–457.

140. Dursteler (*Venetians in Constantinople*, 10–19) gives an excellent
synthesis of the literature on "identity formation" in the early modern Mediterranean. For a medieval vantage, see Epstein, *Purity Lost: Transgressing
Boundaries in the Eastern Mediterranean, 1000–1400* (Baltimore: Johns Hopkins University Press, 2006).

141. Braudel, *The Mediterranean*, 2: 889.

CHAPTER TWO

1. Berenguier et al. to Louis XIII, Marrakech, 4 December 1622, AAE,
Maroc, CC, vol. 1, reprinted in Castries, Cossé Brissac, and Cenival, *SIHM*
(1911), 1st ser., 3: 86–89.

2. The Treaty of Montpellier, signed in October 1622, ended Huguenot autonomy in every part of France except Montauban and La Rochelle.

3. Bergasse and Rambert (*Histoire du commerce de Marseille*, 4: 137–178) list all the goods traded in seventeenth-century Marseille.

4. "Discours abrégé de l'entrée du roy Louis 13 en sa ville de Marseille le 8 [*sic*] novembre 1622, rapporté ici pour servir de mémoire," AMM, AA67 (OC), *Cérémonial de la ville* (1622), ff. 974–980, reprinted by Marie-Claude Canova-Green, "L'Entrée de Louis XIII dans Marseille, le 7 novembre 1622," *Dix-septième siècle* 3, 212 (2001): 523–530.

5. Although the Trinitarians of Marseille sponsored no voyages of redemption during the period 1610–1628, they did arrange for (and presumably pay for) the release of 158 slaves held in Algiers, Tunis, and Constantinople. See app. 2.

6. A 10 January 1622 *arrêt* from the Parlement de Provence (cited in Panzac, *Quarantaines et lazarets: l'Europe et la peste d'Orient [XVIIe–XXe siècles]* [Aix-en-Provence: Edisud, 1986], 32–35; and in Françoise Hildesheimer, *Le Bureau de la santé de Marseille sous l'Ancien régime: le renfermement de la contagion* [Marseille: Fédération historique de Provence, 1980], 21–22) deprived smaller maritime communities of the less expensive and more convenient option of containing disease independently (Etienne-Michel Masse, *Mémoire historique et statistique sur le canton de La Ciotat: Département des Bouches-du-Rhône* [Marseille: Caranud fils, 1842], 197).

7. Berenguier et al. to Louis XIII, 87; quotation from Canova-Green, "L'Entrée de Louis XIII," 530.

8. In 1623, for instance, Marseille demanded the diversion of royal galleys from fighting Protestants on the Atlantic to take on Muslims in the Mediterranean (AMM, BB27, f. 7); in 1625 the Parlement de Provence warned against "the loss of commerce with the Levant, if galleys are not marshaled to prevent the extension of Barbary piracy" (cited in Grammont, *HA*, 144).

9. For reasons that continue to puzzle historians, Richelieu temporarily moved the king's Mediterranean naval base from Marseille to Toulon in 1624. Masson, *Les Galères de France*, 104, 128–129; Alan James, *The Navy and Government in Early Modern France, 1572–1661* (Suffolk, UK: Royal Historical Society, 2004), 97.

10. See, among other depositions left by pilgrims at the chapel at Sainte-Anne d'Auray near Rennes, the one from 12 April 1641 (Archives de la Basilique de Sainte-Anne d'Auray, *Registre des procès-verbaux de faveurs signalées, 1625–1687*, 1: 423). French newspapers described other successful French slave uprisings at sea. See the *Mercure françois* 3 (1613): 18–19; the *Gazette de France* (1645): 1131, 1177, cited in Grammont, "Etudes algériennes: la rédemption," 5–6; and the *Mercure galant* 3 (1673): 207–220, cited in Turbet-Delof, *La Presse périodique française et l'Afrique barbaresque au XVIIe siècle (1611–1715)* (Geneva: Droz, 1973), 143.

11. *Gazette de France* (1634): 487, (1665): 945, cited in Grammont, "Etudes algériennes: la rédemption," 5–6; Rocqueville, *Relations des moeurs*, 95–96; [Nolasque Néant], *Relation de ce qui s'est passé dans les trois voyages que les religieux de l'Ordre de Notre-Dame de la Mercy ont fait dans les etats du roy du Maroc . . .* (Paris: Antoine-Urbain Coustelier, 1724), 182–184. See also Penz, *Les Captifs français*, 305–311.

12. Cited in Earle, *Corsairs of Malta and Barbary*, 54. In assessing premiums, agents considered among other factors season, destination, route, and incidence of piracy. L. A. Boiteux, *La Fortune de mer: le besoin de sécurité et les débuts de l'assurance maritime* (Paris: SEVPEN, 1968), 95–97, 150, 163, 181. For a sample insurance contract, see Plantet, *CDA*, 1: 409 n. 1.

13. Fontenay, "Le Maghreb barbaresque," 17. The August 1681 *Ordonnance de la marine*, while sanctioning insurance against capture (article 9), specifically banned life insurance (article 10) as open to abuse and contrary to good mores. Eighteenth-century commentaries by jurists Robert Joseph Pothier (1777), René Josué Valin (1760), and Balthazard-Marie Emérigon (1783) determined that insurers still had to pay even if the captive died in chains, fled, or won release by some other means, but disallowed further claims in case of recapture or death on the return voyage.

14. Emérigon, *Traité des assurances et des contrats à la grosse*, 2 vols. (Marseille: Jean Mossy, 1783), 1: 532; Hyacinthe Boniface, *Arrests notables de la cour du Parlement de Provence, cours des comptes, aydes & finances du même païs*, 5 vols. (Lyon: Veuve d'Horace Molin, 1708), 5: 463–466.

15. Grandchamp, *FT*, 7: 184.

16. Based on chancery records reproduced in Grandchamp, *FT*, Maurice Eisenbeth calculates that Jews in Tunis loaned ransom funds to Christians 136 times from 1599 to 1699. "Les Juifs en Algérie et en Tunisie à l'époque turque (1516–1830)," *RA* 96 (1952): 358. Devoulx, writing under the name J. M. Haddey, lists ransom payments by Jewish merchants in Algiers throughout *Le Livre d'or des israélites algériens: recueil de renseignements inédits et authentiques sur les principaux négociants juifs d'Alger pendant la période turque* (Algiers: A. Bouyer, 1871).

17. For instance, on 17 April 1635, "trésorier général" François d'Anthoine left one thousand livres to ransom slaves native to Marseille (Archives communales d'Aix-en-Provence, CC595, f. 666 v); in 1661 a Knight of Malta left money to ransom a prisoner in Tripoli (Archives départementales de l'Ardèche, 1J372); and in the 1690s, one M. de Pupin left twenty-five thousand écus for the redemption of captives from Marseille (AMM, GGL105).

18. Slave H. Guiran to his father, Tunis, 18 April 1640, ACT, GG52.

19. Several early modern French jurists cite Justinian's *Novellae* 115, chap. 3, which lists among causes for disinheritance "the inhuman refusal of a son to oblige himself for the deliverance of his father," as Balthasar Débezieux puts it in *Arrests notables de la cour du Parlement de Provence* . . . (Paris: P. G. Mercier et al., 1750), 554. See also Weiss, "Humble Petitioners and Able Contractors: French Women as Intermediaries in the Redemption of Captives," in Kaiser, *Le Commerce des captifs*, 333–344.

20. Arnaud de la Rouvière, *Traité de la révocation et nullité des donations, legs, institutions, fidéicommis & élections* . . . (Toulouse: N. Caranove, 1738), 37–38; Pothier, *Oeuvres de Pothier*, 2nd ed., 10 vols., ed. Jean Joseph Bugnet (Paris: Cosse, 1861), 8: 26.

21. Claude de Ferrière, *La Jurisprudence du Code de Justinien* . . . , 2 vols. (Paris: J. Cochart, 1684), 1: 426–427, citing *arrêts* from 1627 and 1644.

22. According to Boniface (*Arrests notables*, 3: 801–806), the Roman Digest (and the 1681 naval ordinance) "gives them this liberty when it regards taking their family members out of enemy hands" (804).

23. Slave Pierre Calabre to his wife, Algiers, 24 September 1634, ADV, 3E8/15. See also slave Alexandre Anglés to his mother in Frontignan, from a galley near Smyrna, 8 July 1670, ADH, 50H50.

24. According to Marthe Folain Le Bras, Roman law initially allowed married women to retain full capacity to act juridically. *Un Projet d'ordonnance du chancelier Daguesseau: étude de quelques incapacités de donner et de recevoir sous l'Ancien régime* (Paris: Sirey, 1941), 298–300. Contact with Germanic law influenced customary codes, however, and by the sixteenth century made married women incapable. See François Bourjon citing a sixteenth-century *arrêt* from the Parlement of Paris and the opinions of several predecessors. Married female minors, Bourjon noted, still needed permission from a judge. *Le Droit commun de la France et la Coutume de Paris réduits en principes . . .* , 2nd ed., 2 vols. (Paris: Grangé et Cellot, 1770), 2: 585–586.

25. This pact (from October 1671) and similar ones (from November 1663 and February 1668) are cited in Grandchamp, *FT*, 4: 166; 7: 76, 136, 174–175.

26. ADBR, 9B2, f. 1238, cited in Busquet, *Inventaire sommaire*, 4: 62. The chevalier de Romilly was ransomed through the efforts of consul Jean Le Vacher. See Grandchamp, *FT*, 7: xi–xii, 78–82.

27. Louis Merle, "Notes et documents: rachat de prisonniers faits par les barbaresques au XVIIe siècle," *Revue du Bas Poitou* 71, 2 (1960): 142–143.

28. Georges d'Avenel, *Histoire économique de la propriété, des salaries, des denrées, et de tous les prix en général depuis l'an 1200 jusqu'en l'an 1800*, 7 vols. (Paris: Imprimerie nationale, 1894–1926), 3: 541, 4: 269–271. On Christian slave prices in North Africa generally, see Mathiex, "Trafic et prix de l'homme."

29. ADIV, C2653, f. 85 r, cited in Michel Duval, "Des Bretons chez les barbaresques: les Etats de Bretagne à leur secours!" *Dalc'homp Soñj* 14 (1986): 10. Other examples of female petitioners in seventeenth-century France include Louise Lucas of Nantes (Archives départementales de Loire-Atlantique, 4E2/21, 4E2/1760, cited in Julie Hardwick, *The Practice of Patriarchy: Gender and the Politics of Household Authority in Early Modern France* [University Park: Pennsylvania State University Press, 1998], 129) and Catherine Dartille of Biarritz (Archives municipales de Bayonne, GG256, cited in J. B. Daranatz, "Captifs basques et béarnais rachetés en Afrique au XVIIe et XVIIIe siècles," *Guere Herria* 7, 4 [1927]: 323). On female petitioners in seventeenth-century England, see Matar, "Wives, Captive Husbands and Turks: The First Women Petitioners in Caroline England," *Explorations in Renaissance Culture* 23 (1997): iii–29.

30. Both religious confraternities and, at least in the eighteenth century, secular ones allocated money for the redemption of captives. On Freemason efforts in 1781, see Pierre-Yves Beaurepaire, "Correspondances, passeports et signalements maçonniques: un dispositif de reconnaissance fraternelle et de gestion de la mobilité au XVIIIe siècle," in Moatti and Kaiser, *Gens de passage*, 389.

31. On Protestant redemption networks, see Paul de Félice, *Les Protestants*

d'autrefois: vie intérieure des églises, moeurs et usages, 4 vols. (Paris: Fischbacher, 1896–1898), 1: 118; Robert Petitpré, "Tentative de rachat de deux captifs chaumois an Maroc en 1636," *Bulletin de la Société Olona*, 97–98 (1981):
16–18; Petitpré, "Retour très probable de Jean Blay esclave au Maroc, à la
Chaume: incidents auxquels il a mêlé avec le curé du lieu en 1640," *Bulletin
de la Société Olona*, 102 (1982): 18–20; and *Actes des synodes*, 28th Synod,
Charenton, 26 December 1644 to 26 January 1645 (The Hague: n.p., 1710), 2:
677–678, reprinted in *Bulletin de la Société de Histoire du Protestantisme français* (hereafter *BSHPF*) 13 (1864): 119. See also Charles Serfass, "Les Esclaves
chrétiens au Maroc du XVIe au XVIIe siècles," *BSHPF* 79 (1930): 234–235; and
ADCM, E113, reproduced by Gaston Tortat, "Un Livre de raison, 1639–1668:
journal de Samuel Robert, lieutenant particulier en l'élection de Saintes," *Archives historiques de la Saintonge et de l'Aunis* 11 (1883): 328.

32. Contract to transport fifteen thousand livres to Salé and Tetouan between
the Trinitarians and Protestant merchants Nicolas Bonnereau and Pierre Beri-
gier, La Rochelle, 30 August 1653, ADCM, Minutes Cherbonnier, cited in Marcel Delafosse, "Les Rochelais au Maroc au XVIIe siècle: commerce et rachat
de captifs," *Revue d'histoire des colonies* 35 (1948): 79–82. See also Castries,
Cossé Brissac, and Cenival, *SIHM* (1911), 1st ser., 3: 688 and following pages;
as well as [Nazaire Arnoux and Jean Héron], *La Miraculeuse rédemption des
captifs faite à Salé, coste de Barbarie . . .* (Paris: Julien Jacquin, 1654).

33. Castries, Cossé Brissac, and Cenival, *SIHM* (1953), 2nd ser., 5: 572–529;
(1960), 2nd ser., 6: 633 n. 1, 804 n. 1. Also see La Faye et al., *Relation en forme
du journal*, 28 n. 1, 62–63, 70–71.

34. Dan, *Histoire de Barbarie* (1649), 144; Lucien Hérault, *Les Larmes et
clameurs des Chrestiens, François de nation, captifs en la ville d'Alger en Barbarie . . .* (Paris: D. Houssaye, 1643), 33; Pierre Michelin et al., *Le Tableau de
Piété envers les Captifs . . .* (Châlons-en-Champagne: Jean Bouchard, 1668),
214 and following pages; [Comelin and de La Motte], *Etat des Royaumes*, 106.

35. Citing Grandchamp, *FT*, Eisenbeth ("Les Juifs en Algérie," 358–359) calculates 403 redemptions executed by Jews based in Tunis from 1610 to 1702.
Devoulx, *Le Livre d'or*, shows the overwhelming majority of orders from Venice
and Livorno but also from Lisbon, Genoa, Naples, and Hamburg. Jonathan
Israel ("Crypto-Judaism in 17th-Century France: An Economic and Religious
Bridge between the Hispanic World and the Sephardic Diaspora," in *Diasporas
within a Diaspora: Jews, Crypto-Jews, and the World of Maritime Empires,
1540–1740* [Leiden, Netherlands: Brill, 2002], 263–264) highlights two 1625
contracts (from the Gemeentearchief Amsterdam, 646B, pp. 1250–1251), and
"Amsterdam Notarial Deeds Pertaining to the Portuguese Jews in Amsterdam
before 1639," no. 3349, demonstrating the collaboration of Jews in Amsterdam,
Bayonne, and Salé to buy back slaves from France's Basque region. Alexander H.
de Groot ("Ottoman North Africa and the Dutch Republic in the Seventeenth
and Eighteenth Centuries," *ROMM* 39 [1985]: 133, 139) lists the names of some
of the most active Jewish families in slave redemption.

36. Among many examples, see Claude Auxcousteaux de Fercourt, *Relation
de l'esclavage des sieurs de Fercourt et Regnard, pris sur mer par les corsaires*

d'Alger (1678–79) (Toulouse: E. Privat, 1905), 51; and Héron, *Relation du voyage que R.P. Héron supérieur-ministre de Chateaubriand en Bretagne, a fait en la ville d'Alger* . . . (Paris: Julien Jaquin, 1660), 13–18.

37. Letters patent from 1543 exempted Marseille from the *droit d'aubaine*, which denied resident aliens the benefits of inheritance, allowing the king to seize their property at death. So as not to drive away foreigners whose trade brought in wealth, Francis I agreed that they might reside in the city without naturalization and gain sovereign status by marrying locally. Augustin Fabre, *Histoire de Marseille*, 2 vols. (Marseille: Marius Olive, 1829) 2: 79. More generally, on the treatment of foreigners in early modern France, see Peter Sahlins, *Unnaturally French: Foreign Citizens in the Old Regime and After* (Ithaca, NY: Cornell University Press, 2004).

38. Two thousand casualties a day, according to consul Claude Severt, Tunis, 23 April 1622, ACCM, AA511 (OC), cited in Plantet, *CBT*, 1: 59. Plague was still raging in 1624.

39. In a 1623 letter, dey Yusuf informed the Marseille consuls that in the previous "13 moons," he had turned over 182 French slaves to the resident consul in Tunis. ACCM, AA544 (OC), reprinted in Plantet, *CBT*, 1: 61.

40. Bey Osta-Morat to Napollon, Tunis, 3 January, ACCM, AA544 (OC), reprinted in Plantet, *CBT*, 1: 94–95; consul Lange Martin to CCM, Tunis, 11 April 1629, ACCM, AA514 (OC), reprinted in Plantet, *CBT*, 1: 96–95, and 10 April 1630, ACCM, AA514 (OC), reprinted in Plantet, *CBT*, 1: 103; envoy Anthoine Bérengier to CCM, Tunis, 4 July 1629, ACCM, AA544 (OC), reprinted in Plantet, *CBT*, 1: 100–101; Marseille aldermen to Louis XIII, Marseille, 4 January 1631, AAE, MD, Afrique, vol. 8, f. 23, reprinted in Plantet, *CBT*, 1: 104–105 n. 2. See also Napollon to CCM, Bastion, 1 June 1629, reprinted in Grammont, "Relations," 296–297.

41. Grammont, "Etudes algériennes: la rédemption," 18; Napollon to [?], Algiers, 14 December 1626, CADN, CA, vol. 1, ff. 18, 20.

42. *Arrêt* dated 6 November 1627, cited in Plantet, *CDA*, 1: 29 n. 2.

43. For the details of Toulon's loans, see ACT, BB55, GG52, cited in Gustave Lambert, "L'Oeuvre de la rédemption des captifs à Toulon," *Revue de Marseille et de Provence* 10 (1864): 360–361.

44. "Procès verbal . . . des consuls et délégués des communautés du littoral provençal," 14 March 1628, ACC, GG33, now filed at ADBR, 139E.

45. Hard-won contributions from Toulon, La Ciotat, Six-Fours, Cassis, Cannes, Martigues, Marseille, and the king came to 82,190 livres, but Napollon spent 272,435 livres on ransom. Marseille also gave 30,000 livres to the duc de Guise "for the Turks of Algiers and two cannons taken from his galley." Plantet, *CDA*, 1: 34–35 n. 2; Grammont, "Etudes algériennes: la rédemption," 18; ACCM, AA462 (OC), and AMM, Délibérations, 25 August 1628, cited in Masson, *Histoire du commerce*, 50; quittance from the Marseille consuls, 12 September 1628, reproduced in Grammont, "Relations," 113–114.

46. Consul Balthazar de Vias to Richelieu, Marseille, 10 August 1627, CADN, CA, vol. 1, ff. 23–24.

47. For the text of the 1628 treaty, see Rouard de Card, *TF*, 15–19. A slightly

different wording of the sixth clause on apostasy appears in Dan, *Histoire de Barbarie* (1637), 135–136.

48. Napollon to Marseille consuls, Bastion, 4 July and 20 December 1629, reprinted in Grammont, "Relations," 201–202, 306–307.

49. Ambassador Comte de Césy, 23 April 1627, ACCM, AA143 (OC), cited in Masson, *Histoire du commerce*, 42.

50. Slightly different chronologies appear in Féraud, *AT*, 106; Mercier, *Histoire de l'Afrique septentrionale*, 3: 217; and Masson, *Histoire du commerce*, 42 n. 1.

51. French slaves, Tripoli, 25 January and 5 April 1631; Captain Jean Beau, Tripoli, 8 May 1634, all in ACCM, AA555 (OC), cited in Masson, *Histoire du commerce*, 42–43.

52. Though some historians date the establishment of Marseille's health bureau to this outbreak, Hildesheimer (*Le Bureau de la santé*, 17–20) demonstrates that the city had been appointing officers to monitor plague at least since the fifteenth century. What occurred in 1630 was the renovation of the city's "old infirmaries."

53. Benoist Pierre, "Le Père Joseph, l'empire Ottoman et la Méditerranée au début du XVIIe siècle," *CM* 71, 2 (2005), http://cdlm.revues.org/document968 .html; Pierre, *Le Père Joseph: l'éminence grise de Richelieu* (Paris: Perrin, 2007), chap. 7.

54. Penz, *Les Captifs français*, 25–29.

55. Later detailed in François d'Angers, *Histoire de la Mission des Pères capucins de la province de Touraine au royaume de Maroque en Afrique . . .* (Niort: Veuve Jean Bureau, 1644).

56. Interpreter Jean Armand (formerly Mustafa), a Muslim convert, is the presumptive author of *Voyages d'Afrique faits par le commandement du Roy où sont contenus les navigations Français entreprises en 1629 et 1630 . . .* (Paris: Nicolas Trabouilliet, 1631). Penz, *Les Captifs français*, 25–38; Castries, *Agents et voyageurs français au Maroc, 1530–1660* (Paris: Ernest Leroux, 1911), lxxii.

57. A 1618 book by a friar from Toulouse, for example, argued that the king who sponsored the Mercedarians was really French since he was born in Montpellier, that the order's founder Nolasque had French parents, and that the white cross on the Mercedarian banner was a quintessentially French symbol. Jean Latomy, *Histoire de la fondation de l'ordre de Nostre Dame de la Mercy pour la rédemption des captifs* (Paris: Sebastien Huré, 1618), 52–53.

58. Jean Vallery-Radot, "Note sur les estampes gravées par Mellan et Van Thulden pour les ordres rédempteurs de Notre-Dame de la Merci et des Trinitaires," *Bulletin philologique et historique du Comité des travaux historiques et scientifiques* (1955): 419.

59. The Mercedarians clearly did not promptly pay off the debt contracted by François Dathia, head of the Paris convent. In 1634 English merchants laid claim to the order's Parisian properties. Penz, *Les Captifs français*, 44; Castries, Cossé Brissac, and Cenival, *SIHM* (1911), 1st ser., 3: 513; *Histoire de l'ordre sacré*, 809–811; AN, LL1556, ff. 342–343, cited in Cocard, *Les Pères de la Merci*, 203.

60. In October 1629, the governor of Salé agreed to a five-month truce and

the return of all French captives at market price. But it took another year, another trip by Razilly and Chalard (Dathia remained in Morocco during the interim), and the capture of three Saletian vessels to jump-start the release of slaves. A second truce with Salé was signed on 3 September 1630. Penz, *Les Captifs français*, 38–40.

61. Earlier Trinitarian processions in France commemorating the return of Christian captives from eastern Europe and the Iberian Peninsula include a 1448 Parisian march before a ransom mission to Granada and a 1456 celebration afterward, as well as performances in Arles, Arras, and Paris to commemorate the 1602 deliverance of 76–80 captives from Gran, Hungary. Alexandre Tuetey, ed., *Journal d'un bourgeois de Paris, 1405–1449* (Paris: H. Champion, 1881), 338; Pierre de Vaissière, *De Roberti Gaguini, ministri generalis ordinis Sanctae Trinitatis, vita et operibus* (Chartres: Durandi, 1896), 8 vols., translated and cited by Deslandres, *OT*, 1: 398; Calixte de la Providence, *Corsaires et rédempteurs: ou Récit des souffrances des anciens captifs et des travaux entrepris pour leur délivrance* (hereafter *CR*) (Lille: Desclée de Brouwer, 1884), 315; Alonso, *LC*, 1: 202 n.

62. On at least forty-three slave processions organized from the seventeenth century until 1785, see my "From Barbary to France: Processions of Redemption and Early-Modern Cultural Identity," in *La Liberazione dei "captivi" tra Christianità e Islam: oltre la crociata e il gihad tolleranza e servizi umanitario (Rome, Sept. 16–19 1998)*, ed. Giulio Cipollone (Vatican City: Archivio Segreto Vaticano, 2000), 789–805; Chantal de La Véronne, "Quelques processions de captifs en France à leur retour du Maroc, d'Algérie ou de Tunis," *ROMM* 8, 1 (1970): 131–142; and app. 2.

63. Article 21 of the Mercedarians' 1272 Constitutions reads as follows: "Captives ransomed by the brothers are immediately to swear an oath . . . that they will not leave the service of the order until the time assigned by the master or by those who have redeemed them has passed. During that time assigned to them, let them shave off their beards and let the brother who directs them provide appropriately for their needs without any complaints. When the assigned time is completed, let their beards be shaved and their hair cut. They are to be given new clothing according to the season it is and suitable provision, so that they may return to their lands with cheer and happiness." Translated from Catalan by Brodman, *Ransoming Captives*, 134.

64. Alonso (*LC*, 1: 295, 324) cites sixteenth-century processions in Salamanca and Valencia, respectively. Torres analyzes other Spanish ones (*Prisioneros de los infieles*, 99–115). On 21 September 1559, the French ambassador to Lisbon, Jean Nicot, recounted the arrival of "about 200 captives that had been purchased from Algiers by the mercy of this city. . . . Each of them carried at the end of a stick a piece of bread the size of an orange, of which they were given three to live." BN, NAF 6638, f. 163, cited in Jacques Wilhelm, "Captifs chrétiens à Alger," *Revue des sciences politiques* 56 (1933): 134. On features of Italian slave processions of this period, see Ricci, "Crypto-identities," 44.

65. After 120 slaves disembarked in Brouage on 27 September 1630, according to Penz (*Les Captifs français*, 41), all but one (with a musket injury) participated in this religious and patriotic ceremony.

66. Latomy, *Histoire de la fondation*, 169–174; *Histoire de l'ordre sacré*, 808–811. Rather than an account of his Moroccan voyage of redemption, Dathia published a biography of the founder: *Abrégé de la vie de S. Pierre Nolasque* ... (Paris: Louis Feugé, 1631).

67. Penz, *Les Captifs français*, 41–44; French captives to Louis XIII, Safi, 30 November 1630, AN, Marine B7 49, reprinted in Castries, Cossé Brissac, and Cenival, *SIHM* (1911), 1st ser., 3: 356.

68. On the role of David and Moses Pallache (nephews to the eponymous Samuel) in helping and hindering peacemaking and slave liberating, see García-Arenal and Gerard Wiegers, *A Man of Three Worlds: Samuel Pallache, a Moroccan Jew in Catholic and Protestant Europe*, trans. Martin Beagles (Baltimore: Johns Hopkins University Press, 2003), 114–117.

69. Penz, *Les Captifs français*, 44–46. According to Haim Zeev Hirschberg, David Pallache helped organize the 1631 release of 180 French captives transferred from Marrakech to Safi in exchange for one hundred thousand livres worth of fabric. *A History of the Jews in North Africa*, 3 vols. (Leiden, Netherlands: Brill, 1974–1981), 2: 225, 228.

70. *Mercure françois* 17 (1631): 174–185; 18 (1632): 78; Pierre, *Le Père Joseph*, 201, 204.

71. Theodor van Thulden, *Revelatio ordinis s[anctis]s[i]mae Trinitatis redemptionis captivorum sub Innocentio tertio, anno 1198* (Paris: n.p., 1633). On these images, see Emmanuelle Bermès, "Le Couvent des Mathurins de Paris et l'estampe au XVIIe siècle" (Thèse, Ecole nationale des Chartes, 2001); and Le Fur, "La Renaissance d'un apostolat." Despite Trinitarian efforts, however, it was a multinational Mercedarian mission that next managed to free a few Frenchmen. *Les Noms et qualitez de quatre-vingt-dix-sept chrestiens captifs* ... (Paris: Bureau d'Adresse, 1634).

72. Philippe d'Estampes, seigneur de l'Isle-Antry, in Algiers to protest violations of the 1628 treaty, informed his superiors of ten thousand slaves in North Africa; he advocated negotiating with Tunis and Tripoli and returning all Algerian galley slaves from France. Marseille, 11 December 1631, CADN, CA, vol. 1, ff. 50–53. Because the general of the galleys was demanding one thousand écus for each of the 150 Turks he was supposed to relinquish, Napollon told Richelieu, the dey of Algiers was holding on to 150 French captives. It should not come down to so little money to rescue men who have suffered for so long, he wrote. Bastion, 26 April 1632, CADN, CA, vol. 1, f. 60.

73. Brother Gaspard de Crest, slave, to the Marseille city council, Tunis, 10 April 1629, ACCM, G43; slaves Damours et al. to Louis XIII, Tunis, 26 May 1631, AAE, MD, Afrique, vol. 8, f. 24, reprinted in Plantet, *CBT*, 1: 113.

74. "Voyage et inspection de M. [Henri] de Séguiran sur les côtes de Provence en 1633," reprinted in Eugène Sue, ed., *Correspondance de Henri d'Escoubleau de Sourdis* ..., 3 vols. (Paris: Crapelet, 1839), 3: 276, 300. Dan (*Histoire de Barbarie* [1637], 284–286, 313–314) counted eighty vessels and 1,339 French slaves who landed in Algiers between 1629 and 1634, and a total of 25,000 Christian captives (1,500 French, 8,000 renegades) in Algiers; 7,000 Christian captives (3,000–4,000 renegades) in Tunis; 400–500 Christian captives (100

renegades) in Tripoli; and 1,500 Christian captives in Salé (430 French, 300 renegades).

75. CCM deputy Jéhan Blanchard to [Richelieu?], Algiers, 11 February 1634, CADN, CA, vol. 1, f. 64. The French slaves themselves also petitioned the CCM to let the Muslim oarsmen go free. Algiers, 4 September 1635, ACCM, G40.

76. Sanson Le Page, Napollon's successor at the Bastion, made the trip to Algiers with Dan. See Grammont, "Relations," 418–424. See also AMM, Délibérations, 29 September 1634, cited in Masson, *Histoire du commerce,* 38 n. 3.

77. The Franco-Moroccan treaty was signed in Safi by Sultan Mulay al-Sharif and du Chalard on 18 May 1635 (Rouard de Card, *TF,* 311–314), then approved by the inhabitants of Salé in September. Du Chalard traded 27 Muslim rowers for 28 French captives in Marrakech, paid for 215, borrowed for 40, and pledged for 333, who were conditionally released from their chains. In addition, he liberated 60, mostly Breton slaves who had come up with their own ransoms. Royal disgrace was not du Chalard's only problem: a lawsuit brought by the Estates of Brittany accused him of spending four times what they had allocated to ransom 97 Bretons (Penz, *Les Captifs français,* 48–51).

78. *Déclaration royale justifiant par le danger barbaresque l'établissement d'une nouvelle escadre de galères* (Paris: Estienne Richer, 1637), 923–925; Grammont, "Relations," 424–425, 427–428.

79. *Mémoires donnés par le bailli de Forbin . . .* (1639), ADBR, fonds Coriolis, 62/28, cote provisoire, and BN, Collection Dupuy 569, f. 193, cited in Masson, *Les Galères de France,* 106. Turbet-Delof (*La Presse périodique,* 14) takes an even more cynical view of antipiracy policies, writing that the real reason for building up the galleys was not to "cleanse the sea of corsairs and conserve the security of our coasts," as a 7 May 1635 royal edict declared, but to fight the Spanish. He deems an article on the subject from the *Mercure françois* ([1637]: 923–925) an example of "fake maurophobia," which, in fact, served to "camouflage anti-Spanish preparations."

80. In 1637, for example, the families of several Marseille captives made their own ransom arrangements with Isaac Pallache (Castries, Cossé Brissac, and Cenival, *SIHM* [1911], 1st ser., 3: 562). By 1639, the 333 French captives du Chalard left behind had diminished to 150. When the Trinitarians arrived in Salé in 1642, they freed the last 41 who remained. No royal emissary returned to Morocco during the 1640s or 1650s. The Trinitarians, by contrast, conducted another voyage to Morocco, rescuing 43 captives from Salé but leaving 35 in Tetouan behind (Penz, *Les Captifs français,* 53–62).

81. Charles-Roux, *FA,* 127; Plantet, *CDA,* 1: 45–46 n. 2. According to both Plantet (*CBT,* 1: 125–126 n. 2) and Grammont (*HA,* 160–162), the capture of two Algerian boats and liberation of seventy-five Christians during the 1637 siege led by de Sourdis and vice-admiral Théodore de Mantin provided the direct impetus for the Bastion's destruction. Correspondence among Louis XIII, de Sourdis, and Bastion de France director and envoy Le Page shows a concern that every French renegade in Algiers had converted of his own volition. Sue, *Correspondance,* 2: 386–411; Grammont, "Relations," 429–438.

82. *La Rédemption des captifs faite par les religieux de l'ordre de la Sainte-Trinité* . . . (Paris: Jean Petit-Pas, 1635); Dan, *Histoire de Barbarie* (1637), 63–68.

83. Le Fur makes this observation in "La Renaissance d'un apostolat."

84. On the Te Deum, see Kate Van Orden, *Music, Discipline and Arms in Early Modern France* (Chicago: University of Chicago Press, 2005), chap. 4.

85. As Clifford Geertz notes, the most important component of a procession always stands at the center. "Centers, Kings and Charisma: Reflections on the Symbolics of Power," in *Local Knowledge: Further Essays in Interpretive Anthropology* (New York: Basic Books, 1983), chap. 6.

86. On the *processions générales*, see, for example, Robert Darnton, "A Bourgeois Puts His World in Order: The City as Text," in *The Great Cat Massacre and Other Episodes in French Cultural History* (New York: Vintage Books, 1985), 107–143.

87. Dan, *Histoire de Barbarie* (1649), 199.

88. Dan, *Histoire de Barbarie* (1637), 64–66.

89. On the symbolism of processions on the Ile de la Cité during the Wars of Religion, see Barbara B. Diefendorf, *Beneath the Cross: Catholics and Huguenots in Sixteenth-Century Paris* (Oxford: Oxford University Press, 1991), 43–44.

90. Dan, *Histoire de Barbarie* (1637), table of contents; see also pp. 2, 375, 392. On the idea of "purifying oneself with clothing," see Ricci, "Crypto-identities," 43–44.

91. An *arrêt*, dated 24 July 1636, confirmed 6 August 1638 (excerpted in Castries, Cossé Brissac, and Cenival, *SIHM* [1911], 1st ser., 3: 563–567) and several times afterward, gave the Mercedarians dominion over Brittany, Languedoc, Guyenne, Angoulême, Saintonge, Quercy, Béarn, and Provence. The Trinitarians, in turn, received control over the Ile-de-France, Gâtinais, Orléanais, Perche, Maine, Anjou, Picardy, Normandy, Champagne, Dauphiné, Burgundy, Nivernais, Lyonnais, Forez, Beaujolais, Limousin, Marche, Périgord, and l'Agenais. Deslandres, *OT*, 1: 366–369.

92. In 1641, 1642, 1643, 1644, 1645, 1653, 1654, 1655, 1658, and 1659. See app. 2.

93. See app. 1.

94. Sue, *Correspondance*, 414–434.

95. Chevalier du Saillant et al. to Marseille, Algiers, [late 1639], ACCM, AA507 (OC), reprinted in Grammont, "Relations," 438–441.

96. Lucien Peytraud discusses the seizure and settlement of Saint Christopher (known as Saint Kitts) in 1625. *L'Esclavage aux Antilles françaises avant 1789, d'après des documents inédits des archives coloniales* (Paris: Hachette, 1897), 4–9. Numerous authors cite Jean-Baptiste Labat on Louis XIII's decision to allow slavery. Labat, *Nouveau voyage aux isles de l'Amérique* . . . , 6 vols. (Paris: n.p., 1722), 4: 114. Within a decade, Jacques Bouton attested to a "good number" of "blacks or Moors" working alongside indentured servants in Martinique and elsewhere. *Relation d'un établissement de françois depuis l'an 1635 en l'isle de Martinique, l'une des Antilles de l'Amérique* (Paris: Sébastien Cramoisy, 1640), 98, cited in Peabody, "'A Nation Born to Slavery': Missionaries

and Racial Discourse in Seventeenth-Century French Antilles," *Journal of Social History* 38, 1 (2004): 114–115.

97. "Gentilhomme ordinaire de la chambre du Roi" Jean-Baptiste de Coquiel, later appointed governor of the Bastion de France, signed articles renewing France's commercial concessions on 7 July 1640 (Rouard de Card, *TF*, 22–26). On the stalled negotiations to exchange thirty-six Turks for two hundred Frenchmen (which may have been achieved in 1648) and other details, see Plantet, *CDA*, 1: 46 n. 1, 55 n. 1; CADN, CA, vol. 1, ff. 74–78; and Grammont, *HA*, 164–165.

98. In 1639 Marseille merchant Marc David ransomed thirty-five to forty Provençals for the CCM, and between January and March 1640 Coquiel sent home seventy French subjects. On paper, Louis XIII had ordered the release of all Tunisian galley slaves, whose number had diminished to just five. But between 1641 and 1645, the CCM was still spurning requests by Tunisian deys for their return. ACCM, G50. For unknown reasons, dey Ahmad set free thirteen French slaves in April 1641, but then Tunisian corsairs captured twelve Marseille boats in 1642. Plantet, *CBT*, 1: 135–145.

99. On the 1642–1646 mission to Tripoli by the Recollet Fathers, see Féraud, *AT*, 115–116.

100. [Gabriel Perboyre], *Mémoires de la Congrégation de la Mission*, 9 vols. (Paris: A la maison principale de la Congrégation de la Mission, 1863–1866), 2: esp. 14.

101. According to deliberations of the CCM, Marseille, 18 February 1655, 2 June 1656, the chamber would ransom properly bellicose slaves and pay compensation to the families of those who perished. ACCM, B2, ff. 304 v, 582 r, cited in Joseph Fournier, *Inventaire des archives de la Chambre de commerce de Marseille* (Marseille: Chambre de Commerce, 1940), 124, 143.

102. Slave Augier Ollier to CCM and slave Pierre Roman to CCM, Tripoli, 20 March 1655, ACCM, G44.

103. Hérault, *Les Larmes et clameurs*, 15.

104. Hérault (*Les Larmes et clameurs*, 33) claimed to have ransomed 126 natives of Saintonge and Poitiers, some of whom may well have been Protestant, and 33 Protestants, all of whom may well have been French. In a more palatable, revisionist version, however, Dan (*Histoire de Barbarie* [1649], 144) claimed that Hérault had agreed to accept alms from Protestants in La Rochelle but then "this father, not considering this money worth waiting for, departed on the road to Marseille."

105. Both orders had slaves swear to God or sign a notarized document promising attendance. For a Mercedarian example from Algiers, 12 April 1644, see Lambert, "L'Oeuvre de la redemption," 366–369; for a Trinitarian one from Tunis, 23 April 1674, see Grandchamp, *FT*, 7: 232. On the dual character of seventeenth-century charity, see Jones, *The Charitable Imperative: Hospitals and Nursing in Ancien Regime and Revolutionary France* (London: Routledge, 1989), 7; and Davis, *Society and Culture in Early Modern France* (Stanford: Stanford University Press, 1975), 289 n. 161.

106. Treasury records, 10 June 1644, ACC, now 139E at the ADBR, CC180.

107. See, for example, Dan, *Histoire de Barbarie* (1637), 481; [Auvry], *Le Miroir de la charité*, 28; Michelin et al., *Le Tableau de Piété*, 52–53; and on the part of a 1656 observer in Marseille, "Les Statuts municipaux et coustumes anciennes de la ville de Marseille, par François d'Aix," Marseille, 1656, cited in Fabre, *Histoire des hôpitaux et des institutions de bienfaisance de Marseille*, 2 vols. (Marseille: Jules Barille, 1854–1855), 2: 308.

108. In 1650, for example, Louis XIV renewed the exemptions from certain public charges enjoyed by ransom collectors (*marguilliers*). Alexandre Germain, "Oeuvre de la rédemption des captifs à Montpellier," *Publications de la Société archéologique de Montpellier* 30 (1863): 195.

109. Arlette Farge, *Fragile Lives: Violence, Power and Solidarity in Eighteenth-Century Paris*, trans. Carol Shelton (Cambridge, MA: Harvard University Press, 1993), 174.

110. *L'Eminente charité de la rédemption des captifs faite par les religieux de l'Ordre de la Sainte Trinité* . . . (Paris: Veuve Jean Petitpas, 1641), 34, 45.

111. Address to Queen Regent in Hérault, *Les Larmes et clameurs*, 4–5.

112. Hérault, *Les Larmes et clameurs*, 5. As king, Louis XIV, with his mother, Anne of Austria, held his first audience in 1644, receiving several slaves ransomed from Algiers. Edmond Egreville, *La Vive Foy et le recit fidelle de que c'est passé dans le voyage de la rédemption des captifs françois, faicte en Alger* . . . (Paris: Louis Feugé, 1645), 79–80. On the Royal Touch, see Marc Léopold Benjamin Bloch, *The Royal Touch: Sacred Monarchy and Scrofula in England and France*, trans. J. E. Anderson (London: Routledge, 1973).

113. [Etienne Carneaux], *Les Captifs délivrés par les RR. PP. de l'ordre de la très sainte Trinité* . . . (Paris: François Noël, 1654). On a similar note, see [Arnoux and Héron], *La Miraculeuse rédemption*, 47.

114. Dan, *Histoire de Barbarie* (1649), 352; Boyer, "Continuation des mémoires des voyages du feu Père Hérault en Barbarie pour la rédemption qu'il a escrit luy même estant à Alger l'an 1645 ainsi qui s'en suit," *ROMM* 19 (1975): 38.

115. Baptismal act of a "turc de nation" who "attended mass after having been baptized" in the Vendée (27 April 1647, ADV, Actes de baptêmes de l'église de la Bruffière), cited in Mathorez, *Les Etrangers en France*, 1: 178. In Spain, the penultimate redemption procession in Madrid often featured "the baptism of one Muslim or another." Torres, *Prisioneros de los infieles*, 104.

116. "Effet merveilleux de grâce dans la conversion d'un Turc . . . d'Alger," (n.d. [after April 1641]), BN, Fonds latins 11708. See also the baptism of a family of "three Turks" on 19 October 1642 at the Carmelite convent at Place Maubert, as announced in the *Gazette de France* (1642): 1016, cited in Turbet-Delof, *Bibliographie critique*, 126.

117. Léonce Coutoure ("Baptême d'un Turc à Orthez," *Revue de Gascogne* 21 [1880]: 90) excerpts the original *Récit de la conversion admirable d'un Turc More, baptisé par Monsieur Emanuel du Chateau* . . . (Toulouse: F. Boude, 1644). Other publicly celebrated Muslim conversions of the period include "Ali, son of Soliman, who married in Landéda in 1643" (Henri Bourde de La Rogerie and J. Lemoine, eds., *Inventaire sommaire des Archives départementales antérieures à 1790, Finistère*, 4 vols. [Quimper: A. Jaouen, 1889–1933], 3: xcviii n. 7);

"the abjuration of the Muslim faith by Estienne Marcassa, age 14-to-15 years" in Nantes (1647, AMN, GG187, cited in Mathorez, *Les Etrangers en France*, 1: 178); and Gaspard Villeneuve, "Turc natif de Constantinople," by a Carmelite monk in Fayence in July 1650 (J. J. Letrait, A. Degioanni, and R. Le Minor, eds., *Répertoire des registres paroissiaux et de l'état civil jusqu'en 1814* [Draguignan: Lanteaume, 1963], vii).

118. La Rochelle, 3 March 1655, ADCM, E40, cited in Mathorez, *Les Etrangers en France*, 1: 180.

119. On 9 February and 6 March 1656, two Muslims, one Tunisian, and one Saletian were baptized by the Capuchins at the main cathedral in Rennes. ADIV, 3E/Register 245/1 (thanks to archivist Bruno Ibled for these references). See also *Gazette de France* (1656): 442, 992, which reported the baptisms of an "African Turk" at Saint-Nicholas-du-Chardonnet and a Tunisian at the church of the Saint-Jacques hospital in Paris the same year, cited in Turbet-Delof, *L'Afrique barbaresque*, 126–127.

120. Roche, *Humeurs vagabondes*, 371.

121. Zysberg, *Marseille au temps du Roi-Soleil: la ville, les galères, l'arsenal* (Marseille: Jeanne Lafitte, 2007), 55–60.

CHAPTER THREE

1. Héron, *Relation du voyage*, provides the most detailed description of the voyage that ransomed fifty-seven to fifty-nine French slaves (and repatriated as many as eighty) from Algiers and displayed them in Barcelona, Perpignan, Narbonne, Montpellier, Arles, Marseille, Lambesc, Avignon, Valence, Vienne, Lyon, Orléans, and Paris. For additional sources, see app. 2.

2. "Le Livre de raison du notaire Etienne Borrelly, 1654 à 1717," *Mémoires de l'Académie de Nîmes* 8 (1885): 233.

3. On the historiographical consensus that effective governance by "absolutist" monarchs rested on cooperation, not just domination, see William Beik, "Review Article: The Absolutism of Louis XIV as Social Collaboration," *Past and Present* 188 (2005): 195–224.

4. On these related developments—the erection of citadel Saint-Nicolas (1660–1664), the return of the galleys from Toulon (1661–1665), the planning and building of a new arsenal (1666–1669), the construction of Fort Saint-Jean (1668–1669), the receipt of a commercial monopoly (1669), and the expansion and modernization of the city lazaret (1663–1669)—see Zysberg, *Marseille au temps du Roi-Soleil*; and Junko Thérèse Takeda, "French Absolutism, Marseillais Civic Humanism and the Languages of the Public Good," *Historical Journal* 49, 3 (2006): 707–734. On the development of Marseille's plague surveillance system in the 1660s and the convincing argument that the city's commercial monopoly derived from its earlier public health one, see Hildesheimer, *Le Bureau de la santé*, 21–23.

5. See app. 1.

6. See Colley, *Captives*, part 1, on captivity as reflecting weakness rather than proto-imperialism.

7. Philip McCluskey rebuts traditional arguments about the revival of crusading motives (as opposed to maneuvers) during the early years of Louis XIV's reign. "Commerce Before Crusade? France, the Ottoman Empire and the Barbary Pirates (1661–1669)," *French History* 23, 1 (2009): 1–21.

8. Scholars continue to debate the truth status of particular accounts. See, for example, Sylvie Requemora, "Le Voyageur mystificateur ou les ruses de l'écriture viatique dans la seconde moitié du XVIIe siècle: le cas de l'Odyssée de René Chastelet des Boys," in *Ecriture de la ruse*, ed. Elzbieta Grodek (Amsterdam: Rodopi, 2000), 163–186. Accepting that all storytelling is ruse and thus assuming that every Barbary captivity narrative contains elements of invention, I include in my purview those featuring individuals (nine Catholics, two Huguenots)—Emanuel d'Aranda, René Chastelet des Boys, François de Rocqueville, Jean Gallonyé, Germain Moüette, Pierre Daulier, Antoine Quartier, Jean Bonnet, Pierre Girard, Claude Auxcousteaux de Fercourt, Isaac Brassard—whose slavery and liberation can at minimum be independently corroborated.

9. On the "literature of roguery" in early modern Italy, see Ricci, "Crypto-identities," 39–54. On dissimulation as a tactic of the weak against the powerful, see, among others, Rosario Villari, *Elogio della dissimulazione: la lotta politica nel Seicento* (Rome: Laterza, 1987), 3–48; and Jean-Pierre Cavaillé, *Dis/simulations: Jules-César Vanini, François La Mothe Le Vayer, Gabriel Naudé, Louis Machon et Torquato Accetto; religion, morale et politique au XVIIe siècle* (Paris: H. Champion, 2002), 11–38.

10. Virtually every press that put out Barbary captivity narratives was associated with royal or religious authority by geographic proximity. Some had direct ties to the crown. Olivier de Varennes, Parisian publisher of the *Mercure françois*, for example, released two accounts of Algerian slavery, one ostensibly factual (Rocqueville, *Relations des moeurs*), the other obviously fictional (Le sieur de la Martinière, *L'Heureux esclave ou Relation des aventures du sieur de la Martinière* . . . [1674]), which plagiarized the writings of a Trinitarian, an explorer, and a former slave. Roger Chartier and Henri-Jean Martin, eds., *Histoire de l'édition française*, 4 vols. (Paris: Promodis, 1982–1986), 2: 263; Turbet-Delof, *Bibliographie critique*, 205–206.

11. Perez Zagorin, *Ways of Lying: Dissimulation, Persecution, and Conformity in Early Modern Europe* (Cambridge, MA: Harvard University Press, 1990).

12. *Gazette de France* (1660): 463; Plantet, *CBT*, 1: 151–164; Bernard Bachelot, *Louis XIV en Algérie: Gigeri 1664* (Monaco: Rocher, 2003), 56–60.

13. Memorandum from Chevalier Paul "on what needs to be done to ruin Alger, Tunis, et Tripoli," 1661, AN, Marine B7 2, f. 109, cited in Charles-Roux, *FA*, 146.

14. François de Vendôme, duc de Beaufort, to French consul in Majorca, n.p., 25 April 1662, reprinted in Georg Bernhard Depping, ed., *Correspondance administrative sous le règne de Louis XIV*, 4 vols. (Paris: Imprimerie nationale, 1850–1855), 4: 884 n. 1; Louis XIV to Beaufort, n.p., 19 May 1662, and Colbert to naval intendant Louis Testard de La Guette in Toulon, n.p., 8 December 1662, AN, Marine, Recueil de diverses lettres, ff. 1, 184, reprinted in Pierre

Clément, *Lettres, instructions et mémoires de Colbert*, 7 vols. (Paris: Imprimerie impériale, 1861–1873), vol. 3, pt. 1: 3, 27–28.

15. Quartier (*L'Esclave religieux*, 2) described himself as unable "to resist the violence of my curiosity." On sixteenth-century iterations of the perils of curiosity, especially as it involved capture by Turks, see Wes Williams, "'Out of the Frying Pan . . .': Curiosity, Danger and the Poetics of Witness in the Renaissance Traveller's Tale," in *Curiosity and Wonder from the Renaissance to the Enlightenment*, ed. R. J. W. Evans and Alexander Marr (Aldershot, UK: Ashgate, 2006), 21–42.

16. Quartier, *L'Esclave religieux*, avertissement. Turbet-Delof (*L'Afrique barbaresque*, 248) points to evidence that Quartier—identified as F.A.Q.—composed the narrative in 1681 but only received permission to publish in 1690. He also cites the royal privilege giving the full title, which appears nowhere on the book itself: *L'Esclave Religieux, qui raconte les peines qu'il a souffertes dans Tripoly; pendant huit années de Captivité, ses avantures, avec un fidele Recit de tout ce qui s'est passé de plus remarquable dans ce Royaume, pendant le séjour qu'il a fait en Affrique*. Turbet-Delof, "Le Père mercédaire A. Quartier et sa chronique tripoline des années 1660–1668," *CT* 8, 77–78 (1972): 51. Cocard published a new annotated edition as "Antoine Quartier (vers 1632–1702): voyageur, captif, mercédaire; un précurseur de l'orientalisme, au XVIIème siècle," *Analecta mercedaria* 22 (2003): 123–301.

17. Aranda, *Relation de la captivité et liberté du Sieur Emanuel de Aranda mené esclave à Alger en l'an 1640, & mis en liberté l'an 1642* (Brussels: Jean Mommart, 1656), was reprinted the next year under a more elaborately evocative title: *Relation de la captivité du Sieur Emanuel d'Aranda: où sont descriptes les miseres, les ruses, & les finesses des esclaves & des corsaires d'Alger; ensemble les conquestes de Barberousse dans l'Afrique, & plusieurs autres particularités digne de remarque* (Paris: Gervais Clovsier, 1657). A relative best seller, it went through additional French editions (1662, 1665, and 1671) and appeared in English (1666, 1796) and Dutch (1666, 1682) translation. By contrast, Chastelet des Boys, *L'Odyssée ou Diversité d'Avantures, Rencontres et Voyages en Europe, Asie et Affrique* (La Flèche: Gervais Laboë, 1660), was only reproduced once, in 1665.

18. On the topologies of romance, see, among others, Fredric Jameson, "Magical Narratives: Romance as Genre," *New Literary History* 7, 1 (1975): 135–163; Northrop Frye, *The Secular Scripture: A Study in the Structure of Romance* (Cambridge, MA: Harvard University Press, 1976); Patricia A. Parker, *Inescapable Romance: Studies in the Poetics of a Mode* (Princeton, NJ: Princeton University Press, 1979); and Barbara Fuchs, *Romance* (New York: Routledge, 2004).

19. Quartier, *L'Esclave religieux*, 105–107.

20. Quartier, *L'Esclave religieux*, 72–73.

21. "The scourge of the cities of Marseille, La Ciotat, and Toulon," Quartier wrote, "are wicked enough to enslave family and friends as retaliation for not having ransomed them." *L'Esclave religieux*, 24, and echoing this explanation on 91, 174.

22. Quartier, *L'Esclave religieux*, 97–98, 248–254.
23. Quartier, *L'Esclave religieux*, 41, 111.
24. Quartier, *L'Esclave religieux*, 211–214.
25. On "downward travesty [as] comic rather than provocative," see Terry Castle, *Masquerade and Civilization: The Carnivalesque in Eighteenth-Century English Culture and Fiction* (Stanford: Stanford University Press, 1986), 91; and on passing as a Jew, see Ricci, "Crypto-identities," 46–47.
26. Quartier, *L'Esclave religieux*, 98–101. In Moüette's narrative (*Relation de la captivité*, 31–33), a merchant from Bayonne took advantage of the Jews of Salé in a similar manner, wagering four hundred écus that the messiah would not be born in Holland within the year. Girard (*HCRT*, vol. 2, f. 70–71b) devotes several pages to the reception of Sabbatai Sevi in Tripoli.
27. Quartier, *L'Esclave religieux*, 214.
28. Quartier, *L'Esclave religieux*, 189.
29. According to the *Gazette de France* (1662): 1202, reporting from Marseille on 26 November (cited in Grammont, "Etudes algériennes: l'esclavage," 40), several Christian slaves were on the point of executing a plot against Algiers with the help of ten thousand Moors. Though tortured and then buried alive, a Dominican participant refused to identify his accomplices.
30. Instructions from General Superior René Alméras from 1668 emphasized that "it is more important to prevent several slaves from perverting themselves than to convert a single renegade." [Perboyre], *Mémoires*, 2: 276.
31. When Lazarist Philippe de Vacher completed his tour of duty as consul to Algiers, he repatriated seventy French slaves. During periods of plague, his brother cared for Protestant slaves alongside Catholic and through his charitable example claimed to have brought some of them back to the Church. [Perboyre], *Mémoires*, 2: 220, 306, 316, 319; Bonet-Maury, "Les Précurseurs français du Cardinal Lavergerie dans l'Afrique musulman," *Revue des deux mondes* 36 (1896): 923.
32. Regarding the defection of Catholic slaves, see, for example, Grandchamp, *FT*, 6: xiii, 248, 253.
33. [Auvry], *Le Miroir de la charité*, 186–188. On the publishing run, see ADH, 50H94, cited in Cocard, *Les Pères de la Merci*, 221.
34. Plague hit southern France and North Africa in 1662–1663. See Biraben, *Les Hommes et la peste*, 1: 377–388, 433–438. According to Grammont (*HA*, 182), it killed more than ten thousand Christian slaves in Algiers.
35. Vergé-Franceschi reports that the initial assault cost 400 French lives and generated rumors of Muslim cannibalism; 550 men later drowned. *Abraham Duquesne: Huguenot et marin du Roi-Soleil* (Paris: Editions France-Empire, 1992), 199–205. See also Charles Monchicourt, "L'Expédition de Djidjelli," *Revue maritime* 137–138 (1898): 464–492, 41–71; Turbet-Delof, *A propos de trois impressions bordelaises: l'affaire de Djidjelli (1664) dans la presse française du temps* (Bordeaux: Taffard, 1968), 3 n. 2; and Turbet-Delof, *Bibliographie critique*, 171 n. 197.
36. Sieur le Grain to the marine ministry, Algiers, 10 December 1664, AN, Marine B7 49, f. 235.

37. The text of both the official treaty signed on 25 November 1665 and the secret accord signed the following day are reproduced in Plantet, *CBT*, 1: 182–192. The second one specified that all French subjects enslaved in Tunis would be freed in exchange for all Tunisian janissaries and soldiers held in France, and that the remaining slaves could be ransomed for 175 piastres each. Controversially, it also offered to take a Tunisian official back to France to verify that all Tunisian captives had been freed. The details of negotiating their freedom fell to the queen's page, Jacques Dumolin, seigneur de la Grange; Antoine Audoire, commander of the Mercedarians; and the chevalier Laurent d'Arvieux, who later served as consul to Aleppo and Algiers. Armed with a census of the remaining French captives, they bought them back in several batches. In January 1666 Louis XIV ordered the lieutenants of the Provence admiralty to publicize his intention to liberate all French slaves in Tunis and order anyone with family members in captivity to declare the "names, ages, and status of said captives." Extract from the registers of the Conseil d'Etat, Paris, 4 January 1666, ACCM, G39. For the financial details, including a royal grant and collections by the Communautés de Provence and the Mercedarians, see Plantet, *CBT*, 1: 199, 204–205 n. 3, 219–220 n. 3; *Histoire de l'ordre sacré*, 945; and Michelin et al., *Le Tableau de Piété*, 110–112.

38. A 1663 census by Algerian consul Dubordieu (Algiers, 3 December 1663, BN, CCC483, f. 466) counted just one woman (seized near Saint-Tropez) and excluded seven renegades. General commissary André-François Trubert signed the treaty with Algiers on 17 May 1666 (see Rouard de Card, *TF*, 32–36, for the text) and ransomed 1,127 French subjects (CADN, CA, cited in Plantet, *CDA*, 1: 61 n. 2).

39. The Trinitarians liberated fifty-five to fifty-seven captives from Algiers in September 1667; between April and October 1667 the Mercedarians released thirty-eight to thirty-nine captives and brought back another five hundred ransomed by the king. See app. 2.

40. Colbert informed Beaufort of the king's eighty-thousand-livre donation both to execute the treaty with Tunis and to buy back soldiers seized during the retreat from Djidjelli but told him to be discreet so that slaves and their relatives would not hold back contributions. Paris, 18 February 1666, AN, Marine B2 5, f. 202, cited in Plantet, *CBT*, 1: 202. These financial arrangements had repercussions for the next several years. In 1669, for example, the CCM brought a lawsuit against a certain Descamps, who refused to pay back the sum lent for his ransom. Marseille, 1669, ACCM, G40.

41. Twelve thousand livres were earmarked to ransom the Knight of Malta, by the Estates of Brittany, Vannes, 4 November 1667, ADIV, C2657, f. 243.

42. Doléances from the Etats de Provence, Aix-en-Provence, December 1666, ADBR, C2066.

43. Lambert, "L'Oeuvre de la rédemption," 523; ACC, BB11, at ADBR, 139E, cited in Maurice Raimbault, ed., *Inventaire sommaire des archives communales et hospitalières de Cassis antérieures à 1790* (Marseille: Barlatier, 1904), 18; G. Arnaud d'Agnel, "Rôle des soixante-quatorze esclaves provençaux échangés

ou rachetés à Alger par le Sieur de Trubert publiés avec un commentaire historique," *Bulletin historique et philologique* (1905): 215–224.

44. Galley intendant Nicolas Arnoul to Colbert, 11 May 1669, AN, Marine B6 78, f. 186, cited in Zysberg, "Galères et galériens du royaume de France," in *Le Genti del mare Mediterraneo*, ed. Rosalba Ragosta, 2 vols. (Naples: Lucio Pironti, 1981), 2: 790. In a 1665 letter to Colbert, la rade de La Goulette (1 December 1665, AN, Marine B4 2, f. 470), Beaufort had floated the idea of making indentured sailors from freed slaves; in its deliberations (17 December 1665, ACCM, B3, f. 559, cited in Fournier, *Inventaire*, 176), the CCM accepted as a given "the king needing sailors to equip his vessels." Royal instructions the following year calculated that a typical ransom debt would take two to four years to pay off. Saint-Germain-en-Laye, 9 February 1666, AAE, MD, Afrique, vol. 8, f. 124, cited in Plantet, *CBT*, 1: 195, 200.

45. Arvieux, *Mémoires*, 4: 4–5, cited in Turbet-Delof, *L'Afrique barbaresque*, 189–190.

46. Michelin et al., *Le Tableau de Piété*, 160.

47. Pierre Guillebert, *Le Paranymphe de la rédemption* . . . (Troyes: François Icquard, 1667), 5–6.

48. James de Rothschild, ed., *Les Continuateurs de Loret: lettres en vers de la Gravette de Mayolas, Robinet, Boursault, Perdou de Subligny, Laurent et autres (1665–1689)*, 3 vols. (Paris: Demascène Morgand and Charles Fatout, 1881–1883), 2: 490.

49. ADBR, C3632, for example, contains a file devoted to the "passage de la chaîne" from 1760 to 1783, which details the number of men and lists the location and duration of each stop. See also Masson, *Les Galères de France*, 276; Zysberg, *Les Galériens*, 21–44.

50. Lawrence Bryant, *The King and the City in the Parisian Royal Entry Ceremony: Politics, Ritual and Art in the Renaissance* (Geneva: Droz, 1986), 130, 24; Michael Wintroub, *A Savage Mirror: Power, Identity and Knowledge in Early Modern France* (Stanford: Stanford University Press, 2006), chap. 3.

51. Eugène François Joseph Taillar, *Chroniques de Douai*, 3 vols. (Douai: Dechristé, 1875–1877), 3: 7, cited in Deslandres, *OT*, 1: 400 n. 5.

52. Michelin et al., *Le Tableau de Piété*, 214 and following pages.

53. Protestant slaves to members of the Reformed Church of Lyon, Tripoli, 20 February 1670, Bibliothèque municipale de Lyon, MS Coste 447. A Mercedarian mission, led by Jean Plantier and Victor de Saint-Paul of Digne-en-Provence, had ransomed and repatriated twenty-five men the year before. Féraud, *AT*, 136.

54. M. F. Cumont ("Les Antiquités de la Tripolitaine au XVIIIe siècle," *Rivista della Tripolitania* 2 [1925–1926]: 151–167) identifies the name and profession of the anonymous author who recounted his Tripolitan slavery from 1668 to 1676 ([Girard], *HCRT*). For more on this individual—who was captured aboard the Marseillais-commanded *La Neptune* and later became a protégé of British consul Nathaniel Bradley—and his manuscript, see La Roncière, "Une Histoire de Bornou au XVIIe siècle par un chirurgien français captif à Tripoli," *Revue de l'histoire des colonies* 7 (1919): 73–88; Paolo Toschi, *Le Fonti inedite della storia della Tripolitania* (Intra, Italy: A. Airoldi, 1934): 116–126; Bono,

"Fonti inedite di storia della Tripolitania," *Libia* 1, 2 (1953): 117–121; and Ettore Rossi, *Storia di Tripoli e della Tripolitania: dalla conquista araba al 1911*, ed. Maria Nallino (Rome: Istituto per l'Oriente, 1968), 191–194.

55. Colbert reprimanded intendant Pierre Arnoul in 1666 for allowing a Tunisian envoy named Ramadan to tour the galleys, writing that it would be prejudicial to French interests and warning him not to make the same mistake with Algiers. Paris, 18 February 1666, AN, Marine B2 5, f. 209, cited in Plantet, *CBT*, 1: 202. On capturing Turks and instigating a break with England, see Instructions to Louis-Victor de Rochechouart, comte de Vivonne, Saint-Germain-en-Laye, 27 April 1665, and Instructions to Trubert, Saint-Germain-en-Laye, 6 March 1668, CADN, CA, vol. 1, ff. 109–110, 115.

56. Molly Greene, *A Shared World: Christians and Muslims in the Early Modern Mediterranean* (Princeton, NJ: Princeton University Press, 2000), 74–77.

57. Colbert to MM. Tersmitt and Pagez, owners of the *St. Louis*, [1669], AN, Marine B2 9, f. 170, cited in McCluskey, "Commerce Before Crusade?" 10 n. 49.

58. Pasha Isma'il of Algiers to Trubert, Algiers, 26 November 1668, and to Louis XIV, Algiers, 6 December 1668, reproduced in Plantet, *CDA*, 1: 62–65. See also Colbert to Melchior de Harod de Senevas, marquis de Saint-Romain, ambassador to Lisbon, 27 October 1669, reprinted in Depping, *Correspondance*, 3: 497–498.

59. Hajj Muhammad, dey of Tunis, to Louis XIV, Tunis, 1668, AAE, Tunis, cited in Plantet, *CBT*, 1: 245.

60. Louis XIV to Vivonne, Paris, 11 January 1669, AN, Marine B2 7, f. 142; consul Jean Ambrozin to Colbert, Tunis, 10 October 1669, AAE, MD, Afrique, vol. 8, f. 160, cited in Plantet, *CBT*, 1: 247, 248–249.

61. Guénot in preface to Galland, *Histoire de l'esclavage*, 5–6.

62. Galland, *Histoire de l'esclavage*, 27–30.

63. This could be Ragep Vicard, mentioned in chap. 2 of this volume and Grandchamp, *FT*, 7: 184.

64. Galland, *Histoire de l'esclavage*, 34–35. On Dom Philippe, see Arvieux, *Mémoires*, 3: 505–523; Quartier, *L'Esclave religieux*, 119–125; Jean Coste, "Un Prince tunisien converti," *Revue de l'histoire de missions* 11 (1934): 481–493; Grandchamp and Marthe de Bacquencourt, "Documents divers concernant Don Philippe, prince tunisien deux fois renégat (1646–1686)," *Revue tunisienne* 40 (1938): 55–77, 289–312; Grandchamp, "La Fuite de Tunis et le baptême de Don Philippe à Palerme (13 mars–6 mai 1646)," *RA* 84 (1940): 118–132; Plantet, *CBT*, 1: 169–171, 224; and Jean de Thévenot, *Relation d'un voyage fait au Levant . . .* , 3 vols. (Paris: Louis Billaine, 1665–1684), 1: 540–548.

65. Galland, *Histoire de l'esclavage*, 39, 58–59.

66. Galland, *Histoire de l'esclavage*, 46–47.

67. Galland, *Histoire de l'esclavage*, 93–133.

68. An even more fictionalized account of another Provençal slave in Tunis appeared in the late seventeenth century: Louis Marot, *Relation de quelques aventures maritimes de L.M.P.R.D.G.F [Pilote Réal Des Galères de France]*

(Paris: Gervais Clouzier, 1673). But more than a hundred years passed before the public finally read about Jean Bonnet's adventures—first in the journal *Magasin encyclopédique* in 1809 and the following year in a separate imprint. The editor of this 1810 version changed the ending, excising Bonnet's payback to finish with a tender portrait of the captive embracing his family. Guénot in preface to Galland, *Histoire de l'esclavage*, 5–12; see also pp. 134–135 for original ending.

69. Galland, *Histoire de l'esclavage*, 134; Plantet, *CBT*, 1: 268–273 (for the text of the treaty, signed in La Goulette on 28 June 1672); app. 1. In Algiers a show of strength in 1670 led to the reconfirmation of the 1666 accord and a redemption led by Flemish Trinitarians. Grammont, *HA*, 219–221; app. 2.

70. Seven hundred French slaves to Michel Le Tellier, Tripoli, 12 October 1673, reproduced in [Girard], *HCRT*, vol. 2, f. 202; Féraud, *AT*, 132–134, 141–142.

71. For details of France's lukewarm military and diplomatic efforts to liberate slaves from Tripoli in the 1670s, England's bombardment, and the plague that killed six hundred Christian captives in the regency from 1675 to 1676, see Féraud, *AT*, 131–133, 140–142, 145–147 (who relies primarily on [Girard], *HCRT*). For the spotty references to Trinitarian and Mercedarian activities in this period, see app. 2.

72. Charles-Roux, *FA*, 168.

73. Gallonyé, author of *Histoire d'une esclave*, was twenty when captured in October 1670 and twenty-four when ransomed. Moüette, enslaved at eighteen, wrote *Relation de la captivité* after eleven years of captivity in Salé, Fez, Alcazar, and Meknes.

74. See Jacques Gosse, captive in Fez, to his brothers and sisters in La Rochelle (forwarded to Colbert), Fez, 20 August 1670; Gosse and eleven French captives to Colbert, n.d. [before 9 November 1671], AAE, CC, Carton: Rachat des esclaves, 1649 à 1609, and AN, AE B3 316, pièce 10, reproduced in Castries, Cossé Brissac, and Cenival, *SIHM* (1922), 2nd ser., 1: 324–325, 396–397. Also, memorandum from the French slaves in Fez, 1672, AAE, MD, Maroc, vol. 2, f. 84 r–85 r.

75. Penz, *Les Captifs français*, 67–72.

76. The only French captive count for 1672 has 130 in Fez, but there well may have been more in other Moroccan cities. See app. 1.

77. The Mercedarian mission departed from Bayonne and rescued fifty-two to fifty-six slaves in 1674 and another nineteen in 1676 for an average price of seven hundred livres. See app. 2. According to Leïla Maziane, 78 percent of the captives were ransomed within five years, a rate that plummeted in subsequent decades. "Les Captifs européens en terre marocaine aux XVIIe et XVIIIe siècles," *CM* 65 (2002), http://cdlm.revues.org/index45.html.

78. Gallonyé's ransom was by far the most expensive, at 1,762 livres and 10 sols, roughly equivalent to six years' salary for a day laborer, according to Emile Levasseur, *Les Prix: aperçu de l'histoire économique de la valeur et du revenu de la terre en France, du commencement du XIIIe siècle à la fin du XVIIIe* (Paris: Chamerot & Renouard, 1893), 68.

79. Gallonyé, *Histoire d'une esclave*, dedication, preface.

80. Moüette, *Relation de la captivité*, 100–102.
81. Moüette, *Relation de la captivité*, 60–61.
82. Moüette, *Relation de la captivité*, 58.
83. Moüette, *Relation de la captivité*, 67, 93–97.
84. Moüette, *Relation de la captivité*, 84, 161–164. Versions of this tale also appear in Quartier, *L'Esclave religieux*, 79–80, 223–224.
85. Moüette, *Relation de la captivité*, 281–282.
86. Moüette, *Relation de la captivité*, 265, 281.
87. Castle, *Masquerade and Civilization*, 90.
88. Moüette, *Relation de la captivité*, 27–28.
89. After the failure of another French blockade in 1680 and the example of two hundred Spanish captives ransomed from Meknes, Calault de Villalain of Blois sent a frustrated letter to the French ambassador in Madrid, asking him to plead the case of four hundred French slaves with the king. Meknes, 29 June 1680, reprinted in Castries, Cossé Brissac, and Cenival, *SIHM* (1922), 2nd ser., 1: 494–496.
90. Dey Hajji Muhammad to Louis XIV, Algiers, 2 October 1673, reprinted in Plantet, *CDA*, 1: 70–71.
91. See the first article of the peace treaty signed in Algiers on 19 September 1628 granting refuge to Muslim slaves escaping enemy lands, cited in Dan, *Histoire de Barbarie* (1637), 134–135.
92. Seignelay to galley intendant Pierre Arnoul, Versailles, 9 April 1674, ACCM, AA6 (OC), reproduced in Grammont, "Un Académicien (Jean Foy Vaillant) captif à Alger (1674–1675)," *RA* 26 (1882): 315; Louis XIV and Colbert to Jean Rouillé de Meslay, intendant of Provence, Besançon, 23 May 1674, AMM, GGL154; Arvieux (about to become consul to Algiers) to Colbert, Marseille, 12 and 23 May, Aix-en-Provence, 26 May 1674, AN, AE B1 115, ff. 205–214, cited in Mohammed Touili, *Correspondance des consuls de France à Alger, 1642–1792: inventaire analytique des articles A.E. BI 115 à 145* (Paris: Centre historique des Archives nationales, 2001), 20.
93. The Protestant doctor Jacob Spon recounted this episode in *Voyage d'Italie, de Dalmatie, de Grèce et du Levant, fait en 1675 & 1676 . . .* , 3 vols. (Lyon: Antoine Cellier le fils, 1678), 2: 15 and following pages. Although other passengers had to wait until 1676 to be released, a Parisian renegade took fifty piastres to intercede with the dey and secure Vaillant's liberation. Cited in Grammont, "Un Académicien," 317–320, 387–388.
94. One document attests to processions held in September 1675, but no list of ransomed slaves has been found. Alonso, *LC*, 1: 226–227.
95. "Projet pour racheter toutes les ans à perpétuité les François qui seront en captivité," [1650], AN, B7 205, f. 27, cited in Robert Capot-Rey, "La Politique français et le Maghreb méditerranéen (1643–1685)," *RA* 75 (1934): 203. As he points out, the document probably dates to at least 1675, the year that the "Invalides de la Marine" was established.
96. Deslandres, *L'Eglise et le rachat des captifs* (Paris: B. Blond, 1902), 17.
97. Until 1676 Colbert had hesitated even to trade crippled oarsmen for old French captives for fear they would reveal the true number of Algerians and Tu-

nisians enslaved in France and provoke more corsair attacks. Colbert to Arnoul, Versailles, 18 August 1673, 31 August 1674; Colbert to galley intendant Jean-Baptiste-Nicolas Brodart, Saint-Germain, 12 November 1676, all in AN, Ordres du roi concernant les galères, f. 166 (1673), f. 119 (1674), f. 155 (1676), reprinted in Clément, *Lettres,* 3: 501–504, 525, 38–40; Le Vacher to CCM, Algiers, 21 February 1676, reprinted in Teissier, "Correspondance du Père Jean Le Vacher, consul de France à Alger, faisant connaître le vrai motif de la rupture de la paix entre la France et la Régence d'Alger (1676–1683)," *Mélanges historiques* 4 (1882): 765.

98. A change in policy, according to ACCM, Fonds Arnoul 28 (destroyed in 1944), cited in Masson, *Les Galères de France,* 28.

99. The number of galleys in the royal fleet grew from twenty-one to forty between 1671 and 1694. See correspondence between Colbert and galley intendants Arnoul and Brodart in Clément, *Lettres,* 3: 173–175, 364, 390–394, 502–504, 571–574; ACCM, G50: "Esclaves turcs et barbaresques détenus sur les galères de France ou en transit par Marseille, 1597–1693"; Bamford, *Fighting Ships,* 138–172; and Zysberg, *Les Galériens,* 67–69, 281, annex 2.

100. Anne-Hilarion de Corentin, comte de Tourville, blockaded Algiers in 1679; Abraham Duquesne passed by in September 1680; and admirals Hayet and Virelle appeared in 1681. Grammont, *HA,* 246–248. On François Durieu, a merchant from Bordeaux seized from an English vessel in 1680, see *Archives historiques du département de la Gironde* 159 (1914): 366–369.

101. On the march of mothers in La Ciotat in December 1677 and slave Pierre Choland to his father in the same town, Algiers, 10 April 1679, see ACCM, G40.

102. Alonso (*LC,* 1: 227) found a single reference to a mission to Algiers organized by Trinitarian leaders from Lisieux and Regniowez, confirmed in BN, NAF 22136, but no list of the fifty ransomed slaves survives.

103. Fercourt's manuscript survived in the personal library of M. le comte de Troussoure and was excerpted in two nineteenth-century journals, then published as *Relation de l'esclavage* (1905).

104. Fercourt, *Relation de l'esclavage,* 50.

105. Jean-François Regnard fictionalized his Algerian experience in 1709, but *La Provençale* was not published until after his death. It finally appeared in *Les Oeuvres de M. Regnard,* 5 vols. (Paris: Veuve de P. Ribou, 1731).

106. Quartier, *L'Esclave religieux,* 230–238.

107. According to the official account, published by Louis Desmay, the group included twenty Bretons and nine Normans; nine from Bordeaux, Saintes, and Bayonne; seven from Luçon, Poitiers, and La Rochelle; eight from Marseille and Toulon; two from Martigues; two from Paris; two from Chartres; one from Orléans; one from Dunkirk; two from Auvergne; three from Guyenne; and five from Languedoc. *Relation nouvelle et particulière du voyage des RR. PP. de la Mercy aux royaumes de Fez et du Maroc . . .* (Paris: Veuve Gervais Clouzier, 1682), 130–144. See also app. 2.

108. Quartier, *L'Esclave religieux,* 280–283.

109. Quartier journeyed to Saint Maxim, Cavaillon, Pont Saint Esprit,

Vienne, Lyon, Dijon, Paris, Rennes, and Grenoble, where he claimed to have spent two weeks trying to reason with a Huguenot mother not to abandon in Tripolitan slavery her son who converted to Catholicism during the plague. *L'Esclave religieux*, 275–276, 287.

110. Moüette, *Relation de la captivité*, 159–160.

111. Moüette, *Relation de la captivité*, 160–161. Moüette, age thirty, "native of . . . Bonnelle 9 leagues from Paris, diocese of Chartres," also appears among the redeemed captives listed in the *Catalogue des esclaves chrestiens* . . . (Paris: Christophe Journel, 1681).

112. Edward Whiting Fox, *History in Geographic Perspective: The Other France* (New York: Norton, 1971). On contradictory royal policies toward immigration and citizenship, reflecting competing interests for France's mobility and immobility, see Sahlins, *Unnaturally French*, esp. 53–56.

113. Michèle Longino comes to the former conclusion, in part I think because she conflates French visions of the Levant and North Africa. *Orientalism in French Classical Drama* (Cambridge: Cambridge University Press, 2002).

114. Moüette, *Relation de la captivité*, 304. The same year that his captivity memoirs appeared, Moüette also published *Histoire des conquests de Mouley Archy, connu sous le nom de roy de Tafilet, et de Mouley Ismaël ou Seméin* . . . (Paris: Edme Couterot, 1683).

CHAPTER FOUR

1. Captain Soulreys [ra'is?] Mehmet of Algiers to galley intendant Jean-Louis Girardin de Vauvré, "A Marseille sur la galère," 4 July 1681, AN, Marine B3 37, f. 113. At the time, there may have been no more than eighty-three Algerians on the galleys. [Perboyre], *Mémoires*, 2: 338.

2. Dusault to Colbert, Algiers, 7 December 1681, AN, AE BI 115, ff. 320–321, cited in Touili, *Correspondance*, 27; Grammont, *HA*, 206–207; Masson, *Histoire du commerce*, 228.

3. Laurens Gracier to CCM, Algiers, 14 November 1681, ACCM, G41.

4. Bastion de France director Denis Dusault not only complained about the choice (Clément Ribard, "Prisonniers protestants en Barbarie," *BSHPF* 14 [1865]: 134) but objected to bombing Algiers in the first place. Instead, he recommended setting the regency against England and Holland so that "France will have a monopoly over commerce in the Levant and Barbary and get rich off the losses of other nations." Grammont, *HA*, 207; Capot-Rey, "La Politique française," 482.

5. Although Sultan Mehmet IV compelled the French ambassador in Constantinople to pay reparations, Louis XIV counted the raid on Chios successful enough to strike a commemorative medal (Musée national de la Marine, 5 ME 25, ph. 536 bis) and commission a painting by Jan Karel Donatus Van Beecq (*La Cannonade de Scio*, [post-1681], Musée de la Marine Brest). By a 27 November 1681 treaty (preserved at the ACCM, CC156 [OC], and AAE, MD, Afrique, vol. 2, ff. 76–79), Tripoli pledged to unfetter French and foreign slaves apprehended on French ships and to allow newly appointed consul Pierre de la Magdeleine to

ransom compatriots taken from foreign vessels. Sue, *Histoire de la marine française*, 2nd ed., 4 vols. (Paris: Dépôt de la librairie, 1845), 3: 375–381; Féraud, *AT*, 153–158; Masson, *Histoire des établissements*, 170; Vergé-Franceschi, *Abraham Duquesne*, 298–299; Poumarède, "La France et les barbaresques," 139–143.

6. Term employed by Moroccan traveler Ibn Zakour, cited in Matar, *Britain and Barbary*, 129.

7. The epidemic continued into 1683 when, according to consul Jean Le Vacher, several people were dying per day, most of the population was living off grass, and masters could no longer supply their slaves with bread. [Perboyre], *Mémoires*, 2: 317, 1681.

8. Designed by the Basque engineer Bernard Renau d'Eliçagaray (or d'Elissagaray), nicknamed Petit-Renau, these new weapons were meant to throw explosives about 1,350 meters. G. N. Clark, "Barbary Corsairs in the Seventeenth Century," *Cambridge Historical Journal* 8, 1 (1944): 30; Grammont, *HA*, 207–208; Vergé-Franceschi, *Abraham Duquesne*, 303 (he estimated seven hundred killed and one hundred houses destroyed).

9. On 4 November 1681, the CCM had advised the marine ministry about the suspected machinations of a Livornese Jew living in Marseille and a Jewish merchant in Holland with business interests in Algiers (AN, AE BIII 33, f. 252). Its rationale for asking the king to drive all Jews from the city was threefold: usury, trade in pilfered goods, and espionage. Teissier, *La Chambre de commerce de Marseille . . .* (Marseille: Barlatier et Barthelet, 1892), 43. The royal edict of expulsion, following an investigation order by Colbert to Thomas-Alexandre Morant, intendant of Provence (Saint-Germain, 20 November 1681, reprinted in Clément, *Lettres*, 6: 159), was delivered from Saint-Cloud on 2 May 1682 (ACCM, G5, cited in Eisenbeth, "Les Juifs en Algérie," 354).

10. These numbers come from the 3 July 1683 account by Eliçagary addressed to Seignelay from the harbor at Algiers, reproduced in Sue, *Histoire de la marine* 3: 418–423, which noted the delivery of four women: three from Messina and one from Marseille. Some of the freed slaves were sick, according to Philippe de Villette-Mursay, who transported them to Toulon. *Mes campagnes de mer sous Louis XIV: avec un dictionnaire des personnages et des batailles*, ed. Vergé-Franceschi (Paris: Tallandier, 1991), 179–180. Relatives of ninety-four Provençals received instructions to send linens and clothing before their arrival. AMM, GGL105.

11. Lucien Misermont offers the most complete assessment of Le Vacher's execution. "Les Français mis à bouche du canon à Alger en 1683 avec le consul Jean Le Vacher, et le canon appelé *Consulaire*," *Revue des études historiques* 20 (1917): 475–497. In 1830, according to Plantet (*CDA*, 1: 84–85 n. 2), the French government transported the cannon to Brest, where it still adorned the port at the end of the nineteenth century. In June 1912, the Comité du vieil Alger installed a commemorative plaque.

12. John Stoye, *The Siege of Vienna: The Last Great Trial between Cross and Crescent* (New York: Pegasus Books, 2007), esp. 188–189. Louis XIV endured a storm of criticism for not allying with fellow Christian princes to protect Vienna. See, for example, Jean Coppin, *Le Bouclier de l'Europe, ou La Guerre*

Sainte . . . (Lyon: A. Briasson, 1686), cited in Dominique Carnoy, *Représenta-*
tions de l'Islam dans la France du XVIIe siècle: la ville des tentations (Paris:
L'Harmattan, 1998), 19.

13. Also see the description of a Charles Dominique Van Beecq canvas for
Château de Marly, *Le Bombardement d'Alger* (cited in Vergé-Franceschi, *Abra-*
ham Duquesne, 310). Marc Perachon, *Remerciement au roi. Poème conte-*
nant un éloge historique de sa Majesté . . . (Paris: Veuve de Sébastien Mabre
Cramoisy, 1689), cited in Turbet-Delof, *Bibliographie critique*, 245–346 n. 263.

14. Jean Bénigne Bossuet, "Oraison funèbre de Marie-Thérèse d'Autriche"
(Saint-Denis, 1 September 1683), reproduced in *Oraisons funèbres de Bossuet*,
ed. Abel François Villemain and Jean Joseph François Dussault (Paris: Firmin
Didot, 1858), 122. In "Bossuet et la question d'Alger" (*Dix-septième siècle* 100
[1973]: 65 n. 10), Turbet-Delof shows that Bossuet lifted part of these lines from
Luis del Mármol Carvajal, *L'Afrique de Marmol, de la traduction de Nicolas*
Perrot sieur d'Ablancourt . . . (Paris: Thomas Jolly, 1667), 2: 342.

15. France was still trying to use Ottoman channels for slave liberation and
corsair suppression: one quarter of all *firmans* (decrees) issued between 1684
and 1685 by Sultan Mulay Isma'il ibn Sharif at the request of ambassador Gabriel Joseph de Lavergne, comte de Guilleragues, concerned these subjects.
"Liste des commandemens obtenus à la Porte par Mr le comte de Guilleragues
. . . ," AN, AE BI 378, ff. 458–466 v, cited in Poumarède, "La France et les barbaresques," 125.

16. On 25 April 1684, Anne-Hilarion de Costentin, comte de Tourville,
signed the peace treaty (reproduced in Rouard de Card, *TF*, 45–52) on Louis
XIV's behalf. A letter from Dusault to secretary of state and marine minister
Jean-Baptiste Colbert, marquis de Seignelay (Algiers, 1 August 1684), estimated
the number of French slaves in Algiers at 300 and put the number of healthy
Turks on the galleys at 246 and invalids at 54. Cited in [Perboyre], *Mémoires*,
2: 376. Despite peace negotiations, Algerian corsairs were still taking French
prizes (see slave Olivier François to M. Nappollon, Algiers, 15 April 1684,
ACCM, G41).

17. In his speech at Versailles, 4 July 1684, Algerian ambassador Hajj Ja'far
Agha apologized to Louis XIV for Le Vacher's execution. Plantet, *CDA*, 1: 90–
92, reported in the *Gazette de France* (1684): 396, 406.

18. Amfreville escorted the Algerian ambassador with 200 able-bodied and
196 crippled rowers to Algiers in November 1684, returning to Toulon with a
second ambassador, Hajj Mehemet, 400 French sailors, and captain Choiseul-
Beaupré in December. Jean Peter, *Les Barbaresques sous Louis XIV: le duel*
entre Alger et la Marine du Roi (1681–1698) (Paris: Economica, 1997), 73–74;
Villette-Mursay, *Mes campagnes*, 245; Plantet, *CDA*, 1: 96 n. 2, 98 n. 1; *Ga-*
zette de France (1685): 143. Meanwhile, the minister had good reason to order
galley general Louis Victor de Rochechouart, duc de Mortemart, "to reduce as
much as possible the contact the Algerian ambassador has with the Turks on
the galleys." As dey Hajj Hussein complained to Louis XIV in March 1685,
only fifty-one of the returned rowers were "our Janissaries . . . the other slaves
. . . are foreigners who do not belong to us at all." AN, Marine, Registres de

dépêches, 1684, f. 109; Archives coloniales de la Marine (Compagnies du Bastion de France, 1639–1731), cited in Plantet, *CDA*, 1: 111 n. 2, 96–98.

19. Sources disagree about the captives rescued by Tourville in May 1685. Were they seventy-five French captives bought out of the interior (Grammont, *HA*, 211)? Or seventy-five Algerian oarsmen traded for seventy-five French captives (*Gazette de France* [1685]: 190, cited in Plantet, *CDA*, 1: 105 n. 2)? Were they fifty-six non-French Christians traded for an equal number of Turks, whom the dey called "foreign Muslims" ([Perboyre], *Mémoires*, 2: 377; dey Hajj Hussein to Seignelay, Algiers, 1685, reprinted in Plantet, *CDA*, 1: 105–108)? Or, in "order to do good for slaves of various Europe states," did Louis XIV send Tourville with "40 Turks and janissaries" to trade for "75 Christian slaves of diverse nations who had been taken under foreign flag"—who included Spanish, Italian, Hamburgers, Flemish, Genoese, Greek priests, Capuchin monks, women, and children (*Mercure galant* [July 1685]: 11–16, cited in Peter, *Les Barbaresques*, 61)? The dey himself attested that while his country had liberated even English and Dutch slaves taken from French boats, France had released "invalid foreign slaves useless for all service." Dey Hajj Hussein to Seignelay, Algiers, March 1685, Archives coloniales de la Marine (Compagnies du Bastion de France, 1639–1731), reprinted in Plantet, *CDA*, 1: 99–102.

20. Furnished with royal passports—see ADBR, 50H30, for an example—four Trinitarians traveled to Tunis and Algiers in 1685 (see app. 2). Alonso (*LC*, 1: 228) has the Trinitarian procession arriving in Paris on 20 March 1686, but a letter from Father du Rosel to the Prince of Condé dated 21 October 1685 described a Mercedarian one in Versailles the day before (cited in Etienne Allaire, *La Bruyère dans la Maison de Condé*, 2 vols. [Paris: Firmin Didot, 1886], 1: 336). On the former slave Jacques Noblet, a Huguenot from Rouen who made it into Dutch exile, see Philippe Legendre, *Histoire de la persécution faite à l'église de Rouen sur la fin du dernier siècle* (Rotterdam: Jean Malherbe, 1704; reprint, Rouen: Léon Deshays, 1875), 26–35.

21. *Mercure galant* (July 1685): 17–18, cited in Peter, *Les Barbaresques*, 63.

22. In January 1686 dey Hajj Hussein protested that while he had released all his French slaves plus another thirty-six Christians, he was still owed fifty-six Turks. In September 1686, having discovered ten to twelve French captives in the possession of individuals, the dey handed them over to naval commissary Jean-Baptiste Céloron, sieur de Blainville. Dey Hajj Hussein to Louis XIV, Algiers, January 1686; divan of Algiers to Louis XIV, Algiers, 21 September 1686, AN, Marine B7 210, reprinted in Plantet, *CDA*, 1: 114–117, 120–123.

23. According to Boyer ("La Chiourme turque"), 5 of 257 Turks purchased for the galleys between 1685 and 1687 had already been baptized.

24. Copy of a translated letter from Agy Abdallah, slave on the *Patronne de France*, to the dey of Tunis, Marseille, February 1685, ACCM, G50.

25. "Déclaration portant que les Mahométans et idolâtres qui voudront se convertir ne pourront être instruits que dans la religion catholique," Versailles, 25 January 1683 (registered at the Parlement of Paris, 13 February 1683), reproduced in François André Isambert, ed., *Recueil général des anciennes lois françaises depuis l'an 420 jusqu'à la révolution de 1789*, 29 vols. (Paris: Belin-

Leprieur; Verdier, 1821–1833), 19: 414 r–415 r. On 6 February 1685, Louis XIV ordered the intendant of Languedoc to enforce the law by sending "une mauresse" being raised in the "RPR" to a convent at royal expense. Depping, *Correspondance*, 4: 359 n. 1.

26. For reproductions of the frontispieces of the *Almanach royal français* from the years 1686 and 1687, see Arkoun, *Histoire de l'islam*, 406, 440. The *Gazette de France* (1680): 156 and (1686): 108 published accounts of Muslims embracing Catholicism. Baptismal records and correspondence also confirm numerous conversions during the 1680s and 1690s and accompanying alarm on the part of North African leaders. See, for example, Registres paroissiaux d'Avon, 13 September 1681, cited in Grimaldi-Hierholtz, *Les Trinitaires de Fontainebleau et d'Avon* (Fontainebleau: Centre d'études culturelles, civiques et sociales de Seine-et-Marne, 1990), 63–64; Letrait, Degioanni, and Le Minor, *Répertoire des registres*, vii (on the baptism of Amet from Tunis, June 1682); deliberations by the "Prieux de la rédemption des esclaves," Marseille, 6 March 1686, AMM, GGL105; register of baptism and of municipal ceremonies, Marseille, 20 June 1686, ADBR, 201E117, and AMM, 1e div., 7e sect., AG, *Cérémonial*, Reg. 1, f. 935 (OC), cited in Louis Méry and F. Guindon, eds., *Histoire analytique et chronologique des actes et des délibérations du corps et du conseil de la municipalité de Marseille . . .* , 8 vols. (Marseille: Faissat-Demonchy, 1841–1873), 8: 345–346 (on a renegade's son, Jean Paul Turc, who fled Algiers for Marseille and took the name of the city as his own); Marseille, 21 May 1690, f. 968 r, cited in Méry and Guindon, *Histoire analytique*, 8: 410 (conversion of a Turk from Algiers); as well as 7 May 1691, ADBR, 139E/GG2 and 1695, Paroisse de Saint-Malo, cited in Mathorez, *Les Etrangers en France*, 1: 179.

27. The *Mercure galant* recorded the repudiation of Islam by renegades in 1687 (378, 285), 1688 (196), and 1689 (163), cited in Turbet-Delof, *L'Afrique barbaresque*, 150.

28. Statement from the Marseille municipal magistrates, Marseille, 14 November 1687, ACCM, G6.

29. Marine minister Jérôme Phélypeaux, comte de Pontchartrain, to consul Luce in Cyprus, Versailles, 6 July 1701, AN, Marine B7 68, f. 288. See the Parlement of Provence's ruling against thirty-four-year-old mason and Turkish galley slave Sha'bān Mattelin, judged a relapsed heretic, Marseille, 16 January 1700, ADBR (Annex Aix), B5570, 1700, ff. 45–48, cited and discussed in Boyer, "La Chiourme turque," 53–74.

30. In February 1682, the Tripolitans released 125 slaves taken from a boat from Marseille, 127 working aboard Tripolitan vessels, and 18 cabin boys. The French agreed to pay fifty piastres per slave seized from warships and one hundred piastres per slave seized elsewhere, according to Féraud, *AT*, 157–158; and F. Elie de La Primaudaie, "Le Littoral de la Tripolitaine: commerce, navigation, géographie comparée," *Nouvelles annales des voyages, de la géographie, de l'histoire et de l'archéologie* 11, 3 (1865): 298. In his journal, British consul Thomas Baker noted the release of eighty French slaves on 16 February 1682 (44b); on 20 December 1682, he made reference to the deliverance of another ninety (58a), reprinted in Pennell, *Piracy and Diplomacy*, 137–138, 153.

31. Sieur de Bonnecorse, son of a Marseille municipal officer, spent ten days in the bagne before being placed under house arrest at the French consulate with his boat's seventeen-man crew. Louis XIV's letter is attached to the CCM deliberations of 25 January 1683, ACCM, BB3 (OC). The aftermath is related by Mercedarian Jean Plantier to the CCM, Tunis, 7 December 1682, ACCM, AA544 (OC), and Magdeleine to the CCM, Tripoli, 13 December 1682, 25 March 1683, ACCM, AA547 (OC), cited in Masson, *Histoire du commerce*, 229; 12 April 1683, AAE, Tripoli, cited in Masson, *Histoire des établissements*, 170, 171 n 2. "Journal of Thomas Baker" (Tripoli, 20 November, 29 November 1682, 1 February 1683, 57a–59a) gives an account of the events leading up to the November 1683 declaration of war; he also lists "the Damages these Corsars have ye Navigation of Xdome," for the years 1682 and 1683 (60a, 67a), reprinted in Pennell, *Piracy and Diplomacy*, 153–155, 156, 166–167.

32. Arvieux claimed to have received news of Duquesne's assault on Tripoli via Cairo (*Mémoires*, 6: 403; Masson, *Histoire du commerce*, 229–230). I am not convinced, however, that the attack took place, as neither the English consul's journal nor the French translator's account mentions it, while later authors make only vague references. See, for example, Eugène Pélissier de Reynaud, "La Régence de Tripoli," *Revue des deux mondes* 12 (1855): 19.

33. Abu Salim 'Abd Allah ibn Muhammad 'Ayyashi, *Voyages dans le sud de l'Algérie et des états barbaresques de l'ouest et de l'est*, trans. Berbrugger (Paris: Imprimerie royale, 1846), 109–113.

34. Known as Trik, the ninety-two- (or ninety-four-) year-old Hajj Muhammad was dey of Algiers from 1671 to 1682. Louis XIV to Estrées, Versailles, 8 April, 13 April; Seignelay to Estrées, Versailles, 19 April; Estrées to Seignelay, roads of Tripoli, 21 June; dey Hajj Abdallah to Estrées, Tripoli, 23 June; Estrées to Seignelay, roads of Tripoli, 30 June 1685, AAE, Afrique, 1685, vol. 2, cited in Sue, *Histoire de la marine* 3: 501–505, 512–522. See also Elie de La Primaudaie, "Le Littoral de la Tripolitaine," 304–308; Féraud, *AT*, 161–162; Peter, *Les Barbaresques*, 87–93.

35. In a 30 June letter to Seignelay, Estrées claimed to have taken on board 180 slaves; on 10 July 1685, he maintained that the Tripolitans had released about 225. Except for 40 he had kept to navigate and 10 he had sent home to Venice, the rest were bound for Toulon. Cited in Sue, *Histoire de la marine française* 4: 520, 529. Between 1692 and 1697, royal interpreter François Pétis de la Croix wrote and amended several accounts of his 1685 voyage to Tripoli. Annie Berthier reproduces two versions (one from BN, NAF 7488, ff. 291–313; the other from Bayerische Staatsbibliothek Munich, Mss Gall. 729) in "Tripoli de Barbarie à la fin du XVIIe siècle d'après un mémoire inédit de François Pétis de la Croix," *Anatolia Moderna Yeni Andalou* 6 (1997): 13–30.

36. After signing the Franco-Tripolitan treaty on 29 June 1685 (see ACCM, CC156, and AAE, MD, Afrique 2: 29–35, for the text), Estrées left one of his scribes, sieur Martineng (or Martinet), as provisionary consul. Féraud, *AT*, 162–163. It was his successor, Claude Lemaire, who became responsible for enforcing the treaty's provisions. He protested the detention of five French boys who apostatized without the requisite three-day waiting period and took collection of

additional French slaves. CCM to marine ministry, Marseille, 13 March 1686, AN, AE BIII 34, f. 105; "Note des esclaves françois que le divan de Tripoli a remise au Sr Lemaire," 27 September 1686, and roll of French slaves, attached to an 8 November 1686 memorandum, AN, AE BI 1088, ff. 14–16.

37. Panzac, *CB*, 29; Charles-Roux, *FA*, 183.

38. Procureur du roi Boissineau to the procureur général, Nantes, 2 July 1686, cited in Benjamin Vaurigaud, *Essai sur l'histoire des Eglises reformées de Bretagne, 1535–1808*, 3 vols. (Paris: Joël Cherbuliez, 1870), 3: 109–110.

39. As in the case of a Protestant boy from Dieppe who "promised to abjure" but also two committed adherents of the "RPR." English and Dutch agents ransomed others. Piolle, "Mémoires de cette année, 1687," Algiers, 30 January 1687; "Mémoires depuis ma dernière," Algiers, 29 November 1687, AN, AE BI 115, f. 3; and BI 116, ff. 68–70, cited in Touili, *Correspondance*, 43.

40. Mortemart to the divan of Algiers, Bay of Cadiz, 20 July 1687, AN, Marine B7 213, reprinted in Plantet, *CDA*, 1: 143. See also Peter, *Les Barbaresques*, 109, who refers to Mortemart's finding "numerous RPR."

41. Piolle, "Mémoires depuis ma précédente . . . ," Algiers, 18 July 1687, AN, AE BI 116, ff. 24–26, cited in Touili, *Correspondance*, 40.

42. Jean Claude, *Les Plaintes des protestans, cruellement opprimez dans le royaume de France* (Cologne: Pierre Marteau, 1686; reprint, London: Delage, 1707), 158–159.

43. English, Dutch, and German Protestants all fund-raised for Huguenots enslaved in North Africa. One of the responsibilities of pastors-extraordinary in Rotterdam, for example, was overseeing such collections. GAR, "Livres des Actes du Consistoire," 19 July and 15 August 1688, A, ff. 166, 169, cited in Gerald Cerny, *Theology, Politics, and Letters at the Crossroads of European Civilization: Jacques Basnage and the Baylean Huguenot Refugees in the Dutch Republic* (Dordrecht, Netherlands: Martinus Nijhoff, 1987), 69–70. Besides soliciting ransom funds in Rotterdam, Pierre Jurieu appealed to a fellow exiled minister in Berlin and readers of his *Lettres pastorales* (15 December 1688 issue cited in F. R. J. Knetsch, *Pierre Jurieu: Theoloog en politikus der refuge* (Kampen, Netherlands: J. H. Kok, 1967), 279; thanks to Catherine Scallen for the translation). English Protestants apparently contributed enough for there to be leftover funds in 1691. *Proceeding of the Huguenot Society of London* 5 (1898): 352, citing PRO, Treasury Papers, 21: 36, f. 169. For additional signs of English and Dutch intercession on behalf of Huguenots in North Africa, see PRO, State Papers, 71/15/103 and 71/15/10, cited in Matar and Vitkus, *Piracy, Slavery, and Redemption*, 33, 50 n. 180.

44. According to H. de France, who edited and reprinted Brassard's manuscript, the original bears the stamp "Holland" and the address "monsieur La Mothe Salinières, to deliver to mademoiselle Brassard" in Bordeaux. Written or dictated when its author was ninety-two, the account remained in the Combes-Brassard family archives until a descendant began circulating it among friends. Brassard, "Relation de la captivité de M. Brassard à Alger," ed. H. de France, *BSHPF* 27 (1878): 349–350, 353–354. According to Jacques Pannier, Brassard was born in 1620, making him sixty-six or sixty-seven when he was captured.

"Les Protestants français et l'Algérie," *BSHPF* 79 (1930): 151–164. See also Bonet-Maury, "Les Précurseurs," 926.

45. Daniel Poyen to "Messieurs les Pasteurs & Anciens des Eglises Françoises," Algiers, 10 November 1687, printed in Knetsch, "Deux lettres des protestants captifs à Alger, de 1687," *BSHPF* 110 (1964): 55–58. One Huguenot slave who rejected Islam in favor of Catholicism was the ship captain M. Hurtain, according to the ship scribe who recorded the funeral oration before his burial at sea. Quoted in Moureau, "Quand l'histoire se fait littérature: de l'aventure personnelle au récit de captive et au-delà," in *Captifs en Méditerranée*, 26–27.

46. Occasional Algerian attacks preceded the all-out declaration of war, prompting the French government to send emissaries in August 1686 (Blainville, who received a few French captives and promises to release another ten to twelve held by individuals) and in January 1687 (Mortemart). Divan of Algiers to Louis XIV and dey Ibrahim Khodja to Seignelay, Algiers, 21 September 1686, AN, Marine B7 210, reprinted in Plantet, *CDA*, 1: 121–122, 123–125, 141 n. 1. See Pierre Duval to Périllé in Sale, aboard *l'Oranger*, 9 March 1686, ACCM, AA557 (OC), reprinted in Castries, Cossé Brissac, and Cenival, *SIHM* (1924), 2nd ser., 2: 554–556.

47. In December 1687, two months after Hajj Hussein impounded eleven French vessels at port and sold off 372 new French slaves at 225 livres a head, Amfreville captured an Algerian warship, *Le Lion d'or*, freeing 46 French slaves and capturing 180 Turks. Dusault to Seignelay, 19 September 1687, cited in Plantet, *CDA*, 1: 148 n. 1; Villette-Mursay, *Mes campagnes*, 245; Peter, *Les Barbaresques*, 111.

48. Brassard, "Relation de la captivité," 353. For another description of these executions, see [Perboyre], *Mémoires*, 2: 463–470. Among the participants in France's 1688 campaign against Algiers were some recalcitrant Huguenots impressed onto the royal galleys. Seignelay to galley intendant Michel Bégon, 18 April 1688, Archives de la marine à Rochefort, cited in Henry Lehr, *Les Protestants d'autrefois: sur mer et outre-mer* (Paris: Fischbacher, 1907), 233.

49. Consul André Piolle was so badly beaten that he died before he could be blasted from a cannon. Apart from the apostolic vicar, another Lazarist, and a nobleman, the victims included five captains, three skippers, six clerks, and twenty-five sailors. *Relation de ce qui s'est passé devant Alger en 1688* (n.d.), cited in Turbet-Delof, *Bibliographie critique*, 238; Brassard, "Relation de la captivité," 354; letter from future British consul Robert Cole, reproduced in Robert Lambert Playfair, *The Scourge of Christendom: Annals of British relations with Algiers Prior to the French Conquest* (London: Smith, Elder, 1884), 157.

50. Peter, *Les Barbaresques*, 117–123.

51. Panzac, *CB*, 31; John B. Wolf, *The Barbary Coast: Algiers under the Turks, 1500 to 1830* (New York: Norton, 1979), 266–267.

52. Auger Sorhainde, agent of the Compagnie du Cap-Nègre and later consul to Tunis, spent five days in Algiers in April 1689. On naval commissary Guillaume Marcel's first trip to the regency, he signed a new treaty (dated 24 September 1689, reproduced in Rouard de Card, *TF*, 52–60), which agreed to free Turks and Moors for 150 and 100 piastres, respectively. Divan of Algiers to

Seignelay, Algiers, 5 January 1690, Archives coloniales de la Marine (Compagnies du Bastion de France, 1639–1731). On Marcel's second trip to Algiers, which lasted from December 1689 until the following June, he brought 113 Turks and 100 sailor outfits for the French slaves, who "were entirely naked," with the intention of ransoming them for 180 piastres each. Vauvré to Seignelay, 8 December 1689, AN, Marine B7 213; Marcel to Seignelay, Toulon, 25 June 1690, AN, AE BI 116, ff. 279–280, cited in Plantet, *CDA*, 1: 163; 165 n. 1; 185 n. 2, 292 n. 3. Also see Grammont, *HA*, 213–214 and app. 1.

53. See Marcel's 16 November 1689 instructions (copy from Versailles, AN, AE BI 116, ff. 163–165) and Marcel to Seignelay, 14 February 1690 (AN, AE BI 116, ff. 236–242), discussed in Bonet-Maury, "La France et la rédemption," 911, 914–915. Also, dey Hajj Sha'bān to Louis XIV, Algiers, 23 July 1691, AN, Marine B7 214 and 215, reprinted in Plantet, *CDA*, 1: 306–307.

54. See "Extrait du mémoire de S. Marcel sur la suitte de sa négociation," n.d., AN, AE BI 116, ff. 167–172 and app. 2.

55. *Avis au public touchant la rédemption des captifs du royaume de Maroc* (Paris: Antoine-Urbain Coustelier, 1723). There is some disagreement about the number of French captives ransomed during the Mercedarian voyage from February to April 1690 and whether the friars had enough time to organize a procession in Marseille. See app. 2.

56. Marcel to Seignelay, Algiers, 11 April 1690, AAE, CA; dey Hajj Sha'bān to Louis XIV, Algiers, 12 April 1690, AN, Marine B7 213 and 214, cited in Plantet, *CDA*, 1: 216–220, 244, n. 1. Consul René Lemaire to CCM, Algiers, 11 December 1690, ACCM, AA490 (OC), reprinted in Grammont, *Correspondance des consuls d'Alger, 1690–1742* (Algiers: Adolphe Jourdan, 1890), 14.

57. Dissatisfied with available methods for corresponding with Versailles, Lemaire informed Seignelay (AN, AE BI 116, ff. 284–289, cited in Touili, *Correspondance*, 49) and the CCM (Algiers, 15 July 1690, ACCM, AA470 [OC], cited in Eugène Vaillé, *Histoire générale des postes françaises*, 7 vols. [Paris: Presses universitaires de la France, 1947–1955], 4: 491) that he had armed a boat "to serve solely as a postilion to go from here to France and from France to here."

58. Slave Antoine Broglia to CCM, Algiers, 30 August 1690; slave Jean-François Finier to his father, Algiers, 3 November 1690, AMM, GGL106.

59. Lemaire to CCM, Algiers, 25 January 1691, reprinted in Grammont, Correspondance. "Requête du divan d'Alger au très puissant empereur de France, en Considération de la Paix," presented at Versailles, 26 July 1690, AN, Marine B7 214 (on release of galley slaves); Dusault to Pontchartrain, 16 May 1691, AAE, CA, cited in Plantet, *CDA*, 1: 252 (on "Requête"). "Etat de la recette de la dépense du sieur Dusault . . . ," 10 March 1693, cited in Plantet, *CDA*, 1: 383 n. 1 (on treaty); 1: 296 n. 1. Algerian ambassador Muhammad al-Amin, who arrived in Toulon in June 1690, had still not obtained satisfaction in January 1691, as evidenced by his increasingly enraged and despairing correspondence; he returned to Algiers six months later. For several letters from different dates from and to this ambassador, see AN, Marine B7 214, B7 215; Archives coloniales de la Marine (Compagnies du Bastion de France, 1639–1731), all reproduced in Plantet, *CDA*, 1: 254–293, 303–305 n. 2.

60. Twenty slaves were dying a day in July 1691, according to dey Hajj Sha'bān to Louis XIV, Algiers, 23 July 1691, AN, Marine B7 214 and 215, cited in Plantet, *CDA*, 1: 312. Already explaining the high price of slaves on 30 December 1690, Dusault told Pontchartrain that "plague has killed 2000 slaves; which makes [the remaining ones] expensive." Cited in Bonet-Maury, "La France et la rédemption," 918.

61. Dusault to Pontchartrain, Algiers, 30 December 1691, 22 March 1692; Pontchartrain to Dusault, Versailles, 6 February 1692, AN, AE BI 116, ff. 407–424, 449–450, 467–481, cited in Touili, *Correspondance*, 55, 56, 58, and discussed in Bonet-Maury, "La France et la rédemption," 907.

62. For the details of the drawn-out negotiations and shuttling of French captives and Algerian rowers between 1691 and 1692, and Dusault's suggestion, approved by Pontchartrain, that Turks from the galleys be replaced by French turncoats seized in the service of Venice, see AN, AE BI 116, esp. ff. 365–368, 377–378.

63. See app. 2.

64. Call for families to provide ransoms for relatives in captivity (400 livres for captains and masters; 350 livres for pilots and master gunners; 260 livres for surgeons, clerks, officers, and sailors), Toulon, 16 January 1690; "Extrait du Rôlle Général des Esclaves . . . ," [1690] (which contains 154 names and an explanation of why 42 of them do not count as Marseillais); intendant of Provence Pierre-Cardin Lebret to the échevins of Marseille, Aix-en-Provence, 9 May, 31 September, 4 and 24 October 1690, 31 January 1691; François-Roger Robert to the échevins of Marseille, Toulon, December 1690, AMM, GGL106; letters from consuls to intendants of Provence, [1690], ACT, cited in Lambert, "L'Oeuvre de la redemption," 532–533; census extract dated 4 October 1690; ACC, GG37, now filed at ADBR, 139 E.

65. Arrêt from the Conseil d'Etat, Versailles, 26 February 1691, Archives municipales de Saint-Malo, BB15, f. 63 r.

66. For example, René Lemaire to Pontchartrain, Algiers, 15 February 1694 (four French "refugees" up for sale not turned over to the consul); Dusault to Pontchartrain, Toulon lazaret, 21 March 1698 (eight Protestants among French slaves, four with ransom orders from Holland); consul Philippe-Jacques Durand to Pontchartrain, Algiers, 10 January 1701 (census of seven Huguenots seized from a Dutch ship), AN, AE BI 117, ff. 96–97, 377–381; BI 118, ff. 121–124, cited in Touili, *Correspondance*, 68, 86, 98–99.

67. [Comelin and La Motte], *Etat des Royaumes*, 106. This account went through a second edition in 1704 and two more in 1714. Besides sixty-four French and foreign slaves, the Trinitarians' 1700 redemptive voyage to Algiers, Tunis, and Tripoli brought back a two-foot-high crucifix. See app. 2.

68. Trinitarian general Desuignes to intendant Barrentin, Dunkirk, 1 March 1700, Service historique de l'Armée de la Terre, A1 1733, f. 15; AAE, MD, Alger, vol. 15, ff. 9–12.

69. Grimaldi-Hierholtz, *Les Trinitaires de Fontainebleau*, 105; *Mercure galant* (October 1700): 56–62; Philippe de Courcillon Dangeau, *Journal du marquis de Dangeau . . .* , ed. Eudore Soulié et al., 19 vols. (Paris: Firmin Didot,

1854–1860), 7: 314; Durand to Pontchartrain, 14 October 1700, AN, AE BI 118, ff. 109–112, cited in Touili, *Correspondance*, 106.

70. Two Tripolitan ambassadors, Khalīl and Khezer-Agha, asked after the six hostages taken to France as part of the 1685 treaty. Louis XIV repatriated them eight months later. Féraud, *AT*, 170–174.

71. Consul Louis Lemaire to CCM, 6 March, ACCM, AA547 (OC), cited in Masson, *Histoire du commerce*, 291; to Sorhainde, Tripoli, 22 March 1692, AAE, Tunis, cited in Plantet, *CBT*, 1: 467 n. 2; Féraud, *AT*, 178–180.

72. Féraud, *AT*, 180–182; copy of letter from slave Estienne Tourve to CCM, Tripoli, 17 March 1693, ACCM, G44.

73. The dey agreed to release 40 French slaves for free and 310 for ransom, signing a new treaty with Dusault on 27 May 1693. Féraud, *AT*, 182–184; Dusault to Pontchartrain, 17 January 1693, AN, AE BI 117, ff. 1–3, cited in Plantet, *CDA*, 1: 396–397 n. 3; *Gazette de France* (1693): 115, cited in Plantet, *CBT*, 1: 471 n. 1. See Rouard de Card, *TF*, 253–255, for selected text.

74. Féraud, *AT*, 184–185; Royal order, Versailles, 12 January 1694, to send back seventy-four Turks to Tripoli, followed by their names; Pontchartrain to galley intendant M. de Vauban, Fontainebleau, 26 October 1694, with the names of thirty-seven more "Turcs de Tripoli" to be liberated, AN, Marine B6 26, ff. 8 v–10; ff. 447–448; Pontchartrain to CCM, Versailles, 29 February 1696, "Etat des Esclaves tripolins . . . ," ACCM, G51.

75. The passenger in question, Muhammad ibn Shoukir, had been plotting to overthrow the government of Tunis. Fearing discovery, he pretended to leave on pilgrimage to Mecca, planning to take refuge in Algiers. Instead, he was captured and taken to Toulon. Bey Muhammad II sent two ambassadors to France in June 1689, but the king did not grant them an audience until January. Plantet, *CBT*, 1: 417–418 n. 1, 427 n. 1.

76. See 1690–1692 correspondence among Sorhainde, Pontchartrain, and the directors of the Compagnie du Cap-Nègre, as well as the "Convention du 16 décembre 1691," AAE, Salle de Traités, reprinted in Plantet, *CBT*, 1: 434–463.

77. *Gazette de France* (15 July 1681), cited in Penz, *Les Captifs français*, 95–97.

78. This letter from Mulay Isma'il to Louis XIV, 15 September 1681 (AAE, Maroc, CC, vol. 1, f. 104, cited in Nékrouf, *Une Amitié orageuse*, 78–81), has been the subject of much historical conjecture. See also Penz, *Les Captifs français*, 98–100.

79. For the text and discussion, see Castries, Cossé Brissac, and Cenival, *SIHM* (1922), 2nd ser., 1: 608–627.

80. Penz, *Les Captifs français*, 107–108; Muhammad ibn "Ha'ider" to Ali "Mercher," Marseille, 9 May 1682, reproduced in Castries, Cossé Brissac, and Cenival, *SIHM* (1922), 2nd ser., 1: 691–693.

81. Colbert to Saint-Armand, Versailles, 3 June 1682, cited in Masson, *Histoire des établissements*, 196 n. 3.

82. Moroccan galley slaves to Mulay Isma'il, Marseille, 23 April and 9 May 1682, reproduced in Castries, Cossé Brissac, and Cenival, *SIHM* (1922), 2nd ser., 1: 691–693.

83. Penz, *Les Captifs français*, 111–124.

84. Slave Gabriel de Blandières to Seignelay, 10 December 1684, cited in Penz, *Les Captifs français*, 125–128.

85. See app. 1 and consul Jean Périllé to Seignelay, Salé, 27 May 1687, AAE, Maroc, CC, vol. 1, ff. 313–315, reproduced in Castries, Cossé Brissac, and Cenival, *SIHM* (1927), 2nd ser., 3: 84.

86. Penz, *Les Captifs français*, 167–169; AN, Marine B2 66, f. 190.

87. Brussin et al. to Pontchartrain, Meknes, 12 February 1691, AAE, Maroc, CC, Carton: Rachat des esclaves, Barbarie, 1649 à 1709 and AN, AE BIII 316, f. 22, cited in Castries, Cossé Brissac, and Cenival, *SIHM* (1927), 2nd ser., 3: 342–344.

88. J. M. Lopez, "El Cristianismo en Marruecos," *Mauritania* (1931–1937), cited in Maziane, *Salé et ses corsaires (1666–1727): un port de course marocain au XVIIe siècle* (Mont-Saint-Aignan: Publications des Universités de Rouen et du Havre; Caen: Presses universitaires de Caen, 2007), 276.

89. In 1692 Mulay Isma'il agreed to revisit the issue of an exchange, as long as he received galley slaves from Salé, Rabat, Tetouan, Alcazar, and Meknes, but not Marrakech, whom he considered rebels. He also did not want back anyone who had been enslaved for longer than ten years. Penz, *Les Captifs français*, 189–196. For an example of such an exchange, which also included payment of four hundred livres, concluded 26 October 1694, see AN, Marine B6 26, f. 447.

90. On the number of slaves, see app. 1. In 1694 the French captives received 5,200 livres altogether; in 1696 they received 9 livres and 5 sols each. Penz, *Les Captifs français*, 202–223, 321.

91. Estelle to Pontchartrain about Pierre Ballé, Salé, 29 September 1695; with list of slaves, Meknes, Salé, 3 January 1696, and Salé, 20 June 1698, AAE, Maroc, CC, vol. 2, ff. 254–255, 269–271, 427–429, reprinted in Castries, Cossé Brissac, and Cenival, *SIHM* (1931), 2nd ser., 4: 358–360, 376–383, 630–632. According to the *Mercure historique* (September 1699), the number of free Huguenots in Salé was so high that they requested a pastor from the Netherlands (reproduced in *BSHPF* 13 [1854]: 119). See also Jean-Louis Miège, "Aspects de la course marocaine du XVIIe au XIXe siècle," in Vergé-Franceschi and Graziani, *La Guerre de course*, 47.

92. The daughter in question was Marie-Anne, princesse de Conti. Penz, *Les Captifs français*, chap. 7.

93. Germain Cavelier to his mother in Honfleur, Meknes, 3 September 1702, AN, AE B1 827, ff. 170–171 v, reprinted in Castries, Cossé Brissac, and Cenival, *SIHM* (1960), 2nd ser., 6: 282–285. On English negotiations for Huguenot captives, starting in 1694 and culminating in 1705–1706, see P. G. Rogers, *A History of Anglo-Moroccan Relations to 1900* (London: Foreign and Commonwealth Office, 1970), 66–77; and Castries, Cossé Brissac, and Cenival, *SIHM* (1960), 2nd ser., 6: 18 n.

94. Majordomo in 1703, he was finally ransomed in 1725 at age sixty-one after forty years of slavery. See La Faye et al., *Relation en forme du journal*, 157.

95. Mercedarian Alexis Forton to Pontchartrain about Jean-Baptiste Brouillet, 1704, AN, AE BIII 316, cited in Castries, Cossé Brissac, and Cenival, *SIHM*

(1960), 2nd ser., 6: 633 n. 1, 804 n. 1. The next February this Huguenot merchant wrote a condolatory letter to his coreligionists enslaved in Meknes, cited in Penz, *Personnalités et familles françaises d'Afrique du Nord, Maroc (1588–1814)* (Paris: Editions SGAF, 1948), 104.

96. Charles Eliot of Normandy, identified as "reformé" on French censuses in 1696 and 1698, appears on the list of slaves ransomed by the Trinitarians in 1708 (Penz, *Personnalités et familles*, 95).

97. Nolasque Néant, one of the two Mercedarians involved in the joint Moroccan voyages of 1704–1705, 1708–1709, and 1711–1712 (which liberated nine to twelve, thirty-four to forty-five, and twenty to twenty-two French slaves, respectively [see app. 2]), left a description of an October 1712 Trinitarian performance in Aix-en-Provence. According to his *Relation de ce qui s'est passé*, 391–393, between them the orders seem to have mounted processions only in Marseille, Aix, Avignon, and Lyon.

98. In *Histoire du règne de Mouley Ismael, roy du Maroc . . .* (Rouen: Guillaume Bouhart, 1714; abridged version, Paris: Mercure de France, 2002), 100–116, Dominique Busnot claimed that Mulay Isma'il had killed six hundred French slaves. On book 2, chap. 14, "Panurge among the Turks," see Timothy Hampton, "'Turkish Dogs': Rabelais, Erasmus, and the Rhetoric of Alterity," *Representations* 41 (1993): 58–82.

99. According to Simon Ockley, England's King Charles II had been promised the liberation of some French Protestants along with the remainder of his subjects in Morocco. *An Account of south-west Barbary . . .* (London: J. Bowyer and H. Clements, 1713), 123.

100. See app. 2. On the Huguenot merchant Etienne Pillet who took the name Abd al-Hadi in 1724 after thirty-five years in Morocco, see Castries, Cossé Brissac, and Cenival, *SIHM* (1953), 2nd ser., 5: 527–529; and La Faye et al., *Relation en forme du journal*, 28 n. 1, 62–63, 70–71.

101. The Trinitarian voyage of 1724–1725 managed only to exchange 15 elderly Moroccans for 17 Frenchmen, leaving 113 others behind. The Mercedarian one of 1729 unshackled just two more (see apps. 1 and 2). On the cooperative 1737 redemption, separate processions in Toulouse and Montpellier, and the joint performance in Paris, see Deslandres, *OT*, 1: 370; Germain, "Oeuvre de la rédemption"; *L'Ordre et la marche de la Procession des Captifs, rachetés dans le Royaume de Maroc . . .* (Paris: Veuve Delormel, 1737).

102. This ratio (set down in an 11 February 1687 ordinance) was achieved between 2 May 1685 and 30 August 1687 when 2,040 of 7,970 rowers were identified as Turks. Boyer, "La Chiourme turque," 55–56.

103. The year 1687 found about twenty-five thousand black slaves in the French West Indies (James S. Pritchard, *In Search of Empire: The French in the Americas, 1670–1730* [Cambridge: Cambridge University Press, 2004], app. 2, 428); approximately two thousand Muslims (ibid.), and between three hundred and six hundred Huguenots on the French galleys (Lehr, *Les Protestants d'autrefois*, 220; La Roncière, *Histoire de la marine*, 4: 18 n. 2).

104. *Le Dictionnaire de l'Académie françoise*, 2 vols. (Paris: Veuve de J. B. Coignard, 1694), 1: 385. The most comprehensive analysis of the *Code noir* is

Louis Sala-Molins, *Le Code noir ou le calvaire de Canaan* (Paris: Presses universitaires de France, 1987).

105. Antoine Furetière, *Dictionnaire universel . . .* , 3 vols. (The Hague: Arnout & Reinier Leers, 1690), 2: n.p. According to Lucette Valensi and Simone Delesalle, the first information on the Atlantic slave trade published anywhere in France appeared in 1675 in Jacques Savary's *Le Parfait négociant.* "Le Mot 'nègre' dans les dictionnaires français d'Ancien régime: histoire et lexicographie," *Langue française, 'Langage et histoire'* 15 (1972): 79–104.

106. Pontchartrain to Governor of Martinique d'Esragny, 4 October 1691, AN, Colonies B14, f. 312, cited in Peabody, *"There Are No Slaves in France,"* 12.

107. Pontchartrain to Sr. Marin, Fontainebleau, 20 October 1694, AN, Marine B6 26, f. 431; Bamford, *Fighting Ships,* 154–160.

108. Simon Michel Treuvé, ed., *Le Dictionnaire des cas de conscience . . .* , 2 vols. (Paris: J. B. Cignard and H. L. Guérin, 1733), 1: Article *Esclaves,* col. 1437 and following, cited in Russell Parsons Jameson, *Montesquieu et l'esclavage: étude sur les origines de l'opinion antiesclavagiste en France au XVIIIe siècle* (New York: B. Franklin, 1971), 130–132.

CHAPTER FIVE

1. According to consul Antoine-Gabriel Durand, writing from Algiers on 1 August 1702, plague had left forty-five victims in its wake. AN, AE BI 118, ff. 257–262, cited in Touili, *Correspondance,* 108.

2. *Dictionnaire universel françois et latin,* 2 vols. (Trévoux: Estienne Ganeau, 1704), was the first in which the word *nègre* referred not only to people from a geographic region or a species of fish but also to dark-skinned slaves (cited in Valensi and Delesalle, "Le Mot 'nègre,'" 86).

3. According to Pritchard (*In Search of Empire,* 12), the black slave population of the French Caribbean reached about seventy-seven thousand by 1715.

4. The number of Ottoman and Moroccan slaves in France had already fallen by 20 percent. See app. 1.

5. Durand to CCM, Algiers, 15 June 1702, ACCM, AA471 (OC), cited in Grammont, *Correspondance,* 94–95.

6. Translated copy of letter from Pierre Burin to his parents in St. Pé, Algiers, 3 October 1708; Durand to CCM, Algiers, 15 June 1702, ACCM, AA471 (OC), cited in Grammont, *Correspondance,* 94–95; Basque captive Haristeguy to Pontchartrain, Algiers, 4 October 1709, AN, AE BI 119, ff. 244, 250–251, excerpted in Touili, *Correspondance,* 143.

7. For examples of treaty violations and captures, see Sorhainde to Pontchartrain, Tunis, 24 November 1703, 2 August 1704, 2 May and 26 November 1706; Louis XIV to the divan of Tunis, Marly, 15 October 1710, AE, CT, reprinted in Plantet, *CBT,* 2: vi–viii, 21–22, 33, 35, 47–48.

8. The treaty, signed 16 December 1710 by frigate captain Guillaume L'Aigle and the rulers of Tunis (see Plantet, *CBT,* 2: 57–59, for text), differs from the 1685 one only in explicitly barring foreigners from selling French slaves in Tunis. "Ordonnance portant défense de commercer en Tunisie pendant six mois,"

Versailles, 31 October 1714, AN, Marine B7 93, f. 79, cited in Plantet, *CBT*, 2: 86–87.

9. Rodolfo Micacchi, "I Rapporti tra il Regno di Francia e la Reggenza di Tripoli di Barberia nella prima metà del secolo XVIII," *Rivista delle colonie italiane* 8 (1934): 73–74.

10. Permission for the Mercedarians to take collection from the bishop of Saint-Malo, Dinan, 1 December 1714, ADIV, G72.

11. Papal orders for sermons preaching the redemption of captives began in 1675 and were renewed in 1709 and 1711. Deslandres, *L'Eglise*, 17.

12. French slaves to Philippe, duc d'Orléans, Salé, 17 April 1717, AN, AE BIII 317, f. 161.

13. Bishops from every corner of France printed up pastoral letters (*mandements*) ordering collections for the seventy-four French slaves in Morea but warned the conseil de Marine of extremely small yields. AN, Marine B1 3, f. 159; B1 12, ff. 31, 153; B3 239, ff. 77–88, 159–188; B7 93, ff. 330 v, 361 v, 404; and AE BIII 317, ff. 152–154, 168–206. See also ADAM, G1292.

14. The knights had complained to the Grand Master in 1711 that "the brothers of the Redemption . . . refused to help us with our money or with the sums the king gave him: they say that we are rich." Their release was finally negotiated in 1716 for upwards of twenty-two thousand livres. Following some legal wrangling, d'Esparron was exempted from participating in any processions. Consul Jean de Clairambault to conseil de Marine, Algiers, 20 January 1717, AN, AE BI 120, ff. 44–47, cited in Touili, *Correspondance*, 170; Fabre, *Histoire des hôpitaux*, 2: 320–322; Devoulx, "Relevé des principaux français qui ont résidé à Alger," *RA* 16 (1872): 365; Engel, *L'Ordre de Malte*, 167–171.

15. The treaty, signed on 7 December 1719 by Dusault and the leaders of Algiers, is preserved at AN, Marine B7 534. See also Charles-Roux, *FA*, 209.

16. The 1719–1720 Trinitarian mission freed between fifty-eight and sixty-three French slaves. See app. 2.

17. The 1719–1720 Mercedarian mission to Algiers freed between twenty-six and thirty-five French slaves. See app. 2.

18. Conseil de Marine to galley intendant Pierre Arnoul, Paris, 6 April 1718, ACCM, G39.

19. Dusault to conseil de Marine, Algiers, 12 December 1719, AN, AE BI 120, ff. 316–317, cited in Touili, *Correspondance*, 194; *Ordre de la Procession des esclaves rachetés au Royaume d'Alger* (Paris: C. L. Thiboust, 1720), 4–8; [Comelin, La Motte, and Joseph Bernard], *Voyage pour la redemption des captifs . . .* (Paris: Louis-Anne Sevestre, 1721), 16–46; Jacques Philippe Laugier de Tassy, *Histoire du royaume d'Alger . . .* , ed. Noël Laveau and André Nouschi (Paris: Loysel, 1992), 89–91.

20. The Trinitarians initially rejected the dey's page as a "foreigner and Lutheran" but were prevailed upon to repatriate the boy from Hamburg regardless of confession. [Comelin, La Motte, and Bernard], *Voyage*, 134. The slaves had origins in, among other places, Paris, Prague, Périgord and Palermo, Dunkirk, Amsterdam, Hamburg, Ostend, and Bruges. Ibid., preface.

21. Procession description, Paris, 14 May 1720, Dangeau, *Journal*, 18: 286;

Jean Buvat, *Journal de la régence (1715–1723)*, ed. Emile Compardon, 2 vols. (Paris: H. Plon, 1865), 2: 88.

22. [Comelin, La Motte, and Bernard], *Voyage*, 151–152, xii–lv.

23. See app. 2.

24. Consul Pierre-Victor Michel had asked the court to intercede, but after more than a year without response a frustrated dey Mustafa pledged to lock up all the French residents of Tunis if his subjects were not returned within two months (1717–1720 correspondence from AE, CT and AN, Marine B7 103, f. 102 and B7 106 f. 25, reprinted in Plantet, *CBT*, 2: 106–107, 108, 114, 116–117, 120–122, 124–125). From Algiers dey Muhammad sent an ambassador to Paris in protest and threatened consul Jean Baume with the same (1717–1718 correspondence from AN, AE BI 120, cited in Touili, *Correspondance*, 175; Plantet, *CDA*, 2: 99–100 n. 3). A letter from the enslaved Algerians (Syracuse, 27 January 1717, reprinted in M. Le Roy, *Etat général et particulier du royaume et de la ville d'Alger, de son gouvernement, de ses forces de terre et de mer* [The Hague: Antoine Van Dole, 1750], 204) held the dey responsible for the "sins that may be committed" against Muslim women and children in chains.

25. Text of the 1720 treaty reproduced in Plantet, *CBT*, 2: 124–128. See also Alphonse Rousseau, *Annales tunisiennes, ou Aperçu historique sur la régence de Tunis* (hereafter *ATN*) (Algiers: Bastide, 1864), 104–105; Charles-Roux, *FA*, 209; Abel Boutin, *Anciennes relations commerciales et diplomatiques de la France avec la Barbarie (1516–1830)* (Paris: Pedone, 1902), 532.

26. Angry that Dusault had spent funds left over from Algiers on foreigners in Tunis, the Mercedarians of Guyenne, Languedoc, and Provence demanded (and were denied) reimbursal from his brother and heir (20 August 1722, AN, AE BIII 317, ff. 237–243).

27. The May 1720 letters patent are reproduced in Victor Forot, "Les Marguilliers des Mathurins en Limousin," *Bulletin de la Société scientifique, historique et archéologique de la Corrèze* 30 (1908): 512–514. See also [Comelin, La Motte, and Bernard], *Voyage*, xvii, liv–lv.

28. Civil unrest and conflict with its neighbors had prevented Tripoli from making war on France until 1715. That year, while a Tripolitan delegation was visiting Versailles, corsairs seized a boat from Marseille and the cycle of violence started up again. Féraud, *AT*, 185–217. See Rouard de Card, *TF*, 255–262, for the 4 July 1720 Franco-Tripolitan treaty.

29. Dusault to conseil de Marine, Tunis, 23 January 1720, AE, CT; conseil de Marine to Dusault, Paris, 24 June 1720, AN, Marine B7 108, f. 122, cited in Plantet, *CBT*, 2: 132 and n. 1.

30. He appointed his brother to distribute the money. Plantet, *CDA*, 2: xliv; *CBT*, 1: 413 n. 1. See also "Placet de M. Dusault, docteur en Sorbonne," Paris, 22 May 1733, AN, AE BI 123, ff. 59–60, cited in Touili, *Correspondance*, 265.

31. La Faye et al., *Relation en forme du journal*, 148, 154–161; Durand to marine minister Jean-Frédéric Phélypeaux, comte de Maurepas, Algiers, 11 July and 24 July 1725, AN, AE BI 121, ff. 185–194, ff. 197–198, cited in Touili, *Correspondance*, 214–215.

32. Gatien Courtilz de Sandras, *Mémoires de madame la marquise de Frêne* (Amsterdam: Jean Malherbe, 1701). Editions of this book also appeared in 1702, 1706, 1714, 1722, 1734, and 1753.

33. Alain-René Lesage, "The Captives," chap. 20 in *Le Diable boiteux* (Paris: La Veuve Barbin, 1707). Quotation from English translation, *The Devil Upon Two Sticks* (Edinburgh: A. Donaldson and J. Reid, 1762), 261–274.

34. Laugier de Tassy held the French consular post to Algiers for five months in 1718. His *Histoire du royaume d'Alger avec l'état présent de son gouvernement, de ses forces de terre et de mer, de ses revenus, police, justice politique et commerce* (Amsterdam: Henri du Sauzet, 1725), was reprinted in 1727, reissued in Paris in 1757 under the more ominous title *Histoire des Etats barbaresques qui exercent la piraterie*, reprinted in 1830, translated into Dutch in 1725 and Spanish in 1733; and misattributed and translated into English in 1750. Citations are from the modern reprint (1992), 169–170.

35. Ockley, *Relation des estâts de Fez et de Maroc, écrite par un Anglois qui y a été longtems esclave*, trans. Eustache Guillemeau (Paris: Pissot, 1726), excerpted in Albert Savine, *Dans les fers du Moghreb: récits de chrétiens esclaves au Maroc (XVIIe et XVIIIe siècles)* (Paris: Société des éditions Louis-Michaud, 1912), 32 n. 1.

36. René Louiche Desfontaines and Jean-André Peyssonnel, *Voyages dans les Régences de Tunis et d'Alger*, ed. Adolphe Dureau de la Malle, 2 vols. (Paris: Gide, 1838). Citations are from the modern reprint of Peyssonnel, *Voyages dans les régences de Tunis et d'Alger*, ed. Valensi (Paris: La Découverte, 1987), 56–57. At roughly the same time, French scientist Charles-Marie de La Condamine, 111–112) and the German doctor J. E. Hebenstreit favorably compared the lives of Christian slaves in North Africa to those of French sailors and fishermen and Muslim rowers, respectively. Condamine, BN, MF no. 2582, suppl., excerpted in Claude-Antoine Rozet et al., *Algérie, Etats Tripolitains, Tunis* (Paris: Firmin Didot, 1850); Hebenstreit, "Voyage à Alger, Tunis et Tripoli entrepris aux frais et par ordre de Frédéric-Auguste, roi de Pologne, etc., en 1732," *Nouvelles annales de voyages et des sciences géographiques* 46 (1830): 23–24.

37. On the number of Christian slaves, see app. 1. On the number of sub-Saharan African slaves in French colonies in the 1720s, see Frédéric Régent, *La France et ses esclaves: de la colonisation aux abolitions (1620–1848)* (Paris: Bernard Grasset, 2007), 335–337.

38. According to the editor, this passage was added pre-1712. Jean Barbot, *Barbot on Guinea: The Writings of Jean Barbot, West Africa, 1678–1712*, 2 vols., ed. Paul Edward Hedley Hair, Adam Jones, and Robin Law (London: Hakluyt Society, 1992), 2: 782.

39. Voltaire [François-Marie Arouet], *Candide, ou l'Optimisme . . .* (London: n.p., 1759), chaps. 11, 12, and 19; "Alger" and "Esclaves" in *Dictionnaire philosophique* (5th ed., 1765), in *Oeuvres de Voltaire*, ed. Adrien-Jean-Quentin Beuchot, 72 vols. (Paris: Lefèvre, 1829–1840), 26: 176–179; 29: 197–208.

40. Simon Nicolas Henri Linguet, *Théorie des loix civiles . . .* , 2 vols. (London [Paris?]: n.p., 1767), 2: 352–353.

41. Jean-Jacques Rousseau, *Une Grève d'esclaves à Alger au XVIIIe siècle*

avec Emile et Sophie ou les Solitaires de Jean-Jacques Rousseau, ed. Michel Launay (Paris: Jean-Paul Rocher, 1998), 80. For further discussion of the work (many thanks to J. B. Shank for alerting me to it), composed during the 1760s and 1770s, see ibid., 94–102; and Nadine Bérenguier, "L'Infortune des alliances: contrat, mariage et fiction au dix-huitième siècle," *Studies on Voltaire and the Eighteenth Century* 329 (1995): 395. A French artillery officer of Hungarian descent, Baron François de Tott, who visited Tunis during roughly the same period, made a similar argument in *Mémoires du baron de Tott, sur les Turcs et les Tartares,* 4 vols. (Amsterdam: n.p., 1784–1785), 4: 132–133.

42. Henri Bernardin de Saint Pierre, *Empsaël et Zoraïde, ou les blancs esclaves des noirs au Maroc,* ed. Roger Little (Exeter, UK: University of Exeter Press, 1995). According to the introduction, the play was likely begun in 1771 but not completed until 1792–1793.

43. [Diderot] in Guillaume-Thomas Raynal, *Histoire philosophique et politique des établissements et du commerce des Européens dans les deux Indes,* 4th ed., 10 vols. (Geneva: Jean-Leonard Pellet, 1780), book 11, chap. 22, quoted and translated by Sankar Muthu, *Enlightenment against Empire* (Princeton, NJ: Princeton University Press, 2003), 109. "It should not fall . . . to Negro killers, to exclaim against the misfortunes of Christian captives," wrote Pierre Joseph André Roubaud, *Histoire générale de l'Asie, de l'Afrique, de l'Amérique . . . ,* 15 vols. (Paris: Des Ventes de la Doué, 1770–1775), 11: 364. On Roubaud's influence on Diderot's stance toward slavery, see Ann Thomson, "Diderot, Roubaud et l'esclavage," *Recherches sur Diderot et sur l'Encyclopédie* 35 (2003): 69–93.

44. For an analogous tactic in the United States, see Lofti Ben Rejeb, "America's Captive Freemen in North Africa: The Comparative Method in Abolitionist Persuasion," *Slavery and Abolition* 9 (1988): 57–71.

45. See, for instance, Protestant refugee Jacques Bernard, editor of *Nouvelles de la République des Lettres* ([1704], pt. 2, 662), cited in Jameson, *Montesquieu et l'esclavage,* 186–187.

46. For a discussion of this phenomenon as pertains to Malta, see Wettinger, *Slavery in the Islands of Malta,* 53–62. For earlier and later eighteenth-century manifestations in Algiers, see AN, AE BI 119, BI 120, and BI 123, cited in Touili, *Correspondance,* 122–200; in Tripoli, see Féraud, *AT,* 189–190.

47. Féraud, *AT,* 218–220; Albert Vandal, *Une Ambassade française en Orient sous Louis XV: la mission du marquis de Villeneuve, 1728–1741,* 2nd ed. (Paris: E. Plon, Nourrit, 1887), 93.

48. The Franco-Tunisian treaty, signed 1 July 1728, followed reports of Tunisian corsairs cruising near French shores and the arrival of Tunisian ambassadors (held as hostages in Chalon-sur-Saône) to preempt a French declaration of war. The terms required a formal apology to Louis XV; the payment of a large indemnity; and the release of any French slaves taken under foreign flag, any foreigners taken under French flag, and twelve additional Catholic slaves, selected by the French consul and an officer of the divan. It also held that in the future, any Tunisian corsair caught near the coast of France might be sold for the king's profit. Rousseau, *ATN,* 108–110; Plantet, *CBT,* 2: 220–221; Micacchi, "I Rapporti," 163–164.

49. AN, AE B1 1092, ff. 403–428; Féraud, *AT*, 221–225; Seton Dearden, *A Nest of Corsairs: The Fighting Karamanlis of the Barbary Coast* (London: John Murray, 1976), 47–52; Micacchi, "I Rapporti," 164–182; Vandal, *Une Ambassade française*, 94–105.

50. Jean-Antoine Roux to his parents in Saint-Tropez, Tripoli, 30 July 1728, AN, AE BIII 317, f. 271; copy of letter from enslaved captain Ignace Guirard, Tripoli, 6 and 7 November 1728, AN, AE BIII 46, f. 89.

51. Seven enslaved Provençal captains to the marine minister, Tripoli, 6 November 1728, AN, AE BI 1092, ff. 440–441.

52. Same to CCM, Tripoli, 4 December 1728, ACCM, G44.

53. Same to CCM, Tripoli, 22 February 1729, ACCM, G44. Thirteen French slaves from Tripoli were sent to Tunis and then sold in Algiers, where the dey presented them to Durand as a token of friendship. Dey Abdi to Louis XV, Algiers, 25 June 1729; Maurepas to dey Abdi, Versailles, 24 August 1729, cited in Plantet, *CDA*, 2: 137, 142.

54. Cited in Pélissier de Reynaud, "La Régence de Tripoli," 19. For the full text of the 9 June 1729 treaty, see Rouard de Card, *TF*, 263–272.

55. See counter commemorating peace with the Tripoli pirates in the collection of the National Maritime Museum, London, images E2890-1 and E2890-2.

56. Féraud, *AT*, 226–227; Dearden, *A Nest of Corsairs*, 53–55; Micacchi, "I Rapporti," 274–276; Rouard de Card, *TF*, 263–272.

57. Six enslaved Provençal captains to CCM, Tripoli, 29 April 1729, ACCM, G44; list of Christian slaves released to M. de Bandeville, Toulon, 5 April 1729, AN, Marine B3 332, f. 237; Mercedarian Bernard Alexis Forton to marine minister, Cahors, 16 March 1729; Bureau de la Rédemption to marine minister, Marseille, 17 June 1729, AN, AE BIII 318, ff. 4, 125; consul J. de Raimondis, seigneur d'Allons, Tripoli, 11 August 1729, AN, AE BI 1093; Louis XV to dey Abdi of Algiers, Versailles, 24 August 1729, CADN, vol. 2, f. 68.

58. Raimondis to marine minister, Tripoli, 22 August 1729, AN, AE BI 1093.

59. The "Déclaration du Roy portant qu'il ne sera laissé aucun mousse dans les échelles du Levant et Barbarie" given at Versailles on 12 October 1730 (ADBR, B3404, f. 908), registered in Algiers on 26 February 1731, reprinted in Devoulx, *Les Archives du Consulat général de France à Alger . . .* (Algiers: Bastide, 1865), 32–33.

60. Anonymous memorandum, Marseille, 25 February 1729, AN, AE B1 1093, cited in Mathiex, "Sur la marine marchande barbaresque au XVIIIe siècle," *AESC* 13 (1958): 89.

61. Deposition by Gerosme Cavalery of Antibes before the Toulon Admiralty, 1 September 1727, CADN, CA, vol. 2, ff. 2–3; Durand to conseil de Marine, Algiers, 21 February 1721, AN, AE BI 121, ff. 1–2, cited in Touili, *Correspondance*, 201.

62. Forton to Barthélémy Fau, 31 July 1728, ADG, H162 (4), cited in Cocard, "Les Pères de la Merci dans le royaume de France depuis le Concile de Trente jusqu'à la fin de l'Ancien régime" (hereafter "PM"), 2 vols. (Thèse troisième cycle, Université d'Angers, 1982), 2: 327.

63. *Ordre de la Procession et de la Marche des quarante-six Captifs rachetez*

. . . (Paris: Louis Sevestre, 1729); Regnard in Versailles to Mellier in Nantes, 17 July 1729, AMN, II 44, f. 146; Daranatz, "Captifs basques," 317–319; Cocard, *Les Pères de la Merci*, 221, citing ADH, 50H94.

64. *Ordre de la Procession des captifs, rachetés* . . . (Paris: Veuve Delormel, 1730). See also app. 2.

65. "Mémoire pour servir d'instruction au Chevalier de Caylus, capitaine de vaisseau," Marly, 9 April 1731, AN, Marine B2 288, f. 229, cited in Plantet, *CBT*, 2: 260–261; Rousseau, *ATN*, 111.

66. On René Duguay-Trouin's mission, see Berbrugger, ed., "Un Voyage de Paris à Alger en 1731 par le Sieur Tollot," *RA* 11 (1867): 417–434; Henri Begouën, "La Condamine: Tunis, Le Bardo, Catharge (extraits inédits du 'Journal de mon voyage au Levant' [21 mai–6 octobre 1731])," *Revue tunisienne* 5 (1898): 71–94; dey Abdi to Maurepas, Algiers, 21 June 1731, reprinted in Plantet, *CDA*, 2: 150 n. 2, 152–154; Louis-Paul Blanc, "Les Sétois face à face avec les corsaires et les pirates," *Bulletin de la Société d'études scientifiques de Sète et sa région* 3 (1971): 165–168; and CADN, CA, vol. 2, ff. 127–138.

67. Captain and crew of *La Marguerade* of Vannes, which left for Africa en route to Jamaica on 21 October 1749. Jean Mettas, *Répertoire des expéditions négrières françaises au XVIIIe siècle: ports autres que Nantes*, 2 vols., ed. Serge Daget and Michèle Daget (Paris: Société française d'histoire d'outre-mer, 1978–1984), 2: 785.

68. See app. 2.

69. Copy of letter from André Stanya [Stagno] and his crew to Maurepas, accompanying note to consul Benoît Le Maire, Algiers, 10 June 1733, CADN, CA, vol. 2, ff. 189–191; consul Alexis-Jean Eustache Taibout de Marigny, Algiers, 6 January 1736, AN, AE BI 124, ff. 5–6, cited in Touili, *Correspondance*, 286.

70. Jean-Victor-Laurent, baron d'Arreger's narrative of his five years' captivity, composed in Madrid in 1741, was reprinted as "Un Captif à Alger au XVIIIe siècle," ed. by L. Pingaud, *Revue historique* 13 (1880): 325–339. Apparently, an emissary of an Algerian mufti was sent to Toulon in an attempt to negotiate Arreger's liberation. Copy of a letter from the marquis de Villeneuve to Lemaire, 18 March 1734, AN, AE BI 123, f. 190; Taibout to Maurepas, 31 January 1738, AN, AE BI 124, ff. 165–167, cited in Touili, *Correspondance*, 275, 301.

71. On this and other crises, see AN, AE BI 122–124, cited in Touili, *Correspondance*, 254, 271, 276, 284–285, 318–320; Grammont, *HA*, 241–242.

72. Jacques Boyer de Saint-Gervais, *Mémoires historiques qui concernent le gouvernement de Tunis* . . . (Paris: Ganeau fils, 1736), 85–86, 280–281.

73. Consul Jean-Louis Gautier to Maurepas, Tunis, 1 April 1737; to Maurepas, Tunis, 25 January 1738, 26 May 1739, AE, *CT*. On hand kissing, see "Délibération de la nation française à Tunis," 9 March 1740, Archives de la résidence française à Tunis, Registre des délibérations, vol. 16, p. 91, cited in Plantet, *CBT*, 2: 303, 309, 313, 315–316; see also Rousseau, *ATN*, 122–123.

74. Plantet, *CBT*, 2: 322–323.

75. *Lettre d'un comédien, à un de ses amis, touchant sa captivité et celle de vingt-six de ses camarades, chez les corsaires de Tunis* . . . (Paris: Pierre Clément, 1741), which reads as pure fiction, is given some credence by studies of the

Hus family, whose name does appear in the text. The multigenerational troupe, which performed all over France in the 1730s, apparently disappeared from the stage for two years after 1741. See Jean-Philippe Van Aelbrouck, "Comment faire de l'ordre dans une dynastie de comédiens? Le cas de la famille Hus éclairé par des documents d'archives," in *Proceedings of the Second International CESAR Conference (June 2006)*, http://www.cesar.org.uk/cesar2/conferences/cesar_conference_2006/VAelbrouck_paper06.html.

76. Some of the inhabitants managed to flee to La Calle and the Sardinian island of Saint Pierre (Rousseau, *ATN*, 127). After 100 of these slaves were exchanged in 1751, 540 remained. Five years later they were transferred to Algiers, from where 300 were ransomed in 1768 (Bono, *I Corsari barbareschi*, 315).

77. In his "Mémoire sur la prise de l'isle de Tabarque," Tunis, 22 June 1741, Cap Nègre dragoman Alexandre Napoly specified that the bey "had all women, girls, and young children locked up in his harem and the boys in the slave *bagne* where they were made to work." See also vice-consul Louis Crozet to Maurepas, Tunis, 30 September 1741, AE, *CT*, reprinted in Plantet, *CBT*, 2: 324–328, 331–332. By contrast, the historical reflections of a military inspector named Poiron maintained that the French residents of Cap Nègre arrived in Tunis as prisoners, not slaves, and were not housed in the bagnes. Reprinted by Jean Serres, ed., *Mémoires concernans l'état présent du Royaume de Tunis par M. Poiron* (Paris: Ernest Leroux, 1925), cited by Rousseau, *ATN*, 128 n. 1.

78. Crozet to Maurepas, Tunis, 20 July 1742. See also Grammont, *HA*, 243–244. Poiron counted 100 dead, 60 wounded, and 150 enslaved; cited in Rousseau, *ATN*, 137.

79. Rousseau, *ATN*, 141–143.

80. The treaty and secret convention, signed on 9 November 1742 by the Marseille squire and royal commissary François Fort, are reprinted in Plantet, *CBT*, 2: 362–366.

81. Christian Windler makes this point in *La Diplomatie comme expérience de l'autre: consuls français au Maghreb (1700–1840)* (Geneva: Droz, 2002), 446.

82. Some French deserters from Ceuta also landed in Moroccan slavery. See La Faye et al., *Relation en forme du journal*, 67–68.

83. "Advertimientos del . . . Fr. Ysidro de Valcaçar sobre cosas de Berbería . . . 1608," Real Academia de Historia (Madrid), MS 9-6436, cited in Friedman, *Spanish Captives*, 46; James Leander Cathcart, *The Captives, Eleven Years a Prisoner in Algiers*, ed. J. B. Newark (La Porte, IN: Herald Print, 1899), excerpted in Baepler, *White Slaves, African Masters*, 125–126.

84. Between 1742 and 1750, Oran and Ceuta lost over seven hundred men to North African captivity. Archivo General de Simancas, Guerra Moderna, leg. 1531, expediente de 1744; leg. 1532, expediente de 1750, cited in Friedman, *Spanish Captives*, 46–47; and Pike, *Penal Servitude*, 122, table 7.4. Pike notes (123–125) that rates reached their peak in the late 1760s and early 1770s before starting to decline in the last two decades of the century, in part thanks to new laws and tactics.

85. Louis XV, like Louis XIV, commonly commuted the death sentences of young deserters, sending them to the Caribbean instead. André Corvisier,

L'Armée française de la fin du XVIIe siècle au ministère de Choiseul, 2 vols. (Paris: Presses universitaires de France, 1964), 2: 720. See, for example, marine minister César Gabriel de Choiseul-Chevigny, duc de Praslin, to CCM, Versailles, 14 September 1767, ACCM, G41.

86. Consul Pierre Thomas to Maurepas, Algiers, 10 March 1749; memorandum from Lazarist Arnould Bossu, Algiers, 29 October 1749 (forwarded 31 October 1749 with another letter from Thomas to Maurepas), AN, AE BI 126, ff. 211–212, 288–294, cited in Touili, *Correspondance*, 365, 371–372.

87. The Trinitarians and Mercedarians arrived in Algiers in mid-September 1750 and in October left for Marseille with 172 men, the totality of the French slaves. In various publications, the Trinitarians took credit for 105–106 captives and the Mercedarians for 66, listing the names of foreigners separately from the rest. See app. 2.

88. Marine minister Antoine-Louis, comte de Jouy Rouillé, 2 November 1750, Archives de la Marine de Marseille, 1750, lettre 90, reprinted in Deslandres, *OT*, 2: 415; Mercedarian general Gobain to Rouillé, Paris, 6 and 18 December 1751; Trinitarian general Febvre to Rouillé, Paris, 22 January 1751, AN, AE BIII 318, pp. 169, 170, 173.

89. Michel Foucault, *Madness and Civilization: A History of Insanity in an Age of Reason*, trans. Richard Howard (London: Routledge, 2001), chap. 2; Jones, *Charity and Bienfaisance: The Treatment of the Poor in the Montpellier Region, 1740–1815* (Cambridge: Cambridge University Press, 1982), 139–154; Deslandres, *OT*, 1: 370. The promulgation of the "Ordonnance du Roy portant ce qui devra être observé par rapport aux Maronites & autres Chrêtiens Orientaux & aux Esclaves rachetés qui se trouvèrent dans le Royaume," Versailles, 8 January 1753 (registered in Marseille, 6 February 1753), ACCM, G39, seems to have directly followed the expulsion of an impostor Arabian prince named Mustafa. See correspondence from November and December 1762 between Praslin, the intendant of Provence, and the municipal consuls of Marseille at ADBR, C2502.

90. Consul André-Alexandre Lemaire to Rouillé, Algiers, 29 November and 27 December 1751, AN, AE BI 13, ff. 248–249, 260–261, cited in Touili, *Correspondance*, 397, 399. Though the French deserters seem to have been repatriated after their redemption, the Spanish ones stood trial—and three were hanged as "mute preachers against this scandal." Between 1753 and 1755, only 37 men deserted from Oran and Ceuta. Archivo General de Simancas, Guerra Moderna, leg. 1533, expediente de 1755, cited in Friedman, *Spanish Captives*, 47.

91. The plague, which was killing fifty people per day in July 1752, killed seventeen hundred in the single month of May 1753, spreading from Moors to Jews, Turks, and Christian slaves. Besides famously flattening Lisbon, the November 1755 earthquake destroyed most of the buildings in Algiers. Lemaire to Rouillé, Algiers, 2 May and 21 July 1752; 12 April, 25 May, and 11 July 1753, AN, AE BI 14, ff. 42–45, 51–54, 119–122, 130–135, cited in Touili, *Correspondance*, 402, 403, 407, 409.

92. I have found no archival evidence to confirm the 1753 slave revolt reported in the *Gazette de France* ([20 October 1753]: 496) and cited as fact by Grammont (*HA*, 247) among others.

93. In fall 1756, the Algerian army returned from Tunis with 944 Christian slaves, including 306 women and children. Journal of Jean-Antoine Vallière, Algiers, 29 November 1756, reprinted in Lucien Chaillou, *Textes pour servir à l'histoire de l'Algérie au XVIIIe siècle suivis de la guerre de quinze heures* (Toulon: author, 1979), 141; Teissier, *Inventaire*, 52. Also, see app. 1.

94. "Assemblée de la Nation" minutes from 12 April 1760 describe the controversy over Pierre de la Philippe of Saint-Jean-de-Luz, to whom the dey accused consul Joseph-Barthélemy Pérou of delivering a false passport. Lazarist *vicaire apostolique* Théodore de Groiselle was left in charge; he distributed alms to the regency's Christian slaves with funds from the Compagnie royale d'Afrique. Devoulx, *Les Archives*, 86–94.

95. This rumor is suspiciously similar to one reported by Vallière in his journal on 3 November 1756 spread by two slaves ransomed from Naples (Chaillou, *Textes pour servir*, 141). An internal investigation found that there had never been a mosque in Toulon, that the cemetery where Muslims prayed was intact, and that the *qadi* had been chained for stealing. Still, two years later, the chapels of Algiers remained shuttered in retaliation. Dey 'Ali to marine minister Nicolas-René Berryer, Algiers, 12 December 1760; Berryer to Groiselle, and to dey 'Ali, Versailles, 30 March 1761, reprinted in Plantet, *CDA*, 2: 258–259, 260. Intendant Charles-Martin d'Hurson to CCM, Toulon, 19 February, 5 and 12 March 1761, ACCM, G6. See also Régis Bernard, "Les Cimetières des 'esclaves turcs' des arsenaux de Marseille et de Toulon au XVIIIe siècle," *Revue des mondes musulmans et de la Méditerranée* 99–100 (2002): 205–217.

96. On the amnesties of 1757 and 1761, see Pritchard, *Louis XV's Navy, 1748–1762: A Study of Organization and Administration* (Kingston, ON: McGill–Queen's University Press, 1987), 75–87. Groiselle to Berryer, Algiers, 28 January, and Berryer to Groiselle, Versailles, 30 March 1761; Groiselle to secretary of state Etienne-François de Choiseul, duc de Stainville, Algiers, 30 September 1762, AN, AE BI 130, ff. 174–175, 187–190, 342–343, cited in Touili, *Correspondance*, 478, 481, 501.

97. News of the slave revolt in Algiers, published in the *Gazette de France* ([8 March 1763]: 98), was picked up by English-language broadsides like the *Annual Register* (6 [1763]: 60, cited in Charles Sumner, "White Slavery in the Barbary States" [1853], in *The Works of Charles Sumner*, 15 vols. [Boston: Lee and Shepard, 1870–1883], 1: 421); and the *Gentleman's Magazine* (33 [March 1763]: 142, cited in John W. Blassingame, "Some Precursors of the *Amistad* Revolt," *Connecticut Scholar: Occasional Papers of the Connecticut Humanities Council* 10 [1992]: 26–36).

98. Marine secretary César-Gabriel, compte de Choiseul-Chevigny, duc de Praslin, to dey 'Ali, Versailles, 30 April and 7 May; Fontainebleau, 17 October and 16 December; dey 'Ali to Praslin, Algiers, 14 November 1763, 17 January and 4 June 1764; fleet commander Louis de Fabry to dey 'Ali, on board the commanding vessel, 8 January 1764 in Plantet, *CDA*, 2: 271–293. See also Devoulx, *Les Archives*, 112. For the text of the 16 January 1764 Franco-Algerian accord signed by Fabry, see Rouard de Card, *TF*, 79–80. On the Oraners ransomed from Algiers, see Touili, *Correspondance*, 522. For a census of the twenty "Es-

claves Turcs natifs d'Alger" dispatched from Toulon on 24 May 1764, see AN, Marine B3 564, f. 82.

99. Consul Etienne-Lazare-Barthélemy de Saizieu to Praslin, Tunis, 8 October 1763, reprinted in Plantet, *CBT*, 2: 598.

100. Serres, *Mémoires*, 17.

101. Julien, *History of North Africa*, 330–331. For examples of Frenchmen liberated by bey 'Ali and a Tunisian captain publicly chastised, see consul Jean-Baptiste-Joseph-Michel de Grou de Salauze to Praslin, Tunis, 15 December 1762, 14 February 1763; and Saizieu to same, Tunis, 22 July 1763, 13 October 1764. The bey's refusal to punish the perpetrators of a recent descent near Antibes, however, prompted a visit from the fleet of Joseph de Bauffremont, prince de Listenois. Praslin to Saizieu, Versailles, 24 June 1765; Saizieu to Praslin, Tunis, 14 January 1766; Journal of Listenois, Tunis, 7 July 1766, reprinted in Plantet, *CBT*, 2: 588, 590, 595, 614–615, 625, 630–631, 634–637.

102. Saizieu to Praslin, Tunis, 1 and 30 July 1763, AAE, *CT*, and the 21 May 1765 convention providing that "Moroccan corsairs who drop anchor in the ports of the kingdom of Tunis will be required to leave after twenty-four hours, and that at no time and under no pretext will they sell vessels [or] merchandise of other effects seized from the French," AAE, Salle des traités, all reproduced in Plantet, *CBT*, 2: 594, 596, 623.

103. On France's protection of individual foreigners, see, for example, the case of Corsican Jean-Baptiste Biasini: copy of a letter from Biasini to minister, Algiers, 1758, CADN, CA, vol. 4, f. 100; Pérou to Berryer, Algiers, 24 February 1759; Groiselle to Berryer, Algiers, 28 January 1761; apostolic vicar Charles Ludovic La Pie de Sévigny to captain Fabry, Algiers, 19 January 1764, AN, AE BI 130, ff. 25–26 bis, ff. 174–175, BI 131, ff. 197–198, cited in Touili, *Correspondance*, 462, 479, 518.

104. In 1766 an edict ordered the Trinitarians to close small convents, and a commission debated whether to merge with their competitors; in 1768, their three branches regrouped. In 1769 Mercedarian convents started to shut down too. Ledermann, "Les Frères de N.D. de la Merci," 44–47; Deslandres, *OT*, 1: 20–21, 293–294; Cocard, "PM," 2: 413–414.

105. See app. 2. See also [Praslin to Saizieu], Versailles, 9 January 1769, Archives de la Résidence française à Tunis, Registre des délibérations de la nation, n. II, XXIV, p. 26, reprinted in Plantet, *CBT*, 2: 662–663.

106. Saizieu to Praslin, Tunis, 28 February; commander Jean-Joseph de Rafélis de Broves to Praslin, Tunis, 22 August 1769; bey 'Ali to Saizieu, Tunis, 12 February 1770, reprinted in Plantet, *CBT*, 2: 666, 669, 675.

107. François-René de Forbin, chevalier d'Oppède, traveled to Tunis in May 1770 with one frigate and two xebecs and instructions to avoid the bloody retributions of previous eras by evacuating the consul (Saizieu) and his family. He was joined a week later by nineteen warships. The French fleet besieged the port and then, following the usual pattern, sent an envoy on shore with the king's demands. See correspondence among Louis XV, Oppède, Broves, Saizieu, Lions, Praslin, Tunisian negotiator Mustafa Khodja, bey 'Ali, and the divan of Tunis, reprinted in Plantet, *CBT*, 2: 677–714.

108. Article 2, Le Bardo, 25 August 1770, reprinted in Plantet, *CBT*, 2: 715.

109. Ibrahim Effendi and an entourage of thirteen arrived in Toulon in November and, accompanied by Saizieu, traveled via Lyon to Paris and Versailles. See 1770 correspondence among Saizieu, Praslin, and Abbé Joseph-Marie Terray, reprinted in Plantet, *CBT*, 2: 730–733.

110. Capuchin father Santi de Lizzano to Louis XV, Tunis, 22 October 1770; Broves to Praslin, Toulon, 8 November 1770, reprinted in Plantet, *CBT*, 2: xxxix, 725, 730.

111. Treaty renewal, Le Bardo, 3 June 1774, reprinted in Plantet, *CBT*, 3: 32–33.

112. See app. 1.

113. See introduction and correspondence among Sartine, Saizieu, Louis XVI, and bey 'Ali, reprinted in Plantet, *CBT*, 3: vi–vii, 52–55, 56 n. 1, 63, 68, 72. See also "Journal historique de l'ambassade de Suleiman Aga," January 1777, AN, AE BIII 13, ff. 5–6. On the symbolics of Franco–North African gift exchange, see Windler, "Diplomatie et interculturalité: les consuls français à Tunis, 1700–1840," *Revue d'histoire moderne et contemporaine* 50, 4 (2003): 79–84.

114. In fact, the number of free Corsicans in Tunis—twenty-four men, twenty women, and fifteen children—outnumbered the number of metropolitan members of the French *nation*. Saizieu to Sartine, Tunis, 16 March 1778, AN, AE BI 1149, cited in Windler, "Representing a State in a Segmentary Society: French Consuls in Tunis from the Ancien Régime to the Restoration," *Journal of Modern History* 73 (2001): 253; and in Windler, *La Diplomatie*, 190.

115. On Mercedarian and Trinitarian involvement in the redemption of seventy-four to seventy-eight Corsicans (including six women and thirteen children) from Tunis and Algiers, paid for with a hundred thousand livres grant from the king (Sartine to CCM, 17 May 1779, ACCM, AA100 [OC], cited in Teissier, *Inventaire*, 66), see app. 2; Vincent de Caraffa, ed., "Journal du rachat des captifs d'Alger et de Tunis en 1779," *Bulletin de la Société des sciences historiques et naturelles de la Corse* 62–63 (1886): 165–218; and Santoni, "Le Rachat des Corses esclaves à Tunis en 1779," presented at the Congrès national des sociétés historiques et scientifiques: relations, échanges et coopération en Méditerranée, Bastia, Corsica, 2003, http://halshs.archives-ouvertes.fr/view_by_stamp .php?&halsid=7deb1tv1anctoh766j8vjuq9e4&label=SHS&langue=fr&action _todo=view&id=halshs-00162606&version=1.

116. In 1776 French consul Robert-Louis Langoisseur de La Vallée had appealed to the king's royal "benevolence and humanity" to free the captive Corsicans as an act "of justice toward unfortunates who have become his children by the happy reunion of their country and his crown" (report on captive redemption, Algiers, 1 December 1776, AAE, ADP, box 8, vol. 200, no. 4). Their ransom was paid with the aid of Jewish intermediaries and loans (19 January and 8 March 1779, CADN, CA, vol. 7, ff. 157–158; vol. 8, ff. 25–26). In recognition, a group of them offered to arm a galliot against the English. Chancellor Renaudot to Sartine, Marseille, 23 July 1779, AN, AE BI 138, ff. 233–236, cited in Touili, *Correspondance*, 682.

117. See the 1778–1779 correspondence among "Omar du bey de Tunis," Mustafa-Khodja, Sartine, Saizieu, and vice-consul Jacques-Philippe Devoise reprinted in Plantet, *CBT*, 3: 77–79, 102–114. See also Caraffa, "Journal du rachat," 173.

118. Caraffa, "Journal du rachat," 179–191. The nine deserters hailed from Lorraine, Montpellier, Meaux, Lambesc, and Bordeaux. Antoine Hiltebrand, enslaved at the end of 1772, had been recommended for redemption in July 1775. AN, AE BIII 319, f. 94.

119. Trinitarians Gache and Dorvau and Mercedarians de Villa and Chevillard to the CCM, Bastia, 14 September 1779, AN, AE BIII 320, f. 64. See also Caraffa, "Journal du rachat," 192–201.

120. Durocher to Castries, Tunis, 9 September 1781, AN, AE BI 1150, cited in Windler, "Representing a State," 254. Capuchin registers from 1782 list ten "French Corsican families," Archivo Storico della Congregazione "De Propaganda Fide," Rome, *Scritture riferite nei Congressi-Barbaria*, vol. 8, f. 268 r, cited in Windler, *La Diplomatie*, 190.

121. For example, Sartine to La Vallée, Versailles, 12 December 1774, CADN, CA, vol. 4, ff. 106–107; Boynes and then Sartine to CCM, Marly, 20 June 1771, and Versailles, 24 December 1774, ACCM, G51. See also, correspondence among the marine ministry, the intendant of Provence, the Marseille city council, and the consul to Algiers dated 1776, 1779, 1782, and 1785 in the "Police des Levantines" file at ADBR, C2502. And for 1778–1779: AN, AE BIII 14, ff. 190–191; BIII 15, f. 218, cited in Hélène Desmet-Grégoire, *Le "Divan" magique: l'Orient turc en France au XVIIIe siècle* (Paris: L'Harmattan, 1994), 26. Another important site of tension in the years 1774 and 1775 had to do with access to the Muslim cemetery of Marseille. See ACCM, 6; CADN, CA, vol. 6, ff. 11–14; Marcel Emerit, "L'Essai d'une marine marchande barbaresque au XVIIIe siècle," *CT* 11 (1955): 368; and Bernard, "Les Cimetières," 205–217.

122. Whereas counts of French Oraners at the beginning of the decade hovered around 150, after 1775 estimates came in around 400 and never much less than 300 (app. 1).

123. Slave Jean-Eléanore Dumont to Sartine, Algiers, February 1780, AN, AE BIII 320, f. 69.

124. Consul Jean-Antoine Vallière to Praslin, Algiers, 4 October 1769, AN, Marine B1 133, ff. 298–299; slave Jean-Baptiste La Croix to Sartine, Algiers, 11 July 1778, 4 May 1779, AN, AE BIII 320, ff. 11, 34.

125. Slave Alexandre Mercier to Castries, Algiers, 25 August 1785, AN, AE BIII 321, f. 71; Mercier with slave Jean Filion to Castries, Algiers, 12 June 1776, AN, AE BIII 319, f. 162.

126. Slave Rémi Conor to Castries, Algiers, 27 October 1784, AN, AE BIII 321, f. 96.

127. Report on captive redemption, La Vallée, Algiers, 1 December 1776, AAE, ADP, box 8, vol. 200, no. 4.

128. Slave Jean Mauri to Sartine, Algiers, [1778], AN, AE BIII 320, f. 14 (inside).

129. Slave L. Reinet Dalard to Castries, Algiers, May 28, 1781, AN, AE BIII

320, f. 76; sieur Romain to the prince de Montbary, Mascara [1782], AN, AE BIII 321, f. 6; Mercedarian general Chevillard to Castries, Auxerre, 15 September 1784, AN, AE BIII 321, f. 74; consul Jean-Baptiste-Michel de Kercy to Castries, Algiers, 29 April 1784, AN, AE BI 141, ff. 50–56, cited in Touili, *Correspondance*, 728.

130. Notes from M. D. Sr. D, January 1775, AN, AE BIII 32, f. 3; Sartine to intendant of Provence Charles-Baptiste des Galois de la Tour, Versailles, 18 August 1777, ADBR, C4288.

131. La Vallée to Boynes, Algiers, 20 March 1772, AN, AE BI 135, ff. 43–70; to Sartine, 4 September 1776, AN, AE BI 137, ff. 95–97, cited in Touili, *Correspondance*, 606–607; La Vallée, "Dissertation sur les esclaves chrétiens et sur les moyens d'opérer leur rachat," Algiers, 16 August 1772, reprinted in Chaillou, *Textes pour servir*, 45–47; report on captive redemption, La Vallée, Algiers, 1 December 1776, AAE, ADP, box 8, vol. 200, no. 4.

132. La Vallée to Boynes, Algiers, 30 June; "Bulletin," 30 December 1774, AN, AE BI 136, ff. 108–111, 151, cited in Touili, *Correspondance*, 634, 637; *Gazette de France* (13 February 1775): 57.

133. La Vallée to CCM, ACCM, AA487 (OC), cited in Grammont, *HA*, 331–333.

134. La Vallée to Castries, Algiers, 20 November 1781 (P.S. 15 January 1782), AN, AE BI 139, ff. 220–228, cited in Touili, *Correspondance*, 701. Writing to Algiers after an audience with the severely scarred apostolic vicar Claude Cosson, Castries ordered that his French savior—Jean Péricard, otherwise known as "La Fleur"—be ransomed and that the two Neapolitans receive cash rewards. Castries to La Vallée, 16 June 1782, CADN, CA, vol. 10, ff. 81–82. See also Jean Casenave, "Un Consul français à Alger au XVIIIe siècle: Langoisseur de la Vallée," *RA* 78 (1936): 114–120.

135. Castries to La Vallée, 16 June 1782, CADN, CA, vol. 10, ff. 81–82.

136. As early as 1744, the Trinitarian general had acknowledged "rogues who run around the provinces, even disguised as members of our order" (cited in Forot, "Les Marguilliers," 524), and in early 1759, a printed pamphlet had warned "the Public . . . that only members of the two orders will be taking collection during the processions" (*Liste des LXX captives françois rachetés* . . . [Paris: Veuve Delormel et Fils, 1759]). In 1774 and again in 1777 the king ordered his intendant in Provence "to take the necessary measures to eliminate false collectors who surprise the charity of his subjects and deprive the redemptive orders of the aid he intends to accord them." Sartine to La Tour, Versailles, 24 February 1777, ADBR 4288.

137. Anonymous reports, 1783 [first undated, second received 29 May 1783], AAE, ADP, box 8, vol. 200, nos. 6 and 7.

138. See app. 1.

139. For the various sums, see *Lettres-Patentes du Roi qui confirment que l'Oeuvre de la Rédemption établie à Marseille pour le rachat des Captifs . . .* (Aix-en-Provence: A. David, 1784); Castries to CCM, Versailles, 26 April and 12 December 1784, 20 March, 23 April, 1 May, 22 May, and 19 June 1785, ACCM G42.

140. Chevalier de Ligondé to CCM, aboard *La Minerve*, 9 July 1785, ACCM, G42.

141. Commissaries of the redemption to CCM, "Infirmeries de Marseille," 2 August 1785, ACCM, G42; Charles-Auguste-Joseph Lambert, *Histoire de la ville de Mussy-l'Evêque* (Chaumont: C. Cavaniol, 1878), 153.

142. La Tour to Laurens, 8 August 1785, ADBR, 4288.

143. Trinitarian and Mercedarian commissaries to La Tour, Lazaret of Marseille, 2 August 1785, ADBR, C4288.

144. *Voyage dans les états barbaresques de Maroc, Alger, Tunis et Tripoly* . . . (Paris: Guillot, 1785), vii, 193. On sentimentality as way of expressing conditional identification in an imperial context, see Lynn Festa, *Sentimental Figures of Empire in Eighteenth-Century Britain and France* (Baltimore: Johns Hopkins University Press, 2006).

145. [Jacques Grasset de Saint-Sauveur with [?] Sylvain Maréchal], *La Belle captive, ou Histoire véritable du naufrage & de la captivité de Mlle. Adeline* . . . (Paris: Remy & Musier, 1785; 2nd ed., Paris: J. B. G. Musier, 1786), 100–101. Jean Louis Hubert Simon Deperthes, editor of the *Histoire des naufrages* . . . (3 vols. [Paris: Cuchet, 1788–1789], 3: 125–126 n.) called the book "a deception against the public during the last procession of captives."

146. *Affiches et annonces de Toulouse* (22 June): 98; (31 August): 137–138; (14 September): 146; (28 September): 156; (5 October): 158; (12 October 1785): 163. A court case involving a slave ransomed as François Dastague but claiming to be Arnaud Lamaure is featured as "DXIVe cause. Esclave racheté qui reclame son nom" in Nicolas Toussaint Lemoyne Dessessarts, ed., *Causes célèbres, curieuses et intéressantes, de toutes les cours souveraines du royaume, avec les jugemens qui les ont décidées [nouv. ser]* (Paris: P. G. Simon, 1775–1789), 164: 1–215.

147. *Affiches du Dauphiné* (9 September 1785), reprinted in "Un Episode dauphinois du rachat des Captifs avant la Révolution," *Annales dauphinoises* 4 (1903): 279–281. On the September 27 procession in Poitiers, see *Affiches du Poitou* (1785): 158, cited in Charles Auguste Auber, "Histoire de la cathédrale de Poitiers," *Mémoires de la Société des antiquaires de l'Ouest et des musées de Poitiers* 16 (1849): 413.

148. *Mandement de Monseigneur l'archevêque de Paris, qui permet de faire des quêtes pour la Rédemption* . . . (Paris: Claude Simon, 1785), 6–7.

149. *Rédemption des Captifs: Complainte sur les maux qu'endurent les Chrétiens Captifs* . . . (Paris: Valleyre l'aîné, 1785), 2, 4.

150. Frère Déduit, *Détail historique et remarquable des peins & de tourmens affreux que les turcs d'Alger* . . . (Paris: Cailleau, 1785), 5, 7.

151. *Hommage à l'oeuvre de la rédemption des captifs* (Paris: Demonville, [1785]), 4.

152. [Louis Petit de Bachaumont], *Mémoires secrets pour servir à l'histoire de la République des Lettres* . . . , 36 vols. (London: J. Adamson, 1777–1789), 30: 27. Anna Francesca Cradock, an English observer who watched the procession standing on a chair in a café by the Palais-Royal, provided description without judgment. *Journal de Madame Cradock: Voyage en France, 1783–1786*, trans.

O. Delphin Balleyguier (Paris: Perrin, 1896), 318. The menu from the banquet is preserved at AN, S4277–4278.

153. Raynal, BN, FF 6429, f. 121 v, cited in Deslandres, *OT*, 2: 471. Interestingly, Jacques Peuchet, the posthumous editor of Raynal's *Histoire philosophique et politique des établissements et du commerce des Européens dans l'Afrique septentrionale* (2 vols. [Paris: Pierre Maumnus, 1826], 2: 132), which reproduced the same passage, excised this last judgmental phrase, replacing it with "this kingdom."

154. *Nécessité de supprimer et d'éteindre les ordres religieux en France, prouvée par l'histoire philosophique du monachisme . . .* , 2 vols. (London [Paris?]: n.p., 1789), 2: 104, 130–131.

155. Alexandre Moreau de Jonnès, "Mémoires," ed. F.-A. Aulard, *La Révolution française* 19 (1890): 363. He later wrote *Recherches statistiques sur l'esclavage colonial et sur les moyens de le supprimer* (Paris: Bourgogne et Martinet, 1842).

156. Jacques-Marie Trichaud, *Histoire de la sainte l'eglise d'Arles*, 4 vols. (Paris: Etienne Giraud, 1857–1864), 4: 275; AN, S4278, no. 10, cited in Deslandres, *OT*, 1: 421; Trinitarian and Mercedarian officials to the CCM, September 1785 to March 1786, ACCM, G42.

157. Laurent Pierre Bérenger, *Les Soirées provençales, ou Lettres de M. Bérenger, écrites à ses amis pendant ses voyages dans sa patrie*, 3 vols. (Paris: Nyon l'aîné, 1786), 1: 181–185.

CHAPTER SIX

1. Deslandres, *OT*, 1: 306. In the last week of January 1790, Jewish revolutionary Abraham Spire reported a National Assembly discussion of "patriotic gifts" by the French merchants of Constantinople and Tunis to ransom all the French slaves so they might "profit from liberty" in their homeland. Abraham Spire, *Le Journal révolutionnaire d'Abraham Spire*, ed. Simon Schwarzfuchs ([Lagrasse]: Institut Alain de Rothschild/Verdier, 1989), 118, cited in Ronald Schechter, *Obstinate Hebrews: Representations of Jews in France, 1715–1815* (Berkeley: University of California Press, 2003), 183. Given the redemptive orders' impoverishment, marine minister Antoine Jean-Marie Thévenard told consul to Algiers Philippe Vallière that he would ask for the appropriation of public funds. Paris, 29 July 1791, CADN, CA, vol. 18, ff. 72–75.

2. According to former consul to Algiers Kercy, writing in 1791, the great majority of the remaining 150 French slaves were "fugitives from Oran, mostly bad subjects." Gabriel Esquer, ed., *Reconnaissance des villes, forts et batteries d'Alger par le chef de bataillon Boutin (1808), suivie des Mémoires sur l'Alger par les consuls de Kercy (1791) et Dubois-Thainville (1809)* (Paris: H. Champion, 1927), 111. For additional estimates, see app. 1.

3. By adopting a new flag in the winter of 1790, the National Assembly potentially exposed French travelers in the Mediterranean to additional risks of capture at the hands of Tunisian corsairs, whose bey initially refused to recognize the substitution as legitimate. Windler, *La Diplomatie*, 353–354.

4. Marine minister Antoine-François Bertrand de Molleville to the Legislative Assembly, Paris, 24 December 1791, reprinted in *Archives parlementaires de 1787 à 1860: recueil complet des débats législatifs & politiques des chambres françaises, imprimé par ordre du Sénat et de la Chambre des députés* (hereafter *AP*), 1st ser., 99 vols. (Paris: P. Dupont, 1879–1914), 36: 347.

5. According to this census, the combined efforts of the Trinitarians and Mercedarians had yielded 2,351 French slaves in 187 years for an average of 42½ per annum. In the new revolutionary political climate, the authors warned against favoritism toward captives from wealthy families but approved discrimination against Oraners and other French deserters from Spanish presidios. Notes about the redemptive orders (attached to 29 December 1791 document), BN, NAF 21136, ff. 265–270. Research continued into the following year, as attested by the 16 April 1792 "Etat des sommes dues à l'oeuvre de la rédemption particulière des pauvres esclaves de Marseille & son terroir . . . ," ADBR, reproduced in French Revolution Research Collection, 9.5.164.

6. Jean-Baptiste Jamon, *Rapport à l'assemblée nationale . . . sur le rachat de tous les françois captifs chez les puissances barbaresques . . .* (Paris: Imprimerie nationale, 1792), 5. This text, read on 5 March 1792, also appears in the AP, 1st ser., 39: 397–398. It was discussed and then reread on 10 and 21 March. AP, 1st ser., 39: 529; 40: 199. For the resulting decree, see Sylvain Lebeau, ed., *Recueil des lois relatives à la marine et aux colonies*, 9 vols. (Paris: Imprimerie de la République, 1797–1810; reprint, French Revolution Research Collection, 1992), 2: 408.

7. Jamon, "Rapport à l'assemblée nationale." On the matter of secular discomfort with the spiritual connotations of charity, see Jones, *Charity and Bienfaisance*, esp. 166. Another 1792 decree ordered that an Italian and a Frenchman claiming to be ransom collectors, picked up in the department of Aube, turn over 496 livres and 10 sols "to be used for the redemption of captives." Lebeau, *Recueil des lois*, 431–432.

8. Pernille Røge effectively demonstrates that the roots of France's *mission civilisatrice* predate the Revolution. "'La Clef de commerce': The Changing Role of Africa in France's Atlantic Empire, ca. 1760–1797," *History of European Ideas* 34, 4 (2008): 431–443. On evolving attitudes toward colonies in the 1790s and afterward, see Anna Plassart, "'Un Imperialiste Liberal'? Jean-Baptiste Say on Colonies and the Extra-European World," *French Historical Studies* 32, 2 (2009): 223–250.

9. Slave Mathieu Meissonnier et al. to CCM, Algiers, 4 April 1792, AMM, GGL106.

10. Vallière to Thévenard, 11 October 1791, AN, AE BI 144, f. 167 v, cited in Windler, *La Diplomatie*, 376.

11. Vallière to CCM, Algiers, 28 July 1791, and to Molleville, Algiers, 3 December 1791, AN, AE BI 144, ff. 144, 188–189, cited in Touili, *Correspondance*, 780, 785; Thévenard to Vallière, Paris, 16 September 1791, CADN, CA, vol. 18, ff. 99–103. See also marine minister Jean de La Coste to the CCM and to Vallière, Paris, 14 May 1792, ACCM, J1885, and AN, AE BI 145, ff. 175–177.

12. Copy of letter from slaves Messonnier et al., Algiers, 12 August 1792,

AN, AE BIII 321, f. 159. Marine minister Gaspard Monge told the consul of his satisfaction with the outcome and promised to speak to the revolutionary legislature about the remaining French slaves. Paris, 11 September 1792, AN, AE BI 145, ff. 218–219.

13. In fact, Marseille's "Oeuvre de la rédemption" was still pleading the slaves' case during the fall and winter of 1792–1793. Marseille, 24 August 1792, 2 and 26 October 1792, 4 January 1793, AN, AE BIII 321, ff. 158–161. Only in July 1793 did Marseille's provisional "Bureau de commerce" receive orders to loan eighty-five thousand livres to Vallière for a ransom payment. Minister of foreign affairs François Deforgues, 21 July 1793, ACCM, AA122 (OC), cited in Teissier, *Inventaire*, 76–77. A group letter to the foreign affairs minister (enclosing a 5 June 1793 response from the Committee of Petitions and Correspondences of the National Convention), dated Algiers, 20 August 1793, demonstrates that their fate had still not been resolved. This time, 150 "legitimate Frenchmen" complained of plague and misery. By December, one of the Marseillais had indeed succumbed (AAE, CC, Algiers, vol. 32, ff. 59–60, 70).

14. As demonstrated by Panzac (*CB*, summarized 66), the outbreak of the Revolutionary Wars coincided with a spike in North African corsairing activity, which peaked in 1798, declined between 1806 and 1813, and enjoyed a short renaissance from 1814 to 1815 before almost entirely disappearing after 1816.

15. Vallière to the marine ministry, Algiers, 25 July 1792 (forwarded to the Legislative Assembly, 4 August 1792), AN, BI 145, ff. 175–177.

16. Delegates from Beaugency, 6 May 1793 [2?], AN, Assemblée législative, Dossier Loiret, no. 43, D.X.L. 3645, cited in Suzanne Moreau-Rendu, *Les Captifs libérés et le couvent Saint-Mathurin de Paris* (Paris: Editions latines, 1974), 231–232. A letter from M. Curtuis, captain of the Nazareth Battalion, read on 16 September 1792, had the same idea; reprinted in *AP* (1896), 1st ser., 50: 58.

17. As late as June and July 1791, municipalities were forwarding the baptismal records of natives (Vallabreque, 21, 22, and 24 June 1791; Marseille, 21 July 1791, ACCM, G42). A 20 September 1792 decree, however, instituted civil registration. See Gérard Noiriel, "The Identification of the Citizen: The Birth of Republican Civil Status in France," in Caplan and Toppey, *Documenting Individual Identity*, 28–48; and Denis, *Une Histoire de l'identité*.

18. Georges Grosjean, *La Maîtrise de la Méditerranée et la Tunisie pendant la révolution française (1789–1802): étude d'histoire diplomatique et navale* (Paris: Chapelot, 1914), 169–170. On the evolution of such protection, see Francis Rey, *La Protection diplomatique et consulaire dans les échelles du Levant et de Barbarie* (Paris: L. Larose, 1899), 305–384, esp. 345–348.

19. See, for example, Vallière to the foreign affairs minister, Algiers, 4 February and 20 December 1793, and one of the minister's responses, Paris, 19 August 1793, AAE, CC, Algiers, vol. 32, ff. 14, 53.

20. On the edict to end racial discrimination, proclaimed on 28 March and signed into law on 4 April 1792, see Laurent Dubois, *A Colony of Citizens: Revolution and Slave Emancipation in the French Caribbean, 1787–1804* (Chapel Hill: University of North Carolina Press, 2004), 112–114; and David Geggus,

"Racial Equality, Slavery and Colonial Secession during the Constituent Assembly," *American Historical Review* 94, 5 (1989): 1290–1308.

21. Decree of the National Convention, 19 November 1792, *AP*, 1st ser., 53: 474. On the "debate on expansion" during the Revolutionary Wars, see Marc Belissa, *Fraternité universelle et intérêt national (1713–1795): les cosmopolitiques du droit des gens* (Paris: Kimé, 1998), esp. 328–347, 422–439; and Andrew J. S. Jainchill, *Reimagining Politics after the Terror: The Republican Origins of French Liberalism* (Ithaca, NY: Cornell University Press, 2008), chap. 4.

22. "Extrait du procès verbal de l'assemblée des trois corps administratifs et des commissaires des sections . . . ," Marseille, 10 October; Monge to the "administrateurs du Bureau provisoire de Marseille," Paris, 22 October 1792, ACCM, G51. For further articulation of this policy, see Rapport sur Tunis, February 1793, AN, AE BI 38, ff. 38 v–39 r, cited in Windler, *La Diplomatie*, 380.

23. Despite a 21 November 1792 declaration "that the French Republic does not intend to purchase with presents the friendship of the Regency [of Algiers], nor to sell its own," the Committee of Public Safety decided on 14 May 1793 to send gifts valued at 180,000 livres, chosen from a national cache of impounded luxury objects. François-Alphonse Aulard, ed., *Recueil des actes du Comité de salut public: avec la correspondance officielle des représentants en mission et le registre du Conseil exécutif provisoire*, 27 vols. (Paris: Imprimerie nationale, 1889–1923), 3: 254, 414.

24. On French interventions to free Algerian slaves from Genoa, see Pascal Even, "Un Episode des relations de la France avec la régence d'Alger, au début de la Révolution: la mission du capitaine Doumergues en 1791," *Revue d'histoire diplomatique* 98 (1984): 50–70; and Moleville to CCM, 22 November 1791, ACCM, G51. Highlighting the connection between preserving Franco–North African amity and protecting the food supply, on 7 June 1793 the Committee of Public Safety resolved to demand that the leaders of Algiers and Tunis ban their respective corsairs from molesting cargoes of grain on foreign vessels destined for French ports. Aulard, *Recueil des actes*, 4: 163–164, 477.

25. The elite Société des amis de noirs to the contrary, only a handful of the sixty thousand cahiers de doléances composed in 1789 took on the issue of colonial slavery. Claude Wanquet, *La France et la première abolition de l'esclavage, 1794–1802: le cas des colonies orientales, Ile de France (Maurice) et la Réunion* (Paris: Karthala, 1998), 16–17; Seymour Drescher, *Capitalism and Antislavery: British Mobilization in Comparative Perspective* (New York: Oxford University Press, 1987), 53–54.

26. Jean-Claude Halpern, "Les Fêtes révolutionnaires et l'abolition de l'esclavage en l'an II," in Marcel Dorigny, ed., *Les Abolitions de l'esclavage: de L. F. Sonthonax à V. Schoelcher, 1793, 1794, 1848* (Saint-Denis: Presses universitaires de Vincennes, 1995), 187–198.

27. On the absence of French slaves in Tripoli around 1783 and a description of the arrival of a new republican consul in April 1793, accompanied by an impromptu trial of his predecessor and the planting of a liberty tree, see Miss Tully, *Letters Written during a Ten Years' Residence at the Court of*

Tripoli . . . , ed. Dearden (London: Arthur Barker, 1957), 61, 335. As one of the only French citizens left in the regency after 1794, consul Alphonse Guys had few occasions to intervene on behalf of enslaved countrymen. Exceptionally, in 1796, he claimed a Frenchman born in Guadeloupe, part of the crew of a seized American ship. Marie-Agnès Vallette, "L'Echelle de Tripoli de Barbarie: 1786–1802," Mémoire de DES, Université de Paris II, 1975, 68, 80.

28. Maurice Degros, "Les Consulats de France sous la Révolution: les états barbaresques," *Revue d'histoire diplomatique* 105 (1991): 111–113; Plantet, *Les Consuls de France avant la conquête (1579–1830)* (Paris: Messageries Hachette, 1930), 301; Charles-Roux, *Les Travaux d'Herculais ou une extraordinaire mission en Barbarie* (Paris: Société de l'Histoire des colonies françaises, 1926); Grammont, *HA*, 277–279. See app. 2 for slave numbers.

29. French slaves to Saint-André, Algiers, 19 October 1796, 25 May 1798, and [1798, exact date unknown], CADN, CA, vol. 20, ff. 185–186; vol. 22, ff. 108, 149. See also ff. 150, 152, 154, 156–161.

30. This passage follows the reasoning in Sarah C. Maza, *Private Lives and Public Affairs: The Causes Célèbres of Prerevolutionary France* (Berkeley: University of California Press, 1993), chap. 1.

31. That Spain was in the process of ransoming Oraners (excluding anyone born outside its territories) and that Naples and the United States had just freed their slaves (see Richard Bordeaux Parker, *Uncle Sam in Barbary: A Diplomatic History* [Gainesville: University Press of Florida, 2004], 96–124) made France's inaction all the more galling. After a furious mob of French slaves found the consul absent from his city residence, one of them—armed with a billhook and a knife—tracked him down at his country villa. Saint-André to foreign affairs ministry, Algiers, 26 September, 6 October, and 20 November 1796; 14 and 15 March 1797, AAE, CC, Algiers, vol. 33, ff. 3 v, 9, 12–13, 15, 43, 140, 145 v.

32. Epstein, *Speaking of Slavery*, 52–53. French administrators later discovered a tradition among all social strata in Liguria's mountain regions: time spent as *batti birbbi*—or impostor ransom collectors—fleecing charity for nonexistent Barbary captives from unsuspecting donors in Italy, France, Spain, and Portugal. Michael Broers, *The Politics of Religion in Napoleonic Italy: The War against God, 1801–1814* (London: Routledge, 2002), 18.

33. According to Saint-André, writing to the foreign ministry, the dey of Algiers did not seem particularly moved during the presentation of thirty-two of his subjects freed from Genoa. Algiers, 13 August 1797, AAE, CC, Algiers, vol. 33, f. 247.

34. Bonaparte to Directory president Paul Barras, Paris, 28 December 1797, accompanying letter from the Tunisian bey with the names of eighteen French slaves he released, reprinted in Berbrugger, "La Régence d'Alger sous le Consulat et sous l'Empire," *RA* 19 (1875): 18–19. Consul Jacques-Philippe Devoise had specifically instructed all free and captive Corsicans to swear allegiance to France at the Chancellery or else risk being considered English. Devoise to foreign minister Charles Maurice de Talleyrand-Périgord, Tunis, 7 January 1798, reprinted in Plantet, *CBT*, 3: 341. The bey of Tunis finally agreed to liberate a group of Corfiotes (former subjects of Venice) after France seized a Tunisian

corsair crew at the end of December. Maria Ghazali, "La Régence de Tunis et l'esclavage en Méditerranée à la fin du XVIIIème siècle d'après les sources consulaires espagnoles," *CM* 65 (2002): 5, 12–13; Grosjean, *La Maîtrise de la Méditerranée*, 231–232.

35. Former consul Saizieu to the Directory, 23 October 1797, AAE, CC, Tunis, 1797–1798, cited in Charles-Roux, *FA*, 376–381.

36. Talleyrand referred to liberation of eighty-nine Algerians from Zante in a letter to Moltedo, Paris, 23 July 1798, CADN, CA, vol. 22, ff. 147–148.

37. Already in 1795 France's consul sought a policy for Oran deserters from Belgium and Sardinia requesting protection from their "new *patrie*" (Saint-André to foreign affairs ministry, Algiers, 27 September 1795, AAE, CC, Algiers, vol. 33, f. 3 v). In 1797 the Directory demanded that Algerian corsairs stop assaulting Corsicans—whom the dey still judged British subjects—and release all French and Italians taken under French flag in exchange for any Algerians detained by the Venetians in Corfu during the French invasion. It also received pleas from Genoese and Tuscans enslaved in Algiers. "Procès-verbaux du Directoire exécutive," 6 February, 5 April, and 25 September 1797, AN, AF III 432, plaquette 2470, pp. 1–3; AF III 442, plaquette 2571, pp. 29–57; AF* III 9, ff. 11 r–13 r; AN, AF III 467, plaquette 2854, p. 1, cited in Pierre-Dominique Cheynet, ed., *Les Procès-verbaux du Directoire exécutive, an V–an VIII . . .*, 10 vols. (Paris: Centre historique des archives nationales, 2000), 1: 47, 134; 3: 8–9, 14.

38. Triplicate letter from slave Christophe Visovick to Barras, Algiers, 14 March 1798, AN, 171 AP 1 17, p. 75, ff. 1–3. Talleyrand confirmed this account in another letter to Moltedo, Paris, 29 March 1798, CADN, CA, vol. 22, ff. 41–42.

39. Slave Pietro Giovanni Vigo to Saint-André, Algiers, 13 May 1798, CADN, CA, vol. 22, f. 84. He also addressed the consul on 10 May and 19 May, ff. 78, 86.

40. Talleyrand referred to seventeen Venetians and eighteen Italians in a letter to Moltedo, Paris, 17 June 1798, CADN, CA, vol. 22, ff. 130–131. For confirmation of the Algerian dey's nonrecognition of French sovereignty over these men, see Agence de l'Afrique representative Astoin Sielve to citoyen Guibert in Annaba, Algiers, 4 and 19 July 1798, reprinted in Berbrugger, "La Régence d'Alger," 15, 88 (1871): 258–259.

41. Bonaparte had predicted that Malta would "sooner or later belong to Britain if we are stupid enough not to forestall them." Cited in Earle, *Corsairs of Malta and Barbary*, 270.

42. For the text of the 16 June 1798 edict, see Wettinger, *Slavery in the Islands of Malta*, 586–587. Two days before, the Directory asked for a list by country of the Muslim slaves in Malta so that French diplomatic agents in North Africa might secure the release of Maltese slaves there. AN, AF* III 11, ff. 186 v–189 r, cited in Cheynet, *Procès verbaux*, 6: 15.

43. Devoulx, *Les Archives*, 131–132.

44. Former consul Bonaventure Beaussier to Talleyrand, Tunis, 25 June, and Devoise to Napoleon Bonaparte, Tunis, 15 July 1798, reprinted in Plantet, *CBT*, 3: 351–352, 354; Hannibal P. Scicluna, *Actes et documents relatifs à l'histoire*

de l'occupation française de Malte pendant les années 1798–1800 et à la fête du 14 juillet 1798 à Malte . . . , 3rd ed. (Valletta, Malta: A. C. Aquilina, 1979), 156–157.

45. Napoleon's 2 July 1798 proclamation, cited in Grigsby, *Extremities*, 105.

46. *Journal de Paris* (2 February 1799): 587, (4 February 1799): 597; Berbrugger, "La Régence d'Alger," 15, 89 (1871): 330–334; 15, 90 (1871): 411–413; 16, 91 (1872): 2–16; Degros, "Les Consulats de France," 125; app. 2 of this book.

47. "Procès-verbaux du Directoire exécutive," 26 January 1799, AN, AF III 572, plaquette 3890, pp. 7–8, cited in Cheynet, *Procès verbaux*, 7: 118; finance minister to department of Alpes-Maritimes administrators, 27 January 1799, ADAM, L0015; *Journal de Paris* (1 March 1799): 703. The department of Hérault received instructions to draw up a census of Muslims in the area, a proposal that drew resistance from at least some local officials. ADH, 1799, L892.

48. On the revival of corsairing in Tunis, see Panzac, *CB*, 65–66.

49. Robert Eisner, *Travelers to an Antique Land: The History and Literature of Travel to Greece* (Ann Arbor: University of Michigan Press, 1991), 96; François Charles Hugues Laurent Pouqueville, *Voyage en Morée, à Constantinople, en Albanie* . . . , 3 vols. (Paris: Gabon, 1805), esp. 1: 1–9, 58–59.

50. On the seizure of Jean-Pierre Lacombe-Saint-Michel and his brief captivity in Tunis, see Cheynet, *Procès verbaux*, 5: 129 n. 2; 9: 25. For the number of French slaves in Tunis from 1799 to 1800, see app. 1. For their treatment, see Windler, *La Diplomatie*, 382–383; Degros, "Les Consulats de France," 115–116.

51. Talleyrand to Devoise, Paris, 14 April, 4 August, and 19 September 1799; Devoise to bey Hammuda, Tunis, 17 June 1799; Devoise to Talleyrand, Tunis, 26 November 1799, reprinted in Plantet, *CBT*, 3: 384, 391, 396, 399, 400.

52. On this attack, led by Mohammed Roumelli—purportedly the cuckolded (and converted) husband of a local woman—and the long-term ransom negotiations, see Gaston Loth, "Le Pillage de Saint-Pierre de Sardaigne par les corsaires tunisiens en 1798," *Revue tunisienne* 12 (1905): 9–14; the account by French physician Louis Frank (member of the Egyptian expedition and then physician to bey Hammuda of Tunis) in Rozet et al., *Algérie, Etats Tripolitains, Tunis*, 125–127; Bono, *I Corsari barbareschi*, 180–183, 329–330; Khelifa Chater, *Dépendance et mutations précoloniales: la régence de Tunis de 1815 à 1857* (Tunis: Université de Tunis, 1984), 221; and Panzac, *CB*, 81, 102. See also Devoise to Talleyrand, Tunis, 18 September and 27 October 1798, 22 June 1799, 22 April 1803; Talleyrand to Devoise, Paris, 28 January 1799, reprinted in Plantet, *CBT*, 3: 360, 365, 377, 392, 451.

53. While the 1801 treaty simply stated that "Frenchmen cannot be held as slaves in the Kingdom of Algiers under any circumstance or pretext," the 1802 one stipulated that "any individual from a country that by conquest or treaty was united with the states of the French Republic and who finds himself captive in the Kingdom of Tunis will be set free." Rouard de Card, *TF*, 205, 279. Different phrasing in Turkish gave authorities a pretext for continuing to detain slaves from recently annexed territories. Olivier Gaborieau, "Corsaires barbaresques, esclaves chrétiens et diplomatie française à Tunis de 1790 à 1830" (Mémoire de maîtrise, Université de Nantes, 1990), 85.

54. On the May and July 1802 decrees that maintained and reimposed slavery, see the essays in Yves Bénot and Dorigny, eds., *Rétablissement de l'esclavage dans les colonies françaises, 1802: ruptures et continuités de la politique colonial française, 1800–1830; aux origines de Haïti* (Paris: Maisonneuve & Larose, 2003).

55. Bonaparte to Talleyrand, Paris, 30 October 1801, reprinted in *Correspondance de Napoléon 1er* (hereafter *CN*), 32 vols. (Paris: H. Plon, J. Dumaine, 1858–1870), 7: 308. Talleyrand repeated this phrase in a letter to French ambassador Louis-Guillaume Otto, 20 November 1801, cited in Bénot, "Bonaparte et la démence coloniale (1799–1804)," in *Mourir pour les Antilles: indépendance nègre ou esclavage, 1802–1804*, ed. Michel L. Martin, Lucien-René Abénon, and Alain Yacou (Paris: Editions caribéennes, 1991), 22.

56. Devoise, "Mémoire sur un projet d'expédition contre Tunis," Tunis, 26 May 1801, AN, 327 AP 1, cited in Windler, *La Diplomatie*, 379.

57. Bonaparte to Talleyrand (Third annex to *dépêches* d'Amiens), Paris, 19 February 1802, reprinted in *CN*, 7: 391.

58. London *Times* (29 August 1802): 2; *Mercure de France* (April 1802), cited in Bénot, "Une Préhistoire de l'expédition d'Alger," in Bénot and Dorigny, *Rétablissement de l'esclavage*, 539.

59. Saint-André, "Le commissaire général du gouvernement dans les nouveaux départements de la rive gauche du Rhin, au ministre de la marine et des colonies," Mayence, 27 July 1802, reproduced in *Correspondance de Napoléon avec le ministre de la marine depuis 1804 jusqu'en avril 1815*, 2 vols. (Paris: Delloye et V. Lecou, 1837), 1: 232–273. For Kercy's 1791 statement, see Esquer, *Reconnaissance des villes*, 93–120.

60. On Devoise's demand for the liberty of thirty-six slaves from Piedmont and the islands of Elba and Caprera in February and August 1802, see Rousseau, *ATN*, 239, 243. As Devoise told Talleyrand (Tunis, 19 November 1802, reprinted in Plantet, *CBT*, 3: 444), the bey professed to have been unaware of Caprera's annexation to France. For Devoise's claim over anyone from the Cisalpine Republic in March 1802 and the emancipation of a single woman from Milan, see Plantet, *CBT*, 3: 432. For a relatively polite letter from Bonaparte to bey Hammuda of Tunis, dated 7 May 1802, see *CN*, 7: 456.

61. Despite Dubois-Thainville's assiduous efforts to recover all the victims during the winter, by summer many still remained unaccounted for. Bonaparte to Talleyrand, Paris, 7 July 1802; to dey Mustafa of Algiers and to the foreign minister, 27 July 1802, reprinted in *CN*, 7: 513–514, 535–536. The ultimatum was delivered by "adjudant du palais" Pierre Hulin, traveling with the fleet of admiral Corentin-Urbain de Leissègues, on 7 August 1802. André Auzoux, "La Mission de l'amiral Leissègues à Alger et à Tunis," *Revue des études napoléoniennes* 13 (1918): 65–95.

62. Pierre-Paul Thédenat to Talleyrand, "Coup d'oeil sur la Régence d'Alger," 19 August 1802, AAE, MD, Alger, excerpted and analyzed in Charles-Roux, *FA*, 413–423.

63. Bonaparte to Talleyrand, Paris, 16, 18, and 29 July 1802; to the pope, Paris, 28 August 1802; to the emperor of Russia, Paris, 29 August 1802, reprinted in *CN*, 7: 520, 522, 542; 8: 8–9, 11. From Algiers, admiral Leissègues

sailed to Tunis, where he successfully pushed for the release of twenty-two Sardinian slaves born of Corsican mothers and disciplined some of his sailors, caught trying to smuggle out additional captive Neapolitans dressed in French uniform. Auzoux, "La Mission de l'amiral Leissègues," 79, 92–93. As of 1802–1803, the dey of Algiers counted no slaves from metropolitan France but acknowledged eighty-nine Genoese, sixteen Corsicans, and nine Romans. See app. 1; and the London *Times* (16 September 1802): 2.

64. On Bonaparte's instructions, France's consul Beaussier had been negotiating with pasha Qaramanli for the release of about three hundred American captives. American consul general to Tunis William Eaton's overland march from Alexandria to the Tripolitan port of Derna, along with a $60,000 payment, finally ended the four-year-long war between the United States and Tripoli in June 1805. Parker, *Uncle Sam in Barbary*, 133–147; Michael Kitzen, *Tripoli and the United States at War: A History of American Relations with the Barbary States, 1785–1805* (Jefferson, NC: McFarland, 1993).

65. For a captivity narrative by the Milanese (thus French) antiquarian and priest F. Caroni, captured and released in 1804, see "Relation d'un court voyage d'un antiquaire amateur (F. Caroni) surpris par les corsaires, conduit en Barbarie et heureusement rapatrié (1804)," ed. and trans. Marthe Conor and Grandchamp, *Revue tunisienne* 23 (1916): 287–294, 393–403; 24 (1917): 30–54, 96–122.

66. Napoleon to Joseph Bonaparte, Saint-Cloud, 21 May 1806, reprinted in *CN*, 12: 388. Jean-Guillaume-Antoine Cuvelier's *A-t-il deux femmes? ou les Corsaires barbaresques, mélodrame en 3 actes . . .* ([Paris: Barban, 1803], 43) had concluded similarly, with the protagonist announcing his wish "that these scoundrels [Barbary corsairs] be dragged to Naples and that this happy country remember that they owe their deliverance from these audacious pirates to the French."

67. Napoleon Bonaparte to Jérôme Bonaparte, Genoa, 5 July 1805; to Decrès, Fontainebleau, 17 July 1805, reprinted in *CN*, 11: 8–9, 20–21.

68. Decrès to Jérôme, Paris, 11 September 1805, in Albert Du Casse, *Les Rois frères de Napoléon Ier: documents inédits relatifs au premier empire* (Paris: Germer Baillière, 1883), 191. Both the *Gazette de Gênes* (15 September 1805, cited in *Mémoires et correspondance du roi Jérôme et de la reine Catherine*, 7 vols. [Paris: E. Dentu, 1861–1866], 1: 346–348) and Glenn J. Lamar (*Jérôme Bonaparte: The War Years, 1800–1815* [Westport, CT: Greenwood Press, 2000], 22–23) refer to the release of 231 slaves. Bonaparte himself, by contrast, claimed 520 (to Charles-François Lebrun, Saint-Cloud, 10 September 1805, reprinted in *CN*, 11: 184). Despite the bluster, the emperor had actually agreed to give the dey an eighty-thousand-piastre present for the return of the slaves (Devoise to Hammuda bey, Tunis, 24 June 1806, reprinted in Plantet, *CBT*, 3: 465–467).

69. See app. 1. Devoise agreed to pay one thousand piastres each for the slaves, he informed Talleyrand from Tunis on 14 July 1806; on 30 January 1809, he told foreign affairs minister Jean-Baptiste de Nompere de Champagny, duc de Cadore, that the bey was still claiming nonpayment of what he considered their ransom. See Plantet, *CBT*, 3: 464–465 n. 1, 467–468, 482.

70. On dey Mustafa of Algiers's continuing refusal to recognize France's annexation of Genoa, see Devoulx, *Les Archives*, 145. On the passage of the brick *Le Requin* to reclaim 106–123 Italian slaves from Algiers, see Bonaparte to Cadore, Paris, 2 February 1808; to Decrès, Paris, 6 February and 24 March 1808, reprinted in *CN*, 16: 305, 308, 435–436. The number of captive Neapolitans in Algiers skyrocketed from 365 in 1802 to 634 in 1811 (Panzac, *CB*, 99). On the origins and French performances in 1817 and 1830 of Giaocchino Rossini's *La Italiana in Algeri*, see Yacine Daddi Addoun, "L'Abolition de l'esclavage en Algérie: 1816–1871" (PhD diss., York University, 2010), 53–55.

71. Napoleon to Joseph Bonaparte, Saint-Cloud, 21 July 1806, reprinted in *CN*, 2: 571. On Britain's Mediterranean expansion from 1806 to 1809, see Michela d'Angelo, "In the 'English' Mediterranean (1511–1815)," *Journal of Mediterranean Studies* 12, 2 (2002): 281; Charles-Roux, *FA*, 440–442.

72. The resulting report prepared by Vincent-Yves Boutin in May 1808 (reprinted in Esquer, *Reconnaissance des villes*, 18–91) was used in preparation for the invasion of Algiers in 1830. Grammont, *HA*, 291. Bonaparte to Decrès, Bayonne, 18 April 1808; to foreign affairs minister Champagny, Bayonne, 21 April and 29 May 1808, reprinted in *CN*, 17: 21, 29, 229. On [Antoine Bruguière de Sorsum], *Les Captifs d'Alger . . .* (Cassel: Imprimerie royale, 1808) (performed on 14 November), see Fernand Baldensperger, *Alfred De Vigny: contribution à sa biographie intellectuelle* (Paris: Hachette, 1932), 34.

73. Devoise, "Mémoire sur Tunis," 1809, AN, 327, AP 6, cited in Rachida Tlili, "Les Projets de conquête en direction du Maghreb sous la Révolution et l'Empire," in Bénot and Dorigny, *Rétablissement de l'esclavage*, 497. The French physician Frank made a similar observation in contrasting the respective destinies of *nègres* and *européens* in Tunis. Rozet et al., *Algérie, Etats Tripolitains, Tunis*, 115–118, 127–129.

74. Dubois-Thainville, "Sur Alger," Paris, 18 November 1809, AAE, MD, vol. 10, f. 261, reprinted in Esquer, *Reconnaissance des villes*, 133–150.

CHAPTER SEVEN

1. Much of the scholarship on American captives in Barbary fails to draw a distinction between experiences in urban north and pastoral northwest Africa. One recent dissertation that does is Christine Sears, "A Different Kind of Slavery: American Captives in Barbary 1776–1830," PhD diss., University of Delaware, 2007. I have found no estimates for the number of shipwrecks in Algerian territory, but from the mid-eighteenth to the early nineteenth century, there are records of at least thirty European ones, five of them French, along the Atlantic coast of Morocco. Maurice Barbier, ed., *Trois français au Sahara occidental (1784–1786)* (Paris: L'Harmattan, 1984), 26–27; James Grey Jackson, *An Account of the Empire of Marocco and the District of Suse . . .* (London: W. Bulmer, 1809), 234. Olivier Vergniot extrapolates that a maximum of five hundred Europeans were taken captive in the Sahara. "De la distance en histoire: Maroc—Sahara occidental; les captifs du hasard (XVIIe–XXe siècles)," *ROMM* 48 (1988): 100.

2. French captive Charles Cochelet recounted meeting a French renegade who had shipwrecked at age fourteen and supported his family manufacturing gunpowder. *Naufrage du brick français, La Sophie, perdu le 30 mai 1819, sur la côte occidentale d'Afrique . . .*, 2 vols. (Paris: P. Mongie ainé, 1821), 1: xiii. Jackson asserted that out of two hundred English captives taken into the Sahara, about twenty of the younger ones died or converted. *Account of the Empire*, 235. Saugnier profiled a Marseillais in Marrakech who had converted to avoid five hundred lashes and reported the presence in Mogador of 250 French renegades, formerly deserters from Spanish presidios. *Relations de plusieurs voyages à la côte d'Afrique, à Maroc, au Sénégal, à Gorée, à Galam, etc . . .* (Paris: Gueffier jeune, 1791), 52, 62.

3. The construction of Mogador with slave labor was reportedly supervised by a renegade engineer from either Avignon or Roussillon (Théodore Cornut) who later returned to France. Chénier, *Recherches historiques sur les Maures*, 3: 40 n. 1. See also Pierre-Raymond de Brisson, *Histoire du naufrage et captivité de Monsieur de Brisson, Officier de l'Administration de Colonies*, ed. Attilio Gaudio (Paris: Nouvelles éditions latines, 1984), annex 14.

4. On the history of Senegal—its coastal outposts ruled by French chartered companies from 1626 to 1758, then occupied by Britain until 1778, then various iterations of the French state until 1809, then Britain again until 1817, then France until 1960—see Abdoulaye Bathily, *Les Portes d'or: le royaume de Galam (Sénégal) de l'ère musulmane au temps de négriers (VIIIe–XVIIIe siècle)* (Paris: L'Harmattan, 1989); and Boubacar Barry, *Senegambia and the Atlantic Slave Trade*, trans. Ayi Kwei Armah (Cambridge: Cambridge University Press, 1998).

5. These include "Journal du voyage et du séjour que fit au Maroc Pierre-Julien Dupuy," AAE, MD, vol. 2, ff. 436–455, discussed in Jacques Caillé, "Les Naufragés de la 'Louise' au Maroc et l'ambassade de Tahar Fennich à la cour de France en 1777–1778," *Revue d'histoire diplomatique* 78, 3 (1964): 225–264; Adrien Jacques Follie, *Mémoire d'un françois qui sort de l'Esclavage* (Amsterdam et se trouve à Paris: Laporte, 1785); Brisson, *Histoire du Naufrage et de la captivité de M. de Brisson . . .* (Geneva: Barde, Manget; Paris: Royez, 1789); Saugnier, *Relations de plusieurs voyages* (1791); Jean Baptiste Henri Savigny and Alexandre Corréard, *Naufrage de la frégate la Méduse, faisant partie de l'expédition du Sénégal, en 1816 . . .* (Paris: Hocquet, 1817); Pierre Joseph Dumont, *Histoire de l'esclavage en Afrique: (pendant trente-quatre ans) de P. J. Dumont, natif de Paris, maintenant a l'Hospice royal des incurables*, edited by J. S. Quesne (Paris: Pillet ainé, 1819); Cochelet, *Naufrage du brick français* (1821); and Charlotte-Adelaïde Dard, *La Chaumière africaine, ou, Histoire d'une famille française jetée sur la côte occidentale de l'Afrique, à la suite du naufrage de la frégate La Méduse* (Dijon: Noellat, 1824).

6. See Janice E. Thomson, *Mercenaries, Pirates, and Sovereigns: State-Building and Extraterritorial Violence in Early Modern Europe* (Princeton, NJ: Princeton University Press, 1994); Oded Löwenheim, "'Do Ourselves Credit and Render a Lasting Service to Mankind': British Moral Prestige, Humanitarian

Intervention and the Barbary Pirates," *International Studies Quarterly* 47, 1 (2003): 23–48.

7. A joint Trinitarian-Mercedarian redemption had around 1760 paid four thousand to six thousand livres each for seventy captives, a portion from Aix-en-Provence. See app. 2 for scanty references.

8. Moroccan and French sources cite varying numbers of casualties and captives: three hundred killed or wounded, forty-seven captured (Bidé de Maurville); two thousand lost, fifteen enslaved (Chénier); eighty killed, fifty captured (Al-Sadraati); five hundred killed or wounded, sixty captured (Al-Qadiri), cited in Amina Aouchar, "Le Bombardement de Salé et de Larache de juin 1765, à travers les textes marocains et français," *Maroc Europe* 11 (1997–1998): 187. See also Auzoux, "L'Affaire de Larache," *Revue de l'histoire des colonies françaises* 16 (1928): 505–524; and François Dessertenne, "L'Affaire de Larache, 27 juin 1765, un épisode de la négociation franco-marocaine sur la piraterie," *Revue historique des armées* 166 (1987): 4–12.

9. In an attempt to exact more money from the redemptive orders, the sultan had transferred the French slaves from Safi to Mogador in the summer of 1765. A Marseillais merchant living in Safi, Jean-Jacques Salva, accepted ten thousand livres for his role in redeeming the French slaves for the Trinitarians and Mercedarians and twelve Flemish ones for a Spanish father. For the specifics of redemption, see app. 2. On Neptune's status, see especially *L'Ordre et la marche de la procession des captifs françois rachetés . . .* (Paris: P. de Lormel, 1765); and Penz, *Personnalités et familles*, 188 (citing a manuscript from the Bibliothèque d'Arles, Ms 270).

10. For example, copy of letter from François Joseph Hippolyte Bidé de Maurville to his father in Rochefort, Saffi, 24 March 1761, AN, AE BIII 319, p. 56.

11. Bidé de Maurville, *Relation de l'affaire de Larache* (Amsterdam: n.p., 1775), 36, 60–64, 85–112, 127–138, 215–216, 230–244. According to Chénier (*Recherches historiques*, 3: 131), the relatively few renegades in Morocco during this period were deserters from the Spanish presidios.

12. Estimates of the number of French slaves held in Morocco in 1766 to 1767 range from 200 to 300, with 115 in Mogador (see app. 1).

13. In 1767 Pierre-Claude Hocdenault, comte de Breugnon, took up negotiations that had until then been conducted via merchant intermediaries, agreeing to pay two thousand piastres per Larache victim and seven hundred for anyone else. See Pierre Grillon, *Un Chargé d'affaires au Maroc: la correspondance du consul Louis Chénier, 1767–1782* (Paris: SEVPEN, 1970), 70–74, 79. Four Moors liberated from Sardinia through the efforts of the CCM were delivered to the sultan, according to a letter dated Mogador, 5 October 1767. AAE, Maroc, CC, vol. 8, cited in Penz, *Personnalités et familles*, 88.

14. On the financial arrangements, see anonymous, 1766, AAE, Maroc, vol. 3, f. 62–65 v, reprinted in Deslandres, *OT*, 2: 430; ACCM, AA83 (OC), cited in Teissier, *Inventaire*, 58; L'Averdy to La Tour, Versailles, 21 December 1766, ADBR, C4288; extracts of an 18 November 1766 letter from Praslin to M. le

Controlleur general and a 21 December 1766 letter from L'Averdy to the Duc d'Aiguillon, Rennes, 9 May 1767, ADF, C82; and Providence, *CR*, 415.

15. A circular from the bishop of Dol in Brittany, for example, reprinted a note from foreign affairs secretary Louis-Phélypeaux, comte de Saint-Florentin, with instructions from Louis XV, 1 February 1766, ADIV, G164.

16. This rough estimate comes from adding population figures cited in Régent, *La France et ses esclaves*, 335–337. It does not take into account the black slaves in France's Indian Ocean colonies.

17. The 4th edition of the *Dictionnaire de l'Académie française*, published in 1762, clarifies under the listing "nègre, esse": "to treat someone like a negro, that is to say, to treat someone like a slave." For further discussion, see Valensi and Delesalle, "Le Mot 'nègre,'" 79–104. On the popularization of Georges-Louis Leclerc, comte de Buffon's ideas in eighteenth-century France, see Peabody, "There Are No Slaves in France," chap. 4.

18. Unwilling to sanction a Protestant-Catholic union, French officials allowed the woman to stay behind under the pretext of helping the new consul set up his household. On the origins and fates of the 194–200 ransomed slaves and the text of the 28 May 1767 treaty, see app. 2; Penz, *Personnalités et familles*, 167, 170; and Chénier, *Journal du Consulat général de France à Maroc (1767–1785)*, ed. Penz (Casablanca: Imprimeries réunies, 1943), 10, 16–23. Interestingly, it lacks an explicit clause about the redemption of slaves, the inclusion of which, Jacques Caillé conjectures, rulers might have found humiliating. "L'Ambassade du comte de Breugnon à Marrakech en 1767," *Revue d'histoire diplomatique* 75 (1961): 253, 257; 76 (1962): 59–60, 62–63.

19. According to Dean King, the name "Bojador" comes from the Arabic *abu khatar* (father of danger). *Skeletons on the Zahara* (New York: Little, Brown, 2004), 40. On 27 June 1786 marine minister Castries sent orders to the La Rochelle Chamber of Commerce that captains were to sail closer to the Canaries than that portion of the African coast or risk losing their commissions. Archives de la Chambre de Commerce de la Rochelle, carton 19, dossier 1, cited in Penz, *Personnalités et familles*, 57.

20. For letters from consul Louis de Chénier to marine minister Sartine about the fate of Nicolas Crochemare, see Grillon, *Un Chargé d'affaires*, esp. 364–368, 426, 587. On the fates of shipwrecked Europeans, Chénier later wrote (in *Recherches historiques*, 3: 45), "To the shame of humanity, they are sold and resold, and frequently swapped for camels, or other beasts in the markets of the desert."

21. Etienne d'Audibert-Caille, who briefly represented American interests in Morocco, volunteered to trade the enslaved French crewmembers for Moroccan slaves in Malta, a proposal both Dupuy and Chénier rejected. His 1788 memorandum to the Société des amis des noirs was forwarded to the Directory eleven years later. Penz, *Personnalités et familles*, 8–9; Priscilla H. Roberts and James N. Tull, "Moroccan Sultan Sidi Muhammad Ibn Abdallah's Diplomatic Initiatives toward the United States, 1777–1786," *Proceedings of the American Philosophical Society* 143, 2 (1999): 245–247.

22. The ship was headed for "Angola," which as Geggus points out referred to the whole West African coast. "The French Slave Trade: An Overview," *William and Mary Quarterly* 58, 1 (2001): 122.

23. For further analysis of this episode and the resulting Moroccan diplomatic mission, based on a combination of consular correspondence, contemporary newspaper reports, and Dupuy's unpublished journal, see Caillé, "Les Naufragés de la 'Louise.'" Though writing in the 1770s, Chénier referred to the *Louise* as a vessel (*navire*) (e.g., Grillon, *Un Chargé d'affaires*, 405, 409), a decade later he plainly acknowledged its role in "the Negro trade" (*Recherches historiques*, 45 n. 1).

24. Of the *Louise* crewmembers that remained in the desert, one escaped but died of fevers in Mogador and the others were subsequently rescued. Caillé, "Les Naufragés de la 'Louise,'" 249. After his release, Dupuy petitioned for and received a state pension. "Travail du roy," 4 February 1778, AN, AE BIII 14, f. 13.

25. I borrow the phrase "jihad at sea" from Mohamed El Mansour. He argues that redeeming Muslims constituted a form of compensatory holy war during the late eighteenth and early nineteenth centuries (*Morocco in the Reign of Mawlay Sulayman* [Outwell, UK: Middle East and North African Studies Press, 1990], 109–111), whereas Panzac (*CB*, 23) stresses the Moroccan sultan's search for political advantage. Thwarted in France, Mulay Suleiman had better success at the courts of Spain, Naples, and Malta, from which another emissary ransomed 512 slaves in 1782 (Thomas Freller, "'The Shining of the Moon': The Mediterranean Tour of Muhammad Ibn Uthman, Envoy of Morocco, in 1782," *Journal of Mediterranean Studies* 12, 2 [2002]: 307–326; Mariano Arribas Palau, "Rescate de cautivos musulmanes en Malta por Muhammad ibn 'Utman," *Hespéris-Tamuda* 10 [1969]: 273–329) and another 600 in 1789 (Arribas Palau, "Un Rescate de 600 musulmanes cautivos en Malta [1788–1789]," *Hespéris-Tamuda* 25 [1987]: 33–39). On liberation efforts in 1790, see Marie-Joseph Raymond Thomassy, *Des Relations politiques et commerciales de la France avec le Maroc* (Paris: Arthur Bertrand, 1842), 211–212.

26. On the shipwreck of the *Epreuve* in January 1782, see "Enregistrement d'un Consulat fait à Mogador par le nommé Philippe Blanc de Marseille et le Capitaine Jacques Audibert," reprinted in Penz, *Journal du consulat*, 206–211.

27. Follie, *Mémoire d'un françois*, 9–10.

28. While Barbier (*Trois français au Sahara*, 29 nn. 42–43, 28 nn. 34–35) found a dossier on Follie at the Archives nationales (E 186) and biographical details in nineteenth-century bibliographies, he located no information about Saugnier, whose first name remains a mystery. Saugnier's journals were edited and published by Jean-Benjamin Laborde, a court functionary interested in North Africa. In a recent critical edition, François Bessire corroborates Saugnier's account with additional material but maintains that the entire book could not have come from a single source and conjectures that its true author was Follie, in collaboration with Laborde. Bessire, ed., in the preface to Saugnier, *Relations de plusieurs voyages à la côte d'Afrique, à Maroc, au Sénégal, à Gorée, à Galam.*

Tirée des journaux de M. Saugnier (Saint-Etienne: Publications de l'Université de Saint-Etienne, 2005). Whatever the case, someone named Saugnier did sign a deposition taken by vice-consul Henri-Noël Mure in Salé on 22 July 1784 (reprinted in Penz, *Journal du consulat*, 220).

29. Follie's account appeared in English translation in 1786 and in German translation in 1795; a second, truncated French edition came out in 1792. Saugnier's was reprinted under slightly different titles in 1792 and 1799 and immediately translated into English and Dutch.

30. On cannibal legends in early modern Europe, see especially Peter Hulme, *Colonial Encounters: Europe and the Native Caribbean, 1492–1797* (New York: Routledge, 1992), 13–87.

31. Saugnier, *Relations de plusieurs voyages*, 26.

32. Saugnier, *Relations de plusieurs voyages*, 40. On eighteenth-century French depictions of Bedouins, see Sarga Moussa, "Une Peur vaincue: l'émergence du mythe bédouin chez les voyageurs français du XVIIIe siècle," in *La Peur au XVIIIe siècle: discours, représentations, pratiques*, ed. Jacques Berchtold and Michel Porret (Geneva: Droz, 1994), 193–212; and Moussa, "Le Bédouin, le voyageur et le philosophe," *Dix-huitième siècle* 28 (1996): 141–158.

33. Saugnier, *Relations de plusieurs voyages*, 42–66. In Thomas Pellow, *La Relation de Thomas Pellow: une lecture du Maroc au 18 siècle* ([Paris: Editions Recherche sur les civilisations, 1983], 73 n. 29, 86 n. 81), editor Magali Morsy identifies various members of the ben 'Attar clan as high-ranking members of Morocco's Jewish community.

34. Follie, *Mémoire d'un françois*, 92–94.

35. According to Barbier (*Trois français au Sahara*, 34–35 n. 56), the 1799 edition no longer mentioned the slave trade in its title after the 4 February 1794 decree that abolished slavery in the colonies.

36. Saugnier, *Relations de plusieurs voyages*, 165–167.

37. For the notion of colonial knowledge gained through captivity, I am particularly grateful to Snader, *Caught between Worlds*, 62–93.

38. Saugnier, *Relations de plusieurs voyages*, 175–176.

39. Saugnier, *Relations de plusieurs voyages*, 260–341.

40. Saugnier, *Relations de plusieurs voyages*, 327.

41. On Follie, see Barbier, *Trois français au Sahara*, 31–34.

42. Particularly suggestive in linking cannibalism and colonialism are the introductions to two books: Maggie Kilgour, *From Communion to Cannibalism: An Anatomy of Metaphors of Incorporation* (Princeton, NJ: Princeton University Press, 1995); and Kristen Guest, ed., *Eating Their Words: Cannibalism and the Boundaries of Cultural Identity* (Albany: SUNY Press, 2001).

43. According to Robin Blackburn, the export of sugar from British and French slave colonies jumped from 150,000 tons in 1760 to 290,000 tons in 1787–1790. *The Overthrow of Colonial Slavery, 1776–1848* (London: Verso, 1988), 12. Geggus ("The French Slave Trade," 126) writes that at the system's height in 1790, forty thousand black Africans landed in Saint-Domingue alone.

44. *Histoire du Naufrage et de la captivité de M. de Brisson* (1789) also appeared in English, Portuguese, and Polish. Barbier (*Trois français au Sahara*, 37)

identifies the tribes that held Brisson as the Ouled Bou Sba and the Ouled Delim. The captain of Brisson's ship, Pierre Le Turc, believed transferred to Algiers, was still missing in 1792. AN, AE BI 138, f. 49, and BIII 321, f. 155.

45. William Lemprière (*Voyage dans l'empire de Maroc et le royaume de Fez, fait pendant les années 1790 et 1791*, trans. M. de Sainte-Suzanne [Paris: Tavernier, 1801], chap. 10) relates the 1789–1790 Saharan captivity of James Irving (called "Irwing"), whose own writings recently appeared as *Slave Captain: The Career of James Irving in the Liverpool Slave Trade*, ed. Suzanne Schwarz (Liverpool: Liverpool University Press, 2008).

46. Pedagogy, argues Blum, represented one of the primary goals of such accounts in the United States. "Pirated Tars, Piratical Texts: Barbary Captivity and American Sea Narratives," *Early American Studies* 1, 2 (2003): 133–158.

47. Jean-Baptiste-Léonard Durand, *Voyage au Sénégal ou Mémoires historiques, philosophiques et politiques sur les découvertes, les établissemens et le commerce des Européens dans les mers de l'Océan atlantique* . . . (Paris: Henri Agasse, 1802), 2, followed by a summary of Brisson's captivity narrative, 2–20.

48. On ideas for alternative forms of colonization without slavery in South America and Africa, see Bernard Gainot, "La Décade et la 'colonisation nouvelle,'" *Annales historiques de la Révolution française* 339 (2005): 99–116; Røge, "La Clef de commerce"; Plassart, "'Un Imperialiste Liberal'?"; and Marion F. Godfroy-Tayart de Borms, "La Guerre de Sept ans et ses consequences atlantiques: Kourou ou l'apparition d'un nouveau systeme colonial," *French Historical Studies* 32, 2 (2009): 167–191.

49. René Claude Geoffroy de Villeneuve, *L'Afrique, ou histoire, moeurs, usages et coutumes des Africains*, 4 vols. (Paris: Nepveu, 1814), 1: 17, 25, 29, 42, 109–110, 127–129.

50. Théodore Géricault's monumental 1819 painting *Le Radeau de la Méduse*, which now hangs in the Louvre, has generated a massive amount of scholarship. Most inspiring for this chapter was Grigsby, *Extremities*, chap. 4. Savigny and Corréard's first account of what transpired after the sinking of the *Medusa* appeared in the *Journal des débats* (1 October 1816): 4. Their subsequent, more detailed narrative—*Naufrage de la frégate La Méduse* (1817)—was reprinted and expanded in 1818 and 1821 and quickly translated into English, German, and Dutch.

51. Paulin d'Anglas de Praviel, *Relation nouvelle et impartiale du naufrage de la Frégate La Méduse* . . . (Paris: Le Normant, 1818); citations from Jean de Bonnot, ed., *Relation complète du naufrage de la frégate la Méduse* . . . (Paris: J. de Bonnot, 1968), 286–292.

52. Gaspard-Théodore Mollien, *Découverte des sources du Sénégal et de la Gambie en 1818; précédée d'un Récit inédit du naufrage de la Méduse* (Paris: C. Delagrave, 1889), 30.

53. Charlotte-Adelaïde Dard, *La Chaumière africaine, ou, Histoire d'une famille française jetée sur la côte occidentale de l'Afrique, à la suite du naufrage de la frégate La Méduse* (Dijon: Noellat, 1824), 72–73, 92–93.

54. Paul Charles Léonard Alexandre Rang des Adrets [Sander Rang], *Naufrage de "La Méduse," voyage au Sénégal* (Paris: EPI, 1946), 54.

55. M. Brédif, "Le Naufrage de la 'Méduse,'" *Revue de Paris* 14, 3 (1907): 800.

56. Mollien, *Découverte des sources du Sénégal*, 31, 35.

57. Dard, *La Chaumière africaine*, 96, 118–119.

58. Praviel in Bonnot, *Relation complète du naufrage*, 295–296, 299–302.

59. Few scholars have taken notice of Dumont's account. Two who did, Grammont and Emerit, found it riddled with inaccuracies, but neither questioned its basic claims. Yet the letter about "Pierre Eléonore Dumont," which Emerit cites as corroboration, in fact concerned another man. Grammont, "Etudes algériennes: l'esclavage," 4; Thédenat, "Les Aventures de Thédenat, esclave et ministre d'un bey d'Afrique (XVIIIe siècle) (Mémoires de Thédenat)," edited by Emerit, *RA* 92 (1948): 152.

60. Dumont, *Histoire de l'esclavage*, 114–118, 132; Dumont, *Narrative of thirty-four years slavery . . .* , edited by J. S. Quesne (London: Sir Richard Phillips, 1819). The French house that published the first edition in 1819 released three subsequent ones in 1819, 1820, and 1824. A Spanish translation came out in 1829.

61. Dumont, *Histoire de l'esclavage*, 33–34, 38–39.

62. Dumont, *Histoire de l'esclavage*, 43–45, 48–50, 57–58, 73.

63. Dumont, *Histoire de l'esclavage*, frontispieces, 4–6, 14, 67, 132, 141. The Paris *Constitutionnel* ([27 November 1816]: 2) did testify to Dumont's passage through Dijon. From Baltimore, the *Niles' Weekly Register* ([22 August 1818]: 462–463) also reported the strange story of "Peter Dumon" (thanks to Seth Rockman for this reference).

64. Dumont, *Histoire de l'esclavage*, 77, 85, 90.

65. Dumont, *Histoire de l'esclavage*, 1, 50, 96.

66. Dumont, *Histoire de l'esclavage*, 49, 57, 67.

67. Dumont, *Histoire de l'esclavage*, 56–57, 91–93.

68. Dumont, *Narrative of thirty-four years slavery*, vi; *Histoire de l'esclavage*, 10.

69. Castries, "Le Maroc d'autre fois," 852. For additional proposals, see Charles-Roux, *FA*; and Thomson, "Arguments for the Conquest of Algiers."

70. William Sidney Smith, *Mémoire sur la nécessité et les moyens de faire cesser les pirateries des états barbaresques* (Paris: Le Normant, 1814), 1–2.

71. Smith, *Mémoire sur la nécessité*, 2. In their *Réclamation de l'ordre souverain de S.-Jean-de-Jérusalem . . .* ([Paris: Le Normant, 1815], 5), the Knights of Malta stressed the need for an independent corps dedicated to containing this "indestructible race of pirates."

72. At his 29 December 1814 "pic-nic dinner" and ball in Vienna, for example, Smith took collection for a silver candelabrum to grace the Holy Sepulcher in Jerusalem and reminded visitors of the Christian slaves in North Africa. Tom Pocock, *A Thirst for Glory: The Life of Admiral Sir Sidney Smith* (London: Aurum Press, 1996), 221, 224; Pocock, *Breaking the Chains: The Royal Navy's War on White Slavery* (Annapolis, MD: Naval Institute Press, 2006), 16–17; Hilde Spiel, ed., *The Congress of Vienna: An Eyewitness Account*, trans. Richard H. Weber (Philadelphia: Chilton, 1968), 109–113.

73. Examples include London's *Naval Chronicle* 16 (June 1816): 119, 151–152 (cited in Pocock, *Breaking the Chains*, 18–19, 71); the *Niles' Weekly Register* (16 March 1816): 40–41; (24 August 1816): 434; and the London *Times* (2 January 1816): 4; (11 January 1816): 4.

74. Among the names on a list of subscribers to Smith's organization for the years 1815 to 1816 were the emperor of Russia and the kings of Denmark, Prussia, and Bavaria (Bibliothèque de l'Arsenal, Manuscripts, 6339, Papiers de l'abbé Henri Grégoire, 19, ff. 93–94). Asked to become "a member of our illustrious society of knights liberators of slaves in Africa," even the Ottoman sultan responded with an anti-corsairing firman to the Algerian dey. John Barrow, ed., *The Life and Correspondence of Admiral Sir William Sidney Smith*, 2 vols. (London: R. Bentley, 1848), 2: 383; Devoulx, *Le Raïs Hamidou: notice biographique sur le plus célèbre corsaire algérien du XIIIe siècle de l'hégire* . . . (Algiers: Dubos frères, 1858), 62.

75. Thurlow Smith, *Relation des atrocités commises par les corsaires barbaresques* . . . (Paris: A. Belin, n.d.); Chevaliers libérateurs des esclaves blancs en Afrique, *Souscription pour opérer l'abolition de l'esclavage des blancs aussibien que des noirs, en Afrique* . . . ([Paris]: [Les Chevaliers], [1816]).

76. For correspondence from these and other European leaders and diplomats, see Edward Howard, *Memoirs of Sir Sidney Smith, K.C.B., &c.*, 2 vols. (London: R. Bentley, 1839), 2: 314–333; and Laura Veccia Vaglieri, "Santa Sede e Barbareschi dal 1814 al 1819," *Oriente Moderno* 12, 10 (1932): 466 n. 3, 472 n. 1. The letter expressing the position of the Sardinian king was independently printed and circulated. Alessandro Carlo Filiberto, Count de Vallesa, *Lettre de M. le comte de Vallaise, ministre de S.M. le roi de Sardaigne, à Sir Sidney Smith* . . . (Paris: Le Normant, 1814).

77. Domenico Alberto Azuni, *Recherches pour servir à l'histoire de la piraterie* . . . (Genoa: A. Ponthenier, 1816), viii, 109–111, 120, 129–130.

78. *Edinburgh Review* 26 (1816): 452–454, 457.

79. *Quarterly Review* 15 (1816): 140–148. As reported in France's royalist paper, the *Journal des débats* ([19 August 1816]: 1–2), the *Times* ([1 July 1816]: 2; [13 August 1816]: 3) endorsed its competitor's overall argument.

80. Jean Guillaume Hyde de Neuville, *Memoirs of Baron Hyde de Neuville: Outlaw, Exile, Ambassador*, trans. Frances Jackson, 2 vols. (London: Sands, 1913), 2: 6. See also Filippo Pananti, *Relation d'un séjour à Alger . . . les rapports des états barbaresques avec les puissances chrétiennes, et l'importance pour celles-ci de les subjuguer*, trans. Henri La Salle (Paris: Le Normant, 1820), 598.

81. Comte Jules de Polignac, "Note sur l'expédition projetée contre les barbaresques," 19 September 1814, AAE, MD, Afrique, vol. 6, discussed in Charles-Roux, *FA*, 500–503.

82. Henri Grégoire, *De la traite de l'esclavage des noirs et des blancs* (Paris: Adrien Egron, 1815), 57–58 (thanks to Alyssa Sepinwall for this reference).

83. Devoise to Talleyrand, Lazaret of Toulon, 5 September 1814, AE, *CT*, cited in Plantet, *CBT*, 3: 523. Devoise to Talleyrand, Tunis, 22 March 1816, cited in Grandchamp, "Les Français paient la caisse (mai 1816)," *La Tunisie française*, 17 July 1941, in "Autour du Consulat de France à Tunis (1577–1881):

articles parus dans la Tunisie française (novembre 1940–juin 1942)," *Revue tunisienne* 44 (1943): 98–99. The *Journal des débats* of 19 August 1816 repeated this contention, based on remarks in the *Quarterly Review* (15 [1816]: 140–148).

84. François-René de Chateaubriand, "Position relative aux puissances barbaresques," presented to the Chamber of Peers, 9 April 1816, reprinted in *Oeuvres complètes*, 12 vols. (Paris: Garnier, 1859–1861), 8: 237–238.

85. Löwenheim ("Do Ourselves Credit") primarily attributes Britain's decision to assault Algiers to its desire to maintain a consistent policy against the slave trade, whether white or black. Nicholas B. Harding ("North African Piracy, the Hanoverian Carrying Trade, and the British State, 1728–1828," *Historical Journal* 43, 1 [2000]: 25–47) instead stresses the effect of imperial rivalry with France—more specifically, the urge to keep possession of Sardinia as a buffer against French expansion in Italy and to seek recognition from North Africa of British dominion over the Ionian Islands. Shame at the American precedent also served as inspiration, argue Chater (*Dépendance et mutations précoloniales*, 239–241) and Léon Galibert (*L'Algérie, ancienne et moderne depuis les premiers établissements des Carthaginois jusqu'à la prise de la Smalah d'Abd-el-Kader* [Paris: Furne, 1844], 245–246). According to Loth ("Le Pillage de Saint-Pierre," 14), so did continuing horror over the 1798 attack on Sardinia.

86. On the U.S. naval appearance at Algiers in 1815, which compelled the dey to release his American captives, renounce tributes, and pay compensation, see Frank Lambert, *The Barbary Wars: American Independence in the Atlantic World* (New York: Hill and Wang, 2005).

87. Between 158 and 160 slaves, including several women and 2–3 Frenchmen, were captured and the island sacked by a Tunisian fleet flying false English colors in mid-October 1815. Talleyrand to Devoise, Paris, 26 December 1815, reprinted in Plantet, *CBT*, 3: 544–545; Corrado Masi, "Chroniques de l'ancien temps (1815–1859)," trans. Grandchamp, *Revue tunisienne* 21 (1935): 85–89; Panzac, *CB*, 228.

88. Devoise to Talleyrand, Tunis, 25 April 1816, AE, *CT*, reprinted in Plantet, *CBT*, 3: 549–550.

89. Algiers released 357 (out of 1,000) Sicilians and 40 Sardinians; Tunis released 267 Sicilians, 257 Genoese, and, later, 80 Romans; Tripoli released 414 Neapolitans and Sicilians, 140 Sardinians and Genoese, and a few Germans and Romans. K. J. Douglas-Morris and Roger Perkins, *Gunfire in Barbary: Admiral Lord Exmouth's Battle with the Corsairs of Algiers in 1816: The Story of the Suppression of White Christian Slavery* (Havant, UK: Kenneth Mason, 1982), 67–68; Devoise to Richelieu, Tunis, 30 October 1816, reprinted in Plantet, *CBT*, 3: 552.

90. The 31 May 1816 massacre was reported in the *Times* on 21 June 1816 and in the *Journal des débats* on 9 July and 22 September 1817. See also G. A. Jackson, *Algiers: being a complete picture of the Barbary states . . .* (London: R. Edwards, 1817), 286–287.

91. On the 28 August 1816 London meeting, derailed by discussions of Barbary corsairing and captivity, see Daget, *La Répression de la traite des noirs au*

XIXe siècle: les actions des croisières françaises sur les côtes occidentaux de l'Afrique (1817–1850) (Paris: Karthala, 1997), 38.

92. Dumont, *Histoire de l'esclavage*, 110–112. In an account first published in 1817, the Dutch slave Gerrit Metzon described the exodus of, in his estimation, about eleven hundred Christian slaves in much the same terms but, significantly, mentioned nothing about a massacre. "Journal de captivité à Alger (1814–1816)," trans. G. H. Bousquet and G. W. Bousquet-Mirandolle, *Annales de l'Institut d'Etudes orientales de la Faculté des Lettres* 12 (1954): 77–80.

93. The declaration's text was printed in the *Journal des débats* ([5 October 1816]: 1), and the peace treaty signed two days later. Douglas-Morris and Perkins, *Gunfire in Barbary*, 144–145; Panzac, *CB*, 241–243; Archives d'Outre Mer, 15 MI 14, vol. 13, cited in Abdeljelil Temimi, "Le Bombardement d'Alger en 1816," in *Recherches et documents d'histoire maghrébine: la Tunisie, l'Algérie et la Tripolitaine de 1816 à 1871* (Tunis: l'Université de Tunis, 1971), 215 n. 33.

94. This breakdown of national origins was culled from several published lists.

95. For one song example, see Edward Osler, *The Life of Admiral Viscount Exmouth* (London: Smith, Elder, 1835), 342.

96. Abraham V. Salamé, *A narrative of the expedition to Algiers in the year 1816 . . .* (London: J. Murray, 1819), 22–23, 224–225.

97. Smith only learned of Exmouth's success during an audience with Louis XVIII. Though his organization's primary raison d'être had vanished, he continued to sign up "knights liberators" to pursue more modest objectives, including the recovery of shipwreck victims held in the Sahara. Pocock, *A Thirst for Glory*, 228–229; Barrow, *Life and Correspondence*, 374–377; Institution antipirate des chevaliers libérateurs des esclaves blancs en Afrique, *Circulaire aux augustes et illustres fondateurs et autres souscripteurs* ([Paris?]: n.p., [1816]); *Constitutionnel* (13 September 1816): 2. See Pananti's vigorous defense in the 1817 Italian original (*Avventure et Observazioni di Filippo Pananti sopra la coste di Barberia*, 2 vols. [Florence: Léonardo Ciordetti, 1817], 2: 534–535, 544–545), embellished in Edward Blaquière's 1818 English translation, with its more didactive title (*Narrative of a residence in Algiers . . . observations on the relations of the Barbary States with the Christian powers; and the necessity and importance of their complete subjugation* [London: H. Colburn, 1818], xxi, 434–436).

98. Several sources expressed renewed anxiety over the enslavement of European men: the *Constitutionnel* (11 December 1816): 1, 3; the *Journal des débats* (28 May 1817): 2; the London *Times* (6 October 1818): 2; and Devoise to Talleyrand, 15 June 1816, reprinted in Plantet, *CBT*, 3: 550. In 1817, Smith also publicized the case of a Sardinian girl forced to convert and enter the harem of the Algerian dey, who upon his death left evidence of designs on the daughters of the British and Spanish consuls. Playfair, *The Scourge of Christendom*, 282–283.

99. June 1817 memorandum to the German Diet, reprinted in the *Times* (16 July 1817): 3. The French *Journal des débats* ([30 January, 23 February, 28 May, 18 June 1818]: 1; [12 and 13 April, 24 May 1819]: 1) also reported

the spread of plague in North Africa. Meanwhile, Gould Francis Leckie's *An Historical Research into the Nature of the Balance of Power in Europe* ([London: Taylor and Hessey, 1817], 362–363; translated by W. E. Gauttier d' Arc as *De l'Equilibre du pouvoir en Europe* [Paris: Maradan, 1819], 361) linked disease to despotism among the "semibarbarous race of Turcoman Tartars" whose three-hundred-year reign over North Africa had "polluted the soil" and whose "fanaticism and ignorance urge them to refuse all rational precautions against a contagious disease."

100. News of consular murder was reported in the *Times* on 7 June 1817 (2) and confirmed on 10 June 1817 (2) by a letter from Smith. The *Journal des débats* picked up the story the following February and discredited it by the end of the month ([5 and 15 February 1818]: 1; [20 February 1818]: 2). See also Barrow, *Life and Correspondence*, 378.

101. A royal decree dated 7 January 1817 banned the importation of slaves into the French colonies, a 5 April 1818 law specified penalties, and a 24 June 1818 ordinance established a system of West African coastal patrols to intercept slave traders. These French laws and the phrase from the Great Powers' February 1815 declaration abolishing the slave trade are cited in Paule Brasseur, "Le Sénégal et sa lente intégration au mouvement abolitionniste (1815–1830)," in Bénot and Dorigny, *Rétablissement de l'esclavage*, 377.

102. C[harles] S[icard], *Mémoire sur les états barbaresques, nécessité et moyens de mettre fin à leurs pirateries . . .* (Marseille: Ricard, 1819), 4, 48–51.

103. Address by prime minister Armand-Emmanuel du Plessis, duc de Richelieu, at the Congress of Aix-la-Chapelle, 1818, quoted in Julien, *Histoire d'Algérie contemporaine: la conquête et les débuts de la colonisation*, 2 vols. (Paris: Presses universitaires de France, 1964), 1: 30.

104. Protocol of 20 November 1818 from the Congress of Aix-la-Chapelle, reprinted in Plantet, *CBT*, 3: 563–564 n. 3. The French commander was Admiral Jean Pierre Edmond Jurien de la Gravière, author of *Les Corsaires barbaresques*. For Tripoli's response, see Edgard Le Marchand, *L'Europe et la conquête d'Alger d'après des documents originaux tirés des archives de l'Etat* (Paris: Perin, 1913), 36–37, 41–47; Micacchi, *La Tripolitania sotto il dominio dei Caramanli* (Verbania, Italy: A. Airoldi, 1936), 203–204 n. 2. The episode is also discussed in Charles-Roux, *FA*, 516–520.

105. Dumont, *Histoire de l'esclavage*, 93–96. Pananti's French translator disagreed (*Relation d'un séjour à Alger*, 611), calling Algiers a country that "even a second order power could destroy."

106. Robert Adams, *Nouveau voyage dans l'intérieur de l'Afrique fait en 1810, 1811, 1812, 1813 et 1824 . . .*, trans. le Chevalier de Fransans (Paris: L. G. Michaud, 1817). In a recent critical English edition, Charles Hansford Adams argues convincingly that its details were fabricated and casts doubt on the identity of "Robert Adams." *The Narrative of Robert Adams, a Barbary Captive* (Cambridge: Cambridge University Press, 2005), preface.

107. James Riley, *Naufrage du brigantin américain le Commerce perdu sur la côte occidentale d'Afrique . . .*, trans. M. Peltier, 2 vols. (Paris: Le Normant, 1818). It was bound with excerpts from the Saharan narratives of James Gray

Jackson (1814), Robert Adams (1817), and Hector Black (1815). In addition to these books, the *Nouvelles annales des voyages* (8–9 [1821]: 321–353, 285–312) made available the 1810 English account about Alexander Scott, "Relation de la captivité d'Alexandre Scott chez les Arabes du grand désert pendant une période d'environ six années," originally published by William Lawson and Thomas Stewart Traill, "drawn up through conversations with Scott," as "Account of the Captivity of Alexander Scott among the Wandering Arabs of the Great African Desert . . . ," *Edinburgh Philosophical Journal* 4 (1821): 38–54, 225–235.

108. Cochelet, *Naufrage du brick français*, 1: 22–24, 28–29. Seeking consolation, some of Cochelet's companions observed that their hair "was not entirely woolly"; others remarked that "their skin was less black than that of true negroes." But Cochelet was not convinced. He remained apprehensive about remaining among "such uncivilized hosts."

109. Dumont, *Histoire de l'esclavage*, 143–144; Pananti, *Relation d'un séjour à Alger*, 611.

CHAPTER EIGHT

1. While nineteenth-century explanations for France's Algerian invasion in 1830 (discussed in the introduction) took for granted the notion of conquest as emancipation, later ones (generally brief) highlight shorter-term causes, primarily the desire to wipe away a financial debt and preserve the Bourbon monarchy. See, for example, Julien, *Histoire d'Algérie contemporaine*, vol. 1, chap. 1; John Ruedy, *Modern Algeria: The Origins and Development of a Nation*, 2nd ed. (Bloomington: Indiana University Press, 2005), 45–50.

2. In Britain, the prolific philhellene Edward Blaquière, credited with convincing Lord Byron to volunteer his body along with his pen to the cause (Douglas Dakin, *The Greek Struggle for Independence, 1821–1833* [Berkeley: University of California Press, 1973], 107), had earlier published an epistolary narrative sympathetic to the Christian slaves of Tunis (*Letters from the Mediterranean: Containing a Civil and Political Account of Sicily, Tripoly, Tunis, and Malta: with Biographical Sketches*, 2 vols. [London: H. Colburn, 1813], esp. 2: 205–218) and translated Pananti's pro-colonial Algerian captivity account from Italian (*Narrative of a residence in Algiers* [1818]). In France, the travel writings of ex-Tripolitan slave François Pouqueville (*Voyage à Morée . . .* , 3 vols. [Paris: Gabon, 1805] and *Voyage dans la Grèce . . .* , 5 vols. [Paris: Firmin Didot, 1820–1821]) inspired Graecophile poetry and painting. Nina M. Athanassoglou-Kallmyer, *French Images from the Greek War of Independence, 1821–1830: Art and Politics under the Restoration* (New Haven, CT: Yale University Press, 1989), 15.

3. On the ideological origins of French philhellenism and its articulations in travel writing and philosophy, see Dimitri Nicolaïdis, *D'une Grèce à l'autre: représentations des Grecs modernes par la France révolutionnaire* (Paris: Les Belles lettres, 1992); and Olga Augustinos, *French Odysseys: Greece in French Travel Literature from the Renaissance to the Romantic Era* (Baltimore: Johns Hopkins University Press, 1994).

4. *Constitutionnel* (3 July 1822), cited in Athanassoglou-Kallmyer, *French Images*; Boime, *Art in an Age of Counterrevolution*, 202.

5. William St. Clair, *That Greece Might Still Be Free: The Philhellenes in the War of Independence* (London: Oxford University Press, 1972), 80–81; Consul Francis Werry to Levant Company, Smyrna, 2 and 17 May 1822, in Philip Pandely Argenti, ed., *The Massacres of Chios Described in Contemporary Diplomatic Reports* ([London]: John Lane, 1932), 38–39. In 1823 England undertook a mission to release the Greek slaves from Tunis; Polignac asked French consul general Mathieu de Lesseps to intercede on behalf of the Danes. G. Davies, "Greek Slaves at Tunis in 1823," *English Historical Review* 34 (1919): 84–89.

6. Victor-Joseph Jouy and Antoine Jay, *Salon d'Horace Vernet. Analyse historique et pittoresque des quarante-cinq tableaux exposés chez lui en 1822* (Paris: Ponthieu, 1822), 51, cited in Grigsby, *Extremities*, 293, 367 n. 23.

7. The ordinance, registered on either 16 or 18 January, sought to halt a practice condemned by the liberal *Constitutionnel* on 25 January 1823. In their correspondence with Ottoman and Tunisian authorities, English officials insisted on putting Greek captives in the category of "white slaves" rather than allowing them to be considered domestic servants. Under intense pressure, the bey of Tunis finally agreed that until the cessation of hostilities, he would treat the sixty to seventy Greeks in his possession as prisoners of war rather than slaves. Davies, "Greek Slaves," 84–89.

8. Pierre Echinard, *Grecs et philhellènes à Marseille de la Révolution française à l'Indépendance de la Grèce* (Marseille: P. Echinard, 1973), 185.

9. For a fuller articulation of this reading of Delacroix's *Chios*, see Grigsby, *Extremities*, chap. 5. See also Athanassoglou-Kallmyer, *French Images*, 29–35; and Elizabeth Fraser, *Delacroix, Art and Patrimony in Post-Revolutionary France* (Cambridge: Cambridge University Press, 2004), chap. 2, who puts greater emphasis on the sexual pollution of Christian (white) families and French paternalism in seeking to protect them.

10. Chateaubriand, "Note sur la Grèce" (1825), in *Oeuvres complètes*, 5: 45.

11. Chateaubriand, "Avant-propos," *Itinéraire de Paris à Jérusalem* (Paris: Didier, 1848), 1: 17.

12. Chateaubriand, "Opinion sur le projet de loi relative à la répression des délits commis dans les échelles du Levant," Address to the Chamber of Peers, Paris, 13 March 1826, reprinted in *Oeuvres complètes*, 5: 56–58. According to Chateaubriand, Christian ship captains who preached abolition while abetting the enslavement of Greeks were hypocrites and traitors to their religion and their race. "What double abomination!" he thundered in the preface to the third edition of "Note sur la Grèce" (1827), reprinted in *Oeuvres complètes*, 5: 42.

13. Alexis de Noailles made his proposal on 23 May 1826, and debate continued into the following day. Hyde de Neuville, General Sébastiani, Baron de Puymaurin, Casmir Périer, and Benjamin Constant spoke in favor of the proposal. The baron de Dudon, Bacot de Romand, and finance minister de Villèle spoke against it. *AP*, 2nd ser. (1881), 48: 231–248.

14. That Sidney Smith's "noble enterprise" had "become an object of derision" before "fall[ing] into oblivion" pained Raynal's posthumous editor Peuchet

(*Histoire des Deux Indes*, 4th ed., 12 vols. [Paris: A. Costes, 1820–1821], 11: 58, cited in Bénot, "Un Préhistoire de l'expédition d'Alger," 542). Writing in 1826, he saw a glimmer of hope that "a day will come . . . where France will no longer have to groan knowing that it suffers the existence of a market where Frenchmen are sold at its doors." Peuchet in Raynal, *Histoire philosophique* (1826), 1: 110.

15. "Quêtes en faveur des grecs," *La Pandore* (6 June 1826), cited in Fridériki Tabaki-Iona, *Poésie philhellénique et périodiques de la Restauration* (Athens: Société des archives helléniques, littéraires et historiques, 1993), 66–67.

16. The overall take was thirty-six thousand francs, close to the amount sought by Noailles. Loukia Droulia, Dimitri Nicolaïdis, Fani-Maria Tsigakou, et al., eds., *La Grèce en révolte: Delacroix et les peintres français, 1815–1848* (Paris: Réunion des musées nationaux, 1996), 54; Grigsby, *Extremities*, 309.

17. The archbishop of Corfu, cited in a letter from Comité grec delegate J. G. Eynard in *Journal des débats* (11 June 1826). Also see an eyewitness account of mass enslavement published in *L'Etoile* (13 June 1826), reprinted in Dimakis, *La Presse française face à la chute de Missolonghi et à la bataille navale de Navarin: Recherches sur les sources du philhellénisme français* (Salonika, Greece: Institute for Balkan Studies, 1976), 293–295.

18. This interpretation of Delacroix's *Missolonghi* relies on Grigsby, *Extremities*, chap. 6.

19. For example, A. Guiraud, "Missolonghi," printed in the *Journal des débats* (10 June 1826): 1a–b, cited in Boime, *Art in an Age of Counterrevolution*, 219, and reprinted in Dimakis, *Presse française*, 291–292; E. Michelet, "La Jeune captive de Missolonghi," printed in the *Journal politique et littéraire de Toulouse* (13 July 1826), cited in Tabaki-Iona, *Poésie philhellénique*, 106–107. Most famously, Victor Hugo's "Les Têtes du Sérail"—printed in the *Journal des débats* on June 13, quoted in Grigsby, *Extremities*, 298, 368 n. 41—described "impure eunuchs" as witnesses to "the hour when [the sultan's] foul pleasures / Have reclaimed our sisters, our daughters, our wives."

20. Dominique Cante and Loukia Droulia (in Droulia, Nicolaïdis, et al., *Grèce en révolte*, 74, 251) cite both the *Indicateur* (21 May 1827) and the Salon, which showed that the painting by Charles Brocas opened in November 1827.

21. Daget, "L'Abolition de la traite des noirs en France de 1814 à 1831," *Cahiers d'études africaines* 11, 41 (1971): 43–44; *Journal de la Société de la morale chrétienne* 9 (1829): 18–19, reporting on a 27 September 1827 meeting in Marseille, cited in Grigsby, *Extremities*, 309, 370 n 71. Also Echinard, *Grecs et philhellènes*, 227–228.

22. Hirschberg, *A History of the Jews*, 2: 30, 32; Morton Rosenstock, "The House of Bacri and Busnach," *Jewish Social Studies* 14 (1952): 343–364.

23. Marc-Antoine Jullien, "Grèce: Situation morale du pays—Premiers besoins de la nation grecque, voeux et espérances de ses amis," *Revue encyclopédique* 36 (October 1827): 234.

24. News of the victory at Navarino on 20 October 1827 reached France in early November. *Constitutionnel* (10 November 1827): 1a–b; *Gazette de France* (14 November 1827): 3a, reprinted in Dimakis, *Presse française*, 344, 367.

25. The *Journal des débats* printed several stanzas of Hugo's poem "Navarin" (published whole in *Les Orientales* [1829]) on December 1. Cited in Grigsby, *Extremities*, 305–306, 370 n. 65.

26. René Julien Chatelain, *Mémoire sur les moyens à employer pour punir Alger et détruire la piraterie des puissances barbaresques* . . . (Paris: Anselin, 1828), 2.

27. Marseille delegate Pierre-Honoré de Roux to the Chamber of Deputies, 13 May 1828, *AP*, 2nd ser. (1883), 54: 31–32, also discussed in Julien, "La Question d'Alger devant les Chambres sous la Restauration," *RA* 63 (1922): 299–303.

28. Julien, "La Question d'Alger," *RA* 63 (1922): 425–450. See also his *Histoire d'Algérie contemporaine*, 1: 32–37.

29. Polignac, Paris, 4 February 1830, AAE, MD, vols. 5, 6, 7, cited in Esquer, *Le Commencements d'un empire: la prise d'Alger*, 2nd ed. (Paris: Larose, 1929), 145.

30. Jacques W. MacCarthy in Thomas Shaw, *Voyage dans la régence d'Alger* . . . , trans. MacCarthy (Paris: Marlin, 1830), 5–6. According to Thomas Xavier Bianchi, who accompanied the final French delegation to Algiers in 1829 and in 1830 translated American consul William Shaler's 1826 Algerian narrative as *Esquisse de l'état d'Alger, considéré sous les rapports politique, historique et civil* . . . (Paris: Ladvocat, 1830), "The public is avidly looking for works about [Algiers]. . . . Only this eagerness can explain the appearance during the past two months of diverse writings about Algiers, one of which is already in its third edition" (i–ii). The book in question was MacCarthy's new French rendering of Thomas Shaw, *Travels, or observations relating to several parts of Barbary and the Levant* (Oxford: Printed at the Theatre, 1738), with additional passages from Laugier de Tassy (1725), Walter Croker (*The cruelties of the Algerine pirates* . . . , 3rd ed. [London: W. Hone, 1816]), and Pananti (1817).

31. Charles X to the Chamber of Deputies, Paris, 2 March 1830, reprinted in *AP*, 2nd ser. (1886), 61: 543.

32. At the 10 July 1829 session of the Chamber of Deputies, Alexandre de Laborde had insisted, "If necessity requires it, we will undertake this expedition which, executed with care and sufficient forces, cannot help but succeed. France will thus accomplish under this reign what was vainly attempted by Charles V, Louis XIV, and the naval forces of England; she will show Europe that when one insults an old lion, he can still shake his mane and make laurels fall." Cited in *Au Roi et Aux Chambres, sur les véritables causes de la rupture avec Alger et sur l'expédition qui se prépare* (Paris: Truchy, 1830), 44–45, 81–82, 103–104, 109. This important brochure is analyzed by Thomson, "Arguments for the Conquest of Algiers," 112; and Sessions, "Making Colonial France: Culture, National Identity and the Colonization of Algeria, 1830–1851," PhD diss., University of Pennsylvania, 2005, 41. According to Julien, citing Nettement, Laborde's pamphlet was released in April 1830. "L'Opposition et la guerre d'Alger à la veille de la conquête," *Bulletin trimestriel de la Société de géographie et d'archéologie d'Oran* 61 (1921): 23 n. 3.

33. Haussez to the Chamber of Deputies, Paris, 16 March 1830, *AP*, 2nd ser.

(1886), 61: 594. This phrasing was repeated in the official *Moniteur* of 20 April 1830.

34. *Journal des débats* (7 March 1830), cited in Julien, "L'Opposition et la guerre d'Alger," 28.

35. On the liberal side: *Courrier français* (16 and 26 April, 6 June 1830); *National* (27 May 1830); Laborde, *Au Roi et Aux Chambres*, 46. Responding to liberal critiques: *Moniteur* (8 July 1830); *Aperçu historique, statistique et topographique sur l'état d'Alger . . .*, 3rd ed. (Paris: C. Picquet, 1830), 31–32. See also Julien, *Histoire d'Algérie contemporaine*, 1: 47.

36. Sessions, *Empire of Virtue*, chap. 1.

37. *Journal du Havre* (1830), cited in Esquer, *Le Commencements d'un empire*, 196–197; Jean-Charles-Léonard Simonde de Sismondi, "De l'expédition contre Alger," *Revue encyclopédique* 46 (May 1830): 273–296, esp. 279–284.

38. M. Renaudot, *Alger. Tableau du royaume, de la ville d'Alger et de ses environs . . .*, 4th ed. (Paris: P. Mongie ainé, 1830), 176, 181. This book, which went through four French editions in 1830, was also translated into German and published in Stuttgart and Leipzig. See also Capitaine Contremoulins, *Souvenir d'un officier français, prisonnier en Barbarie pendant les années 1811, 1812, 1813 et 1814 . . .* (Paris: Anselin, 1830), esp. 11–13.

39. Edward W. Said, *Orientalism* (New York: Vintage Books, 1979), 81–88. Among the writers accompanying the invading army was Jean-Toussaint Merle. Known in Paris as a playwright, he carried a printing press to Algiers, produced two numbers of *L'Estafette d'Alger* and recounted his Algerian experience in *Anecdotes historiques et politiques pour servir à l'histoire de la Conquête d'Alger en 1830* (Paris: G.-A. Dentu, 1831). Julien, *Histoire d'Algérie contemporaine*, 1: 49–58. See also Esquer, "Les Débuts de la presse algérienne: Jean-Toussaint Merle et 'L'Estafette de Sidi Ferruch,'" *RA* 70 (1929): 254–318.

40. Alexandre-Martin Lomon, *Souvenirs de l'Algérie: captivité de l'amiral Bonard et de l'amiral Bruat en Algérie* (Paris: J. Hetzel, 1863). The journal of the English consul records a total of 109 killed, with 85 heads and 73 prisoners arriving in Algiers on 20 and 21 May, respectively. Henri Noguères, *L'Expédition d'Alger 1830* (Paris: René Julliard, [1962]), 126.

41. Proclamation by General Louis de Bourmont, 10 May 1830, cited in A. M. Perrot, *La Conquête d'Alger, ou Relation de la campagne d'Afrique . . .* (Paris: H. Langlois fils, 1830), 38.

42. Merle, *Anecdotes historiques et politiques*, 127.

43. *Abrégé ou aperçu de l'histoire d'Alger et des nations barbaresques en général . . .* (Bordeaux: J. Lebreton, 1830), x. This anonymous author, plagiarizing Sidney Smith (unless it is Sidney Smith) and Chateaubriand, remarked that "various governments in abolishing the black slave trade seem to have indicated the object of a greater triumph for our emulation: ceasing the slavery of whites, which is no less odious and criminal" (xiv). He also noted, "It is in France that the First Crusade was preached; it is in France that should be raised the standard of the last" (xv).

44. Perrot (*La Conquête d'Alger*, 86–88) provides a list of eighty shipwreck victims found in the bagne on 23 May 1830.

45. Théodore de Quatrebarbes, *Souvenirs de la campagne d'Afrique*, 2nd ed. (Paris: G.-A. Dentu, 1831), 63. The figure recorded in the Tunisian registers is cited in Boyer, *La Vie quotidienne à Alger à la veille de l'intervention française* (Paris: Hachette, 1963), 24; and in multiple modern accounts (see app. 1). The *Journal des débats* reported the deliverance of the Toulonnais on 22 July 1830.

46. George Simon Frederick Pfeiffer, *Meine Reisen und meine fufjaehrigen Gefangenschaft in Argier* (Giessen, 1832), which describes the author's captivity from 1825 to 1830, was translated into English in 1832 and Dutch in 1834 and 1835 but only paraphrased in French during the 1870s: "La Prise d'Alger racontée par un captif," ed. and trans. Alfred Michel, *RA* 19 (1875): 471–482; 20 (1876): 30–41, 112–127, 220–231. My citations come from the American edition: *The Voyages and Five Years' Captivity in Algiers of Doctor G. S. F. Pfeiffer . . .* , trans. Israel Daniel Rupp (Harrisburg, PA: John Winebrenner, 1836), 223, 239.

47. Emile Barbier and Louis Prévost, *Sur la conquête d'Alger: le baron d'Haussez, ministre de la marine de Charles X, et le vicomte de Saint-Priest, duc d'Almazan, ambassadeur de France en Espagne* (Rouen: J. Lecerf, 1930), 53; *Journal des débats* (10 July 1830); *Constitutionnel* (11 July 1830), cited in Julien, *Histoire d'Algérie contemporaine*, 1: 61–62.

48. The "Jacobins" of the *Cercle Pythéas* celebrated the conquest of Algiers on July 11. Pierre Guiral, "L'Opinion marseillaise et les débats de l'entreprise algérienne (1830–1841)," *Revue historique* 214 (1955): 10.

49. Barbier and Prévost, *Sur la conquête d'Alger*, 54. *Gazette de France* (13 July 1830), translated and reprinted in the *Times* (15 July 1830): 4. Smith's presence was also noted by *L'Ami de la religion* 64 (1830): 315.

50. According to the "Image of France, 1795–1880" database (http://www .lib.uchicago.edu/efts/ARTFL/projects/mckee/), the colored engraving received authorization for publication on 24 July 1830. The engraver, Jean-Pierre-Marie Jazet, also popularized the works of Jacques-Louis David, Antoine-Jean Gros, and Horace Vernet.

Bibliography

MANUSCRIPTS

Departmental Archives

Archives départementales des Bouches-du-Rhône (Marseille), Séries B, 2B, 9B, C, 5E, 14E, 139E, 193E, H
Archives départementales de Charente-Maritime (La Rochelle), Série B
Archives départementales des Côtes-d'Armor (Saint-Brieuc), Série 20 G
Archives départementales du Finistère (Quimper), Séries B, C, E
Archives départementales de la Gironde (Bordeaux), Séries IB, B
Archives départementales de l'Hérault (Montpellier), Séries C, H, L, 39 M, Sète CC and GG, Frontignan, II 8
Archives départementales d'Ille-et-Vilaine (Rennes), Séries B, G, C, 3E
Archives départementales de Loire-Atlantique (Nantes), Série B, C, G, H
Archives départementales du Morbihan (Vannes), Série H
Archives départementales de la Vendée (La Roche-sur-Yon), Série E

Municipal Archives

Archives communales d'Aix-en-Provence, Séries BB, CC, GG
Archives communales d'Hennebont, Série GG
Archives communales de Saint-Malo, Séries BB, GG
Archives communales de Six-Fours, Série GG
Archives communales de Toulon, Séries BB, DD, FF, GG
Archives municipales de Bayonne, Séries BB, CC, GG
Archives municipales de Fréjus, Série BB
Archives municipales de Marseille, Série AA, BB, DD, EE, FF, GGL, HH
Archives municipales de Nantes, Série CC, EE, GG, HH
Archives municipales de Rennes, Série BB

Other Archives

Archives des Affaires étrangères (Paris), Mémoires et documents Afrique, Algérie, Maroc, Tunisie, Turquie, France; Affaires diverses politiques France; Contrôle des étrangers

Archives de la Basilique de Sainte-Anne d'Auray, Registre des procès-verbaux de faveurs signalées, 1625–1687

Archives de la Chambre de commerce de Marseille, Séries F, G, H, J

Archives nationales (Paris), Séries G (G5, G7, G8), L, LL, M, MM, S, A (A2, A3, A4), Marine (B1, B2, B3, B7), 171 AP (Papiers Barras), 284 AP (Archives Sièyes), Affaires Etrangères (BI, BIII)

Bibliothèque nationale (Paris), Fonds françaises, Nouvelles acquisitions françaises, Collection Clairambault, Collections Colbert, Collections Dupuy, Collection Moreau, Fonds latins

Centre des Archives diplomatiques de Nantes, Archives des postes diplomatiques et consulaires, Alger, Tripoli de Barbarie, Protectorat Tunisie

Service historique de l'Armée de Terre (Vincennes), Série A1

Service historique de la Marine à Toulon, Série O

Service historique de la Marine à Vincennes, Manuscrits

PUBLISHED PRIMARY SOURCES

Newspapers

Affiches et annonces de Toulouse
Associated Press
Constitutionnel
Courrier français
Gazette de France
Journal des débats
Journal de Paris
Mercure de France

Mercure françois
Mercure gallant
Moniteur
National
Niles' Weekly Register
Times (London)
Washington Post

Barbary Captivity Narratives

Adams, Robert. *The Narrative of Robert Adams, a Barbary Captive.* Edited by Charles Hansford Adams. Cambridge: Cambridge University Press, 2005.

———. *Nouveau voyage dans l'intérieur de l'Afrique, fait en 1810, 1811, 1812, 1813 et 1824 ou Relation de Robert Adams, Américain des Etats-Unis: Contenant les détails de son naufrage sur la côte occidentale de l'Afrique; de sa captivité, pendant trois années, chez les Arabes du Sahara ou Grand Désert; et de son séjour dans la ville de Tombuctoo.* Translated by le Chevalier de Frasans. Paris: L. G. Michaud, 1817.

Aranda, Emanuel d'. *Les Captifs d'Alger.* Edited by Latifa Z'Rari. Paris: Jean-Paul Rocher, 1997.

———. *Relation de la captivité du Sieur Emanuel d'Aranda: ou sont descriptes les miseres, les ruses, & les finesses des esclaves & des corsaires d'Alger; ensemble les conquestes de Barberousse dans l'Afrique, & plusieurs autres particularites digne de remarque.* Paris: Gervais Clovsier, 1657.

Arreger, Jean-Victor-Laurent de. "Un Captif à Alger au XVIIIe siècle." Edited by L. Pingaud. *Revue historique* 13 (1880): 325–339.

Barbier, Maurice, ed. *Trois français au Sahara occidental (1784–1786).* Paris: L'Harmattan, 1984.

Bidé de Maurville, François Joseph Hippolyte. *Relation de l'affaire de Larache.* Amsterdam: n.p., 1775.

Bonnot, Jean de, ed. *Relation complète du naufrage de la frégate la Méduse, faisant partie de l'expédition du Sénégal en 1816: témoignages écrits de MM. A. Corréard, et H. Savigny, d'Anglas de Praviel, Paul C. L. Alexandre Rang des Adrets, dit Sander Rang, tous rescapés du naufrage.* Paris: J. de Bonnot, 1968.

Brassard, Isaac. "Relation de la captivité de M. Brassard à Alger." Edited by H. de France. *Bulletin de la Société de Histoire du Protestantisme français* 27 (1878): 349–355.

Brisson, Pierre-Raymond de. *Histoire du naufrage et captivité de Monsieur de Brisson, Officier de l'Administration de Colonies.* Edited by Attilio Gaudio. Paris: Nouvelles éditions latines, 1984.

———. *Histoire du Naufrage et de la captivité de M. de Brisson, officier d'administration des Colonies: avec la description des deserts d'Afrique, depuis le Senegal jusqu'a Maroc.* Geneva: Barde, Manget; Paris: Royez, 1789.

Brooks, Francis. *Navigation faite en Barbarie, contenant diverses choses curieuses, et de quelle manière il fut pris sur mer par trahison et mené en esclavage, les aventures qu'il y a eues et comment, après dix années de servitude, il s'échappa.* Utrecht: Etienne Neaulme, 1737.

Carey, Matthew. *A Short Account of Algiers, and of its several wars against Spain, France, England, Holland, Venice, and other powers of Europe, from the usurpation of Barbarossa and the invasion of the Emperor Charles V. to the present time. With a concise view of the origin of the rupture between Algiers and the United States . . . To which is added, a copious appendix, containing letters from Captains Penrose, M'Shane, and sundry other American captives, with a description of the treatment those prisoners experience.* 2nd ed. Philadelphia: Matthew Carey, 1794.

Caroni, F. "Relation d'un court voyage d'un antiquaire amateur (F. Caroni) surpris par les corsaires, conduit en Barbarie et heureusement rapatrié (1804)." Edited and translated by Marthe Conor and Pierre Grandchamp. *Revue tunisienne* 23 (1916): 287–294, 393–403; 24 (1916): 30–54, 96–122.

Chastelet des Boys, René. *L'Odyssée ou Diversité d'Avantures, Rencontres et Voyages en Europe, Asie et Affrique. Divisée en quatre parties.* 2nd ed. La Flèche: Gervais Laboë, 1665.

———. "L'Odyssée ou diversité d'aventures, encontres en Europe, Asie et Afrique par le sieur du Chastelet des Boys [1665]." Edited by Louis Piesse.

Revue africaine 10 (1866): 91–101, 257–268; 11 (1867): 157–167; 12 (1868): 14–32, 350–363, 436–454; 13 (1869): 193–199; 14 (1870): 371–383.

Chetwood, William Rufus, and Richard Castelman. *Les Voyages et aventures du capitaine Robert Boyle; où l'on trouve l'histoire de Mademoiselle Villars, avec qui il se sauva de Barbarie; celle d'un Esclave Italien, & celle de Dom Pedro Aquilo, qui fournit des exemples des coups les plus surprenans de la fortune; avec La relation du voyage & de la conservation miraculeuse du sieur Castelman, où l'on voit, une description de la Pensylvanie, & de Philadelphie, sa capitale.* Amsterdam: Westeins & Smith, 1730.

Cochelet, Charles. *Naufrage du brick français, La Sophie, perdu le 30 mai 1819, sur la côte occidentale d'Afrique, et captivité d'une partie des naufragés dans le Désert de Sahara; avec de nouveaux renseignemens sur la ville de Timectou.* 2 vols. Paris: P. Mongie ainé, 1821.

Dard, Charlotte-Adelaïde. *La Chaumière africaine, ou, Histoire d'une famille française jetée sur la côte occidentale de l'Afrique, à la suite du naufrage de la frégate La Méduse.* Dijon: Noellat, 1824.

Dumont, Pierre Joseph. *Histoire de l'esclavage en Afrique: (pendant trente-quatre ans) de P. J. Dumont, natif de Paris, maintenant à l'Hospice royal des incurables.* Edited by J. S. Quesne. Paris: Pillet ainé, 1819.

———. *Narrative of thirty-four years slavery and travels in Africa.* Edited by J. S. Quesne. London: Sir Richard Phillips, 1819.

Durand, Jean-Baptiste-Léonard. *Voyage au Sénégal ou Mémoires historiques, philosophiques et politiques sur les découvertes, les établissemens et le commerce des Européens dans les mers de l'Océan atlantique: depuis le Cap-Blanc jusqu'à la rivière de Serre-Lionne inclusivement; suivis de la Relation d'un voyage par terre de l'île Saint-Louis à Galam; et du texte arabe de Trois traités de commerce faits par l'auteur avec les princes du pays.* Paris: Henri Agasse, 1802.

Fercourt, Claude Auxcousteaux de. *Relation de l'esclavage des sieurs de Fercourt et Regnard, pris sur mer par les corsaires d'Alger (1678–79).* Toulouse: E. Privat, 1905.

Follie, Adrien Jacques. *Mémoire d'un françois qui sort de l'Esclavage.* Amsterdam and Paris: Laporte, 1785.

Foucques, Guillaume. *Mémoires portants plusieurs advertissemens presentez au Roy par le Cappitaine Foucques, Capitaine ordinaire de sa Maiesté en la marine du Ponant. Apres estre delivré de captivité des Turcs, pour le soulagement des François, & autres nations Chrestiennes, marchands, & matelots, qui se trafiquent sur mer: Avec une description des grands cruautez, & prises des Chrestiens par les pyrates Turcs de la ville de Thunes, par l'intelligence qu'ils ont auec certains François renegats.* Paris: Guillaume Marrette, 1609.

Galland, Antoine. *Histoire de l'esclavage d'un marchand de la ville de Cassis, à Tunis.* Edited by Catherine Guénot and Nadia Vasquez. Paris: Editions de la bibliothèque, 1992.

Gallonyé, Jean. *Histoire d'une esclave qui a été quatre années dans les prisons de Sallé en Afrique: Avec un abbregé de la vie du Roy Taffilette.* Lyon: Rolin Glaize, 1679.

Gramaye, Jean-Baptiste. *Alger XVIe–XVIIe siècle: journal de Jean-Baptiste Gramaye, 'évêque d'Afrique.'* Edited by Abd El Hadi Ben Mansour. Paris: Editions de Cerf, 1998.

Knight, Francis. *A relation of seaven yeares slaverie under the Turkes of Argeire, suffered by an English captive merchant. Wherein is also conteined all memorable passages, fights, and accidents, which happined in that citie, and at sea with their shippes and gallies during that time. Together with a description of the sufferings of the miserable captives under that mercilesse tyrannie. Whereunto is added a second booke conteining a discription of Argeire, with its originall manner of government, increase, and present flourishing estate.* London: T. Cotes, 1640.

Laranda, Viletta. *Neapolitan Captive: Interesting Narrative of the Captivity and Suffering of Miss Viletta Laranda, A Native of Naples, Who, with a Brother, was a passenger on board a Neapolitan vessel wrecked near Oran, on the Barbary coast, September 1829, and who soon after was unfortunately made a Captive of by a wandering clan of Bedowen Arabs, on their return from Algiers to the Deserts—and eleven months after providentially rescued from Barbarian Bondage by the commander of a detached Regiment of the victorious French Army.* New York: Charles C. Henderson, 1830.

Lettre d'un comédien, à un de ses amis, touchant sa captivité et celle de vingt-six de ses camarades, chez les corsaires de Tunis, et ce qu'ils sont obligés de faire pour adoucir leurs peines; avec une description historique et exacte de Gênes, d'où ils sortaient lorsqu'ils ont été pris. Paris: Pierre Clément, 1741.

Lisdam, Henry du. *L'Esclavage du brave chevalier François de Vintimille, des comtes de Marseille et Olieule, à présent commandeur de Planté et Cadaillon, où l'on peut voir plusieurs rencontres de guerre dignes de remarque.* Lyon: C. Morillon, 1608.

Lomon, Alexandre-Martin. *Souvenirs de l'Algérie. Captivité de l'amiral Bonard et de l'amiral Bruat en Algérie.* Paris: J. Hetzel, 1863.

Marot, Louis. *Relation de quelques aventures maritimes de L.M.P.R.D.G.F [Louis Marot, pilote réal des galères de France].* Paris: Gervais Clouzier, 1673.

Mascarenhas, João de Carvalho. *Esclave à Alger: récit de captivité de João Mascarenhas (1621–1626).* Edited by Paul Teyssier. Paris: Chandeigne, 1993.

Metzon, Gerrit. "Journal de captivité à Alger (1814–1816)" [1817]. Translated by G. H. Bousquet and G. W. Bousquet-Mirandolle. *Annales de l'Institut d'Etudes orientales de la Faculté des Lettres* 12 (1954): 43–83.

Mollien, Gaspard-Théodore. *Découverte des sources du Sénégal et de la Gambie en 1818; précédée d'un Récit inédit du naufrage de la Méduse.* Paris: C. Delagrave, 1889.

Moüette, Germain. *Histoire des conquests de Mouley Archy, connu sous le nom de roy de Tafilet, et de Mouley Ismaël ou Seméin, son frère et son successeur à présent régnant, tous deux rois de Fez, de Maroc, de Tafilet, de Sus, etc., contenant une description de ces royaumes, des loix, des coustumes et des moeurs des habitants, avec une carte du païs, à laquelle on a joint les plans des principales villes et fortresses de Fez, dessinées sur les lieux par le sieur G. Moüette, qui a demeuré captif pendant onze années.* Paris: Edme Couterot, 1683.

————. *Relation de la captivité du Sr Moüette dans les royaumes de Fez et de Maroc, où il a demeuré pendant onze ans. Où l'on voit les Persecutions qui y sont arrivées aux Chrêtiens captifs, sous les Regnes de Mouley Archy, & de Mouley Seméin son Successeur regnant aujourd'huy, et les travaux ordinaires ausquels on les occupe. Avec un Traité du Commerce, & de la maniere que les Negocians s'y doivent comporter: Ensemble des termes principaux de la Langue qui est la plus en usage dans le Païs.* Paris: Jean Cochart, 1683.

Nicholson, Thomas. *An Affecting Narative of the Captivity and Sufferings of Thomas Nicholson [A Native of New Jersey] Who has been Six Years a Prisoner among the Algerine, And from whom he fortunately made his escape a few months previous to Commodore Decatur's late Expedition. To which is added, a Concise Description of Algiers of the Customs, Manners, etc of the Natives—and some particulars of Commodore Decatur's Late Expedition, Against the Barbary Powers.* Boston: G. Walker, 1816.

Ockley, Simon. *An account of southwest Barbary: containing what is most remarkable in the territories of the king of Fez and Morocco. Written by a person who had been a slave there . . . To which are added, two letters. . . .* London: J. Bowyer and H. Clements, 1713.

Pananti, Filippo. *Avventure et Observazioni di Filippo Pananti sopra la coste di Barberia.* 2 vols. Florence: Léonardo Ciordetti, 1817.

————. *Narrative of a residence in Algiers: comprising a geographical and historical account of the regency; biographical sketches of the dey and his ministers; anecdotes of the late war; observations on the relations of the Barbary States with the Christian powers; and the necessity and importance of their complete subjugation.* Translated by Edward Blaquière. London: H. Colburn, 1818.

————. *Relation d'un séjour à Alger, contenant des observations sur l'état actuel de cette régence, les rapports des états barbaresques avec les puissances chrétiennes, et l'importance pour celles-ci de les subjuguer.* Translated by Henri La Salle. Paris: Le Normant, 1820.

Pellow, Thomas. *La Relation de Thomas Pellow: une lecture du Maroc au 18e siècle.* Edited by Magali Morsy. Paris: Editions Recherche sur les civilisations, 1983.

Pfeiffer, G. Simon Friedrich. "La Prise d'Alger racontée par un captif." Edited and translated by Alfred Michel. *Revue africaine* 19 (1875): 471–482; 20 (1876): 30–41, 112–127, 220–231.

————. *The Voyages and Five Years' Captivity in Algiers, of Doctor G. S. F. Pfeiffer: With an Appendix, Giving a True Description of the Customs, Manners, and Habits of the Different Inhabitants of the Country of Algiers.* Translated by Israel Daniel Rupp. Harrisburg, PA: J. Winebrenner, 1836.

Phelps, Thomas. *A True Account of the Captivity of Thomas Phelps at Machaness in Barbary: and of his strange escape in company of Edmund Baxter and others, as also of the burning two of the greatest pyrat-ships belonging to that kingdom in the River of Mamora upon the thirteenth day of June 1685.* London: H. Hills jun., 1685.

Quartier, Antoine. "Antoine Quartier (vers 1632–1702): voyageur, captif, mercédaire; un précurseur de l'orientalisme, au XVIIème siècle." Edited by Hughes Cocard. *Analecta mercedaria* 22 (2003): 123–301.

———. *L'Esclave religieux et ses avantures.* Paris: Daniel Hortemels, 1690.

Rang des Adrets, Paul Charles Léonard Alexandre [Sander Rang]. *Naufrage de "La Méduse," voyage au Sénégal.* Paris: E.P.I., 1946.

Regnard, Jean-François. *La Provençale* [1709]. In *Les Oeuvres de M. Regnard.* 5 vols. Paris: Veuve de P. Ribou, 1731.

Riley, James. *Naufrage du brigantin américain le Commerce perdu sur la côte occidentale d'Afrique au mois d'août 1815; accompagné de la Description de Tombuctoo et de la grande ville de Wassanah, inconnue jusqu'à ce jour.* Translated by M. Peltier. 2 vols. Paris: Le Normant, 1818.

Rocqueville, [François] le sieur de. *Relations des moeurs et du gouvernement des Turcs d'Alger. Par le sieur de Rocqueville.* Paris: Olivier de Varennes, 1675.

[Saint-Sauveur, Jacques Grasset de, with [?] Sylvain Maréchal]. *La Belle captive, ou Histoire véritable du naufrage & de la captivité de Mlle. Adeline, comtesse de St. Fargel, âgée de 16 ans, dans une des parties du royaume d'Alger, en 1782.* Paris: Remy & Musier, 1785; 2nd ed., Paris: J. B. G. Musier, 1786.

Saugnier. *Relations de plusieurs voyages à la côte d'Afrique, à Maroc, au Sénégal, à Gorée, à Galam.* Edited by François Bessire. Saint-Etienne: Publications de l'Université de Saint-Etienne, 2005.

———. *Relations de plusieurs voyages à la côte d'Afrique, à Maroc, au Sénégal, à Gorée, à Galam, etc. Avec des détails intéressans pour ceux qui se destinent à la traite de nègres, de l'or de l'ivorie, etc. Tirés des journaux de M. Saugnier, qui a été long-temps Esclave des Maures, et de l'Empereur de Maroc. . . .* Paris: Gueffier jeune, 1791.

Savigny, Jean Baptiste Henri, and Alexandre Corréard. *Naufrage de la frégate la Méduse, faisant partie de l'expédition du Sénégal, en 1816: relation contenant les événements qui ont eu lieu sur le radeau, dans le désert de Saaara, à Saint-Louis, et au camp de Daccard; suivie d'un examen sous les rapports agricoles de la partie occidentale de la côte d'Afrique, depuis le Cap-Blanc jusqu'à l'embouchure de la Gambie.* Paris: Hocquet, 1817.

Scott, Alexander. "Relation de la captivité d'Alexandre Scott chez les Arabes du grand désert pendant une période d'environ six années." *Nouvelles annales des voyages, de la géographie, de l'histoire et de l'archéologie* 8–9 (1821): 321–353, 285–312. Originally published as William Lawson and Thomas Stewart Traill, "Account of the Captivity of Alexander Scott among the Wandering Arabs of the Great African Desert for a period of nearly Six Years. With Geographical Observations on his Routes, and Remarks on the Currents of the Ocean on the North-Western Coast of Africa, by Major Rennell, F.R.S. &c&c&c." *Edinburgh Philosophical Journal* 4 (1821): 38–54, 225–235.

Thédenat, [Pierre-Paul]. "Les Aventures de Thédenat, esclave et ministre d'un bey d'Afrique (XVIIIe siècle) (Mémoires de Thédenat)." Edited by Marcel Emerit. *Revue africaine* 92 (1948): 143–184, 331–362.

Voyage dans les états barbaresques de Maroc, Alger, Tunis et Tripoly; ou lettres d'un des captifs qui viennent d'être rachetés par MM. les Chanoines réguliers de la Sainte-Trinité; suivies d'une notice sur leur rachat, & du Catalogue de leurs noms. Paris: Guillot, 1785.

Barbary Redemption Narratives

[Arnoux, Nazaire, and Jean Héron]. La Miraculeuse rédemption des captifs faite à Salé, coste de Barbarie, sous les heureux auspices du sacre du Roy très chrestien par les religieux de l'Ordre de la Très-Sainte-Trinité, vulgairement appellez Maturins. Paris: Julien Jacquin, 1654.

Auvry, Michel. Le Miroir de la charité chrestienne ou Relation du voyage que les Religieux de l'Ordre de Nôtre Dame de la Mercy du Royaume de France ont fait l'année dernière 1662. en la ville d'Alger, d'où ils ont ramené environ une centaine de Chrétiens esclaves. Aix-en-Provence: Jean-Baptiste & Etienne Roize, 1663.

Busnot, Dominique. Histoire du regne de Mouley Ismael, roy de Maroc, Fez, Tafilet, Souz, &c. De la revolte & fin tragique de plusieurs de ses enfans & de ses femmes. Des affreux supplices de plusieurs de ses officiers & sujets. De son genie, de sa politique & de la maniere dont il gouverne son empire. De la cruelle persecution que souffrent les esclaves chrétiens dans ses etats, avec le recit de trois voyages à Miquenez & Ceuta pour leur redemption, & plusieurs entretiens sur la tradition de l'eglise pour leur soulagement. Rouen: Guillaume Bouhart, 1714. Abridged version published as Histoire du règne de Moulay Ismaïl. Paris: Mercure de France, 2002.

Caraffa, Vincent de, ed. "Journal du rachat des captifs d'Alger et de Tunis en 1779." Bulletin de la Société des sciences historiques et naturelles de la Corse 62–63 (1886): 165–218.

Carneaux, Etienne. Les Captifs délivrés par les RR. PP. de l'ordre de la très sainte Trinité, dits Mathurins, présentés au roi le treizième septembre 1654. Paris: François Noël, 1654.

[Comelin, François, and Philémon de La Motte]. Etat des Royaumes de Barbarie, Tripoly, Tunis et Alger, contenant l'Histoire naturelle et Politique de ces Pais, la maniere dont les Turcs y traitent les esclaves, comme on les rachete, & diverses avantures curieuses. Avec la Tradition de l'Eglise pour le rachat ou le soulagement des Captifs. Rouen: Guillaume Behourt, 1703.

[Comelin, François, Philémon de La Motte, and Joseph Bernard]. Voyage pour la redemption des captifs aux royaumes d'Alger et de Tunis, fait en 1720. Paris: Louis-Anne Sevestre, 1721.

Dan, Pierre. Histoire de Barbarie et de ses corsaires, divisée en six livres, où il est traité de leur Gouvernemens, de leurs Moeurs, de leurs Cruautés, de leurs Brigandages, de leurs Sortilèges & de plusieurs autres particularités remarquables. Ensemble des grandes misères & des cruels tourmens qu'endurent les Chrestiens Captifs parmi ces Infidèles. Paris: Pierre Rocolet, 1637; 2nd ed. 1649.

Dathia, François. Abrégé de la vie de S. Pierre Nolasque, fondateur et religieux de l'ordre de Notre-Dame de la Mercy de la Rédemption des captifs. Paris: Louis Feugé, 1631.

Desmay, Louis. *Relation nouvelle et particulière du voyage des RR. PP. de la Mercy aux royaumes de Fez et du Maroc, pour la rédemption des chrétiens captifs négociée en l'année 1681 avec Moulé Ismaël, roy de Fez et de Maroc régnant aujourd'huy*. Paris: Veuve Gervais Clouzier, 1682.

Egreville, Edmond. *La Vive Foy et le recit fidelle de ce qui c'est passé dans le voyage de la Redemption des Captifs François, faicte en Alger par les Peres de l'Ordre de Nostre-Dame de la Mercy Redemption des Captifs, les mois de Mars & d'Avril 1644*. Paris: Louis Feugé, 1645.

Fau, Barthélémy, and Paschal La Caze. *Rédemption faite au royaumes de Maroc et d'Alger, depuis le mois de septembre 1727 jusqu'au mois de Mai 1729*. Reprinted in Charles Braquehaye, "Description de la ville d'Alger, écrite à 1729, par le R. P. Fau." *Revue tunisienne* 14 (1907): 237–243.

Hérault, Lucien. *Les Larmes et clameurs des Chrestiens, François de nation, captifs en la ville d'Alger en Barbarie. Addresses à la Reyne Regente, Mère de Louis Roy de France et de Navarre*. Paris: D. Houssaye, 1643.

———. *Les Victoires de la charité. La Relation des Voyages de Barbarie faits en Alger par le R.P. Lucien Herault, pour le Rachapt des François Esclaves aux années 1643. & 1645. Ensemble ce qui s'est passé en sa Captivité, Emprisonnement & Mort arrivée audit Alger le 28. Janvier 1646*. Paris: Louis Boulanger, 1646.

———. *Récit veritable du arrivée au port de Marseille, de cinquante esclaves chrestiens françois de nation racheptez des mains des infidèles turcs et barbares, par les religieux reformez de l'ordre de la Ste Trinité*. Paris: Jean Petrimal, 1643.

Héron, Jean. *Relation du voyage que R.P. Héron supérieur-ministre de Chateaubriand en Bretagne, a fait en la ville d'Alger, côte de Barbarie; d'où il a retiré cinquante-cinq captifs de la main des Turques et remis en liberté*. Paris: Julien Jaquin, 1660.

Jehannot, Guillaume. *Voyage à Constantinople pour le rachat des captifs*. Paris: Veuve Delormel, 1732.

La Faye, Jean de, Denis Mackar, Augustin d'Arcisas, and Henry Le Roy. *Relation en forme du journal du voiage pour la redemption des captifs aux roiaumes de Maroc et d'Alger pendant les annees 1723, 1724 & 1725*. Paris: Louis Sevestre, 1726.

———. *Relation en forme du journal du voyage pour la redemption des captifs aux roiaumes de Maroc et d'Alger pendant les annees 1723, 1724 et 1725*. Edited by Ahmed Farouk. Paris: Bouchène, 2000.

Michelin, Pierre, Guillaume Basire, Antoine Dachier, and Victor Le Beau. *Le Tableau de Piété envers les Captifs: ou Abregé contenant, avec plusieurs remarques, deux Relations de trois Redemptions de Captifs faites en Afrique, aux Villes & Royaumes de Tunis & d'Alger en Barbarie, és années 1666. & 1667. par les Religieux de l'Ordre de la Tres-Sainte Trinité (apellez vulgairement à Paris Maturins), des quatre Provinces qui composent leur Chapitre General en France. Ensemble Le Martyre du Venerable Frere Pierre de la Conception, Religieux du mesme Ordre, souffert audit Alger le 19. Juin de l'année derniere 1667*. Châlons-en-Champagne: Jean Bouchard, 1668.

[Néant, Nolasque]. *Relation de ce qui s'est passé dans les trois voyages que les religieux de l'Ordre de Nostre-Dame de la Mercy ont faits dans les etats du roy de Maroc pour la Redemption des Captifs en 1704, 1708 & 1712.* Paris: Antoine-Urbain Coustelier, 1724.

Relation succincte de plusieurs avantures arrivées dans le cours de la redemption des captifs, suivie depuis M.DCC.IV. jusqu'à M.DCC.XII. n.p.: n.p., n.d.

Relation véritable, contenant le rachapt de plusieurs captifs qui estoient detenus a rancon dans la ville d'Alger: Avec une lettre envoyée par l'Ambassadeur de France, touchant les grandes persecutions que les Turcs font souffrir aux Chrestiens. Paris: Veuve Du Pont, 1672.

Thulden, Theodor van. *Revelatio ordinis s[anctis]s[i]mae Trinitatis redemptionis captivorum sub Innocentio tertio, anno 1198.* Paris: n.p., 1633.

Slave Catalogs and Processions

Avis au public touchant la rédemption des captifs du royaume de Maroc. Paris: Antoine-Urbain Coustelier, 1723.

Catalogue des esclaves chrestiens, rachetez aux mois de fevrier et mars de cette Année 1681. aux Villes de Fez, Miguenz, Salé, et Toutoüan en Barbarie, par les Peres de la Mercy Redemption des Captifs, deputez de la Congregation de Paris, & de la Province de Guyenne, & Languedoc, partis de Marseille, avec le Passeport que le Roy leur accorda en Octobre dernier, & qui après avoir consolé les Captifs en differentes Villes du Royaume de Fez & Maroc, & en avoir racheté soixante & quinze [corrected 18], tous François, sont arrivez à Marseille le 26. jour de May. Paris: Christophe Journel, 1681.

L'Eminente charité de la Rédemption des Captifs, faicte par les Religieux de l'Ordre de la Saincte Trinité, & du nombre des Esclaves Racheptez, par ledit Ordre, presenté a nostre Saint Pere le Pape Urbain VIII. Avignon: Jacques Bramereau, 1644.

L'Eminente charité de la Rédemption des captifs faite par les religieux de l'Ordre de la Sainte Trinité, dits les Mathurins, en l'année 1641. Ensemble l'Ordre de la Procession d'iceux captifs faite à Paris le 23 mai 1641. Paris: Veuve Jean Petitpas, 1641.

Liste des captifs françois rachetés dans le royaume d'Alger, le mois d'Octobre 1750, par les RR. PP. Jacques Houllier & Melchior Heraud, députés de l'ordre royal & militaire de Notre-Dame de la Mercy, institué pour la rédemption de captifs. Rennes: Joseph Vatar, 1751.

Liste des Esclaves Chrestiens rachetez dans les Royaumes de Maroc & d'Alger en 1728 & 1729 par les Reverends Peres Germain Beguin & Jean Olive, Commissaires Généraux députez de la Congregation de l'Ordre de Notre-Dame de la Mercy, Rédemption des Captifs, du Couvent de Paris. Paris: Louis Sevestre, 1729.

Liste des esclaves françois rachetés par les charités travaux des Reverends Peres de l'Ordre de la Saincte Trinité des Provences de France. Qui ont este a leur arrivée dans cette ville d'Arles accompagnés des Religieux de la Communauté de ladite Ville, & des Messieurs les Penitens noirs aggregés a la Con-

frerie de la Redemption rendre graces dans la venerable Eglise Metropolitaine St. Thropine avec grande sollemnité, ou le R.P. Estienne Boymaux de l'Ordre des Freres Mineurs a fait l'exhortation sur le sujet de cette eminente charité le 29 septembre mil six cens soisante & quinze. Arles: Claude et Jacques Mesnier, 1675.

Liste des Esclaves rachetés a Tunis et a Alger. Et conduits en Corse par les RR. PP. André Gache, Procureur-Général de la Rédemption, Ministre de la Maison de Pontharme, & Charles-Gaspard Dorvaus, Docteur de Sorbonne, Ministre de la Maison de Metz, & Provincial de la Province de Champagne, Commissaires Députés de l'Ordre des Chamoines Réguliers de la Ste. Trinité, & les RR. PP. Dominique Paul de Villa, Docteur en Théologie, Provincial de la Province de Toulouse, & Cloud Chevillard, Vicaire-Général de la Con- grégation de Paris, Commissaires Députés de l'Ordre de Notre-Dame de la Mercy, en 1779. Paris: P. M. Delaguette, 1779.

Liste des LXX captives françois rachetés par les RR. PP. Pierre-George, Minis- tre de Beauvoir, sur Mer, de l'Ordre de la Tres-Sainte Trinité, & Jean-Jacques Aubert, Prieur du Collége de l'Ordre de Notre-Dame de la Mercy, Docteurs de Sorbonne, Commissaires députés desdits Ordres, réunis pour la Rédemp- tion des Captifs, dans le Royaume de Maroc, Fez & Sallé. Paris: Veuve Delormel et fils, 1759.

Noms des cent cinq esclaves chrestiens racheptés au Royaume d'Alger en l'année 1750, par les RR. PP. Alexandre la Maniere, Jean Montour & Mi- chel Gairoard, Commissaires Générauc des Chanoines Réguliers de l'Ordre de Sainte Trinité, Redemption des Captifs, dits Mathurins. Paris: Veuve Delormel, 1750.

Les Noms et qualitez de quatre-vingt-dix-sept chrestiens captifs, racheptez cette année par les Religieux de l'ordre de Nostre Dame de la Merci. Paris: Bureau d'Adresse, 1634.

Ordre de la marche de la procession des captifs rachetés par les deux ordres de la Rédemption, scavoir celui des Chamoines Réguliers de la Sainte Trinité dit Mathurins et celui de Notre-Dame de la Mercy sortant de l'Abbaye de St-Anthoine pour se rendre en l'Eglise Cathédrale de Notre-Dame de Paris, le 17 octobre 1785. Paris: Basset, 1785.

Ordre de la procession des captifs français rachetés en la ville de Constantino- ple en 1731 par les religieux Mathurins de l'ordre de la Sainte-Trinité, qui se fera le mardi 15 janvier 1732. . . . Liste des esclaves chrétiens rachetés à Con- stantinople par le R. P. Guillaume Jehannot. . . . Paris: Veuve Delormel, 1732.

Ordre de la procession des captifs rachetés au royaume d'Alger, au mois de novembre 1729, par les religieux Maturins de l'ordre de la Sainte Trinité; qui se fera le . . . 28 mars 1730, aux . . . Minimes de la place royale. Paris: Veuve Delormel, 1730.

Ordre de la Procession des esclaves rachetés au Royaume d'Alger, par les Reli- gieux de la Trinité, & Redemption des Captifs, dits Mathurins. Qui se sera le Lundy 13 May 1720, en l'Abbaye Royale de Saint Antoine, & le lende- main matin en l'Eglise des R.P. Feuillants ruë Saint Honnore. Paris: C. L. Thiboust, 1720.

Ordre de la Procession des esclaves rachetés aux Royaumes de Maroc, &
d'Alger, par les Religieux Trinitaires ou Maturins. Qui se sera Lundi 22. Octobre 1725. en l'Abbaye Royale de Saint Antoine, & le lendemain matin en
l'Eglise des RR. PP. Theatins. Paris: V. Lamesle & P. Delormel, 1725.

Ordre de la Procession et de la Marche des quarante-six Captifs rachetez dans
les Royaumes de Maroc et d'Alger, par le Religieux de la Mercy, Rédemption
des Captifs. Qui se sera Lundy prochain dix-huit du présent Mois de Juillet,
& les deux jours suivans; le Lundy dix-huit Juillet, de l'Eglise de l'Abbaye de
saint Antoine à Nostre-Dame; le Mardy dix-neuf du même Mois, en l'Eglise
de saint Sulpice, & le Mercredy vingt en l'Eglise de saint Eustache. Paris:
Louis Sevestre, 1729.

Ordre de la Procession et de la marche des soixante-six Captifs rachetés dans
le Royaume d'Alger, au mois d'Octobre 1750, par les Religieux de l'Ordre
Royal et Militaire de Notre-Dame de la Mercy, institué pour la Redemption
des Captifs. Paris: C. F. Simon, 1750.

L'Ordre et la marche de la procession des captifs françois rachetés dans le royaume du Maroc, le 23 Août 1765, par les ordres de la Sainte-Trinité, dit des
Mathurins, & de Notre-Dame de la Merci, qui se fera Lundi 20 Janvier 1766,
en l'Eglise de l'Abbaye Royale de Sainte Antoine. Le Mardi 21 dudit mois, en
celle de l'Ordre Royal & Militaire de Notre-Dame de la Merci, Rédemption
des Captifs, au Marais. Et le Mercredi 22 dudit mois, en celle des Chanoines
Réguliers de la Sainte-Trinité, Rédemption des Captifs, dits Mathurins. Paris:
P. de Lormel, 1765.

L'Ordre et la marche de la Procession des Captifs, rachetés dans le Royaume de
Maroc, le 25 Août 1737. Qui se fera cejourd'huy Mercredy 4 Décembre 1737,
en l'Eglise des RR. PP. Celestins, le lendemain matin en l'Eglise des RR. PP.
Jacobins de la rüe S. Honoré; par les Religieux Maturins, rüe S. Jacques, &
les Religieux de la Mercy, Redemption des Captifs, au Marais. Paris: Veuve
Delormel, 1737.

L'Ordre et la Marche de la Procession des Captifs Rachetés dans le Royaume
de Maroc, le 11 Août 1754. par les Ordres réunis de la Sainte Trinité, &
de Notre-Dame de la Mercy; Qui se fera ce jourd'hui Samedi 14 Décembre
1754. en l'Eglise des R.R. P.P. Minimes. Le Lundi suivant 16 dudit mois, en
celle de l'Ordre Royal & Militaire de Notre-Dame de la Mercy, au Marais. Et
le Mardi 17. en celles des Chanoines Réguliers de la Sainte Trinité, Redemption des Captifs, dits Mathurins. Paris: Veuve Delormel, 1754.

Redemption des Captifs: Complainte sur les maux qu'endurent les Chrétiens Captifs, sou la domination des Mahométan barbares, & sur le rachat
qui vient d'être fait par les Chanoines Réguliers de la Sainte-Trinité, dits
Mathurins, & les Reverens Peres de la Merci, de trois cent treize Captifs
Français, venant du Royaume d'Alger, dont une partie doivent venir incessam-
ment à Paris, pour y marcher en Procession solennellement. Paris: Valleyre
l'ainé, 1785.

La Rédemption des captifs faite par les religieux de l'ordre de la Sainte-Trinité,
dit les Mathurins. Ensemble l'ordre de la processions d'iceux captifs faite à
Paris le 20 mai 1635. Paris: Jean Petit-Pas, 1635.

Redemption des quatre-vingts captifs françois. Ordre de la Procession qui a été faite a Lyon le 2 Décembre 1765, par MM. les Chanoines Réguliers de la Sainte Trinité & les Religieux de la Mercy, à l'occasion des quatre-vingts Esclaves François rachetés a Maroc par les deux Ordres de la Rédemption. Lyon: Aimé Delaroche, 1765.

Relation de la Procession solennelle que les Reverends Peres de l'Ordre de la Trinité & Redemption des Captifs ont fait a Montpellier le 23. juin avec quarante-cinq Esclaves rachetez dans le Royaume de Tunis, au mois de Mai de cette année 1720. par le R.P. Joseph Bernard, Religieux du mesme Ordre. Toulouse: Claude-Gilles Lecamus, 1720.

Additional Published Primary Sources

Abrégé ou aperçu de l'histoire d'Alger et des nations barbaresques en général, par un ami de la justice et de l'humanité. Bordeaux: J. Lebreton, 1830.

Africanus, Leo. *Description de l'Afrique.* Edited by Alexis Epaulard. 2 vols. Paris: Librairie d'Amérique et d'Orient, 1980.

Angers, François d'. *Histoire de la Mission des Pères capucins de la province de Touraine au royaume de Maroque en Afrique, par les ordres du R.P. Joseph de Paris, prédicateur capucin, commissaire apostolique des missions étrangères.* Niort: Veuve Jean Bureau, 1644.

Aperçu historique, statistique et topographique sur l'état d'Alger, à l'usage de l'armée expéditionnaire d'Afrique, avec cartes, vues et costumes; rédigé au dépot général de la guerre. 3rd ed. Paris: C. Picquet, 1830.

Archives historiques du département de la Gironde 49 (1914): 366–369.

Archives parlementaires de 1787 à 1860: recueil complet des débats législatifs & politiques des chambres françaises, imprimé par ordre du Sénat et de la Chambre des députés. 2 ser. 99 vols. Paris: P. Dupont, 1879–1914.

Arcos, Thomas d'. "Lettres inédites de Thomas d'Arcos à Peiresc." Edited by Philippe Tamizey de Larroque. *Revue africaine* 32 (1888): 161–195, 289–302.

Arcs, Anselme des. *Mémoires pour servir à l'histoire de la mission des Capucins dans la régence de Tunis, 1624–1865.* Edited by Apollinaire de Valence. Rome: Archives générales de l'ordre des Capucins, 1889.

Argenti, Philip Pandely, ed. *The Massacres of Chios Described in Contemporary Diplomatic Reports.* [London]: John Lane, 1932.

Armand, Jean [Mustapha]. *Voyages d'Afrique faits par le commandement du Roy où sont contenus les navigations Français entreprises en 1629 et 1630, sous la conduite de M. le commandeur de Razilly, ès costes occidentales des royaumes de Fez et de Maroc; le traité de paix fait avec les habitants de Salé et le délivrance de plusieurs esclaves français. Ensemble la description des susdits royaumes, villes, coutumes, religions, moeurs et commodités de ceux dudit pays. Le tout illustré de curieuses observations par Jean Armand, Turc de nation, chirurgien de Mgr le comte de Soissons.* Paris: Nicolas Trabouilliet, 1631.

Arvieux, Laurent d'. *Memoires du chevalier d'Arvieux, envoyé extraordinaire du Roy à la Porte, Consul d'Alep, d'Alger, de Tripoli, & autre Echelles du Le-*

vant contenant Ses Voyages à Constantinople dans l'Asie, la Syrie, la Pales-
tine, l'Egypte & la Barbarie, la description de ces Païs, les Religions, les
moeurs, les Coûtumes, le Négoce de ces Peuples, & leurs Gouvernemens,
l'Histoire naturelle & les événemens les plus considérables, recüeillis de ses
Memoires originaux, & mis en ordre avec des réfléxions. Edited by Jean-
Baptiste Labat. 6 vols. Paris: Charles-Jean-Baptiste Delespine, 1735.

Aulard, François-Alphonse. *Recueil des actes du Comité de salut public: avec*
la correspondance officielle des représentants en mission et le registre du
Conseil exécutif provisoire. 27 vols. Paris: Imprimerie nationale, 1889–1923.

Avenel, Denis Louis Martial, ed. *Lettres, instructions diplomatiques et pa-*
piers d'Etat du Cardinal de Richelieu. 8 vols. Paris: Imprimerie impériale,
1853–1877.

'Ayyashi, Abu Salim 'Abd Allah ibn Muhammad. *Voyages dans le sud de*
l'Algérie et des états barbaresques de l'ouest et de l'est. Translated by Adrien
Berbrugger. Paris: Imprimerie royale, 1846.

Azuni, Domenico Alberto. *Recherches pour servir à l'histoire de la piraterie,*
avec un précis des moyens propres à l'extirpation des pirates barbaresques.
Genoa: A. Ponthenier, 1816.

[Bachaumont, Louis Petit de]. *Mémoires secrets pour servir à l'histoire de la*
République des Lettres en France depuis 1762 jusqu'à nos jours. 36 vols.
London: J. Adamson, 1777–1789.

Barbot, Jean. *Barbot on Guinea: The Writings of Jean Barbot, West Africa,*
1678–1712. 2 vols. Edited by Paul Edward Hedley Hair, Adam Jones, and
Robin Law. London: Hakluyt Society, 1992.

Bérenger, Laurent Pierre. *Les Soirées provençales ou Lettres de M. Bérenger*
écrites à ses amis pendant ses voyages dans sa patrie. 3 vols. Paris: Nyon aîné,
1786.

Blaquière, Edward. *Letters from the Mediterranean: Containing a Civil and*
Political Account of Sicily, Tripoly, Tunis, and Malta: with Biographical
Sketches. 2 vols. London: H. Colburn, 1813.

Blyth, Stephen Cleveland. *History of the War between the United States and*
Tripoli, and Other Barbary Powers to which is prefixed, A Geographical,
Religious and Political History of the Barbary States in General. Salem, MA:
Salem Gazette Office, 1806.

Boniface, Hyacinthe. *Arrests notables de la cour du Parlement de Provence,*
cours des comptes, aydes & finances du même païs. 5 vols. Lyon: Veuve
d'Horace Molin, 1708.

Bossuet, Jacques Bénigne. *Oraisons funèbres de Bossuet.* Edited by Abel François Villemain and Jean Joseph François Dussault. Paris: Firmin Didot, 1858.

Bourde de La Rogerie, Henri, and J. Lemoine, eds. *Inventaire sommaire des*
Archives départementales antérieures à 1790, Finistère. 4 vols. Quimper:
A. Jaouen, 1889–1933.

Bourdeille, Pierre de. *Oeuvres complètes de Pierre de Bourdeille, seigneur*
de Brantôme, ed. Ludovic Lalanne. 11 vols. Paris: Veuve J. Renouard,
1864–1882.

Bourjon, François. *Le Droit commun de la France, et la Coutume de Paris réduits en principes, tirés des loix, des Ordonnances, des Arrêts, des Juris-consultes & des Auteurs, & mis dans l'ordre d'un Commentaire complet & méthodique sur cette Coutume. Contenant, dans cet ordre, les usages du Châtelet sur les liquidations, les comptes, les partages, les substitutions, les dîmes, & toutes autres matières.* 2nd ed. 2 vols. Paris: Grangé et Cellot, 1770.

Bréard, Charles. *Documents relatifs à la marine normande et ses armements au XVIe siècles, pour le Canada, l'Afrique, les Antilles, le Brésil et les Indes.* Rouen: A. Lestringant, 1889.

Brèves, François Savary de. *Relation des voyages de Monsieur de Breves tant en Grece, Terre-Saincte et Aegypte, qu'aux royaumes de Tunis & Arger. Ensemble, Un traicté faict l'an 1604. entre le Roy Henry le Grand, & l'Empereur des Turcs, et trois discours dudit sieur.* Paris: Nicolas Gasse, 1628.

Busquet, Raoul, ed. *Inventaire sommaire des Archives départementales antérieures à 1790, Bouches-du-Rhône.* 4 vols. Marseille: Archives des Bouches-du-Rhône, 1932.

Buvat, Jean. *Journal de la régence (1715–1723).* Edited by Emile Campardon. 2 vols. Paris: H. Plon, 1865.

Castries, Henry de, Philippe de Cossé Brissac, and Pierre de Cenival, eds. *Les Sources inédites de l'histoire du Maroc de 1530 à 1845.* 3 ser. 30 vols. Paris: Paul Geunther, 1905–1960.

Charrière, Ernest, ed. *Négociations de la France dans le Levant, 1515–1589.* 4 vols. Paris: Imprimerie nationale, 1848–1860.

Chateaubriand, François-René de. *Oeuvres complètes.* 12 vols. Paris: Garnier, 1859–1861.

Chatelain, René Julien. *Mémoire sur les moyens à employer pour punir Alger et détruire la piraterie des puissances barbaresques; précédé d'un précis historique sur le caractère, les moeurs et la manière de combattre des Musulmans habitant la côté d'Afrique, et d'un coup-d'oeil sur les expéditions françaises tentées contre eux à diverses époques.* Paris: Anselin, 1828.

Chénier, Louis de. *Journal du Consulat général de France à Maroc (1767–1785).* Edited by Charles Penz. Casablanca: Imprimeries réunies, 1943.

———. *Recherches historiques sur les Maures, et histoire de l'empire du Maroc. . . .* 3 vols. Paris: author, 1787.

Chevaliers libérateurs des esclaves blancs en Afrique. *Souscription pour opérer l'abolition de l'esclavage des blancs aussi-bien que des noirs, en Afrique: extrait du rapport général. Paris, ce 22 juin, 1816.* [Paris]: [Les Chevaliers], 1816.

Cheynet, Pierre-Dominique, ed. *Les Procès-verbaux du Directoire Exécutif, an V–an VIII: inventaire des registres des délibérations et des minutes des arrêtés, lettres et actes du Directoire faisant suite au Recueil des actes du Directoire Exécutif d'Antonin Debidour.* 10 vols. Paris: Centre historique des archives nationales, 2000.

Claude, Jean. *Les Plaintes des protestans, cruellement opprimez dans le royaume de France.* Cologne: Pierre Marteau, 1686; reprint, London: Delage, 1707.

Clément, Pierre, ed. *Lettres, instructions et mémoires de Colbert.* 7 vols. Paris: Imprimerie impériale, 1861–1873.

Contremoulins, Capitaine. *Souvenir d'un officier français, prisonnier en Barbarie pendant les années 1811, 1812, 1813 et 1814: situation civile et militaire de ce pays, moeurs, gouvernement, armée, positions militaires, productions indigènes, climat, moyens de s'en rendre maître et de s'y maintenir, plan d'attaque, de conquête et de colonisation, projet d'organisation d'une armée d'expédition, stratégie nouvelle et seule praticable pour assurer le succès de cette entreprise. Ouvrage indispensable de militaires de tous grades et de toutes armes qui feront partie de l'armée d'expédition d'Alger*. Paris: Anselin, 1830.

Contreras, Alonso de. *The Life of Captain Alonso de Contreras, Knight of the Military Order of St. John, Native of Madrid, Written by Himself (1582 to 1633)*. Translated by Catherine Alison Phillips. New York: A. A. Knopf, [1926].

Correspondance de Napoléon avec le ministre de la marine depuis 1804 jusqu'en avril 1815. 2 vols. Paris: Delloye et V. Lecou, 1837.

Correspondance de Napoléon Ier. 32 vols. Paris: H. Plon, 1858–1870.

Courtilz de Sandras, Gatien. *Mémoires de madame la marquise de Frêne*. Amsterdam: Jean Malherbe, 1701.

Cradock, Anna Francesca. *Journal de Madame Cradock: Voyage en France, 1783–1786*. Translated by O. Delphin Balleyguier. Paris: Perrin, 1896.

Cuvelier, Jean-Guillaume-Antoine. *A-t-il deux femmes? ou les Corsaires barbaresques, mélodrame en 3 actes, paroles de J.-G.-A. Cuvelier et J.-M. B***, musique arrangée par L. Morange*. Paris: Barban, 1803.

Dangeau, Philippe de Courcillon. *Journal du marquis de Dangeau, avec les additions du duc de Saint-Simon*. Edited by Eudore Soulié et al. 19 vols. Paris: Firmin Didot, 1854–1860.

Débezieux, Balthasar. *Arrests notables de la cour du Parlement de Provence, recueillis par feu messire Balthazar Debezieux, seigneur de Valmousse, Conseiller du Roi & Président en la Chambre des Enquêtes au même Parlement. Sur diverses matières ecclésiastiques, civiles & criminelles; avec les motifs des juges qui les ont rendus. Ouvrage divisé en 9 livres qui serviront de continuation aux deux compilations de Boniface. Avec une table des livres, titres, chapitres & paragraphes, & une dernière fort ample des matières par ordre alphabétique. Le tout par le soin de Me Sauveur Eiriés, avocat au même Parlement*. Paris: P. G. Mercier et al., 1750.

Déclaration royale justifiant par le danger barbaresque l'établissement d'une nouvelle escadre de galères. Paris: Estienne Richer, 1637.

Déduit, Frère. *Détail historique et remarquable des peins & de tourmens affreux que les turcs d'Alger, de Tunis & de Maroc font souffrir journellement aux esclaves chrétiens; suivi d'une complainte & d'un choeur triomphal sur la délivrance des captifs rachetés en 1785, par les RR. PP. Mathurins & de la Merci*. Paris: Cailleau, 1785.

Depping, Georg Bernhard, ed. *Correspondance administrative sous le règne de Louis XIV*. 4 vols. Paris: Imprimerie nationale, 1850–1855.

Desfontaines, René Louiche, and Jean-André Peyssonnel. *Voyages dans les Régences de Tunis et d'Alger*. Edited by Adolphe Dureau de la Malle. 2 vols. Paris: Gide, 1838.

Devoulx, Albert. *Les Archives du Consulat général de France à Alger, recueil de documents inédits concernant soit les relations politiques de la France soit les rapports commerciaux de Marseille avec l'ancienne régence d'Alger.* Algiers: Bastide, 1865.

————. [J. M. Haddey]. *Le Livre d'or des israélites algériens: recueil de renseignements inédits et authentiques sur les principaux négociants juifs d'Alger pendant la période turque.* Algiers: A. Bouyer, 1871.

————. *Le Raïs Hamidou: notice biographique sur le plus célèbre corsaire algérien du XIIIe siècle de l'hégire, d'après des documents authentiques et pour la plupart inédits.* Algiers: Dubos frères, 1858.

————. "Le Registre des prises maritimes." *Revue africaine* 15 (1871): 70–79, 149–160, 184–201, 285–299, 341–352, 447–457; 16 (1872): 70–77, 233–240, 340–342.

————. "Relevé des principaux français qui ont résidé à Alger." *Revue africaine* 16 (1872): 357–387, 420–450.

————. *Tachrifat: recueil de notices historiques sur l'administration de l'ancienne Régence d'Alger.* Algiers: Imprimerie du gouvernement, 1852.

Le Dictionnaire de l'Académie françoise. 2 vols. Paris: Veuve de J. B. Coignard, 1694.

Du Casse, Albert. *Les Rois frères de Napoléon Ier: documents inédits relatifs au premier empire.* Paris: Germer Baillière, 1883.

Emérigon, Balthazard-Marie. *Traité des assurances et des contrats à la grosse.* 2 vols. Marseille: Jean Mossy, 1783.

Esquer, Gabriel. *Iconographie historique de l'Algérie depuis le XVIe siècle jusqu'à 1871.* 3 vols. Paris: Plon, 1929.

————. *Reconnaissance des villes, forts et batteries d'Alger par le chef de bataillon Boutin (1808), suivie des Mémoires sur l'Alger par les consuls de Kercy (1791) et Dubois-Thainville (1809).* Paris: H. Champion, 1927.

Ferrière, Claude de. *La Jurisprudence du Code de Justinien, conférée avec les ordonnances royaux, les coutumes de France et les décisions des cours souveraines.* 2 vols. Paris: J. Cochart, 1684.

Flassan, Gaëtan de Raxis de. *Histoire générale et raisonnée de la diplomatie française; ou de la politique de la France, depuis la fondation de la monarchie, jusqu'à la fin du règne de Louis XVI; avec des tables chronologiques de tous les traités conclus par la France.* 7 vols. Paris: Treuttel et Würtz, 1809–1811.

Fleury, Rosset de. *Mandement de Mgr. l'Eveque de Chartres, qui permet de faire de quêtes pour la redemption des François captifs au Royaume de Maroc.* Chartres: Hammerville, 1766.

Fournier, Joseph. *Inventaire des archives de la Chambre de commerce de Marseille.* Marseille: Chambre de commerce, 1940.

Furetière, Antoine. *Dictionnaire universel, contenant généralement tous les mots françois tant vieux que modernes, et les Termes de toutes les sciences et des arts.* 3 vols. The Hague: Arnout & Reinier Leers, 1690.

Gaufreteau, Jean de. *Chronique bordeloise.* 2 vols. Bordeaux: Charles Lefébvre, 1877.

Gorani, Giuseppe. *Recherches sur la science du gouvernement.* 2 vols. Paris: Guillaume Junior, 1792.

Grammont, Henri Delmas de. *Correspondance des consuls d'Alger, 1690–1742.* Algiers: Adolphe Jourdan, 1890.

Grandchamp, Pierre, ed. *La France en Tunisie.* 10 vols. Tunis: J. Aloccio, 1920–1937.

Grégoire, Henri. *De la traite de l'esclavage des noirs et des blancs.* Paris: Adrien Egron, 1815.

Guillebert, Pierre. *Le Paranymphe de la rédemption ou l'heureuse arrivées des chrestiens captifs en la ville de Troyes.* Troyes: François Icquard, 1667.

Haëdo, Diego de. *Topographie et histoire générale d'Alger.* Translated by Dr. Monnereau and Adrien Berbrugger. Paris: Bouchène, 1998.

Hebenstreit, J. E. "Voyage à Alger, Tunis et Tripoli entrepris aux frais et par ordre de Frédéric-Auguste, roi de Pologne, etc., en 1732." *Nouvelles annales de voyages et des sciences géographiques* 46 (1830): 5–90.

Histoire de l'ordre sacré, royal et militaire de Notre-Dame de la Merci, rédemption des captifs, dédiée au roi: Composée par les révérends Pères de la Merci de la congrégation de Paris. Amiens: Guislain Le Bel, 1685.

Hommage à l'oeuvre de la rédemption des captifs. Paris: Demonville, 1785.

Humbert, Jean-Emile, and Giampietro Vieusseux. *Les Barbaresques et les chrétiens.* Florence: Tipografia Coppini, 1983.

Hyde de Neuville, Jean Guillaume. *Memoirs of Baron Hyde de Neuville: Outlaw, Exile, Ambassador.* Translated by Frances Jackson. 2 vols. London: Sands, 1913.

Institution antipirate des chevaliers libérateurs des esclaves blancs en Afrique. Circulaire aux augustes et illustres fondateurs et autres souscripteurs. [Paris?]: n.p., [1816].

Isambert, François André, ed. *Recueil général des anciennes lois françaises depuis l'an 420 jusqu'à la révolution de 1789.* 29 vols. Paris: Belin-Leprieur; Verdier, 1821–1833.

Jackson, G. A. *Algiers: being a complete picture of the Barbary states; their government, laws, religion, and natural productions; and containing a sketch of their various revolutions, a description of the domestic manners and customs of the Moors, Arabs, and Turks; an account of the four great capitals of Algiers, Tripoli, Tunis, and Morocco, and a narrative of the various attacks upon Algiers, by the European states; including a faithful detail of the late glorious victory of Lord Exmouth.* London: R. Edwards, 1817.

Jackson, James Grey. *An Account of the Empire of Marocco, and the district of Suse; Compiled from Miscellaneous Observations Made During a Long Residence in, and Various Journeys Through, these Countries. To which is Added, An Accurate and Interesting Account of Timbuctoo, the Great Emporium of Central Africa.* London: W. Bulmer, 1809.

Jamon, Jean-Baptiste. *Rapport à l'assemblée nationale, au nom du comité des secours publics, tant sur le rachat de tous les françois captifs chez les puissances barbaresques que sous celui de tout étranger qui étant au service d'un françois ou employés sur les bâtimens de la nation, serait tombé en captivité par J. B. Jamon, député du département de la Haute-Loire, le 6 mars 1792.* Paris: Imprimerie nationale, 1792.

Jonnès, Alexandre Moreau de. "Mémoires." Edited by F.-A. Aulard. *La Révolution française* 19 (1890): 352–367.

Jullien, Marc-Antoine. "Grèce: Situation morale du pays—Premiers besoins de la nation grecque, voeux et espérances de ses amis." *Revue encyclopédique* 36 (October 1827): 233–236.

Knetsch, F. R. J. "Deux lettres des protestants captifs à Alger, de 1687." *Bulletin de la Société de l'histoire du Protestantisme français* 110 (1964): 54–59.

[Knights of Malta]. *Réclamation de l'ordre souverain de S.-Jean-de-Jérusalem, adressée au roi de France et aux deux Chambres, dans l'intérêt général de l'ordre et dans l'intérêt particulier des trois langues françaises.* Paris: Le Normant, 1815.

Laborde, Alexandre de. *Au Roi et Aux Chambres, sur les véritables causes de la rupture avec Alger et sur l'expédition qui se prépare.* Paris: Truchy, 1830.

Latomy, Jean. *Histoire de la fondation de l'ordre de Nostre Dame de la Mercy pour la rédemption des captifs.* Paris: Sebastien Huré, 1618.

Lauguier de Tassy, Jacques Philippe. *Histoire du royaume d'Alger: avec l'état présent de son gouvernement, de ses forces de terre et de mer, de ses revenus, police, justice, politique et commerce.* Edited by Noël Laveau and André Nouschi. Paris: Loysel, 1992.

———. *Histoire du royaume d'Alger avec l'état présent de son gouvernement, de ses forces de terre et de mer, de ses revenus, police, justice politique et commerce.* Amsterdam: Henri du Sauzet, 1725.

La Véronne, Chantal de, ed. *Documents inédits sur l'histoire du Maroc: sources françaises.* 2 vols. Paris: Paul Geunther, 1975.

Lebeau, Sylvain, ed. *Recueil des lois relatives à la marine et aux colonies.* 9 vols. Paris: Imprimerie de la République, 1797–1810; reprint, French Revolution Research Collection, 1992.

Leckie, Gould Francis. *De l'Equilibre du pouvoir en Europe.* Translated by W. E. Gauttier d'Arc. Paris: Maradan, 1819.

———. *An Historical Research into the Nature of the Balance of Power in Europe.* London: Taylor and Hessey, 1817.

Lemprière, William. *Voyage dans l'empire de Maroc et le royaume de Fez, fait pendant les années 1790 et 1791.* Translated by M. de Sainte-Suzanne. Paris: Tavernier, 1801.

Le Roy, M. *Etat général et particulier du royaume et de la ville d'Alger, de son gouvernement, de ses forces de terre et de mer.* The Hague: Antoine Van Dole, 1750.

Lesage, Alain-René. *The Devil Upon Two Sticks.* Edinburgh: A. Donaldson and J. Reid, 1762.

———. *Le Diable boiteux.* Paris: La Veuve Barbin, 1707.

Letrait, J. J., A. Degioanni, and R. Le Minor, eds. *Répertoire des registres paroissiaux et de l'état civil jusqu'en 1814.* Draguignan: Lanteaume, 1963.

Lettres-Patentes du Roi qui confirment que l'Oeuvre de la Rédemption établie à Marseille pour le rachat des Captifs. . . . Aix-en-Provence: A. David, 1784.

Linguet, Simon Nicolas Henri. *Théorie des loix civiles, ou principes fondamentaux de la société.* 2 vols. London [Paris]: n.p., 1767.

Lurbe, Gabriel de. *Chronique bordeloise.* Bordeaux: S. Millanges, 1594; 2nd ed., Bordeaux: Simon Boé, 1703.

MacGill, Thomas. *Nouveau voyage à Tunis.* Translated by Alexandre L. Ragueneau de la Chesnaye. Paris: C. L. F. Panckoucke, 1815.

Mandement de Monseigneur l'archevêque de Paris, qui permet de faire des quêtes pour la Rédemption des François Captifs dans la Régence d'Alger. Paris: Claude Simon, 1785.

Masi, Corrado. "Chroniques de l'ancien temps (1815–1859)." Translated by Pierre Grandchamp. *Revue tunisienne* 21 (1935): 83–122.

Maurand, Jérôme. *Itinéraire de Jérome Maurand d'Antibes à Constantinople (1544).* Edited by Léon Dorez. Paris: Ernest Leroux, 1901.

Mémoires et correspondance du roi Jérôme et de la reine Catherine. 7 vols. Paris: E. Dentu, 1861–1866.

Méry, Louis, and F. Guindon. *Histoire analytique et chronologique des actes et des délibérations du corps et du conseil de la municipalité de Marseille, depuis le Xme siècle jusqu'à nos jours.* 8 vols. Marseille: Faissat-Demonchy, 1841–1873.

Minto, Gilbert Elliot, Earl of. "Correspondance de Sir Gilbert Elliot, Vice-Roi de Corse, avec le Gouvernement anglais." Translated by Sébastien de Caraffa. *Bulletin de la Société des sciences historiques et naturelles de la Corse* 12 (1892): 1–556.

Morgan, John. *A Complete History of Algiers. To which is prefixed, an epitome of the general history of Barbary, from the earliest times: Interspersed with many curious Passages and Remarks, not touched on by any writer whatever.* London: J. Bettenham, 1731.

Nécessité de supprimer et d'éteindre les ordres religieux en France, prouvée par l'histoire philosophique du monachisme. . . . 2 vols. London [Paris?], n.p.: 1789.

Nicolay, Nicolas de. *Les Quatre premiers livres des navigations et pérégrinations orientales: avec les figures au naturel tant d'hommes que de femmes selon la diversité des nations.* Lyon: G. Roville, 1568.

Noah, Mordecai M. *Travels in England, France, Spain and the Barbary States in the years 1813–14 and 15.* New York: Kirk and Mercein, 1819.

Paris, Louis, ed. *Négociations, lettres et pièces diverses relatives au règne de François II, tirées du portefeuille de Sébastien de l'Aubespine, évêque de Limoges.* Paris: Imprimerie royale, 1841.

Pasquier, Etienne. *Les Oeuvres d'Estienne Pasquier: contenant ses recherches de la France; son Plaidoyé pour M. le duc de Lorraine; celuy de Me Versoris, pour les jesuites, contre l'Université de Paris; Clarorum virorum ad Steph. Pasquierium Carmina; Epigrammatum libri sexe, Epitaphiorum liber; Iconum liber, cum nonnullis Theod. Pasquierii in Francorum regum icones notis, ses lettres, ses oeuvres meslées, et les lettres de Nicolas Pasquier, fils d'Etienne.* 2 vols. Amsterdam: Aux depens de la compagnie des librairies associez, 1723.

Peiresc, Nicolas Claude Fabri de. *Lettres de Peiresc.* Edited by Philippe Tamizey de Larroque. 7 vols. Paris: Imprimerie nationale, 1888–1898.

Perrot, A. M., ed. *La Conquête d'Alger, ou Relation de la campagne d'Afrique, comprenant les motifs de la guerre, les détails des préparatifs de l'expédition et des événemens qui ont précédé le débarquement, la composition de l'armée de terre et de l'armée navale, les noms des officiers supérieurs, et un précis des opérations militaries.* Paris: H. Langlois fils, 1830.

Pignon-Reix, Jean. "Un Document inédit sur les relations franco-tunisiennes au début du XVIIe siècle." *Revue de l'Occident musulman et de la Méditerranée* 20 (1975): 105–130.

Plantet, Eugène, ed. *Correspondance des beys de Tunis et des consuls de France avec la cour, 1577–1830.* 3 vols. Paris: Félix Alcan, 1893–1899.

——, ed. *Correspondance des deys d'Alger avec la cour de France, 1579–1833.* 2 vols. Paris: Félix Alcan, 1889.

Pothier, Robert Joseph. *Oeuvres de Pothier.* Edited by Jean Joseph Bugnet. 2nd ed. 10 vols. Paris: Cosse, 1861.

Quatrebarbes, Théodore de. *Souvenirs de la campagne d'Afrique.* 2nd ed. Paris: G.-A. Dentu, 1831.

Raimbault, Maurice, ed. *Inventaire sommaires des archives communales et hospitalières de Cassis antérieures à 1790.* Marseille: Barlatier, 1904.

Raynal, Guillaume-Thomas. *Histoire philosophique et politique des établissemens et du commerce des Européens dans l'Afrique septentrionale.* Edited by Jacques Peuchet. 2 vols. Paris: Pierre Maumus, 1826.

Renaudot, M. *Alger. Tableau du royaume, de la ville d'Alger et de ses environs, état de son commerce, de ses forces de terre et de mer, description des moeurs et des usages du pays; précédés d'une introduction historique sur les différentes expéditions d'Alger depuis Charles-Quint jusqu'a nos jours.* 4th ed. Paris: P. Mongie aîné, 1830.

Rothschild, James de, ed. *Les Continuateurs de Loret: lettres en vers de la Gravette de Mayolas, Robinet, Boursault, Perdou de Subligny, Laurent et autres (1665–1689).* 3 vols. Paris: Damascène Morgand and Charles Fatout, 1881–1883.

Roubaud, Pierre Joseph André. *Histoire générale de l'Asie, de l'Afrique, de l'Amérique, contenant des Discours sur l'Histoire Ancienne des Peuples de ces Contrées, leur Histoire Moderne & la Description des lieux, avec des Remarques sur leur Histoire Naturelle, & des Observations sur les Religions, les Gouvernemens, les Sciences, les Arts, le Commerce, les Coutumes, les Moeurs, les Caracteres, &c des Nations.* 15 vols. Paris: Des-Ventes de la Doué, 1770–1775.

Rousseau, Jean-Jacques. *Une Grève d'esclaves à Alger au XVIIIe siècle avec Emile et Sophie ou les Solitaires de Jean-Jacques Rousseau.* Edited by Michel Launay. Paris: Jean-Paul Rocher, 1998.

Rouvière, Arnaud de la. *Traité de la revocation et nullité des donations, legs, institutions, fidéicommis & élections d'heritiers par l'ingratitude, l'incapacité & l'indignité des donataires héritiers, légataires, substitués & élûs à une succession.* Toulouse: N. Caranove, 1738.

Ruffi, Antoine de. *Histoire de la ville de Marseille.* 2nd ed. 2 vols. Marseille: Henri Martel, 1696.

Saint-Gervais, Jacques Boyer de. *Mémoires historiques qui concernent le gouvernement de Tunis, avec des réflexions sur la conduite d'un consul et un détail du commerce.* Paris: Ganeau fils, 1736.

Saint Pierre, Bernardin de. *Empsaël et Zoraïde, ou les blancs esclaves des noirs au Maroc.* Edited by Roger Little. Exeter, UK: University of Exeter Press, 1995.

Salamé, Abraham V. *A narrative of the expedition to Algiers in the year 1816, under the command of the Right Hon. Admiral Lord Viscount Exmouth. By Mr. A. Salamé.* London: J. Murray, 1819.

Scicluna, Hannibal P. *Actes et documents relatifs à l'histoire de l'occupation française de Malte pendant les années 1798–1800 et à la fête du 14 juillet 1798 à Malte: d'après des documents pour la plupart inédits des archives de Malte.* 3rd ed. Valletta, Malta: A. C. Aquilina, 1979.

Serres, Jean. *Mémoires concernans l'état présent du Royaume de Tunis par M. Poiron.* Paris: Ernest Leroux, 1925.

Shaler, William. *Esquisse de l'état d'Alger considéré sous les rapports politique, historique et civil contenant un tableau sur la géographie, la population, le gouvernement, les revenues, le commerce, l'agriculture, les arts, les manufactures, les tribus, les moeurs, les usages, le langage, les événemens politiques et récens de ce pays.* Translated by Thomas Xavier Bianchi. Paris: Ladvocat, 1830.

———. *Sketches of Algiers, Political, Historical and Civil, containing an account of the Geography, Population, Government, Revenues, Commerce, Agriculture, Arts, Civil Institutions, Tribes, Manners, Language and Recent Political History of that Country.* Boston: Century, 1826.

Shaw, Thomas. *Travels or Observations Relating to Several Parts of Barbary and the Levant.* 3rd ed. 2 vols. Edinburgh: J. Ritchie, 1808.

———. *Voyage dans la régence d'Alger, ou Description géographique, physique, philologique, etc. de cet état par le Docteur Shaw.* Translated by Jacques W. MacCarthy. Paris: Marlin, 1830.

S[icard], C[harles]. *Mémoire sur les états barbaresques, nécessité et moyens de mettre fin à leurs pirateries: Lu en séance academique, le 20 août 1818.* Marseille: Ricard, 1819.

Sismondi, Jean-Charles-Léonard Simonde de. "De l'expédition contre Alger." *Revue encyclopédique* 46 (May 1830): 273–296.

Smith, Thurlow. *Relation des atrocités commises par les corsaires barbaresques dans l'Adriatique et autres parties de la Méditerranée au commencement de l'année 1815, faite à Sir Sidney Smith par le Capne Thurlow Smith, de la marine royale britannique.* Paris: A. Belin, n.d.

Smith, William Sidney. *Mémoire sur la nécessité et les moyens de faire cesser les pirateries des états barbaresques.* Paris: Le Normant, 1814.

[Sorsum, Antoine Bruguière de]. *Les Captifs d'Alger: pièce historique en trois actes et en vers . . . représentée par le théâtre . . . de Gand le 14 novembre 1808.* Cassel: Imprimerie royale, 1808.

Spiel, Hilde, ed. *The Congress of Vienna: An Eyewitness Account.* Translated by Richard H. Weber. Philadelphia: Chilton, 1968.

Spon, Jacob, and George Wheler. *Voyage d'Italie, de Dalmatie, de Grèce et du Levant, fait en 1675 & 1676.* . . . 3 vols. Lyon: Antoine Cellier le fils, 1678.

Sue, Eugène, ed. *Correspondance de Henri d'Escoubleau de Sourdis, archevêque de Bordeaux, chef des conseils du roi en l'armée navale: augmentée des ordres, instructions, et lettres de Louis XIII et du Cardinal de Richelieu a M. de Sourdis concernant les operations des flottes francaises de 1636 a 1642, et accompagnée d'un texte historique, de notes, et d'une introduction sur l'état de la Marine en France sous le ministère du Cardinal de Richelieu.* 3 vols. Paris: Crapelet, 1839.

Teissier, Octave. "Correspondance du Père Jean Le Vacher, consul de France à Alger, faisant connaître le vrai motif de la rupture de la paix entre la France et la Régence d'Alger (1676–1683)." *Mélanges historiques* 4 (1882): 755–784.

———. *Inventaire des archives historiques de la Chambre de commerce de Marseille.* Marseille: Barlatier-Feissat, 1878.

———. *Inventaire sommaire des archives communales antérieures à 1790.* Toulon: V. E. Aurel, 1867.

Testa, Ignace de. *Recueil des traités de la Porte Ottomane, avec les puissances étrangères, depuis le premier traité conclu, en 1536, entre Suléyman I et François jusqu'à nos jours.* 11 vols. Paris: Amyot, Muzard & Leroux, 1864–1911.

Thévenot, Jean de. *Relation d'un voyage fait au Levant, dans laquelle il est curieusement traite des Estats sujets du Grand Seigneur, des moeurs, religions, forces, gouvernemens, politiques, langues & coustumes des habitans de ce grand Empire.* 3 vols. Paris: Louis Billaine, 1665–1684.

Tilimsani, Muhammad ibn Muhammad al-. *Chroniques de la régence d'Alger.* Translated by Alphonse Rousseau. Algiers: Imprimerie du gouvernement, 1841.

Tollot, Jean-Baptiste. *Nouveau voyage fait au Levant es annees 1731–1732: contenant les descriptions d'Alger, Tunis, Triploy de Barbarie, Alexandrie en Egypte, Terre Sainte, Constantinople, &c.* Paris: Durand, 1742.

Tortat, Gaston. "Un Livre de raison, 1639–1668: journal de Samuel Robert, lieutenant particulier en l'élection de Saintes." *Archives historiques de la Saintonge et de l'Aunis* 11 (1883): 323–406.

Tott, François de. *Mémoires du baron de Tott, sur les Turcs et les Tartares.* Amsterdam: n.p., 1784–1785.

Touili, Mohammed. *Correspondance des consuls de France à Alger, 1642–1792: inventaire analytique des articles A.E. BI 115 à 145.* Paris: Centre historique des Archives nationales, 2001.

Tuetey, Alexandre, ed. *Journal d'un bourgeois de Paris, 1405–1449.* Paris: H. Champion, 1881.

Tully, Miss. *Letters Written during a Ten Years' Residence at the Court of Tripoli: Published from the originals in the possession of the family of the late Richard Tully, Esq. the British Consul: Comprising authentic memoirs and anecdotes of the reigning Bashaw, his family and other persons of distinction:*

Also an account of the domestic manners of the Moors, Arabs and Turks. Edited by Seton Dearden. London: Arthur Barker, 1957.

Twohig, Dorothy, ed. *The Papers of George Washington: Presidential Series.* Vol. 3, *June–September 1789.* Charlottesville: University Press of Virginia, 1989.

Vallesa, Alessandro Carlo Filiberto, Count de. *Lettre de M. le comte de Vallaise, ministre de S.M. le roi de Sardaigne, à Sir Sidney Smith [Turin, 5 octobre 1814].* Paris: Le Normant, 1814.

Venture de Paradis, Jean-Michel. *Tunis et Alger au XVIIIe siècle.* Paris: Sindbad, 1983.

Villeneuve, René Claude Geoffroy de. *L'Afrique, ou histoire, moeurs, usages et coutumes des Africains.* 4 vols. Paris: Nepveu, 1814.

Villete-Mursay, Philippe de. *Mes campagnes de mer sous Louis XIV: avec un dictionnaire des personnages et des batailles.* Edited by Michel Vergé-Franceschi. Paris: Tallandier, 1991.

Voltaire [François-Marie Arouet]. *Candide, ou l'Optimisme, traduit de l'allemand de M. de Volt.* London: n.p., 1759.

———. *Dictionnaire philosophique.* In *Oeuvres de Voltaire*, vols. 26 and 29, edited by Adrien-Jean-Quentin Beuchot. 72 vols. Paris: Lefèvre, 1829–1840.

Voyage à Alger, ou Description de cette ville, de ses environs et du royaume d'Alger: avec l'état de son commerce, de ses forces de terre et de mer, son gouvernement et les moeurs et usages des habitans. Translated by Jacques W. MacCarthy. Paris: Lecointe, 1830.

Windus, John. *A Journey to Mequinez, the Residence of the Present Emperor of Fez and Morocco, on the occasion of Commodore Stewart's Embassy thither for the Redemption of the British Captives in the year 1721.* London: J. Tonson, 1725.

al-Zayyani, Abu al-Qasim ibn Ahmad. *Le Maroc de 1631 à 1812: extrait de l'ouvrage intitulé Ettordjeman elmo'arib 'an douel elmachriq ou'lmaghrib: l'interprète qui s'exprime clairement sur les dynasties de l'Orient et de l'Occident.* Paris: Ernest Leroux, 1886.

SECONDARY WORKS

Addoun, Yacine Daddi. "L'Abolition de l'esclavage en Algérie: 1816–1871." PhD diss., York University, 2010.

Allaire, Etienne. *La Bruyère dans la Maison de Condé.* 2 vols. Paris: Firmin-Didot, 1886.

Allier, Raoul. *Une Société secrète au XVIIe siècle: la Compagnie du Très-Saint-Sacrement de l'Autel à Marseille, documents publiés.* Paris: H. Champion, 1909.

Alonso, Bonifacio Porres. *Libertad a los cautivos: actividad redentora de la Orden Trinitaria.* 2 vols. Córdoba: Secretariado Trinitario, 1998.

Angiolini, Franco. *I Cavalieri e il principe: l'Ordine di Santo Stefano e la società toscana in età moderna.* Florence: Edifir, 1996.

————. "Slaves and Slavery in Early Modern Tuscany (1500–1700)." *Italian History and Culture* 3 (1997): 67–86.

Aouchar, Amina. "Le Bombardement de Salé et de Larache de juin 1765, à travers les textes marocains et français." *Maroc Europe* 11 (1997–1998): 171–192.

Arkoun, Mohammed, ed. *Histoire de l'islam et des musulmans en France du Moyen Age à nos jours.* Paris: Albin Michel, 2006.

Arnaud d'Agnel, G. "Rôle des soixante-quatorze esclaves provençaux échangés ou rachetés à Alger par le Sieur de Trubert publiés avec un commentaire historique." *Bulletin historique et philologique* (1905): 215–224.

Arnoulet, François. "L'Oeuvre hospitalière des Trinitaires et des Capucins dans la Régence de Tunis." *Cahiers de Tunisie* 26, 105–106 (1978): 35–47.

Arribas Palau, Mariano. "Rescate de cautivos musulmanes en Malta por Muhammad ibn 'Utman." *Hespéris-Tamuda* 10 (1969): 273–329.

————. "Un Rescate de 600 musulmanes cautivos en Malta (1788–1789)." *Hespéris-Tamuda* 25 (1987): 33–89.

Athanassoglou-Kallmyer, Nina M. *French Images from the Greek War of Independence, 1821–1830: Art and Politics under the Restoration.* New Haven, CT: Yale University Press, 1989.

Auber, Charles Auguste. "Histoire de la cathédrale de Poitiers." Special issue, *Bulletin de la Société des antiquaires de l'Ouest et des musées de Poitiers* 16 (1849).

Audisio, Gabriel. "Recherches sur l'origine et la signification du mot 'bagne.'" *Revue africaine* 101 (1957): 363–380.

————. "Renégats marseillais (1591–1595)." *Provence historique* 46, 185 (1996): 305–331.

Augustinos, Olga. *French Odysseys: Greece in French Travel Literature from the Renaissance to the Romantic Era.* Baltimore: Johns Hopkins University Press, 1994.

Auzoux, André. "L'Affaire de Larache." *Revue de l'histoire des colonies françaises* 16 (1928): 505–524.

————. "La Mission de l'amiral Leissègues à Alger et à Tunis." *Revue des études napoléoniennes* 13 (1918): 65–95.

Avenel, Georges d'. *Histoire économique de la propriété, des salaries, des denrées, et de tous les prix en général depuis l'an 1200 jusqu'en l'an 1800.* 7 vols. Paris: Imprimerie nationale, 1894–1926.

Avramescu, Cătălin. *An Intellectual History of Cannibalism.* Translated by Alistair Ian Blyth. Princeton, NJ: Princeton University Press, 2009.

Aymard, Maurice. "Chiourmes et galères dans la seconde moitié du XVIe siècle." In *Il Mediterraneo nella seconda metà dei '500 alla luci di Lepanto,* edited by Gino Benzoni, 71–94. Florence: L. S. Olschki, 1974.

Bachelot, Bernard. *Louis XIV en Algérie: Gigeri 1664.* Monaco: Rocher, 2003.

Baepler, Paul Michel, ed. *White Slaves, African Masters: An Anthology of American Barbary Captivity Narratives.* Chicago: University of Chicago Press, 1999.

Baldensperger, Fernand. *Alfred De Vigny: contribution à sa biographie intellectuelle.* Paris: Hachette, 1932.

Bamford, Paul. *Fighting Ships and Prisons: The Mediterranean Galleys of France in the Age of Louis XIV.* Minneapolis: University of Minnesota Press, 1973.

Barbier, Emile, and Louis Prévost. *Sur la conquête d'Alger: le baron d'Haussez, ministre de la marine de Charles X, et le vicomte de Saint-Priest, duc d'Almazan, ambassadeur de France en Espagne.* Rouen: J. Lecerf, 1930.

Barrow, John. *The Life and Correspondence of Admiral Sir William Sidney Smith.* 2 vols. London: R. Bentley, 1848.

Barry, Boubacar. *Senegambia and the Atlantic Slave Trade.* Translated by Ayi Kwei Armah. Cambridge: Cambridge University Press, 1998.

Bashan, Eliezer. "Le Rachat des captifs dans la société juive méditerranéenne du XIVe au XIXe siècle." In *La Société juive à travers l'histoire,* edited by Shmuel Trigano, 4: 463–472. Paris: Fayard, 1993.

———. *Shivyah u-fedut ba-hevrah ha-yehudit be-artsot ha-Yam ha-tikhon (1391–1830).* Ramat-Gan, Israel: Hotsa'at Universitat Bar-Ilan, 1980.

Bathily, Abdoulaye. *Les Portes d'or: le royaume de Galam (Sénégal) de l'ère musulmane au temps de négriers (VIIIe–XVIIIe siècle).* Paris: L'Harmattan, 1989.

Beaurepaire, Pierre-Yves. "Correspondances, passeports et signalements maçonniques: un dispositif de reconnaissance fraternelle et de gestion de la mobilité au XVIIIe siècle." In *Gens de passage en Méditerranée, de l'Antiquité á l'époque moderne: procédures de contrôle et d'identification,* edited by Claude Moatti and Wolfgang Kaiser, 387–398. Paris: Maisonneuve & Larose, 2007.

Begouën, Henri. "La Condamine: Tunis, Le Bardo, Catharge (extraits inédits du 'Journal de mon voyage au Levant' [21 mai–6 octobre 1731])." *Revue tunisienne* 5 (1898): 71–94.

Beik, William. "Review Article: The Absolutism of Louis XIV as Social Collaboration." *Past and Present* 188 (2005): 195–224.

Belhamissi, Moulay. *Alger, l'Europe et la guerre secrète (1518–1830).* Algiers: Dahlab, 1999.

———. *Les Captifs algériens et l'Europe chrétienne, 1581–1836.* Algiers: Entreprise nationale du livre, 1988.

Belissa, Marc. *Fraternité universelle et intérêt national (1713–1795): les cosmopolitiques du droit des gens.* Paris: Kimé, 1998.

Bély, Lucien, ed. *Dictionnaire de l'Ancien régime: royaume de France, XVIe–XVIIIe siècle.* Paris: Presses universitaires de France, 1996.

Bennassar, Bartolomé, and Lucille Bennassar. *Les Chrétiens d'Allah: l'histoire extraordinaire des renégats, XVIe et XVIIe siècles.* Paris: Perrin, 1989.

Bénot, Yves, and Marcel Dorigny, eds. *Rétablissement de l'esclavage dans les colonies françaises, 1802: ruptures et continuités de la politique coloniale française, 1800–1830; aux origines d'Haïti.* Paris: Maisonneuve & Larose, 2003.

Ben Rejeb, Lotfi. "America's Captive Freemen in North Africa: The Comparative Method in Abolitionist Persuasion." *Slavery and Abolition* 9, 1 (1988): 57–71.

Berbrugger, Adrien. "La Régence d'Alger sous le Consulat et sous l'Empire."

Revue africaine 15 (1871): 241–260, 321–334, 401–414; 16 (1872): 1–19; 19 (1875): 16–31, 115–147.

———. "Un Voyage de Paris à Alger en 1731 par le Sieur Tollot." *Revue africaine* 11 (1867): 417–434.

Bérenger, Jean. "La Politique française en Méditerranée au XVIe siècle et l'alliance ottomane." In *La Guerre de course en Méditerranée (1515–1830)*, edited by Michel Vergé-Franceschi and Antoine-Marie Graziani, 9–26. Paris: Presses de l'Université de Paris-Sorbonne, 2000.

Bérenguier, Nadine. "L'Infortune des alliances: contrat, mariage et fiction au dix-huitième siècle." *Studies on Voltaire and the Eighteenth Century* 329 (1995): 271–417.

Bermès, Emmanuelle. "Le Couvent des Mathurins de Paris et l'estampe au XVIIe siècle." Thèse, Ecole nationale de Chartes, 2001.

Bernard, Régis. "Les Cimetières des 'esclaves turcs' des arsenaux de Marseille et de Toulon au XVIIIe siècle." *Revue des mondes musulmans et de la Méditerranée* 99–100 (2002): 205–217.

Berthier, Annie. "Tripoli de Barbarie à la fin du XVIIe siècle d'après un mémoire inédit de François Pétis de la Croix." *Anatolia Moderna Yeni Andalou* 6 (1997): 13–30.

Biraben, Jean-Noël. *Les Hommes et la peste en France et dans les pays européens et méditerranéens.* 2 vols. Paris: Mouton, 1975–1976.

Blackburn, Robin. *The Overthrow of Colonial Slavery, 1776–1848.* London: Verso, 1988.

Blanc, Louis-Paul. "Les Sétois face à face avec les corsaires et les pirates." *Bulletin de la Société d'études scientifiques de Sète et sa région* 3 (1971): 141–200.

Blassingame, John W. "Some Precursors of the *Amistad* Revolt." *Connecticut Scholar: Occasional Papers of the Connecticut Humanities Council* 10 (1992): 26–36.

Bleys, Rudi C. *The Geography of Perversion: Male-to-Male Sexual Behaviour outside the West and the Ethnographic Imagination.* New York: New York University Press, 1995.

Blili, Leïla. "Course et captivité des femmes dans la régence de Tunis aux XVIe et XVIIe siècles." In *Captius i esclaus a l'antiguitat i al món modern: actes del XIX colloqui internacional del GIREA*, edited by María Luisa Sánchez León and Gonçal López Nadal, 259–274. Naples: Jovene, 1996.

Bloch, Marc Léopold Benjamin. *The Royal Touch: Sacred Monarchy and Scrofula in England and France.* Translated by J. E. Anderson. London: Routledge, 1973.

Blum, Hester. "Pirated Tars, Piratical Texts: Barbary Captivity and American Sea Narratives." *Early American Studies* 1, 2 (2003): 133–158.

———. *The View from the Masthead: Maritime Imagination and Antebellum American Sea Narratives.* Chapel Hill: University of North Carolina Press, 2008.

Blumenthal, Debra. *Enemies and Familiars: Slavery and Mastery in Fifteenth-Century Valencia.* Ithaca, NY: Cornell University Press, 2009.

Boime, Albert. *Art in an Age of Counterrevolution, 1815–1848.* Vol. 3 of *A Social History of Modern Art.* Chicago: University of Chicago Press, 2004.

Boiteux, L. A. *La Fortune de mer: le besoin de sécurité et les débuts de l'assurance maritime.* Paris: SEVPEN, 1968.

Bombard, F. "Les Vicaires apostoliques de Tunis et d'Alger (1645–1827)." *Revue tunisienne* 1 (1894): 387–391, 495–498; 2 (1895): 73–76, 259–262, 429–432, 581–586.

Bonaffini, Giuseppe. *Cattivi e redentori nel Mediterraneo tra XVI e XVII secolo.* Palermo: ILA Palma, 2003.

Bonet-Maury, Gaston. "La France et la rédemption des esclaves en Algérie à la fin du XVIIe siècle." *Revue des deux mondes* 35 (1906): 898–923.

———. "Les Précurseurs français du Cardinal Lavergerie dans l'Afrique musulman." *Revue des deux mondes* 36 (1896): 899–932.

Bono, Salvatore. *Les Corsaires en Méditerranée.* Translated by Ahmed Somaï. Paris: Editions Paris-Méditerranée, 1998.

———. *I Corsari barbareschi.* Turin: ERI, Edizioni RAI radiotelevisione italiana, 1964.

———. "Fonti inedite di storia della Tripolitania." *Libia* 1, 2 (1953): 117–121.

———. "Le Maghreb dans l'histoire de la Méditerranée à l'époque barbaresque (XVIe siècle–1830)." *Africa: notiziario dell'Associazione fra le imprese italiane in Africa* 54, 2 (1999): 182–192.

———. *Schiavi musulmani nell'Italia moderna: galeotti, vu' cumpra', domestici.* Naples: Edizioni scientifiche italiane, 1999.

Bookin-Weiner, Jerome B. "The 'Sallee Rovers': Morocco and Its Corsairs in the Seventeenth Century." In *The Middle East and North Africa: Essays in Honor of J. C. Hurewitz*, edited by Reeva S. Simon. New York: Columbia University Press, 1990.

Borms, Marion F. Godfroy-Tayart de. "La Guerre de Sept ans et ses consequences atlantiques: Kourou ou l'apparition d'un nouveau systeme colonial." *French Historical Studies* 32, 2 (2009): 167–191.

Boubaker, Sadok. "Négoce et enrichissement individuel à Tunis du XVIIe siècle au début du XIXe siècle." *Revue d'histoire moderne et contemporaine* 50, 4 (2003): 29–62, 228–229.

———. *La Régence de Tunis au XVIIe siècle: ses relations commerciales avec les ports de l'Europe méditerranéenne, Marseille et Livourne.* Zaghouan, Tunisia: CEROMA, 1987.

Boulle, Pierre H. *Race et esclavage dans la France de l'Ancien régime.* Paris: Perrin, 2007.

Boussion, Abbé. "Les Ordres religieux à Toulon et dans le diocèse de Toulon avant 1789." *Bulletin de la Société des amis du vieux Toulon* 25 (1930): 280–284.

Boutin, Abel. *Anciennes relations commerciales et diplomatiques de la France avec la Barbarie (1516–1830).* Paris: Pedone, 1902.

Boyer, Pierre. "Alger en 1645 d'après les notes du R.P. Hérault." *Revue de l'Occident musulman et de la Méditerranée* 17 (1974): 19–41.

———. "La Chiourme turque des galères de France de 1685 à 1687." *Revue de l'Occident musulman et de la Méditerranée* 6 (1969): 53–74.

———. "Continuation des mémoires des voyages du feu Père Hérault en Barbarie pour la rédemption qu'il a escrit luy même estant à Alger l'an 1645 ainsi qui s'en suit." *Revue de l'Occident musulman et de la Méditerranée* 19 (1975): 29–74.

———. *La Vie quotidienne à Alger à la veille de l'intervention française.* Paris: Hachette, 1963.

Brahimi, Denise. *Opinions et regards européens sur le Maghreb aux XVIIe et XVIIIe siècles.* Algiers: Société nationale d'édition et de diffusion, 1978.

Braude, Benjamin. "The Sons of Noah and the Construction of Ethnic and Geographical Identities in the Medieval and Early Modern Periods." *William and Mary Quarterly* 54 (1997): 103–142.

Braudel, Fernand. *The Mediterranean and the Mediterranean World in the Age of Philip II* [1949]. Translated by Siân Reynolds. 2 vols. New York: Harper and Row, 1966; reprint, Berkeley: University of California Press, 1995.

Brodman, James. *Ransoming Captives in Crusader Spain: The Order of Merced on the Christian-Islamic Frontier.* Philadelphia: University of Pennsylvania Press, 1986.

Broers, Michael. *The Politics of Religion in Napoleonic Italy: The War against God, 1801–1814.* London: Routledge, 2002.

Brogini, Anne. "L'Esclavage au quotidien à Malte au XVIe siècle." *Cahiers de la Méditerranée* 65 (2002). http://cdlm.revues.org/index26.html.

Brooks, James T. *Captives and Cousins: Slavery, Kinship and Community in the Southwest Borderlands.* Chapel Hill: University of North Carolina Press, 2002.

Brunschvig, Robert. "'Abd." In *Encyclopedia of Islam*, 2nd ed., 1: 24–40. Leiden, Netherlands: Brill, 1960.

Bryant, Lawrence. *The King and the City in the Parisian Royal Entry Ceremony: Politics, Ritual and Art in the Renaissance.* Geneva: Droz, 1986.

Burke, Edmund, III. "The Sociology of Islam: The French Tradition." In *Islamic Studies: A Tradition and Its Problems*, edited by Malcolm H. Kerr, 73–99. Santa Monica, CA: Undena, 1980.

Burton, Jonathan. "English Anxiety and the Muslim Power of Conversion: Five Perspectives on 'Turning Turk' in Early Modern Texts." *Journal for Early Modern Cultural Studies* 2, 1 (2002): 35–67.

Buti, Gilbert. "Contrôles sanitaire et militaire dans les ports provençaux aux XVIIIe siècle." In *Gens de passage en Méditerranée, de l'Antiquité á l'époque moderne: procédures de contrôle et d'identification*, edited by Claude Moatti and Wolfgang Kaiser, 155–180. Paris: Maisonneuve & Larose, 2007.

Caillé, Jacques. "L'Ambassade du comte de Breugnon à Marrakech en 1767." *Revue d'histoire diplomatique* 75 (1961): 245–274; 76 (1962): 58–96.

———. "Les Naufragés de la 'Louise' au Maroc et l'ambassade de Tahar Fennich à la cour de France en 1777–1778." *Revue d'histoire diplomatique* 78, 3 (1964): 225–264.

Canova-Green, Marie-Claude. "L'Entrée de Louis XIII dans Marseille, le 7 novembre 1622." *Dix-septième siècle* 3, 212 (2001): 521–533.

Caplan, Jane, and John Toppey, eds. *Documenting Individual Identity: The Development of State Practices in the Modern World.* Princeton, NJ: Princeton University Press, 2001.

Capot-Rey, Robert. "La Politique français et le Maghreb méditerranéen (1643–1685)." *Revue africaine* 75 (1934): 47–61, 175–217, 426–490; 77 (1934): 97–163.

Capponi, Niccolò. *Victory of the West: The Great Christian-Muslim Clash at the Battle of Lepanto.* Cambridge, MA: Da Capo Press, 2007.

Cardaillac, Louis. *Morisques et chrétiens: un affrontement polémique, 1492–1640.* Paris: Klincksieck, 1977.

Carnoy, Dominique. *Représentations de l'Islam dans la France du XVIIe siècle: la ville des tentations.* Paris: L'Harmattan, 1998.

Casenave, Jean. "Un Consul français à Alger au XVIIIe siècle: Langoisseur de la Vallée." *Revue africaine* 78 (1936): 101–122.

Castle, Terry. *Masquerade and Civilization: The Carnivalesque in Eighteenth-Century English Culture and Fiction.* Stanford: Stanford University Press, 1986.

Castries, Henry de. *Agents et voyageurs français au Maroc, 1530–1660.* Paris: Ernest Leroux, 1911.

———. "Le Maroc d'autrefois: les corsaires de Salé." *Revue des deux mondes* 13 (1903): 823–852.

Cavaillé, Jean-Pierre. *Dis/simulations: Jules-César Vanini, François La Mothe Le Vayer, Gabriel Naudé, Louis Machon et Torquato Accetto; religion, morale et politique au XVIIe siècle.* Paris: H. Champion, 2002.

Cerny, Gerald. *Theology, Politics, and Letters at the Crossroads of European Civilization: Jacques Basnage and the Baylean Huguenot Refugees in the Dutch Republic.* Dordrecht, Netherlands: Martinus Nijhoff, 1987.

Chaillou, Lucien. *Textes pour servir à l'histoire de l'Algérie au XVIIIe siècle suivis de la guerre de quinze heures.* Toulon: author, 1979.

Chaix, Gérald, Marie-Luce Demonet, and Robert Sauzet, eds. *La Ville à la Renaissance: espaces, représentations, pouvoirs: actes XXXIXe Colloque international d'études humanistes (1996).* Paris: H. Champion, 2008.

Charles-Roux, François. *France et Afrique du Nord avant 1830: les précurseurs de la conquête.* Paris: Félix Alcan, 1932.

———. *Les Travaux d'Herculais ou une extraordinaire mission en Barbarie.* Paris: Société de l'Histoire des colonies françaises, 1926.

Chartier, Roger, and Henri-Jean Martin, eds. *Histoire de l'édition française.* 4 vols. Paris: Promodis, 1982–1986.

Chater, Khelifa. *Dépendance et mutations précoloniales: la régence de Tunis de 1815 à 1857.* Tunis: Université de Tunis, 1984.

Cipollone, Giulio. *La Liberazione dei "captivi" tra Cristianità e Islam: oltre la crociata e il gihad tolleranza e servizi umanitario (Rome, Sept. 16–19, 1998).* Vatican City: Archivio Segreto Vaticano, 2000.

Clark, G. N. "Barbary Corsairs in the Seventeenth Century." *Cambridge Historical Journal* 8, 1 (1944): 22–35.

Cocard, Hugues. *Les Pères de la Merci en France (1574–1792): un ordre voué à la libération des captifs.* Paris: L'Harmattan, 2007.

———. "Les Pères de la Merci dans le royaume de France depuis le Concile de Trente jusqu'à la fin de l'ancien régime." 2 vols. Thèse troisième cycle, Université d'Angers, 1982.

Cohen, William B. *The French Encounter with Africans: White Response to Blacks, 1530–1880*. Bloomington: Indiana University Press, 2003.

Colley, Linda. *Captives: The Story of Britain's Pursuit of Empire and How Its Soldiers and Civilians Were Held Captive by the Dream of Global Supremacy, 1600–1850*. New York: Pantheon Books, 2002.

———. *The Ordeal of Elizabeth Marsh: A Woman in World History*. New York: Random House, 2008.

Corré, Alan D. *A Glossary of Lingua Franca*. 5th ed. (2005). http://www.uwm.edu/~corre/franca/go.html.

Corvisier, André. *L'Armée française de la fin du XVIIe siècle au ministère de Choiseul*. 2 vols. Paris: Presses universitaires de France, 1964.

Coste, Jean. "Un Prince tunisien converti." *Revue de l'histoire de missions* 11 (1934): 481–493.

Cottias, Myriam, Alessandro Stella, and Bernard Vincent, eds. *Esclavage et dépendances serviles: histoire comparée*. Paris: L'Harmattan, 2006.

Coutoure, Léonce. "Baptême d'un Turc à Orthez." *Revue de Gascogne* 21 (1880): 90.

Cresti, Federico. "Descriptions et iconographie de la ville d'Alger au XVIe siècle." *Revue de l'Occident musulman et de la Méditerranée* 34 (1982): 1–22.

———. "La Population d'Alger et son évolution durant l'époque ottomane: un état des connaissances controversé." *Arabica* 52, 4 (2005): 457–495.

———. "Quelques réflexions sur la population et la structure sociale d'Alger à la période ottoman turque (XVIe–XIXe siècles)." *Cahiers de Tunisie* 34, 137–138 (1986): 151–164.

Cumont, M. F. "Les Antiquités de la Tripolitaine au XVIIIe siècle." *Rivista della Tripolitania* 2 (1925–1926): 151–167.

Daget, Serge. "L'Abolition de la traite des noirs en France de 1814 à 1831." *Cahiers d'études africaines* 11, 41 (1971): 14–58.

———. *La Répression de la traite des noirs au XIXe siècle: les actions des croisières françaises sur les côtes occidentaux de l'Afrique (1817–1850)*. Paris: Karthala, 1997.

Dakhlia, Jocelyne. "Ligne de fuite: impostures et reconstructions identitaires en Méditerranée musulmane à l'époque moderne." In *Gens de passage en Méditerranée, de l'Antiquité á l'époque moderne: procédures de contrôle et d'identification*, edited by Claude Moatti and Wolfgang Kaiser, 427–457. Paris: Maisonneuve & Larose, 2007.

———. *Lingua Franca*. [Arles]: Actes sud, 2008.

———. "'Turcs de profession'? Réinscriptions lignagères et redéfinitions sexuelles des convertis dans les cours maghrébines (XVIe–XIXe siècles)." In *Conversions islamiques: identités religieuses en islam méditerranéen*, edited by Mercedes García-Arenal, 151–171. Paris: Maisonneuve & Larose, 2001.

Dakin, Douglas. *The Greek Struggle for Independence, 1821–1833*. Berkeley: University of California Press, 1973.

D'Angelo, Michela. "In the 'English' Mediterranean (1511–1815)." *Journal of Mediterranean Studies* 12, 2 (2002): 271–285.

Danigo, Joseph-Marie. "Chrétiens aux prises avec les Barbaresques." *Mémoires de la société d'histoire et d'archéologie de Bretagne* 31 (1951): 49–63.

Daranatz, J. B. "Captifs basques et béarnais rachetés en Afrique au XVIIe et XVIIIe siècles." *Guere Herria* 7, 4 (1927): 310–323.

Darnton, Robert. *The Great Cat Massacre and Other Episodes in French Cultural History.* New York: Vintage Books, 1985.

Dávid, Géza, and Pál Fodor, eds. *Ransom Slavery along the Ottoman Borders: Early Fifteenth–Early Eighteenth Centuries.* Leiden, Netherlands: Brill, 2007.

Davies, G. "Greek Slaves at Tunis in 1823." *English Historical Review* 34 (1919): 84–89.

Davis, David Brion. *The Problem of Slavery in Western Culture.* Ithaca, NY: Cornell University Press, 1966.

Davis, Diana K. *Resurrecting the Granary of Rome: Environmental History and French Colonial Expansion in North Africa.* Athens: Ohio University Press, 2007.

Davis, Natalie Zemon. *Society and Culture in Early Modern France.* Stanford: Stanford University Press, 1975.

———. *Trickster Travels: A Sixteenth-Century Muslim between Worlds.* New York: Hill and Wang, 2006.

Davis, Robert C. *Christian Slaves, Muslim Masters: White Slavery in the Mediterranean, the Barbary Coast, and Italy, 1500–1800.* New York: Palgrave Macmillan, 2003.

———. "Counting European Slaves on the Barbary Coast." *Past and Present* 172, 1 (2001): 87–124.

Dearden, Seton. *A Nest of Corsairs: The Fighting Karamanlis of the Barbary Coast.* London: John Murray, 1976.

Debbasch, Yvan. *La Nation française en Tunisie, 1577–1835.* Paris: Sirey, 1957.

Degros, Maurice. "Les Consulats de France sous la Révolution: les états barbaresques." *Revue d'histoire diplomatique* 105 (1991): 103–133.

Delafosse, Marcel. "Les Rochelais au Maroc au XVIIe siècle: commerce et rachat de captifs." *Revue d'histoire des colonies* 35 (1948): 70–83.

Denis, Vincent. *Une Histoire de l'identité: France, 1715–1815.* Seyssel: Champ Vallon, 2008.

Deperthes, Jean Louis Hubert Simon, ed. *Histoire des naufrages, ou Recueil des relations les plus intéressantes des Naufrages, Hivernemens, Délaissemens, Incendies, Famines, & autres Evènemens funestes sur Mer; qui ont été publiées depuis le quinzième siècle jusqu'à présent.* 3 vols. Paris: Cuchet, 1788.

Deslandres, Paul. *L'Eglise et le rachat des captifs.* Paris: B. Blond, 1902.

———. *L'Ordre des Trinitaires pour le rachat des captifs.* 2 vols. Toulouse: Privat, 1903.

Desmet-Grégoire, Hélène. *Le "Divan" magique: l'Orient turc en France au XVIIIe siècle.* Paris: L'Harmattan, 1994.

Dessertenne, François. "L'Affaire de Larache, 27 juin 1765, un épisode de la négociation franco-marocaine sur la piraterie." *Revue historique des armées* 166 (1987): 4–12.

Dessessarts, Nicolas Toussaint Lemoyne, ed. *Causes célèbres, curieuses et inté-ressantes, de toutes les cours souveraines du royaume, avec les jugemens qui les ont décidées [nouv. ser].* Vol. 164. Paris: P. G. Simon, 1773.

Devy, René. "Le Couvent narbonnais de la Merci." *Bulletin de la Commission archéologique et littéraire de Narbonne* 35 (1973): 61–72.

Dew, Nicholas. "Reading Travels in the Culture of Curiosity: Thevenot's Collection of Voyages." *Journal of Early Modern History* 10 (2006): 39–59.

Dewald, Jonathan. *Aristocratic Experience and the Origins of Modern Culture: France, 1570–1715.* Berkeley: University of California Press, 1993.

Diefendorf, Barbara B. *Beneath the Cross: Catholics and Huguenots in Sixteenth-Century Paris.* Oxford: Oxford University Press, 1991.

Dimakis, Jean. *La Presse française face à la chute de Missolonghi et à la bataille navale de Navarin: recherches sur les sources du philhellénisme français.* Salonika, Greece: Institute for Balkan Studies, 1976.

Dimopoulos, Aristide G. *L'Opinion publique française et la révolution grecque (1821–1827).* Nancy: V. Idoux, 1962.

Dorigny, Marcel, ed. *Les Abolitions de l'esclavage: de L. F. Sonthonax à V. Schoelcher, 1793, 1794, 1848.* Saint-Denis: Presses universitaires de Vincennes, 1995.

Douglas-Morris, K. J., and Roger Perkins. *Gunfire in Barbary: Admiral Lord Exmouth's Battle with the Corsairs of Algiers in 1816: The Story of the Suppression of White Christian Slavery.* Havant, UK: Kenneth Mason, 1982.

Drescher, Seymour. *Capitalism and Antislavery: British Mobilization in Comparative Perspective.* New York: Oxford University Press, 1987.

Droulia, Loukia, Dimitri Nicolaïdis, Fani-Maria Tsigakou, et al., eds. *La Grèce en révolte: Delacroix et les peintres français, 1815–1848.* Paris: Réunion des musées nationaux, 1996.

Dubois, Laurent. *A Colony of Citizens: Revolution and Slave Emancipation in the French Caribbean, 1787–1804.* Chapel Hill: University of North Carolina Press, 2004.

Duprat, Anne, and Emilie Picherot, eds. *Récits d'Orient dans les littératures d'Europe, XVIe–XIXe siècles.* Paris: Presses de l'Université de Paris-Sorbonne, 2008.

Dupuy, Emile. *Etudes d'histoire d'Amérique: américains et barbaresques (1776–1824).* Paris: R. Roger & F. Chernoviz, 1910.

Dursteler, Eric R. *Venetians in Constantinople: Nation, Identity, and Coexistence in the Early Modern Mediterranean.* Baltimore: Johns Hopkins University Press, 2006.

Duval, Michel. "Des Bretons chez les barbaresques: les Etats de Bretagne à leur secours!" *Dalc'homp Soñj* 14 (1986): 9–11.

Earle, Peter. *Corsairs of Malta and Barbary.* London: Sidgwick & Jackson, 1970.

Echinard, Pierre. *Grecs et philhellènes à Marseille de la Révolution française à l'Independence de la Grèce.* Marseille: P. Echinard, 1973.

Eisenbeth, Maurice. "Les Juifs en Algérie et en Tunisie à l'époque turque (1516–1830)." *Revue africaine* 96 (1952): 114–187, 343–384.

Eisner, Robert. *Travelers to an Antique Land: The History and Literature of Travel to Greece.* Ann Arbor: University of Michigan Press, 1991.

Ekin, Des. *The Stolen Village: Baltimore and the Barbary Pirates.* Dublin: O'Brien Press, 2006.

El Hamel, Chouki. "'Race,' Slavery and Islam and Maghribi Mediterranean Thought: The Question of the Haratin in Morocco." *Journal of North African Studies* 7, 3 (2002): 29–52.

———. "The Register of the Slaves of Sultan Mawlay Isma'il of Morocco at the Turn of the Eighteenth Century." *Journal of African History* 51, 1 (2010): 89–98.

Elie de La Primaudaie, F. "Le Littoral de la Tripolitaine: commerce, navigation, géographie comparée." *Nouvelles annales des voyages, de la géographie, de l'histoire et de l'archéologie* 11, 3 (1865): 5–69, 141–222, 279–323.

El Mansour, Mohamed. *Morocco in the Reign of Mawlay Sulayman.* Outwell, UK: Middle East and North African Studies Press, 1990.

El-Rouayheb, Khaled. *Before Homosexuality in the Arab-Islamic World, 1500–1800.* Chicago: University of Chicago Press, 2005.

Emerit, Marcel. "Un Astronome français à Alger en 1729." *Revue africaine* 84 (1940): 249–256.

———. "L'Essai d'une marine marchande barbaresque au XVIIIe siècle." *Cahiers de Tunisie* 11 (1955): 363–370.

Engel, Claire-Elaine. *L'Ordre de Malte en Méditerranée (1530–1798).* Monaco: Editions du Rocher, 1957.

"Un Episode dauphinois du rachat des Captifs avant la Révolution." *Annales dauphinoises* 4 (1903): 279–281.

Epstein, Steven A. *Purity Lost: Transgressing Boundaries in the Eastern Mediterranean, 1000–1400.* Baltimore: Johns Hopkins University Press, 2006.

———. *Speaking of Slavery: Color, Ethnicity and Human Bondage in Italy.* Ithaca, NY: Cornell University Press, 2001.

Erdem, Hakan. *Slavery in the Ottoman Empire and Its Demise, 1800–1909.* New York: St. Martin's, 1996.

Esquer, Gabriel. *Le Commencements d'un empire: la prise d'Alger.* 2nd ed. Paris: Larose, 1929.

———. "Les Débuts de la presse algérienne: Jean-Toussaint Merle et 'L'Estafette de Sidi Ferruch.'" *Revue africaine* 70 (1929): 254–318.

Even, Pascal. "Un Episode des relations de la France avec la régence d'Alger, au début de la Révolution: la mission du capitaine Doumergues en 1791." *Revue d'histoire diplomatique* 98 (1984): 47–76.

Fabre, Augustin. *Histoire de Marseille,* 2 vols. Marseille: Marius Olive, 1829.

———. *Histoire des hôpitaux et des institutions de bienfaisance de Marseille.* 2 vols. Marseille: Jules Barile, 1854–1855.

Farge, Arlette. *Fragile Lives: Violence, Power and Solidarity in Eighteenth-Century Paris.* Translated by Carol Shelton. Cambridge, MA: Harvard University Press, 1993.

Faur, José. *In the Shadow of History: Jews and Conversos at the Dawn of Modernity.* Albany: SUNY Press, 1992.

Félice, Paul de. *Les Protestants d'autrefois: vie intérieure des églises, moeurs et usages.* 4 vols. Paris: Fischbacher, 1896–1898.

Féraud, Charles L. *Annales tripolitaines publiées avec une introduction et des notes par Augustin Bernard.* Tunis: Tournier; Paris: Vuibert, 1927; reprint, Paris: Bouchène, 2005.

Festa, Lynn Mary. *Sentimental Figures of Empire in Eighteenth-Century Britain and France.* Baltimore: Johns Hopkins University Press, 2006.

Finkelman, Paul, and Joseph Calder Miller, eds. *Macmillan Encyclopedia of World Slavery.* 2 vols. New York: Simon & Schuster Macmillan, 1998.

Fishbein, Rand H. "Echoes from the Barbary Coast." *National Interest* (Winter 2001–2002): 47–51.

Fisher, Godfrey. *Barbary Legend: War, Trade, and Piracy in North Africa, 1415–1830.* Oxford: Clarendon Press, 1957.

Folayan, Kola. *Tripoli during the Reign of Yusuf Pasha Qaramanli.* Ile-Ife, Nigeria: University of Ife Press, 1979.

Fontenay, Michel. "Corsaires de la foi ou rentiers du sol? Les Chevaliers de Malte dans le 'corso' méditerranéen au XVIIe siècle." *Revue d'histoire moderne et contemporaine* 35 (1988): 361–384.

———. "Le Maghreb barbaresque et l'esclavage méditerranéen aux XVIe et XVIIe siècles." *Cahiers de Tunisie* 44, 3–4 (1991): 7–43.

———. "La Place de la course dans l'économie portuaire: l'exemple de Malte et des portes barbaresques." *Annales: economies, sociétés, civilisations* 43, 6 (1988): 1321–1347.

———. "Routes et modalités du commerce des esclaves dans la Méditerranée des temps modernes (XVIe, XVIIe et XVIIIe siècles)." *Revue historique* 640, 4 (2006): 813–830.

Forot, Victor. "Les Marguilliers des Mathurins en Limousin." *Bulletin de la Société scientifique, historique et archéologique de la Corrèze* 30 (1908): 507–527.

Foucault, Michel. *Madness and Civilization: A History of Insanity in an Age of Reason.* Translated by Richard Howard. London: Routledge, 2001.

Fox, Edward Whiting. *History in Geographic Perspective: The Other France.* New York: Norton, 1971.

Fraser, Elizabeth. *Delacroix, Art and Patrimony in Post-Revolutionary France.* Cambridge: Cambridge University Press, 2004.

Freller, Thomas. "'The Shining of the Moon': The Mediterranean Tour of Muhammad Ibn Uthman, Envoy of Morocco, in 1782." *Journal of Mediterranean Studies* 12, 2 (2002): 307–326.

Friedman, Ellen G. "Christian Captives at 'Hard Labor' in Algiers, 16th–18th Centuries." *International Journal of African Historical Studies* 13 (1980): 616–632.

———. *Spanish Captives in North Africa in the Early Modern Age.* Madison: University of Wisconsin Press, 1983.

———. "Trinitarian Hospitals in Algiers: An Early Example of Health Care for Prisoners of War." *Catholic Historical Review* 66, 4 (1980): 551–564.

Friedman, Yvonne. *Encounter between Enemies: Captivity and Ransom in the Latin Kingdom of Jerusalem.* Leiden, Netherlands: Brill, 2002.

Frye, Northrop. *The Secular Scripture: A Study of the Structure of Romance.* Cambridge, MA: Harvard University Press, 1976.

Fuchs, Barbara. *Mimesis and Empire: The New World, Islam, and European Identities.* Cambridge: Cambridge University Press, 2001.

———. *Passing for Spain: Cervantes and the Fictions of Identity.* Urbana: University of Illinois Press, 2003.

———. *Romance.* New York: Routledge, 2004.

Gaborieau, Olivier. "Corsaires barbaresques, esclaves chrétiens et diplomatie française à Tunis de 1790 à 1830." Mémoire de maîtrise, Université de Nantes, 1990.

Gaffarel, Paul. *La Conquête de l'Algérie jusqu'à la prise de Constantine.* Paris: Firmin-Didot, 1888.

Gainot, Bernard. "La Décade et la 'colonisation nouvelle.'" *Annales historiques de la Révolution française* 339 (2005): 99–116.

Galibert, Léon. *L'Algérie, ancienne et moderne depuis les premiers établissements des Carthaginois jusqu'à la prise de la Smalah d'Abd-el-Kader.* Paris: Furne, 1844.

Garcés, María Antonia. *Cervantes in Algiers: A Captive's Tale.* Nashville: Vanderbilt University Press, 2002.

García-Arenal, Mercedes, ed. *Conversions islamiques: identités religieuses en islam méditerranéen.* Paris: Maisonneuve & Larose, 2001.

García-Arenal, Mercedes, and Gerard Wiegers. *A Man of Three Worlds: Samuel Pallache, a Moroccan Jew in Catholic and Protestant Europe.* Baltimore: Johns Hopkins University Press, 2003.

Garrot, Henri. *Histoire générale de l'Algérie.* Algiers: P. Crescenzo, 1910.

Gaudin, R. "Le Rachat des captifs français en pays barbaresques." *Mémoires de la société archéologique et historique de la Charente* (1954): 101–122.

Geertz, Clifford. *Local Knowledge: Further Essays in Interpretive Anthropology.* New York: Basic Books, 1983.

Geggus, David. "The French Slave Trade: An Overview." *William and Mary Quarterly* 58, 1 (2001): 119–138.

———. "Racial Equality, Slavery, and Colonial Secession during the Constituent Assembly." *American Historical Review* 94, 5 (1989): 1290–1308.

Germain, Alexandre. "Oeuvre de la rédemption des captifs à Montpellier." *Publications de la Société archéologique de Montpellier* 30 (1863): 165–198.

Ghazali, Maria. "La Régence de Tunis et l'esclavage en Méditerranée à la fin du XVIIIe siècle d'après les sources consulaires espagnoles." *Cahiers de la Méditerranée* 65 (2002). http://cdlm.revues.org/index43.html.

Ginio, Eyal. "Piracy and Redemption in the Aegean Sea during the First Half of the Eighteenth Century." *Turcica* 33 (2001): 135–147.

Giraudias, Etienne. *Etude historique sur les lois somptuaires.* Poitiers: Oudin, 1910.

Godard, Léon. *Description et histoire du Maroc comprenant la géographie et la statistique de ce pays d'après les renseignements les plus récents.* Paris: C. Tanera, 1860.

Gonzalez-Raymond, Anita. *La Croix et le croissant: les inquisiteurs des îles face à l'Islam, 1550–1700*. Paris: Editions de CNRS, 1992.

Grammont, Henri Delmas de. "Un Académicien (Jean Foy Vaillant) captif à Alger (1674–1675)." *Revue africaine* 26 (1882): 309–320, 387–396.

———. "Certificat des souffrances du Père Sébastien." *Revue africaine* 35 (1891): 98–108.

———. "Etudes algériennes: la course, l'esclavage, la rédemption." *Revue historique* 25–27 (1884–1885): 1–42, 1–44, 1–37.

———. *Histoire d'Alger sous la domination turque (1515–1830)*. Paris: Ernest Leroux, 1887; reprint, Paris: Bouchène, 2002.

———. *Histoire du massacre des Turcs à Marseille en 1620*. Paris: H. Champion, 1879.

———. "Relations entre la France et la Régence d'Alger au XVIIe siècle. Les deux canons de Simon Dansa (1606–1628). La mission de Sanson Napollon (1628–1683). La mission de Sanson, Le Page et les agents intérimaires (1633–1646)." *Revue africaine* 23 (1879): 5–32, 95–114, 134–160, 295–320, 367–392, 409–448.

Grandchamp, Pierre. "Autour du Consulat de France à Tunis (1577–1881): articles parus dans la Tunisie française (novembre 1940–juin 1942)." *Revue tunisienne* 44 (1943): 1–266.

———. "La Fuite de Tunis et le baptême de Don Philippe à Palerme (13 mars–6 mai 1646)." *Revue africaine* 84 (1940): 118–132.

———. "Une Mission délicate en Barbarie au XVIIe siècle: Jean-Baptiste Salvago, drogman vénitien à Alger et à Tunis (1625)." *Revue tunisienne* 8 (1937): 299–322, 471–501.

Grandchamp, Pierre, and Marthe de Bacquencourt. "Documents divers concernant Don Philippe, prince tunisien deux fois renégat (1646–1686)." *Revue tunisienne* 40 (1938): 55–77, 289–312.

Greene, Molly. "Beyond the Northern Invasion: The Mediterranean in the Seventeenth Century." *Past and Present* 174, 1 (2002): 42–71.

———. *A Shared World: Christians and Muslims in the Early Modern Mediterranean*. Princeton, NJ: Princeton University Press, 2000.

Grigsby, Darcy Grimaldo. *Extremities: Painting Empire in Post-Revolutionary France*. New Haven, CT: Yale University Press, 2002.

Grillon, Pierre. *Un Chargé d'affaires au Maroc: la correspondance du consul Louis Chénier, 1767–1782*. 2 vols. Paris: SEVPEN, 1970.

———. "Origines et fondation du Consulat de France à Alger (1564–1582)." *Revue d'histoire diplomatique* 78 (1964): 97–117.

Grimaldi-Hierholtz, Roseline. *L'Ordre des Trinitaires: histoire et spiritualité*. Paris: Sarment-Fayard, 1994.

———. *Les Trinitaires de Fontainebleau et d'Avon*. Fontainebleau: Centre d'études culturelles, civiques et sociales de Seine-et-Marne, 1990.

Groebner, Valentin. *Who Are You? Identification, Deception and Surveillance in Early Modern Europe*. New York: Zone Books, 2007.

Groot, Alexander H. de. "Ottoman North Africa and the Dutch Republic in the

Seventeenth and Eighteenth Centuries." *Revue de l'Occident musulman et de la Méditerranée* 39 (1985): 131–147.

Grosjean, Georges. *La Maîtrise de la Méditerranée et la Tunisie pendant la révolution française (1789–1802): étude d'histoire diplomatique et navale.* Paris: Chapelot, 1914.

Guest, Kristen, ed. *Eating Their Words: Cannibalism and the Boundaries of Cultural Identity.* Albany: SUNY Press, 2001.

Guiral, Pierre. "L'Opinion marseillaise et les débats de l'entreprise algérienne (1830–1841)." *Revue historique* 214 (1955): 9–34.

Hampton, Timothy. "'Turkish Dogs': Rabelais, Erasmus, and the Rhetoric of Alterity." *Representations* 41 (1993): 58–82.

Harding, Nicholas B. "North African Piracy, the Hanoverian Carrying Trade, and the British State, 1728–1828." *Historical Journal* 43, 1 (2000): 25–47.

Hardwick, Julie. *The Practice of Patriarchy: Gender and the Politics of Household Authority in Early Modern France.* University Park: Pennsylvania State University Press, 1998.

Harrak, Fatima. "Mawlay Isma'il's Jaysh al-'Abīd: Reassessment of a Military Experience." In *Slave Elites in the Middle East and Africa: A Comparative Study*, edited by Toru Miura and John Edward Philips, 177–196. London: Kegan Paul, 2000.

Heers, Jacques. *Les Barbaresques: la course et la guerre en Méditerranée, XIVe–XVIe siècle.* Paris: Perrin, 2001.

———. *Esclaves et domestiques au Moyen Age dans le monde méditerranéen.* Paris: Fayard, 1981.

Heinrich, Pierre. *L'Alliance franco-algérienne au XVIe siècle.* Lyon: Veuve Mougin-Rusand, 1898.

Helgason, Thornsteinn. "Historical Narrative as Collective Therapy: The Case of the Turkish Raid in Iceland." *Scandinavian Journal of History* 22 (1997): 275–289.

Herzfeld, Michael. "Practical Mediterraneanism: Excuses for Everything, from Epistemology to Eating." In *Rethinking the Mediterranean*, edited by William Vernon Harris, 45–63. Oxford: Oxford University Press, 2005.

Hildesheimer, Françoise. *Le Bureau de la santé de Marseille sous l'Ancien régime: le renfermement de la contagion.* Marseille: Fédération historique de Provence, 1980.

Hirschberg, Haim Zeev. *A History of the Jews in North Africa.* 3 vols. Leiden, Netherlands: Brill, 1974–1981.

"Histoire du massacre des Turcs à Marseille en 1620." In *Documents de l'histoire de Provence*, edited by Edouard Baratier, 191–193. Toulouse: Privat, 1971.

Hoexter, Miriam. *Endowments, Rulers and Community: Waqf al-Haramayn in Ottoman Algiers.* Leiden, Netherlands: Brill, 1998.

Howard, Edward. *Memoirs of Sir Sidney Smith, K.C.B., &c.* 2 vols. London: R. Bentley, 1839.

Hulme, Peter. *Colonial Encounters: Europe and the Native Caribbean, 1492–1797.* New York: Routledge, 1992.

Huntington, Samuel. "The Clash of Civilizations." *Foreign Affairs* 72, 3 (1993): 22–49.

Hunwick, John, and Eve Trout Powell, eds. *The African Diaspora in the Mediterranean Lands of Islam*. Princeton, NJ: Markus Wiener, 2002.

Isom-Verhaaren, Christine. "'Barbarossa and His Army Who Came to Succor All of Us': Ottoman and French Views of Their Joint Campaign of 1543–1544." *French Historical Studies* 30, 3 (2007): 395–425.

Israel, Jonathan. "Crypto-Judaism in 17th-Century France: An Economic and Religious Bridge between the Hispanic World and the Sephardic Diaspora." In *Diasporas within a Diaspora: Jews, Crypto-Jews, and the World of Maritime Empires, 1540–1740*, 245–268. Leiden, Netherlands: Brill, 2002.

Jainchill, Andrew J. S. *Reimagining Politics after the Terror: The Republican Origins of French Liberalism*. Ithaca, NY: Cornell University Press, 2008.

James, Alan. *The Navy and Government in Early Modern France, 1572–1661*. Suffolk, UK: Royal Historical Society, 2004.

Jameson, Fredric. "Magical Narratives: Romance as Genre." *New Literary History* 7, 1 (1975): 135–163.

Jameson, Russell Parsons. *Montesquieu et l'esclavage: étude sur les origines de l'opinion antiesclavagiste en France au XVIIIe siècle*. New York: B. Franklin, 1971.

Jensen, De Lamar. "The Ottoman Turks in Sixteenth Century French Diplomacy." *Sixteenth Century Journal* 16, 4 (1985): 451–470.

Jones, Colin. *The Charitable Imperative: Hospitals and Nursing in Ancien Regime and Revolutionary France*. London: Routledge, 1989.

———. *Charity and Bienfaisance: The Treatment of the Poor in the Montpellier Region 1740–1815*. Cambridge: Cambridge University Press, 1982.

———. "Plague and Its Metaphors in Early Modern France." *Representations* 53 (1996): 97–127.

Jouanna, Arlette. *L'Idée de race en France au XVIe siècle et au début du XVIIe siècle, 1498–1614*. Paris: H. Champion, 1976.

Julien, Charles-André. *Histoire d'Algérie contemporaine: la conquête et les débuts de la colonisation*. 2 vols. Paris: Presses universitaires de France, 1964.

———. *History of North Africa (Tunisia, Algeria, Morocco) from the Arab Conquest to 1830*. Translated John Petrie. New York: Praeger, 1970.

———. "Marseille et la question d'Alger à la veille de la conquête." *Revue africaine* 60 (1919): 16–61.

———. "L'Opposition et la guerre d'Alger à la veille de la conquête." *Bulletin trimestriel de la Société de géographie et d'archéologie d'Oran* 61 (1921): 21–44.

———. "La Question d'Alger devant les Chambres sous la Restauration." *Revue africaine* 63 (1922): 270–305, 425–456.

———. *La Question d'Alger devant l'opinion, 1827 à 1830*. Oran: Fouque, 1922.

Jurien de la Gravière, Jean Pierre Edmond. *Les Corsaires barbaresques et la marine de Soliman le Grand*. Paris: E. Plon, Nourrit, 1887.

Kaiser, Wolfgang. "Les 'Hommes de crédit' dans les rachats des captifs proven-
    çaux, XVIe–XVIIe siècles." In *Le Commerce des captifs: les intermédiaires
    dans l'échange et le rachat des prisonniers en Méditerranée, XVe–XVIIIe
    siècle*, edited by Kaiser, 291–319. Rome: Ecole française de Rome, 2008.
———. *Marseille au temps des troubles, 1559–1596: morphologie sociale et
    luttes de factions*. Paris: Editions de l'EHESS, 1992.
———. "Négocier la liberté: missions françaises pour l'échange et le rachat de
    captifs au Maghreb (XVIIe siècle)." In *La Mobilité des personnes en Méditer-
    ranée de l'antiquité à l'époque moderne: procédures de contrôle et documents
    d'identification*, edited by Claudia Moatti. Rome: Ecole française de Rome,
    2004.
———. "Les Paradoxes d'une ville frontière: conflits et compromis à Marseille
    au XVIe siècle." In *La Ville à la Renaissance: espaces, représentations, pou-
    voirs*, edited by Gérald Chaix, Marie-Luce Demonet, and Robert Sauzet.
    Paris: H. Champion, 2008.
———. "Vérifier les histoires, localiser les personnes: l'identification comme pro-
    cessus de communication en Méditerranée (XVIe–XVIIe siècles)." In *Gens de
    passage en Méditerranée de l'Antiquité à l'époque moderne: procédures de
    contrôle et d'identification*, edited by Claude Moatti and Wolfgang Kaiser,
    369–386. Paris: Maisonneuve & Larose, 2007.
———, ed. *Le Commerce des captifs: les intermédiaires dans l'échange et le
    rachat des prisonniers en Méditerranée, XVe–XVIIIe siècle*. Rome: Ecole
    française de Rome, 2008.
Kilgour, Maggie. *From Communion to Cannibalism: An Anatomy of Meta-
    phors of Incorporation*. Princeton, NJ: Princeton University Press, 1995.
King, Dean. *Skeletons on the Zahara*. New York: Little, Brown, 2004.
Kitzen, Michael. *Tripoli and the United States at War: A History of American Re-
    lations with the Barbary States, 1785–1805*. Jefferson, NC: McFarland, 1993.
Knetsch, F. R. J. *Pierre Jurieu: Theoloog en politikus der refuge*. Kampen, Neth-
    erlands: J. H. Kok, 1967.
Koehler, Henry. *L'Eglise chrétienne du Maroc et la Mission franciscaine (1221–
    1790)*. Paris: Société d'éditions franciscaines, 1934.
———. "Quelques points d'histoire sur les captifs chrétiens de Meknès." *Hés-
    peris* 8 (1928): 177–187.
Koufinkana, Marcel. *Les Esclaves noirs en France sous l'Ancien régime (XVIe–
    XVIIIe siècles)*. Paris: L'Harmattan, 2008.
Krieken, Gérard van. *Corsaires et marchands: les relations entre Alger et le
    Pays-Bays, 1604–1830*. Paris: Bouchène, 2002.
Lamar, Glenn J. *Jérôme Bonaparte: The War Years, 1800–1815*. Westport, CT:
    Greenwood Press, 2000.
Lambert, Charles-Auguste-Joseph. *Histoire de la ville de Mussy-l'Evêque*.
    Chaumont: C. Cavaniol, 1878.
Lambert, Frank. *The Barbary Wars: American Independence in the Atlantic
    World*. New York: Hill and Wang, 2005.
Lambert, Gustave. "L'Oeuvre de la rédemption des captifs à Toulon." *Revue de
    Marseille et de Provence* 10 (1864): 324–332, 353–369, 401–413, 523–539.

La Roncière, Charles de. "Une Histoire de Bornou au XVIIe siècle par un chirurgien français captif à Tripoli." *Revue de l'histoire des colonies* 7 (1919): 73–88.

———. *Histoire de la marine française.* 6 vols. Paris: E. Plon, Nourrit, 1899–1932.

———. *Nègres et négriers.* Paris: Editions des Portiques, 1933.

Larquié, Claude. "Captifs chrétiens et esclaves maghrébins au XVIIIe siècle: une tentative de comparaison." In *Captius i esclaus a l'antiguitat i al món modern: actes del XIX colloqui internacional del GIREA . . .*, edited by María Luisa Sánchez León and Gonçal López Nadal, 347–364. Naples: Jovene, 1996.

La Véronne, Chantal de. "Quelques processions de captifs en France à leur retour du Maroc, d'Algérie ou de Tunis." *Revue de l'Occident musulman et de la Méditerranée* 8, 1 (1970): 131–142.

Le Bras, Marthe Folain. *Un Projet d'ordonnance du chancelier Daguesseau: étude de quelques incapacités de donner et de recevoir sous l'Ancien régime.* Paris: Sirey, 1941.

Leclercq, Jules. "Les Corsaires algériens en Islande en 1627." *Bulletin de la Classe des lettres et des sciences morales et politiques (Académie royale de Belgique)* 12 (1926): 312–324.

Ledermann, Emile. "Les Frères de N.D. de la Merci et la rédemption des captifs." Bachelier en théologie, Université de Paris, 1898.

Le Fur, Erwan. "La Renaissance d'un apostolat: l'Ordre de la Trinité et la rédemption des captifs dans les années 1630." *Cahiers de la Méditerranée* 66 (2003). http://cdlm.revues.org/index110.html.

Legendre, Philippe. *Histoire de la persécution faite à l'église de Rouen sur la fin du dernier siècle.* Rotterdam: Jean Malherbe, 1704; reprint, Rouen: Léon Deshays, 1875.

Lehr, Henry. *Les Protestants d'autrefois: sur mer et outre mer.* Paris: Fischbacher, 1907.

Leiner, Frederick C. *The End of Barbary Terror.* New York: Oxford University Press, 2006.

Le Marchand, Edgard. *L'Europe et la conquête d'Alger d'après des documents originaux tirés des archives de l'Etat.* Paris: Perin, 1913.

Lespès, René. *Alger, étude de géographie et d'histoire urbaines.* Paris: Félix Alcan, 1930.

Lesure, Michel. "Les Relations franco-ottomanes à l'épreuve des guerres de religion (1560–1594)." In *L'Empire ottoman, la République de Turquie et la France*, edited by Hâmit Batu and Jean-Louis Bacqué-Grammont, 38–57. Istanbul: Isis, 1986.

Levasseur, Émile. *Les Prix: aperçu de l'histoire économique de la valeur et du revenu de la terre en France, du commencement du XIIIe siècle à la fin du XVIIIe.* Paris: Chamerot & Renouard, 1893.

Lewis, Bernard. "Corsairs in Iceland." *Revue de l'Occident musulman et de la Méditerranée* 16 (1973): 139–144.

———. *Race and Slavery in the Middle East: An Historical Enquiry.* New York: Oxford University Press, 1990.

"Le Livre de raison du notaire Etienne Borrelly, 1654 à 1717." *Mémoires de l'Académie de Nîmes* 8 (1885): 222–298.

Longino, Michèle. *Orientalism in French Classical Drama.* Cambridge: Cambridge University Press, 2002.

Loth, Gaston. *Arnoldo Soler: chargé d'affaires d'Espagne à Tunis et sa correspondance, 1808–1810.* Tunis: Société anonyme de l'imprimerie rapide, 1905.

———. "Le Pillage de Saint-Pierre de Sardaigne par les corsaires tunisiens en 1798." *Revue tunisienne* 12 (1905): 9–14.

Löwenheim, Oded. "'Do Ourselves Credit and Render a Lasting Service to Mankind': British Moral Prestige, Humanitarian Intervention and the Barbary Pirates." *International Studies Quarterly* 47, 1 (2003): 23–48.

———. *Predators and Parasites: Persistent Agents of Transnational Harm and Great Power Authority.* Ann Arbor: University of Michigan Press, 2006.

MacMaster, Neil. "The Torture Controversy (1998–2002): Towards a 'New History' of the Algerian War?" *Modern and Contemporary France* 10, 4 (2002): 449–459.

Martin, Michel L., Lucien-René Abénon, and Alain Yacou. *Mourir pour les Antilles: indépendance nègre ou esclavage, 1802–1804.* Paris: Editions caribéennes, 1991.

Masse, Etienne-Michel. *Mémoire historique et statistique sur le canton de La Ciotat: département des Bouches-du-Rhône.* Marseille: Caranud fils, 1842.

Masson, Paul. *Les Galères de France, 1481–1781: Marseille, port de guerre.* Paris: Hachette, 1938.

———. *Histoire des établissements et du commerce français dans l'Afrique barbaresque (1560–1793): Algérie, Tunisie, Tripolitaine, Maroc.* Paris: Hachette, 1903.

———. *Histoire du commerce français dans le Levant au XVIIe siècle.* Paris: Hachette, 1896.

Matar, Nabil. "The Barbary Corsairs, King Charles and the Civil War." *Seventeenth Century* 16, 2 (2001): 239–258.

———. *Britain and Barbary, 1589–1689.* Gainesville: University Press of Florida, 2005.

———. *Islam and Britain, 1558–1685.* Cambridge: Cambridge University Press, 1998.

———. *Turks, Moors and Englishmen in the Age of Discovery.* New York: Columbia University Press, 1999.

———. "'Turning Turk': Conversion to Islam in English Renaissance Thought." *Durham University Journal* 86, 55 (1994): 33–41.

———. "Wives, Captive Husbands and Turks: The First Women Petitioners in Caroline England." *Explorations in Renaissance Culture* 23 (1997): iii–29.

Mathiex, Jean. "Sur la marine marchande barbaresque au XVIIIe siècle." *Annales: economies, sociétés, civilisations* 13 (1958): 87–93.

———. "Trafic et prix de l'homme en Méditerranée au XVIIIe siècle." *Annales: economies, sociétés, civilisations* 9 (1954): 157–164.

Mathorez, Jules. "Les Eléments de population orientale en France: Sarrasins, Maures et Turcs." *Revue des études historiques* 2 (1917): 191–203.

————. *Les Etrangers en France sous l'Ancien régime: histoire de la formation de la population française.* 2 vols. Paris: Edouard Champion, 1919.

Maza, Sarah C. *Private Lives and Public Affairs: The Causes Célèbres of Prerevolutionary France.* Berkeley: University of California Press, 1993.

Maziane, Leïla. "Les Captifs européens en terre marocaine aux XVIIe et XVIIIe siècles." *Cahiers de la Méditerranée* 65 (2002). http://cdlm.revues.org/index45.html.

————. *Salé et ses corsaires (1666–1727): un port de course marocain au XVIIe siècle.* Mont-Saint-Aignan: Publications des Universités de Rouen et du Havre; Caen: Presses universitaires de Caen, 2007.

McCloy, Shelby Thomas. *The Negro in France.* [Lexington]: University of Kentucky Press, 1961.

McCluskey, Philip. "Commerce Before Crusade? France, the Ottoman Empire and the Barbary Pirates (1661–1669)." *French History* 23, 1 (2009): 1–21.

Meakin, Budgett. *The Moorish Empire: A Historical Epitome.* London: Swan Sonnenschein, 1899.

Meillassoux, Claude. *The Anthropology of Slavery: The Womb of Iron and Gold.* Chicago: University of Chicago Press, 1991.

Mercier, Ernest. *Histoire de l'Afrique septentrionale (Berbérie) depuis les temps les plus reculés jusqu'à la conquête française.* 3 vols. Paris: Ernest Leroux, 1888–1891.

Merle, Jean-Toussaint. *Anecdotes historiques et politiques pour servir à l'histoire de la Conquête d'Alger en 1830.* Paris: G.-A. Dentu, 1831.

Merle, Louis. "Notes et documents: rachat de prisonniers faits par les barbaresques au XVIIe siècle." *Revue du Bas-Poitou* 71, 2 (1960): 142–143.

Merouche, Lemnouar. *Recherches sur l'Algérie à l'époque ottomane.* 2 vols. Paris: Bouchène, 2002–2007.

Mesnage, Joseph. *Le Christianisme en Afrique.* 3 vols. Algiers: Adolpe Jourdan, 1914–1915.

Mettas, Jean. *Répertoire des expéditions négrières françaises au XVIIIe siècle: ports autres que Nantes.* 2 vols. Edited by Serge Daget and Michèle Daget. Paris: Société française d'histoire d'outre-mer, 1978–1984.

Micacchi, Rodolfo. "I Rapporti tra il Regno di Francia e la Reggenza di Tripoli di Barberia nella prima metà del secolo XVIII." *Rivista delle colonie italiane* 8 (1934): 65–81, 159–182, 247–276.

————. *La Tripolitania sotto il dominio dei Caramanli.* Verbania, Italy: A. Airoldi, 1936.

Miège, Jean-Louis. "Aspects de la course marocaine du XVIIe au XIXe siècle." In *La Guerre de course en Méditerranée (1515–1830)*, edited by Antoine-Marie Graziani and Michel Vergé-Franceschi, 39–71. Paris: Presses de l'Université de Paris-Sorbonne, 2000.

Miller, Kathryn A. *Guardians of Islam: Religious Authority and Muslim Communities of Late Medieval Spain.* New York: Columbia University Press, 2008.

Mireur, Frédéric. "Ligue des ports de Provence contre les pirates barbaresques en 1585–1586." *Mélanges historiques* 5 (1886): 601–638.

Misermont, Lucien. "Les Français mis à bouche du canon à Alger en 1683 avec le consul Jean Le Vacher, et le canon appelé Consulaire." *Revue des études historiques* 20 (1917): 475–497.

Moalla, Asma. *The Regency of Tunis and the Ottoman Porte, 1777–1814: Army and Government of a North-African Ottoman Eyālet at the End of the Eighteenth Century*. New York: Routledge, 2004.

Monchicourt, Charles. "L'Expédition de Djidjelli." *Revue maritime* 137–138 (1898): 464–492, 41–71.

Monlaü, Jean. *Les Etats barbaresques*. Paris: Presses universitaires de France, 1973.

Mooney, Chris. "The Barbary Analogy." American Prospect Online. 16 October 2001. http://www.prospect.org/cs/articles?article=the_barbary_analogy.

Moreau-Rendu, Suzanne. *Les Captifs libérés et le couvent Saint-Mathurin de Paris*. Paris: Editions latines, 1974.

Moudine, Mohamed. "Le Rachat des esclaves musulmans en Europe méridionale du XIIIe siècle à la fin du XVIIIe siècle: le cas du Maroc." Doctorat, Université de Provence, Aix-Marseille I, 1996.

Moureau, François, ed. *Captifs en Méditerranée (XVIe–XVIIIe siècles): histoires, récits, legends*. Paris: Presses de l'Université de Paris-Sorbonne, 2008.

Moussa, Sarga. "Le Bédouin, le voyageur et le philosophe." *Dix-huitième siècle* 28 (1996): 141–158.

———. "Une Peur vaincue: l'émergence du mythe bédouin chez les voyageurs français du XVIIIe siècle." In *La Peur au XVIIIe siècle: discours, représentations, pratiques*, edited by Jacques Berchtold and Michel Porret, 193–212. Geneva: Droz, 1994.

Muthu, Sankar. *Enlightenment against Empire*. Princeton, NJ: Princeton University Press, 2003.

Nékrouf, Younès. *Une Amitié orageuse: Moulay Ismaïl et Louis XIV*. Paris: Albin Michel, 1987.

Nicolaïdis, Dimitri. *D'une Grèce à l'autre: représentations des Grecs modernes par la France révolutionnaire*. Paris: Les Belles Lettres, 1992.

Noguères, Henri. *L'Expédition d'Alger 1830*. Paris: René Julliard, [1962].

Noirel, Gérard. "The Identification of the Citizen: The Birth of Republican Civil Status in France." In *Documenting Individual Identity: The Development of State Practices in the Modern World*, edited by Jane Caplan and John Toppey, 28–48. Princeton, NJ: Princeton University Press, 2001.

Nordman, Daniel. "Sauf-conduits et passeports." In *Dictionnaire de l'Ancien régime: royaume de France, XVIe–XVIIIe siècle*, edited by Lucien Bély, 1123–1124. Paris: Presses universitaires de France, 1996.

Nys, Ernest. *Etudes de droit international et de droit politique*. 2 vols. Brussels: Alfred Castaigne, 1896–1901.

Osler, Edward. *The Life of Admiral Viscount Exmouth*. London: Smith, Elder, 1835.

Pannier, Jacques. "Les Protestants français et l'Algérie." *Bulletin de la Société de Histoire du Protestantisme français* 79 (1930): 146–203.

Panzac, Daniel. *Les Corsaires barbaresques: la fin d'une épopée, 1800–1820*. Paris: CNRS Editions, 1999.

————. *Quarantaines et lazarets: l'Europe et la peste d'Orient (XVIIe–XXe siècles)*. Aix-en-Provence: Edisud, 1986.

Parker, Patricia A. *Inescapable Romance: Studies in the Poetics of a Mode*. Princeton, NJ: Princeton University Press, 1979.

Parker, Richard Bordeaux. *Uncle Sam in Barbary: A Diplomatic History*. Gainesville: University Press of Florida, 2004.

Patterson, Orlando. *Slavery and Social Death: A Comparative Study*. Cambridge, MA: Harvard University Press, 1982.

Peabody, Sue. "'A Nation Born to Slavery': Missionaries and Racial Discourse in Seventeenth-Century French Antilles." *Journal of Social History* 38, 1 (2004): 113–126.

————. *"There Are No Slaves in France": The Political Culture of Race and Slavery in the Ancien Régime*. New York: Oxford University Press, 1996.

Pennell, C. R., ed. *Piracy and Diplomacy in Seventeenth-Century North Africa: The Journal of Thomas Baker, English Consul in Tripoli, 1677–1685*. Rutherford, NJ: Fairleigh Dickinson University Press, 1989.

Penz, Charles. *Les Captifs français du Maroc au XVII siècle, 1577–1699*. Rabat, Morocco: Imprimerie officielle, 1944.

————. *Journal du consulat de France à Maroc, paraphé par Louis Chénier*. Casablanca: Imprimeries réunies, 1943.

————. *Personnalités et familles françaises d'Afrique du Nord, Maroc (1588–1814)*. Paris: Editions S.G.A.F., 1948.

[Perboyre, Gabriel]. *Mémoires de la Congrégation de la Mission*. 9 vols. Paris: A la maison principale de la Congrégation de la Mission, 1863–1866.

Peskin, Lawrence A. *Captives and Countrymen: Barbary Slavery and the American Public, 1785–1816*. Baltimore: Johns Hopkins University Press, 2009.

Peter, Jean. *Les Barbaresques sous Louis XIV: le duel entre Alger et la Marine du Roi (1681–1698)*. Paris: Economica, 1997.

Petitpré, Robert. "Retour très probable de Jean Blay esclave au Maroc, à la Chaume: incidents auxquels il a mêlé avec le curé du lieu en 1640." *Bulletin de la Société Olona* 102 (1982): 18–20.

————. "Tentative de rachat de deux captifs chaumois an Maroc en 1636." *Bulletin de la Société Olona* 97–98 (1981): 16–18.

Pey, Marc-André. "Tripoli de Barbarie sous les dernier Karamanli (1754–1835): essai de monographie d'un régence à la fin de l'ère barbaresque." Thèse troisième cycle, Université d'Aix-en-Provence, 1977.

Peyssonnel, Jean-André. *Voyages dans les régences de Tunis et d'Alger*. Edited by Lucette Valensi. Paris: La Découverte, 1987.

Peytraud, Lucien. *L'Esclavage aux Antilles françaises avant 1789, d'après des documents inédits des archives coloniales*. Paris: Hachette, 1897.

Pierre, Benoist. *Le Père Joseph: l'éminence grise de Richelieu*. Paris: Perrin, 2007.

————. "Le Père Joseph, l'empire Ottoman et la Méditerranée au début du XVIIe siècle." *Cahiers de la Méditerranée* 71, 2 (2005). http://cdlm.revues.org/index968.html.

Pignon, Jean. "L'Esclavage en Tunisie de 1590 à 1620." *Revue tunisienne* 32 (1930): 18–37; 34 (1932): 345–377.

———. "Une Expédition marseillaise sur les côtes barbaresques (1616). L'armement Vincheguerre." In *Maghreb et Sahara: études géographiques offertes à Jean Despois*, edited by Xavier de Planhol, 307–320. Paris: Société de géographie, 1973.

Pike, Ruth. *Penal Servitude in Early Modern Spain.* Madison: University of Wisconsin Press, 1983.

Pillorget, René. "Un Incident diplomatique franco-turc sous Louis XIII: le massacre d'une ambassade de la Régence d'Alger (14 mars 1620)." *Revue d'histoire diplomatique* 88 (1974): 44–58.

Plantet, Eugène. *Les Consuls de France avant la conquête (1579–1830).* Paris: Messageries Hachette, 1930.

Plassart, Anna. "'Un Imperialiste Liberal'? Jean-Baptiste Say on Colonies and the Extra-European World." *French Historical Studies* 32, 2 (2009): 223–250.

Playfair, Robert Lambert. *The Scourge of Christendom: Annals of British relations with Algiers Prior to the French Conquest.* London: Smith, Elder, 1884.

Pocock, Tom. *Breaking the Chains: The Royal Navy's War on White Slavery.* Annapolis, MD: Naval Institute Press, 2006.

———. *A Thirst for Glory: The Life of Admiral Sir Sidney Smith.* London: Aurum Press, 1996.

Popkin, Richard H. "Epicureanism and Skepticism in the Early Seventeenth Century." In *Philomathes: Studies and Essays in the Humanities in Memory of Philip Merlan*, edited by Robert B. Palmer and Robert Hamerton-Kelly, 346–357. The Hague: Martinus Nijhoff, 1971.

Poumarède, Géraud. "La France et les barbaresques: police des mers et relations internationales en Méditerranée (XVIe–XVIIe siècles)." *Revue d'histoire maritime* 4 (2005): 117–146.

———. "Naissance d'une institution royale: les consuls de la nation française en Levant et en Barbarie au XVIe et XVIIe siècles." *Annuaire-bulletin de la Société de l'histoire de France* (2001): 65–128.

———. *Pour en finir avec la croisade: mythes et réalités de la lutte contre les Turcs aux XVIe et XVIIe siècles.* Paris: Presses universitaires de France, 2004.

Pouqueville, François Charles Hughes Laurent. *Voyage dans la Grèce: comprenant la description ancienne et moderne de l'Épire, de l'Illyrie grecque, de la Macédoine Cisaxienne, d'une partie de la Triballie, de la Thessalie, de l'Arcarnie, de l'Étolie ancienne et Épicète, de la Locride Hespérienne, de la Doride, et du Péloponèse; avec des considérations sur l'archéologie, la numismatique, les moeurs, les arts, l'industrie et le commerce des habitants de ces provinces.* 5 vols. Paris: Firmin Didot, 1820–1821.

———. *Voyage en Morée, à Constantinople, en Albanie et dans plusieurs autres parties de l'Empire othoman pendant les années 1798, 1799, 1800 et 1801.* 3 vols. Paris: Gabon, 1805.

Pritchard, James S. *In Search of Empire: The French in the Americas, 1670–1730.* Cambridge: Cambridge University Press, 2004.

Providence, Calixte de la. *Corsaires et rédempteurs: ou Récit des souffrances des anciens captifs et des travaux entrepris pour leur délivrance.* Lille: Desclée de Brouwer, 1884.

Ragosta, Rosalba. *Le Genti del mare Mediterraneo.* 2 vols. Naples: Lucio Pironti, 1981.

Rambert, Gaston, ed. *Histoire du commerce de Marseille.* 8 vols. Paris: Plon, 1949–1966.

"Recate de cautivos en Malta por Muammad b. Utmàn." *Hésperis-Tamuda* 10 (1969): 273–329.

Régent, Frédéric. *La France et ses esclaves: de la colonisation aux abolitions (1620–1848).* Paris: Bernard Grasset, 2007.

Requemora, Sylvie. "Le Voyageur mystificateur ou les ruses de l'écriture viatique dans la seconde moitié du XVIIe siècle: le cas de l'Odyssée de René Chastelet des Boys." In *Ecriture de la ruse,* edited by Elzbieta Grodek, 163–186. Amsterdam: Rodopi, 2000.

Rey, Francis. *La Protection diplomatique et consulaire dans les échelles du Levant et de Barbarie.* Paris: L. Larose, 1899.

Reynaud, Eugène Pélissier de. "La Régence de Tripoli." *Revue des deux mondes* 12 (1855): 5–48.

Ribard, Clément. "Prisonniers protestants en Barbarie." *Bulletin de la Société de Histoire du Protestantisme français* 14 (1865): 131–135.

Ricard, Robert. "Ibero-Africana: le père Jérôme Gratien de la Mère de Dieu et sa captivité à Tunis (1593-1595)." *Revue africaine* 89 (1945): 190–200.

Ricci, Giovanni. "Crypto-identities: Disguised Turks, Christians and Jews." In *Finding Europe: Discourses on Margins, Communities, Images,* edited by Anthony Molho and Diogo Ramada Curto, 39–54. New York: Berghahn Books, 2007.

Riggio, Achille. "Un Censimento di schiavi in Tunisia ottocentesca." *Archivio storico per la Calabria e la Lucania* 8 (1938): 333–342.

———. "Esclaves et missionnaires en Barbarie, 1672–1682." *Revue africaine* 93 (1949): 38–64.

Ritchie, Robert C. *Captain Kidd and the War against the Pirates.* Cambridge, MA: Harvard University Press, 1986.

Roberts, Priscilla H., and Richard S. Roberts. *Thomas Barclay (1728–1793): Consul in France, Diplomat in Barbary.* Bethlehem, PA: Lehigh University Press, 2008.

Roberts, Priscilla H., and James N. Tull. "Moroccan Sultan Sidi Muhammad Ibn Abdallah's Diplomatic Initiatives toward the United States, 1777–1786." *Proceedings of the American Philosophical Society* 143, 2 (1999): 233–265.

Roche, Daniel. *The Culture of Clothing: Dress and Fashion in the Ancien Régime.* Translated by Jean Birrell. Cambridge: Cambridge University Press, 1996.

———. *Humeurs vagabondes: de la circulation des hommes et de l'utilité des voyages.* Paris: Fayard, 2003.

Rodriguez, Jarbel. *Captives and Their Saviors in the Medieval Crown of Aragon.* Washington, DC: Catholic University of America Press, 2007.

Røge, Pernille. "'La Clef de commerce': The Changing Role of Africa in France's Atlantic Empire, ca. 1760–1797." *History of European Ideas* 34, 4 (2008): 431–443.

Rogers, P. G. *A History of Anglo-Moroccan Relations to 1900.* London: Foreign and Commonwealth Office, 1970.

Romano, Aurora. "Schiavi siciliani e traffici monetari nel Mediterraneo del XVII secolo." In *Rapporti diplomatici e scambi commerciali nel Mediterraneo moderno*, edited by Mirella Mafrici, 275–303. Soveria Mannelli, Italy: Rubbettino editore: 2004.

Rosenstock, Morton. "The House of Bacri and Busnach." *Jewish Social Studies* 14 (1952): 343–364.

Rossi, Ettore. *Storia di Tripoli e della Tripolitania: dalla conquista araba al 1911.* Edited by Maria Nallino. Rome: Istituto per l'Oriente, 1968.

Rostagno, Lucia. *Mi faccio turco: esperienze ed immagini dell'Islam nell'Italia moderna.* Rome: Istituto per l'Oriente, 1983.

Rotalier, Charles de. *Histoire d'Alger et de la piraterie des Turcs dans la Méditerranée à dater du seizième siècle.* 2 vols. Paris: Paulin, 1841.

Rothman, E. Natalie. "Becoming Venetian: Conversion and Transformation in the Seventeenth-Century Mediterranean." *Mediterranean Historical Review* 21, 1 (2006): 39–75.

Rouard de Card, Edgard. *Traités de la France avec les pays de l'Afrique du Nord: Algérie, Tunisie, Tripolitaine, Maroc.* Paris: A. Pedone, 1906.

Rouillard, Clarence Dana. *The Turk in French History, Thought, and Literature.* Paris: Boivin, 1941.

Rousseau, Alphonse. *Annales tunisiennes, ou Aperçu historique sur la régence de Tunis.* Algiers: Bastide, 1864.

Rozet, Claude-Antoine, Antoine-Michel Carette, Ferdinand Hoefer, and Louis Frank. *Algérie, Etats Tripolitains, Tunis.* Paris: Firmin Didot, 1850.

Rudt de Collenberg, Wipertus H. *Esclavage et rançons des chrétiens en méditerranée, 1570–1600 d'après les "litterae hortetoriae" de l'Archivo Segreto Vaticano.* Paris: Le Léopard d'Or, 1987.

Ruedy, John. *Modern Algeria: The Origins and Development of a Nation.* 2nd ed. Bloomington: Indiana University Press, 2005.

Sahlins, Peter. *Unnaturally French: Foreign Citizens in the Old Regime and After.* Ithaca, NY: Cornell University Press, 2004.

Said, Edward W. *Orientalism.* New York: Vintage Books, 1979.

Sala-Molins, Louis. *Le Code noir ou le calvaire de Canaan.* Paris: Presses universitaires de France, 1987.

Santoni, Pierre. "Le Passage des morisques en Provence (1610–1613)." *Provence historique* 46, 185 (1996): 333–383.

———. "Le Rachat des Corses esclaves à Tunis en 1779." Presented at the Congrès national des sociétés historiques et scientifiques: relations, échanges et coopération en Méditerranée, Bastia, Corsica, 2003. http://halshs.archives-ouvertes.fr/view_by_stamp.php?&halsid=7deb1tv1anctoh766j8vjuq9e4&label=SHS&langue=fr&action_todo=view&id=halshs-00162606&version=1.

Savine, Albert. *Dans les fers du Moghreb: récits de chrétiens esclaves au Maroc (XVIIe et XVIIIe siècles).* Paris: Société des éditions Louis-Michaud, 1912.

Scaraffia, Lucetta. *Rinnegati: per una storia dell'identita' occidentale.* 2nd ed. Bari, Italy: Laterza, 2002.

Schechter, Ronald. *Obstinate Hebrews: Representations of Jews in France, 1715–1815.* Berkeley: University of California Press, 2003.

Schen, Claire S. "Breaching 'Community' in Britain: Captives, Renegades, and the Redeemed." In *Defining Community in Early Modern Europe*, edited by Michaël Halvorson and Karen E. Spierling, 229–246. Aldershot, UK: Ashgate, 2008.

Schneider, Robert A. *The Ceremonial City: Toulouse Observed, 1738–1780.* Princeton, NJ: Princeton University Press, 1997.

Sears, Christine E. "A Different Kind of Slavery: American Captives in Barbary, 1776–1830." PhD diss., University of Delaware, 2007.

Sebag, Paul. *La Course tunisienne au XVIIe siècle.* Tunis: IBLA, 2001.

———. *La Régence de Tunis à la fin de dix-septième siècle.* Paris: L'Harmattan, 1993.

Serfass, Charles. "Les Esclaves chrétiens au Maroc du XVIe au XVIIe siècles." *Bulletin de la Société de Histoire du Protestantisme français* 79 (1930): 216–244.

Serval, Pierre. *La Ténébreuse histoire de la prise d'Alger.* Paris: La Table Ronde, 1980.

Sessions, Jennifer. *Empire of Virtue: Colonialism and Political Culture in Nineteenth-Century France and Algeria* (Ithaca, NY: Cornell University Press, forthcoming).

———. "Making Colonial France: Culture, National Identity and the Colonization of Algeria, 1830–1851." PhD diss., University of Pennsylvania, 2005.

Shepard, Todd. *The Invention of Decolonization: The Algerian War and the Remaking of France.* Ithaca, NY: Cornell University Press, 2006.

Shuval, Tal. *La Ville d'Alger ver la fin du XVIIIe siècle: population et cadre urbain.* Paris: CNRS Editions, 1998.

Silverstein, Paul A. "The New Barbarians: Piracy and Terrorism on the North African Frontier." *New Centennial Review* 5, 1 (2005): 179–212.

Skilliter, Susan A. "Catherine de' Medici's Turkish Ladies in Waiting: A Dilemma in Franco-Ottoman Diplomatic Relations." *Turcica* 7 (1975): 188–204.

Snader, Joe. *Caught between Worlds: British Captivity Narratives in Fact and Fiction.* Lexington: University Press of Kentucky, 2000.

Soucek, Svet. "Remarks on Some Western and Turkish Sources Dealing with the Barbarossa Brothers." *Güney-Doğu Avrupa Araştırmaları Dergisi* 1 (1972): 63–76.

Starna, William A., and Ralph Watkins. "Northern Iroquoian Slavery." *Ethnohistory* 38, 1 (1991): 34–57.

St. Clair, William. *That Greece Might Still Be Free: The Philhellenes in the War of Independence.* London: Oxford University Press, 1972.

Stella, Alessandro. "Les Galères dans la Méditerranée (XVe–XVIIIe siècles): miroir des mises en servitude." In *Esclavage et dépendances serviles: histoire comparée*, edited by Myriam Cottias, Alessandro Stella, and Bernard Vincent, 265–282. Paris: L'Harmattan, 2006.

———. *Histoires d'esclaves dans la péninsule ibérique.* Paris: Editions de l'EHESS, 2000.

Stewart, Devin J. "Taqiyyah as Performance: The Travels of Baha' al-Din al'Amili in the Ottoman Empire (991–93/1583–85)." In *Law and Society in Islam*, edited by Devin J. Stewart, Baber Johansen, and Amy Singer, 1–70. Princeton, NJ: Markus Wiener, 1995.

Stora, Benjamin. *La Gangrène et l'oubli: la mémoire de la guerre de l'Algérie*. Paris: La Découverte, 1998.

Stoye, John. *The Siege of Vienna: The Last Great Trial between Cross and Crescent*. New York: Pegasus Books, 2007.

Sue, Eugène. *Histoire de la marine française*. 2nd ed. 4 vols. Paris: Dépôt de la librairie, 1845.

Sumner, Charles. *The Works of Charles Sumner*. 15 vols. Boston: Lee and Shepard, 1870–1883.

Sweet, James H. "The Iberian Roots of American Racist Thought." *William and Mary Quarterly* 54, 1 (1997): 143–166.

Tabaki-Iona, Fridériki. *Poésie philhellénique et périodiques de la Restauration*. Athens: Société des archives helléniques, littéraires et historiques, 1993.

Takeda, Junko Thérèse. "French Absolutism, Marseillais Civic Humanism and the Languages of the Public Good." *Historical Journal* 49, 3 (2006): 707–734.

Teissier, Octave. *La Chambre de commerce de Marseille: son origin—sa mission création des premiers comptoirs français dans les échelles du Levant développement du commerce général et de la richesse nationale*. Marseille: Barlatier et Barthelet, 1892.

Temimi, Abdeljelil. "Le Bombardement d'Alger en 1816." In *Recherches et documents d'histoire maghrébine: la Tunisie, l'Algérie et la Tripolitaine de 1816 à 1871*, 209–239. Tunis: l'Université de Tunis, 1971.

Tenenti, Alberto. *Naufrages, corsaires, et assurances maritimes à Venise, 1592–1609*. Paris: SEVPEN, 1959.

———. *Piracy and the Decline of Venice, 1580–1615*. Berkeley: University of California Press, 1967.

Thomassy, Marie-Joseph Raymond. *Des Relations politiques et commerciales de la France avec le Maroc*. Paris: Arthur Bertrand, 1842.

Thomson, Ann. "Arguments for the Conquest of Algiers in the Late Eighteenth and Early Nineteenth Centuries." *Maghreb Review* 14, 1–2 (1989): 108–118.

———. *Barbary and Enlightenment: European Attitudes toward the Maghreb in the 18th Century*. Leiden, Netherlands: Brill, 1987.

———. "Diderot, Roubaud et l'esclavage." *Recherches sur Diderot et sur l'Encyclopédie* 35 (2003): 69–93.

Thomson, Janice E. *Mercenaries, Pirates, and Sovereigns: State-Building and Extraterritorial Violence in Early Modern Europe*. Princeton, NJ: Princeton University Press, 1994.

Tigier, Hervé. *La Bretagne de bon aloi: répertoire des arrêts sur remontrance du parlement de Bretagne, 1554–1789*. Rennes: Archives départementales d'Ille-et-Vilaine, 1987.

Tolbert, Jane. "Ambiguity and Conversion in the Correspondence of Nicolas-Claude Fabri de Peiresc and Thomas D'Arcos, 1630–1637." *Journal of Early Modern History* 13, 1 (2009): 1–24.

Toledano, Ehud R. *As If Silent and Absent: Bonds of Enslavement in the Islamic Middle East.* New Haven, CT: Yale University Press, 2007.

Tonnelé, Jean. "Les Corsaires algériens." *Revue historique de l'armée* 9 (1953): 25–37.

Torres, José Antonio Martínez. *Prisioneros de los infieles: vida y rescates de los cautivos cristianos en el Mediterráneo musulmán siglos XVI–XVII.* Barcelona: Ediciones Bellaterra, 2004.

Toschi, Paolo. *Le Fonti inedite di storia della Tripolitania.* Intra, Italy: A. Airoldi, 1934.

Trichaud, Jacques-Marie. *Histoire de la sainte eglise d'Arles.* 4 vols. Paris: Etienne Giraud, 1857–1864.

Turbet-Delof, Guy. *L'Afrique barbaresque dans la littérature française au XVIe et XVIIe siècles.* Geneva: Droz, 1973.

———. *A propos de trois impressions bordelaises: l'affaire de Djidjelli (1664) dans la presse française du temps.* Bordeaux: Taffard, 1968.

———. *Bibliographie critique du Maghreb dans la littérature française (1532–1715).* Algiers: Société nationale de l'édition et de diffusion, 1976.

———. "Bossuet et la question d'Alger." *Dix-septième siècle* 100 (1973): 63–67.

———. "Le Père mercédaire A. Quartier et sa chronique tripoline des années 1660–1668." *Cahiers de Tunisie* 8, 77–78 (1972): 51–58.

———. *La Presse périodique française et l'Afrique barbaresque au XVIIe siècle (1611–1715).* Geneva: Droz, 1973.

Vaglieri, Laura Veccia. "Santa Sede e Barbareschi dal 1814 al 1819." *Oriente Moderno* 12, 10 (1932): 465–484.

Vaillé, Eugène. *Histoire générale des postes françaises.* 7 vols. Paris: Presses universitaires de la France, 1947–1955.

Valensi, Lucette. "Esclaves chrétiens et esclaves noirs à Tunis au XVIIIe siècle." *Annales: economies, sociétés, civilisations* 6 (1967): 1267–1288.

Valensi, Lucette, and Simone Delesalle. "Le Mot 'nègre' dans les dictionnaires français d'Ancien régime: histoire et lexicographie." *Langue française, 'Langage et histoire'* 15 (1972): 79–104.

Vallery-Radot, Jean. "Note sur les estampes gravées par Mellan et Van Thulden pour les ordres rédempteurs de Notre-Dame de la Merci et des Trinitaires." *Bulletin philologique et historique du Comité des travaux historiques et scientifiques* (1955): 417–421.

Vallette, Marie-Agnès. "L'Echelle de Tripoli de Barbarie: 1786–1802." Mémoire de DES, Université de Paris II, 1975.

Van Aelbrouck, Jean-Pierre. "Comment faire de l'ordre dans une dynastie de comédiens? Le Cas de la famille Hus éclairé par des documents d'archives." In *Proceedings of the Second International CESAR Conference (June 2006).* http://www.cesar.org.uk/cesar2/conferences/cesar_conference_2006/VAelbrouck_paper06.html.

Vandal, Albert. *Une Ambassade française en Orient sous Louis XV: la mission du marquis de Villeneuve, 1728–1741.* 2nd ed. Paris: E. Plon, Nourrit, 1887.

Van Koningsveld, Pieter Sjoerd. "Muslim Slaves and Captives in Western Europe during the Late Middle Ages." *Islam and Christian-Muslim Relations* 6, 1 (1995): 5–23.

Van Orden, Kate. *Music, Discipline and Arms in Early Modern France*. Chicago: University of Chicago Press, 2005.

Vatin, Nicolas. "A propos de la captivité à Rhodes d'Oruç Re'îs dans les Gazavât-ı Hayrü-d-dîn Pasa." In *Turcica et Islamica: studi in memoria di Aldo Gallotta*, 2: 995–1011. Naples: Università degli studi di Napoli "L'Orientale," 2003.

Vaurigaud, Benjamin. *Essai sur l'histoire des églises réformées de Bretagne, 1535–1808*. 3 vols. Paris: Joël Cherbuliez, 1870.

Veinstein, Gilles. "Le Mythe des capitulations de 1536." In *Histoire de l'islam et des musulmans en France du Moyen Age à nos jours*, edited by Mohammed Arkoun, 354. Paris: Albin Michel, 2006.

Verdier, Léon. "L'Esclavage musulman en Algérie du XVe au XIXe siècles." Doctorat, Université de Paris, 1948.

Vergé-Franceschi, Michel. *Abraham Duquesne: huguenot et marin du Roi-Soleil*. Paris: Editions France-Empire, 1992.

———. *Chronique maritime de la France d'Ancien régime, 1492–1792*. Paris: SEDES, 1998.

———. *Toulon, port royal, 1481–1789*. Paris: Tallandier, 2002.

Vergé-Franceschi, Michel, and Antoine-Marie Graziani, eds. *La Guerre de course en Méditerranée (1515–1830)*. Paris: Presses de l'Université de Paris-Sorbonne, 2000.

Vergniot, Olivier. "De la distance en histoire: Maroc–Sahara occidental: les captifs du hasard (XVIIe–XXe siècles)." *Revue de l'Occident musulman et de la Méditerranée* 48 (1988): 96–125.

Verlinden, Charles. *L'Esclavage dans l'Europe médiévale: péninsule ibérique-France*. Bruges: De Tempel, 1955.

———. "The Transfer of Colonial Techniques from the Mediterranean to the Atlantic." In *The Beginnings of Modern Colonization*, translated by Yvonne Freccero, 3–32. Ithaca, NY: Cornell University Press, [1970].

Vertot d'Aubeuf, René Aubert de. *Histoire des Chevaliers de Malte, d'après l'abbé de Vertot*. 2nd ed. Tours: A. D. Mame, 1839.

Villari, Rosario. *Elogio della dissimulazione: la lotta politica nel Seicento*. Rome: Laterza, 1987.

Vincent, Bernard. "La Vie affective des esclaves de la péninsule ibérique XVIe–XIXe siècle." In *Familia y mentalidades*, edited by Angel Rodríguez Sánchez and Antonio Peñafiel Ramón, 31–39. Murcia, Spain: Universidad de Murcia, 1977.

Vitkus, Daniel J., ed. *Piracy, Slavery, and Redemption: Barbary Captivity Narratives from Early Modern England*. New York: Columbia University Press, 2001.

———. *Turning Turk: English Theater and the Multicultural Mediterranean, 1570–1630*. New York: Palgrave Macmillan, 2003.

Vovard, André. *Les Turqueries dans la littérature française: le cycle barbaresque*. Toulouse: Privat, 1959.

Wanquet, Claude. *La France et la première abolition de l'esclavage, 1794–1802*:

le cas des colonies orientales, Ile de France (Maurice) et la Réunion. Paris: Karthala, 1998.

Watbled, Ernest. "Aperçu sur les premiers consulats dans le Levant et les états barbaresques." *Revue africaine* 16 (1872): 20–34.

———. "La France et les barbaresques au XVIe siècle." *Nouvelle Revue* 84 (1893): 368–388.

Weiss, Gillian. "Barbary Captivity and the French Idea of Freedom." *French Historical Studies* 28, 2 (2005): 231–264.

———. "From Barbary to France: Processions of Redemption and Early-Modern Cultural Identity." In *La Liberazione dei "captivi" tra Cristianità e Islam: oltre la crociata e il gihad tolleranza e servizi umanitario (Rome, Sept. 16–19 1998)*, edited by Giulio Cipollone, 789–805. Vatican City: Archivio Segreto Vaticano, 2000.

———. "Humble Petitioners and Able Contractors: French Women as Intermediaries in the Redemption of Captives." In *Le Commerce des captifs: les intermédiaires dans l'échange et le rachat des prisonniers en Méditerranée (XVI–XVIII siècles)*, edited by Wolfgang Kaiser, 333–344. Rome: Ecole française de Rome, 2008.

Wettinger, Godfrey. *Slavery in the Islands of Malta and Gozo ca. 1000–1812.* San Gwann, Malta: Publishers Enterprises Group, 2002.

Wheelan, Joseph. *Jefferson's War: America's First War on Terror, 1801–1805.* New York: Carroll & Graf, 2003.

Wilhelm, Jacques. "Captifs chrétiens à Alger." *Revue des sciences politiques* 56 (1933): 127–137.

Williams, Wes. "'Out of the Frying Pan . . .': Curiosity, Danger and the Poetics of Witness in the Renaissance Traveller's Tale." In *Curiosity and Wonder from the Renaissance to the Enlightenment*, edited by R. J. W. Evans and Alexander Marr, 21–42. Aldershot, UK: Ashgate, 2006.

Windler, Christian. *La Diplomatie comme expérience de l'autre: consuls français au Maghreb (1700–1840).* Geneva: Droz, 2002.

———. "Diplomatie et interculturalité: les consuls français à Tunis, 1700–1840." *Revue d'histoire moderne et contemporaine* 50, 4 (2003): 63–91.

———. "Representing a State in a Segmentary Society: French Consuls in Tunis from the Ancien Régime to the Restoration." *Journal of Modern History* 73 (2001): 233–274.

Wintroub, Michael. *A Savage Mirror: Power, Identity and Knowledge in Early Modern France.* Stanford: Stanford University Press, 2006.

Wolf, John B. *The Barbary Coast: Algiers under the Turks, 1500 to 1830.* New York: Norton, 1979.

Yerushalmi, Yosef Hayim. *From Spanish Court to Italian Ghetto: Isaac Cardoso, a Study in Seventeenth-Century Marranism and Jewish Apologetics.* Seattle: University of Washington Press, 1981.

Zagorin, Perez. *Ways of Lying: Dissimulation, Persecution, and Conformity in Early Modern Europe.* Cambridge, MA: Harvard University Press, 1990.

Ze'evi, Dror. *Producing Desire: Changing Sexual Discourse in the Ottoman Middle East, 1500–1900.* Berkeley: University of California Press, 2006.

Zonza, Christian. "Henri du Lisdam: la captivité au carrefour du roman et de la philosophie dans les premières années du XVIIe siècle." In *Captifs en Méditerranée (XVIe–XVIIIe siècles): histoires, récits, légendes*, edited by François Moureau. Paris: Presses de l'Université de Paris-Sorbonne, 2008.

———. "Le Récit de captivité entre fiction et histoire." In *Récits d'Orient dans les littératures d'Europe: XVIe–XIXe siècles*, edited by Anne Duprat and Emilie Picherot, 145–160. Paris: Presses de l'Université de Paris-Sorbonne, 2008.

Zysberg, André. "Galères et galériens du royaume de France." In *Le Genti del mare Mediterraneo*, edited by Rosalba Ragosta. 2 vols.; 2: 787–809. Naples: Lucio Pironti, 1981.

———. *Les Galériens: vies et destins de 60,000 forçats sur les galères de France, 1680–1748*. Paris: Editions du Seuil, 1987.

———. *Marseille au temps du Roi-Soleil: la ville, les galères, l'arsenal*. Marseille: Jeanne Lafitte, 2007.

Index

Page numbers in italic indicate illustrations.